D0074665

BL
1033
H384
2004

INTRODUCTION TO
ASIAN
RELIGIONS

Alamance Community College
Library
P.O. Box 8000
Graham, NC 27253

INTRODUCTION TO
ASIAN
RELIGIONS

BRADLEY K. HAWKINS

PEARSON

Longman

1185 Avenue of The Americas, New York

This book is dedicated to Susan, Donovan, and Aidan

and

to the memory of Ninian Smart (1927–2001)
scholar, gentleman, and dear friend

Vice President and Publisher: Priscilla McGeehon
Director of Marketing: Tim Stookesbury
Marketing Manager: Wendy Albert
Cover Design Manager: Nancy Danahy
Cover Designer: Andrew Shoolbred
Picture Researcher: Julia Ruxton
Maps: Andrea Fairbrass
Printed in Hong Kong

This book was designed and produced by Laurence King Publishing Ltd, London
Copyright © 2004 Laurence King Publishing

For permission to use copyrighted material, grateful acknowledgment is made to
the copyright holders on pp. 398–9, which are hereby made part of the copyright page.

CIP data is on file at the Library of Congress, and will be added in reprint.

All rights reserved. No part of this publication may be reproduced, stored in a retrieval
system, or transmitted in any form or by any means, electronic, mechanical, photocopying,
recording, or otherwise, without the written permission of the publisher.

Please visit our website at http.//www.ablongman.com

ISBN 0-321-17289-2

10 9 8 7 6 5 4 3 2 1

Contents

Preface

I must admit at the outset that I am old-fashioned. While I applaud the myriad of new teaching materials such as audio-visual material, computer programs, the Internet, and the like that are now available to teachers of religion, I firmly believe in the Asian concept that the most meaningful educational experiences are the result of a personal interaction between student and teacher. It is this philosophy that has guided the writing of the present text. It is self-evident that no textbook of any manageable size could be written that would exhaustively treat the magnificent diversity of Asian religious experience. Choices of methodological emphasis, what topics are to be included or excluded, to what depth these topics should be treated, and to what extent one should involve the beginning student in an examination of the many still unresolved scholarly debates associated with the study of Asian religions are all questions that need to be considered when deciding how to structure the tremendous mass of data available on the religions of Asia. Clearly, instructors of the subject will hold different opinions on all of these issues.

Moreover, every class is unique in the mix of its students and the specific expertise of its instructor, not to mention the necessity of contending with the numerous unexpected factors that affect the conduct and evolution of each individual class from term to term. It is impossible to predict what aspects of the study of the Asian traditions will fire the imagination of the students and emerge at any given point as a living concern in the classroom, either for an individual or the group at large. Instructors must be the facilitators and sculptors of this educational experience, since they mediate between the purely intellectual facts of the study and the dreams, aspirations, and concerns of the students. It is through the teacher's inspiration and technical knowledge that students transcend the dry facts of Asian religion and come to understand it for what it truly is—a vital and living force in the lives of much of the human race.

This text, then, is designed to support the instructor's efforts in bringing the Asian religions to life for the students who will use it. As such, it makes no pretense of being exhaustive in its treatment of Asian religious phenomena, nor of being "inspirational" in its own right. Rather it aims at providing a framework within which instructors are free to develop their exposition of the material in the manner most appropriate to their own expertise and inclinations, and the conditions of their individual classrooms. With this goal in mind, I have chosen to present the religions of Asia in a primarily historical manner. As a historian of religion I believe that, far from being a static ahistorical phenomenon, religion is a living and evolving organism, and that examination of the overall historical development of the Asian religions is the clearest way for the beginning student to gain an overview of these thought systems and their place in their societies. Readers of this text will also find that my presentation is conditioned by the assumption that religions are both influenced by the physical and social environments in which they develop and in turn influence those environments.

This should not be taken to mean that I hold the reductionist viewpoint that all religion is nothing more than an outgrowth of human society and the human psyche. But given the intellectual boundaries within which the process of academic analysis takes place, scholars are committed to working with data as it presents itself, and it must be recognized that data can often be interpreted from a secular materialist point of view as well as in a spiritual manner. Nor does this method of interpretation necessarily negate the transcendental origins and possibilities advocated by the religious traditions themselves. As my grandfather used to observe, "The Lord moves in mysterious ways His wonders to perform."

Even though the text is primarily structured along historical lines, the tremendous mass of information demands further organization. Consequently, I have divided the book into three main sections—South and Southeast Asia, China, and Northeast Asia. The pan-Asian religions such as Shamanism and Islam are examined at appropriate points throughout the narrative.

Such wide diversity of geographic and cultural areas creates considerable challenges in transliterating the various languages of Asia into English. Since this is a textbook for beginners, I have chosen to use simple phonetic transliteration for the Indic languages. (In more advanced texts, Indic terms and names are transliterated using the excellent system that has been developed for these languages.) Likewise, I have simplified the transliteration of most of the other Asian languages encountered in the text. For Korean, I have adhered to the McCune-Reischauer system with the exception of using "ö" and "ü" to indicate the short sounds of those vowels. In the case of Chinese, I have used Pinyin; however, since so many seminal books on Chinese religion use the significantly different Wade-Giles system, I have also given that form of transliteration when words or names are encountered in the text for the first time.

We live in a world full of electronic information resources, and present-day instructors and students of Asian religions have an immense volume of multimedia material no further away than their computers. I have chosen to use some of these newly available resources to construct what one might describe as a "counter text." Whereas the printed text concentrates primarily on the systematic presentation of the historical and intellectual development of the Asian religions—subjects that are treated very unevenly in the Internet material that I have reviewed—most of the electronic sources quoted in the text are linked to sites that give the students the "feel" of the various religions. This material will hopefully convey a fuller understanding and appreciation of the non-intellectual components of the various Asian traditions that make them so appealing to their devotees. It is where phenomenological information on festivals, rituals, and so forth is to be found, and here many of the literary and artistic expressions of the various religions are presented. Writings drawn from the various religious traditions of Asia are also printed at the end of this text, to provide immediate access to a representative selection of primary sources.

Finally, no book is written in isolation, and certainly not a book that covers such an immense field of knowledge as a broad study of the religions of Asia. Consequently, I would like at this point to acknowledge some of those who have contributed to its development. First and foremost, I am indebted to my *doktorvater* and friend, the late Ninian Smart. His encyclopedic knowledge of the various religious traditions of the world, and his deep sympathy and affection for the human beings who practice them, informs every sentence of this book. It is only fitting that it should be dedicated to his memory.

Likewise, I owe much to my other teachers. At the University of California, Santa Barbara, Wade Clark Roof and Barbara Holdrege were always generous with their advice and support. At Loyola University in New Orleans, Stephen J. Duffy and Robert Gnuse introduced me to the rich treasures of the Jesuit scholarly tradition. I would be remiss if I did not pay homage to the five people at the University of Toronto who solidified my determination to become a scholar and opened my eyes to the marvels of Asia. N. K. Wagle, Aziz Ahmad, and A. L. Basham introduced me to the wonder that is India. J. S. Brownlee awakened a lifelong interest in the culture and history of Japan, while Clifford Leech, the great Shakespearean expert, presented me with the perfect paradigm of the scholar and gentleman.

In more immediate terms, I would like to thank the reviewers of the present volume. All of them were exceedingly generous with their time and advice and made many useful comments that have greatly improved the text. They include Christopher Key Chapple, Loyola Marymount University; Kathleen Erndl, Florida State University; Terry Kleeman, University of Colorado at Boulder; Carol Anderson, Kalamazoo College; Anne Monius, University of Virginia; Mario Poceski, University of Florida; Jay Williams, Hamilton College; and Jane Marie Law, Cornell University. I am particularly indebted to Dr. Jennie Klein, who was most generous in sharing her rich knowledge of Internet sources with me.

I also owe a special debt to Kate Tuckett, Melanie White, and Julia Ruxton of Laurence King Publishing in London for their patient assistance to an often irascible author, and to Priscilla McGeehon of Longman Publishing. Robert W. Reid, Sophia Kaszuba, and Bill Falshaw were there when the intricacies of Asian religion overwhelmed me, as were many other friends such as Gene O'Toole. My mother, Audrey M. Hawkins, and my sister Lynn were always supportive of my interests and ambitions, even though these led me much farther from our northern Ontario hometown than they would have liked. Here in southern California, my father-in-law Ru Nguyen and my mother-in-law Quynh Nguyen (the best cook in the world) have kept me well fed and at the same time taught me a great deal about the family-oriented dimensions of Asian religion.

But most of all, I am indebted to my wife Susan, and my two sons Donovan and Aidan. Scholarship is not a nine-to-five job, and often it is our families who bear the brunt of our eccentric work habits. Mine does so with grace and good humor, and I love them all the more for it.

Bradley K. Hawkins
California State University, Long Beach

అయిరావతము మీంద దేవదృతుు యయుఫంఇ యయుటఇ విహ్లుఖుర్తు

Indra riding on Airavat, western Bengal, probably Bunkura district, 19th century. Indra was considered to be the king of the gods by the Vedic Aryans. The largest number of hymns in the Rig Veda are dedicated to him.

PART ONE

◆

The Religions of South and Southeast Asia

CHAPTER ONE

The Foundations of the Study of Religion in Asia

Students of Asian religion face real difficulties in understanding the nature and development of Asian religions. Asia is the largest continent in the world and displays tremendous geographical and cultural diversity. Moreover, the difficulty of reconstructing a coherent historical chronology for many parts of the region means that our knowledge of the ebb and flow of Asian history is uneven at best. All of this contributes to Asia's tremendous religious diversity. This means that the analysis of Asian religious phenomena is much more complex than is the case with other religious traditions. Monotheistic religions such as Christianity, Judaism, and Islam have similar generic characteristics—there is a God, He is the one God, the Creator of the visible world, and there is no other. He is all-powerful and knows all that occurs in His domain. Even though He is favorably disposed toward humanity. He is also just and punishes those who disobey His moral order. Human beings have one life in which they can choose to follow the dictates of God or not. God's "rules" are known because they have been "revealed" to selected human beings. The consequence of disobeying the dictates of God is eternal damnation. Following God's decrees results in eternal life in an abode of everlasting bliss.

While some of these characteristics can be seen in the religions of Asia, none of them matches the tenets of the monotheistic religions very closely. Hindus and Daoists, for example, believe in many gods. In some Asian religions, many people, including some Hindus, believe that there is an all-powerful God who controls human destiny; but there are also other Hindus who hold that there are no gods at all! Buddhism does not teach the existence of any Supreme Being, although some branches of the religion postulate the existence of enlightened beings who, in their attitudes and powers, are the functional equivalents of the gods of other religions. None of the major religions of Asia teaches that the visible world was God's creation. Indeed, this central preoccupation of monotheism is of little or no interest for the Asian religions. In their systems of thought, the world is self-existent and eternal.

In addition, there is considerable divergence in Asian perceptions of the interaction of the divine with the mundane world of the senses. Buddhists believe that there are inflexible universal laws that affect human destiny and cannot be abridged or contravened. Some Hindus believe that God is favorably inclined toward humans, but others hold ideas essentially similar to Buddhists. Whereas Daoists feel that human destiny can be affected by religious rituals, many Confucians do not. No Asian religion postulates an absolute and permanent judgment at the end of life. Some Chinese thought systems such as Confucianism possess only the vaguest conceptions of the afterlife, and efforts are concentrated on this present life. Daoism, on the other hand, has an elaborate conception of the afterlife, and a huge ritual arsenal designed to affect the individual's fate there. As for the Indian religions, they all hold to the concept that human beings are caught in a constant cycle of birth and rebirth. Actions in this life will have inescapable consequences in the next one.

In Asian religions, human knowledge of the divine is seen to come from different sources. Some traditions believe in a concept of revelation that is much the same as that espoused by practitioners of the monotheistic religions—namely that God reveals Himself to humanity through the inspired utterances of prophets. These utterances are recorded, and provide an absolute and inflexible guide to the will of God and humanity's necessary responses to that will. Other Asian traditions believe that knowledge of the divine comes through other means, such as introspection and meditation. Yet others, such as Confucianism, have little interest in things outside of the world of humanity. They acknowledge the existence of the supernatural, but believe that the human being's primary attention should be concentrated on this world, not the next. All this can lead the student of Asian religious traditions to wonder whether any order can be imposed on the relevant data that allows for a systematic examination of Asian religions in a coherent and meaningful way.

As with all other academic disciplines, the study of religion has its own methods of organizing its analysis of its subject material. Unlike other disciplines, however, the study of religion does not easily fit into any single methodological or subjective framework. Whereas sociology, for example, always deals only with questions of the individual in social interaction, the study of religion can encompass history, philosophy, ethics, sociology, literary and linguistic analysis, and numerous other studies as well—sometimes using all of these possible approaches simultaneously! This has led frequently to confusion, all the more so since the study of religion often transcends both temporal and geographical boundaries as well. Thus students of comparative religion may well find themselves grappling with, say, the importance of revelation as a religious category in the widely different contexts of European Christianity, Indian Hinduism, Chinese Confucianism, and indigenous South American religions. Given this wide variety of variables, it is imperative to establish some methodological framework if the study of religion in general, and in this case of Asian religions, is to proceed in an orderly manner.

In the present study, history provides the framework within which these Asian traditions are examined. There are two major reasons for this. The first is the interrelatedness of these traditions. Despite geographical and cultural separations, many of the religions of Asia developed either as a direct result of influences from different regions, or in reaction to such influences. A good illustration of this principle is Daoism, which was clearly a product of Chinese culture. However, much of its later development was predicated on its interactions with Buddhism, a faith that originated in India but which greatly influenced the course of Chinese religious history. The second reason for using a historical matrix as the framework for the study of religion is the nature of religion itself. It is not a static entity, but rather a dynamic, ever-changing one. Thus to say that Buddhists, for example, believe in a particular doctrine needs to be qualified by saying that Buddhists at a particular time and place believed in a particular doctrine. There are, of course, significant similarities between the various regional and doctrinal schools of Buddhism, but the understanding and expression of these similarities differ greatly from area to area and time to time.

Asia: The Geographical Setting

As with other world faiths, Asian religions are greatly influenced by the physical environment in which they exist, and one must understand this interaction in order in turn to understand them. Asia is the largest continent in the world, and it is not surprising that it should display considerable geographical diversity, not only in physical terrain, but also in climate, vegetation, and population distribution. In turn, all these factors affect what might be called human geography. They contribute to differences in economics, social diversity, and, eventually, religious expression. Asia can be divided into a series of discrete geographical zones. By far the largest of these is "Inner Asia." This zone stretches across the top of Asia from the eastern borders of Europe to the former Soviet Pacific Maritime Region (now the Pacific coast of Russia), and from Tibet to the Arctic Ocean. It is a harsh, unforgiving land of endless forests and grass plains broken up at intervals by large, shallow rivers and medium-sized mountain ranges. Owing to the harsh, extreme climate of hot summers and freezing winters, agriculture is virtually impossible. The inhabitants have tended to subsist by hunting and gathering or herding. At present, the region is mainly utilized for the harvesting of raw materials, although some efforts have been made to establish urban centers. In general, however, Inner Asia has played a very minor role in the cultural history of Asia as a whole.

The great civilizations of Asia have grown up on the peripheries of the Asian land mass. There are four major cultural regions, each with its own particular conditions, that have given rise to clearly defined clusters of cultures. Of these regions, only three—South, Southeast, and East Asia—directly concern us. Southwest Asia, while being an important center for the development of human culture, is the home of the great monotheistic religions of Islam, Judaism, and Christianity. As such, the study of this region's religious history is generally considered in connection with European religious history, although Islam is very widespread throughout Asia, as well as in Africa.

Although nowadays we tend to think of South Asia as being restricted to the modern countries of India and Pakistan, in antiquity this region was much greater in extent. It would have included not only present-day India and Pakistan, but also Bangladesh, Sri Lanka, Nepal, Tibet, Afghanistan, and the newly independent republics of Central Asia as well. Premodern South Asia displayed marked similarities in culture and religious expression despite possessing significant geographical diversity. The northern parts of the region are extremely mountainous, the Himalayas being the highest mountains in the world. South Asia's mountains have tended to separate much of it from the rest of the Asian landmass, restricting access to and from the area. These northern regions tend to be dry, and a number of deserts, including the Thar Desert in northwestern India, the desert of Taklamakan in Central Asia, and the high deserts of the Tibetan plateau, have also served as roadblocks to the access of peoples into South Asia.

The most important climatic feature of South Asia is the monsoon, the regular cyclical pattern of rainfall that defines the region's pattern of agriculture. The monsoon climate allows for the growing of rice in the southern and eastern parts of the region, but produces only enough rain in the north and west to allow for the growing of wheat and barley. In terms of indigenous vegetation, the monsoon contributed to the growth of lush semitropical forests in Peninsular South Asia which, in combination with such physical features as mountain ranges and large rivers, made travel difficult. This contributed to the development of a series of distinct cultural zones within the region, and of considerable diversity within the general parameters of the core cultural and religious tradition.

The situation in Southeast Asia was at once similar to, and very different from, South Asia. Like the latter, Southeast Asia is bordered in the north by mountains that separate it both from East Asia and from South Asia. But unlike both these regions, Southeast Asia has numerous islands and long stretches of coastline linked by the sea. Consequently, its various regions were not as cut off from one another as were those of South and East Asia, although there are clear distinctions between the cultures of Island Southeast Asia and Mainland Southeast Asia. Southeast Asia was also within the influence of the monsoon climate, but most of it received sufficient rain to allow for rice cultivation. Sandwiched between South and East Asia, Southeast Asia borrowed cultural elements from both. Nevertheless, it evolved its own distinctive culture and its own religious traditions.

At the eastern end of the Asian landmass lies East Asia, a region composed primarily of China, Japan, and Korea. Here again, physical features such as mountains and deserts separate this region from other parts of Asia. Although possessing long coastlines, East Asia tended to be inward looking and not particularly interested in long-distance trade, although at times its countries carried on considerable trade between themselves and also with adjacent Southeast Asia. Because of its large size and sharp regional divisions, caused by its internal mountain ranges and large rivers, China displayed the most diversity. The southern part of the country resembled Southeast Asia, with its warm wet climate and rice agriculture, while the north was much drier and grew wheat, barley, and millet. Japan's climate was more moderate; but the extremely rugged nature of its topography sharply limited its agricultural potential, making it more dependent on the ocean for food. Korea, with a much more extreme climate, was in a very similar position.

Asia: The Historical Setting

Just as the geography of Asia has influenced the development of its people, so too has its history. Unfortunately, our understanding of Asian history is very uneven. In some regions, such as East Asia, it is relatively complete. In others, such as South and Southeast Asia, there are serious gaps in our knowledge of the region's development, affecting our understanding of how Asian religious traditions evolved. The most complete historical records come from East Asia, more specifically China. Here a tradition of historical study developed as an aid to practical considerations of government. The Chinese, believing that people could learn from historical precedent, began to keep detailed records from about 1500 B.C.E., as witnessed by their recently discovered archives of **oracle bones**. Consequently, students of East Asian religion have at their disposal a wealth of written material that is the envy of their colleagues in other areas of Asian religious studies.

At the other end of the spectrum is Southeast Asia. Here the only historical documentation for most of the region's history is, until a relatively late date, either archaeological or inscriptional. These two sources of information are by their very nature uneven—to say the least. To make matters worse, we know from Chinese sources that the various Southeast Asian peoples kept records, which may have been extensive. But these were apparently recorded on perishable material that has decayed in the hot, wet Southeast Asian climate. Whatever their possible value might have been to the study of religion in Southeast Asia, they are at present lost to scholars.

Finally, there is South Asia, the historiography of which is conditioned by two factors. The first is the South Asian tendency—visible, as we shall see, in their religious traditions as well—to preserve important facts in the memory rather than commit them to paper. The second factor has to do with the South Asian concept of time. Whereas European and Chinese thinking tends to see time as linear, in the South Asian tradition it is seen as cyclical. If such a viewpoint is adopted, then no event is of unique importance in itself. This greatly diminishes the importance and value of history and the attention paid to it by local scholars. In addition, given the regional diversity of South Asian culture, native historians tended to date their material based on local events rather than on some commonly agreed chronological scale. This makes it extremely difficult to establish a coherent timeline for early South Asian history, a problem that again spills over into the study of religion in the region.

The Archaic Roots of Asian Religion

The origins of religion in human history remain a deep mystery. There are, however, some tantalizing hints to be found in the archaeological record, for example the very fact that there have been purposeful burials of human remains. Even among the Neanderthals we find that the dead were interred with flowers and artifacts, suggesting that those left behind may have believed that the dead had gone on to some other existence. But beyond the suggestion of this possibility we can not go. It was not until human beings began to decorate the walls of caves with paintings and to establish ritual sites that we are able to speculate further on the human religious impulse. The first students of these cave-dwelling artists' religion thought that it must have been akin to the shamanic religions that form the basis of all later Asian religions, and which are still extant in much of their original form in northern Asia. However, later scholars have made a significant case against this theory, suggesting that rather than following a shamanic pattern, Paleolithic religion was shaped by two predominant ideas: the cyclical nature of time and fertility. The dialectic between these two concepts found expression in the cult of the earth goddess with her menstrual cycle that united the cycles of the moon and the birth of children, both of which were central to the lives of early humans. Our ancestors depended on the annual migrations of beast, fish, and fowl as well as on the cycles of plant growth in order to live. Consequently, a decline in these food sources would inevitably lead to the death of those who depended on them.

Human fertility was also critical to the survival of the race. Modern humans, masters of the earth and all its riches, forget how tenuous human dominance of the environment has been for most of the history of our species' existence. Early humans probably lived in small, isolated bands that interacted relatively little with one another. The number of people in a group directly affected the life-sustaining activities of hunting and gathering as well as the ability to fight off predators, both animal and human. The more hands there were to draw on, the greater the chances of survival. This factor, combined with very high rates of infant and mother mortality, would have led to a natural interest in human fertility and the strong desire to influence it positively wherever possible. The natural result of the interaction of these concerns with the human religious impulse no doubt led to a cult of the protective and nurturing "Mother Goddess," which made considerable, albeit often hidden or downplayed, contributions to the great religious traditions of the world and still has force in many cultures to this day. Undoubtedly, appeals were also made to divine figures associated with particular animal groups—some of which may have been male as well as female. Speculations such as these may be very interesting in a general sense, but they do not describe shamanic religion, the first recognizable constellation of religious beliefs associated with Asia.[1]

Shamanic religion is a difficult phenomenon to categorize neatly. The term itself comes from *saman*, a word that has its origins among the Tungusic herders of northeastern Asia and which means either "one who is excited" or "to know." Shaman refers to the most prominent religious specialist in the tradition, but in many cultures practicing shamanic religion there are subsidiary religious figures as well. The people of Northeast Asia are the only people who practice Shamanism in the strict sense of the word. But although Shamanism *per se* still exists only among these few remaining hunters and gatherers, a set of religious ideas and practices which we may loosely term "shamanic religion" often persists elsewhere in Asia, acting as a sort of counterpoint to the more formalized "high" religions. Indeed, there is often considerable hostility between the priests of these religions and the practitioners of local shamanic traditions.

Shamanic religion may be said to be more of a worldview than a formal religion. Its essential nature flows from a belief that all things are, in some sense, imbued with a life force and, to a limited extent, consciousness. Thus the world of the shamanic peoples is one inhabited by myriad spirits who can affect people's lives for good or ill. This worldview is, in a sense, scientific, stemming from shamanic peoples' understanding of the concept of cause and effect: if something happens for which there is no visible cause, such as an illness or bad luck, it must necessarily follow that there is an invisible agent that is causing the visible disturbance, and that there are consequently whole worlds invisible to the average person. The specific details of how these worlds are organized and distributed differs from tribe to tribe. However, all shamanic groups believe, on the basis of observed phenomena, that there are individuals who can perceive these hidden worlds. Such a person is thought to be able, with the proper training, to intercede with the unseen beings to mitigate and deflect their antagonism, or to gain their assistance and goodwill so as to help their fellow tribespeople. Interestingly enough, there seems to be little general gender differentiation in who can perform this function. Shamanic societies are equally divided between those in which the shamans are women and those in which they are men. Male dominance of the formal structures of religion seems to come at a later stage of religious development in Asia.

The Selection and Training of Shamans

Shamans can best be defined as individuals who, by virtue of their ability to see and interact with the unseen worlds of the spirits, intercede for the members of their tribe with those spirits. They accomplish this through entering what might be termed "altered states of consciousness"—a term that should be disassociated from the way in which it and others like it were used by members of the counter culture of the 1960s. For shamans, there is nothing enjoyable in such states. As Mircea Eliade, the great scholar of shamanic religion, has observed, these states may be achieved through "techniques of ecstasy." However, "ecstasy" refers not to a state of bliss, but rather to a sense of moving beyond and above one's self and entering into a state of heightened or intensified feeling and perception. To interact successfully with the worlds of the spirits and their inhabitants, natural talent is needed—but this is not in itself enough. The shaman must undertake a rigorous course of training, and this may be quite lengthy. It is a great mistake to think that just because a society is at a relatively simple stage of economic development it is therefore correspondingly intellectually primitive and uncomplicated. Indeed, such societies often have very complex cosmological infrastructures, and the shaman, by virtue of his or her central place in tribal life, is the chief custodian, interpreter, and manipulator of this infrastructure.

How are such important religious figures chosen? First of all, the position is seldom self-selecting. A person does not decide one day that he or she wants to become a shaman. Nor is the position in most cases hereditary: the children of shamans do not automatically follow their parents' calling. Usually, the spirits themselves are seen as the primary agents of choice. People know they have been chosen by the spirits through a number of means. For example, candidates may be set off from the tribal group by some anomaly such as physical appearance. If, say, an entire tribe is dark haired and five foot in height except for one individual who is blond and six foot tall, then this can be interpreted as indicating that some special destiny might be in store for him or her. Likewise, if a person survives a normally fatal accident or illness, this too may indicate a special destiny. Other indications of a shamanic calling include experiencing dreams or visions in which symbols of the spirits figure prominently. Or a person will feel more estranged from the social group and may withdraw from it in order to spend time in solitude in the forest or some other uninhabited place. In hunting and gathering societies, where the areas outside the village or encampment are seen as dangerous and frightening—not the oases of tranquillity and peace that modern city dwellers believe them to be—this behavior is considered strange in the extreme.

When it is decided that certain individuals are destined to be shamans, their journeys are only beginning. Now comes an extended period of apprenticeship training with a recognized shaman. Candidates pay for such training by working for and serving their teachers, helping with both day-to-day chores and ritual work. In return, the shamans teach the young apprentices the cosmology and myths of the tribe, the various herbal and medicinal lore particular to the region, and the proper rituals and meditative techniques designed to enhance their ability to travel and function in the spirit world.

Of these various lessons, the first, and in some ways the most important, is in the cosmology and myths of the tribe. All societies have core values that are passed on from generation to generation through the medium of stories and shamanic societies are no different. In America, for example, the virtue of truth is exemplified by the probably apocryphal story of George Washington cutting down the cherry tree. The myths of a tribe function simultaneously as explanations of how the world came into being and why it is as it is, as repositories of the values and mores of the group, and as paradigms for how people should lead their lives. Myths are the foundations upon which all other shamanic studies are based. Since virtually no shamanic societies over time have possessed writing systems, all the tribal myths—as well as all other shamanic knowledge—must be memorized. Since the amount of material to be learned might well have been extensive, the task of committing it to memory could often be quite lengthy.[2]

The next component of shamanic knowledge is the art of interpreting dreams and visions. The centrality of this study stems from the way in which the spirits prefer to communicate with human beings. The spirits prefer to communicate through dreams and visions, although in some regions, such as Southeast Asia, mediums might be possessed by the spirits and serve as their earthly mouthpieces.

Consequently, the study of dreams has two major components: how to cultivate dreams in order to find out specific information; and how to interpret such dreams. In case it is thought that this is an antiquated way of understanding reality, we need look no further for its validity in modern life than the teachings of Sigmund Freud and C. G. Jung. Although these modern practitioners of dream interpretation would claim a psychological rather than a spiritual underpinning for their theories, in practical terms the uses and applications of dream symbolism are much the same for shamans as for modern psychologists. This underlines another important function of the shaman, namely that of communal "psychologist" in his or her tribal setting.

The Spirits in Shamanism

The next phase of the shaman's training is to learn about the spirits that inhabit the unseen worlds that surround his or her tribe. He or she had to know the spirits' names, their likes and dislikes, and how they can be either appeased or controlled as the situation demands. If we remember that shamanic societies see spirits everywhere—in trees, animals, and even peculiar rock formations and waterfalls— then we can see that this can be a lengthy undertaking. Moreover, it is an intensely local study, since by their very nature all spirits are always local. Shamanic cultures might have some vague concept of a supreme spirit, but such a spirit is usually seen as the original Creator of the world who is now remote and disinclined to get involved in the day-to-day round of terrestrial existence. It is the local spirits that influence human life, and thus have to be controlled one way or another. To move to a different region is to encounter an entirely new group of spirits with entirely different powers. But interaction with the spirits is not just a matter of knowledge, it is also a matter of self control.

By their very nature, the spirits possess considerable knowledge about the inner state of the shaman. Moreover, since they resemble human beings in that they do not appreciate being cajoled or forced to do things against their will, they can be expected to use their knowledge of the shaman's inner doubts, fears, and anxieties in any spiritual confrontation. Consequently, it is of the utmost importance that shamans be totally aware of their shortcomings and psychological idiosyncrasies before attempting any confrontations with the spirit world. This is accomplished in a number of ways, for example through ascetic practices that aim to strengthen and purify practitioners by forcing them to confront the negative aspects of their psyche. Many of these practices will become familiar as we examine the other belief systems of Asia, where they constantly recur in the continent's high religions. They include sexual continence (at least for limited periods), fasting, ritual bathing of various sorts, and sleep deprivation. These practices are combined with solitude and what we today would term "meditative techniques." The cumulative result is what might be described as "primitive psychoanalysis." This inner journeying takes place under the tutelage and guidance of the shaman's teacher, but it is still a very dangerous enterprise. All human beings have within them areas of the psyche that are, to be blunt, just plain nasty. To confront these negative qualities and to integrate them into a coherent psychological whole is empowering; but the history of religion is littered with numerous examples of instances where such attempts have led not to successful integration but to madness.

Ideally, however, the shaman's psychological practices lead to a breakthrough event that marks the end of the long apprenticeship. This event can take a number of forms. It could be the phenomenon of the blinding white light by which the shaman is engulfed and transformed, experiencing the light as something infinitely benevolent and comforting. But the experience can be much less pleasant. Sometimes there is the experience of rebirth in a new body. Here, shamans experience their own deaths (sometimes accompanied by dismemberment), burials, and then resurrection after the transformation of their material body into a new, tougher form. It is interesting to note that similar experiences have been reported by contemporary Westerners using psychedelic drugs or meditation, as well as by meditators in many Asian traditions.

Shamanic Religion in the Social Context

On the shamans' return to their tribes, they take up their public duties of spiritual intercession on their tribes' behalf. This usually revolves around the key ritual of making the shamanic journey to the inner worlds to deal with the spirits in their own realm. This journey is always fraught with difficulties, and so careful planning and proper ritual must be carried out in its execution. The first thing that must be done is to ensure the purity of the shaman. This is done through the usual mediums of fasting, ritual bathing, isolation, and sexual abstinence. Next, a ritual space must be created to represent the spirit world, and in which the inner journey will take place. Through their training, shamans supposedly acquire the ability to enter the altered state of consciousness required by such a journey, but their entry is often aided by the use of special clothes, dancing, and drumming.[3] Drugs are frequently used as well: there are over a hundred hallucinogenic plant species spread throughout the world. Once in the trance state, the shamans travel through the spirit world in search of the appropriate spirit. While in this state, they are to some extent capable of controlling the images and experiences that occur. They experience an increased sense of concentration, but decreased awareness of the environment. They also exhibit increased mental energy and a variety of emotional states, and they can communicate with those around them through an organized use of imagery consistent with tribal cosmology and the purpose of the journey.

When the spirit is contacted, the shamans must make a decision as to how to proceed. Essentially, there are only two ways to deal with spirits—one is to bribe them, the other is to force them to do what is desired. Of the two, bribery is preferable since it is less onerous for the shaman. Since the spirits are generally conceived as being motivated in ways similar to human beings, this ploy generally takes the form of ritual deference and the exchange of material goods. Each spirit is held to have its own likes and dislikes in food and drink, so offerings of the appropriate victuals are always part of the exchange. In modern times, some spirits have developed a taste for cigars, cigarettes, and imported liquors, as well as a variety of fabrics and other luxury goods. Since misfortune in shamanic societies is often associated with offending the spirits, these gifts are usually accompanied by profuse apologies for any intended or unintended offense that may have been given to the spirit. Should the spirit fail to be mollified by these offerings, then shamans are compelled to confront the spirit and force it to their will. This is seen as a chancy business and much less likely to succeed.

At present, shamanic religion is often mistakenly seen as the primitive, unevolved expression of the universal religious impulse that has been superseded by more evolved expressions of that impulse except in a few wild and inaccessible regions of the Asian continent. But such a viewpoint masks both the considerable influence that shamanic ideas have had on the predominant religious traditions of the region as well as the very real appeal that shamanic-based religious rituals continue to have in today's world. The high religions of Asia tend to deal with what might be called the great questions of life. Why are we here? What is the purpose of human existence? What is our fate at death? It is to these high traditions that people turn if tormented by such existential concerns. But, as we have seen, these questions are seldom addressed by the shamanic tradition, which is more concerned with practical questions. How can I cure my daughter's fever? How can I improve the rice harvest? How can I convince Nguyen Diep Ngoc, the local village beauty, to marry me? For problems such as these, the still-functioning shamanic traditions that permeate Asia do offer solutions.

How these elements are integrated into people's greater religious lives differs from one tradition to another. In many societies in Asia, shamanistic elements have been absorbed wholesale into the high religious traditions, as is the case with Hinduism. Sometimes they exist as what might be called a "shadow religion," which runs parallel with the official high religion, complete with its own cadre of religious specialists—as is found all over Southeast Asia. And sometimes, as in the case of Shinto or some expressions of Chinese religion, shamanic religion evolved directly into a later tradition, although these traditions usually received considerable influences from elsewhere as well. Consequently, it would be unwise to consider shamanic religion as a dead or dying religious phenomenon of only passing historical interest. In some ways, its ideology and practices are still very much a functioning element, either overtly or covertly, in the practical faith of the Asian continent, and show no signs of disappearing in the new millennium.[4]

Website References

1. A good overview of Shamanism, particularly in its Mongolian form, is found at
   www.geocities.com/RainForest/Vines/2146/mongolia/cms.htm

2. Some examples of shamanic myths can be found at
   www.geocities.com/Athens/Oracle/8226/mythology.html

3. www.shamanicdimensions.net/archives/siberia.html gives some good examples of shamanic costumes.

4. www.geocities.com/Athens/Oracle/8226/sibshamanism.html is a good general source of information on a variety of shamanic topics.

CHAPTER TWO

The Beginnings of South Asian Religion

Without a doubt, India presents today's students of Asian religions with their most daunting challenge. Not only is Indian religion richly diverse and complex in its own right, but India is also the homeland of two great religions, Hinduism and Buddhism, that each spread far beyond its borders. Although these religions were modified and adapted to their respective new environments, they still preserved an Indian "flavor" that underlay all subsequent indigenous developments. Consequently, it is useful to start our inquiry into the great religious traditions of Asia with India and the source tradition from which all other indigenous Indian religions ultimately evolved.

The Problem of Defining "Hinduism"

Having resolved to do this, we are immediately confronted with a simple but extremely difficult problem. How are we to conceptualize and categorize this source tradition and the various religious expressions of India that developed from it? Traditionally, we have termed this "Hinduism," but how is this to be defined? In most religious traditions, no matter how much and in what way the various branches diverge from one another, there is usually a core set of doctrines and beliefs that are common to all. In the monotheistic religions, for example, there is a general uniform agreement as to the nature of God and to the content and status of the core scriptural foundations of the religion.

While a trained eye can see something of this uniformity in the source religious tradition of India, it is by no means so clear cut. Indeed, one of the things that perplexed early European scholars of Indian religion and which caused them to view the Indian tradition as primitive "unevolved" religion was the broad spectrum of basic beliefs that a person could hold and still be considered a faithful adherent to the Indian tradition. As we shall see, there are numerous continuities running throughout the Hindu tradition, but its basic presuppositions were so different from the cultural worldview of these early colonial scholars that these continuities were, in effect, invisible. Thus, for example, a devout Indian can believe that there is one god (in the monotheistic sense of the word espoused by Christians, Jews, and Muslims), many gods, or no gods at all. This has led to considerable difficulty in defining the basic parameters of this tradition, with some scholars arguing that there is no such thing as "Hinduism." Rather, they contend, there is a constellation of "Hinduisms" sharing a common cultural matrix, but different enough from one another to be considered separate religions. Consequently, although we will refer to the core Indian tradition in the following discussions as "Hinduism" for convenience, the student must keep in mind that the term is a conventional shorthand that by no means suggests doctrinal or practical uniformity.

Geographical and Cultural Divergence in the Indic Cultural Region

This problem of defining Hinduism is made ever more difficult by the fact that Indian culture, in the broad sense of the word, covers a large geographical area and embraces a huge number of very different sociocultural and linguistic groups. Traditionally, Indian culture has for several thousand years dominated the area that now contains the present-day states of Afghanistan, Pakistan, Nepal, Bangladesh, and Sri Lanka, as well as India itself. As even a cursory glance at a map of the region makes clear immediately, this includes a wide variety of geographical and climatic regions.

Perhaps the clearest division in Indian cultural geography is between the northern part of the region and the south. The people of the north speak Indo-European languages derived from the language spoken by immigrants who drifted into India from the plains of southern Russia some four thousand years ago. Early European scholars were fascinated by these languages since they were distant relatives of their own English, French, and German. In the south, on the other hand, the languages, called collectively Dravidian, were of a different type, and completely unrelated to the northern Indo-European languages. Likewise, the geography and climate of the south gave rise to agricultural and economic pursuits very different from those practiced in the north. However, the division between north and south was not the only one found in the Indian cultural region, which was crisscrossed with mountain ranges and huge river systems. These, combined with the thick jungle forests that covered the area in earlier days and which are now almost completely gone—victims of one of the densest populations in the world—served to divide the region into clearly defined subregions. These tended to develop their own distinctive languages and cultures defined by local conditions.

It is not surprising to find that these regions also developed local variations of Hinduism that in turn were often so pronounced as to cause some scholars of Hinduism to talk of a Great Tradition and a Little Tradition. The Great Tradition was seen as the Pan-Indic expression of Hinduism that remained relatively consistent across the various regions of the area and was expressed through the medium of the sacred language Sanskrit. The Little Tradition referred to the many regional expressions of Hinduism that often diverged rather significantly from one another and expressed themselves in the vernacular languages of their home region. These scholars saw that the interplay between the Great and Little Traditions gives modern Hinduism its rich nuanced textures. While this interpretation is by no means universally accepted, Hinduism often displays a clear distinction between local and culturewide traditions.

The Core Components of the Hindu Tradition

Religions are a complex interweaving of ideas, practices, morality, and socio-historical factors. Nowhere is this more evident than in South Asia. Here, the student of religion faces particular problems of interpretation stemming from the region's long history and extreme sociolinguistic complexity. With a documented history of over 8,500 years and the presence of Indo-European, Dravidian, Sino-Tibetan, and Austro-Asiatic language groups, South Asia represents one of the richest repositories of religious experience in the world. Four relatively distinct strands make up the earliest contributions to its rich religious tapestry. The first of these, and by far the most indistinct, is the religious tradition of the prehistoric inhabitants of the region. Since it has been populated more or less consistently for almost five hundred thousand years, these prehistoric religious traditions must have been very extensive at one time. At present, however, it is virtually impossible to recreate with any sense of certainty the religious systems of any of these very early peoples. At best, we can look to some archaeological remains and to the religious practices still extant among the *adivasis*, the marginal tribal peoples of South Asia, although this must be done with great care since religions are fluid entities that evolve and inter-penetrate one another over time and so such use of ethnographic analogy must be done with great care.

It is difficult to isolate the cultural elements that made up this indigenous Indian culture, but it probably had two major parts to it: an Australoid component dating from perhaps as long ago as about 50,000 B.C.E. with a culture similar in many respects to that of the present-day Australian aborigines; and a more recent Austro-Asiatic cultural component dating from about 8000 B.C.E. Now restricted to a few isolated tribal units, these sociolinguistic groups were once considerably more widespread in the southern, central, and northeastern areas of South Asia. Recent scholarship suggests that speakers of Australoid and Austro-Asiatic languages had far greater influence on the now dominant Indo-European and Dravidian peoples than previously supposed. It is not unreasonable to postulate that their influence went beyond the merely linguistic and that it added elements of Australoid and Austro-Asiatic religion to the South Asian tradition. Some scholars think that this contribution was fairly substantial. S. K. Chatterji, for example, has suggested that the Austro-Asiatic peoples imported the worship of the **linga**, the predominate symbol of the god Shiva, to India. Shrines containing lingas are still found in almost every small village and town throughout the non-Muslim areas of South Asia.

The second and much richer strand of the South Asian religious tradition comes from the so-called Indus Valley or Harappan civilization that flourished in the northwest of the region around the Indus River from about 6500 B.C.E. At present, we believe that this culture covered eight hundred thousand square kilometers—although ongoing excavations of its archaeological remains seem to suggest that it extended farther than this and that its influences may have been far more widespread.

The third strand of tradition is currently found in the southern third of the Indian peninsula. Here, the old and well-developed culture of the Dravidian peoples still exercises considerable influence. Possessing a complex religious system that predates Indo-European influences in the area, Dravidian culture, which may or may not preserve features of the Indus Valley culture, has made significant contributions to the development of South Asian religion as a whole.

Finally, there is the fourth, the Indo-European or Aryan, strand, which has

Shiva shrine beneath a pipal tree. Small shrines such as this are found in every village and town throughout India, and are characteristic of local Indian religion.

traditionally been accorded the greatest attention by academics since within it were composed and preserved the earliest literary remains of the South Asian tradition. For this reason, and because of its linguistic associations with the languages of the European colonial powers that dominated the region for some two hundred and fifty years, the Indo-European strand has traditionally been viewed by scholars as the fundamental core of the South Asian religious tradition.[1] But as we explore the Hindu tradition in the following pages, it will become evident that this strand has little or nothing to do with many important parts of the tradition.

The Indus Valley Culture and its Religion

It is virtually impossible to isolate the *adivasi* cultural elements in modern Hinduism, but it is not so difficult to do so for the Indus Valley culture. The major reason for this is that we have a wealth of archaeological material associated with the Indus culture, particularly the material found in the great cities of Mohenjo-Daro and Harappa, which we do not have for the tribal cultures that preceded it and which continued to flourish on its peripheries. Even so, our interpretations of Indus culture must be at best tentative. It is unwise to claim, as some scholars have, that any element of modern Hinduism that cannot be traced back to Aryan sources must be by default an element of the earlier Indus culture. Certainly, the available evidence is tantalizingly suggestive, but the interpretation of it should be approached

The Indus Valley civilization and the migration of the Indo-Aryan peoples. The Indus Valley civilization and the Aryan settlements in northwest India represent the wellsprings of Hindu religious tradition.

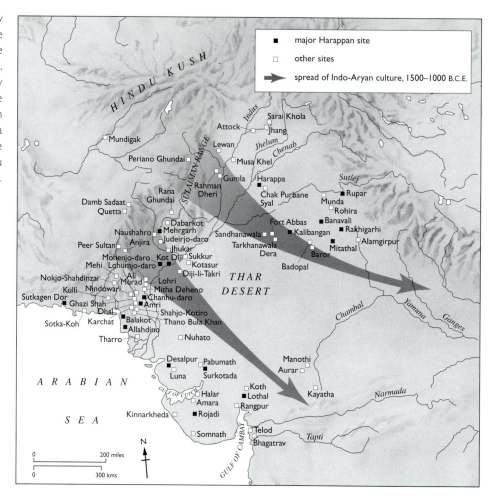

with caution. Even the physical anthropology of the inhabitants of the Indus culture is in doubt, since the remains exhibit diverse ethnic groups, including Dravidian, Australoid, Austro-Asiatic, and even Aryan, all of which are still present in living Indian populations. Since more evidence is coming to light daily, we can reasonably hope to be able to make more definite judgments at a later date.

Recent excavations at such sites as Harappa, Kalibangan, and Lothal have given archaeologists some interesting surprises. The first of these concerns the age of the Indus civilization. Originally it was thought to have come into existence about 1,000 to 1,200 years later than the more well-known civilizations of Egypt and Mesopotamia. However, new evidence seems to suggest that the Indus civilization's development was contemporaneous with those other early cultures or might even have preceded them. The earliest evidence of food production and associated urbanization seems to date from about 6500 to 5000 B.C.E. These early villages grew wheat, barley, peas, melons, cotton, and a variety of other crops as well as raising humped cattle, goats, sheep, pigs, and dogs. By c. 5000 to 2600 B.C.E., the culture had moved down from the hills where it originated and had become centered in the Indus Valley. Here was rich silt agricultural land that needed no deep plowing and there was abundant water. The civilization that grew up in this fertile river valley began to spread widely across present-day Pakistan, northwestern India, and per-haps into Central Asia as well. The period between 2600 and 1900 B.C.E. saw the rise of great urban centers along the Indus River and elsewhere that were supported by the surplus of their surrounding farms.[2]

After 1900 B.C.E., the civilization seems to have collapsed. The reasons for this are still being debated. At first, archaeologists, interpreting references in early Aryan literature, thought that the new Aryan inhabitants of northern India had entered the Indus region as a conquering horde and had destroyed its great cities. Certainly, the Aryans' references to dark, snub-nosed peoples who were phallic worshippers and to the Aryan destruction of enemy fortresses seemed very convincing. But archaeological data does not support the case. There is some evidence in Harappa that a horse-using people occupied part of the city near the end of its existence, but what their relationship was to the earlier inhabitants and what role they played in the city's demise is very unclear. More likely, the Indus civilization disintegrated under its own weight after some disastrous shift in the ecology of the region, rather than because of external invasion. New geological studies in the region suggest that shifts in land elevation occurred frequently. That, or perhaps a rise in sea levels, could have slowed the flow of the Indus River. This in turn would have caused the extensive irrigation system to silt up and the surrounding agricultural land to become salinated. The resulting loss of food-producing capacity would have destroyed the Indus civilization just as thoroughly as any invasion.

The second fact that has surprised archaeologists is the geographical extent of the culture. At first it was believed to have flourished only in the Indus Valley and the immediately surrounding area, but recent excavations show a different picture. Indus remains dating from the height of the civilization have been found as far north as Shortugai in Central Asia, as far east as the Ganges River, as far west as Sutkagen Dor in Iran, and as far south as the headwaters of the Godavari River in the north-ern Deccan. Indus trade goods have been found even farther afield in Mesopotamia and around the Persian Gulf. In addition, some of the materials used in the manu-facture of Indus trade goods, such as lapis lazuli from Afghanistan and gold from South India, suggest well-developed trade contacts beyond the civilization's formal borders. In short, it is evident that the Indus civilization was a major entity.

It should not surprise us, therefore, to learn that at its height the Indus civiliza-tion had a highly developed, socially stratified culture complete with a complex urban society that boasted centrally planned urban communities, large public build-ings, a centralized authority, craft specialization, a complex irrigation system, and indoor plumbing. The Indus people also possessed a system of writing that is mostly found on steatite intaglio seals, which were probably used to identify the owners of trade goods. Regrettably, this writing has yet to give up its secrets, since samples of it are limited and of short length. It is unlikely that these seals would convey much factual information, but they would furnish us with a much better idea of the lin-guistic affiliations of the inhabitants of the Indus cities, and thus possibly their reli-gious ideas. In the absence of such knowledge, we must rely on the material remains of the culture, and these can often be ambiguous.[3]

Although scant, these archaeological remains are still of great interest. The archi-tecture of the Indus cities clearly shows that they were divided between private res-idences and public areas. The cities have citadels that probably served as the headquarters for the ruling class, and perhaps for a religious elite as well. Some scholars have conjectured that large structures resembling swimming pools found in the center of several cities were used for ritual bathing and purification rites. Given the present-day Hindu emphasis on ritual purification through bathing in sacred rivers and on ritual purity in general, there may be some validity in this interpretation. Certainly, the Aryans who came to India at a later date from water-poor Central Asia would have had little contact with bathing in any form, as witnessed by the conduct of later steppe-dwelling peoples such as the Mongols. It is more likely that the practice of bathing would have originated in the much wetter region of India.[4]

Another architectural feature of some Indus cities such as Kalibangan has stirred up considerable controversy. These are the so-called "fire altars." As we shall see below, fire played a considerable role in early Aryan religion. Indeed, the *yajna*, or sacrifice, was the central feature of public Hindu worship. The appearance of these "altars" has caused some scholars to speculate that the inhabitants of the Indus cities were Aryans. This in turn has led to even greater speculation about the ultimate origins of the Aryan peoples and other related topics. Since most of these speculations lie outside the scope of the present discussion, we must regretfully pass over them in silence.

When we turn to the material evidence of the Indus seals and other small artifacts, such as small pieces of art that may or may not have had religious significance, we find some very fertile ground for conjecture. A number of the seals have depictions of animals and plants that still possess religious significance in modern folk Hinduism, for example representations of the hump-backed Brahma bull. Modern Hindus venerate cows and, given the prominence of these animals in the earliest Aryan scriptures, it was long assumed that the Aryans, a herding people, brought this reverence for the cow with them. But the existence of the Indus material seems

The Great Bath, Mohenjo-daro. Although the precise function of this structure is still debated, it may have been used for communal religious purification. Ritual purification still plays a great role in modern Hinduism.

to cast some doubt on this theory, or at least on the exclusively Aryan origins of cow veneration. Cows were of equal or even greater value in agricultural societies than in herding cultures because of their many uses in the processes of agricultural production. They were probably of such great value that they were protected and not eaten, their dairy products and contributions to agricultural labor far outweighing their value as a source of food. The Aryans, on the other hand, are constantly seen as sacrificing and eating their cattle, as would be expected in a herding culture.

We might ask ourselves how the Indus people viewed the final fate of human beings. Burial practices show us that they believed in some form of survival after death and that they buried their dead—unlike later Indians who practiced cremation. Along with the deceased were interred pots containing food, which suggests a belief in the afterlife. Yet another feature seen in the material remains of the Indus culture that is carried over into later Indian religions is an emphasis on sacred trees, primarily the pipal, the sacred fig tree. There is an extant Indus seal that shows a deity seated in a pipal tree, at the base of which stands a stool with a human head on it. It has been suggested that this represents a human sacrifice to a tree spirit. These tree spirits, called *yakshas*, are still worshipped in rural India today. Moreover, the line of figures represented at the bottom of the seal suggests that this sacrifice was a corporate cultic act rather than an individual one. It is unclear whether this particular tree spirit is male or female, but there are numerous female representations found in the Indus material remains. It is likely that the agricultural Indus people worshipped a female deity or deities associated with the fertility of the earth. This would be consistent with the evidence from other contemporary agricultural societies and is in marked contrast to the later Aryans, whose religion was centered on male sky gods. For the Aryans, female deities existed only as consorts to the gods. It is interesting to observe that later artistic renderings of Hindu goddesses seem to follow the artistic conventions of the Indus valley.

We should also note the existence of a particular Indus Valley deity who is represented on various seals and who has been associated with the Hindu god Shiva, a popular god of the present day who did not figure in Aryan religion until a relatively late date. This Indus deity is shown seated in a cross-legged "yogic" position. His head is that of a buffalo, and he is sometimes shown surrounded by animals. This has led to identifying the deity as Pachupati, the lord of the animals, a later epithet of Shiva. Some scholars have interpreted this figure as having an erection, which would be consistent with modern representations of Shiva in the form of the linga, a stylized representation of the male sex organ. This might well signify that the Indus deity was the consort of a goddess, responsible for the fertility of the land and all living things on it—such an interpretation is buttressed by the numerous representations of bulls in Indus art, the bull being naturally associated with fertility in many cultures. Considerable speculation has been lavished on the image of this Indus deity and its significance in Indian religious history. Many scholars would see it as sure proof that the figure of Shiva is a pre-Aryan god who was later adopted by the Aryans when they came to India. However, a very similar image can be seen on a caldron dating from the first century B.C.E. that was retrieved from the Danish bog of Gundestrup and which is clearly of Indo-European provenance. This suggests that considerably more scholarly work needs to be done before any definitive statements can be made concerning the nature of the Indus figure and its implications for early Indian religion.

But intriguing as it is, the Indus civilization is by no means the only pre-Aryan culture in India that could have contributed to the development of modern Hinduism. In central India, at Daimabad, about fifty miles east of Mumbai in

Indus seal, *Lord of the Beasts*, 3rd millennium B.C.E. Some scholars believe that this seal shows evidence of religious practices such as yoga that predate the arrival of the Aryan people into India.

Maharashtra state, archaeologists have unearthed the remains of a culture that flourished in the region in about 1200 B.C.E. Here they found another image of a male with an erect phallus, this time cast in bronze, along with metal figures of various animals and representations (on pottery) of wolves or dogs. The high value of bronze in primitive societies suggests the various figures had some religious significance. The religious status of the canine figures is less apparent. Farther south and east at Piklihalb in the modern state of Karnataka, there are remains of a culture of cattle herders. These people kept their herds in communal pens and decorated the rocks near their settlement with pictures of cattle. From this, one might again deduce that the current religious reverence paid to the cow in India is not necessarily of Aryan origin, as has commonly been supposed.

Finally, it is interesting to note the presence of a megalithic culture dating from about 1500 B.C.E. in extreme southern India and parts of northeastern and eastern India, where large stone pillars have survived.[5] These were associated with a variety of burial practices and may originally have served as stone tombs for interring the dead or as repositories for their bones. They may have had other functions as well, as they did in Southeast Asia. Megaliths continued to be erected by tribal peoples until almost the present and it is interesting to speculate about their origins and religious functions. In Southeast Asia the megalithic culture was far more widespread, and the geographical placement of the Indian remains suggests possible influence from that region. Again, however, much work needs to be done before any judgments can be made.

The Vedas: The Earliest Religious Literature of India

To mention Hinduism and the Aryans in the same sentence might be considered a little premature, since the religion of these nomadic immigrants, who entered north-western India sometime between 2000 and 1500 B.C.E., is, as we have seen, only one of a number of the strands in the evolution of Hinduism. But the Aryan religion is the best known of these early strands, and it has traditionally been the practice to refer to it as the principal foundation for the present-day constellation of religious practices that have been collectively termed Hinduism. Indeed, one of the tests used to separate a Hindu from believers of other similar religions, such as Jainism or Buddhism, has been to see whether or not a person believed in the Vedas, the sacred texts of the early Aryans.

The Vedas represent not only the oldest literary remains of Hinduism, but also of Indo-European religion as a whole, and are thus important for the study not only of Indian religion but of the roots of European religion as well. The Vedas were originally written in Vedic Sanskrit, an early form of the Sanskrit language that became the common language of Hindu religious literature up to the present day. Sanskrit is far from being a dead language. In a recent Indian census, some five hundred thousand people listed it as their mother tongue.[6]

The contents of the Vedas, which comprise hymns, folk beliefs, and ceremonial chants, were considered so sacred that they could not be committed to writing, which would have been impossible in any event, given the Aryans' lack of an alphabet. Even during later times, the contents of the Vedas were thought to possess such magical power that they were memorized verbatim and passed from generation to generation continuously until parts of them were finally written down in the third century B.C.E. By that time, four collections were considered to be authoritative: the Rig Veda, the Sama Veda, the Yajur Veda, and the Atharva Veda. These four texts, known collectively as the Samhitas, are considered to be supernatural texts revealed to human beings through the Aryan prophets or poet-priests known as *rishis*.

Of these texts, the oldest is the Rig Veda. Considerable ink has been spilled concerning the dating of this text. Max Müller, the great nineteenth-century Indologist, assigned the first hymns of the Rig Veda to about 1500 B.C.E. However, Indian scholars have long suggested a much earlier dating of these hymns, and some modern European and American scholars have sided with these opinions. It seems likely, given internal linguistic evidence, that an earlier date of 2000 B.C.E. might not be out of line, and some hymns of the collection might be even earlier. In all, the Rig Veda contains 1,028 hymns of varying length, style, subject matter, and prosody, amounting in total to some 10,552 verses. These, in turn, were organized into ten books or *mandalas*. The oldest stratum of the work is found in books two through seven, each of which seems to have been composed by a separate priestly family. Books one, eight, nine, and ten are clearly of later composition.

It would be unwise to think that because the Rig Veda is the earliest of the Vedas it is a primitive work. Many of its hymns are very complex metrically and often subtle in their analysis of the human condition.[7] They clearly represent a tradition that has been developing for some time. Indeed, there is considerable discussion as to whether or not this text originated in India. Certainly large parts of it did, as witnessed by the numerous geographical references to locations in northwestern India. But other references, including those to geographical areas not readily identifiable within the Indian context, and to animals such as the lion, which were unknown to the Indian subcontinent, suggest that at least some of the hymns were composed before the Aryans reached that locale. The text itself was used extensively in the Vedic sacrificial rituals by the *hotri* priest, whose duty it was to invoke the gods by chanting their praises. Consequently, the majority of the hymns found in the Rig Veda are songs of praise to the deities, particularly Indra and Agni. But interspersed with these hymns are prayers for concord, marriage, children, and prosperity as well as magical formulas and rules for performing domestic rituals.

The other Vedas tend to be more or less derivative of the Rig Veda. The Sama Veda consists of various hymns, usually taken from the Rig Veda, that were used by a different class of priests during the sacrifice. Much shorter than the Rig Veda, it has some two thousand verses. Likewise, the Yajur Veda was used by yet another group of priests and contained two thousand **mantras** or specific formulas for recitation at the sacrifice. The Yajur Veda was divided into the Black Yajur Veda and the White Yajur Veda. The White Yajur Veda contains only the ritual formulas themselves, but in the Black Yajur the mantras were accompanied by brief explanations of their meanings and their place in the ritual. This might be seen as the beginning of the extensive Vedic commentarial tradition.

The Atharva Veda appears to have been composed possibly as late as 500 B.C.E. This has caused many Indian scholars to exclude it from the category of revelation enjoyed by the first three Vedas. Attributed to the Vedic sage Atharvan, this work contains six thousand verses of hymns and incantations. Some scholars believe that parts of the text came from pre-Aryan sources. While the Rig Veda was, and remains, the province of a small religious elite, the Atharva Veda seems to have had a much wider audience since it deals with the day-to-day concerns of the average person. Its appeal to local deities and its presentation of simple rituals that did not require the presence of a priest further strengthens this impression. It is in the Atharva Veda, as well as in the last book of the Rig Veda, that we see the beginnings of the Indian philosophical tradition. Here are found a series of speculative hymns on the nature of the universe and the ultimate fate of human beings.

Finally, we should note that in later times considerable subsidiary literature came to be attached to each Veda. First, there were one or two **Brahmanas**, or ritual handbooks, associated with each of the Vedic texts, which began to be composed around 900 B.C.E., and continued to be produced and refined for several hundred years thereafter. Although in the main rather dry and of little interest to anyone not directly involved in the performance of the Vedic sacrifices themselves, some of the Brahmana literature contains the seeds of later Indian thought—for example the Shatapatha Brahmana, traditionally ascribed to the ancient Indian sage Yajnavalkya. Also included in the commentarial literature were the Aranyakas, which attempted to interpret the sacrificial rituals in more spiritual, personal ways. Finally came the numerous Upanishads, discussed in more detail below, which became the foundations of much of later Indian philosophical thought. In addition, there were the Upavedas, which dealt with the technical subjects associated with the Vedas, such as how they should be chanted; and the Vedangas, which outlined practical programs for applying the Vedas to daily life.

The Vedas had such a central place in Hindu thinking that allegiance to them as revealed literature, in some sense at least, is one of the few central dogmas of present-day Hinduism. Believed to have existed throughout all eternity, they and their attendant literature are the only texts termed **shruti**, literally "that which is heard." *Shruti* corresponds approximately to the Euro-American concept of "revelation," communication given directly to humanity by God, which in early India came through the agency of the *rishis*, the inspired poet-priests of the early Aryans, and contained otherwise unknowable information concerning the divine will for humanity.

Although *shruti* does not precisely correspond to revelation, it does carry the same sense of supreme and unquestionable authority. Hindus may discuss *shruti*, debate its meaning, comment on and build philosophical systems based upon it, no matter how widely divergent they may be; but what they cannot do is question the authority of the Vedas or their supernatural origins. This, combined with a belief in the magical power inherent in the words of the Vedic texts themselves, served to ensure that the Vedas were passed down to the present day relatively intact. That is not to say that the meanings of the texts continued to be perfectly understood. The earliest gloss on the Rig Veda, that of Yaska, dating from the sixth century B.C.E., shows that even at that early date the exact meaning of many of the words of the text was becoming obscure.

But the value of the Vedas to modern scholars of Hinduism is undeniable, since they provide the only literary sources we possess concerning the life and thought of the early Aryan immigrants to India. Moreover, they represent one of the primary sources for our understanding of the origins of the peoples who came to dominate Europe and much of South Asia. But there is still considerable debate regarding the origins of the Indo-Europeans, the parent stock of the Aryans. The current consensus is that they originated on the steppes of southern Russia from where they dispersed in all directions, eventually colonizing Europe, parts of the Middle East, and northern India and finally spreading as far as the borders of China. Certainly, the material culture of the Aryans described in their sacred scriptures would seem to bear this hypothesis out. Here, the Aryans are portrayed as a conglomerate of nomadic herding tribes, sometimes fighting common enemies, sometimes each other, who enjoy the simple pleasures of life, such as eating, drinking, and gambling. There seems to have been little puritanism among these early Aryans, and women appear to have enjoyed a marked degree of freedom that their modern descendants in India would envy.

The Aryan peoples, as depicted in Vedic literature, seem to have had an extremely simple cosmology. The heavens were the residence of the major gods—the Sanskrit word for god was ***deva***, literally "the shining one"—and of the souls of those human beings who had lived a good life or made the appropriate sacrifices. Between the heavens and the earth lay the *antarikshaloka*, or "middle heavens," inhabited by birds, clouds, and demigods. Below the earth was the House of Clay, where demons and the spirits of those who had transgressed the natural order dwelled. In contrast to present-day Indian religions, the early Aryans seem not to have believed in a constant series of rebirths but in the concept of a single lifetime. Death brought no judgment, only a dim half life that could be avoided by joining the gods in heaven. A person accomplished this, just as he or she achieved other material goals, such as increase in the herds, the birth of sons, and success in battle, through the medium of the *yajna*, the sacrifice.

The Gods of the Aryans

The gods of the early Aryans were seen as each possessing a particular function known as a *vrata*. These *vratas* were associated with the powers of nature—for example the god Agni's *vrata* was associated with fire, Indra's with rain, and Varuna's with water. The gods worked together to preserve ***rita***, the balance of the cosmos, and opposing them were the ***asuras***, the demons of chaos and darkness from under the earth. The guardian of *rita* in the early books of the Rig Veda is Varuna, the god of the waters. In one version of the Hindu creation myth, found in Rig Veda VI, 7, the waters had been contained by the demon Vritra. Indra, the god of rain and of war, then slew Vritra and released the waters, which were then placed in the keeping of Varuna. This god is described as living in a luxurious palace in the sky to which his agents bring reports concerning events on earth—an image that some scholars believe comes from an Aryan memory of the rulers of the great empires of Mesopotamia that lay to the south of their original homeland. When human beings transgress the natural order, Varuna punishes them with disease, misfortune, or, in extreme cases, an afterlife in the House of Clay. Those who follow the dictates of *rita* enjoy prosperity, many sons, and a joyful afterlife.

Although Varuna is seen as the leader of the gods in the early parts of the Rig Veda, he is soon superseded by Indra, the god of war and rain. Mentioned in some two hundred and fifty hymns, Indra is described in terms that could just as easily have been applied to a human Aryan chieftain. He glories in war, hunting, and feasting. Seated on his war elephant Airavat, he was seen as leading the Aryans and their gods against the dark-skinned original inhabitants of India, the *dasas*. Despite his central importance to Indian religious thought during the Vedic period, the worship of Indra has almost completely disappeared from India in the present day, being replaced by veneration for other gods such as Shiva and Vishnu.

Indra is able to consume tremendous quantities of **soma**, the divine intoxicant of the gods. It is not surprising, therefore, that the rites and sacrifices dedicated to him should have a strong feasting component associated with them. It is interesting to note that the nature of the *soma* on which Indra becomes inebriated has been a subject of considerable debate. *Soma* was ritually consumed at the great Vedic sacrifices where it appears to have imparted supernatural strength and visions of the gods to those who drank it. Many plants have been suggested as being the *soma* plant that was pressed out, filtered through a sheepskin, and mixed with milk before being consumed. The most likely plant is the fly agaric mushroom (*Amanita muscaria*) that grows wild throughout northern Asia. This fungus is used extensively by the shamanic religions of the region, and it seems likely that the Aryans of Central Asia would have been no exception. It would also explain why the clearly hallucinogenic drink of the Vedas was replaced by non-intoxicating substitutes in India, where it is simply too warm for the fly agaric mushroom to grow. Thus, as the Aryans lost contact with their Central Asian homeland, they would also have lost access to the mushroom and needed to find replacements. So powerful was *soma* in the early Aryans' religious imagination that later in their history, after it had ceased to be a central element in the sacrifices, *soma* was elevated to the rank of a god in its own right as god of the moon. The moon, associated with ecstatic behavior and prophetic visions in other Aryan religions as well, was seen to mimic the effects of *soma*.

The only Vedic god who has survived in any recognizable form to the present day is Agni, the god of fire. The second most popular of the gods, with some two hundred hymns dedicated to him in the Rig Veda, Agni manifested himself in many forms to the ancient Aryans. He was the lightning that lit up thunderclouds, the sun, and the fire of the sacrificial altar. As the messenger of the gods who transformed the sacrifice into smoke and carried it up to the gods in heaven, Agni was the intermediary between heaven and earth. The great public sacrifices were not the only sacrifices performed by the early Aryans—there were also the humble daily sacrifices of ghee, or clarified butter, which still take place in devout households—and, as a key participant in these rituals, Agni has retained his status as an important deity—emphasized in the first hymn of the first book of the Rig Veda, where the poet sings in a typical manner:

I extol Agni, the household priest, the divine minister of the sacrifice, the chief
priests, the bestower of blessings.
May that Agni, who is extolled by ancient and modern seers, conduct the gods here.
Through Agni may one gain day by day wealth and welfare which is glorious and
replete with heroic sons.
O Agni, the sacrifice and ritual which you encompass on every side, that indeed
goes to the gods.
May Agni, the chief priest, who possesses the insight of a sage, who is truthful,
widely renowned, and divine, come here with the gods.
O Agni, O Angiras [messenger], whatever prosperity you bring to the pious is indeed
in accordance with your true function.
O Agni, illuminator of darkness, day by day we approach you with holy thought
bringing homage to you,
Presiding at ritual functions, the brightly shining custodian of the cosmic order
[*rita*], thriving in your own realm.
O Agni, be easy of access to us as a father to his son. Join us for our well-being.

SOURCE: Ainslie T. Embree, *Sources of Indian Tradition*, vol i, 2nd ed. (New York: Columbia
University Press, 1988), p. 9

On the whole, the Aryans were on very good terms with all their gods except
Rudra, whose name means "the ruddy one." Rudra was seen as the god of the storm
in its most destructive aspect and was also linked with the storm spirits known as
the Maruts. As such, he was feared and respected rather than admired, as the other
gods were. The few Vedic hymns to Rudra implore him to stay away and cause no
harm, separate rites were also held for him at the great public sacrifices, and he was
not invited to participate at the main ritual feast that concluded the ceremonies.
Conversely, Rudra was seen as the god of medicine and was closely associated with
soma. All this ambivalence is very reminiscent of that associated with Shiva in the
present day, and many scholars see in Rudra the prototype of this later god. In support of this claim in the *Shatarudiya* section of the Yajur Veda, numerous epithets are
given to Rudra, such as Nilakantha, Pashupati, and Nilagriva, which are later associated with Shiva.

The Foundations of the Traditional Hindu Social Order

From the foregoing we can see that, as was the case with most other early peoples, the
Aryans tended to see the gods as larger versions of themselves. Thus, they reasoned,
the gods would respond to the same incentives as themselves, namely praise and the
giving of gifts. From these two sources grew the increasingly complex Vedic rituals
that marked this first phase in the development of Hinduism. The earliest sacrifices
must have been relatively simple affairs conducted by the sacrificer himself in the
open air. Today, Hinduism is associated with magnificent temples, but this is a fairly
late development. The Vedic sources make clear that originally the rituals required
little more than some open space and the building of a small, simple fire altar.

But as time went on, the rituals became more complex. An interesting result of this
was the development of the religious specialists who still dominate Hindu religious
life today, the **Brahmins**. However, it should be noted that there were other religious
specialists as well, notably the *munis*, silent sages who were particularly associated

with Rudra, and not with the other gods of the pantheon and their sacrificial cults. These *munis* appear to have followed a form of religion that was at odds with the sacrificial cult of the Brahmins and which has been termed the religion of the Shramanas or Ascetics. Some scholars have seen this tradition as the roots of the ascetic-meditative aspect of Hinduism that flowered just after the end of the Vedic period. Certainly, the term *muni* came to be used to designate holy men in the non-Hindu religions that arose later in India. It should be noted that the association of the term Brahmin with the priesthood seems to be a relatively late development, and occurs only once in the Rig Veda in a very late hymn (X, 90). But the Brahmins were only one of several divisions in Aryan society, and these divisions seem to be only a replication of a feature of Indo-European society that was to be found in Ireland, early Greece and Rome, the Germanic and Scandinavian regions, and, indeed, wherever Indo-European speaking peoples settled. Some academics have argued that this social division was a reflection of Indo-European religious thinking.

We must note that the Aryan social order was somewhat unique to India. Whereas in other Indo-European societies there were three social groups, in India there were four. At the top of the social order were the religious specialists, the Brahmins, followed by the rulers/warriors—the **kshatriyas**. The general mass of the peoples, from which came the farmers, artisans, and tradespeople, were designated as **vaishyas**. Finally came a fourth class that had no formal existence in any other Indo-European community: the **shudras** or servant class. Georges Dumezil theorized that the three-class society was normative, with the fourfold division of Indian society being a local adaptation of the older tripartite system.

Dumezil also postulated that each of the three Indo-European classes represented a vital function of society, which was reflected in Indo-European myth and religion. The Brahmin or priestly class was associated with rulership and the preservation of cosmic and secular order. The warriors held the monopoly on physical force and hence on rulership, while the common people were the producers that sustained the other two classes. Dumezil then connected the classes and their functions with the mythology of the proto-Indo-Europeans. Among other things, he postulated that there was conflict from time to time between the various classes of Aryan society, particularly between the priests and warriors, who each saw themselves as the paramount leaders of society. This conflict was certainly present in India and was to manifest itself in religiously interesting ways in later times. Each of these classes had its distinctive features—including what animals were appropriate for sacrifice and what color was associated with their particular group. This linkage with colors may be the origins of the Sanskrit term for the class system, *varna*, which earlier theorists of religion interpreted in terms of a social differentiation based on race, with the darker Dravidian peoples being relegated to a lower social stratum. Current research has tended to support the non-racial origins of the system, yet it must be noted that skin color is still a factor in social interaction in India.

The Structure of the Vedic Sacrifice

Originally, Aryan religion seems to have been practiced primarily in the home. We read of rituals such as the *darshapurnamasa* performed on the days of the new and the full moon. Likewise every four months there was the *caturmasya* ritual. These sacrifices were inexpensive and priestly involvement was minimal. Indeed, even today, much of the daily ritual that undergirds Hindu devotion is performed at the altar in the home, not in the temple. In addition, there are a number of what one might describe as rites of passage described in the Vedic literature. A wedding hymn shows that the Aryans viewed marriage as a serious religious rite, complete with many features which are still found in the Hindu marriage ceremony. The dead may have been cremated, as in modern Hindu practice, but there seem to be references to other types of funerals as well. It is possible that only the wealthy were burned. Although we have no direct evidence, it is likely that memorial ceremonies honoring the ancestors were performed, perhaps akin to the present-day *shradda* ceremony. It is also likely that other ceremonies linked to daily life were enacted but, falling outside the compass of the Vedic literature, were not recorded for posterity.

From humble beginnings, the Vedic sacrifice grew to become the center of Aryan religious life. As it did so, its complexity increased. Originally performed by the individual who would benefit from its enactment, the sacrifice was soon the exclusive province of the Brahmins. The primary figure in the ritual was the *purohita*, literally "the one who is placed in front," whose job it was to supervise the entire conduct of the sacrifice. The *purohita* was usually responsible for all the public religious functions of the tribe. He ensured fertility, success in war, and the general good fortune of the group through sacrifices and other rituals. He was assisted at the sacrifices by the *ritvij* whose job it was to ensure that the smallest details of the ritual were performed correctly. Likewise the *hotri* priest was responsible for the correct chanting of the complex hymns associated with the ritual. These main priests were assisted by many others in such sacrifices as the yearly *agnishtoma* ritual designed to cleanse people of their transgressions, the great royal ceremonies of the *rajasuya* coronation sacrifice, and the *vajapeya* sacrifice for the rejuvenation of the king's power. These were grand affairs involving everyone in the tribe, not just the ruler on whom they focused. Since most of the great sacrifices involved public feasting, they presented the tribe with an opportunity to renew the bonds of their corporate identity and to discuss matters of tribal importance.

The grandest of all the great public royal sacrifices was undoubtedly the **ashvamedha** or horse sacrifice, which is spoken of throughout the Vedas and in other early religious literature. Horses held a special place in the Indo-European imagination, and the importance of the horse is clearly seen in all their successor cultures. The importance of the horse sacrifice in India seems to have increased as the powers of the rulers increased, since it was intimately associated with the exercise of political power. The sacrificial ceremony itself was only the last stage in a complicated ritual drama that took almost a year to perform.

In the year before the actual sacrifice various rituals took place and, in the spring, four Brahmin priests selected a stallion from the king's herd. Preliminary rituals were performed, then the stallion was freed to wander the land at will. The horse was followed by some four hundred warriors whose duty it was to prevent it from associating with mares, as well as by a hundred other horses, who acted as a sort of honor guard. It was also the warriors' duty to prevent anyone from interfering with the stallion's progress. Since all of the land that the stallion walked upon was considered to become the property, either literally or symbolically, of the king sponsoring the rite, neighboring rulers had an interest in preventing the stallion from entering their territory. There are instances on record where the performance of the horse sacrifice led to war between kingdoms.

Finally, the stallion was returned to the royal capital for the ultimate ceremony, which lasted three days. During this time, the stallion pulled the royal chariot and performed other ritual acts. There was a large-scale sacrifice of various animals that led up to the climactic smothering of the stallion. But the ceremonies did not conclude with the death of the horse. The creature's corpse was covered with cloths and, beneath them, the king's chief queen performed ritual intercourse with the dead animal, to the accompaniment of obscene remarks from the assembled priests and nobility. Finally, the horse was dismembered into three portions, each dedicated to a different god.

As the size of the kingdoms of India grew, the *ashvamedha* sacrifice was performed less and less frequently, although there are occasional records of its performance up to 1000 C.E. The same may be said of all the public sacrifices of the Vedic period. As they increased in complexity and expense, so too did they become more and more inaccessible to the lower levels of Aryan society. At the same time, the tribal structure of this society was breaking down as the beginnings of complex state formation proceeded. For this and other reasons, the religion of the Aryans began to change as well. We shall consider the nature and impact of these changes in the next chapter.

Website References

1. www.cofah.utsa.edu/drinka/pie/pie.html discusses the origins of the Indo-European languages and culture.

2. The Indus Valley culture in general is discussed at www.harappa.com/har/har0.html

3. For further discussion of the Indus Valley script, see www.harappa.com/script/maha2.html

4. A good overview of what an Indus Valley city was like is found at www.harappa.com/har/moen0/html

5. lab2.cc.wmich.edu/~zagarell/meg.htm presents a good discussion of another early Indian culture.

6. For a brief introduction to Sanskrit, see archarya.iitm.ac.in/sanskrit/lessons/lessons.html

7. For a literal translation of the text of the Rig Veda, see www.sacred-texts.com/hin/rigveda/

CHAPTER THREE

◆

The Emergence of the Hindu Wisdom Tradition

As Vedic religion began to evolve into the complex of interacting religious traditions that we now collectively term Hinduism, its literature began to evolve and expand as well. But the Vedas always retained in the Hindu religious mind a special place that has never been superseded. They became a special class of literature all to themselves that, as we have seen, was termed by Hindu theologians *shruti*, "that which is heard." This reflected the belief that the Vedas were revealed literature on a par with the Christian Bible or the Muslim Qur'an.

The Upanishads

Attached to the four Vedas were their commentarial literature, of which the most important texts for the development of the later traditions were those known as the Upanishads. The word Upanishad comes from a Sanskrit compound that means "to sit near," and it reflects the early Indian practice of sitting near the feet of a revered teacher, or guru, who passed on the oral teachings that he had received from his own teachers. The Upanishads generally took the form of dialogues between individuals and their teachers and probably reflect the original teaching method that produced them. It is interesting to note that some of these texts may well predate the Socratic dialogues of Plato, the father of Euro-American philosophy, whose ideas and pedagogic methods closely parallel them. The Upanishads are clearly a later, more developed phase of the philosophical speculation that we can see originating in the later Vedas.

In the tenth and last book of the Rig Veda, we read that:

There was no nonexistence; and there was no existence at that time. There was neither the mid-space nor the heaven beyond. What stirred? And in whose control? Was there water? The abyss was deep.
Neither death nor deathlessness was there then. There was no sign of day or night. That One breathed without wind through its independent power. There was nothing other than it.
Darkness there was, hidden by the darkness, in the beginning. A signless ocean was

everything here. The potential that was hidden by emptiness—that One born by the power of heat. (X, 129:1–3)

SOURCE: Embree, *Sources of Indian Tradition*, p. 21

But even the author of this examination of the origins of the world doubted what could be known about such beginnings, as the conclusion of this hymn shows:

Who really knows? Who shall here proclaim it?—whence things came to be, whence this creation. The gods are on this side, along with the creation of this [world]. So then who does know whence it came to be?
This creation, whence it came to be, whether it was made or not—he who is its overseer in the highest heaven, he surely knows. Or if he does not know . . . ?
(X, 129:6–7)

SOURCE: Embree, *Sources of Indian Tradition*, p. 21

This hymn demonstrates an early interest in Hinduism focusing on that which we would now call philosophy. This is evident in later Vedic material as well. There are a few isolated philosophical references in the Brahmanas and in the later Aranyakas, but the true flowering of this phase of Indian religious development is in the Upanishads.

It must be kept in mind at the outset that the Upanishads are a diverse set of texts with a variety of viewpoints produced over an extended period of time. There are considered to be some 108 principal Upanishads, but that number could well be doubled if other texts that claim to be of equal authenticity were included. The date of the principal texts is debated, but scholars would generally put the initial composition of the most philosophically important Upanishads between about 900 and 200 B.C.E. However, so-called "Upanishads" continued to be produced long after the classical period, and there is even one mentioning London and the British presence. Barring prescient knowledge of the future (which the text claims), it is evident that this latter text was composed after the Europeans reached South Asia in the seventeenth century.

Despite their differences, the genuinely early Upanishads, such as the Brihadaranyaka, the Chandogya, the Taittiraya, and the Mandukya, display many common themes that were to become established principles in Indian religious thought. First and foremost of these themes was their reinterpretation of the formal sacrificial cult of the Brahmins. As such, the Upanishads represent the beginnings of the second great strand of Hinduism—that of the pursuit of *jnana* or knowledge. By this is meant not knowledge in the sense of knowing facts such as the boiling point of water or the earth's distance from the sun, but rather a deep, intuitive, existential knowledge of Reality. Such understanding cannot be communicated in words, but must be won through extreme effort. The goal of the Upanishads was not to intellectualize about Reality but to discover its true nature and the methods by which it could be known, thus winning liberation from the cycle of life and death.[1]

Samsara and Karma: The Foundations of the Wisdom Tradition

The Upanishads also contain the first references to some of the most fundamental of Hindu religious concepts. Prominent among these is *samsara*, the belief in an endless cycle of human reincarnation. Reincarnation is so much a part of modern Indian religious thought, being found not only in Hinduism but in Buddhism,

Jainism, and Sikhism as well, that people assume that it has always been integral to Hinduism. But this is clearly not the case. The early Aryans do not show any signs of having believed that the soul is constantly born and reborn into an endless series of bodies and lives. Instead, they seemed to have seen this life as the only one that there is. Indeed, as we have seen, they were extremely vague as to what came after this life and generally concentrated their efforts more on the enjoyment of their present existence rather than on securing any future benefits after death. Some sacrifices did aim at securing a place for the sacrificer in "heaven" after death, but the general mass of the Aryan peoples seemed to have situated their life goals in a more worldly context. This included the pursuit of wealth (*artha*), love (*kama*), and an ethical and appropriate lifestyle (**dharma**).

Between the end of the period of the composition of the Vedas and the beginning of the period of the composition of the Upanishads, the orientation of the Aryans appears to have altered radically. It now appears that reincarnation became the accepted understanding of the human fate after death. But why? Some scholars believe that the Aryans adopted this idea from the Austric or Dravidian peoples they came in contact with as they expanded farther into the Indian subcontinent. Others think that reincarnation arose spontaneously from the observation of the cyclical natural world of India, with its monsoon climate and abundant native flora and fauna so different from the austere Central Asian plains from where the Indo-Europeans had originated.

Whatever the case, the Indian understanding of reincarnation was not a source of comfort. Far from rejoicing in the prospect of an endless series of lives, the Indians abhorred the idea. To them, life was far more pain than pleasure. Even pleasure was seen as a type of pain, since it was temporary and threw the underlying pain of life into even starker relief when it disappeared. Again, one might speculate on the origins of this pessimistic strand in Indian religious thought. Perhaps it was the result of social change. The old Aryan tribal social system was disappearing at this time and being replaced by a much more impersonal state system in which the individual had far less access to his leaders than had previously been the case. Perhaps population pressures and the general change from a herding to an agricultural economy led to a more precarious settled life style that exposed the individual to greater psychological pressures than before. Whatever the reason, the rather bleak doctrine of reincarnation spread rapidly during this period and became universal in Indian thought. Consequently, to the three original human goals of achieving *artha*, *kama*, and *dharma* was added a fourth, **moksha**—liberation from the cycle of life and death.

Fortunately, the concept of reincarnation was somewhat mitigated by another idea that became universal during this period: **karma**. The word literally means "work" or "action," but the idea it represents is somewhat more complex. In the earlier Hindu thought, karma had referred to the "action" of performing the ritual sacrifices. In the emerging wisdom tradition, karma took on an ethical meaning, referring to the belief that all actions had inevitable and inescapable results. Hence good actions had good results, and bad actions had bad ones. What was especially interesting about karmic actions, however, was that they need not bear fruit in this life alone. Rather, they could and did have effects in future lives as well. They were seen as being particularly important in determining one's next rebirth. Thus those born in a low **caste** could, through diligent attention to the duties imposed by their station in life, be reborn in a higher caste or in better economic circumstances. While some might see this as a form of social control, it could equally be seen as source of hope and encouragement for people whose current condition offered them little of either.

Brahman and *Atman*: The Immortal Constituents of Reality

It was on these foundations that the Upanishads based their subsequent analysis of reality, which centered on two fundamental concepts. The first of these was **Brahman**, the universal principle that was held to undergird and support Reality. The second was **atman**, the individual soul. These concepts complemented each other, and it is only through understanding their nature and interrelationship that we can understand the Upanishads' doctrine of liberation from the cycle of birth and death.

Brahman, the foundation of both the seen and the unseen world, being by its very nature beyond the realm of human language, was something that the ancient Indian philosophers had considerable difficulty in discussing. Consequently, they tended to resort to description by negation. A example of this is the description of *Brahman* in the Mundaka Upanishad (I, 1.6):

> What cannot be seen, what cannot be grasped,
>   Without color, without sight or hearing,
>   Without hands or feet;
> What is eternal and all-pervading,
>   extremely minute, present everywhere—
> That is the immutable,
>   which the wise fully perceive.

SOURCE: Patrick Olivelle (trans.), *The Early Upanishads* (Oxford: Oxford University Press), p. 437

Brahman completely filled and animated the sensible world. In the Chandogya Upanishad, the sage Uddalaka observes to his son Shvetaketu, while showing him the infinitesimal seed of the fig tree, "My son, from the very essence of the fig, which you do not see, this great tree exists." After having the boy dissolve salt in water and taste it, the sage points out that, like the salt, *Brahman* pervades all things in the visible world. He concludes, "It is the true self, Shvetaketu, and that you are."

However, despite sharing many attributes with the Judaic, Islamic, and Christian concepts of a supreme being, the Indian concept of *Brahman* differs significantly as well. Perhaps the greatest of these differences is the Indian belief in the impersonality of *Brahman*. The monotheistic religions see ultimate Reality as being personal, i.e. a supreme being or Person, while the Indians saw it as an impersonal force or set of natural forces. Thus, for example, where the monotheistic religions hold that the world originated through the conscious willed act of God, the Indians saw creation as a spontaneous manifestation of ultimate Reality.

The other great concept of the Upanishads was that of *atman*. In the Chandogya Upanishad (XIV, 2–4) the nature of *atman* is clearly outlined:

> This self (*atman*) of mine that lies deep in my heart—it is made of mind; the vital functions (*prana*) are its physical form; luminous is its appearance; the real is its intention; space is its essence (*atman*); it contains all action, all desires. All smells, and all tastes; it has captured this whole world; it neither speaks nor pays any heed ... it is smaller than a grain of rice or barley ... but it is ... larger even than all [the] worlds put together ... It is *brahman*. On departing from here after death, I will become that.

SOURCE: Olivelle, *The Early Upanishads*, p. 209

Again, one can see important similarities between this idea and that of the soul in monotheistic religions. Both ideas envisage every human being as possessing an immortal component that transcends the perishable body that contains it. But here again there are important differences. In the Indian tradition, the idea that the soul is unswayed by the emotions and needs of the body was paramount. In the monotheistic religions, the soul is seen as being ruled by passion. Not so for the Indians, who held the soul to be above the turmoils that beset the physical body. Moreover, the Upanishads mark out a new direction for the Indian religious quest. The goal of religious experience now became the search for the soul and *Brahman*, the ground from which it sprang. Increasingly, *atman* came to be identified with *Brahman*. The relationship between the two was likened to that between a fire and a spark from that fire. The two shared identity, in that they were both in themselves fire, but they were also unique in that they were also physically separated and thus independent entities.

What separated the individual from knowing his or her true self, and thus achieving liberation, was illusion (**maya**)—the illusion that *Brahman* and *atman* differed. This led to ignorance (**avidya**) of the true nature of Reality, which in turn led to wrong actions and the inevitable karmic consequences that flowed from them. All in all, this was the chain of events that bound individuals to the endless, painful cycle of birth and death (*samsara*). The way to sunder that chain was through proper understanding (*jnana*) of Reality. But such deep "gut level" understanding was difficult to attain, and so a series of methods was developed to assist the seekers of truth in their quest. Their goal was to penetrate appearances, delve into the depths of the human being, and eventually reach the core of that being wherein resided the ultimate and eternal bliss that was the true ground of Reality. But still it may be asked: how is this to be done? The practical aspects of how to accomplish the theoretical goals of the teachers of the Upanishads occasioned considerable debate. However, two main strands of practice emerged fairly early in the development of the tradition.

Tapas, Asceticism, and Liberation

The first of these practices was the use of asceticism. Asceticism (from the Greek verb *askein*, meaning "to train"—as for an athletic contest) is a common practice in all of the world's religions. Every religion believes that the physical body in some way impedes spiritual development. In some forms of Christianity (under the influence of Hellenistic Greek philosophical thought), this was seen as being a result of the inherent sinfulness of the physical world. While not all Christians, then or now, accepted this dismal vision of the natural world, it was to have a very significant effect on Christian thinking and practice for many centuries. Asceticism was to have important effects on Hindu thought as well, but it proceeded from a very different set of first principles.

In Hinduism, the natural world was not seen as sinful so much as inadequate. Consequently, there was never any question of atonement for sin in Hindu asceticism. Rather, asceticism was seen as a means of overcoming an obstacle to the realization of the true nature of the Real. The development of this doctrine rested on earlier theories of the nature of the sacrifice. Briefly, these centered on the concept of *tapas* (literally "heat"). The source of this idea seems to be very old, certainly stretching back to early Vedic times. *Tapas* was seen as the energy generated by sacrificial ritual and the force that moved the universe and influenced the cosmic balance. It was not a great step to see this energy as analogous to the energy generated by the practices of the dedicated ascetics through the "sacrifice" of bodily comforts.

Ascetic practices that generated *tapas* were many and varied. At one end of the scale were those practices that Hinduism held in common with other religions, the foremost being celibacy. Sexual abstinence has always been seen by the world's religions as an absolute prerequisite for serious religious development. The layperson might combine religion and sexuality, but never the seriously devoted seeker of the Absolute. Why should this be so? Perhaps it was the very strength of the sexual drive itself, the indulgence of which produces pleasures both more immediate and more intense than the more subtle delights of religion. More likely, however, it was the fruits of sexual intercourse—namely children and all the duties and joys associated with them—that were seen as the major impediment arising from the gratification of the sensual urges. All this results in a much closer association with the world, quite the opposite of the severing of worldly ties advocated by most religions. It can of course be argued that a closer identification with the divine results from a closer identification with creation, but, as classically understood, it was the opposite that was seen as the greater good, in Hinduism as elsewhere. Just as abstaining from sexual activity was seen as essential, so too was abstaining from other bodily pleasures. The true seekers after the divine were enjoined to eat little and to take no joy in whatever they did eat. Likewise, they should minimize their sleep and fill their hours with religious exercises and, in some traditions, but not the Hindu one, by engaging in manual labor.

The emerging Hindu tradition advocated these practices as well. However, it went even further than this, based on its understanding of the place of *tapas* in the quest for religious liberation. *Tapas* had come to be seen as a sort of "spiritual rocket fuel" that could, if generated in sufficient quantities, "blast" the *atman* out of the cycle of life and death, thereby reuniting it with *Brahman*. Nor were the uses of *tapas* limited solely to the great matters of liberation. *Tapas* could also be employed for much more mundane ends. It could compel the gods to grant its possessor a variety of boons, including material wealth and worldly power. Unlike most other traditions, including later Hinduism, purity of motive and right intentions were seen as playing little part in the accumulation of *tapas*. It was sufficient simply to perform the appropriate actions, which worked on the principle that *tapas* behaved somewhat like water: if one dammed up its flow of energy through physical austerities, it would accumulate and could then subsequently be used as the motivating force in the production of tangible results.

The "damming" of *tapas* was accomplished through denial of the body. In point of fact, the more severe such denial was, the more effective it was seen to be in generating *tapas*. Thus Hindu followers of these practices controlled the mind through **japa** (the repetition of a name of God or a short mantra) or religious singing (*bhajana*). They controlled their breath through the practice of *pranayama*. Most significantly, they controlled the body through fasting, lack of sleep, and other physical austerities of an often ferocious nature. This type of Hinduism has worked its way into the Euro-American popular imagination through literature and films. The depiction of a scantly clad, brown figure in a turban lying on a bed of nails is the direct heir of the Hindu concept of *tapas*, although purveyors of this image have no idea of its philosophical underpinnings.

Nor are such ascetic practices simply a legacy of the past. Even today in India there are followers of these ancient ideas. Ascetics can still be found who never sleep lying down, who have stood on one leg for years, or have kept one arm elevated until it has withered away, and so forth. These practices are not only painful, but necessarily need to be practiced over a long period of time. The Hindu gods did not take lightly the attempts of mere mortals to compel them into action. There are numerous stories concerning the gods' efforts to prevent mortals from achieving their supernatural goals. This was usually done by tricking the ascetic into abandoning his practice, even if only temporarily. If this was accomplished, then all the practitioner's previous effort counted for nothing—all his accumulated *tapas* immediately dissipated and he would be required to start again at the beginning. But some thinkers in the Hindu wisdom tradition apparently did not see asceticism as an end in itself. While they agreed with the idea that asceticism had practical value in the search for wisdom, these thinkers held that such practices were only useful as a preparation for deeper experiential inquiry into Reality. For them, this was to be accomplished through meditation.

Meditation: Liberation Through Knowledge of Reality

In the Upanishads, there is the story of Indra, the king of the gods, going to the sage Prajapati in order to find out the nature of truth. Prajapati has the god purify himself for thirty-two years and, at the end of this period, consents to teach him the nature of the self. At first, Indra is shown a vision of the physical body, but he is not so foolish as to identify it with the true self. Next he is shown the self in dreams, that is to say, the self that exists in the mind. Once again, he realizes that this is not the true self, since the mental self can suffer pains, doubts, anxieties, and so forth that are incompatible with the nature of the true self. Then Prajapati, who is skillfully leading Indra toward the true teaching, tells him that the self exists in the state of dreamless sleep. But Indra objects that this would be the same as death, which clearly it is not. Prajapati finally reveals that there is a fourth state that transcends all the previous states, and that it is here that the true self resides. Here all illusionary duality ceases. To reach this true self is to reestablish the identity of the individual *atman* and *Brahman*. This is done through meditation.

Many people in the West have tended to view all meditation as being the same, namely the entering into a state of withdrawal from the sensible world. This does not appear to be what actually takes place in meditation. Studies done in the 1970s on meditators in a variety of traditions show that there are some very real physical differences in brainwave patterns between the various styles of meditation. For Hindus, meditation is envisioned as a systematic withdrawal of the senses from interaction with the material world. While this might appear to the uninitiated as constituting unconsciousness, the Hindu would argue that in fact it entails entering into greater consciousness. What meditators encounter when they withdraw their minds from the turmoil of the senses is consciousness in the higher sense of the word. To withdraw the senses from the limited temporal world is to open the mind to the greater world of the truly Real.

So much for the theory: how was this done in practice? We know from Buddhist sources that there were numerous teachers of meditation at the time of the Buddha in about the sixth century B.C.E., since the Buddha lists the various teachers under whom he studied before perfecting his own meditative method. But for our present purposes, it is sufficient to note certain broad themes as mentioned in what is perhaps the most important of the texts of the ascetic tradition, the Yoga Sutra, the classic work of Patanjali. The first of these techniques is *pranayama*, the control of the breath. Throughout human history, the breath has been associated with life. Early man did not need a medical degree to realize that when people stopped breathing they were dead. The association of breath and life was thus not a difficult step to take. It is not surprising that the early Hindu seekers after wisdom believed that to control the breath was to harness the energy that was the ultimate source of life. This control of the breath consisted of suppressing the natural rhythm of breathing. The point of the exercise was to slow the pace of breathing until respiration almost ceased. Some modern practitioners of this ancient art have been scientifically observed to slow their breathing to the point where it is almost imperceptible. While this is an impressive physical feat, its spiritual value is perhaps questionable. The second major technique of Hindu meditation was the withdrawal of the senses, or *pratyahara*. As the Yoga Sutra (II, 54) puts it, "When the senses do not have any contact with their objects and follow, as it were, the nature of the mind ..." As we have seen, this is taken to mean that the mind is no longer cloaked in illusory sense data. This, in turn, leads to the crucial third step of the process, *samyama*.

In the Yoga Sutra, *samyama* is described as being composed of three elements. The first of these is *dharana*, the fixation of the mind on one thing, often a particular part of the body. As anyone who has tried to meditate knows, this is much easier said than done. The nature of the mind is, as the early Indian philosophers in all traditions observed, in constant flux. Consequently, concentrating on anything single-mindedly is extremely difficult and takes considerable effort. Next comes *dhyana*, the deepening and elaboration of that effort, by which objects other than that which is the focus of concentration are eliminated from consciousness. Finally, there is **samadhi**, the complete identification of the knower and the known, where all duality and separation ceases. Once the full state of *samadhi* is reached, then liberation is achieved.

Samnyasa and the Hindu Stages of Life

As we have noted, it became apparent to Hindu religious thinkers very early that the serious pursuit of religious goals was incompatible with the demands of normal life. Consequently, it was held that for people truly to undertake the religious quest, they would have to renounce (*samyasa*) their prospects of family life. Then as now, there were a certain number of persons for whom such a sacrifice was acceptable. But for the majority of the Indian population such a sacrifice was either undesirable or unfeasible due to family responsibilities. Did this mean that most people were excluded from the religious pursuits? The response to this question was the development of an idealized Hindu life pattern in which people could both fulfill their obligations to society through earning a living and raising a family, while also pursuing religious goals. The key to the proper conduct of a human life lay in this concept of the four stages of life, each with its appropriate functions and goals, lived out within the framework of the caste system described in the previous chapter. This overarching model for human existence was known as **varnashramadharma**.

The first of these stages of life was **brahmacharya**, the stage of the celibate student, which lasted up to about the age of fifteen. During this stage, the individual was expected to study the arts and crafts appropriate to his caste and station in life. For Brahmins this meant study of the scriptures and the rites and rituals at which they were expected to preside. For the warriors, it was the study of martial arts and statecraft. For the *vaishyas*, studies consisted of learning their family trade—be it farming, pottery making, tailoring, or whatever—and the same applied to the *shu-dras*. The *brahmacharya* stage was followed by the **grihastya** stage, that of the house-holder. This stage, which lasted to about the age of forty or forty-five, was the period in which the individual married, had children, and played an active role in society. During this stage, far from being frowned upon as it was in later stages of life, a person's behaviour was considered praiseworthy if he was successful in acquiring material wealth for his extended family. Nor was it seen as wrong for him to enjoy the sweet-tasting pleasures of the world, such as food and sex, so long as they were enjoyed discreetly and in moderation.

It was in the third stage, **vanaprastha**, that individuals began to turn away from worldly pleasures and pursuits in order to concentrate on religious interests. Having performed the appropriate rituals during the householder stage, they were now able to leave these duties to their families and concentrate on their own spiritual development. Typically, they withdrew to a secluded part of their family homes or, less often, to the edge of the forest. There they engaged in religious practices designed to achieve liberation from the cycle of life and death, or at least ensure a better rebirth in the next life. This is not to say that they completely cut themselves off from the rest of their families. They still interacted with them, particularly their grandchildren, but they maintained a certain psychic distance which ideally fostered their religious development. The last stage of life, that of **samnyasin**, was not one that many people embraced. This meant renouncing one's family and leaving home completely to wander as a mendicant.

From these early beginnings in the late Vedic period of c. 1000 B.C.E., the Hindu wisdom tradition continued to evolve as people began to consider the implications of the ideas contained in the Upanishads as well as other Hindu texts. Also, like their counterparts in the West, Indian thinkers began to elaborate and build on these ideas and, as a result, six principal schools of philosophy developed in India. These are still studied and utilized today.

Website References

1. www.digiserve.com/mystic/Hindu/Upanishads/index.html gives a number of translated examples from the Upanishads.

CHAPTER FOUR

◆

The Six Schools of Indian Philosophy

The philosophical study of religion in the ancient world was not universal, since only Greece, India, and China can be said to have evolved philosophical systems of religious investigation in the strict sense of the word. Nor, truth to tell, was philosophical speculation of great interest to anyone other than a very small number of practitioners in any particular tradition. But it is important to examine the philosophical arguments of the various traditions in order to gain the deepest possible understanding of the intellectual principles that shaped them, and which, in turn, they helped to shape. This is particularly true in the case of India, which was in the forefront of applying philosophical thought to the analysis of the human condition.[1]

Indian philosophy is traditionally seen as being divided into six principal schools of thought known as the *Shaddarshanas*, the Six Viewpoints. These are further grouped into three pairs of complementary schools: Samkhya and Yoga; Nyaya and Vaisheshika; and Mimamsa and Vedanta. Of these schools, only Vedanta could be said to have any substantial influence in modern-day Hinduism, but all these systems have made significant contributions at one time or another to the development of Hindu philosophy. As with all matters to do with chronology in India, there is considerable difficulty in establishing the relative antiquity of each of these schools. However, internal evidence seems to suggest that the earliest of the six schools was Samkhya, and it is with this school that we shall start.

Samkhya and Yoga

As with all religious philosophy in India, Samkhya was primarily concerned with the practical goal of liberation from the cycle of life and death. Growing out of the wisdom tradition, it held that this liberation was to be achieved through existential knowledge of Reality. The core text of this tradition, the *Samkhyakarika* of the philosopher Ishvara Krishna, observes in verses one and two that "from torment by three-fold misery the inquiry into the means of terminating it" consists of "the discriminative knowledge of the evolved, the unevolved and the knower [as] the means of surpassing all sorrow." There is still considerable debate over the origins of the

Samkhya school. Some scholars believe that it had its origins in the teachings of the Upanishads, while others think that it represents the culmination of philosophical speculations that were taking place independent of the Vedic tradition. Whatever the case, many scholars believe that Samkhya was the first distinct Indian philosophical school to emerge.

Samkhya displays some marked differences from the Vedic tradition. It was purportedly founded by the philosopher Kapila in the fourth or fifth century B.C.E., although the *Samkhyakarika* can be dated no earlier than the third century C.E. But, unlike the monistic traditions of the roughly contemporaneous Upanishads where *Brahman* and *atman* are seen as essentially the same, Samkhya is profoundly dualistic. It is the understanding of the interaction of the two fundamental building blocks of Reality, **purusha** (spirit) and **prakriti** (matter), that forms the basis of Samkhya, the "enumeration" or "counting" of the results of this interaction. The sum of this analysis is that Samkhya sees the visible world as the product of an organic evolutionary process in which matter and spirit become intertwined although not interpenetrating.

Central to Samkhya's vision of the religious quest was its concept of causality. Samkhya had a very orderly worldview: things did not just happen, but were the result of causes either proximate or remote. This idea of causes, called *satkaryavada* in Samkhya, saw Reality as a constantly evolving interactive fabric of interconnected causes and effects. As proof of this, the great Samkhyan philosopher Ishvara Krishna claimed in verse nine of his *Samkhyakarika* that "the effect (of an action) exists before the operation of (its) cause: a) because of the nonproductivity of non-being, b) because of the need for material cause, c) because of the impossibility of all things coming from all things, d) because something can only produce what it is capable of producing, and e) because the effect is nondifferent from the cause" (*Samkhyakarika* 9).

We might wonder why so much emphasis is placed on the interconnection of causes and effects. The answer to this question lies in the Samkhyan presupposition, perhaps based on the doctrines of the Upanishads, that all Reality is ultimately the same despite the seemingly endless variety of forms and attributes. If, as the Samkhyans contend, everything stems from a single ultimate cause, and effects are in fact identical to the causes from which they are produced, then Reality—which stems from the interaction of a single undifferentiated primordial material (*prakriti*) with an original cause—must be a unified whole.

But what, then, is the nature of that single cause which supposedly triggered the evolution of the current plurality of material forms? Samkhya's answer to this question is that first of all *prakriti* must possess the necessary capacity to transform itself. This capacity resulted from *prakriti* being composed of three strands known as **gunas**. The three *gunas* were termed *sattva*, *rajas*, and *tamas*. The different proportions of each of them in all material forms accounted for the differences between the forms. *Sattva* was seen as being buoyant and shining—and was the essence that brought *prakriti* into existence and caused it to continue in existence. *Rajas* was the principle of activity that initiated change within matter, while *tamas* was the principle of stolidness and inertia that produced equilibrium. But these *gunas* only provided the possibility of change and transformation, not the transformation itself.

In order to understand the primary cause of transformation, we need to consider another key concept in Samkhya—*purusha*. This, according to the *Samkhyakarika* (19), is "the opposite of the unmanifest *prakriti* [and is] witness, isolated, indifferent, a spectator, and inactive." By this is meant that *purusha* was: (a) never observed (being itself the observer); (b) free from, rather than bound by, *prakriti*; (c) not moved by pleasure or pain; (d) unmoved by the ebb and flow of events; and

(e) eternal and unchanging. In all ways separate from *prakriti*, *purusha* nevertheless "illuminated" matter in the same way that light illuminates a pool of water. Another analogy is that *purusha* is reflected in *prakriti* in the same way that a rose is reflected in a mirror. In both cases, it is an illusion to think that the illumination or reflection is the thing itself. Herein lies the Samkhyan understanding of the nature of bondage to the cycle of life and death—the mistaken belief that *purusha* is *prakriti*. It is, simply put, ignorance of the true nature of Reality.

But it is the interaction of *purusha* and *prakriti* that is the first cause for the transformation and evolution of the material world and results in the appearance of *buddhi* (intelligence). This in turn gives rise to self-awareness and thereby creates the apparent separation of one being from another. This process of evolution eventually leads to the development of the material world as we experience it. The essence of this whole process lies in the Samkhyan view that *purusha* somehow upset the primordial equilibrium of the *gunas* that make up *prakriti*, thus initiating the motion that resulted in the differentiation of *prakriti*. So much for the Samkhyan analysis of the origins and nature of the material world, but how is one to be liberated from it? This is something that does not concern Samkhya *per se*. It was left up to the thinkers of the Yoga school to take Samkhyan philosophical theory and put it into practice.

Yoga is another Indian thought system that appears to be of great antiquity. It was traditionally held to have been founded by Patanjali, author of the Yoga Sutra, also in the fourth or fifth century B.C.E. However, all the extant manuscript copies of the Yoga Sutra are from a later time—about 200 B.C.E. Nevertheless, the ancient origins of many yogic practices are indisputable. The Tejobindu Upanishad contains much of the Yoga Sutra word for word, and some scholars see in the few remaining seals of the Indus Valley civilization tantalizing suggestions of later yogic themes. Suffice it to say here that elements of Yoga have a long history in Indian religious thought, as witnessed by their inclusion in the Upanishadic literature. However, it is Yoga Sutra, the core text of the formal philosophical school, that forms the classical foundation of the school and not its Upanishadic antecedents.[2]

Patanjali opens the text with a concise definition of his goal, "Now the exposition of yoga. Yoga is the restriction of the fluctuations of the mind stuff (*citta*). Then the [self] abides in itself. At other times, it takes the same form as the fluctuations [of the *citta*]" (I, 1–4). By *citta* Patanjali meant a person's mental processes which he thought had the ability to give form to matter. Patanjali believed that if the fluctuations of these mental processes could be stilled, then the true and unbound nature of *purusha* could be discerned—in much the same way as one could see the bottom of a pond whose waters were not muddied up by constant movement.

The goal of realizing the true nature of *purusha* was complicated by a number of factors that promoted bondage to the world. The first of these was ignorance (*avidya*), a result of the self's tendency to want to forget its own nature and consequently remain in *prakriti*. The second was the urge to maintain an ego (*asmita*) distinct from other egos. The third was *raga*, the desire for involvement with, and possession of, objects of experience and the pleasures associated with them. The fourth factor was *dvesha*, the aversion to anything that might threaten the bodily self. This, taken with *raga*, resulted in a pushing and pulling of the individual that caused constant mental agitation. Finally, there was the fifth force, *abhinivesha*, the will to live forever, or what we would now term the existential fear of death.

The good news from the yogic standpoint was that these hindrances to liberation from material existence could be overcome. Patanjali proceeded to set forth an eight-step program by which this liberation could be achieved. The first step was moral restraint (*yama*). This served as the foundation upon which all subsequent efforts were founded. There were five moral restraints, but all flowed from *ahimsa* (non-harming), the first and most important one. *Ahimsa* is the radical expression of compassionate love for all creation as manifested in the complete avoidance of causing harm to anything. From *ahimsa* arose the restraint of avoiding speech that would hurt others, of not taking that which did not belong to you, of eliminating the desire to possess things, and the avoidance of sexual activity that would harm other people.

These negative prohibitions were buttressed by, and found their perfect expression in, the five spiritual observances (*niyama*). The first of these was to observe purity in thought, word, and deed. To purify one's self was to cut off the roots of bad actions and the karmic consequences of such action. Next came the virtue of being satisfied with whatever one possessed—be it much or little. The third spiritual observance was to practice asceticism, thus establishing self-control through self-denial. Fourth came study. This meant that the yogic practitioner must be open both to instruction and to following the directions of his teacher and the texts of his tradition. Finally, Yoga called for devotion to one or more of the Hindu gods and goddesses as well as reverence for one's teacher. This reverence for the divine is a distinct feature of Yoga that is not found in the atheistic Samkya doctrine with which it is associated.

On the dual foundations of *yama* and *niyama*, a practitioner could begin the actual religious practices of the Yoga school that constitute the remaining six of Yoga's eight steps. The third and fourth steps were the **asanas** (postures) and *pranayama* (breath control). Aiming to restrain the body and bring its natural processes under control, both these practices probably developed out of Shamanism and earlier Indian speculation concerning the sources of the life principle. By the time of Patanjali, however, they had become established as spiritual techniques grounded in Samkhyan thought. The various physical postures were seen as ways of controlling the body and, in some later schools of Yoga, ways of channeling and utilizing life energies. Breath control, on the other hand, was seen as a very effective technique for entering meditative states.

Padma-asana. The *asanas* were believed to unlock spiritual energy that could be used both for acquiring magical powers and for achieving release from the cycle of life and death.

In this 18th-century miniature, we see a yogi practising an exercise, attended by a servant. One of the goals of yoga is to withdraw the senses from the physical world to perceive the immortal inner *atman*.

पद्मासन२

The fifth step in yogic practice was *pratyahara* (withdrawing the senses). By detaching one's self from the objects of the material world, one could calm the mind and achieve the sixth step, *dharana* (concentration). This in turn gave rise to the seventh step, meditation on the nonduality of reality (*dhyana*). Finally, one could aspire to the eighth and final step on the yogic path, *samadhi*. This was the stage at which all movement of the mind ceased and the true nature of *purusha* could be discerned. At this point, the yogi was freed from the cycle of life and death, achieving *moksha*—true and final liberation.

Nyaya and Vaisheshika

India has always been regarded primarily as a religious culture, and rightly so. But it would be both unfair and untrue to suggest that Indian philosophers did not give any consideration to the physical world around them and dismissed it out of hand as unimportant. No philosophical stance developed in Euro-American philosophy is without its counterpart in Indian thought, up to and including atheism, existentialism, and materialism. If later Indian civilization chose to reject these ideas, it was not out of ignorance, but as a considered choice of values. That these ideas exist and flourish in Euro-American society does not point out the poverty of Indian intellectual life so much as shedding light on modern Euro-American philosophical priorities and concerns. Just as Thales and other early Greek philosophers such as Pythagoras, Democritus, and Heraclitus spent much of their time considering the natural world and its beginnings, so too did many Indian philosophers. From their deliberations emerged the Indian schools of epistemology and metaphysics known as Nyaya and Vaisheshika.

Although Nyaya has had a more lasting influence on Indian thought, the foundation on which it constructed its system of logic is more readily apparent if we begin our inquiry with Vaisheshika. The age of Vaisheshika, as is the case with all the schools of Indian philosophy, is debatable. The core text of the school, the Vaisheshika Sutra attributed to Kanada, is thought to predate Buddhism, but the most complete exposition of the system is found in the Dashapadartha Shastra, a text that dates from the sixth century C.E. In essence, Vaisheshika saw the material world as being composed of eternal and indivisible atoms (*anu*) of four primary substances—earth, air, fire, and water. There was also a fifth element, ether (*akasha*), which is eternal, inert, and not capable of joining with any other element. These atoms combined with one another according to both natural laws and *adrishta*, the will of Ishvara (God). These different combinations of atoms could be analyzed through the examination of their specific qualities, which were divided by Vaisheshika thinkers into six categories.

The first of these categories was substance, which in Vaisheshika terms formed the necessary substratum for all other qualities and actions. Vaisheshika distinguished nine different kinds of substance: earth, water, light, air, ether, time, space, self, and mind. Substance was known either by direct perception through the senses or else by inference from direct perception—a viewpoint entirely consistent with the modern scientific method. Thus time was inferred by the fact that a person directly experiencing the here and now could also conceive of the future. Hence what lies between the present and the future must be time; and, since it cannot be reduced to anything else, time must itself be a substance in its own right. So too the same principle applies to the other substances.

The next Vaisheshika category is quality—what medieval European scholastics termed "accidents." These included color, smell, sound, number, happiness, size, distance, lightness, fluidity, and so forth. Linked to this category was motion, the third category, by which the Vaisheshika philosophers used to explain the changes that substances underwent. The similarities in things were attributed to universals, the fourth category. In contrast to this stood the fifth category—particularity. Finally, there was the sixth category—inherence. This was used to analyze how the various categories of perception cohered in a given object as a whole. Outside the six categories stood a seventh—nonexistence—which was held to necessarily exist on the premise that negation was possible, as it obviously was.

While Vaisheshika emphasized the kinds of things that existed as objects of knowledge, Nyaya emphasized the nature of the acts of knowing such objects. The key text of the tradition, the Nyaya Sutras attributed to Gautama (a later philosopher not to be confused with the person of the Buddha), may well have their roots as far back as the fourth century B.C.E. The starting point of Nyaya is the self, since knowledge implies a knower. Following Vaisheshika, the Nyaya school saw the self as a distinct substance which was endowed with knowledge, feeling, and volition. It was self-evident to the followers of Nyaya that the self must be separate and distinct from all other objects perceived by it. Further, since the self is a unique substance—consciousness being only a quality of that substance—consciousness is not the self *per se*. For the followers of Nyaya, liberation entailed the elimination of this consciousness that they believed bound the self to other objects. Only then could the self exist as the self without confusion.

As with all the schools of thought under consideration, Nyaya had a program for achieving liberation. For Nyaya, this involved investigating what could, in fact, be definitively known. By knowledge, the Nyaya philosophers meant knowledge arising from the contact of the senses with objects of knowledge. All other forms of knowledge (**pramanas**) must, therefore, have at least some basis in physical perception, even if at some degree removed. But how was perception to be tested in relation to reality? We know from modern psychology that the evidence of the senses is not always to be trusted. Nyaya's answer to this problem lay in experiential practice. A bowl of a white granulated substance in a restaurant might look like sugar, but only by experiencing it through taste, would it be possible to say definitively that it was sugar and not salt. Although perception (*pratyaksha*) was the basic form of knowledge for Nyaya, the school also recognized three other forms of knowledge: inference (*anumana*), analogy (*upamana*), and verbal testimony (*shabda*). Inference could be of three types. The first was from cause to effect; the second from effect to cause; and the third from common characteristics. Analogy was knowing something from its similarity to a known thing. Finally, verbal testimony depended on the word of a trusted authority on something that transcended one's own experience.

For the Nyaya school, inference could only be established through the application of syllogistic reasoning. A Nyaya syllogism had five components—as opposed to the three used in Aristotelian logic. These were: (1) a starting proposition to be proved; (2) the experience that established the proof; (3) the example that illustrated the proof; (4) corroboration of the proof by a perceived fact; and (5) the inference that could be made from this perceived fact (which should correspond to the initial proposition). So, for example: (1) the hill in the distance is on fire (even though I can see no fire on the hill); (2) this is because I can see smoke; (3) wherever there is smoke, there is fire, e.g. a campfire; (4) the hill in the distance has smoke and smoke is always accompanied by fire; so (5) the hill in the distance is on fire.

Comparison was based on similarity of a known object to an unknown one. But verbal testimony stood somewhat outside the orbit of the other three sources of knowledge. This was a result of Nyaya's desire, shared by the other five classical philosophical schools, to retain the Vedas as valid sources of religious knowledge. For testimony to be a valid form of knowledge, three criteria needed to be met. First, the person delivering the testimony had to be absolutely honest and reliable. Next, the person needed to actually know, through one of the other three forms of knowledge, that to which he or she was testifying. Finally, the hearer needed to understand exactly what was being heard.

So much then, for Nyaya and Vaisheshika. But neither they nor Samkhya and Yoga became the intellectual basis for modern Hinduism (although they continued to exert considerable influence on Indian thought). That distinction belongs to the last two of the *Shaddarshanas*—Mimamsa and, most especially, Vedanta.

Mimamsa and Vedanta

Mimamsa and Vedanta take the Vedas as their starting point and accept as a given the revealed nature of its text and its authority as scripture. Of the two, Mimamsa is the older school and is often referred to as Purva (Old) Mimamsa to differentiate it from Uttara (New) Mimamsa, another name for Vedanta. Of all the six philosophical schools of India, Mimamsa and Vedanta come closest to what would be termed "theology" in Euro-American thought. Both of them initiate their inquiry into the nature of Reality on the basis of terse, almost aphoristic core texts. For the Mimamsa school this was the Mimamsa Sutra, which is attributed to Jaimini and dates from about 200 B.C.E. But it was the commentaries on this text, such as those of the later philosophers Prabhakara and Kumarila Bhatta, that brought Mimamsa philosophy to its fullest flowering. The essence of Mimamsa was the pursuit of *dharma*. This is a very slippery term that carries with it a multitude of meanings in Sanskrit and the Indian languages descended from it. Mimamsa, however, had a clear definition of what *dharma* meant: for Jaimini, as for subsequent Mimamsa philosophers, "*dharma* is that which is indicated by Vedic injunctions for the attainment of the good" (Mimamsa Sutra I, 1–2).

For the followers of Mimamsa, despite their belief in a supernatural order, this foundational assumption of the goal of philosophy did not necessarily imply the existence of a supreme being. Indeed, there are Mimamsa philosophers who have constructed elaborate arguments *against* the existence of God. Rather, this school held to the idea of the eternal existence of the world and thought that it was the performance of Vedic sacrifice, or more specifically the *apurva* or essence generated by such sacrifice, that was the only real permanent agent for sustaining the cosmos. Like those of all Indian schools, Mimamsa philosophers preached liberation from the world and, for them, this was intimately associated with the act of sacrifice, the object of which was to attain heaven. By this was meant some vague and ill-defined form of liberation whereby the individual no longer assumed a physical form. Since the Vedas insisted that this was accomplished through the agency of the sacrifice, Mimamsa turned to this as the main subject of its study. Consequently, the appeal of Mimamsa, by its very nature, was limited mostly to Brahmins.

The same cannot be said for Vedanta. This school, which has universal applicability to the religious life of a broad spectrum of Indian society, has come to form the philosophical underpinnings, in one form or another, of most contemporary

Hindu thought. As with Mimamsa, Vedanta has a core text that is more important as a vehicle for commentarial literature than for any intrinsic merit of its own. This is the Brahma Sutra of Badarayana, which is supposedly a commentary on the Upanishads. The problem with the 550 aphorisms of this text, some of which are only a word or two in length, is that they are often literally incomprehensible without a commentary. Of the numerous commentaries that have been written on the Brahma Sutra, three stand out—those of Shankara, Ramanuja, and Madhva. Each of these has, in turn, given rise to a distinct subschool of Vedanta, although the radical differences of interpretation espoused by each of their founders would in most other circumstances have resulted in the establishment of totally new and separate philosophical schools. It is best to start our inquiry with Shankara, both because his was the earliest of the Vedanta schools and because the thought of his two great successors was in large part a reaction to his philosophical system.

Shankara was born, as were Ramanuja and Madhva, in southern India. The date of his birth and the length of his life are matters for scholarly debate, but it is certain that he was flourishing in about 800 C.E. Like his successors, he founded his philosophy on the essential unity of Reality, relying on such Upanishadic aphorisms as "*atman* being known ... everything is known" (Chandogya Upanishad VI, 2.1); "there was only Being at the beginning, it was one without second" (Mundaka Upanishad II, 2.11); and "this self is the *Brahman*" (Brihadaranyaka Upanishad II, 5.19). Since the Upanishads were for Shankara integral parts of the Vedas, and thus revealed truth, he felt no need to question their primary hypothesis, namely that all of Reality was one. This is the philosophical stance known in Euro-American thought as monism. If the truth of Reality had already been revealed in the Upanishads, then Shankara's task, as he saw it, was to explain this truth philosophically, and to show how it was not contrary to either reason or experience.[3]

Shankara began his analysis with the proposition that *Brahman* is the Reality that underlies the appearances of the empirical physical world. But *Brahman* is not these appearances *per se*: it is something other than that which can be apprehended by the senses or the mind. Consequently, Shankara dismissed Nyaya, Vaisheshika, and Mimamsa on the grounds that all these systems held sense data, or reasoning based on such data, as being necessary to prove or disprove the nature of Reality. In Shankara's opinion, Reality (*Brahman*) could only be "proved" by the testimony of scripture, or by direct experience gained through yogic practices. It followed, then, that all the perceptual data of the senses must be inaccurate, since it did not disclose true Reality. It was, in fact, all illusory.

Of course this viewpoint directly contradicts the evidence of the senses. Human beings perceive a world of multiple objects that are in constant flux and affected by change. Shankara denied both the real existence of these multiple objects and their changing—since *Brahman* is eternal and unchanging. How did he justify such a view? Shankara did not dispute the *appearance* of change. Rather he argued that it does not constitute a true reality, drawing an analogy with things experienced in dreams. These things may seem real to the dreamer at the time, and they may have a physiological effect or even prompt the dreamer into action. For example, a person terrified of snakes might dream of one and have very real physical fear reactions as a result. But this experience does not make the dream snake real. Likewise, argued Shankara, objects in the material world may appear real, but when sited within the higher reality of *Brahman*, they are seen to be unreal. Hence our experience of the pains and pleasures of the material world is merely an illusion, a distortion of *Brahman*, the true Reality. In the final analysis, Reality is a unified whole and it is this perspective that has led to Shankara's system being termed **Advaita** or Nonduality.

Despite Shankara's powerful logic, many of his successors felt uneasy with his summary dismissal of the perceived world. One of these later Vedanta philosophers was Ramanuja, who lived in the eleventh century C.E. He attempted to reconcile Shankara and the evidence of the senses. His school, Vishishtadvaita—Qualified Nondualism—did not see *Brahman* as distinct from the empirical world of the senses, but rather viewed the world as part of *Brahman*, although *Brahman* transcended the world that it contained. For Ramanuja, *Brahman* was an organic unity of consciousness and the various objects apprehended by it. As he wrote in *Vedarthasangraha* (81):

> The supreme *Brahman* is the self of all. The sentient and the nonsentient entities constitute Its body. The body is an entity and has being only by virtue of its being the mode of the soul of which it is the body. The body and the soul, though characterized by different attributes, do not get mixed up. From all this follows the central teaching the *Brahman*, with all the nonsentient and sentient entities as its modes, is the ultimate.
>
> SOURCE: S. S. Raghavacar (trans.), *Vedarthasangraha* by Ramanuja (Mysore: Ramakrishna Math, 1956), p. 97

Given Ramanuja's primary analogy—that *Brahman* permeates and animates the material world but is not limited to it—he necessarily had to concede the reality of matter in its own right. But, following Samkhya, he held that this matter had no form, motion, or purpose in its own right. It acquired these characteristics through its relationship to *Brahman*.[4]

The final school of Vedanta is the one that most closely mirrors the basic theology of the world's monotheistic religions. This is the **Dvaita**, or Dualism, of Madhva, who lived in the thirteenth century C.E. For Madhva, the experienced material world and *Brahman* are completely separate and distinct. He based this viewpoint on two basic facts. The first was that of the senses. The second was the philosophical concept that since individuals were, by definition in Indian thought, caught up in suffering and endless reincarnation, then they must be separate from *Brahman*, since *Brahman* neither suffers nor is incarnated. However, Madhva was reluctant to give up the traditional Vedanta emphasis on the unity of *Brahman*, and so held that although everything is separate from *Brahman*, all depend on it for their existence.[5]

As we have seen from the brief summary above, many of the principal Indian systems of thought such as Samkhya, Yoga, Nyaya, and Vaisheshika were essentially atheistic in their worldview, as were many branches of Mimamsa, at least in the sense of denying a Supreme Being possessing what we would term individual personality. It is only Vedanta that is uncompromisingly theistic in the sense of positing a Supreme Reality that subsumes all other realities (although Indian philosophers held serious doubts about Shankara's Advaita Vedanta). Yet, at present, all these systems except Vedanta have been reduced to the status of quaint curiosities of little interest to any except a few scholars. Why did Vedanta triumph as a practical system of thought while the others faltered?

One part of the answer to this question is that Vedanta offered a truly integrated intellectual approach to the fundamental questions that interested Indian philosophers. It united in a much more organic way than had previously been the case the metaphysical, epistemological and theological aspects of the Indian philosophical enterprise. At the same time, it was sufficiently flexible to allow for differences of opinion, and to combat the other philosophical schools that were vying for the Indian intellectual's allegiance. Vedanta, without demanding an unreasonable adherence to revelation, provided a seamless explanation of the world and of the human condition. At the same time, it allowed for the expression of the various understandings of the Divine that had constituted the Hindu religious spectrum.

The various schools of Vedanta provided a rationale for the various modes of Hindu worship. Although particularly weighted toward the wisdom tradition and faith (the sacrificial aspects of the religion being better explained by the Mimamsa school), Vedanta was able to philosophically justify most types of religious practice in the way that the more rigorously philosophical schools such as Samkhya, Nyaya and Vaisheshika could not. Only Yoga offered an alternative practical program, and it lacked the intellectual suppleness of Vedanta. In the end, it was Vedanta that most effectively combined practice and theory within the Hindu religious matrix.

But the real answer to this question of why Vedanta triumphed over the other schools of Hindu philosophy most probably lies in essential human nature. For the vast majority of human beings, relationship is the centre of our existence. But for relationship to exist, there must be another being with whom to relate. It would follow from this that human beings can relate most comfortably to an Ultimate Reality that is not a vague philosophical principle, but rather a "person" in the broad sense of the term. Indian religious thought was open ended enough to allow for a plurality of expressions of the nature of the Divine. But only Vedanta philosophy could truly accommodate the human need for seeing the Divine in personal terms. The many ways in which this unquenching thirst for the personification of the Divine found other expressions in Indian popular culture is the subject that will concern us in the next chapter.

Website References

1. For Indian philosophy in general, see **www.philo.demon.co.uk/Darshana.htm**

2. A translation of the Yoga Sutra can be found at
   www.digiserve.com/mystic/Hindu/Yoga/index.html

3. **www.advaita-vedanta.org/avhp/** has information on Shankara and on Advaita Vedanta in general.

4. Information on Ramanuja and links to some of his writings can be found at
   home.att.net/~s-prasad/ramanuja.htm

5. **www.dvaita.net/** and **www.dvaita.org/index/shtml** discuss Madhva and Dvaita Vedanta.

CHAPTER FIVE

◆

Hindu Devotionalism

So far, we have focused on the historical and philosophical expressions of the Hindu tradition and, to a lesser extent, on its ritual and social nature. But religion, if it is to transcend the merely formal and become a living force in its milieu, must speak to the hearts, not just the minds, of its practitioners. This is as true for Hinduism as for any other tradition, and it is therefore no surprise to find that the vast majority of present-day Hindus interact with the divine on an emotional rather than a purely intellectual level. This emotional approach is the third great strand of Hinduism and is known as **bhakti** or faith. It naturally follows that the idea of faith implies faith in someone or something, and one of the few facts that the average Euro-American knows about Hinduism is that it has a huge number of gods and goddesses.[1]

But here, again, the natural human impulse toward personal relationship is at work, producing a sort of natural discrimination. Just as it is not possible for people to have complete and utter faith in everyone they meet, so too is it impossible to have such faith in a multitude of heavenly beings. Devout Hindus tend to place their faith in a particular personal god (*ishtadeva*) or, at most, a small group of related gods. This has resulted in a sort of functional monotheism. Thus over time, Hinduism has reduced the number of gods that are actually invoked by its adherents to a very few. Moreover, under the influence of Hindu philosophical thought, the idea that all gods and goddesses are simply manifestations of a single divine principle has grown into a generally accepted truth. But this divine principle, if it is to be apprehended in an effective manner, must be personalized. In modern India, two modes of personality are generally ascribed to the divine: one is termed Shiva, the other Vishnu.[2]

The Worship of Shiva

Although Vishnu commands the loyalties of the majority of Hindus—about 60 percent of India's Hindus as opposed to about 40 percent for Shiva—we will begin our discussion of this aspect of Hinduism with Shiva for a variety of reasons. The first is that Shiva is clearly the older entity, but exactly how old is a matter of considerable debate. Some scholars would see in the seals of the Indus Valley civilization the first sparks of Shaivite iconography. As we have already seen, there are depictions of a human figure with a buffalo head seated in what some have seen as a yogic posture and surrounded by animals. Since Shiva is strongly associated with Yoga in the Indian tradition, and since one of his epithets is Pachupati, the Lord of Beasts, this interpretation seems credible. We might be able to decide the matter once and for all if we could decipher the Indus script, since these seals carry an inscription that might reveal the name of the figure portrayed, but at present this is impossible.

Whether or not the worship of Shiva dates back to the cities of the Indus, most scholars doubt very much that he has an Indo-European provenance. Some would connect his origins with the Tamil peoples of southern India, since his name appears close to a Tamil name meaning "the graceful one." Nevertheless the Aryan worship of Shiva seems to have an ancient provenance, since he is associated with the god Rudra found in the Vedas. However, Rudra was not a god that the ancient Indo-Europeans of India venerated willingly, but was a god to be feared. His portion of the sacrifice was granted grudgingly and the rituals associated with it were performed well away from the main sacrificial site. Rudra was the god of the storm wind and the darkness. But he was also the god of magic and medicine. As a result, there developed a profound ambivalence toward him. He could heal or kill, save or destroy, apparently without rhyme or reason. This ambivalence continues to the present day among devotees of Shiva. He is at once majestic and terrifying, ascetic and erotic, benevolent and despotic. In fact, it is these polarities and dichotomies that define Shiva in the minds of his worshippers.

Post-Vedic references to Shiva abound. He is mentioned in Panini's early work on Sanskrit grammar, and the earliest Greek accounts of India by Megasthenes in the third century B.C.E. speak of Indian worshippers of Dionysus who were possibly Shaivites. Likewise, there are numerous references to Shiva in the great Indian epics—the *Mahabharata* and the *Ramayana*. The *Mahabharata* contains several hymns to the god as well as references to four distinct sects of his worshippers. The *Ramayana* also contains numerous myths concerning Shiva. The more modern sources of Shaivism are the Shiva Puranas and the Agamas. Although themselves of relatively recent composition, they contain much ancient material.

The earliest group of organized Shiva worship may appear in the Atharva Veda. Here are described the Vratyas, a sect who seem to fall outside of the Brahmanic traditions of the dominant Aryan religion, although they are depicted in terms that suggest that they were ethnically Aryans. Many hymns in this section use names for the deity associated with this group that are later applied to Shiva. Similar undercurrents can be seen elsewhere in the Vedic literature. The emergence of a positive Shaivite philosophy may be seen in the Shvetashvatara Upanishad, where internal evidence seems to indicate a relatively late date of composition. This text propounds a theology of Shiva as *Brahman*. It holds that "the immortal and imperishable Hara [Lord] exercises complete control over the perishable *prakriti* and the powerless *jiva* [soul, spirit]: the radiant Hara is one alone." Essentially Advaitin or nondualistic in nature, the same Upanishad teaches that "one attains peace on realizing that self-effulgent, adorable Lord, the bestower of blessings, who, though one, presides over all the various aspects of *prakriti* and into whom this universe dissolves, and in whom it appears in manifold forms" (VI, 11).

But without a doubt, the most beloved expressions of Shaivite literature are the hymns of the Nayanmar saints of southern India that eschew philosophical speculation in favour of absolute and wholehearted adoration of the deity. The best known of these saints was Manikkavacakar, the author of the *Tiruvacakam*, in which he sings (XXV, 8–10):

I shall raise my hands in prayer to you [Shiva]; I shall clasp your holy feet and call your name.
I shall melt like wax before the flame, incessantly calling out, "My Beloved Father."
I shall behold your effulgent glory. In joyful bliss shall I join the society of the true devotees.
Then I shall look up to hear you say with your beauteous lips: "Fear not!" The assurance of your all-embracing love alone sets my soul at ease and peace.

SOURCE: Ratna Navaratnam (trans.), from *Tiruvacakam* (Mumbai: Bharatiya Vidya Bhavan, 1963), p. 181

Manikkavacakar and the other Nayanmars did far more to rekindle the flame of devotion among the common people of southern India who had left Hinduism for Jainism and Buddhism than all the philosophical treatises ever written.

The wealth of Shaivite mythology and devotionalism also found expression in art. Perhaps the earliest representation of the deity was the linga. The origins of this image are clearly phallic, with the image representing the erect male organ and its associated power to create and destroy. But it would be unfair to characterize modern Shaivites as worshipping the phallus. Just as the cross, originally a Roman symbol of torture and execution, has been transformed by its association with Christianity into a symbol of hope and redemption, so too the linga has been transformed for devout Hindus into a symbol of the formless yet ever-present nature of the divine. This is not to say that anthropomorphic images of Shiva, such as the famous dancing Shiva, do not abound, but they are seen as incomplete, though devotionally useful, representations of something that defies representation. Likewise, elaborate and ornate temples have arisen—in much the same way as the great cathedrals and mosques have farther west—to house the elaborate rituals of the god and to give form in stone to the impulses of the human heart.[3]

Shaivite Philosophy and Religious Groups

As previously mentioned, the worshippers of Shiva seem to have organized themselves into religious fraternities at a relatively early date in Indian religious history. This may have happened as early as c. 1200 B.C.E. if the references to the Vratyas in the Atharva Veda are interpreted as referring to such groups. It is not surprising, therefore, that a number of different interpretations of who Shiva was and how liberation could be achieved developed as well. The earliest school of what we might call Shaivite theology was that of the Pashupata. This sect was founded by Lakulin, who may have been a real person living in the second century B.C.E. The Pashupata order, while primarily interested in questions of ritual devotion to the god, also furnished the religion's first coherent analysis of the human predicament. According to the principle text of the sect, the Pashupata Sutra, Shiva taught five subjects to human beings: (1) *karya*, the condition of human bondage; (2) *karana*, the nature of the lord and liberator (i.e. Shiva himself); (3) yoga, the way to liberation; (4) *vidhi*, the forms of ritual worship that led to liberation; and (5) *duhkhanta*, literally "the end of suffering" or liberation. The very name of the sect, Pashupata, came from their understanding of the nature of reality: human beings are in bondage to the cycle of life and death, just as an ox (*pashu*, literally "beast") is in bondage to its owner (*pata*) by the noose (*pasha*) of illusion, unrighteousness, attachment, and ignorance. Freedom is achieved through the grace, or freely given help, of Shiva and

Shiva within the cosmic linga, Tamil Nardu, South India, Chola period, c. 900 C.E. The linga is the symbolic representation of Shiva. It may have had its origin in phallic worship, but this aspect of its symbolism is no longer relevant to modern Hindus.

through the worshipper's own efforts. These included the rhythmic repetition of mantras such as the names of Shiva (*japa*), singing hymns to the god (**kirtana**), ascetic practices, ritual worship, and meditation.

More elaborate was the theology of the most important of the Shaivite schools, Shaiva Siddhanta ("the final truth of Shiva"), which attempted to synthesize the various strands of Shaivite devotion into a coherent intellectual system. To do so, it took as its textual foundation works that were primarily from southern India. These included the twenty-eight Shiva Agamas and the poetic works of the Nayanmars, the great popular religious poets of the Tamil country, such as Appar, Jnanasambhandar, Sundaramurti, and Manikkavacakar. Preeminent among these texts was the *Shivajnanabodha*, which was much discussed by later writers. The essence of this group's thought is similar to that of their Pashupata predecessors. Humans are eternally caught in the noose of ignorance if not saved by Shiva, who was conceptualized as the Supreme Reality, possessing independence, purity, self-knowledge, omniscience, freedom from sin, benevolence, omnipotence, and blissfulness. He alone possessed *sat* (being) and *cit* (consciousness). The Shaiva Siddhanta denied the Vaishnavite doctrine of the incarnation of divine **avataras**, since this existence involves elements such as sin and death that are contrary to the essential nature of God. He might appear in an illusory bodily form to teach selected individuals out of his great love for humanity, but he could never be truly incarnated in matter that was anything other than illusion.

Bondage to this world was a result of three factors: *maya*, karma, and *anava*. *Maya* (illusion) was essential to the very nature of the changing, insubstantial world. It was, by definition, illusionary and insufficient. Karma was the iron law of cause and effect which demanded that all actions must have their consequences. Finally, there was *anava* (literally "veil"). This was what has been termed "congenital ignorance" and comes closest to the Christian concept of original sin. The very nature of the world is such that any created thing must necessarily be bound to it. Its components are *moha* (delusion), *mada* (intoxication with the pleasures of the senses), *raga* (passion), *vishada* (depression), *shosha* (dryness or the inability to connect with the Supreme Reality), *vaicitriya* (distraction or lack of attention), and *harsha* (improper happiness). Only by Shiva's gracious love can these indigenous delusions be overcome.

Liberation came from realizing the essence of Shiva (*shivatva*), which lay at the core of all human beings but was concealed as a result of sin. Four elements were seen as necessary for liberation: *vidya* (knowledge of the truth), *kriya* (ritual actions devoted to Shiva), yoga (asceticism), and *carya* (a moral life style). Far from despairing at being born a human being, followers of the Shaiva Siddhanta school rejoiced, because they believed that only as a human being could one achieve liberation by worshipping Shiva, contemplating him with the mind, praising him with the mouth, and exerting the body in his service. The result of these activities was bliss in this life and final liberation from the cycle of life and death in the next.

Of the northern schools of Shaivite theology, the best known is Kashmir Shaivism and its great proponent Abhinavagupta. Today a school in decline, it was in former centuries a driving force in Shaivite thinking, having been called Shaiva-Advaita as a result of its similarities to the philosophical system of Shankara. Like that school, Kashmir Shaivism sees liberation as proceeding from the realization that all reality proceeds from a single divine source, in this case Shiva. The goal of the school is to reaffirm one's identity with the divine Reality. The experience of such unity while still in the body was called *samavesha*, and it was achieved through much the same program as described for the other Shaivite schools above. In trying to convey the nature of this experience, Abhinavagupta wrote, "It is Shiva himself of unimpeded

Devotees of Shiva worshipping the linga. Ritual worship is one of the most common ways to express devotion to the deity. Such devotion to the deities is the predominant mode of religiosity in modern India.

will and pellucid consciousness who is ever sparkling in my heart. It is his highest *shakti* [power, often symbolized as a woman] herself that is ever playing at the edge of my senses. The entire world gleams as the wondrous delight of pure I-consciousness. Indeed I know not what the sound 'world' is supposed to refer to."[4]

The most recent branch of Shaivism is Virashaivism—the "heroic Shiva religion." Founded in its present form by the southern Indian sage Basava in the twelfth century C.E., its roots seem to stretch farther back in time. The Virashaiva school developed a strong missionary ethos and a vigorous social reform agenda. Its followers do not recognize the caste system, and they are considered economically and socially progressive. Their practices include burying rather than burning their dead. Philosophically Vishishtadvaitan in outlook, they are easily recognizable by the linga that they wear around their necks and which they hold to contain the real presence of Shiva.

Devi, the Great Goddess

Of perhaps equal antiquity with the worship of Shiva is the cult of Devi, the Great Goddess. Both a regional and a universal figure in Hinduism, the goddess goes under many names, of which the most widespread are Durga and Kali.[5] The violent iconographic presentation of these two figures in Indian art caused considerable misunderstanding when they were first encountered by representatives of the European colonial powers, and consequently serious study of these extremely important Hindu religious figures did not match early interest in Shiva and Vishnu. However, Durga and Kali, as well as other local expressions of the divine as female, still play a tremendous role in popular piety. Indeed, in some areas of South Asia, such as Bengal and Assam, the worship of the Great Goddess is the predominant form of religious devotion.

The mythology associated with Devi comes from a number of sources, such as the Devi Bhagavata Purana, and sections from other Puranas. But the most famous source of this material is the Devimahatmya section of the Shaivite Markandeya Purana. Here, in section 81, the god Brahma addresses the goddess and says to her:

> By you this universe is borne, by you this world has been created. By you it is protected and you, O Devi, shall consume it at the end . . . You are above all, the supreme Mistress. You are the shakti, the power of all things, sentient and others, you are the soul of everything. Who is capable of praising you, who has given form to all of us, to Vishnu, Shiva and myself?

The Goddess Bahuchraji, Gujurat, western India, 20th century. Many goddesses are very local in nature, and may have followers in only a small area of India. However, this does not diminish their worshippers' devotion.

Here we see the deeply held conviction that the goddess is the creator of, and superior to, all other aspects of creation. This superiority is most clearly exemplified in the myth of Durga and Mahishasura, the buffalo-headed demon who had wrested the dominion of heaven away from the gods. Faced with defeat and the dissolution of the created order, the gods band together to manifest Durga from their own essences and arm her with their own distinctive weapons. She defeats the armies of the demons and kills Mahishasura, thereby saving creation. After this, Durga promises always to protect the world from evil and prophesies that she will be repeatedly incarnated in a variety of guises. The Devimahatmya, which contains the account of this epic battle, is recited every year at the great Bengali festival of Durga Puja.[6]

While the worship of the Great Goddess in her various forms, often referred to collectively as Shaktism, usually followed the patterns of the worship of the other gods, the religious devotion known as Tantra grew up in association with the goddess. The texts that chronicle this devotion—and which are also known as the Tantras—first start appearing in the fourth or fifth century C.E. and are initially associated with Buddhism. Followers of Tantra could be devotees of Vishnu, Shiva, or Devi, although the goddess tended to be the deity predominantly associated with this form of worship. The Tantras identified two modalities for the practice of religious ritual. The first, the "right-handed worship" (*dakshinacara*), involved worship of Devi in the approved Vedic manner. In this, although the worshipper's devotions were directed toward the goddess, the manner of those devotions did not differ from those of one's Shaivite or Vaishnavite neighbors.

Conversely, the "left-handed worship" (*vamacara*) of many tantric practitioners involved the use of taboo materials and actions known as the "five m's" (*pancha makaras*) because their names in Sanskrit start with that letter. They were: fish, meat, wine, parched grain, and sexual intercourse. All these things which were forbidden to ordinary Hindus were believed to possess great spiritual potential that would, if properly applied in conjunction with the appropriate ritual actions and diagrams (*yantras*), awaken the energy dormant at the base of the spine—the *kundalini*. If raised through the seven *chakras* or energy centers that lay along the spine, *kundalini* could instantly propel the practitioner out of the cycle of life and death. But the knowledge of how to achieve this was so dangerous that it was encoded in the Tantras in a highly metaphorical and obscure form known as *samdhyabhasha* (twilight language). Just as it could bring salvation, *kundalini* could also bring damnation.

At present, the worship of the Great Goddess still commands the allegiance of many Hindus. It was legitimized and popularized by such great modern saints as Ramakrishna Paramahamsa, who was a priest of Kali, the popular Bengali manifestation of Durga. At the same time, Ramakrishna explicitly condemned the left-handed path of Tantra. But even today, followers of this path still exist in India. They are, however, greatly outnumbered by worshippers who see in Durga, Kali, and other manifestations of the Great Goddess, as a loving and nurturing incarnation of the divine principle.

The Worship of Vishnu and his *Avataras*

While Shaivism may claim the greater antiquity, it is the worship of Vishnu and his earthly manifestations, his *avataras* or "descents" into a physical body, that engages the religious fervor of the majority of modern Hindus. Like Shaivism, Vaishnavism

Kali astride Shiva, Bengal, late 19th century. Many Hindus see the supreme power that animates the universe as being female. Kali, often depicted in Indian art as the spouse of Shiva, represents the awesome and sometimes frightening aspects of this power.

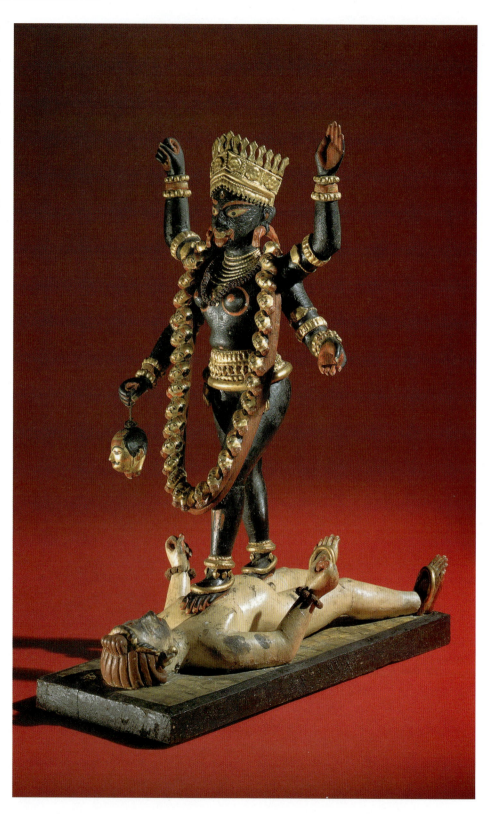

is a melange of Vedic traditions, external influences, and imported ideas from the now defunct cults of formerly separate gods such as Narayana and Vasudeva Krishna. This absorption of disparate religious elements and personages takes place in Shaivism as well, but through the mechanism of making such personages members of Shiva's extended family, either by birth or by marriage. A good example of this is in the figure of Ganesha. This god, widely venerated in South and Southeast Asia by business people and scholars, clearly had his beginnings as a tribal god associated with elephants. In the course of time, however, he came to be seen as a son of Shiva and his consort Parvati, and so part of the Shaivite pantheon.

Vaishnavism's unitive theme is its understanding of Vishnu as savior of the world. This is the predominant motif in the greatest of all Vaishnavite religious works, the Bhagavad Gita, which has rightly been called the Bible of Hinduism. The earliest references to Vishnu as savior seem to come from the Rig Veda (I, 22; I, 154; and VII, 100), where Vishnu is associated with the sun and solar worship. But it is in the Puranic and Epic material that we see this concept reach its richest and fullest flowering.[7]

There are traditionally thought to be ten incarnations or avatars of Vishnu—nine of them have occurred and one has yet to take place. Five of the avatars are in the form of animals and may represent the assimilation of tribal deities into the Vaishnavaite pantheon. Two others, Rama and Krishna, may be folk memories of historical personages who were later deified. The rest are mythical heroes or, in some cases, historical personages. All incarnate in themselves Vishnu's saving love for humanity and his intent to preserve the world. In this regard, Vishnu is often associated with two other gods—Brahma, who represents the creative principle at work in the world, and Shiva, representing destruction—and takes the form of a threefold divinity, *Trimurti*, who embodies the creative, preservative, and destructive aspects of Reality. The actual list of Vishnu's avatars varies, but the following are the most widely recognized.

Crowned Ganesha, Punjab Hills, c. 1720. Ganesha, the god of new enterprises, is a popular deity throughout India. He is only one of a large number of deities that the Hindu faithful can call upon for aid and comfort.

The first is Matsya, the fish, who defeats the demons who have stolen the Vedas and returns them to the Hindu gods. Next is Ekasringa, the unicorn, who saves Manu, the ancestor of the human race, from a flood in which all other humans perish. Kurma the tortoise helps the gods recover the elixir of immortality from the primordial ocean into which it has fallen. Varaha the boar upholds the earth like Atlas in Greek mythology, preventing it from drowning in the cosmic ocean on which it floats. Nrisingha the man-lion saves the devotee Prahlada from being murdered by his own father. Vamana the dwarf defeats the demon Bali and wins the world for himself and humanity. Parashurama—Rama with the battle ax—is the first of Vishnu's human incarnations. He defeats the warrior caste and restores the dignity of the Brahmins. Then in the fullness of time will come the last of the avatars, Kalki, the liberator mounted on a white horse, who will end the present degenerate age of the world and usher in an age of perfection. But it is Rama and Krishna who are the most popular and widely revered of Vishnu's avatars in modern India. Both have their roots in northern India. Rama is associated with the central region of the Ganges River valley, and Krishna with the region somewhat farther west. Originally, both seem to have been worshipped as gods in their own right, but from about the start of the Common Era, their cults were absorbed into the broader worship of Vishnu.

The story of Rama is a perennial theme of Hindu literature and has given rise to a number of hauntingly beautiful works of literature. The most famous of these is the *Ramayana*, attributed to Valmiki. In its present form, which was completed sometime between 200 B.C.E. and 200 C.E., there are some 24,000 verses. Originally written down in Sanskrit, the story was adapted into all the later Indian vernaculars, the most famous version being the sixteenth-century Hindi Ramacaritamanasa of Tulasidasa. Later works, such as the *Adyatma Ramayana*, attempted to carry the story forward beyond the climax of the original work, but it is the *Ramayana* itself that continues to be most revered by Rama's devotees.

The story itself is relatively simple. Rama is the eldest son of Dasharatha, the king of Ayodhya, "the city without war"—a small kingdom in the central Ganges valley. The king has three wives, one of whom persuades him to name her son Bharata as heir to his kingdom and to exile Rama, the rightful heir, to the forest for fourteen years. Rama is a supremely dutiful son and accepts his fate gladly as a way of allowing his father to redeem the promises he made to his scheming wife years earlier. So, in company with both his younger half-brother Lakshmana and his new wife Sita, he goes into exile. Bharata, a man of great moral rectitude in his own right, refuses the kingship but remains as regent on the throne of Ayodhya until such time as Rama returns.

Rama has many adventures in the forest and by killing demons, forest sprites, and assorted hobgoblins, such as Tataka, shown opposite, makes it safe for the hermits and sages who live their holy lives of meditation and austerity there. One day, Rama insults the sister of the king of the demons, Ravana, who, infatuated with Rama's wife Sita, kidnaps her and takes her to his fortress on the island of present-day Sri Lanka. Rama and Lakshmana now undertake an epic quest to rescue Sita, complete with many colorful adventures that continue to thrill audiences today, since adaptations of the *Ramayana* are still performed as sacred plays at fairs, and even as television specials. Along the way, the couple meet Hanuman, the great monkey warrior, who becomes Rama's greatest devotee. Then Rama kills the demon, fulfills the terms of his exile, and returns in triumph to Ayodhya. But troubled by the time his wife Sita has spent alone with King Ravana, Rama exiles her to the forest for the sake of propriety. There she bears him two sons, returns them to their

Rama battling with the demoness Tataka, Kandi, Murshidabad District, Bengal, c. 1800. In this panel the ogress Tataka fights with Rama, who is shown firing an arrow at her, to the left.

father, and is then promptly swallowed up by the earth as a mark of her unsullied purity. Finally, Rama and his brothers physically reenter the body of Vishnu from which they have emanated, and the epic ends.

What we see in the story of Rama is the absorption into the Vishnu cult of a preexisting cult of a divine king, probably of some antiquity. But Rama's own absorption into the Vishnu cult is a relatively late phenomenon—certainly later than the similar absorption of Krishna. Rama's appeal seems to lie in his human rather than divine attributes. His loyalty, devotion to duty, and regard for honor and tradition have a powerful resonance in Hindu hearts. Likewise his wife Sita's qualities of devotion and cheerful submission to her husband's will are taken as models of the ideal Hindu woman. This embodiment of all the Hindu virtues has made Rama the focal point of modern Hindu fundamentalist and nationalist fervor. In February 1992, a group of such Hindus demolished the Babri Masjid, a Muslim mosque in present-day Ayodhya that supposedly stood on the site of Rama's birthplace. The resulting sectarian violence between Hindus and Muslims did little to usher in the Ram Rajya (Rama's Rule)—the Hindu religious state that the fundamentalists ardently desired.

Even more widespread than devotion to Rama is devotion to the other great incarnation of Vishnu—Krishna, the "Black One." As is the case with other avatars, the worship of Krishna is an amalgam of various elements from different sources. Its core seems to be the worship of Vasudeva Krishna, who was worshipped as early as the third century B.C.E. around what is now Mathura in northwestern India. Indeed, many of the most important places mentioned in the Krishna myths are found in this area. Another element is the cult of Krishna Govinda, the Divine Cowherd, perhaps a tribal deity of the Ahir people. Then there are the still later accretions of the Child Krishna material. Finally, there is Krishna the Divine Lover, who is usually associated with Radha, his consort, and the multitude of *gopis* or female cowherds who are his lovers. This element perhaps reflects the influence of Tantric ideas on the cult of Krishna and is again a relatively late development.

In all his manifestations Krishna displays two primary characteristics. The first is his accessibility. He is not a god who dwells in a remote heaven isolated from the needs of his worshippers. He is totally human, and his humanity gives his worshippers a focal point for their devotion. Krishna's second characteristic is his role as savior, a familiar Vaishnavaite theme. In all the myths surrounding him, he is portrayed as the savior of humanity in one way or another. Indeed, even actions which might on the surface seem worldly or even sinful are, when seen from the proper

Jagat Singh worshipping Krishna, Mewar, Rajasthan, c. 1700 C.E. Krishna, in his many aspects, is the most popular avatar of Vishnu and forms the object of *bhakti* devotion for many Hindus.

perspective, really examples of his transcendent love for humanity and vehicles for its liberation. This theme of liberation, closely associated with Krishna on many levels, helped to give rise to the most popular scripture of modern Hinduism, the Bhagavad Gita or "Song of the Lord."

The Bhagavad Gita is itself part of a much longer work, the 100,000-verse-long *Mahabharata*. This huge work, four times as large as the entire Bible, tells the story of the great struggle between the Pandava brothers and their cousins the Kauravas for control of the northwestern kingdom of Hastinapura. It is a veritable compendium of all sorts of information on early India, being composed and reedited a number of times between its origins in about 300 B.C.E. and its final form in 400 C.E. The Bhagavad Gita forms only chapters twenty-three to forty of the *Bhishmaparvan* section of the epic and clearly reflects fairly late developments in Hindu religious thought. But it is fair to say that no other single book has had such an effect on the religious life of modern Hindus.[8]

As with the *Ramayana*, the bare outline of the book is simple. The great Pandava warrior Arjuna, on the eve of the final great battle against the Kauravas, refuses to fight and kill his relatives and friends. His charioteer, Krishna, proceeds to advance arguments as to why such actions, traditionally considered sinful, are in fact justifiable. First, says Krishna, no action affects the inner *atman*, the soul. But Arjuna is from the warrior caste, and it is his duty, his *dharma*, to fight. Whom he fights is immaterial—what is central to his well-being is the performance of duty. If this is done without rancor, then no karma is generated that would harm the *atman* in a future life. This, for Krishna, is the essence of Yoga, the dispassionate performance of all actions with no attachment to their outcomes.

So far the message of the Bhagavad Gita has been a reworking of traditional Samkhya and Yoga philosophy, but in chapters nine through eleven, new elements are added. In these, Krishna reveals himself as the Supreme God. He explains, "I am the father of this world, the mother, the supporter and the grandsire. I am the object of knowledge, the purifier. I am . . . the goal, the upholder, the lord, the witness, the abode, the refuge and the friend . . . I am immortality and also death, I am being as well as nonbeing" (IX, 17–19). Then, in the section that follows (IX, 26–34), Krishna sums up the true path to salvation for Arjuna:

> Whosoever offers to Me with devotion, a leaf, a flower, a fruit or water, that offering of love, of the pure of heart I accept . . . Whatever thou doest, whatever thou eatest, whatever thou offerest, whatever thou givest away, whatever austerities thou dost practice—do that, O Son of Kunti (Arjuna), as an offering to Me. Thus shalt thou be freed from the good and evil results which are the bonds of action . . . I am the same in [alike to] all beings. None is hateful nor dear to me. But those who worship Me with devotion they are in Me and I also in them . . . For Those who take refuge in Me, O Partha (Arjuna), though they are lowly born, women, Vaishyas, as well as Shudras, they also attain to the highest goal . . . On Me fix thy mind; to Me be devoted, worship Me; revere Me; thus having disciplined thyself, with Me as thy goal, shalt thou come.
>
> SOURCE: Sarvipalla Radhakrishnan (trans.), *The Bhagavadgita* (London: George Allen & Unwin, 1960), pp. 245–254

The Bhagavad Gita climaxes by presenting a tremendous epiphany in which Krishna reveals himself to Arjuna as God Transcendent, a terrifying and beautiful vision that never fails to move the reader no matter how many times the passage is read. The book ends with a final promise from Krishna to Arjuna:

Listen again to My supreme word, the most secret of all. Well beloved art thou of Me, therefore I shall tell thee what is good for thee. Fix thy Mind on Me; be devoted to Me; sacrifice to Me; prostrate thyself before Me; then shalt thou come to Me. I promise thee truly, for thou art dear to Me. (XVIII, 64–66)

Vaishnavaite Philosophy and Devotion

For the two greatest Vaishnavaite philosophers, Ramanuja and Madhva, the key to their philosophical speculations lay in the ninth chapter of the Bhagavad Gita. Here, Krishna explains:

By Me all this universe is pervaded through My unmanifested form. All beings abide in me but I am not established in them ... My spirit which is the source of all beings sustains the beings but does not abide in them. (IX, 4–5)

This revelation as to the nature of God made it very clear to these Vaishnavaite thinkers that the Advaita system of Vedanta advanced by Shankara could not be correct. What resulted were the Vishishtadvaita and Dvaita forms of that school which we have examined above. It is interesting, however, to note Ramanuja's conclusions regarding the practical application of his philosophy to the task of salvation. He writes in his *Vedarthasangraha* (126):

The pathway through which the supreme *Brahman* is to be attained is as follows: By an accumulation of great merit the sins of the past lives are destroyed. Thus liberated a person will seek refuge at the feet of the *Purushottama* [the Ultimate Man, an epithet for Vishnu]. Such self-surrender begets an inclination toward Him. Then the aspirant acquires knowledge of reality from the scriptures aided by the instruction of holy teachers. Then by a steady effort the devotee develops in an ever increasing measure the qualities of soul like the control of the mind, sense-control, austerity, purity, forgiveness, sincerity, fearlessness, mercy and non-violence. The devotees continue in the ritual duties and offer their very own self at the lotus-like feet of the *Purushottama*. They ceaselessly worship Him with dedication. The *Purushottama*, who is overflowing with compassion, being pleased with such love, showers His grace on the aspirant, which destroys all inner darkness. In such a devotee there develops devotion, which is valued for its own sake, which is uninterrupted, an absolute delight in itself, and which is meditation that has taken on the character of the most vivid and immediate vision. Through such devotion is the Supreme attained.

SOURCE: Raghavacar (trans.), *Vedarthasamgraha* by Ramanuja, p. 159

One sees a similar emphasis on devotion and complete surrender to the grace of Vishnu in the philosophy of Madhva as well. This teacher, who considered himself to be an incarnation of Vayu, a mediator between Vishnu and the world, saw the human soul as a reflection of the divine. Similar to other Vaishnavaite philosophers in many ways, Madhva was unique in Hindu thought for postulating the doctrine of "predestination," the concept that some souls were destined from the outset to eternal damnation.

With such a philosophical emphasis on devotion to the god, it is not surprising that the great popular movements (*sampradayas*) in Vaishnavism were primarily devotional, rather than doctrinal or ritualistic, in nature. Drawing on later

Krishna Temple in Dvarka. Pilgrimage to locations associated with events in the life of Krishna, or with important Vaishnavaite religious leaders such as Chaitanya, is still a popular activity in modern India.

Vaishnavaite philosophers such as Nimbarka and Vallabha, these schools placed great emphasis on devotion to the head teacher of the group, the **guru**. A number of these influential schools have arisen, the most visible to western eyes being ISKCON, the International Society for Krishna Consciousness, popularly known as the Hari Krishnas. An outgrowth of the followers of the Bengali Gaudia Vaishnavism of the great sixteenth-century teacher Chaitanya, ISKCON continues to demonstrate the vitality, adaptability, and worldwide appeal of the Vaishnavaite religion in the present day.

Website References

1. www.hindunet.org/ covers many aspects of Hindu devotionalism in general.

2. An excellent collection of stories concerning Shiva and Vishnu, and Indian mythology in general, is found at members.tripod.com/~srinivasp/mythology/stories.htm

3. Indian temples are well-illustrated at www.templenet.com/. Good examples of Saivite religious art can be found at www.asia.si.edu/exhibitions/chola.htm

4. www.kheper.auz.com/topics/Trika/Trika.htm has good information on the important Tantric school of Kashmir Shaivism.

5. www.hindupaintings.com/kali.htm has a good discussion of the goddess Kali.

6. Information on the goddess Durga is found at www.hubcom.com/tantric/durga.htm

7. Vishnu and his avatars are discussed at www.hindunet.org/avatars/index.htm

8. eawc.evansville.edu/anthology/gita.htm has a full translation of the Bhagavad Gita.

CHAPTER SIX

◆

Islam and its Influence on Medieval South Asian Religion

Indian history, like that of most other countries, has been defined to some extent by upheavals. In the case of India, however, these have been relatively infrequent. Aside from the Indo-European migrations, there have really been only three major intrusions into the Indian subcontinent proper. The first was the incursions of Central Asian peoples such as the Huns and Kushans, which lasted for about two hundred years between about 100 B.C.E. and 100 C.E. These incursions, triggered by the expansion of China into the borderlands of Central Asia, had little practical effect on Hinduism and introduced to it no new intellectual or ritual elements. Their only effect was to cause a certain hardening of Hindu attitudes, as can be seen from the sharp increase in Hindu texts dealing with social organization, as well as the pro- liferation of caste distinctions within the original fourfold division of society. The fairly modern incursion into India by the British in the middle of the eighteenth century had considerably more impact; but undoubtedly the incursions that had the most profound effect on the religions of the region were those of the Muslims, which began in 1000 C.E. After this date, different Muslim ethnic groups entered and departed from northern India for some seven and a half centuries. But from a reli- gious, rather than a political, perspective, the effects of these Muslim incursions from the Middle East and Central Asia were relatively coherent, since they were always based on the principles of Islam—principles that were often completely at odds with the ideas and values of indigenous Indian religion.

The first Muslim invasions of India had little or nothing to do with spreading the tenets of Islam. They were merely raids on the northwest region of India con- ducted from Afghanistan. What effect they did have was mainly negative. Under the guise of uprooting idolatry, the Muslims destroyed many of the great temples and monasteries of northern India that had flourished for centuries. Even today, the greatest Hindu temples are found in southern India, where the Muslims failed to penetrate until fairly late. Likewise, the great monasteries of the Buddhists were sacked at this time, a blow from which Indian Buddhism never recovered. As time went on, however, the Muslim raiders began to carve out small principalities in the northwest, and these eventually expanded to cover the entire northern half of the subcontinent. The rulers and ruling families of these inherently unstable principalities constantly changed until the advent of the Mughals in 1526 C.E. Under such great rulers as Akbar, Jahangir, and Shah Jahan, the Mughals extended their influence throughout the area now covered by India and Pakistan, and even into Central Asia. In doing so, they created the largest single political unit in the region. In this way, the Islamic culture and politics of the Mughal Empire had a tremendous effect on Hinduism.

The Basic Tenets of Islam

Our solid historical knowledge of the beginnings and growth of Islam is much greater than that of any other world religion, and we know far more about its founder, Muhammad (570–632) than we do about Jesus, the Buddha, or Moses.

Hand-written Qur'an. All Muslims hold the Qur'an to be the revealed word of Allah. As such, it is the absolute guide to human conduct and morals.

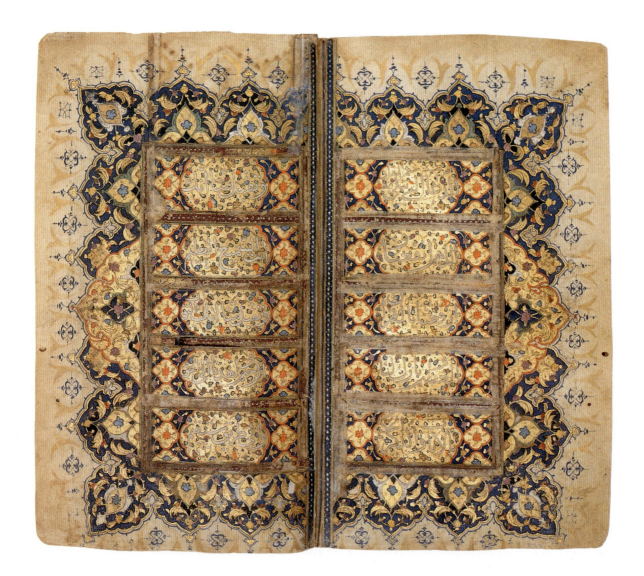

He was born in the Arabian town of Mecca and became an orphan at an early age. Forced to earn a living, he went to work on the caravans that traveled up the west coast of the Arabian peninsula to bring spices and incense to the great empires of Byzantium and Persia. There he came in contact with representatives of Christianity, Judaism, and Zoroastrianism. These encounters awakened in him a desire to know God. When, as a result of a fortunate marriage, he was able to live a life of ease, he devoted his time to religious exercises and prayer. According to Muslim tradition, he was visited in a cave in the hills above Mecca by an angel who revealed to him the Holy Qur'an, the perfect expression of Allah's (God's) will for humanity.[1] The Qur'an is held by Muslims to be Allah's final communication to human beings, and the religion revealed in it, Islam, the definitive word on what must be believed and practiced in order to achieve salvation.[2]

Islam is a rich and complex religion that can not be done justice in the small space that we can allot to it here, but its essence can easily be summarized. It is contained in what the Muslims term "the five pillars of the faith." The first and foremost of these pillars is absolute faith in the unity and power of Allah. For the Muslim, Allah alone is real, all else is His creation and dependent on Him. Creation exists to reflect Allah's glory, and a person's proper relationship to Allah is one of submission to His will, hence the name of the religion, Islam ("submission"—to the will of God), and of its followers, Muslims (those who have submitted). Humanity's task is to follow the will of Allah as presented to his final prophet Muhammad in the Holy Qur'an. Since Allah is the author of creation, nothing in creation is His equal, and He cannot be represented in art in any manner, since that would diminish Him. Of Allah, the Qur'an says (quoting Abdullah Yusuf Ali's translation):

Children learning the Qur'an in Karachi, Pakistan. The traditional method of religious education in Muslim countries has been for children to first commit the Qur'an to memory. Only then is the text itself studied.

Say: He is Allah,
The One and Only;
Allah, the Eternal, Absolute;
He begetteth not,
Nor is he begotten;
And there is none
Like unto Him

SOURCE: Abdullah Yusaf Ali (trans.), *The Meaning of the Holy Qu'ran*, revised ed. (Brentwood, MD: The Amana Corporation, 1989), p. 1714

It is the pious Muslim's duty to know and study the text of the Qur'an, the ultimate guide to life in this world and in the next.

The second pillar of Islam is prayer. The Muslim is enjoined to pray five times a day. These prayers, which take some ten to fifteen minutes to perform, involve prostration and other movement, as well as the recitation of selected verses of the Qur'an. On prayer, the Qur'an teaches:

Guard strictly
Your (habit) of prayer,
Especially the Middle Prayer [of the day];
And stand before Allah
In a devout (frame of mind).

If ye fear (an enemy),
Pray on foot, or riding,
(as may be most convenient),

Indonesian Muslims at prayer. Prayer, which the devout Muslim practices five times a day, is one of the five central tenets of Islam.

But when you are
In security, celebrate
Allah's praises in the manner
He has taught you [with prostrations],
Which ye knew not (before).

SOURCE: Ali (trans.), *The Meaning of the Holy Qu'ran*, p. 98

Once a week on Fridays, the faithful gather for the communal noon prayer at the mosque. The prayers are led by a member of the community, for Islam has no priests. Rather, its leaders are the scholars who interpret the rules of daily life that have developed from the Qur'an, and the sayings and deeds of the prophet Muhammad known as the **hadith**.

The third pillar of Islam is fasting. During the lunar month of Ramadan, Muslims are required, if they are of age and physically able, to fast from sunrise to sunset. This means no food or drink can pass their lips, nor can they smoke, take injections, or have sexual intercourse. In addition, pious Muslims attempt to fast from evil thoughts, actions, and words during this period. The Qur'an praises fasting, and observes:

O ye who believe!
Fasting is prescribed to you
As it was prescribed
To those before you,
That ye may (learn)
Self-restraint.

(Fasting) for a fixed
Number of days;
But if any of you is ill;
Or on a journey,
The prescribed number
(Should be made up)
From days later.
For those who can do it
(with hardship), is a ransom,
The feeding of one
That is indigent.
But he that will give
More, of his own free will—
It is better for him.
And it is better for you
That ye fast,
If ye only know.

SOURCE: Ali (trans.), *The Meaning of the Holy Qu'ßran*, p. 73

This emphasis on almsgiving, an act that is so powerful that it can absolve a person from the obligation of fasting as seen above, is the fourth pillar of Islam. The Qur'an promises that:

If ye loan to Allah
A beautiful loan [i.e. give charity], He

will double it to
Your (credit), and He
Will grant you Forgiveness:
For Allah is most Ready
To appreciate (service),
Most Forbearing ...

SOURCE: Ali (trans.), *The Meaning of the Holy Qu'ran*, p. 1480

Since, for the Muslim, all worldly riches are the gift of Allah, it follows that they are given to human beings for the good of all creation. People are therefore under an obligation to share the bounty that Allah has given them with those less fortunate, and Muslims are obliged to contribute a fixed percentage of their worldly gains to good causes or needy individuals.

Finally, the fifth pillar of Islam enjoins the faithful to make a pilgrimage to Mecca during the month of the ***Hajj*** ("pilgrimage") once in their lives if possible. For, as the Qur'an makes plain:

The first House (of worship)
Appointed for men
Was that at Bakka [another name for Mecca];
Full of blessing
And of guidance
For all kinds of beings:

In it are Signs
Manifest; (for example),
The Station of Abraham;
Whoever enters it
Attains security;
Pilgrimage thereto is a duty
Men owe to Allah—
Those who can afford
The journey; but if any
Deny faith, Allah stands not
In need of any of His creatures.

SOURCE: Ali (trans.), *The Meaning of the Holy Qu'ran*, p. 152

This journey reaffirms the unity and solidity of the Muslim community, the equality of all Muslims, and the unity of humanity. Moreover, it shows a willingness to subordinate one's own will to the will of Allah. Pious Muslims will save for an entire lifetime to make the pilgrimage.[3]

Over the centuries, Islam has spread to every corner of the world. The countries with the largest Muslim populations—Indonesia, Pakistan, India, and Bangladesh—are all found in Asia. Islam aims at providing the structure for all aspects of a person's life, and it has a rich heritage of philosophical and theological development. For our purposes, however, we need be concerned with only one particular aspect of this development. This is the tradition of mystical Islam known as Sufism. Expounded by such great religious philosophers as Al-Ghazali, Rumi, and Ibn Sina, Sufism had a tremendous effect on Hindu religious thought and the development of new religious traditions in India, notably Sikhism. Sufism stresses the primacy of personal experience of the divine over sterile formulaic observances. The communal norms were still seen as important, and good Sufis followed the external tenets of their religion to the letter. But it was the personal interaction with Allah that mattered. This was to be nourished in a number of ways that made up what has been called the Sufi path.[4]

First, the Sufi needed to cultivate repentance. By this was meant not so much a sense of guilt for one's sins, although this was certainly desirable. Rather repentance involved adopting a new attitude toward life whereby the Sufi became mindful of the inherently defective nature of human existence. This defectiveness was not the result of some flaw in creation. Since creation was the work of Allah, it was, by its very nature, pure. It was human willfulness that had corrupted people's relationship to Allah, and it was only through the leading of a virtuous life that this breach could be repaired.

Part of this life of virtue consisted of the practice of abstinence—the second step on the path. Here again, nothing in the material creation was deemed to be inherently evil or unwholesome. These qualities arose only as a result of human use and attitudes. The major problem with the sweet-tasting things of this world was that they were so good and beguiling. Thus people had a tendency to mistake the enjoyment of them for the greater good and happiness of being united with their Creator. To abstain from worldly things was an essential means of recognizing that nothing really belonged to anyone but Allah, and He alone should be sought. The third Sufi virtue—of renunciation—carried the second step—abstinence—of the Sufi path to its logical conclusion. To abstain from the joys and pleasures of the material world was useless if it was not accompanied by a concomitant renunciation of the desire to enjoy and possess them. Needless to say, this was a far harder task than simply denying one's self the enjoyment of these pleasures.

Again, this led the Sufi to the next step on the path: poverty. The Sufis saw no particular virtue in poverty itself. For poverty to be an effective spiritual tool, it needed to proceed from an interior attitude whereby Sufis ardently desired to be united with Allah. This desire naturally led them to do away with everything that might distract their minds from this quest. This not only included property, but also thoughts, wishes, and desires that might distract them from the search for Allah and so separate their souls from Him. Naturally, the foregoing was a difficult process that, because it was in a sense so contrary to human nature, took a great deal of time and effort to accomplish. Hence the fifth step on the Sufi path was the cultivation of patience. True seekers had to throw themselves completely on the mercy of God and to endure all things as the Will of Allah. The problem, of course, was discerning that Will. This was a time-consuming process of reflection and practice. To succeed, Sufis needed to resign themselves to an enormous series of disappointments and false starts. Consequently, patience was essential.

So too was the sixth step, trust in Allah. Human nature, as we have observed, was degraded in the Muslim view by the agency of sin. Human beings had been created to love and serve Allah, but had fallen away from the perfection that they had previously enjoyed as a result of the wrongful use of free will. It was easy, therefore, to despair of the human capacity to regain this lost state of grace. The Sufi needed to cultivate the belief that Allah was able to remedy the deplorable situation in which human beings had placed themselves: they had fallen by sin—and sin was an integral part of human nature—but Allah was all-powerful. His grace would allow Sufis to overcome all obstacles to union with Him that were present in human nature, but this was only granted if their trust in His love, mercy and compassion was great enough.

Finally, the seventh step and culmination of the Sufi path lay in finding satisfaction only in Allah. As one's state of perfection and closeness to Allah increased, so did one's complete satisfaction in doing His will and living only for Him. Thus, in a sense, one participated in the divine conduct of creation, never *becoming* God, as was believed in some branches of Hinduism, but becoming *like* God. This, for the true believer, was the final culmination of human destiny and would bring complete happiness and satisfaction in this life and in the next.

The seven steps of the Sufi path were accomplished through two things. The first was human effort. Allah wanted the best for human beings and offered His grace to them. But for such grace to be effective, people needed to make an effort to grasp it. If they did, Allah provided them with a number of graces. He granted them the power to meditate on Him, as well as the sense of closeness that arose from such meditation. He kindled in the human heart a love of Himself that served to motivate people and draw them toward the Truth. He engendered in them the twin emotions of fear of separation from His grace and a longing for the divine embrace. This would lead to intimacy with Allah, as well as the inner peace that came from it. Finally, Allah granted true seekers the ability to contemplate Him and the confidence in salvation that would eventually lead them home to His embrace.

All of the foregoing was codified and set forth in the works of the great philosophical thinkers of Sufism. Foremost among these was Al-Ghazali (1059–1111). A brilliant youth, Al-Ghazali was appointed in his twenties to teach in the great university of Baghdad, the preeminent Islamic educational institution of its time. But as with many before and after him, the young Al-Ghazali found that academic life stifled his own religious development. In desperation, he turned to Sufism to revive his flagging faith and found the peace and contentment that had eluded him in the academic world. But even if, as they say, you take the person out of the university, it is harder to take the university out of the person. This was certainly true in Al-Ghazali's case, as he proceeded to write a number of volumes that were aimed at discussing the undiscussable. The central point of his explorations of the divine, of which *Revival of Religious Science* is the most enduring and influential, was that Allah was the only true object of knowledge, and that He could only be known through faith. Al-Ghazali firmly took to task those philosophers, such as Ibn Sina, who, influenced by Plato and the Neo-Platonists, relied on natural reason rather than revelation.

In his aptly named book, *The Nonsense of Philosophers*, Al-Ghazali used his considerable philosophical skills to show that conclusions from reason could just as easily be argued in such ways as to lead to completely opposite conclusions. Although this viewpoint, which subordinated human reason to divine revelation, could be refuted (and was by such able critics as Ibn Rushd in his *The Nonsense of Nonsense*), it became enshrined as the "official" philosophy of Islam. Henceforth, the proper employment of reason was not speculation about the natural world, but the defense of orthodox theology and the revelation of scripture. This did not stop other philosophers from their own speculations. Notable among these were Ibn Sina's musings on divine love. Without devaluing the importance of natural reason and the study of the material world, Ibn Sina—said to be the greatest Islamic scientist of his day—gave primacy to the human heart as the truest source of knowledge about Allah. God was reflected in the mirror of the human heart and illuminated the entire world in the process.

For Ibn Sina, Allah was ultimate beauty, as witnessed by His creation. It was beauty's very nature to be self-expressive, as it was Allah's nature to be self-expressive. The perfect expression of beauty, Ibn Sina argued, was love; and love was the

Here we see Ibrahim ibn Adham being helped by a group of angels. The lives of great Sufi saints provided a model of life for later followers of Sufi doctrines.

motivating energy that caused all created reality to seek the source of its being. Human beings, created in the image and likeness of Allah, had within them a divine spark that impelled them to seek reunion with God. This theory of the motivating power of love and the journey to reunion with the divine was more fully worked out by Ibn Arabi (1165–1240), who held that Allah was both immanent and transcendent. For Ibn Arabi, this implied that people, while never becoming Allah, could in a sense merge themselves with Him, just as a drop of water in the ocean was both merged with and separate from that ocean.

This emphasis on the love of Allah had the practical effect of making the Sufis tend not to withdraw from society, but to work within it. They might live severely ascetic personal lives—and many did—but this asceticism had to find its fulfillment in service to the greater community. As an old Sufi saying holds, "Though there are as many paths to God as there are particles in the universe, none is shorter than that of bringing comfort to troubled hearts." Consequently, the Sufis became the great missionaries of Islam. They generally avoided involvement in political issues or sectarian disputes, leaving these to the philosophers and legal experts. Theirs was a mission of communicating the reality of the Real through spiritual guidance and the incarnation of divine love, and many of the great Sufi leaders are still venerated as saints by modern Muslims.

The *Bhakti* Tradition and Hindu-Muslim Syncretism

It is not surprising, therefore, to learn that the Sufis were at the forefront of Islamic missionary activity in India. Organized into formal orders similar to that of the Naqshbandiyyah of Central Asia or the Shadhiliyyah of North Africa, they fanned out across India with a message that resonated deeply with many people. Nor did they stop there. In the fullness of time, they took ship to the areas of Southeast Asia that had been deeply influenced by Indian culture for generations. There they began to propagate Islam, with the result that today Indonesia is the largest Muslim country in the world. At the other end of the Islamic world, Sufis began to penetrate Africa, where, at present, Islam is the fastest-growing religious tradition.

The Muslim message fell on fertile ground in India. Many people, particularly those low in the caste structure, saw in Islam a way to improve their social standing as well as an appealing alternative to the complicated formalism of much of medieval Hinduism. The concept of one God who loved humanity and wished for its salvation was a powerful one when allied to more worldly benefits, such as the Muslim exemption from certain taxes. Consequently, medieval Hinduism found itself on the defensive, both socially and intellectually. Fortunately, it possessed the religious capacity to fight back through the evolving concept of *bhakti*. As we have seen, devotion to a particular god had a long and venerable history in Hinduism. With the advent of Islam, this tradition took on new depth.

The word *bhakti* most likely comes from the Sanskrit root *bhaj-*, meaning "to worship" or "be devoted to." From this comes our English translation "faith" or "devotion." The medieval Indian philosopher Vallabha goes one step further and breaks *bhakti* into two components, *bhaj-* and *kti*. He takes the root, *bhaj-*, to mean "service" and the suffix to indicate "love of." This would mean that *bhakti* is "the love of service [to the divinity]." In any case, *bhakti* has become the predominant manner by which Hindus interact with the divine. Many scholars trace its origins to the Rig Veda. In this, they claim, there are traces of devotional cults worshipping the old

Vedic gods, such as Indra or Varuna. Certainly Varuna is referred to in terms that are very reminiscent of those applied to the *bhakti*-oriented worship of Vishnu.

While the term *bhakti* never specifically appears in the Upanishads, we see in two of them—the Mundaka (III, 2,3) and the Katha (II, 22)—a doctrine of grace not dissimilar to that of the later tradition. As these texts observe, the essence of the human being cannot be reached through insight, learning, or study. It can only be comprehended through divine revelation. Clearly we have here a belief in a personal divinity who interacts with humanity, a being who is Purushottama, the Highest Person (a term often applied to Vishnu in later times). As Hinduism developed, so too did the *bhakti* tradition. At first it was focused on existing divinities such as Shiva and Vishnu. But as time went on, particularly in response to the challenges of Islam, the tradition split into two distinct branches. The first, represented by such groups as the Alvars and the Nayanmars of southern India, continued to refine the old tradition. For them, God was primarily conceived as being **saguna**—possessing form in a way that could be apprehended by human beings. This gave rise to many of the glories of Indian art and architecture, as devotees of God, whether they conceived of Him as Shiva or Vishnu, attempted to capture the transcendental beauty of the Lord.

Another tradition, however, began to appear in the northern parts of India under Muslim domination. This was based on the concept of God as being **nirguna**, without any form that was perceivable to human beings, at least by the physical senses. No doubt influenced by the Muslim concept of the ineffability of God, this group became known as the Sants (Holy Ones). They believed that God transcended any physical form, and they preferred to communicate their direct experiential knowledge of Him through the medium of words. We find in their ranks many of the greatest luminaries of Indian literature, including Kabir, Surdas, Tulsidas, Ramprasad, and Tukaram.[5]

What did these Sants believe? First and foremost, they believed that the path of salvation was open to all, and they denied any attempts to limit God's power or His saving grace, which was extended to all beings. Thus the path of *bhakti* was open to women, outcasts, Muslims, and Hindus alike. Many of these great souls refused to be categorized as either Hindus or Muslims, with the result that they are claimed by both religions. Likewise, some of the greatest of the Sants, such as Nanda and Cokamela, were from the lowest stratum of society, and some, such as Mirabai and Antal, were women. As the great poet Kabir sang:

> It is foolish to ask a saint as to his caste. The *brahmin*, the *kshatriya* [warrior], the *vaishya* [common person] and the *shudra* [servant], all seek but God. The barber has looked for God too, and so has the washerman and the carpenter . . . Hindus and Muslims have equally realized God, there is no scope of distinction in the ultimate aim.
>
> SOURCE: Klaus K. Klostermaier, *A Survey of Hinduism*, 2nd ed. (Albany: State University of New York Press, 1994), pp. 224–225

The Sants systematically denied most of the popular ritual elements of Hinduism. Kabir neatly summarizes their practical approach to religion when he says:

> My true *guru* has shown me the way: I have given up all rites and ceremonies, I bathe no more in holy rivers. I then became aware that I alone was mad, the whole world sane. I had been disturbing those intelligent people! No longer could I live in the dust of subservience; no longer do I ring the temple-bells, nor do I enthrone a

divine image. I no longer offer flowers. Mortification does not please the Lord; we do not reach Him by going naked and torturing ourselves. They who are kind and righteous, who do not get entangled in this world's dealings, who consider all creatures on earth as their own self, they attain to the Immortal, the true God is with them forever. Kabir says: Those attain [true union with God] whose words are pure, who are devoid of pride and self-deceit.

SOURCE: Klostermaier, *A Survey of Hinduism*, p. 225

The divine was to be realized through service to, and love of, other beings, remembrance of God through devotional practices such as meditation, hymn singing (*kirtana*), and repetition of the divine name (*japa*); association with others of like inclinations (**satsang**); and, perhaps most importantly, devotion to the divine guru (*satguru*) through reverence for one's earthly guru. This reverence became especially important for followers of the *nirguna* schools of Hinduism for whom the guru was often seen as a bodily incarnation of the formless God and, as such, worthy of extreme veneration.

As is often the case with new and innovative ideas, the syncretic religion of the Sants aroused considerable resistance from both Muslims and Hindus. The Muslims, many of whom were often in conflict with even the more liberal wings of their own religion, saw the nondenominational stance of the Sants as a threat to the purity of Islam. On the other hand, the Hindus saw it as a denial of the essential truths of their religion and a threat to the very fabric of society. Rejected by both the traditions from which it had sprung, the religion of the Sants had only two directions in which it could progress. One was to modify its more radical elements and bring them more into line with the beliefs of the Hindu or Muslim majorities. The other was to blaze a new trail, one separate from that of either Islam or Hinduism. Some courageous souls did just that. Of such groups formed in this way, the most famous and influential were the followers of Guru Nanak, who later became known as the Sikhs.

Website References

1. The life of the Prophet Muhammad is the subject of www.muhammad.net/

2. Several different translations of the Qur'an can be found at www.stg.brown.edu/webs/quran_browser/pqueasy.shtml

3. The *hadiths* or sayings of the Prophet can be found at wings.buffalo.edu/sa/muslim/isl/hadith1.html

4. www.digiserve.com/mystic/Muslim/ discusses Islamic mysticism.

5. Kabir's work is translated at www.boloji.com/kabir/ Tukaram's life and work is covered at www.neonblue.com/tfs/tukahome.htm Tulsidas and his work are discussed at www.freeindia.org/biographies/tulsi/

CHAPTER SEVEN

◆

Sikhism

Of all of the various religious groups that emerged from the Sant movement, undoubtedly the largest and most enduring were the Sikhs. The Sikhs took the thought of the various religious traditions of India and from it fashioned a new religion that attempted to incorporate the best elements of these faiths in new and unique ways. Guru Nanak (1469–1539), the founder of Sikhism, was born on April 15, 1469, in the town of Talwandi, which lay in the Punjab, a fertile area of northwestern India from which the majority of Sikhs were to come. The Punjab also lay astride the main route used by invaders of India, and so it was usually the first part of the subcontinent to experience new ideas. At the time of Guru Nanak's birth, the region was experiencing a rare period of peace and stability under Muslim rule. Guru Nanak's family were Hindus of the warrior caste. His father, Kalyan Chand, was an accountant for a prosperous local Muslim convert. Nanak's birth was seen as particularly auspicious, since his horoscope predicted he would be a great religious teacher revered by both Muslims and Hindus. Although his father wanted him to go into business, Nanak's own inclinations seem to have been in the direction of poetry and religious matters. He studied Sanskrit, as well as Persian and Arabic, and did well at all of them, but seems to have had little interest in practical subjects.

At the age of eleven, Nanak was supposed to be initiated into the warrior caste, thus becoming "twice-born." To everyone's amazement and consternation, however, he refused to participate in the ceremony. He had by then been influenced by the poetry and thought of the great Sant devotees, such as Kabir. He also began at this time to write poetry that expressed his religious convictions and thoughts on both Hinduism and Islam. Of Islam, he observed:

Let compassion be your mosque,
Let faith be your prayer mat,
Let honest living be your Koran,
Let modesty be the rules of observance,
Let piety be the fasts you keep;
In such wisdom try to become a Muslim:
Right conduct the Ka'ba; Truth the Prophet;
Good deeds your prayers;
Submission to the Lord's Will your rosary;
Nanak, if this you do, the Lord will be your Protector

SOURCE: Patwant Singh, *The Sikhs* (New York: Alfred A. Knopf, 2000), p. 20

He was equally skeptical concerning the mechanical observance of Hindu rituals:

> Pilgrimages, penances, compassion and alms-giving
> Bring a little merit, the size of a sesame seed.
> But he who hears and believes and loves the Name [of God]
> Shall bathe and be made clean
> In a place of pilgrimage within him[self].

SOURCE: Singh, *The Sikhs*, p. 20

Nanak left his home at the age of sixteen to live with his sister and brother-in-law at the regional capital of Sultanpur. There he was employed by the local ruler as a clerk in the treasury. He was diligent in his labor and well liked by the prince, but his mind was clearly elsewhere. He was searching for the direct experience of the divine, for, as he later wrote:

> One may read for years and for years,
> And spend every month of the year in reading only;
> And thus read all one's life,
> Right up to one's last breath.
> Of all things, a contemplative life
> Is really what matters;
> All else is the fret and fever of egoistic minds.

SOURCE: Singh, *The Sikhs*, p. 22

By this time, the core of his faith were clear to Nanak:

> There is but one God. He is all that is.
> He is the Creator of all things and He is all-pervasive.
> He is without fear and without enmity.
> He is timeless, unborn and self-existent.
> He is the Enlightener
> And can be realized by his grace alone.
> He was in the beginning; He was in all ages.
> The True One is, was, O Nanak, and shall forever be.

SOURCE: Singh, *The Sikhs*, p. 27

It was during this period that Nanak began to teach, living in a rented house with two boyhood friends. People began to congregate there to pray, sing hymns (*bhajans*), and meditate. It was also at this time that Nanak married, since he did not believe that true love of God required a person to flee the world, but rather to embrace it. From this marriage, two sons, Srichand and Lakhmidas, were born. But Nanak was restless. If God was one and indivisible, why should His creation be divided into competing faiths? Moreover, why should some of these faiths, notably Hinduism, create further divisions within themselves, such as the caste system? To try to resolve these questions, Nanak felt that he needed to travel and experience other religions at first hand. Accordingly, in the summer of 1469, at the age of twenty-seven, he left home to do just that. First, he traveled to the east, visiting the great Hindu pilgrimage sites of Hardwar, Varanasi, Kamrup in Assam, and Puri in Orissa. From there, he traveled south to Sri Lanka and southern India. Next, he journeyed to Tibet, Mecca, and the great center of Muslim learning, Baghdad. These journeys brought him into contact with many different peoples and his experiences were later collected in the traditional stories of his life, the *janam sakhis*, still read by devout Sikhs to this day.

Accompanied by his faithful Muslim friend Mardana, Nanak traveled for some twenty-eight years. In 1497, however, he settled down for good at Kartapur, north of Lahore on the Ravi River. There he began to attract disciples. The word "disciple" in Punjabi—Nanak's native language—is "Sikh" (a word derived from the Sanskrit *Shishya*), and this became the commonly accepted term for his followers. Nanak entered fully into the lives of his followers, doing his share of the daily tasks. He continued to write religious verse in Punjabi, using the Gurmukhi script to write Hindi rather than the more widespread Devanagari script used in northern India. He produced 974 hymns, which became the core of the Sikh scriptures when they were compiled by his successor, Arjan Das, some sixty-five years later.

Nanak's travels had given him considerable respect for many aspects of Islam and Hinduism, but he was adamantly opposed to those areas that he felt to be contrary to the two religions' nobler impulses. He totally rejected the caste system, and his earliest followers were drawn from a variety of castes, with Khatris of the merchant class and Jat farmers forming the majority of his early disciples. He also dismissed Muslim pretensions of superiority to the Hindu people whom they ruled. He was ahead of his time in many respects, for example in his attitude toward women. As he sings:

> Of woman are we born, of woman conceived,
> To woman engaged, to woman married.
> Woman we befriend, by woman is the civilization continued.
> When woman dies, woman is sought for.
> It is by woman that order is maintained.
> Then why call her evil from whom great men are born?
> From woman is woman born,
> And without woman none could exist.
> The eternal Lord is the only one, O Nanak,
> Who depends not on woman.

SOURCE: Singh, *The Sikhs*, p. 27

One of the ways in which Nanak attempted to break down caste and sexual prejudices was the establishment of the **langar** or common kitchen. Sikhs were expected to cook and eat in common with no regard for caste. It is an institution that is still widely observed today, at least on formal occasions.[1]

Guru Nanak's Successors

Just before his death, Nanak bestowed the leadership of the nascent Sikh community not on his sons, but on his disciple Angad (1504–1552). He was the perfect successor to the founder of the Sikh faith since he saw it as his duty to maintain and strengthen its foundations as they had been bequeathed to him by Nanak. A man of deep and mystical religious faith, he collected Guru Nanak's hymns into a book—to which were later added sixty-two of his own hymns. But perhaps his greatest contribution to Sikhism was his choosing Amar Das (1480–1574) to succeed him on his death in 1552. Although already an old man, Amar Das was a vigorous and far-sighted leader. He organized the scattered Sikh congregations (*sangats*) into twenty-two administrative districts (*manjis*). He formalized the institution of the communal kitchen originated by Nanak, and set the example for other Sikhs by eating there himself. He emancipated women from many of the onerous customs of both Hinduism and Islam, an action that was far in advance of other Indian religions. He forbade *sati*, the practice of widows burning themselves to death on their husbands' funeral pyres, and the wearing of veils. He allowed widows to remarry, and appointed women preachers. Indeed, many of the new *manjis* were led by women.

Amar Das is also remembered for the fact that he was instrumental in establishing the location of Harmandir Sahib (the House of God), the official name of the Golden Temple, at what would become the Sikh holy city of Amritsar in the western Punjab. The temple would be built on the site of a small mud hut that he used as a meditation retreat. Like his predecessors, Amar Das was an indefatigable poet, and 907 of his hymns are to be found in the Guru Granth Sahib, the sacred scripture of the Sikhs. Despite his advanced age on his accession to the office of Guru, he held that office for over twenty years and greatly influenced the shape of the developing faith. Amar Das was succeeded by his son-in-law, Ram Das (1534–1581) in 1574. It was he who began to expand Amar Das's tiny meditation retreat into the Golden Temple.[2]

Ram Das governed the Sikhs for only a short time, and was succeeded by his son Arjan Das (1563–1606). One of the most energetic and farsighted of the Sikh Gurus, he expanded the Golden Temple, whose cornerstone was laid in 1588, and the buildings around it, thus making it the preeminent pilgrimage site for Sikh devotees and the spiritual center of the religion. Knowing that buildings were only an empty show unless they acquired a deeper spiritual significance, Arjan Das next turned his efforts to collating and establishing a definitive edition of the Sikh scriptures, which he gathered from many sources. Pride of place naturally went to the

The Golden Temple in Amritsar. The holiest place in the Sikh religion, the Golden Temple is a central symbol of their faith for Sikhs throughout the world.

writings of Guru Nanak and his successors, and 2,218 of Arjan Das's own works were included. But Arjan Das also included in the anthology works by Kabir, Namdeva, Ravi Das, and a number of Sufi saints. Once compiled, the scriptures were set to music so that they could be sung in the classical *bhajan* style still beloved in India to this day.

The collection became known as the Guru Granth Sahib ("the honorable compilation") and ran to some 1,948 pages containing over 7,000 hymns. It was all written in the Gurmukhi script favored by Nanak, but since many of its poems were composed by non-Punjabis, they are in a variety of different languages such as Old Punjabi, Old Hindi, Marathi, and even Persian. The organizational principle of the text was to present the works of the Gurus in chronological order first, followed by the hymns of the other saints. Arjan Das had the newly compiled scriptures placed in the newly completed Golden Temple on August 16, 1604. In fact, the scriptures continued to expand up to the death of the last Guru, in 1708, when they were officially declared complete. From the date of its installation in the Golden Temple to the present, the Guru Granth Sahib has been brought forth and chanted from dawn to dusk every day in the temple, thus sanctifying the building with the words of revelation of the divine.[3]

Muslim Opposition and the Development of the Khalsa

Arjan Das is also notable for being the first Sikh martyr. The Mughal emperor of his time, Jahangir, lacked the ecumenical openness of his predecessors, being something of a religious bigot. Disturbed by Sikhism's continuing inroads into the Muslim and Hindu communities, Jahangir ordered the arrest of Arjan Das on the pretext that he had aided his, Jahangir's, son's rebellion. Arjan Das was then tortured to death. His calm fortitude is remembered by Sikhs to this day. Unfortunately, this savage act set the seal of enmity on Muslim–Sikh relations that still persists. It also transformed what had previously been a pacific religious movement into a militant one. Arjan Das's son Hargobind (1595–1644) succeeded him, and immediately began to build a military organization. He established training camps for the teaching of archery, swordsmanship, and other martial skills. He established the Akal Takht, the temporal administrative center of Sikhism near the Golden Temple in Amritsar, and emphasized the use of consensual decision making. The Mughals attempted to control this unruly element in their midst, but with only occasional success. In 1628, open warfare broke out, with the Sikhs initially having the best of the fighting. But the vast resources of the Mughal Empire eventually forced Hargobind to flee Amritsar for a nomadic life that ended in the Punjabi foothills of the Himalayas.

Another enduring legacy of Hargobind was the establishment of the institution of the *gurdwara*, the Sikh equivalent of the Christian church, the Hindu temple, or the Jewish synagogue. Sikhs had previously congregated for spiritual purposes, but the establishment of the *gurdwaras*, literally "the door to the Guru (i.e. God)," gave a permanent focal point to local Sikh devotion. Usually a simple whitewashed hall without idols or decorations, the *gurdwara* is dominated at one end by a raised platform covered with silk, on which rests a copy of the Guru Granth Sahib.[4] Here an officiant reads and chants from the book as the rest of the community reverently listens, sitting on carpets strewn around the hall and covered with white cotton sheets. The reading of the scriptures goes on throughout the day until evening, when they are reverently wrapped in silk to await the next day. Thus they are chanted every day of the year in an unending cycle.[5]

Har Rai (1630–1661) succeeded his grandfather Hargobind. He was a saintly man whose interests were more spiritual than temporal. His successor Har Krishan (1656–1664) died of smallpox at a young age. He was in turn succeeded by Guru Hargobind's youngest son, Tegh Bahadur (1621–1675), who, on his accession to the leadership of the Sikhs, began to travel widely, particularly in Bengal and Assam. In 1672, he opposed the Mughal emperor Aurangzeb over the issue of the treatment of Hindus in what is now Kashmir. Tegh Bahadur issued the challenge that if Aurangzeb could convert him to Islam, then the Kashmir Hindus would convert as well. In 1675, however, he was tortured to death in an effort to force him to convert. Tegh Bahadur was succeeded by his son, Gobind Singh (1666–1708), who was to be the last of the human Sikh Gurus—he would be succeeded, as we shall see, by the Guru Granth Sahib.

Only nine when he assumed his father's mantle, Gobind Singh began to train himself for his responsibilities. He learned Sanskrit, Persian, Arabic, and two dialects of Hindi in addition to his native Punjabi. He also undertook extensive military training and studied practical subjects such as astronomy, botany, and Ayurvedic medicine. The Sikhs of this period had to contend not only with Muslim aggression, but with Hindu opposition as well, particularly on the part of the Kangra hill states. But in 1690, the Sikhs allied themselves with rebellious Hindu leaders against the Mughals. As tensions mounted, Guru Gobind Singh issued a command to his followers to assemble for the spring festival of Baisakhi, the Punjabi New Year, in 1694. They were to come bearing arms and with unshorn beards. The Mughals attacked, but were repulsed, and a period of peace ensued during which the Sikhs marshaled their strength.

It was during this period that the final transformation of the Sikhs from a pacific group to a militant warrior sect was accomplished. Guru Gobind Singh now declared Sikhism a *tisar panth*, a third religion completely separate from both Hinduism and Islam. As token of this, he decreed that henceforth the Sikhs would be known as the **Khalsa** or "pure ones." To set themselves apart from followers of other religions, the Sikhs were to adopt what was to become known as "the five Ks." The first of these was *kesh*, long hair. Sikhs were forbidden to cut their hair or trim their beard. Next was *kanga*, the wearing of a comb in the hair to hold it up. This is supplemented by the use of the distinctive Sikh turban whose purpose is to confine a Sikh's unshorn locks. *Kachh*, the third "K," were short underclothes designed to remind the Sikh of the need for continence and moral restraint. Next was the *kara*, a steel bangle worn on the right wrist to symbolize the wheel of *dharma*. Finally there was the *kirpan*, the sword. In the early days of the Khalsa, the sword was a functioning weapon. Today, it is a small symbolic knife. These five Ks remain the distinctive marks of a practicing Sikh.

The transformation of the Sikhs was completed at the Baisakhi festival of March 30, 1699. At that event, Gobind Singh called for volunteers to sacrifice their lives for the Khalsa. After initial hesitation, five Sikhs came forward and were apparently killed. However, it was only a ruse to test the will of the assembled Sikhs. Gobind Singh then proceeded to inaugurate the baptism ritual still followed by the Sikhs. An iron bowl was filled with water into which sugar was stirred with a sword as verses of the Guru Granth Sahib were chanted. This mixture, known as *amrit*, or nectar, was administered to those wishing to be initiated into the Khalsa. At this time as well, Gobind Singh coined the rallying cry of the Sikh religion—"*Sri Wahe Guruji Ka Khalsa, Sri Wahe Guruji Ki Fateh*" ("the Khalsa belong to God, and God's truth will always prevail"). In the first few days, it is estimated that some fifty thousand Sikhs were baptized into the Khalsa. Gobind Singh also fixed the definitive text of the Guru Granth Sahib at this

A priest recites from the Guru Granth Sahib during a religious celebration in Punjab, northern India. Believed to be the closest that human beings can come to perceiving the formless God, the sacred scriptures of Sikhism are constantly recited daily in Sikh *gurdwaras* throughout the world.

time. In remembrance of this great event, all Sikhs were to take the surname Singh ("lion"), if they were men, and Kaur ("princess") if they were women.

The Mughals reacted with unprecedented ferocity, murdering the Guru's two sons (aged eight and six) when they refused to accept Islam. The two sides became implacable enemies, and after the death of Aurangzeb in 1707, the balance of power in the Punjab began to shift in favor of the Sikhs. But the Sikhs were to lose their great leader as well: Gobind Singh was struck down by assassins in 1708 during discussions with the new Mughal emperor, Bahadur Shah, who had been given military support by the Sikhs in his fight for the throne. Just before his death, however, Gobind Singh abolished the human guruship of the Sikhs. In its place was put the authority of the Guru Granth Sahib, and temporal authority was to reside in a five-person council. Gobind Singh's injunction forms the basis of a prayer recited every day after every prayer service:

I have established the Khalsa by God's command
To all Sikhs, this then is the commandment:

Accept the Granth as the Guru.
Acknowledge the Guru Granthji as the visible form of the Gurus.
Those with disciplined minds will find what they seek in it.

The Sikhs and the British

With the abolition of the institution of the human guruship, the Sikhs now entered a new phase of their development—that was to be intimately associated with the rising paramount power in India, the British. At first, these newcomers, centered as they were in eastern India, had little effect on the Sikhs of the extreme northwestern regions of the Punjab. But as the British continued their inexorable push westward they inevitably came in contact with the Sikhs, first in conflict and later in cooperation. But this was still almost a century and a half in the future. The history of the Sikhs during this period is a constant litany of woes. Rather than diminishing after the death of the last Guru in 1708, Muslim persecution of the Sikhs increased. So, too, did Sikh resistance to that persecution. The day-to-day government of the Sikhs now resided in a combination of local assemblies (*sangats*) and a permanent executive, the *panjpiyare* ("the beloved five"), originally the five Sikhs who had offered themselves to Gobind Singh for sacrifice.

The Sikhs' resistance to Muslim and Hindu oppression often hinged on the leadership of charismatic war leaders. The first of these was Banda Singh, who had been appointed to his position by Gobind Singh just before his death. After a series of daring raids that increased Sikh territory, Banda defeated Mughal forces sent to destroy him at the historic battle of Chappar Chiri in 1710. Banda then proclaimed a Sikh state, issuing his own coinage. Next he had to turn his attention to the Hindu rulers of the hill states along his northeastern borders. Although he was captured by the Mughals and executed in 1716, Banda Singh had ensured the survival of the Sikh religion through a combination of military genius and executive acumen. One of his most farsighted decisions was to abolish in areas under Sikh control the *zamindari* system, by which government revenues were collected through the use of intermediary landlords who often controlled large tracts of land and extracted heavy rents from their tenants. With the abolition of this system, Banda Singh made the peasants who worked the land its owners. This both strengthened the peasants' adherence to the Sikh cause and increased the revenues, since the peasants naturally worked harder for themselves than for someone else.

Despite the death of Banda Singh, Sikh resistance continued unabated. Finally in 1733, the Mughals attempted to buy the rebels off by granting them a principality of their own under the nominal control of the Mughal emperor. The *panjpiyare* and the *sangats* chose Kapur Singh to head it. He immediately reorganized the community into *dals* (groups), which allowed for better control and utilization of Sikh resources. The Dal Khalsa, composed of the Budha Dal (warriors over forty) and the Taruna Dal (warriors under that age), were charged with guarding the Sikh holy places, conducting conversions, and harassing the Mughals. The Taruna Dal was further subdivided into five sections, each with its own emblems of authority, headed by a veteran of proven ability. These *dals* administered the territory that they had brought under Sikh control.

As Mughal power continued to erode, Sikh influence in the Punjab increased, although not without considerable sacrifice. The wars between the Muslim Mughals and the Sikhs increased in number and viciousness, with massacres of women and children becoming a common feature of the conflict. The situation was complicated by the increasing frequency after 1739 of foreign invasions from the northwest, from Persia and Afghanistan. The Sikhs had declared the Khalsa an independent state in 1748 when they had wrested control of Amritsar back from the Mughals. In 1753, they declared themselves the rulers of the entire Punjab. They were able to do so through the institution of the *rakhi* system. In return for one fifth of the revenue paid to the state, the Sikhs protected the peasants who had paid them, regardless of their religious affiliations. Such protection was badly needed, as wave after wave of invaders swept over northwestern India between 1740 and 1800. By 1765, the Sikhs were minting their own coins in Amritsar. Meanwhile, the *dals* were evolving into the twelve Sikh *misls*—states under hereditary Sikh chieftains. One of these leaders, Jassa Singh Ahluwalia, even overran the Mughal capital city of Delhi in 1783, departing only after the emperor agreed to pay an annual tribute. While in possession of the city, they built several *gurdwaras* on the sites of the deaths of Sikh martyrs.

The control of the Punjab continued to seesaw until the early 1800s when Ranjit Singh (1780–1839) of the Sukerchakia *misl* united the region into a single state. On his death, his state splintered and was eventually defeated by the British in the two Anglo-Sikh Wars of 1845–46, and 1848–49. Although the Sikhs dealt the British some severe defeats, particularly at the battle of Chillianwala in 1849, the British broke the Sikh power at the subsequent battle of Gujarat. They then incorporated their territory into the emerging British Indian Empire. Despite their hard-fought battles with the British, the Sikhs remained loyal to them during the Indian Mutiny of 1857. This loyalty, along with their native military prowess honed over two centuries of warfare, caused the British to utilize them as soldiers in their Indian armies. Even today, the Indian armed forces contain a disproportionate number of Sikhs.

The arrival of the British in the Punjab brought in its wake a wave of missionaries intent on converting the Sikhs to Christianity. Several Sikh groups sprang up in response. The first, led by Baba Dayal (1783–1855), called for a return to basic Sikh values. Known as the Nirankaris for their devotion to the Formless One (*Nirankar*), this group emphasized an ascetic lifestyle that resonated with many Sikhs. So too did the message of the Kukas, led by Bhai Balak Singh (1799–1862). The Kukas rejected the whole apparatus of British rule and were well organized in twenty-two administrative districts. The most effective of these new groups, however, was the Singh Sabha, founded in 1873 at Amritsar. Soon there were 117 Singh Sabhas across the Punjab. The Singh Sabha and groups like it, such as the Tat Khalsa and the Panch Khalsa Diwan, advocated a return to traditional values. Other groups, such as the Amritsar Singh Sabha, had a broader definition of what was involved in being a Sikh; but eventually a more rigorous form of Sikhism, purged of the Hindu elements that had crept into Sikh usage, became the norm. This led to increased insistence on the equality of women, the establishment of new educational institutions such as the Khalsa College, and the replacement of Hindu rituals by distinctively Sikh ones.

As the calls for Indian independence grew more strident, the Sikhs began to become more militant as well. In 1920, the Shiromani Gurdwara Parbandhak and the Shiromani Akali Dal were founded. Known collectively as the Akalis (after Akali, "Timeless One," a Sikh epithet for God), these groups arose in response to perceived abuses of British authority. Primary among these abuses was the British compliance with the *Mahant* system whereby the various *gurdwaras* were under the control of hereditary caretakers who were often Hindus. Likewise, they objected to the control of the Golden Temple being in the hands of the British Deputy Commissioner of Amritsar, who had appointed an overseer totally anathema to observant Sikhs. After a long struggle, the Sikh Gurdwara Act was passed in 1925, returning the custody of the *gurdwaras* and the Golden Temple to Sikhs. But once the genie had been let out of the bottle, it was not so easily replaced, and Sikhs now played a conspicuous role in the struggle for Indian independence.

Sikhism in Post-Independence India

Regrettably, the story of the Sikhs in post-Independence India has not been a happy one. The terms of independence split the Punjab down the middle, with half going to India and half to the new state of Pakistan. Mass movements of people fleeing both sides of the partition took place and were accompanied by mass murder as old communal scores were settled in blood. The Sikhs, caught between the Muslims and the Hindus, suffered cruelly. Despite this, Sikhs continued to serve in the Indian Army, fighting with valor in Kashmir, and in the several wars that later erupted between India and Pakistan. Meanwhile, the Punjab advanced economically and agriculturally to become one of the richest regions of the country. But the Sikhs were not completely satisfied. While most other regions of the country had been divided into political units based on language and ethnicity, the Punjab was not given that status until relatively late. Moreover, various political actions of the central government were interpreted by many Sikhs as a subtle form of discrimination against them by the Hindu majority. More radical elements of the community now began to call for the establishment of "Khalistan," an autonomous or semi-autonomous Sikh political unit. Needless to say, the government of India did not look favorably on such efforts. As matters progressed, events took yet another tragic turn.

With the hardening of Indian governmental attitudes toward their political aspirations, many Sikhs began to turn away from the moderate position toward more radical leaders. Prominent among these was Jarnail Singh Bhindranwale, a devout, charismatic Sikh seminary professor. As his following increased, he moved his headquarters to the Golden Temple on December 15, 1983. Meanwhile, the more moderate Akali Sikhs, who represented the opinions of the majority of their people and had been negotiating with the central government for over a decade, decided to protest the government's intransigence to their demands by burning a page of the Indian Constitution in public. One thing led to another, and in June 1984, Bhindranwale and his followers clashed with the Indian Army in Amritsar. By the time the smoke had cleared, Bhindranwale was dead, along with some five thousand civilians, the Golden Temple was in ruins, and Sikhs worldwide were stunned and appalled. In October of that year, Indira Gandhi, the Indian prime minister who had ordered the attack, was herself dead—shot down by two Sikh members of her bodyguard, who were immediately killed by their fellows. The Sikh tradition of courage and sacrifice, even if perhaps misplaced, lived on. This triggered severe communal reaction by Hindu extremists and as a result several thousand Sikhs were murdered in a four-day orgy of revenge.

External factors are not the only source of tension in modern Sikhism. Internal dissension is evident in the distinction often drawn within the community between Jat Sikhs and Sikhs of other classes. Indeed, prejudices exist within the Jat community itself based on geographical origin. In the main, the Jats are farmers, while the non-Jats tend to be found in trade, commerce, and the professions. Although the two groups have no diversity in religious beliefs, the trend toward internal divisions in the Khalsa bothers many Sikhs. Despite these difficulties, however, the Sikh religion continues to be a vital growing faith. Now spread throughout the world as a result of Sikh immigration, Sikh *gurdwaras* can be found on every continent in the world except Antarctica. But in its Indian homeland, it must contend—as must all non-Hindu religions—with the growing trend toward Hindu nationalism that threatens to change India from the tolerant pluralistic state envisioned by its founders to a mono-religious entity ruled by "Hindu" principles. It is to the evolution of this phenomenon that we must now turn our attention.

Website References

1. Basic Sikh religious philosophy is explained at www.sikhs.org/philos.htm

2. The Golden Temple can be seen at www.sikh.net/Gurdwara/golden/golden.htm

3. The sacred scriptures of Sikhism are translated at www.sikhs.org/english/frame.html

4. Some examples of famous Sikh *gurdwaras* are found at www.sikhs.org/hgurd.html

5. www.sikhs.org/audio.htm gives audio files of some of the major Sikh prayers.

CHAPTER EIGHT

♦

Hinduism's Changing Relationship with the West

As we have seen, Hinduism's interaction with other religions has not always gone smoothly. Periodically there were outbreaks of sectarian violence toward not only foreign religions, notably Islam, but also against the non-Vedic Indian religions, such as Buddhism and Jainism. One needs look no further than the medieval stories of saints' lives among the various Hindu groups to see evidence of this. Such stories often praise the saint in question for his conversion of a local ruler to the saint's form of Hindu observance. This conversion is often accompanied by the ruler's execution of large numbers of his former coreligionists. The image of Hinduism as a pacific, welcoming, and all-inclusive tradition is largely a modern construct that has more to do with attempts to raise the status of the religion in the eyes of the Euro-American peoples than with any historical reality. Neither, of course, should one view the tradition as excessively bloodthirsty. Rather, it displays negative traits and attitudes that are, unfortunately, common to all religious traditions.

In Hinduism's case, conflict was somewhat mitigated by the attitude of practitioners of other religious traditions toward Indian culture in general. As one of the oldest and most sophisticated of human cultures, Indian civilization held a profound fascination for even Hinduism's harshest critics. The Muslim invaders of India, who absolutely abhorred most aspects of their Indian subjects' native religion, were nevertheless fascinated by Indian art, literature, music, and science. Consequently, there was a constant engagement between Hindu intellectuals and those of other traditions. This facilitated, at least on a simple level, the interchange of ideas and viewpoints between certain segments of the Hindu population and their counterparts from other traditions. Sadly, this interchange did not reach as far as the average Hindu. With the domination of northern India by Muslim rulers after the tenth century C.E., Hinduism became more reactionary and inward looking in an effort to protect itself. While this did not mean a complete cessation of new intellectual activity, as the work of the later Vedanta philosophers amply demonstrates, the average Hindu was little affected by new ideas. As often as not, two parallel Indias—one Hindu, the other Muslim—functioned side by side from this period onward with only minimal contact between them.

This tenuous equilibrium came to an end with the advent of the Europeans. At first, the Portuguese and the Dutch who landed on Indian shores in the mid-sixteenth century were content to have little political and cultural contact with the powerful Mughal Empire that ruled India. Despite a history of conflict between Christianity and Islam, these European newcomers were content with the limited trade that they were allowed to engage in, since that trade, small as it was by Indian standards, could still make them wealthy beyond the dreams of avarice when they sold their cargoes of silks and spices on the docks of Lisbon and Amsterdam. But as time went on, other countries joined the India trade, and these countries, notably England and France, were to have a much more profound and direct impact on India's future. At first, these new countries were also satisfied with simple trading. But as the seventeenth century progressed, two new factors were added to the equation. The first was the rise of the great European colonial empires. The second was the decline of the Mughals.

Initially, France and England were not particularly interested in India. They both made great profits from the India trade, but these were uncertain compared with the lesser but more reliable revenues gained through the direct colonization of the Americas and the Caribbean. French and English influence in India was restricted to a few trading posts/fortresses and their immediate hinterlands. This would likely have remained the case had not a series of dynastic feuds, starting around 1630, begun to erode the power and prestige of the Mughal Empire. This encouraged local Indian rulers to defy the court at Delhi, but it would be almost a hundred years before these vassals rebelled directly against central control. Unfortunately for India, this action coincided with major political changes in Europe and America as well. Since the early seventeenth century, European politics had been dominated by the French, whose influence reached its apogee under Louis XIV, the Sun King. On Louis's death, the political balance of Europe began to shift. During the Seven Years' War (known in American history as the French and Indian War), France lost virtually all her colonies in North America. Hoping to counterbalance this loss, the French began to expand their activities in India through alliances with ambitious former vassals of the Mughals. But the French were blocked in their efforts by a series of brilliant English admirals and generals, and their influence in India soon dwindled to almost nothing. What the French did do, however, was to initiate a new mode of interaction between the Europeans and the Indians in which the Europeans became much more actively involved with Indian political affairs. This was to prove disastrous for Indian independence.

In this initial period of increased political interaction between Indian rulers and the Europeans, conducted not by direct contact between governments but indirectly through the French and English East India companies, the advantages seemed to be all on the Indian side. They craved European munitions and found European military organization to be superior to their own; but this support of their dynastic ambitions required only a small number of European technical advisors who offered no direct threat to their continued rule over their subjects. It thus became the practice of these rulers, starting in southern India but soon spreading northward, to use European or European-trained troops at every opportunity. The Europeans cooperated, partially to purchase the goodwill of their erstwhile landlords and, more significantly, for the hefty cash payments that accompanied such service. However, all this changed fundamentally after a battle fought in western Bengal at the small village of Plassey in 1757. Here, a young East India Company employee by the name of Robert Clive defeated a much larger Mughal army, thus ensuring the independence of the Bengali viceroy. In payment, the new ruler of Bengal bestowed on the East Indian Company the absolute rule of the region situated around the English settlement of Calcutta. The Company now ceased to be a purely commercial vehicle and became an actual Indian ruling state.

Modern Indian religious sites. Modern India is home to a number of religious traditions, including Hinduism, Jainism, and Sikhism. These sites are scattered throughout the whole length and breadth of the subcontinent.

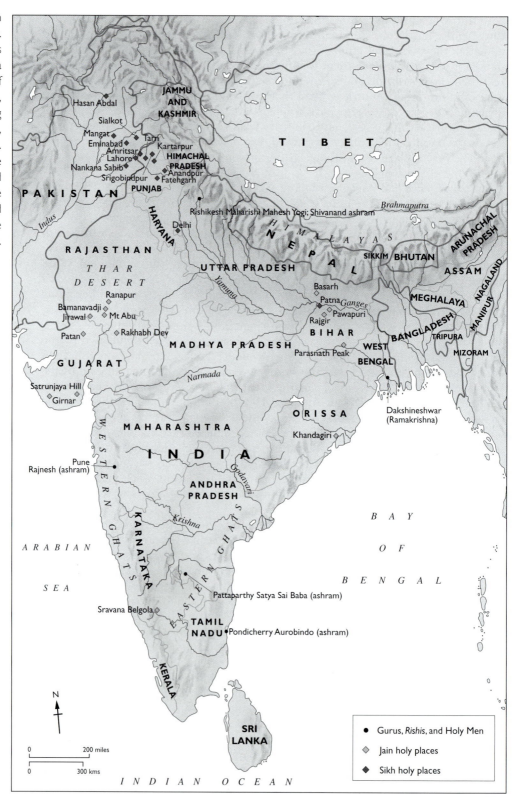

JAMMU AND KASHMIR

Hasan Abdal

Sialkot

T I B E T

Mangat
Eminabad
Amritsar
Lahore
Nankana Sahib
Tarn
Kartarpur
HIMACHAL
PRADESH
Anandpur
Srigobindpur
Fatehgarh

PUNJAB

P A K I S T A N

HARYANA

Indus

Delhi

RAJASTHAN

Brahmaputra

H I M A L A Y A S

N E P A L

SIKKIM   BHUTAN

ARUNACHAL PRADESH

ASSAM

Rishikesh Maharishi Mahesh Yogi; Shivanand ashram

T H A R
D E S E R T

Ranapur
Bamanavadji
Jirawal   Mt Abu

Patan

Rakhabh Dev

UTTAR PRADESH

Yamuna

Basarh
Patna *Ganges*
Rajgir   Pawapuri

MEGHALAYA

NAGALAND

MANIPUR

BANGLADESH

TRIPURA

MIZORAM

BIHAR

MADHYA PRADESH

Narmada

Parasnath Peak

WEST
BENGAL

GUJARAT

Satrunjaya Hill
Girnar

Dakshineshwar
(Ramakrishna)

O R I S S A

MAHARASHTRA

I N D I A

Khandagiri

Pune
Rajnesh (ashram)

W
E
S
T
E
R
N

G
H
A
T
S

Godavari

ANDHRA
PRADESH

Krishna

A R A B I A N

KARNATAKA

B A Y

O F

B E N G A L

S E A

E
A
S
T
E
R
N

G
H
A
T
S

Pattaparthy Satya Sai Baba (ashram)

Sravana Belgola

TAMIL
NADU

Pondicherry Aurobindo (ashram)

KERALA

N

0   200 miles

0   300 kms

SRI
LANKA

I N D I A N   O C E A N

●	Gurus, *Rishis*, and Holy Men
◇	Jain holy places
◆	Sikh holy places

Things went from bad to worse for the rulers of India. After the American Revolution and the loss of their most productive North American colonies, the British began to concentrate their attention on the acquisition of a new colonial empire to feed the needs of their nascent industrial revolution, and the locus of this search became India. By 1850, most of India was under either direct or indirect British control. This of course meant that the British came into close contact with the Indians and their culture, and vice versa. What resulted was a shock for both sides. Given the nature of the British–Indian relationship, it was inevitable that all such interactions would be tinged with political overtones. This was definitely the case with religion.

The Beginnings of the Hindu Reform Movement

Just as the British were beginning their rule over Bengal, a young man was born in the region under their control in the village of Bardwan who was to have a prodigious effect on the course of Indian intellectual development. This was Ram Mohan Roy (1772–1833), a young man of considerable talents who was consequently something of a trial to his conservative Hindu parents. His father had served the Muslim administration of Bengal and wished his son to follow in his footsteps and pursue a similar career. Accordingly, the elder Roy sent his son to the Muslim university of Patna to study the court languages of Arabic and Persian. Ram Mohan mastered these subjects with ease, but also picked up an interest in Sufism, the mystical school of Islam. This resulted in his rebelling against traditional Hindu image worship, and from there he began to question systematically many other tenets of his family's faith.

After an inevitable confrontation, Ram Mohan eventually acceded to his father's wish that he should study Sanskrit and Hindu scriptures at Varanasi, the ancient center of the Hindu faith. At the same time, however, Ram Mohan began studying English in order to qualify for employment with the East India Company. Joining the Company as a revenue officer in the district of Rangpur, he prospered to the extent that in 1814 he was able to retire and devote himself entirely to the study of religion and, more specifically, to the cause of Hindu religious reform. To do this, he felt that he needed to understand the doctrines of Christianity better, so he studied Hebrew and Greek in preparation for a projected translation of the Bible into his native Bengali.

It might be useful at this point to say a word about the propagation of Christianity in India in Ram Mohan Roy's time. Unlike the Spanish and Portuguese, and to a lesser extent the French and Dutch, the English East India Company had no interest whatsoever in spreading the word of Christianity in its domains. Indeed, sentiment within the Company held that this would only serve to destabilize the newly acquired Company lands in India. The Company therefore decided to forbid missionary work in its territories. It was only at the beginning of the nineteenth century, under pressure from evangelical Christian members of the English Parliament, that they reluctantly allowed some missionary work to proceed in their domains.

This issue was symptomatic of a great gulf between British attitudes and those of former foreign rulers of India. The British maintained from an early period a sort of cultural apartheid. Thomas Babington Macaulay, while Secretary of Education for India in the 1830s, made the famous remark that there was more truth and value in a single shelf of English books than in all Indian literature combined. What little interest there was in Indian culture on the British part was directly related to questions of law and governance. Even linguistically, our initial knowledge of Sanskrit exists only because it threw light on the development of European languages. Likewise, there was, after a short period of initial exuberance, virtually no mixing of British and Indian blood through intermarriage—as had previously been the case with other foreign groups. The impression that all this carried to the Indians was that their culture was of absolutely no interest, value or importance to their new rulers. Provided that taxes were paid on time and there were no domestic insurrections, the British seemed quite content never to have to interact with their Indian subjects at all.

The only exceptions were those officials, such as district commissioners, judges and the like, who dealt directly with Indians as part of their jobs, or the missionaries. Ram Mohan Roy was at home with both groups, and consequently had a far better understanding of European thought and mores than any of his contemporaries. At the same time, however, he had a profound understanding and respect for the Upanishadic foundations of his own religion as interpreted through the teachings of the Advaita school of Vedanta. He appreciated the riches of Christian theology and Enlightenment philosophy, but he had no intention of either abandoning Hinduism for Christianity, or joining in a blanket denunciation of the Hindu tradition. This was to cause a certain amount of consternation among Europeans, who could not comprehend how a Hindu scholar could clearly understand and appreciate European thought without embracing it wholeheartedly. Ram Mohan Roy's pamphlet *Precepts of Jesus: The Guide to Peace and Happiness*, an attempt to meld the best features of Hinduism and Christianity, only managed to alienate both Hindus and Christians—as do most attempts to merge ideas from differing religious traditions and cultures.

Where Ram Mohan Roy was most in tune with European sentiment was in his belief in, and campaign for, reform in certain questionable Hindu beliefs that

The Bathing Ghats at Varanasi. Ritual purification by bathing is still a central practice of modern Hinduism, as is pilgrimage to important religious sites such as Varanasi. These practices have no precedent in the early Hindu texts and likely represent practices absorbed into the religion from non-Vedic sources.

claimed to be absolutely essential to salvation but were, in point of fact, simply superstitious customs or ancient social practices masquerading under the guise of revelation. Notable among these was the practice of *sati*, which involved the burning of widows along with their deceased husbands. The British condoned this practice, and when Ram Mohan began his campaign to have it declared illegal and punishable by law, he was actually opposed in his efforts by such notable British figures as the great Indologist H. H. Wilson, who argued for the classic East India Company policy of noninterference in Indian religious affairs. Fortunately, more humane views prevailed, and *sati*, along with similar practices such as female infanticide, was legally forbidden.

Ram Mohan Roy had also wanted to purify Hinduism of image worship since his youth. To this end, he founded in 1828 a new religious movement called the Brahmo Samaj. This movement saw itself as a return to the pure religion of the Upanishads, but in doing so, it also incorporated a considerable Christian influence. Its founder did not see this as being problematic or incompatible with more mainline Hinduism. Regrettably, his more conservative Hindu contemporaries did not share this broadly ecumenical vision, and he and all members of the group were summarily excommunicated from the greater Hindu community. This did not in any way stop Ram Mohan Roy from continuing to exercise his reform activities, which included the founding of English-style schools for Brahmo Samaj children, promoting an education that emphasized a modern scientific system of schooling. After his early death in 1833, Ram Mohan Roy was succeeded in his position of as leader of the Brahmo Samaj by Debendranath Tagore (who was the father of the first Indian Nobel laureate, Rabindranath Tagore). Tagore went on to establish a Bengali-language newspaper as well as a school for Brahmo Samaj missionaries. He was opposed in his more conservative ideas by Keshub Chandra Sen (1836–1884), who advocated more radical departures from mainline Hinduism. Regrettably, this led to a split in the movement and ultimately, its subsequent decline.[1]

Whereas Ram Mohan Roy saw Hindu regeneration as coming through interaction with the new intellectual winds blowing into India from the West, another great reformer, Swami Dayananda Saraswati (1824–1883) wanted to slam the windows firmly shut. Dayananda, who was Gujarati by birth, had lost his faith in Shiva at a young age, and by the age of twenty-four had run away from home in order to discover the truth of existence. He encountered the irascible sage Swami Virajananda Saraswati, who returned the young man to the bosom of Hindu orthodoxy. For Dayananda, this was a strictly Vedic religion shorn of such later accretions as found in the Epics, the Puranas, the Samhitas, and the Agamas. Dayananda only accepted the authority of the Vedas, the Upanishads, the Manusmriti, and a few Dharma Sutras.

Far from being syncretic in outlook, Dayananda vigorously refuted the teachings of both Islam and Christianity. In 1875, he founded the Arya Samaj in Mumbai to combat what he saw as the pernicious incursions of these two religions into Hinduism. His main weapon in this fight was education, and he founded a series of schools (*gurukulas*) as training institutions based on Vedic principles for the education of children. He went even further than this, however, in suggesting that any means used to preserve Hinduism was absolutely justified, even physical violence. On Dayananda's death, the Arya Samaj split into a conservative and a liberal wing. Both groups continued to be active. Increasingly they saw their main opponents as being the Christian missionaries, whom they tried to frustrate by any means at their imagination and disposal.[2]

Vivekananda and the Euro-American Reappraisal of Hinduism

Both the Brahmo Samaj and the Arya Samaj preached reform, but their programs tended to be primarily social and educational in nature. As such, they had only a limited appeal to the vast mass of the Indian population. More widespread was the influence of Ramakrishna (1836–1886), a little Brahmin priest of Kali from Calcutta. On the face of it, this minor priest of the Dakshineshwar Temple just outside Calcutta should have played no role in the greater epic of Hindu civilization. He was an eccentric mystic who did not write any books or found any formal school. Yet the effect that he had on the English-educated youth of Calcutta was nothing short of miraculous. Ramakrishna was a follower of Advaita Vedanta, albeit in a very eclectic manner, who preached the unity of all religions. Under his influence, many middle-class Bengali youth decided to renounce their worldly ambitions and become monks in what was to become known as the Ramakrishna Mission. This group, which has become immensely influential in India through its charitable and educational activities, spoke to the Indian heart more directly than its predecessors, and began to proselytize for a regeneration of Hindu spirituality based on Advaita principles. By far the most well-known of the early members of the Mission was Vivekananda (1863–1902).[3]

Vivekananda believed that Hinduism was essential not only for India but for the whole world. Realizing that his religion was misrepresented and misunderstood in Europe and America, he traveled to both continents to preach a new vision of Hinduism totally at odds with the popular Western understanding of the tradition as nothing more than a hodgepodge of primitive superstitions. At the World Parliament of Religions in Chicago in 1893, he articulated a model of Hinduism that was an alternative to Euro-American materialism. As he wrote in his *Complete Works* (vol. 3, p. 139), "We Hindus have now been placed, under God's providence, in a very critical and responsible position. The nations of the West are coming to us for spiritual help." Elsewhere in the same work (pp. 27–29), he observes, "Once more the world must be conquered by India ... mighty minds will arise, gigantic spiritual minds who will be ready to go forth from India to the ends of the world to teach spirituality and renunciation ... Ours is a religion of which Buddhism with all its greatness is a rebel child and of which Christianity is a very patchy imitation." As part of this movement to bring Hinduism to the wider world, Vivekananda established the Vedanta Society, which still functions in the United States and elsewhere.

This vision of Hinduism as the spiritual teacher of Europe and America gained impetus through the work of two great modern Hindu teachers, Ramana Maharshi (1879–1950) and Swami Shivananda (1887–1964). Both were charismatic figures who embodied in themselves the best of the Hindu tradition. Ramana Maharshi's life and work in particular was popularized by the English writer Paul Bruton, and this triggered the desire to experience such holy men at first hand in many Westerners. Living the life that they preached, and interacting with Euro-American disciples, teachers such as Ramana Maharshi and Shivananda popularized the image of the Indian holy man who possessed an existential wisdom denied to his more worldly Western counterparts. This sent many young people in the 1960s and 1970s to India in search of enlightenment at the hands of Hindu gurus. Many of these seekers eventually found enlightenment, but often not in the form that they had expected.

More representative of modern gurus that appeal to indigenous Indian religious appetites is Sri Sathya Sai Baba (b. 1924). Purportedly the reincarnation of the great Marathi saint Sai Baba of Shirdi, Sathya Sai Baba is a native of Puttapuri in the state of Andhra Pradesh. At a young age he was renowned for creating candies and flowers for his playmates. His followers believe implicitly in his miraculous powers and ability to heal even the most dire of diseases. In addition to producing jewelry, photographs of himself, and *vibhuti* (sacred ash), he is also reputed to be able to bilocate, read thoughts, and prophesy. Indeed, many hold him to be an avatar of God, an idea that he seems to do nothing to dispel.

Mahatma Gandhi and the Politicization of Hinduism

Perhaps the most famous of modern Hindu holy men is Mohandas Karamchand Gandhi (1869–1948). A modern film of his life by Sir Richard Attenborough in the 1980s was a major commercial success and deservedly earned the actor who played

Mahatma Gandhi leaving Meherauli, a Muslim shrine. This is one of the last appearances between the end of his fast and his death. Gandhi's success as a political leader was directly tied to his religious ideals and activities.

Gandhi, Ben Kingsley, an Oscar. This success was partly a result of the cinematic art of the film, fueled by the dramatic events of Gandhi's life, including the achievement of winning India's independence from Britain in 1947. But it also stood as a testimony to Gandhi's unique personality and to the fact that all his actions, and in particular his political actions, were at their core motivated by religious fervor. This, combined with Gandhi's inclusive vision of Hinduism as embracing the best in all religions, has earned him the status of an ecumenical twentieth-century saint in most of the world's religions. But a closer examination of his thought shows that even though he was open to other religions, he saw himself as being definitely and absolutely a Hindu.[4]

Gandhi was born in the Gujarati princely state of Porbandhar. Situated in the western region of Gujarat known as Kathiawar, where many small states had submitted early on to British rule and thus preserved a measure of independence, Porbandhar's ruling family had relied on Gandhi's father to run the day-to-day affairs of the state for many years. His mother was a particularly devout follower of Vishnu who visited the temple daily and rigorously practiced various ascetic disciplines. Gandhi was by all reports a very average student in elementary school. His grades improved in high school, but like many adolescents he rebelled against authority during this period. His rebellion was mainly religious in character. He ate meat, drank alcohol, and smoked cigarettes. Fortunately for the subsequent history of India, Gandhi regained his faith and never relapsed into his "sinful" ways—indeed, he did quite the opposite.

On graduating from high school, Gandhi entered Samaldas College in Bhavnagar to train as a lawyer. His studies failed to prosper, however, and he returned home at a loss as to the next step in his life's journey. It was suggested to him that he should go to England to study, a radical step for orthodox Hindus since it "broke caste"— that is it rendered one ritually impure and ineligible to perform religious rituals unless the impurity was sacramentally removed. Gandhi went to England anyway, completed his studies in law with honors, and was admitted to the British bar. At this time, he met many famous European religious luminaries of the period and interacted with a number of prominent Christians, including Josia Oldfield and Cardinal Manning. As Gandhi later avowed, his trip to England taught him to detest the British colonial government but to love the British people; and the relatively bloodless nature of the Indian independence movement against British rule was in no small degree the result of Gandhi's making this distinction.

Returning to Indian in 1891, Gandhi underwent religious purification and once more became a full member of the Hindu communion. However, he had not completely escaped being infected by pernicious European ideas: he ate oatmeal and cocoa for breakfast, drank and wore European clothes. He began to practice law, but he had one flaw fatal for a barrister—who by definition constantly had to speak in court—in that he was extremely shy and tongue-tied. As a result, he was required to eke out a living preparing legal papers for other lawyers until 1893, when he moved to South Africa. The move was to change his life and world history.

Up until then, Gandhi had led a privileged life and met with little or no racial discrimination. All this changed in South Africa, where racial prejudice was rampant. At one point, Gandhi was ejected from a first-class train compartment for no other reason than that he was "colored." At the same time, Gandhi's interest in religion continued to grow and intensify. He read the Qur'an and Christian literature, but he was especially influenced by the somewhat eccentric Christian socialism of the Russian writer Leo Tolstoy's *The Kingdom of God is Within You*, a book that managed to get Tolstoy excommunicated from his own Russian Orthodox Church. This combination of factors drew Gandhi more and more into the struggle for Indian civil rights in South Africa during the seventeen years he spent there. He moved to Pretoria and was soon acknowledged the moral leader of the South African Indian community. In 1901, he briefly returned to India to report to the All-India Congress of that year on South African conditions.

On a personal level, Gandhi began his "experiments with Truth" in his own life. A dedicated vegetarian, he refused to allow his son to eat eggs and bouillon during a potentially fatal illness. He established a commune based on socialist principles. Members of his family rose at 6:30 A.M. to grind wheat for the day's bread, and Gandhi himself walked the six miles to and from his law office every day while concurrently teaching his children Gujarati. All this simplicity and religious fervor was fed by Gandhi's readings in the Bhagavad Gita, the works of Rabindranath Tagore and Vivekananda, and, especially, John Ruskin's *Unto This Last*. From Ruskin, Gandhi took the beginnings of his belief that individual well-being must be subordinated to the good of all, that all work was of equal value, and that manual labor was the purest form of labor. It was a worldview that exalted the lower classes of society and in particular the Indian peasant. As such, it was to have tremendous resonance in the mind of the average Hindu.

All these influences coalesced into Gandhi's concept of **satyagraha**, passive resistance based on love and nonviolence. As Gandhi's agitation for civil rights increased, the South African government became more and more repressive. In 1908, Gandhi was jailed for the first time along with 155 followers. He urged them to follow prison regulations to the letter, and he himself used his time to study not only religious tomes but political science, economics, and sociology as well. Far from resenting it, Gandhi always appreciated his time in prison. This was fortunate, since he was destined to spend a great deal of time there. In 1909, Gandhi wrote his political manifesto *Hind Swaraj* (*Indian Self-Rule*). In it, he outlined his principle of nonviolent opposition to British rule and also made clear his critique of modern civilization. A Luddite in a loincloth, Gandhi condemned technology, modern medicine, and the mores of the civilization of his time in general. He urged India to turn back the clock and return to a simpler life style close to the earth.

Gandhi put these principles into action in South Africa with the establishment of Tolstoj Farm in 1910. A radical commune, Tolstoj Farm aimed at total self sufficiency. Strangely enough, and perhaps tellingly, its basic regulations were based on those of Pretoria prison. All the communards worked in the fields and attended the religious services of all the religions of its inhabitants. No modern medical procedures were allowed, and all the residents were required to learn a handicraft skill. Gandhi himself learned how to make sandals from an ashram member who had learned the craft while residing in a Trappist monastery. Children did not attend the public school system, but spent their mornings in the fields and their afternoons in study. In the same year Gandhi closed his law practice in order to devote his full attentions to the commune. In 1912, he took a formal vow renouncing all private property. Before this, he had vowed to renounce sex.

By 1915, Gandhi had decided to return to India. He was forty-six years old and, except for a handful of intellectuals, totally unknown in his native land. On the urging of the grand old man of Indian politics, G. K. Gokale (1866–1915), he traveled throughout India familiarizing himself with conditions there. He then settled in his native Gujarat at Wardha, where he established his Satyagraha Ashram. Here again everyone worked in the fields. Dress and food were of the simplest kind and, for three months each year, students were required to walk through India learning from and aiding the poor villagers of the countryside. Children began their education at the age of four, spending ten years studying religion, agriculture, weaving, literature, Sanskrit, Hindi, and a Dravidian language. Gandhi, at considerable financial hardship and loss of prestige to himself, allowed "untouchables"—those at the bottom of society whom Gandhi termed *harijan* or "children of God"—to join the ashram despite upper-caste prejudices. The plight of the untouchables was of constant concern to Gandhi—theirs was a cause that he was passionate about throughout his entire public career.

Gandhi's political agenda was structured on three guiding principles: the search for, and enactment of, truth; nonviolence; and sexual continence. This harking back to the ascetic practices of Indian religion found its fullest expression in Gandhi's "fasts unto death." He carried out these acts of protest a number of times in his career, starting in 1921. Often they were not protesting British repression, but sectarian violence on the part of Hindus; and they were effective because of the witness of Gandhi's own life. The average Indian peasant saw him as the modern embodiment of the great religious figures of old, hence his sobriquet Mahatma ("Great Soul"). Consequently, his actions and opinions carried immense authority in many quarters of Indian society where the arguments of the Europeanized Indian intellectuals fell on stony ground. Gandhi's vision might not always be realistic, for example his belief that all Indians should weave their own cloth, but they could not be ignored. Ultimately, Gandhi was successful, and the British simply packed their bags and left India. Sadly, the India that Gandhi wanted to emerge from this great "act of Truth" was never realized.

Despite the relatively bloodless revolution that he had engineered, the Partition of India resulted in horrific violence in which hundreds of thousands of people on both sides lost their property, their homes, and often their lives. Despite his appreciation for many aspects of Euro-American culture, Gandhi was in the end a traditional Hindu. He might love the Qur'an and the Christian Gospels, but his scriptures of choice were the Ramacaritamanas and the Bhagavad Gita. He believed in most traditional Hindu beliefs, and when he appeared to deviate from them, in such matters as untouchability for example, he firmly believed—as did Ram Mohan Roy and Swami Dayananda before him—that he was being faithful to the older, purer streams of the tradition. His aim was to bring about Ram Rajya, the Kingdom of God on earth, although he understood this term in a much different sense than it would be later used by nationalist politicians. After his assassination in 1948, his mantle descended on Jawaharlal Nehru, an English-educated atheistic socialist who was determined to make India a secular socialist democratic state. This did not sit well with several segments of Indian society.

One of the great ironies of modern Indian history is that the greatest proponent of the modern revival of Hinduism was assassinated by a Hindu. Gandhi's murderer, Nathuram Godse, was a member of a group that espoused a radically Hindu India and had developed out of the Hindu Mahasabha movement, which began in 1910 and built on the work of B. G. Tilak (1856–1920), "the Father of Indian Unrest." Followers of the Hindu Mahasabha believed that, "Hindus have a right to live in peace as Hindus, to legislate, to rule, to govern themselves in accordance with Hindu genius and ideals, and establish by all lawful and legal means a Hindu state based on Hindu Culture and Tradition, so that Hindu ideology and way of life should have a homeland of its own" (quoted in Klostermaier, p. 463). Later leaders who espoused the cause of a Hindu homeland held that whatever means were necessary to achieve this end, including violence, were justified. It was the death-knell for Gandhi's dream of India as the moral leader of humanity, as present-day events in India have proven. This was particularly tragic, since India was the home of several other indigenous religions that had made considerable contributions to world culture, and whose rights and future in the country of their birth are now seen by some people to be threatened to the point of extinction by the rise of Hindu communal politics.[5]

Hinduism in the Twenty-First Century

At the opening of the twenty-first century, Hinduism has become a true world religion, although the vast majority of its practitioners still live in the countries of South Asia. Hindus have spread throughout the world, and have carried their religious culture with them. Hindu temples are now found in many of the world's major cities, and Hindus have made concerted efforts to maintain their traditions and beliefs while still functioning in the technological societies of Europe and America. Moreover, a number of Hindu or quasi-Hindu groups composed mostly of non-Indians have arisen over the last half a century that have attempted to make Hinduism available to Euro-Americans in forms that resonate with their own cultural norms. How successful these groups will be in the long run is still open to question.

With its long history in South Asia, and the dispersal of Hindus throughout the world, what are the prospects for Hinduism in the twenty-first century? As well as its strengths, Hinduism has what might be perceived as its weaknesses. It is still primarily a South Asian tradition, and the powerful role that the caste system still plays in Hindu society hampers its ability to expand beyond its traditional boundaries. Moreover, since Hinduism is not a single unitary religion, but rather a series of interlocking traditions and modes of interaction with the divine, some of which are in direct contradiction of one another, diversity of understanding of what "Hinduism" is, coupled with the ethnic, linguistic, and geographical diversity of

Temple scene in Mathura. Religion in India is still a vital force that plays a great part in the life of the country.

South Asia, has often led to sectarianism and division within the ranks of Hindus themselves. This has led to strained relations with the other religious traditions of the region as well.

But this very diversity could work to Hinduism's advantage in the new millennium. Many of its key concepts have gained a wide acceptance that they did not have only fifty years ago. As the traditional religions of Europe and America struggle in the face of science and materialism, many people have been attracted to the experiential branches of Hinduism such as Yoga by their very lack of pronounced dogma and adherence to any absolute institutional or scriptural authority. Thus Hinduism's very lack of structure could conceivably turn out to be its greatest strength. Klaus Klostermaier neatly sums up the possibilities for the future of Hinduism when he writes,

> It would not be surprising to find Hinduism the dominant religion of the twenty-first century. It would be a religion that doctrinally is less clear-cut than mainstream Christianity, politically less determined than Islam, ethically less heroic than Buddhism, but it would offer something to everybody, it would delight by its richness and depth, it would address people at a depth that has not been reached for a long time by other religions or by the prevailing ideologies. . . . All of us may be already much more Hindu than we think.
>
> SOURCE: Klostermaier, *A Survey of Hinduism*, pp. 475–476

Website References

1. The history and beliefs of the Brahmo Samaj are discussed at www.chanda.freeserve.co.uk/brahmoframe.htm

2. www.punjabilok.com/faith/arya_samaj/arya_samaj.htm gives information on the Arya Samaj.

3. Information on the Ramakrishka Mission can be found at www.vedanta.org/ramak/

4. www.mkgandhi.org/ covers the life and work of M. K. Gandhi.

5. Some aspects of political Hinduism can be seen at //bjp.org/

CHAPTER NINE

✦

Jainism: The First of the *Nastika* Traditions

Sometime about 1000 B.C.E. a division began to arise between those Indian religious thinkers who were content to follow the old religious tradition of sacrifice, the Brahmanic tradition, and those who held that the path to the divine lay more in experiential knowledge. This latter group, which became known as the Shramanas or Ascetics, did not reject earlier traditions outright. Rather, they reinterpreted them in the light of personal experience; and some scholars have suggested that they represent the reassertion of religious ideas and practices that predate the Vedas, whether of Aryan or non-Aryan origin. Whatever the case, the emergence of the Shramanic tradition was to lead to a deeper division in Indian religious thought that lay along the fault line of belief in the Vedas. One group within the emerging knowledge school, while holding to interpretations of the sacred scripture rejected by the sacrificial branch of Hinduism, still felt that the Vedas in some manner or other embodied revelatory truths. This group was to evolve into the Yoga school of philosophy. But the other knowledge-oriented groups rejected this interpretation, saying that, despite the many useful insights contained in the Vedas, they were merely products of the human mind and thus no more nor less sacred than any similar religious speculations. The two groups became known as the *astikas*, those who said the Vedas were divinely revealed; and the *nastikas*, those who said that they were not.

This divergence of opinion marked the point of origin for those religions of India which, while in themselves retaining many features of their parent Hindu tradition, have developed in such ways as to make them separate entities at the same time. Of these, three traditions commend themselves to our attention: **Carvaka** (which is also known as Lokayata), the Indian form of materialism; Jainism; and Buddhism. Of the three, Buddhism has prospered most, becoming one of the world's great religions. Jainism is at present a relatively small tradition, but at one time it claimed the allegiance of a substantial number of inhabitants of South Asia. Moreover, it has subsequently had a considerable influence on the development of modern Hinduism.[1] As for Carvaka, this viewpoint was decisively rejected by later Indian thinkers, but it is important to note its existence in order to refute the charge that Indian philosophy was less thorough in its inquiries than Euro-American philosophy.[2]

Mahavira and the Rise of Jainism

According to Jain legend, Jainism is an ancient religion, having some twenty-three leaders prior to the birth of the first historical leader of the religion, Mahavira ("The Great Hero"), in the sixth century B.C.E. These leaders, known as Tirthamkaras ("Ford-makers"), were credited with having reached enlightenment, but rather than depart existence they had chosen to remain on earth to teach humanity the way to liberation from the cycle of life and death. The biographies ascribed to these august personages had very similar elements: noble birth, renunciation of the world, successful pursuit of the religious quest, and the founding of a religious community. This bare outline of what might be called the Indian religious founder myth was then fleshed out with details of the life of the particular founder. This is a pattern that we see not only in Jainism, but also in the slightly later Buddhist tradition. One might, therefore, reach the conclusion that these stories were just pious fictions. However, the stories of the last two of the twenty-four Jain Ford-makers exhibit enough divergence from this pattern to suggest that, in their cases at least, this mythical framework was augmented by a core of historical facts. The twenty-third Ford-maker, Parshva, is said to have lived some two hundred and fifty years before Mahavira, and it is quite possible that he, not Mahavira, was the original founder of the Jain school of practice.

The Tirthamkaras Rishabhadeva and Mahavira, Orissa, 11th century. Rishabhadeva is considered by Jains to be the first "Ford-maker" of the present cycle of the world. Mahavira is considered to be the last. The twenty-four Ford-makers are venerated by Jains for their efforts to show humanity the way out of the cycle of life and death.

But for all practical purposes, the story of Jainism begins with Prince Vardhamana who was later given the title Mahavira or Jina ("the Conqueror"), a title often applied to the Buddha as well. Mahavira was born at Kundagram in the kingdom of Magadha, northeastern India, in about 600 B.C.E. He was reputedly a Brahmin by caste and member of a royal family ruling a small city state on the lower reaches of the Ganges River. Raised with all the material benefits afforded by his birth, he married and had a daughter, and generally prepared himself to assume the life of an Indian nobleman. It is with the death of his parents, who seem to have been devotees of Parshva's sect, that the life of Mahavira begins to diverge from the ordinary. As the second son of the family, he now approached his brother, the new king, and asked for permission to renounce the world. This was grudgingly granted, and Mahavira became a member of Parshva's mendicant sect. He followed the meditative life style of this group for two years before blazing his own religious trail.

Mahavira appears at this point to have come to a conclusion different from that of his younger contemporary, the Buddha. He concluded that more rigorous asceticism was the best way of making rapid religious progress. Accordingly, he renounced even the small comforts afforded followers of Parshva and became a naked wanderer. He lived this life for the next twelve years, eating a strictly vegetarian diet, staying in no place longer than three days, and practicing meditation. In the thirteenth year of his quest, he was meditating at the foot of a *sala* tree when he achieved *kaivalya*, "aloneness," or what is termed in Buddhism "enlightenment." Now free from the cycle of life and death, he began preaching his doctrine in the area of the lower Ganges valley more or less coterminous with Magadha, although he may have journeyed slightly outside this area, as did his immediate disciples. He is said to have died at the town of Pava, aged seventy-two, probably in about 527 B.C.E.

The Principal Tenets of Jainism

Like all other Indian religions, Jainism started its analysis of reality from the viewpoint that human beings were trapped in an endless, painful cycle of birth and death. This bondage flowed from the nature of the human constitution, which, following Samkhya thinking, Jains held to have two components: the soul (*jiva*) and matter (*pudgala*). In itself, the soul was pure life-force, all-knowing, perfectly happy, full of energy. But when it was associated with matter, as in the case of human existence in this world, it became limited, and consequently experienced unhappiness. Matter was viewed as both the atoms that constitute it and the forces that give form to those atoms. Matter could be "gross," that is visible, as in the case of the perceived physical body; or "subtle," that is invisible, as in the case of the soul. Thus the Jains held the view that the soul was a material thing, albeit of a different composition and nature from that of the outer physical body.

The Jains also thought that karma, "action," added to or subtracted from this subtle soul body. Since the latter continued to exist after the dissolution of the outer physical body, actions had consequences not only in this lifetime, but in the next. The Jains envisioned the universe as being permeated by tiny particles of subtle matter that could be attracted to an embodied soul, thus obscuring its true nature. Liberation from this condition had two components. The first was to prevent the accumulation of any more karmic matter. The second was to cleanse the soul of the matter that it had already accumulated. True existential saving knowledge, the goal of all of the wisdom-based traditions in Indian thought, came from cleansing the *jiva* of the karmic residue that had accumulated around it and was obscuring its true luminosity—just as clouds obscure the sun. The accumulation of karmic matter was conditioned by certain predispositions and attitudes that affected the energy field surrounding the soul. If the soul was ruled by desire of any sort, or by anger and hatred, then conditions were more favorable for the accumulation of karmic matter. Of course all actions and thoughts resulted in karmic deposits, but these negative inclinations made the soul particularly "attractive." Moreover, the process was exponential. The more karmic matter accumulated on the soul, the more was drawn to it, in a sort of law of spiritual gravitational attraction.

The Jains developed an elaborate philosophy regarding karma's nature and effects, and the ways to bypass them. They identified eight forms of karma: four were classified as destructive karmas that had a directly negative effect; and four were nondestructive, in the sense that they simply created the preconditions for particular forms of embodiment. The worst of these karmas were those associated with the desire to do others harm. But there was also a bright spot inherent in Jain philosophy—the belief that no karmic effect was permanent. After a period of time conditioned by the precipitating action and the strength of the passion motivating it, the karma attached to the act played itself out and the matter "fell way" from the soul. Since karmic accretions could be controlled and limited, it was possible eventually to cleanse the soul of their defilements. If this was accomplished, the soul would no longer be fettered to matter and so would be liberated from the cycle of life and death. As with most schools of Indian thought, the Jains had a plan by which this liberation could be accomplished. This was a fourteen-stage program of progressive purification of the soul and the cutting off of the inflows of karmic matter known as the *gunasthanas*. By restraining the body, senses, speech, and mind, and by adhering to the practices of not harming other beings, not stealing, restraining one's sexuality, being truthful, and not desiring things, a person could gain freedom.

But naturally this is not an easy process. At first, the soul is totally immersed in the deluded passions of material existence. Fortunately, there comes the second step on this Jain path when the individual has a sudden fleeting burst of faith, which, even though it soon disappears, triggers a minuscule amount of insight into the true nature of reality. This in turn motivates the seeker to inquire further and leads to the third step of the path, at which the individual, through practice of the Jain virtues—however imperfect such practice might be at this stage—begins to develop a stronger faith. Doubt continues to obscure the soul's capacity for true insight, but this is the first point at which the true nature of the human being and the conditions that bind the soul to matter are realized. This insight has a tremendous purifying effect on the individual; but, if the karmic burden is too heavy, then he or she will revert to step one, rather than progressing to step four.

It is only with the fourth step that the individual experiences the bliss of the soul as it truly is in itself. But since this is the result of the suppression, rather than the elimination, of the karmic defilements, it is only a brief experience, after which the individual reverts again to step two. However, now armed with experiential knowledge, the individual can renew the ascetic program with increased vigor. Eventually this leads to step five, in which the passions are finally brought under at least partial control. Now it is possible to take the formal Jain vows to refrain from destructive actions and intentions. This leads to the sixth step, where there is an increased restraint of the passions. In the seventh step this self-restraint is perfected and one's meditative powers increased.

In step eight, it is now possible to reexperience the ecstatic vision of step four, but at this stage it is experienced in a more purified and intense form. The process of purification continues in step nine, and in step ten it is almost perfected: only the greed of wishing to possess a body remains at what we would term a subconscious level. In steps eleven and twelve, even this most fundamental of human desires is overcome. All the passions have finally been overcome. In step thirteen, the individual experiences uninterruptedly the bliss and knowledge inherent in the soul. But because the soul is still in the body, karma can continue to accumulate. It is only in step fourteen that final liberation is accomplished.

The "Three Jewels" of Jainism: Knowledge, Faith, and Conduct

The Jains believe that the fourteen steps on the path to liberation are attained by means of the "three jewels" of knowledge, faith, and pure conduct. Each of these requires the other two in order to be truly effective. Although faith is seen as the first and foremost of these "jewels," it is based on knowledge. As in all Indian wisdom traditions, the Jains hold that bondage to the cycle of life and death comes, ultimately, from ignorance. This ignorance could, however, be dispelled through the cultivation of knowledge.

The Jains saw the universe as being incredibly complex, replete with innumerable substances possessing innumerable qualities capable of innumerable modifications. Whereas the *astika* Hindu philosophers of the period held to the concept of a single underlying foundation to Reality, or *Brahman*, the Jains held to the epistemological position of **anekanta** or "many-sidedness." Things in themselves are permanent, since substances have real, and not simply contingent, being. But these substances are undergoing constant modification and changes. This led Jain thinkers to their second fundamental position, namely that all mundane, as opposed to existential, knowledge was necessarily conditioned by perspective (*naya*). From this emerged the Jain concept of **syatvada**, the "way of 'maybe.'" By this, they meant that all the claims of knowledge were necessarily based on limited perspective and so could never be more than tentative. This was illustrated by the story of the five blind men and the elephant. On encountering an elephant for the first time, the blind men each touched a different part of the beast. Consequently they each came up with a description of the animal that completely differed from that of their companions. The one who had felt the trunk claimed that the elephant was like a snake: the one who had touched its side claimed that it was like a wall; the one who touched the tail held it to be like a rope; and so forth. Likewise, said the Jains, human knowledge is limited by perspective. This leads, in turn, to the idea of conditional predication.

The Jains held that in any given situation, seven possibilities existed: a condition *A* may exist: *A* might not exist; *A* may both exist and not exist; the conditions for ascertaining whether *A* exists may not be present and thus *A* is unknowable; *A* may be known to exist, but only if certain conditions are present; *A* might be known to not exist, but only if certain conditions are present; finally, *A* might be known to both exist and not exist, but only if certain conditions exist. It is clear from the foregoing that certain knowledge is impossible, given the present conditions in which human beings find themselves. This led the Jains to the question of faith and its place in developing insightful knowledge unfettered by human existence.

The second of the three jewels, faith, is intimately associated with the twenty-four Jain Ford-makers, the last of whom was Mahavira. Since human beings exist in a reality which allows them to perceive only conditional and incomplete knowledge, they need to practice those actions and cultivate those virtues that will lead them to true existential knowledge. But what are these actions and virtues, and how can they be known by man, given the epistemological uncertainty inherent in the human condition? They are known through the teachings of the Ford-makers, beings who have achieved full and unconditional knowledge of reality, and so can now speak to others with the authority born of experience. This is, of course, not sufficient in itself, but faith in the message of the Ford-makers is a necessary first step for a person to embark on the long and arduous journey to true enlightenment. The true motivating force of this journey, however, is the momentary flash of insight (**samyak darshana**) which is achieved at the fourth step of the Jain path, but this will never occur if an individual does not set out on the path. In this sense, then, Jainism, ostensibly an atheistic system of thought—since it does not believe in an omnipotent Creator of the universe who is controlling human destiny accordingly— is just as much based on faith as are the religions of Islam, Judaism, Christianity, or *bhakti* Hinduism.

The practical center of the three jewels is conduct. Since all karmic accretions come from actions and the thoughts that precede and motivate them, conduct is the only way to choke off the influx of karmic material and cleanse the *jiva* of the material already obscuring it. The Jains recognize five primary virtues—"nonharming" (*ahimsa*), truth (*satya*), "nonstealing" (*asteya*), sexual purity (*brahmacarya*), and "nongrasping" (*aparigraha*). These are buttressed and augmented by numerous secondary vows, some of which apply to all Jains, laypersons and monks alike, while others are observed only by the members of the Jain monastic community. The primary Jain virtue is *ahimsa*. It could be argued that all questions of good and evil come down to the question of hurting other living beings (and not just human beings). The Jains see reality as an interconnected web of beings whose primary purpose is to help one another. Thus "nonharming," far from being the simple refraining from causing hurt, has a far deeper positive meaning. It must be carried out at the level both of action and of intent since, as we have seen, intent creates the preconditions for karmic accretion. But harm does not hinge, as it does in Hinduism, solely on intent. Actions that cause harm to others, even if unintentional, are still culpable.

This attitude is often expressed in the Jain scriptures. As this passage from the Acaranga Sutra (I, 1) observes:

> Earth is afflicted and wretched, it is hard to teach, it has no discrimination. Unenlightened men, who suffer from the effects of past deeds, cause great pain in a world full of pain already, for in earth souls are individually embodied. If, thinking to grasp praise, honor, or respect . . . or to achieve a good rebirth, . . . or to win salvation, or to escape pain, a man sins against earth or causes or permits others to do so, . . . he will not gain joy or wisdom. . . . Injury to the earth is like striking, cutting, maiming, or killing a blind man. . . . Knowing this a man should not sin against earth or cause or permit others to do so. He who understands the nature of sin against earth is called a true sage who understands karma . . . All beings . . . in fact all creation, know individually pleasure and displeasure, pain, terror, and sorrow. All are full of fears that come from all directions. And yet there exist people who would cause greater pain to them. . . . A man who is averse from harming even the wind knows the sorrow of all things living. . . . Those whose minds are at peace and who are free from passions do not desire to live [at the expense of others].

SOURCE: Embree, Sources of Indian Tradition, pp. 65–66

Satya, truth, flows from this primary injunction to prevent harm to other beings and means not only not lying, but also avoiding speech that is unkind, harsh, rude, gossipy, slanderous, and so forth. Likewise, "nonstealing" involves avoidance of theft and any form of dishonest business practice. Sexual purity differs according to one's station in life. If one is a monk, then it involves total celibacy. If one is a layperson, it involves limiting relations to those bound by marriage. Finally, there is "non-grasping," perhaps the most difficult of all the vows to fulfill. This is the development of complete detachment from the karmically conditioned world. This means the renunciation not only of physical things but also of the ideas and attitudes that are their foundations.

These primary virtues lead to a host of secondary features of Jainism, two of which we will consider here. The first is radical vegetarianism. Obviously, all human food is gained at the cost of some other being's life. The humble carrot may not be an especially vivacious conversationalist, but by all scientific standards it is a living being. The Jains recognized this, and it presented them with a difficult dilemma: they were under an absolute injunction not to harm any other living being, but they needed to eat food to live. The Jains realized that in the ordinary course of things this meant that they must necessarily incur bad karma if they were to survive. They therefore attempted to minimize this by eating vegetables—the least "alive" of

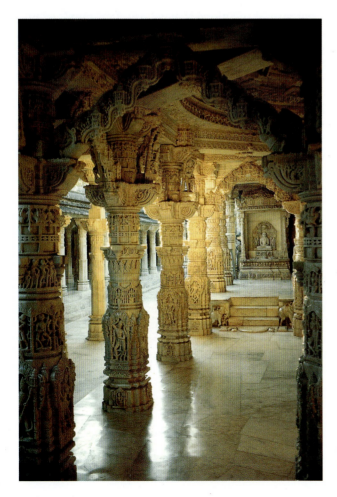

View of the inside of Dillawara Temple, India. Jain temples are some of the earliest examples of Indian temple architecture.

beings. They could also use dairy products, since they were produced with limited harm, but they totally rejected all meat and eggs. Still, there was the lingering taint of harm caused by eating. This, the Jains believed, could be eliminated by *sallekhana*—ritual suicide by fasting to death.

Perhaps the most notable feature of the religion Mahavira founded is its formal organization into a corporate body with recognized group leaders—in effect, a religious order. Although much of early Jain history may be the product of pious imagination, it is clear that some of it at least reflects real events and personalities. One of the most influential of the early Jain leaders, Bhadrabahu, seems to have been a contemporary of the great emperor Ashoka in the third century B.C.E. It was during Bhadrabahu's term as head of the Jain order that Jainism penetrated into southern India. Jainism put down solid roots in the south, and many of its great temples are to be found here. On returning to the north, however, the southern Jains found that their northern coreligionists had become, in their opinion, lax. Eventually, in 79 B.C.E., this led to a schism between the two groups that endures to this day. The more relaxed northern group became known as the Shvetambaras, the "white wearers," who dressed in simple white clothing. The southern group became the Digambaras, the "sky clothed," who maintained the earlier Jain tradition of total nakedness.

The monastic regime of the Jains, which is severe, is open to both men and women. In addition to the five principal virtues mentioned above, the Jain monk or nun undertakes much more rigorous asceticism. As is the case in Christian and Buddhist monasticism, the daily routine of the Jain monk is heavily regulated. Rules exist for every aspect of daily life, down to the amount of food that can be consumed (thirty-two mouthfuls the size of an egg). One of the most important monastic practices is fasting, which can take two forms. One is total fasting, which is by its nature of limited duration. The other is partial fasting, which can go as long as fifty-two days.

Another interesting feature of Jain monasticism is public confession. Again, this is reminiscent of Christianity—except that Christian confession has become a private ritual between the individual and the priest. However, this was not always so: in the early Church, confession was apparently made in public and resembled the Jain rite of public confession. There are ten different levels of expiation of sins, ranging from physical punishments through reduction in monastic seniority, with the most serious being expulsion from the monastic community. Laypersons have a complex set of rules to follow as well. They must confess their faults and follow twelve rules of conduct. Naturally, the five principal virtues apply to them as well.

Jainism is at present a very small piece of the Indian mosaic, but its influence on Hinduism has been very substantial. Indeed, if we were to classify the greatest of the modern Indian religious figures, Gandhi, by his daily activities and beliefs, we would be just as likely to conclude that he was a Jain as that he was a Hindu. Nonviolence, vegetarianism, and other key Hindu concepts clearly have their origins in Jain thought. So too do many aspects of Buddhism, to which we will now turn our attention.

Website References

1. Various aspects of Jainism, both traditional and modern, can be explored at www.cs.colostae.edu/~malaiya/jainhlinks.html and www.umich.edu/~umjains/

2. www.philo.demon.co.uk/Carvaka.htm discusses the often neglected tradition of Indian Materialism.

CHAPTER TEN

Early Buddhism in India

Like Jainism and the knowledge schools of Hinduism, Buddhism emerged out of the period of Indian religious ferment that lasted from about 1000 to 600 B.C.E. Like Jainism, Buddhism is also one of the first religions where we can be reasonably certain that we have at least some reliable information about its founder. Unlike Jainism, however, Buddhism was able to transcend its origins and become a world religion. It was the core teachings of its founder that allowed for this transformation.

The Life of the Buddha

On the face of it, it appears that we have a considerable amount of information concerning the life of Siddhartha of the clan Gautama of the Shakya kingdom, or, as he is better known to history, the Buddha ("Awakened One"), who lived from about 560 to 480 B.C.E. Our knowledge of the Buddha's life comes from a variety of sources. The earliest coherent biography of him was written by the Buddhist poet Ashvagosa in about100 C.E. Previous to this, our knowledge of the Buddha's life can only be pieced together from stray references in the Buddhist scriptures. There is also a type of literature in the scriptures called **Jatakas**, which purport to describe the lives of the Buddha previous to his last incarnation and his enlightenment and subsequent freedom from the round of rebirth and death. Needless to say, interesting as these tales are in illustrating for us the psychological and mythological mindset of the people of the period, they provide us with little or no real factual data about the historical Buddha. In addition, we should recognize that the life story of the Buddha, as we now have it, is in itself a stylized account. As we saw when we examined the biography of the other great religious leader of the period, Mahavira, it seems likely that these Buddhist stories draw on an archetypal Indian religious biography that had as its principal aim not so much the recounting of the factual life of the individual involved as the presentation of that person as an embodiment of a cosmic truth.[1]

Traditionally, the Buddha was believed to have been born in the town of Lumbini, which is now just inside the border of Nepal, northeast of India. His father, Suddhodana, was thought to have been the king of the Shakya clan that inhabited the region, and so the Buddha was born not into the priestly class, but into the warrior/ruler class. His mother, Mahadevi, was believed to have conceived without the need for human intervention and to have died seven days after the birth of her

Dream of Queen Maya, Bharut, 2nd century B.C.E. Buddhists believe that the birth and life of the Buddha was surrounded by miraculous events including his conception without any human agency.

illustrious offspring. He was named Siddhartha Gautama and raised by his aunt Mahaprajapati. Shortly after his birth, according to the customs of his people, a Brahmin priest was consulted so that the young Siddhartha's horoscope could be cast and his future ascertained. The Brahmin then informed his father that the young prince would become either a great king or a great religious leader. His father, wishing his son to follow in the family business of government, decided to shield the boy carefully from experiencing any of the disappointments and disillusionments of the world that were traditionally held to be the catalysts that impelled people to embrace the spiritual life. Consequently, the prince was raised in a privileged environment while being taught the skills needed to be a secular ruler.

In due course, Siddhartha married his cousin Yashodhara, who bore him a son, Rahula. Despite living in the lap of luxury, however, Siddhartha came to wonder about the world beyond the palace gates. One day, at the age of about twenty-nine, he told his charioteer, Channa, that he wanted to go out and see the city. Channa immediately communicated this desire to the king, who asked the young prince to postpone his outing for a day, during which time he arranged for all unpleasant reminders of human mortality, such as the infirm, the elderly, and the feeble-minded of his capital city, to be hidden from his son's sight. Unfortunately for his plans, he missed one old man. The prince, having never seen old age, asked Channa what was wrong with the old man, and was informed that it was only the inevitable onset of age. Disturbed by this, Siddhartha made further trips outside without the knowledge of his father, and during these outings he encountered sickness and death as well. But on his final trip into the world as a prince, he also met a wandering holy man. When he asked Channa who this was, Channa told him that this was someone who had escaped the evils of the world and the cycle of life and death. Deeply impressed, Prince Siddhartha decided to go and do likewise.

In the middle of the night, Siddhartha kissed his sleeping wife and child goodbye, and saddling his favorite horse, he rode away from his life in the secular world forever. At first, he practiced a life of extraordinary austerity common to many of the devotees of the knowledge-based schools of the period. He wandered naked through the countryside in all sorts of weather, fasted continually, did not bathe, went without sleep, and in general performed the *tapas* that were common to the ascetics or **Shramanas** of the period. He also seems to have studied under two famous meditation teachers of the time, Alara Kalama and Udraka Ramaputra, whose names are familiar to us from other religious literature of the period. From these teachers, the Buddha learned how to enter the trance states which mark the practice of yoga. He did not, however, attain the religious insight that he hoped for. Consequently, he redoubled his severe asceticism, determined to achieve enlightenment and to escape from the wheel of birth and death.

One day, as he meditated on the burning sands beside the Ganges, he came to his first major spiritual insight—that the way of severe asceticism did not work! Begging a little food from a passing village woman called Sujata, the Buddha recast his search for enlightenment within what he later termed "the middle way." By this, he meant moderation in all things. One should eat a sufficient amount to maintain one's health, but not too much; one should take enough rest, but not too much; and so forth. This path of moderation was a radical departure from the religious practices of the times. Despite this new regime, however, Siddhartha had still not found his way out of *samsara*. Determined to do so, he sat down to meditate under a Bo tree— the sacred tree depicted on the Indus Valley seals—at Bodh Gaya, a small village in what is now Bihar in India, and swore that he would not get up until he had either gained enlightenment or died. On the full moon night of May in approximately

525 B.C.E., he accomplished his goal and arose, no longer prince Siddhartha Gautama of the Shakyas, but the Buddha—the Awakened One.[2]

After spending many days in meditation, the Buddha was moved by compassion for suffering humanity, and so he decided to go immediately and communicate his insights to others. Over the next forty-five years, as the scriptures tell us, he preached his new message of salvation and gathered a large following of disciples including such famous ones as Ananda, Shariputra, Mahakashyapa, and Mahamaugalyayana. These disciples he organized into the **Sangha**, or Buddhist monastic order, possibly on the already existing model of the Jains. The Buddha developed a complex code of rules, called the *Vinaya*, by which members of the Sangha lived their lives. These codes of conduct probably represent the earliest of the Buddhist scriptural writings. He also explained his teachings in a series of talks or sermons called collectively the Sutras. The *Vinaya* and the Sutras, along with a third group of texts, the Abhidharma or texts of philosophical analysis, make up early Buddhism's canon of sacred scriptures, known collectively as the **Tripitika** ("Three Baskets"), so called because the individual books of the canon, originally written on rolled parchment, were placed into one of three baskets according to their general classification.[3]

The recension that has come down to us is written in Pali, a spoken language of central India that was spoken at, or just after, the time of the Buddha.[4] Written in the language of the common people, these sacred texts were much more accessible than the scriptures of the Brahmins, which were written in Sanskrit—a language that most people at the time of the Buddha no longer spoke or understood. This use of the vernacular language no doubt contributed greatly to the rapid spread of Buddhism throughout northern India before the Buddha's death at the age of about eighty in about 480 B.C.E. We should note, however, that the scriptures were preserved in other languages as well, including Sanskrit, and these other recensions

Sanci, Stupa I, northern Torana. After his death and cremation, the remains of the Buddha were enshrined in stupas for the veneration of the faithful.

often contain interesting differences from the Pali text. Before we leave this subject, we must consider how much of the life story of the Buddha reflects actual facts. Nowadays it is generally agreed that the Buddha was a real person who was born in northern India around 560 B.C.E. and died around 480 B.C.E. No doubt he was from the warrior class and at first lived a relatively comfortable life; but the idea that he was a prince seems to be contradicted by the fact that the region in which he was born was not a monarchy, but rather a sort of republic ruled by councils of nobles. Beyond that, very little can be said with certainty about the actual life of the founder of the religion. What we can discuss with authority is his understanding of the nature of the world and the way to escape it.

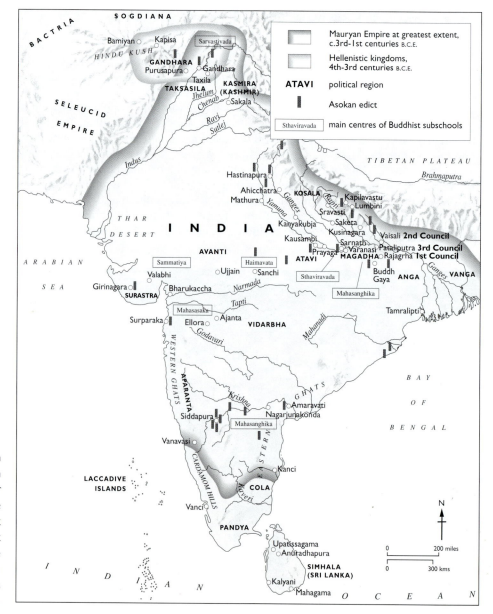

Early Buddhist sites in South Asia. Although Buddhism is no longer a major religion in the land of its birth, ancient India was at some point of its history more Buddhist than Hindu. Ancient Buddhist sites still dot the region.

The Three Marks of Existence and the Four Noble Truths

The Buddha based his analysis of the human condition on three basic perceptions which he termed the "Three Marks of Existence" (**trilaksana**). The first of these marks or characteristics, and the foundation of the entire subsequent Buddhist religious system, is impermanence (**anitya**; Pali, *anicca*). Everything, said the Buddha, is in a constant state of flux. Nothing in the material world is permanent in itself. Things may give the impression of being permanent, but that is only an illusion. Given enough time, everything—mountains, seas, the heavens, and most importantly of all, human beings—will change and cease to be: they are all impermanent. The second mark of existence, unsatisfactoriness (**duhkha**; Pali, *dukkha*, literally "pain"), arose from this impermanence. All things that were not permanent were, in the Buddha's way of thinking, deeply unsatisfactory. In this, his analysis was much the same as that of the great ancient Greek philosopher Plato. To place trust in any material thing was pointless and entirely doomed to failure. The third mark of existence also derived from the first. This was the idea that human beings did not have, as the Buddha's *Brahmanic* contemporaries believed, even any form of permanent material soul (*atman*). For the Buddha, humans were no more than composite beings made up of an ever-shifting cloud of physical and mental components. Thus to talk about an eternal "kernel" of the human being was, in the Buddha's opinion, utterly false since such a self could not be identified. Certain traits and characteristics might possibly persist from one life to another, but not the conscious personality *per se*.

But the Buddha went on from this very pessimistic understanding of the human condition to suggest that there was a way out of this endless cycle. The way to escape *samsara* was the Four Noble Truths (**arya-satya**). As the *Samyutta Nikaya* (5.421 ff.) observes:

> This is the [first] Noble Truth of Sorrow [*duhkha*]. Birth is sorrow, age is sorrow, disease is sorrow, death is sorrow; contact with the unpleasant is sorrow, separation from the pleasant is sorrow, every wish unfulfilled is sorrow . . .
> And this is the [second] Noble Truth of the Arising of Sorrow. It arises from craving [**trishna**, lit. "thirst"], which leads to rebirth, which brings delight and passion and seeks pleasure now here, now there—the craving for sensual pleasure, the craving for continued life, the craving for power.
> And this is the [third] Noble Truth of the Stopping [*nirodha*] of Sorrow. It is the complete stopping of that craving, so that no passion remains, leaving it, being emancipated from it, being released from it, giving no place to it. And this is the [fourth] Noble Truth of the Way which Leads to the Stopping of Sorrow. It is the Noble Eightfold Path [**ashtangika-marga**]—Right Views, Right Resolve, Right Speech, Right Conduct, Right Livelihood, Right Effort, Right Mindfulness, and Right Concentration.

> SOURCE: Embree, *Sources of Indian Tradition*, pp. 100–101

Here, encapsulated in a very few easy-to-remember steps, lies the entire Buddhist program of salvation, designed to break the cycle of **pratityasamutpada** ("interdependent arising"), which was seen as the driving force in binding the individual to the painful cycle of death and rebirth.

Interdependent Arising and the Eightfold Path

As with most other Indian religious traditions, Buddhism held to the belief that all actions had inevitable consequences. Early Buddhists divided these actions and results into twelve interlocking groups, each arising from the one before it and giving rise to the one after it. When taken as a whole, they formed a great wheel upon which hapless individuals revolved endlessly, bound to repeat the whole sorry process for eternity unless they could manage to break this chain of interdependent causation. The key factor binding one to this wheel was ignorance (*avidya*). Ignorance was of two types. The first was negative ignorance, the simple lack of knowledge of the truth. The second was active ignorance, whereby one imposed a false view on data of one sort or another, such as mistaking a rope for a poisonous snake. Just as holding a false view about an object being a snake could have negative results—such as dying of a heart attack from fright—so too did holding wrong views about the nature of Reality, in that it bound one to the cycle of rebirth into this unsatisfactory world.

The basic ignorance that caused this bondage, the Buddhists held, was ignorance of the chain of interdependent causation and the false view that beings and events had a separate permanent nature in themselves. It is for this reason that the Buddhist philosophers listed ignorance as the first of the twelve links in the chain of causation. This led to the second link in the chain: volition. Since individuals are shrouded in ignorance, they will the wrong thing, namely to act as though they were truly separate beings with a permanent and abiding eternal self or soul. Believing themselves to be free agents, individuals then suffer from the supposed assaults of others and the failure of attempts to achieve stability in an unstable world.

From the choices that we make regarding our perceived mode of existence comes the third step in the chain of causation: consciousness. For the Buddhist, consciousness is compared to a monkey jumping restlessly from one branch of a tree to the next. In like manner does human consciousness flit from one object to another, motivated by either attraction to a thing or repulsion by it. This increased activity of the already unstable consciousness now cloaks itself in the body, thus giving rise to the fourth link in the chain of causation.

With the body comes a whole new set of problems. The first of these is the fifth link in the chain—the six senses. Rather than the traditional five senses, the Buddhists held that human beings had six: sight, hearing, touch, taste, smell, and thought. Conditioned by the wrong viewpoint that the world is constructed of enduring separate entities, the senses convey the wrong data to individuals and stimulate either craving or aversion. But the very act of sensing produces contact, the sixth link, with these supposed objects, and contact leads to feelings about them—the seventh link. This all leads to one of the most important links in the chain of interdependent causation: craving. From our feelings about things develops our desire for them. Our modern society seems to confirm the Buddhist analysis of this phenomenon. People are constantly bombarded with information calculated to enflame their desire for things. But even as we get the objects of our desire—such as bigger cars, a beautiful mate, or a Big Mac—we are told that they should want something else in an endless cascade of desire-producing information.

Naturally, in our ignorance, we not only desire these things, but make efforts to obtain them. This is the Buddhist concept of grasping, the ninth link of the chain. These acts and desires of grasping set into motion what the Buddhists term the predisposition to "becoming." By this, they mean that grasping perpetuates itself and the other factors that lead up to it. This, the tenth link in the chain, leads naturally to the eleventh, namely birth, since the greatest craving and grasping is the desire for embodiment so that these impulses can be gratified. Finally, birth leads to its natural concomitants: old age, suffering, and death. But if a person dies in a state of ignorance, this predisposes the foundations of the next lifetime, and so the cycle begins again and repeats endlessly.

The Eightfold Path was the instrument taught by the Buddha as the means to break this endless cycle of interdependent causation. When examined more closely, it can be seen to be divided into three discrete parts. The first, right viewpoint and right intention, both concern what is generally termed faith, that is to say, the underlying core of one's understanding of, and response to, Reality. In order for his program of liberation to be effective, the Buddha knew that its practitioners had to change fundamentally the way in which they perceived the world. This was the purpose of right viewpoint—an orientation away from the understanding of the world as made up of material things that were acted upon, toward an understanding of the world as a series of constantly changing and interacting processes. From this new understanding of the world came the second step on the Eightfold Path: right intention. This was achieved when the individual decided that the Buddhist analysis of existence was correct and determined to follow the Buddhist plan for salvation.

The next three steps on the Eightfold Path were designed to take the insights gained from the first two steps and to put them into practice in the world. Right speech was, as its name implies, based on a proper use of speech, but in the fullest sense it really involved the entire way in which people mentally interacted with one another. Thus one was enjoined not to lie, not to slander, not to backbite—not, in short, to say (or presumably even think) anything which would upset or cause pain to another. This intention of not harming another was also played out in the next step of the path: right action. This involved agreeing not to steal, not to kill, not to use sex improperly—a rule that had different applications depending on whether or not one was a monk—not to use intoxicating substances, and generally not to do anything which would harm or upset another. The fifth step, right livelihood, was closely allied to the fourth in that it forbade making a living by any means that would cause harm to others, such as being an arms or drugs dealer, or a butcher.

But these negative steps were not enough to ensure salvation. The sixth step, right effort, enjoined positive actions as the natural culmination of the moral foundations that had previously been laid. It is only when we come to the last two steps of the Eightfold Path, right mindfulness and right concentration, that we encounter actions that we would consider explicitly religious. Right mindfulness is a uniquely Buddhist spiritual exercise that may rightfully be called the core practical teaching of the tradition. Having established the prerequisites for liberation through the cultivation of a proper attitude and the foundation of a moral life style, right mindfulness aims at directly shattering the chain of causation that binds the individual to the cycle of life and death.

Mindfulness is established through watching one's own thoughts, emotions, and actions, and living life in an extremely deliberate manner. Efforts are then made to strip these things of their emotional content by seeing them as they actually are— mere temporary phenomena without any abiding reality. Right mindfulness was generally restricted in practice to monks, and the practitioner was urged, "when walking, be aware that you are walking; when sitting, be aware that you are sitting; when breathing, be aware that you are breathing." If this exercise is properly pursued, the individual gains not indirect knowledge of the various components of existence, but true existential experience of these objects. The first stage in the

Buddhist's effort to wake up to Reality, this awareness and existential knowledge formed the foundations for the last of the Eightfold Path: right concentration or right meditation.

Buddhist meditation can be further broken down into two interrelated components or processes. The first of these is termed **shamatha** or *samadhi*. *Shamatha* means "calm abiding," while *samadhi* is usually translated as "concentration." Both terms refer to calming and stilling the turbulent mind. If one practices mindfulness, one of the first things one observes is that the mind is in constant movement. Thoughts bubble up unbidden and float through the mind in a constant whirlpool of agitation. In order to penetrate more deeply into the true nature of reality, the Buddhists hold that it is necessary to first calm this fountain of thought. This is the goal of practices designed to induce *shamatha*. But this is only the first component of the program. Next one must practice **vipassana** (Sanskrit, *vipashyana*) or "insight" meditation, which emphasizes "seeing" more deeply as the mind stabilizes. It is through practicing this aspect of meditation that insight finally penetrates Reality, and **Nirvana**, the state of nonreturning to *samsara*, is achieved.[5]

The formal practice of Buddhism came to be anchored on three basic foundations. The first was the figure of the Buddha. The second was the teachings, the **Dharma**, that he had expounded.[6] Finally, there was the Sangha, the order of monks and nuns (*bhikshus* and *bhikshunis*) who followed those teachings.[7] When taken together they were the **triratna**, the "three jewels" of the Buddhist tradition. Of these, the Dhammapada, one of the earliest Buddhist texts, says:

> Blessed is the appearance of the Buddhas.
> Blessed is the teaching of the Dhamma.
> Blessed is the unity of the Order.
> Blessed is the disciplined life of its followers.
> Whosoever honors those worthy of honor,
> The Buddhas or their disciples
> Who have overcome the obstacles (to development),
> And have rid themselves of grief and lamentation,
> Who have attained inner peace
> And have become fearless—
> His merit cannot be measured by anyone ... (XVI, 16–18)

> SOURCE: Ven. Ananda Maitreya (trans.), Rose Kramer (rev.), *The Dhammapada: The Path of Truth* (Berkeley: Parallax Press, 1995), p. 54

Theravada Buddhism and the Formation of the Pali Canon

But like all religious teachings, Buddhism was destined to change and develop as time passed and its influence grew. In the event, it spread widely and developed in a number of interesting ways. However, the early years of Buddhism are shrouded in obscurity. The Sangha, the Buddhist order of monks, survived the death, or Parinirvana, of its founder in about 480 B.C.E., always a critical moment in the history of any religion. But the period between that event and the reemergence of Buddhism into the light of history in about 250 B.C.E. is cloudy. Supposedly, there was a meeting or council held immediately following the Buddha's death at Rajagriha in what is now southern Bihar in India. The major concern at this time

Seated Buddha, Gandhara, 2nd century C.E. Statues of the Buddha meditating and indeed all images of the Buddha, were a fairly late development in Buddhism. Early Buddhist art preferred to represent the Buddha symbolically through such images as a parasol, a footprint and so forth.

was to stabilize the Buddhist scriptures by coming to an agreement as to what were the accepted *Buddhavacana*, the "Words of the Buddha."

For a variety of reasons, no such agreement was forthcoming, although there seems to have been general agreement on the basic message of the Buddha, and certain key texts came to be seen as authoritative, if not exclusive. This means that the Buddhist canon or collection of scriptures remained what scholars of religion term "open," that is, a canon to which additional scriptures can be added. The opposite, a "closed" canon, such as we see in Islam, Judaism, and Christianity, occurs when the majority of religious believers in a given tradition agree to a definite set of scriptures and cease to add later works to it. The Second Buddhist Council at Vaishali in about 380 B.C.E. met because of a dispute over interpretations of the Buddhist scriptures. The problem lay in the meaning of certain monastic rules found in the *Vinaya*. One group, the Mahasanghikas, were more open to a relaxed interpretation of the rules and to a viewpoint that held that an *arhant*, one who had achieved enlightenment in this lifetime, could still be subject to human uncertainties and frailties. Their opponents, the Sthaviras or "Elders," who formed the majority of the Sangha, were much more rigorous in their interpretation of the received tradition. Unable to resolve their differences, the two groups henceforth went their separate ways, with the Sthaviras developing into the first of the great divisions of Buddhism: the **Theravada** school or "The Way of the Elders." Thus, only one hundred years after the death of its founder, Buddhism began to show sectarian tendencies.

Reclining Buddha, Polonnaruwa, Sri Lanka. As Buddhism spread, pious rulers began to erect great monumental representations of the Buddha such as this one. In many of these countries, Buddhism was used to buttress the king's authority and right to rule.

A note must be added here concerning "schism," and its associated term "heresy," in Buddhism. Schism could only take place within the order of monks. For Buddhists, schism meant a disagreement on the manner in which the monastic rules were interpreted and applied. It naturally followed that laypersons were constitutionally incapable of being "schismatic" or "heretical" since they were, by definition, outside monastic institutions and so not bound by their strictures. It is for this reason that we seldom see wholesale warfare between differing factions in Buddhist history, although sectarianism could have significant repercussions when the ruling class held to one form of Buddhism and the monks to another.

On the whole, it does not seem that this division within the Sangha had any particular effect on the expansion of Buddhism or on its continued success among the peoples of India. Nor did subsequent splits in the Sangha over diverse interpretations of the *Vinaya*. Eventually, some eighteen schools, or *nikayas*, emerged in early Indian Buddhism. By 250 B.C.E., Buddhism's popularity in India was extremely high. This popularity became even greater when its tenets were approved and implemented as state policy by one of the greatest of India's rulers, Ashoka Maurya. Over the preceding fifty years, the Mauryan rulers had come to control almost the whole of India and a significant portion of Central Asia. Ashoka, the third of his dynasty and its last great king, had been forced to conduct only one war during his reign. But that experience had so sickened him that he turned away from conquest and espoused a code of morality that was based on Buddhist precedents. In order to promulgate this code of behavior among his subjects, he caused a series of inscriptions that outlined the Buddhist moral code to be carved at strategic places throughout his empire. This is the first tangible evidence we have of how greatly Buddhism had come to influence Indian life and thought.

However, this was not all Ashoka did to advance the Buddhist cause. Under his authority, the Third Council of Buddhism was convened at his capital city of Pataliputra in northeastern India in about 240 B.C.E. Here the assembled Buddhist monks purged the Sangha of monks who were not sincere in their religious professions and attempted, once again without success, to promulgate an authoritative version of the Buddhist scriptures. More important for the future of Buddhism, however, was the decision to expand Buddhist missionary efforts outside of India proper. Given Buddhism's tolerance for local customs, a feature of the religion which had served it well within India, it is no surprise that it was able to establish itself beyond the borders of the subcontinent, particularly with the help of royal patronage.[8]

The reign of Ashoka was in many ways the high watermark of Buddhist influence in India. After the fall of the Mauryan Empire in c. 185 B.C.E., Buddhist influence began to decline. But this decline was by no means swift. Buddhist evangelism continued with notable success, particularly in Sri Lanka, the island that lies just off the southeastern coast of India which used to be known as Ceylon. Sri Lankan kings adopted Buddhism as the state religion in about 200 B.C.E. It is also possible that this period saw the first Buddhist missionaries to Southeast Asia in general, and to the nearby region of Myanmar in particular. Likewise, a number of later Indian rulers were attracted to the religion. Notable among these was Kanishka, a king belonging to a nomadic people who had invaded and subsequently settled in the Mauryan provinces in Central Asia and northwestern India. It was Kanishka who called the Fourth Buddhist Council—and the last—in about 100 C.E. This council, which is not accepted as being canonical by the Theravada school of Buddhists—the modern descendants of the Sthavira party—was yet another doomed attempt to develop an authoritative canon of scripture.

Website References

1. www.buddhanet.net/bt_conts.htm has a number of translations of the influential Jataka stories of the Buddha's previous births.

2. The life of the Buddha is covered at www.buddhanet.net/e-learning/buddhism/bud_ltc.htm

3. An overview of the contents and organization of the Tripitika can be found at www.buddhanet.net/ripitaka.htm

4. www.buddhanet.net/pdf_file/paligram.pdf gives an overview of the Pali language.

5. General aspects of early Indian Buddhist philosophy can be found at www.scils.rutgers.edu/~akhilas/ and www.buddhanet.net/abhidh01.htm

6. www.quangduc.com/English/palisutra/index.html gives the translation of a number of influential discourses of the Buddha.

7. The Sangha and Buddhist monkhood is discussed at www.buddhanet.net/e-learning/budworld/monastics.htm

8. Information on Ashoka and his contribution to the rise of Buddhism in India can be found at www.cs.colostate.edu/~malaiya/ashoka.html and at www.bartleby.com/86/29.html. For information on the great cave temple-monasteries that sprang up soon afterward, see www.indiatravelite.com/feature/bhajakarlacaves.htm and travel.indiamart.com/maharashtra/caves/ajanta-caves.html

CHAPTER ELEVEN

✦

Later Developments in Indian Buddhism

It is during this period of expansion that we see the development of what was to become the second great expression of Buddhism—**Mahayana**. This, however, was not a single school, but rather a general interpretation of the Buddhist teachings that gained its identity by distinguishing itself from the original Theravadin mode of interpretation. Mahayanist tendencies are seen in Buddhism from early times, notably in attempts to emphasize the primacy of the sutras over the other two divisions of the Buddhist scriptures, and the inclination toward viewing the Buddha in a manner that made him indistinguishable from a god.

The Rise of Mahayana Buddhism

The earliest indications that we have for the emergence of a distinct Mahayana tradition date from about 100 B.C.E. Many European and Japanese scholars hold that the rise of Mahayana represented a lay revolt against the control of the religion by monks. These scholars believe that, tired of being "second-class citizens," the ordinary lay Buddhists began to evolve a theology and practice that bypassed the monks and reduced their authority. For these scholars, Mahayana grew up around groups of lay and monastic persons of equal status, whose religious devotion was centered on mounds called **stupas** in which relics of the Buddha were supposedly buried.[1] People began to make pilgrimages to these mounds, just as they would to see a living teacher, and to make offerings for their upkeep. Since monks were not allowed to handle money, these stupas were administered by the laity, and so these laypersons came to control much of the Sangha's wealth.

This interpretation of Mahayana's development does seem to be in accord with general trends in Buddhism at this period. Indeed, only the Theravada literature has no discussion in its version of the *Vinaya* of how to construct a stupa. There are other indications of a shift away from the monastic emphasis, and toward a more lay orientation. The Vimalakirti-nirdesha Sutra, a popular text of the period, shows a shift in emphasis from the renunciate monk to the householder still living in the world. Other sutras of the period speak of **bodhisattvas**, beings who had completed the prerequisites to escape from the cycle of birth and death but had chosen to remain within it to help suffering beings with their tremendous supernatural powers. They, not the monks, were portrayed as the true renunciates and the models that laypersons should emulate. There is also an increased role for laywomen as teachers in Buddhist scriptures of the time.

But this is by no means the whole picture. Other scholars have shown that some of the early Mahayana texts took a positively hostile attitude to the stupa cult. The real religious orientation of members of this group seems to center not around the stupas, although they had a significant place in Buddhist piety of the time, but around new religious texts that were being generated during this period by monks who claimed to be in direct contact with the Buddha. The attachment to these texts seems to have increased to the extent that the books themselves were often formally venerated as embodiments of the Buddha. Moreover, of the Mahayana inscriptions produced during this period, some 70 percent are inscribed on behalf of Buddhist monks and nuns. These inscriptions show that the cult of Buddhist images associated with the rise of Mahayana that developed at this time was a primarily monastic concern, rather than one that took its impetus from the laity. Before this period, the Buddha was never directly represented in art. Rather, images such as footprints or lotus flowers were used to represent him symbolically. It has been suggested that Greek influence, imported to India through Alexander the Great's invasion, was responsible for the shift from symbolic representations of the Buddha to actual physical representations.

Avukana Buddha, near Sigiriya, Sri Lanka. Many different regional artistic styles developed for portraying the Buddha. Scholars can often use these styles as a way of establishing the patterns of Buddhist dispersion in India and beyond.

The impetus that led to the development of Mahayana teachings seems to lie in the changing status of the Buddha. The idea that the Buddha had entered Nirvana, and so was completely separated from the world and his followers, seems to have troubled many later Buddhists. It is human nature to want to have the divine directly available in times of trouble. Consequently, the idea emerged that the Buddha's absence from the world was only an illusion and that he remained accessible to suffering humanity. According to the believers in Mahayana, only the Buddha's gross material body had died. His subtle material body, dwelling on another plane of existence, was still available for consultation to a select few. For these Buddhists, the Buddha was still alive and capable of preaching new truths about the Buddhist religion.

Alongside this concept arose the ideal of the *bodhisattva*. This concept was not a new one in Buddhism, but as the thirst for direct contact with the divine and the need for supernatural intercessors to help with the problems of daily life got stronger among the Buddhists, so too did the cult of the *bodhisattvas*. All the Buddhas—and there were reckoned to be some twenty-three who had preceded the current Buddha—had been *bodhisattvas* immediately prior to their achieving Buddhahood. In the Mahayana tradition, however, the figure of the *bodhisattva* took on an autonomous existence and an independent role. As the Ashtasahasrika Prajnaparamita Sutra (XXII, 402–403) describes this figure:

> The bodhisattva is endowed with wisdom of a kind whereby he looks on all beings as though victims going to the slaughter. And immense compassion grips him. His divine eye sees . . . innumerable beings, and he is filled with great distress at what he sees, for many bear the burden of past deeds which will be punished in purgatory, others will have unfortunate rebirths which will divide them from the Buddha and his teachings, others must soon be slain, others are caught in the net of false doctrine, others cannot find the path [of salvation], while others have gained a favorable rebirth only to lose it.
>
> So he [the *bodhisattva*] pours out his love and compassion upon all those beings, and attends to them, thinking, "I shall become the savior of all beings, and set them free from their sufferings."

SOURCE: Embree, *Sources of Indian Tradition*, p. 160

These *bodhisattvas* were prepared to use any means necessary to accomplish the task that they had set for themselves of bringing beings to the safety of Nirvana, even if these means appeared to the less spiritually developed as being of a questionable moral nature. Consequently, an emphasis grew up in Mahayana Buddhism on the practice of *upaya*, or skillful means. This concept had significant practical implications. When Mahayana Buddhist missionaries left India to propagate Mahayana elsewhere, they carried with them the idea that it was perfectly acceptable to accommodate themselves, like *bodhisattvas*, to local conditions and practices as long as the essentials of Buddhism were taught. Naturally, this made the Buddhist message more congenial to the different societies that they encountered and greatly facilitated its dispersal throughout Asia and beyond.

So, from the first century B.C.E onward, a set of sutras claiming to be the direct word of the Buddha arose within the existing Buddhist community. These scriptures, while taking more notice of lay Buddhists, seems to have been written primarily by monks. It advocated the supremacy of the Buddha and the *bodhisattvas*, as well as the ideal of the promotion of the welfare of all beings rather than simply following the *Dharma* and striving for personal salvation. Cults arose around each of these new sutras with little or no interconnection, each being peculiar to the geographical region in which they originated. Adherents to these new texts felt themselves to be in direct contact with the Buddha, whether through the medium of the new sutras themselves, or through the more direct paths of meditation and dreams. They also seem to have held—in contradiction to other segments of the Buddhist community—that these new sutras were directly connected with the living Buddha himself and so more worthy of veneration than the stupas which contained only the remains of the Buddha's gross material body. On the whole, however, these emerging Mahayanists were a minority in the Buddhist community, and their public behavior did not differ in any significant respect from their non-Mahayana neighbors. It was

Bodhisattva, Fondukistan, 7th–8th century. *Bodhisattvas*, beings who delayed their entry into Nirvana in order to help others, became an important feature of Mahayana Buddhism and objects of popular devotion in their own right.

only later, possibly when they had to compete for declining resources as the reviving Hindu tradition began to eat away at their lay support, that animosity arose between the two groups. In any case, Mahayana Buddhism was only one of several competing ideologies within Indian Buddhism. Its real successes were to come elsewhere, as Buddhism spread to East Asia.[2]

Madhyamika and Yogacara

The rise of the Mahayana form of Buddhism led to the formation of a number of new philosophical schools. We will restrict our present study to the main Indian ones, Madhyamika and Yogacara, leaving the Chinese and Japanese schools for their appropriate chapters below. The first great philosophical school—that of Madhyamika established by Nagarjuna, probably sometime in the first century C.E.—became the foundation upon which many subsequent schools of Buddhist philosophy were founded. Its name, which means the "Middle Way" school, comes from its rejection of both the view that existence is composed of permanent, self-existing entities, and the view that nothing really exists, with everything being no more than an illusion.

The Madhyamika school builds on an earlier Buddhist philosophical tradition called the Prajnaparamita or "Perfection of Wisdom" school. This school, with its emphasis on the *bodhisattva* ideal, is associated with the beginnings of the Mahayana movement. In it, we find two concepts that became central to Nagarjuna's Madhyamika philosophy: the concept of **shunyata** or emptiness, and the belief that the truth of direct experience supersedes the truth of conceptual understanding. The texts of the Perfection of Wisdom school span some eight hundred years from about 200 B.C.E to 600 C.E, and include both early texts, such as the Diamond Sutra (Vajraccedikaprajnaparamita-sutra), and later texts such as the Heart Sutra (Mahaprajnaparamitahridaya-sutra).

The essential message of these texts is that there are three types of knowledge. The first of these is conventional knowledge, which is derived from the senses. The second type, deep knowledge (wisdom), is derived from insight and careful reflection. But it is the third type of knowledge, that of direct realization unmediated by conceptual frameworks, the so-called "perfect wisdom," that leads to liberation. The texts of the Perfection of Wisdom school teach this viewpoint through a three-stage process of construction, deconstruction, and reconstruction. They first state a truth conventionally so that it appears to refer to an independently existing entity or action. Then they show how this statement cannot be true, at least in the sense of possessing an independent existence. Finally, they reconstruct the statement in the light of interdependent causation, thus demonstrating, at least to their own satisfaction, an ultimate truth achieved through direct insight.

The Heart Sutra is a one-page summation of the doctrines of the Perfection of Wisdom school, and is held in such veneration by several Mahayana schools that it is still chanted in its entirety by monks of those schools at least once a day. The key to this text is the concept of emptiness (shunyata). We must be careful in talking about emptiness not to ascribe to it the commonly held English meaning of the opposite of fullness. For the Buddhist philosophers of the Perfection of Wisdom school, and schools such as Madhyamika that built on it, emptiness was a quality in itself and not just the absence of some other quality. What was meant by the term was that things were empty of self-existence. This did not mean that they did not exist, but rather that they did not exist by themselves. Their existence was the result of interdependent causation. The Perfection of Wisdom philosophers were attempting to steer a middle course between the viewpoint of an earlier Buddhist philosophical school, the Sarvastivada school, which ascribed enduring self-existence to a limited number of basic constituents of existence, and those Buddhist philosophers who would see reality as totally illusory. Things really did exist, but only as part of the chain of interdependent causation and not as self-existing independent entities.

The Madhyamika school of Nagarjuna took these insights and developed them further. Nagarjuna's method was similar to that of the Perfection of Wisdom texts that had preceded him. Through using the method of demolishing opposing views by pointing out their inconsistencies, Nagarjuna tried to demonstrate that the absolutist point of view was inconsistent and thus untenable. He then went on to demonstrate that the primary theories of causality, namely (1) effects produce themselves, (2) effects are produced by things other than themselves, (3) effects both produce themselves and are produced by other things, and (4) effects are produced without causes, are all logically inconsistent. But rather than abandon the necessary concept of causality altogether, Nagarjuna proposed a different viewpoint. He suggested that things do have a limited existence due to conditions, but that none of these conditions are self-existent causes. Thus, from the conventional point of view, Nagarjuna sees causation not as a direct response to some causal power, but rather a spontaneous response to fluctuating sets of conditions.

All this had important religious implications. Take, for example, the nature of the human self. On the one hand, applying Nagarjuna's dialectic, no enduring entity called the self could be said to exist in any sense, including even the traditional Buddhist one of a conglomeration of separate components, since that would mean ascribing a real existence to those components. On the other hand, the self could not be said to exist separate from these components, since that would imply that no change in the components would affect the self, and, if this is so, no religious practice could have any effect. This would render all religious practice, and Buddhist religious practice in particular, a moot point. However, Nagarjuna was able, through the use of the concept of emptiness, to reaffirm the basic foundations of the Buddhist worldview as delineated in the Four Noble Truths.

Nagarjuna first refutes the argument that if things are empty of reality, then no truth is possible and the Four Noble Truths are void. He argues that the Buddha taught two truths—a conventional truth and an ultimate truth. The mistake of his opponents, he thinks, is to take emptiness as an ultimate truth. In fact, says Nagarjuna, emptiness is a conventional truth. It is a mere conceptual framework which, given the nature of all conceptional frameworks, is an imperfect attempt to grapple with an indescribable truth. Its real meaning, says Nagarjuna, points to the interconnectedness of all phenomena. Thus emptiness implies interdependent causation, while interdependent causation implies a middle way between affirming and denying the reality of phenomena; and this middle way is the core teaching of the Four Noble Truths. Hence the Four Noble Truths are correct. Nagarjuna's arguments were to have a lasting effect on the dialectic of Mahayana Buddhism. But there were still some outstanding questions that needed to be addressed, such as the understanding of the nature of enlightenment and how to achieve it. These were the questions that engaged the two philosopher brothers, Asanga (c. 365–440 C.E.) and Vasubandhu (c. 380–460 C.E.). Their conclusions led to the foundation of a new school of Buddhism within Mahayana—one which became known as the Yogacara or "Practice of Discipline" school.

Neither Asanga nor Vasubandhu saw themselves as the founders of a new school of Buddhist thought. Rather, they saw their philosophical enterprise as being an expansion and clarification of the implications inherent in the Madhyamika philosophy of Nagarjuna. Yogacara accepted without reservation the idea of emptiness, as well as the corollary that when *bodhisattvas* achieved enlightenment, they would perceive that the apparent dichotomy between Nirvana and *samsara* was nothing more than an illusion born of ignorance. What engaged the interest of Yogacara scholars was the nature of this ignorance and its origins, what constituted enlightenment, and how were ignorance and enlightenment related? All this led to a problem that had plagued Buddhism from its inception. If there was no abiding "person," then what was the motivation to achieve enlightenment, and, if it was achieved, how could one say that there was any substantial link between the entity which had existed before enlightenment and the one existing after? The key to this question, said the Yogacara philosophers, lay in establishing a continuity between the various different states of consciousness. But it was impossible to assert, at least within a Buddhist context, that there even was something which could be a permanent consciousness. Clearly, the Yogacara thinkers had to approach this problem from a different perspective.

They began their analysis of the problem by postulating a threefold theory of knowledge. A thing could be known, they reasoned, as something intellectually apprehended, or as something conditioned by other things, or in its true nature through direct existential knowledge. In the first instance, the thing appears to be a self-existent object in a world of such objects. But this is a mistake. Conceptual concepts are only roadmaps that give an approximate knowledge of an object, not the object itself. When we dig deeper, as in the second instance, we see that the object has no self-existence *per se*, but does exist as part of the flow of interdependent causation. But this is not the ultimate reality either. That can only be apprehended at the third level of realization, the experience of the true essence of the object. Here the dichotomy between subject and object disappears, and perfect knowledge of the object becomes possible. With this perfect knowledge, said the Yogacara thinkers, comes the realization that all things in themselves are empty in the Madhyamika sense of the term.

But knowledge is a function of consciousness—so how does consciousness manage to produce these three forms of knowledge? It does so in two basic ways. One is through ordinary dualistic consciousness and the other is by direct apprehension. We are faced with a problem, however, in that whenever we want to talk about an object, we must necessarily use concepts that do not convey the essential "objectness" of the object. The problem of consciousness eventually led the Yogacara philosophers to make their greatest contribution to Buddhist thought. This was the doctrine of *alayavijnana*, "storehouse consciousness." Yogacara thinkers recognized that there were eight forms of consciousness. The first six were what we would term the senses and thought. The seventh was "defiled consciousness," which organized the first six into a conceptual framework that mistakenly ascribed self-existence to them. The eighth kind of consciousness was the "storehouse consciousness," which formed the true foundation of Reality. To become aware of this consciousness as itself, without any mediating concepts, was what constituted enlightenment according to the Yogacara thinkers, who, from this concept, were able to go on to construct a coherent theory that explained the continuity of consciousness. In this "storehouse consciousness" were collected all the effects associated with karma. Sometimes these were played out immediately, sometimes they "matured" in the storehouse consciousness until they were "ripe." These "seeds of future events" provided the thread of continuity between one state of consciousness and the next.

This concept also served to explain why ignorance existed at all. Ignorance arose because the defiled consciousness mistakes what are the conceptions of things for their reality. Enlightenment arises from the rejection of this viewpoint and by efforts to see things as they are in themselves—empty of essential self and merely a flow of constantly changing conditions. This is accomplished in the classical Buddhist manner through the practice of mindfulness. Thus Yogacara, like all previous and subsequent schools of Buddhist philosophy, returned to the fundamental primacy of the religious experience gained through rigorous practice over mere philosophical speculation.

Tibet and the Development of Vajrayana Buddhism

The development of **Vajrayana** Buddhism, the last great Buddhist form to arise on Indian soil, is intimately intertwined with the development of the country of Tibet. In a very real sense, it is amazing that people can survive in Tibet, let alone prosper as the Tibetans have done. A high, rocky, dry, and desolate region, Tibet has little or no natural resources to attract human inhabitants. Nor does it occupy a particularly strategic geographical position. Nevertheless, it has been, from very early times, the home of nomadic herding peoples. Sometime about 600 C.E., a lineage of kings arose in central Tibet around the city of Lhasa who were able to unite the diverse peoples of the Tibetan plateau under their rulership. The first and greatest of these was Songtsen Gampo (c. 609–649). To cement his position of authority and improve foreign relations, this king married two wives, one from Nepal to the south and one from imperial China to the northeast. Both these wives were Buddhists, and no doubt contributed to the spread of Buddhism in Tibet. More important than this, however, was the fact that as Tibet became more unified, the kings of Lhasa found that the old shamanic religion, Bön-po, could not buttress their political authority to the same degree as Buddhism.

Moreover, Tibet was beginning to look beyond its own borders for the first time. During Songtsen Gampo's reign, envoys were dispatched to India in search of cultural improvements that could be transplanted to Tibet. These envoys returned with a modified form of the Sanskrit script that could be used for writing Tibetan. This was no small feat, given that the Sanskrit script is phonetic and Tibetan is a tonal language akin to Chinese. Meanwhile, enterprising Buddhist missionaries were trekking up the passes of the Himalayas from the Indian plains, and over the eastern mountains from China. The earliest arrival of these missionaries is shrouded in the mists of time, but legend attributes the establishment of Buddhism in Tibet to one particular holy man, the wonder-working Padmasambhava. He emerges from early legends as a larger-than-life figure, possessing awesome magical power acquired through severe austerities, secret rituals, and prolonged meditation. Credited with subduing the dangerous and violent gods of the mountains, he is also said to have been responsible for the building of the Jokhang—the first Buddhist temple in Tibet—at Lhasa during the reign of Songtsen Gampo.

The arrival of Buddhism is more clearly described in the accounts of the mission of Shantarakshita. Invited to Tibet by the second of the Great Religious Kings, Trisong Detsen (c. 704–797), this Indian Tantric master built the Samyé, the other great early temple of Buddhism in Tibet. It was here between 792 and 794 that the direction of Tibetan Buddhism was decided for all time. These years were the period of the so-called Great Debate between Kamalashila, the representative of the Indian Tantric form of Buddhism, and the Chan Buddhist monk Heshang Mahayana from China. When the metaphysical dust had settled, the Tibetans chose in favor of the Indian, rather than the Chinese, form of Buddhism, and henceforth the Buddhism of Tibet was modeled on Indian forms. It is from this period as well that the Tibetans began to invest considerable efforts in retrieving Buddhist texts from India and translating them into their own language. They were so successful at this that many texts that have disappeared from the land of their composition are still available in Tibetan translations.

The development of Tibetan Buddhism proceeded sporadically. The last of the Great Religious Kings, Ralpachen (805–838), was a weak ruler, and perished at the hands of his brother Langdarma. This new king was no friend of Buddhism, and he attempted to eliminate the religion from Tibet. Despite the fact that he was murdered by a Buddhist monk after a brief reign of only four years in 842, his tenure on the Tibetan throne marked the end both of the first transmission of Buddhism to Tibet and of the rule of Tibet by secular kings. At this point, a dark age descended on Tibet for a hundred and fifty years, ending in about 1000. At this point, the second transmission of Buddhism to Tibet began, not in central Tibet, but in the western part of the country. Here the Buddhist teacher Atisha (c. 982–1054) brought new teachings from the university at Vikramashila in India to the region before traveling on to central Tibet. Likewise in eastern Tibet, Tibetans such as Naropa (1016–1100) and Marpa (c. 1012–1096) made the arduous trek to India in search of inspired teachers from whom they could learn the latest trends in Buddhism. With this new influx of ideas came a renewed interest in Buddhist practice, and the major schools of Buddhism in Tibet date their foundations from this time.

The oldest of these schools is the Nyingmapa or "Old Ones" school, which holds that its origins predated this second foundation of Buddhism in the early eleventh century. Its adherents venerate Padmasambhava as their founder and incorporate many indigenous spiritual beliefs that came from the time before the introduction of Buddhism into Tibet. Unlike the other schools of Tibetan Buddhism, the Nyingmapas allow their monks to marry and have families. Organized in only the loosest possible manner, the Nyingmapas are primarily individualists, and concentrated on local community issues such as divination, agricultural rituals, and exorcisms. They are heirs to a somewhat vague tradition and tend to be more involved with Tantric ritual practices than other schools. But it must be remembered that this is a only a difference of degree, since all the Tibetan schools are involved in Tantric practices to a greater or lesser extent.

One of the oldest of the more orthodox schools of Buddhism is the Sakya school, which was founded by Konchog Gyalpo (1034–1102). Named for its principal monastery at Sakya in south-central Tibet, this school is particularly renowned for its teaching system, called the Lamdre, which skillfully interweaves the study of **Tantra** and the Buddhist scriptures, and for its focus on a particular text, the Hevajra Tantra. The Sakya school rapidly began to influence secular as well as spiritual events, and when one of its head monks became the official teacher of the great Sino-Mongol emperor Kublai Khan, the latter vested him with the secular rule of the entire country of Tibet, at that time a province of the Mongol Empire. Thus began the long tradition of Tibet being ruled by the Buddhist monastic orders. This arrangement continued, as we shall see, up to 1951. Unlike other Buddhist schools in Tibet, the leadership of the Sakyapas is hereditary, passing from uncle to nephew in the Khön family.

Another school that has been prominent in Tibetan history is the Kagyu school, which traces its lineage back to Marpa and his famous pupil Milarepa (1052–1135). Both these teachers were well known for their magical attainments, and Milarepa is recognized as the foremost poet of Tibet. The Kagyu school is especially popular in eastern Tibet, an area known as Kham. Therefore, it is not surprising to learn that the head of this school, known as the Black Hat Lama after his distinctive headgear, wielded great secular authority here. The Kagyu were the first to establish the concept of the *tulku*. Briefly put, they believed that on his death the Black Hat Lama was reincarnated and took up residence in a new body. Thus, soon after he had died, monks fanned out over Tibet in order to find this new reincarnation and return him to his rightful place at the head of the order. In much later times, this order was one of the first to recognize the potential for expansion to Europe and America, and the famous contemporary monks Chögyam Trungpa and Chujé Akong belonged to the Kagyu order.

But of all the schools, the most famous is the Gelugpa or Yellow Hat school, headed by the Dalai Lama. Founded as a reform movement at the beginning of the fifteenth century by Tsongkhapa (1357–1419), the Gelugpa school soon became the preeminent school of Buddhism in Tibet, and a disciple of Tsongkhapa, Gendun-drup (1391–1474), was the first head of the school to be titled Dalai Lama. The title passed down to his successors, who, as with the Kagyu, were seen as being at the same time his (Gendun-drup's) reincarnation and the reincarnation of Avalokiteshvara, the *bodhisattva* of compassion. In 1642, the fifth Dalai Lama was appointed ruler of all Tibet, and so matters remained until the Chinese proceeded to drive the present, fourteenth, Dalai Lama out of Tibet in 1959. With the concentration of the administrative power in the hands of the Dalai Lamas, Tibet settled into a relatively peaceful routine and increasingly retreated from the world stage. Content to profess a nominal subordination to the Chinese court, Tibet shunned contact with the outside world until the beginning of the twentieth century when the outside world decided that it would come to Tibet, whether Tibet wished it or not!

Vajrayana: The Way of Ritual Mysticism

Buddhism is no stranger to ritualism. But in most schools of Buddhism this aspect of the religion has tended to remain subordinate to the more central religious practices of meditation and monastic discipline. In about 500 C.E., however, a new set of religious developments was taking place in India, with both Hinduism and Buddhism beginning to exhibit those traits that we now term "Tantric." In Buddhism, Tantra seems to have been an attempt to develop a new form of practice that was more dynamic than static meditations and monastic formalism. In the process, a radical new mode of Buddhism emerged.

Vajrayana Buddhism starts from somewhat different premises than other forms of Buddhism. This difference is not so much one of philosophy but of methodology. Previously, the human body had been looked on as something of a hindrance to the achievement of enlightenment. But this new form of Buddhism, far from dismissing the body as a means of achieving enlightenment, embraced it, and made it central to its religious practices. In the emerging Vajrayana school, the body and all its drives and passions were harnessed to the goal of escaping the cycle of birth and death. According to the *Cittavishuddhiprakarana*:

The jewel of the mind is naturally devoid
   of the color of [impure] ideas,
Originally pure, unoriginated,
   Impersonal and immaculate . . .

[The practitioner of Buddhism] is not Buddha, he is not set free,
   If he does not see the world
As originally pure, unoriginated,
   Impersonal and immaculate.

The mystic duly dwells
   On the manifold merits of his [intrinsic] divinity,
He delights in thoughts of passion,
   And by the enjoyment of passion is set free. . . .

Water in the ear is removed by more water,
   A thorn [in the skin] is removed by another thorn.
So wise men rid themselves of passion,
   By yet more passion.

SOURCE: Embree, *Sources of Indian Tradition*, pp. 195–196

Given this distinctly radical change in viewpoint, the Vajrayana Buddhist monk's training was somewhat different from that of the Theravadin or the Mahayanist monk. The essence of Theravada training lies in the perfection of meditation through monastic discipline and the knowledge of the Pali scriptures. The essence of Mahayanist training, although it may differ somewhat from school to school, is primarily centered on the perfection of meditation through self-discipline

Tibetan New Year ceremony in Jokhang Cathedral, Dharan Sala, India. Tibetan Buddhism places great emphasis on the effective use of ritual to gain enlightenment.

and the knowledge of a given school's core texts. The essence of Vajrayana training is the perfection of meditation through ritual practice and the mastery of the school's core Tantric texts—which are not seen, at least by other forms of Buddhism, as being part of the larger Buddhist canon at all! But this type of study only comes relatively late in the Vajrayanist monk's career. First, he is required to undergo a long period of scriptural study that will serve as a foundation for his ritual studies.

Tantric practices are seen as extremely effective in leading the practitioner to Nirvana, but they are extremely dangerous as well. To approach them without immense preparation is foolhardy and can lead to reincarnation in one of the numerous Buddhist hells. Likewise, Tantric study is not something that can be done on one's own. It can only be learned at the feet of a guru who has personally traveled the path that the practitioners wish to follow, and so can guide them by experience. Indeed, the guru is seen as being of such great importance that he is often venerated as a deity in his own right. Many of these highly developed gurus are seen as being able to reincarnate over and over again at will. Under their guidance, the novice can safely enter the Tantric path.

This path begins with the preliminary practices, which, although they may vary from school to school, have certain common elements. Practitioners must make a hundred thousand prostrations. They must perform a hundred thousand repetitions of various ritual offerings and repetitions of formulas designed to purify and focus the mind. But none of these practices is actual Tantra in itself. These rituals, which necessarily take many years to perform and beyond which many people never go, are designed to test would-be Tantric practitioners and purify them for the work ahead. This being said, they are also thought to have value in themselves, and many people, particularly laypersons, perform them without any thought of progressing beyond to the actual study of Tantra itself, which is generally seen as the preserve of monks and nuns. For these people, the rituals are generating merit and thus conducive to material and spiritual rewards in some future existence.

Having completed these preliminary practices, students are now ready to be initiated by their gurus. This ritual, known as the **abhisheka**, is central to the students' study. Without it, even if they had access to the Tantric texts, their study would be in vain. The *abhisheka* not only authorizes the students' practice, but it empowers it as well. Perhaps more importantly, it places students in the "family" of those who use the texts and thus qualifies them to receive the all-important oral teachings that have passed down from student to teacher concerning the meaning of the text. This is very important. In modern society, we believe that texts should be self-explanatory. But in the Tantric traditions, the text was seen as being much too dangerous to be allowed unimpeded circulation. The knowledge contained in the text could cause real damage. As a result, the texts were often written in a confusing and enigmatic "twilight language" and served not as the core of the teaching, but rather as a sort of memory aid for the teachers and students.

It was at the time of the *abhisheka* that the student received his mantra and the **mandala** of his **yidam** or titular deity. Vajrayanist Buddhists rely on a vast pantheon of gods and goddesses in their ritual practices and meditations. But for the practitioner of Tantra, these deities are not so much actual existing entities as they are archetypal symbols for psychological processes and neuroses. As such, they provide practitioners with a symbolic way of interacting with factors in their own minds. At the time of initiation, the guru, who is experienced with such matters, selects a suitable *yidam* for the student. Likewise, he shows the student the appropriate mantra for that deity. This mantra, usually of Sanskrit origin, encapsulates the essence of the *yidam* and consists of a short phrase that the student can meditate on at all times and in all places in daily life. Through it, students maintain a constant spiritual connection with their deity. The *mandala* is used in more formal religious practice and comprises a very complex drawing that in effect unites the student and the universe through the production of a sacred space. It becomes a sort of symbolic map that describes the journey of the student to the "palace" of the *yidam*. By ritually and meditatively following this map, and overcoming the various obstacles that confront them, students move closer to their ultimate goal of uniting with the *yidam*—the culmination of the student's practice. Through it, one comes to recognize one's identity with ultimate reality, and thus achieves release from the cycle of birth and death.[3]

The Decline of Buddhism in India

The Tantric Buddhism of Tibet represents the last major development of Buddhism in its homeland of India. With the rise of the Gupta dynasty in northern India in about 300 C.E., Buddhism found itself more on the defensive as a now-resurgent Hinduism began to assert itself. By 600, the worship of the gods Shiva and Vishnu began to displace Buddhism in the affections of its followers. This is first evident in

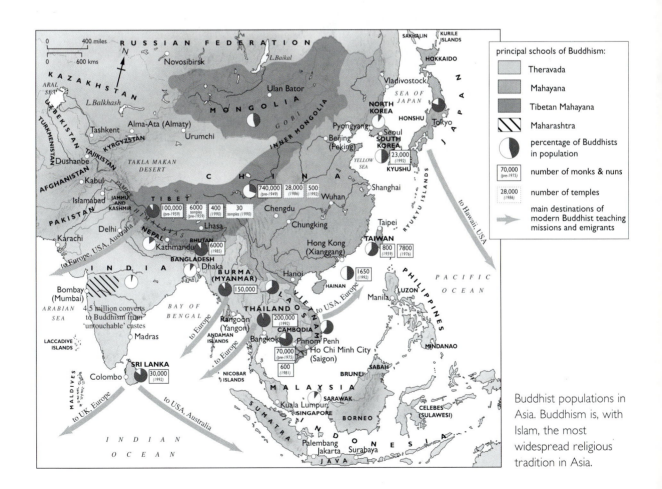

Buddhist populations in Asia. Buddhism is, with Islam, the most widespread religious tradition in Asia.

the southern part of the subcontinent. Before this date, Buddhism had been highly regarded in southern India, and was richly patronized by the Kalabhra rulers of southeastern India. Indeed, this region produced some of the greatest names in Buddhist philosophy during this period, and Buddhist missionaries had left from southern ports to evangelize Southeast Asia and southern China. By about 800, Buddhism was in serious decline in the south, although it continued to maintain a very limited presence up to the seventeenth century.

Buddhism continued to flourish in the northeast of the country, particularly in Bengal, with its large monastery-universities that housed and educated hundreds of monks at a time. Travelers from China reported that these Buddhist places of learning drew students from all over southern and eastern Asia, and that the monarchs of far-away states sent costly gifts earmarked for the maintenance of these elaborate institutions. It was here that the Tantric form of Buddhism evolved, and it was from here that it was exported to Tibet and beyond. In many respects, the Buddhism of the monastery-universities had changed significantly from the rather austere faith expounded by the Buddha. Now, a complex ritual shared space with a highly developed and subtle philosophy, an ever-expanding canon of scripture, and new artistic forms.

Despite this, Buddhism continued, on the whole, to lose ground to its rivals in India. The reasons for this are not completely clear, but certain factors are evident. India after 700 was politically very unstable. With the decline of the Guptas and their immediate successor states, the country dissolved into a patchwork of petty warring states. This meant that inevitably the lot of the common folk became more and more difficult. Their overall standard of living declined as a result of higher taxes brought on by wars and the damage sustained in those wars. This had two results. First, the amount that they could afford to donate to religious causes became

Buddhist *mandala*, Yuan dynasty, c. 1330. Ritual forms of Vajrayana Buddhism became popular throughout Asia from the sixth century onward.

The Buddha, Sultanganj, 7th century. The great monastery-universities of Bengal were the last great flowering of Buddhism in India before its decline and disappearance. This later figure of the Buddha dates from this period.

considerably less than had been the case in more prosperous times. Perhaps more importantly, their religious interests shifted from long-term goals, such as achieving salvation, to more immediate ones. No longer were they mainly interested in long-term release from the cycle of life and death. Rather they wanted a religion that could provide them with tangible results quickly. All this meant that peasant donations to the Buddhists began to drop off as the peasants switched their religious allegiances to the gods of Hinduism.

Even so, Buddhism continued to limp along. But the final blow fell with the Muslim invasions. These invaders swept out of the northwest, inflamed with the dual desire of eliminating idolatry and lining their pockets. The richly endowed Buddhist monastery institutions were easy targets which allowed them to do both. Between 1000 and 1200, wave after wave of Muslim invaders plundered and sacked these last islands of Buddhist influence in India. When the smoke cleared, Buddhism had virtually ceased to exist in the land of its birth. Those few monks who had escaped the wholesale slaughter of their brethren emigrated to less hostile lands. The Buddhist monuments and monasteries were either converted by Muslims and Hindus for their own use, destroyed, or they sank through neglect into jungle-shrouded obscurity. It was not until the coming of the British, some six hundred years later, that these ruins began to give up their secrets, and not until a further hundred and fifty years after this that Buddhism was to reemerge as a living religion in the land of its birth.

Website References

1. The greatest of these stupas, the stupa at Sanchi, is discussed at

   www.buddhanet.net/sanchi.htm and at www.abm.ndirect.co.uk/leftside/arty/stupa.htm

2. buddhism.miningco.com/msub19.htm covers many aspects of Mahayana Buddhism.

3. Vajrayana Buddhism is discussed at www.hawaiian.net/~dsparks/Vajrayana.html

CHAPTER TWELVE

♦

Buddhism in the Modern World Context

As we have seen, it was not until the European powers started to carve out their colonial empires in South and Southeast Asia and meddle in the affairs of the East Asian nations that they began to pay attention to the indigenous belief systems of their conquered populations. But generally, this attention had little or nothing to do with the intrinsic worth of these systems. Rather, these early administrators saw religion as a means of social control.

As time progressed, however, some Europeans came to appreciate Buddhism, Hinduism, and the other Asian religions. As they began to master the classical Asian languages such as Sanskrit, Chinese, Japanese, and Pali, European scholars began to piece together the new and fascinating universe of Buddhist thought.

The Spread of Buddhism in Europe and the United States

These European scholars tended to emerge from the lower ranks of the colonial administrators, who spent most of their days dealing with the problems of governing the common people over whom they ruled. Since there were very few other Europeans to socialize with, these officers often took up studying the local culture as a way to stave off boredom and madness (occasionally unsuccessfully). A good example of this was the case of T. W. Rhys-Davids. An administrator in Sri Lanka, he spent his leisure hours learning Pali, the sacred language of Theravada Buddhism. What he found astonished him. The Buddhism that began to emerge from the texts was not the seemingly superstitious religion that he felt surrounded him, but rather an elegant, subtle philosophical viewpoint that resonated with the logical, scientific philosophy that was coming to dominate European thinking. He became so enthusiastic about his studies that he founded the Pali Text Society with the intention of editing the entire Pali canon and translating it into English—a goal which the society has very nearly achieved.

The next major change in Buddhist-European relations came in 1879, when Sir Edwin Arnold published his famous epic poem, *The Light of Asia*. This was a retelling in English verse of the life of the Buddha, not from an academic standpoint but from the viewpoint of someone who appreciated Buddhist teaching as religious expression. Soon after this, Helen P. Blavatsky and Henry Steele Olcott, the two founders of the syncretic religious movement known as Theosophy, traveled to India and Sri Lanka. In Sri Lanka, they participated in a ceremony that formally accepted them into the Buddhist faith. Although their understanding of Buddhism was somewhat idiosyncratic, these new converts were enthusiastic about it.

Olcott in particular began a campaign to return Sri Lankan Buddhism to its former glories, taking as his model the newly translated philosophical texts of early Buddhism. This "return to the sources" appeared to many Euro-Americans as being similar to the return to the Bible proposed by Protestant reformers of Christianity such as Martin Luther. Consequently, the Buddhism that developed along the lines suggested by Olcott is often termed "Protestant Buddhism." Olcott organized schools and religious associations modeled on the YMCA, and mounted a campaign to counteract the vigorous Christian missionary activities. His efforts bore fruit, and soon the Buddhists were on the offensive. Under such able controversialists as Anagarika Dharmapala (1864–1933), Sri Lankan Buddhists began to rediscover and

Bodhgaya Mahabodhi Temple. This temple supposedly marks the spot where the Buddha achieved enlightenment. Some Hindus believe that the Buddha is an incarnation of Vishnu and so for many years the temple was controlled by Hindu priests. It was only restored to the Buddhists in the early years of the twentieth century through the efforts of Buddhist reformers such as Anagarika Dharmapala.

revitalize their traditions. Dharmapala was particularly successful in his campaign to have the holy places of Buddhism in India, such as the Bodhgaya Mahabodhi Temple, returned to Buddhist control. Nevertheless, Olcott is still remembered with great affection and gratitude in Sri Lanka, where a number of public streets, parks, and monuments bear his name.[1]

But the Theosophists were just the tip of the iceberg, so to speak. From about 1850 onward, Europe and the United States began to enter a period of religious crisis. Increasingly, intellectuals and those who fancied themselves as intellectuals were becoming dissatisfied with Christian claims. Some took issue with the idea that the Bible gave a complete, accurate and literal picture of the origins of humanity and the physical world; others with Christian claims to be in exclusive possession of the means of salvation in this world and the next. Many others simply wanted to replace what they thought of as mere superstition with a more scientific worldview. For many, Buddhism's "sudden" appearance on the intellectual horizon offered an answer to their dilemma.

But these early Euro-American enthusiasts of Buddhism tended to misunderstand it. As we have seen, Buddhism does not deny a realm beyond the senses, nor does it suggest that more powerful beings than humans do not exist. Rather, it simply asserts that *ultimate* salvation lies elsewhere. Early Euro-American adherents to Buddhism tended to interpret Buddhism as being completely atheistic and self-oriented, which is certainly not the case for many, if not most, Buddhists. It is not surprising, therefore, that early converts to Buddhism tended toward Theravada Buddhism, where these "rational" elements are the most pronounced. The first of these converts actually to become a Buddhist monk was the Englishman Allen Bennett (1872–1925), who was ordained in Myanmar. He was soon followed by a number of other Britons and Germans who embraced the monastic life style. But it was not until after the Second World War that other forms of Buddhism began to make their way into Europe and America.

The war itself was the major contributing factor to this new renaissance of interest in non-Theravada Buddhism, since it brought Europeans and Americans into contact with Buddhist countries such as China and Japan. Buddhism from these countries had already made a small beachhead in Hawaii and on the west coast of America; but these immigrant communities, hemmed in by racism and prejudice, tended to keep their religion to themselves. All this changed after the war. The first of the great Buddhist invasions of North America was the Zen craze that swept America in the 1950s. Zen had come to America with the attendance of the Japanese monk Soyen Shaku (1859–1919) at the great World Parliament of Religions held in Chicago in 1893. Here he had met the enthusiastic publisher of religious materials, Paul Carus, and had agreed to send one of his disciples to help Carus with the translation of Japanese Zen Buddhist texts. This disciple was to spend much of his life introducing Zen to the West: his name was D. T. Suzuki (1870–1966) and he was to become the patriarch of Zen studies in the West.

Other Zen masters were to follow Suzuki to America in the period before the Second World War, and they soon gathered small groups of enthusiastic American disciples. But it was the Beatnik generation, which emerged after the war, that took Zen to its heart. Writers from this movement, such as Jack Kerouac, Gary Snyder, and Allen Ginsberg, became ardent publicists for Zen, at least as they understood it. Alan Watts (1915–1973), a peripatetic jack-of-all-religions, also preached the gospel of Zen to an appreciative audience of youthful enthusiasts in California during the late 1950s and 1960s. This initial groundwork led to an influx of traditional Zen teachers into America in the decades that followed. These teachers established Zen training facilities, which taught Zen in the old-fashioned, rigorous Japanese manner. While something of a shock to an earlier generation of seekers, who saw Zen as a "do-your-own-thing" sort of religion, Zen in America has now, as a result of this second wave of teachers, come more into line with traditional expressions of the religion found in Asia. Indeed, a number of Americans have been recognized as Zen masters in their own right, and it might be said that there is a new type of Zen, American Zen, emerging under their guidance.

Nor should the contributions of the Chinese and Korean Zen schools be forgotten. In California, Zen Master Hsüan Hua (b. 1908) founded the Sino-American Buddhist Association and the Gold Mountain Dhyana Monastery, where the training is very traditional and rigorous. Other teachers, such as Sheng Yen Chang, are also spreading the teachings of Chinese Zen to America. Likewise, Korean masters such as Soen Sa Nim (b. 1927) are revealing the treasures of the much underestimated Korean tradition. Soen Sa Nim established the increasingly popular Kwan Um school—named for Kwan Yin, the *bodhisattva* of compassion—in 1972. He was preceded in 1967 by Samu Sunim, with his Toronto-based Zen Lotus Society.

Just as the Second World War marked the beginning of the penetration of Zen into America, so too did the Southeast Asian wars of the late 1960s and 1970s mark the start of a new appreciation of Theravada Buddhism. During this period, American servicemen serving in Vietnam used the neighboring country of Thailand as a rest and recreation spot. There they came in contact with Theravada Buddhism. Likewise, the increased American presence in Southeast Asia led to a growing number of Peace Corps volunteers being sent to the more stable countries in the region. A number of people, including Jack Kornfield and Joel Goldstein, went to these countries and to Sri Lanka to study Buddhism and even to be ordained as Buddhist monks under such great contemporary Theravadin teachers as Ajahn Chah in Thailand and Taungpulu Sayadaw in Myanmar. Eventually, many of them returned to Europe and America, either to reenter lay life or to teach as ordained monks. The Theravada Buddhism that they taught was, however, somewhat different in nature than that found in the countries where they had trained. There, laypersons did not, by and large, meditate. Meditation was something that was done by monks. In America and Europe, however, meditation was to become the primary religious activity of laypersons.

On the other hand, the traditional lay activities associated with Theravada Buddhism in its home countries came virtually to cease in America and Europe. There were few monks on whom to bestow alms, and so this most central of Theravada practices in Asia could not be maintained in America. Moreover, the people most drawn to Theravada Buddhism were often persons who were not comfortable with traditional religion, and most particularly with its institutional and supernatural aspects. Just as had been the case earlier in the century, it was the perception of Theravada Buddhism as an "atheistic" and "scientific" philosophy, rather than as a religion in the traditional sense of the term, that was attractive to this new group of followers.

Many people found the austere meditative practices of Zen and Theravada unappealing and looked for a more colorful Buddhism than these two traditions provided. For them, the answer to their search for religious meaning lay in Vajrayana Tantric Buddhism. This form of Buddhist expression was the least known of the Buddhist schools and the one which came to the West relatively late. Content to remain isolated in its Tibetan homeland, Tantric Buddhism might have remained unappreciated by outsiders had it not been for the national catastrophe that overtook Tibet in 1950. In that year, a newly Communist China decided to reassert the traditional Chinese claim that Tibet was an integral part of China by sending troops to occupy Lhasa, the Tibetan capital. This began the initial exodus of Tibetan monks out of Chinese-occupied territory and into nearby Nepal and India. After 1959, when the present Dalai Lama fled to Dharmasala in northwestern India, the trickle of emigrating monks became a flood.

Right from the first, these monks were faced with a severe problem: the Chinese were systematically destroying their entire religious culture. Horrible stories emerged from Tibet, most of which were, unfortunately, all too true. They told of monasteries burned, monks tortured and killed, and priceless works of art smashed. These activities became even more pronounced in the late 1960s during the Chinese Cultural Revolution when the Chinese attempted to totally eradicate Tibetan cultural identity through the most repressive means possible. The Tibetan monks desperately needed to find a way in which to preserve their cultural inheritance. Replacing their depleted numbers was no real problem, since Tibetans continued to enter the religious life, as many still do today. But how would these monks be supported now that the great Tibetan monasteries and their associated land holdings were gone? What could be done to replace their texts, many of which were unique to the Tibetan tradition? The answers to these dilemmas, the Tibetans swiftly discovered, lay in the West.

Thus in the 1960s Tibetan monks began to teach in the West. The most famous of these early missionaries was Chögyam Trungpa (1939–1987), a *tulku* of the Kagyu order, who established the first Tibetan monastery (*gonpa*) outside Asia: Samyé Ling, in Dumfriesshire, Scotland, in 1967 and wrote the classic text *Cutting Through Spiritual Materialism*. From this humble beginning, Trungpa created the far-flung Vajradhatu organization dedicated to propagating Kagyu Tibetan Buddhism in the West. After a serious car crash, from which he never completely recovered, Trungpa married and left Britain for the United States in 1970. At Boulder, Colorado, he established a new international Vajradhatu organization where he was succeeded as head of the organization by his American disciple Osel Tendzin (1945–1990) whose profligate life style and subsequent death from AIDS underscored the dangers in the unquestioning obedience to the guru taught by the Tibetan tradition.

It was in the United States that Tibetan Buddhism really flourished. In 1951, a group of Kalmyks, fleeing from their former homes in post-war Russia, were allowed to settle in New Jersey. Since the Kalmyks had been for many centuries followers of Tibetan Buddhism, it was here that the first Tibetan Buddhist temple in America was established, presided over by the Gelugpa monk Geshé Wangal (1901–1983). This led to the first formal teaching of Tibetan Buddhism in America when, in 1967, Geshé Wangal's disciple, Geshé Sopa (b. 1923), was invited by the great Canadian Buddhologist Richard Robinson to join the faculty of the newly established Buddhist Studies Program at the University of Wisconsin. Geshé Sopa, in turn, arranged for the Dalai Lama to come to the United States in 1981, and in that year the Dalai Lama presided over a Kalachakra Initiation at which some twelve thousand people were said to have attended. Other Gelugpa leaders who contributed to the development of Tibetan Buddhism in the West at this time were Thubten Yeshé (1935–1984) and his disciple Zopa Rimpoché (b. 1946) who established the Foundation for the Preservation of the Mahayana Tradition in 1971 and Wisdom Publications, a well-respected publishing house now based in Boston. Meanwhile, in the 1980s, Kalu Rimpoché (1905–1989) began to produce the first group of authentically trained Euro-American monks qualified to run their own training establishments.

Nyingmapa Tibetan Buddhism found a new lease of life in America as well. In 1969, Tarthang Tulku established the Tibetan Nyingma Institute in Berkeley, California. He was soon followed by other notable teachers of the school, including its supreme head Dudjom Rimpoché (1904–1987). One of Tarthang Tulku's major projects was to edit and publish the enormous corpus of Nyingmapa scriptures, a goal that is currently well on the way to completion. This, along with other similar publishing ventures, such as Wisdom Publications, has ensured that the immensely rich treasure trove of Tibetan Buddhist scriptures will be carefully preserved for future generations.

Finally, a word must be said concerning Pure Land and the other faith-based forms of Buddhism, which will be discussed in detail in subsequent chapters. The Pure Land school of Buddhism has been part of the American scene since the mid-nineteenth century, when Chinese and Japanese workmen began to be brought to the United States to work on the railroads and in the cane fields of Hawaii. Over the years, this school has acquired many trappings reminiscent of Protestant Christianity, not only in the West but even in the lands of its birth. By and large, it has remained in the Asian community, probably because, to the uninitiated eye, it offers little that differs from the Christian religion of the majority. Most non-Asians who are attracted to Buddhism are drawn to its core message because it is radically different from that of Christianity and Judaism. Thus Pure Land Buddhism, with its many apparent similarities to these traditions, does not seem as appealing to Westerners as more exotic forms of Buddhism. Nevertheless, its traditional followers are still numerous, particularly the Japanese school of Jodo Shin-shu, which in the United States goes by the name of the Buddhist Churches of America.

All in all, Buddhism, in its various forms and guises, is still very much alive and well in the United States and Europe. Indeed, in Hawaii, it is the religion of the majority of the state's people. Nor does this popularity seem likely to wane soon. Those factors which have made Buddhism tremendously appealing to such a broad spectrum of peoples in widely differing cultures still sing their siren song to many people of many different nationalities to this day, and likely will for many years to come.

Buddhism in the Twenty-first Century

Buddhism is no different from other world religions in that it faces challenges in the modern world as well as opportunities. The twentieth century has not been as kind to Buddhism as it has been to Hinduism. Large areas of the Buddhist world have disappeared owing to political and social changes. A good example of this is in China, where Buddhism was once widespread. After the Communists took power, Buddhism was systematically suppressed so that it is difficult today to discern how many Buddhists still remain in that huge country. As we have seen, the Communists carried their dislike of Buddhism to Tibet in 1951, where they attempted to eradicate Buddhism entirely, often by extraordinarily violent means. Likewise during the hideous excesses of the Khmer Rouge in Cambodia between 1975 and 1979, virtually the entire Buddhist monastic order of that Theravadin Buddhist country was murdered by their own countrymen. Many estimate that at the end of this period, out of an initial eighty thousand monks, only a few hundred survived. In China, Cambodia, and Tibet, temples were destroyed, scriptures burned, and valuable pieces of Buddhist art sold to the highest bidder.

Of much greater concern to Buddhist religious figures, however, is a new and far more insidious assault on their beliefs and way of life. This has come through the medium of Euro-American culture. Smuggled in on the backs of Mickey Mouse and Michael Jackson, the Euro-American gospel of consumerism seems to be entirely at odds with Buddhist values, which preach simplicity, tranquillity, and turning away from the relentless acquisition of goods. But the "Coca-Colonization" of Asian societies has left them awash in rock videos, Euro-American nightclubs, and expensive electronic consumer goods. While certainly not bad in themselves, these things weave a not-so-subtle counterpoint to traditional values. They do this by replacing religious ideals with their own vision of the nature of human happiness based on material prosperity, comfort, and entertainment. Along with these cultural values comes the worldview that supports them. The Euro-American scientific materialist worldview, with its discounting of religious values and religious theories of the nature and ends of human existence, has also had a powerful effect on many educated people in Asia.

Need we fear that Buddhism, like so many religions before it, will slowly fade away in the face of these challenges? The answer to this is that such an event is highly unlikely. Over the centuries, Buddhism has shown itself to be highly adaptable to new cultural conditions. As we have seen, it spread from its original home in India throughout most of Asia, coping with new cultures and new languages as it encountered them. In the process, it became an integral part of these cultures. Even now, it is changing and adapting. The Buddhism that came to America and Europe from various Asian cultures is being reconceptualized and revitalized in such a manner as to make it a unique part of these cultures. It is adapting to the changing environment in its homelands as well. For many years seen as being untouched by the normal concerns of secular society, Buddhist groups that are primarily focused on social problems are now springing up. In Thailand, groups headed by monks are addressing environmental concerns stemming from that country's rapid industrialization. In Sri Lanka, monastic organizations are becoming more involved in community health issues in the many tiny villages that dot the island. In the United States, Buddhist teachers are a persuasive voice in many areas of the fight for social justice. All this marks the emergence of an "engaged Buddhism"—based on a melding of personal concerns and social issues—that is successfully bringing the religion into the new world of the twenty-first century.[2]

For many people whose traditional religious faith is not Buddhism, the Buddhist analysis of reality and its practical program for achieving transcendence from the pains of human life is proving very appealing. One of the features of Buddhism which is most attractive to many people, especially those raised in the scientific milieu of Euro-American society, is that Buddhism does away with the idea of the "supernatural"—a split between this world and some unseen, "totally other" world. The universe, says the Buddhist, is a vast system of processes, not things, controlled by unchangeable laws that strictly control human destiny. Salvation, that is to say freedom from the endless cycle of rebirth and death, comes from a recognition of these laws and conformity to their demands.

For the Buddhist, the inexorable laws of cause and effect can no more be changed than the law of gravity repealed. Such a viewpoint is extremely attractive to the Euro-American mind that has been nurtured on scientific principles. Whereas other religions depend on the unproved, and indeed probably unprovable, concept of a supreme deity, Buddhism has no such need. In addition, Buddhist presuppositions seem to mesh much more easily with the generally accepted laws of physics, and these laws themselves increasingly seem to support many Buddhist contentions about the nature of the universe. For many people, Buddhism is an increasingly acceptable religious option because it is so "non-religious."

Another reason that Buddhism maintains its popularity is that it tends toward individual, rather than corporate, expressions of religiosity. Among the Euro-American religions of Christianity and Judaism, the core religious actions are defined as taking place in community. Buddhism, on the other hand, sees religious activity consisting of people's personal actions that may from time to time intersect with those of others. In the increasingly individualistic Internet societies of Europe and America, this is a distinct advantage, particularly as demands on the individual's time increase and the stately seasonal cycles of ritual that mark Judaism and Christianity—geared as they were to the slow pace of agricultural societies—become increasingly impractical in a twenty-four-hours-a-day, seven-days-a-week industrial world. This appreciation of the personal in Buddhism can be seen in other ways as well. Buddhism lacks much of the institutionalized prejudice that exists in other religions. Consequently, people of differing races, genders, sexual orientation, and life styles find a supportive atmosphere in Buddhism that they do not necessarily find in the Euro-American religions.

In Buddhism, individuals can practice as much or as little ritualism as they choose. Whereas the majority of Euro-American religious activity takes place within the context of formal ritual, Buddhists can practice their religion without any recourse to ritual whatsoever, if that is their choice. On the other hand, those who do wish to support their meditation practice with more formal rituals can do so easily. Moreover, Buddhism has a long history of using everyday vernacular language rather than a sacred language that is understood by only a few specialists. This means that the scriptures of the religion are readily available to all its members for study and reflection. Finally, the lack of a mediating priesthood means that each individual Buddhist possesses an equal potential for achieving realization of Nirvana without needing to depend on another.[3]

It seems that in the foreseeable future, Buddhism will remain a compelling advocate for a quieter, gentler, more contemplative world. As long as the problems that mark human existence persist, Buddhism will always find people in every generation for whom its message of hope, peace, and compassion will continue to resonate. It will continue to offer such individuals a way of coping realistically with life's many disappointments and tragedies in a way that can be tailored to each individual case and circumstance.

Website References

1. Buddhism and indigenous religion in Sri Lanka is the subject of
   www.thanhsiang.org/education/dip3-14.htm

2. www.dharmanet.org/engaged.html gives an overview of the emerging "engaged Buddhism" movement.

3. Buddhism outside of Asia is discussed at
   www-user.uni-bremen.de/~religion/baumann/bib-ambu.htm

CHAPTER THIRTEEN

✦

Religion in Southeast Asia

As in the case of South Asia, geography has had an important effect on the development of religion in Southeast Asia as well. This region presents a remarkably diverse topography, split into two roughly equal halves: Mainland Southeast Asia to the north and Island Southeast Asia to the south. Mainland Southeast Asia contains the present-day nations of Vietnam, Laos, Cambodia, Thailand, Myanmar, and Malaysia, and is a land of contrast. Along its northern borders it is fenced in by rugged mountain ranges. Although not as formidable as their Himalayan counterparts farther west, these mountains still present an effective deterrent to invasions from China and Central Asia as well as a refuge for tribal peoples dispossessed from the fertile plains and river valleys farther south. In addition to this main range of mountains, Mainland Southeast Asia is further divided by two other ranges: one runs from north to south, along the border between Vietnam, Cambodia, and Laos; the other forms the border between Myanmar and Thailand. There are also east-west ranges, such as the Dangrek Mountains and the Cardamons in Cambodia. The rugged nature of this mainland region, along with its dense vegetation, broad rivers, and heavy monsoon rains, has hampered communication among the various cultural groups that live there and allowed them to develop their own individual customs.[1]

Between these various mountain ranges flow the great rivers of Southeast Asia, all of which have their genesis in the eastern Himalayas. In Myanmar, the valleys of the Salween and Irrawaddy provide some of the richest agricultural land in the region, as do the Chao Praya (Menam) River in Thailand, the Mekong River in Laos, Cambodia, and southern Vietnam, and the Red River in northern Vietnam. Nor does nature stop there in its gifts to the region. The fertility of the land is increased by its climate. Like India and Island Southeast Asia, Mainland Southeast Asia is the beneficiary of the monsoons. These regular winds drop abundant rainfall on the region. This has allowed for the development of intensive agriculture and, consequently, the agricultural surplus necessary for the growth and development of civilization. Island Southeast Asia presents a somewhat different picture. This region, which today contains the present-day nations of Singapore, Indonesia, Brunei, and the Philippines, is a huge archipelago of volcanic islands. Despite the fertility of its volcanic soil and the regular rains of the monsoon, this region has developed less rapidly than the mainland. Nevertheless, it too has a long religious history.

Four principal sociolinguistic groups can be distinguished in Southeast Asia. The first of these is the Mon-Khmer culture. Members of this group can currently be found throughout the mainland from Myanmar to Vietnam. The second group is the Tai, who were originally inhabitants of northwestern Vietnam and Laos, where many of them still live, but who have now spread widely into Laos, Thailand, and northeastern Myanmar. The third group, the Burmese, are relative newcomers to the region, having drifted down from the eastern mountains of Tibet beginning in the sixth or seventh century C.E. They are localized in the lowlands of Myanmar. The fourth group is Austronesian culture. This cultural group can be seen as comprising two broad divisions. The first of these is the mainland Austronesians, who have been relegated to the highlands of southern Vietnam with a few small pockets living in Cambodia. Although their influence is negligible at present, they were once a considerable force in the history of Southeast Asia and played an important role in the development of its religious traditions. The second Austronesian division is much more widespread and contains the numerous cultural subgroups that have dominated the islands of Southeast Asia and the lower third of the Malay Peninsula for thousands of years, as they still do today. Each of these cultures possesses distinctive religious features, as do their subcultures, but the striking fact about indigenous religious traditions in Southeast Asia is not so much their differences as their similarities. In addition, scattered throughout the mountains of Mainland Southeast Asia are other sociolinguistic groups, such as the Hmong, the Kachins, and the Karins, who are relatively recent immigrants to the region and have had little impact on its cultural development.

One of the great pioneers of the study of Southeast Asia was the French scholar Paul Mus, who believed that, despite their geographical and ethnic diversity all the religions of Southeast Asia possessed a number of common traits. The first of these was the belief in an amorphous local god of the soil who controlled the fertility of the region that he inhabited. Without the cooperation of this god, no crops could be grown and no children would be born. From this belief stemmed the second common feature of the local religion—the idea of a primordial sacrifice that effected a sort of union between a group's ancestral founder and its local god through which the two separate entities merged into one. This ritual act established a permanent and absolute bond between the people and their homeland. The third feature identified by Mus was an ongoing sacrificial cult in which the current political leader of the people continued to be associated with the ancestor/deity, acting as both a medium for the communication of that deity's desires and as a high priest for the sacrifices designed to gain the deity's favor. This cult maintained and renewed the essential bond between the people and their land. Finally, Mus suggested that the symbol for this interaction between the people—as personified by their political leader—and the spiritual principle of the land was symbolized by the use of sacred standing stones identified with the deity, ancestor, and living chieftain simultaneously. This idea was based on the widespread ancient megalithic remains found throughout Southeast Asia.

To these common traits, some others can be added. In indigenous Southeast Asian traditions, both men and women participate equally in religious rituals in a way they do not in the imported religious traditions, which are almost totally controlled by men. There is also an ancient association of divinity with mountains, as well as a profound sense of dualism, which is expressed in a number of ways, such as the sense of dichotomy between the mountains and the sea found among many Southeast Asian groups. Finally there is the most important facet of indigenous Southeast Asian religion: the belief in a vast number of very local spirits and deceased ancestors who influence all aspects of people's lives and who have to be constantly wooed or placated if life is to proceed smoothly.

Burmese Nat, 19th century. Local spirits such as the Nats are still very important in the day-to-day religious life of the various peoples of Southeast Asia.

Prehistoric Religion in Southeast Asia

As in all areas of the world, Southeast Asia shows practices from a very early period that might be termed generically religious. The earliest example of these is associated with the Haobinhian phase of Stone Age tool culture, which was widespread throughout the region for many millennia. At the West Mouth of the Niah Caves in Sarawak archaeologists have found a large number of human burials that have been dated to between 12,000 and 6000 B.C.E. The bodies from a number of these burials had been painted with hematite to give them a blood-red color, and one had a rhinoceros femur as a pillow. In addition, some of the burials included stone tools. Recently, similar burials have been found at Hang Dang and Moc Long caves in northern Vietnam. Here the dead were also buried in a crouching position, covered with red ochre, in association with Haobinhian pebble tools. Most likely, these remains represent the beliefs of the earliest inhabitants of the region, the Australoid-Melanesian peoples, and suggest that they did not see death as the end of a person's existence. With the exception of a few tiny tribal groups, these people have long since moved on to other areas outside of the Southeast Asian region, primarily Oceania and Australia, or they have been absorbed into the present-day population. It may be that these early peoples' religious ideas influenced the new arrivals from southern China who now dominate the region, but if so, these ideas have been integrated into Southeast Asian religious thinking for so long that they are no longer discernible in themselves.

The next major advance in our knowledge of the people of the region comes from Thailand. A burial near the coast, dated to about 2000 B.C.E., reveals burials that suggest from the richness of their grave goods that ranking based on both genealogical considerations and on status was well established in Southeast Asian societies. Parallel to the developments in Thailand were the developments in northern Vietnam that culminated in the culture known to archaeologists as the Dong Son culture. This society was characterized by a particular type of cast-bronze drum, which first seems to have come into existence in about 600 B.C.E. These drums are highly decorated with geometric patterns and scenes that probably represent religious rituals. One such scene shows a group in prayer, another a standing couple embracing. Both these scenes are likely connected with fertility rituals. But there is also another scene that is of special interest. This shows a festival scene in which a pillar is clearly the focal point of devotions being performed by a woman. Given the context of the scene in proximity to other clearly fertility-oriented scenes, it is not unreasonable to assume that this ritual is also involved with fertility, and that both the pillar and the presiding priestess are associated with such worship.

These sacred pillars found on the Dong Son drums may also be associated with the extensive megalithic monuments scattered throughout Southeast Asia. Whatever the origins of the megaliths, and despite the still ongoing archaeological debate over their ethnic affiliations, R. Heine-Geldern's analysis of their religious function remains very plausible. As he wrote:

> With very few and unimportant exceptions, the megaliths are concerned with special notions concerning life after death; . . . the majority are erected in the course of rites destined to protect the soul from the dangers believed to threaten it in the underworld or on its way there, and to assure eternal life either to the persons who erect the monuments as their own memorials while alive, or to those to whom they are erected after their death; . . . at the same time the megaliths are destined to serve as a link between the living and the dead and to enable the former to participate in the wisdom of the dead; . . . they are thought to perpetuate the magic qualities of the persons who had erected them or to whom they had been erected, thereby furthering the fertility of men, livestock and crops and promoting the wealth of future generations.
>
> SOURCE: Heine-Geldern, "Prehistoric Research in the Netherlands Indies" in *Science and Scientists in the Netherlands Indies*, (eds.) Honig and Verdoon (New York: Board for the Netherlands Indies, Surinam and Curacao, 1945), p. 151

The Beginnings of Indian Influences in Eastern Mainland Southeast Asia

Starting from about 200 B.C.E, the history of Southeast Asia begins to come into sharper focus. It is at this time that the Chinese, now unified under the ruling house of the state of Qin, extend their influence to the coasts of the South China Sea. Southeast Asia, its resources, and its peoples now began to feature in the Chinese records as the source of rare and costly merchandise for the Chinese market, and of exotic travellers' tales. Likewise, Indian merchants, wishing to benefit from the region's immense natural resources, began to undertake the long and dangerous sea voyage to these previously unknown shores. The Chinese and the Indians brought with them new ideas and new technologies, and were to change the cultural landscape of Southeast Asia in profound ways.

The first states in Southeast Asia to adopt ideas from India were those of Funan, in what is now southern Cambodia, and Champa, the present-day southern coast of Vietnam. In Champa and Funan, political events continued to be inextricably linked with the religious life of the country, as they had been since prehistoric times. In the

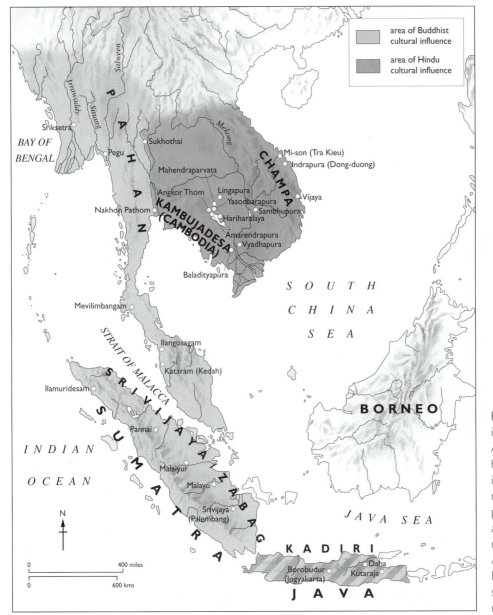

Early Indian religious influences in Southeast Asia. Southeast Asia has been deeply influenced by the religions of India, particularly Hinduism and Buddhism. Early religious sites such as Angkor Wat and Borobudur are still sources of pride in the region.

royal courts of these two states, a form of Hinduism based on the veneration of Shiva as the founding ancestor of the ruling families of the state seems to have predominated. Of the some one hundred and thirty Champan inscriptions that have come down to us, ninety-two refer principally to Shiva and the gods and goddesses associated with him, while only five refer to Brahma, and only three are specifically dedicated to Vishnu. In addition, we find seven inscriptions mentioning the Buddha, two that mention Shiva and Vishnu equally, with some twenty-one inscriptions that do not refer to any god in particular. But it would be unwise to conclude from this that there was a full-scale transfer of local religious allegiance away from domestic deities to the newly arrived Indian ones. In many cases, local gods, and particularly goddesses, reemerged cloaked in a veneer of Indian iconography. The gods of India found a place in Southeast Asia directly proportional to the role that they could play in the development of the sociopolitical institutions of the region.

Shiva was clearly the preeminent god of the Champan aristocracy who produced the inscriptional record, and the references to Shiva's greatness are numerous and fulsome. He came to be regarded as the patron of the country, and both the northern religious sanctuary of Mi-son and the southern one of Po Nagar are dedicated to him. According to one inscription, the very capital was said to be "created by the rays issuing from the pair of feet of Shiva." In another, Shiva is called "the god Shrishanabhadreshvara who is the origin of the kingdom of Champa." Shiva was represented by his symbol, the linga, which served as a token of Shiva's protection of the state. Champan kings, starting with king Bhadravarman in about 350 C.E., vied with one another in constructing magnificent temples to house the lingas that they erected at the beginnings of their reigns.[2] They also allotted large amounts of gold and silver, as well as fortunes in precious stones, to the decoration of the lingas themselves—not for art's sake alone, but for the magical power that they believed flowed from these sacred objects through themselves into the land.

But the veneration of Shiva and his lingas was very much an upper-class affair. The common people persisted in their placation of the local spirits that ruled their lives, and perhaps began to listen to a new group of holy men who had begun to disembark from the ships coming from India—the Buddhist monks. The earliest records that we have concerning Buddhism in mainland Southeast Asia in general, and Champa in particular, are Chinese and Vietnamese written sources. In the *Thien uyen tap anh ngu luc*, a Vietnamese history compiled between the late eleventh and early thirteenth centuries C.E., we read that when questioned about Buddhism in Giao Chau (northern Vietnam) by the Chinese emperor Sui Wendi, the monk Tan Tian explained that:

> Giao Chua has routes leading to India. By the time that Buddhism was introduced into China (c. first century), twenty Buddhist towers had already been built (in Giao Chua), more than 500 monks trained and 15 books of Buddhist sutras translated . . . Then monks like Ma Ha Ky-vuc, Khuong Tang Hoi, Chi Cuong Luong, and Mau Bac went to China to spread Buddhism.

How much can we trust this assertion that Buddhism in Vietnam and Champa, which lay along the same sea route, predated the religion's introduction into China? The question seems to hinge on the date that trade was established with India. This matter is still unclear, but new archaeological discoveries suggest that trade contacts were initiated earlier than previously supposed, possibly in the second century B.C.E. The itinerary of the monk Mahajivika, who is recorded to have been born in India, traveled through the area in the middle of the third century C.E. He gives us a good

Lakshmi, Khmer sculpture. Although the early artistic renderings of divinities were clothed in Indian iconography, they were often associated with indigenous gods and goddesses.

idea of what the route between India and Vietnam would have been like. He traveled to Funan, along the coast controlled by Champa, to northern Vietnam, and then on to southern China and Luoyang. There can be little doubt that even if Buddhism was not the primary religion of Champa, it was widespread. Chinese records report that one of the Chinese invasions of Champa in 605 resulted in 1,350 works on Buddhism being carried off. Likewise there appears to have been considerable royal interest in the religion. King Indravarman III was said to be proficient in its theology, and the occasional king of Champa, such as Jaya Indravarman II, took posthumous Buddhist names.

Specific information concerning the schools of Buddhism in Champa is, unfortunately, uneven at best. Likewise the archaeological record of Buddhism in Champa is sparse. Indigenous Buddhist sculpture does not seem to have been produced much before 600, but, as one might expect in a polity so actively engaged in trade as Champa was, imported Buddhist sculpture has been found. One of the oldest of these figures is the so-called Dong Duong Buddha. This bronze figure, dating from the third or fourth century C.E., is in the style of the artists of southeastern India and Sri Lanka. Some art historians see in this statue an affinity with Mon Buddhist art found in northeastern Thailand. There seems to be other evidence of Mon influence in Champa, and thus, by extension, of the Theravadin Buddhist traditions that commanded the Mons' religious loyalty from the earliest times.

The religious situation in Funan, the other early state of Mainland Southeast Asia, seems to parallel closely the state of affairs found in Champa. The Chinese *History of the Liang* tells us that the people of Funan "worship[ed] the spirits of the sky. They make bronze images of these sky spirits; those that have two faces have four arms; those that have four faces have eight arms. Each hand holds something—sometimes a child, sometimes a bird or a four-legged animal, or else the sun or the moon." It seems that the Chinese chronicler was trying to describe Hindu images. There is evidence that Buddhism flourished here as well, as did Hindu cults other than the worship of Shiva—for example the veneration of Vishnu.

Religion in the Period of the Great Empires (800–1300 C.E.)

By 800 C.E., two sizable empires had emerged in Southeast Asia. One, the Shailendra state, was located on the island of Java in present-day Indonesia and included parts of an earlier major state, Shrivijaya, that had flourished on the neighboring island of Sumatra and the lower Malay Peninsula. The second, and more famous, state was the mainland Khmer Empire of Cambodia, which produced Angkor Wat, one of the architectural wonders of the ancient world. Both states greatly influenced the course of Southeast Asian history, and both left imposing monuments that give us a clear picture of their religious ideas.

In the Shailendra lands, the primary religion, although certainly not the exclusive one, was Buddhism. The Shailendras inaugurated an unparalleled period of monument building in central Java that was to result in the creation of Borobudur, one of the world's great legacies of religious art. However, the brilliance of the Buddhist monuments of Java should not blind us to the fact that this is also a period in which Hinduism made considerable gains in the region as well. Indeed, some scholars believe that Shaivism was better adapted to local conditions and therefore spread

Borobudur. Borobudur, a Buddhist monument, was the first of the great Southeast Asian religious monuments to be constructed.

more rapidly than Buddhism. Given the relatively small area in which Buddhist remains are found, as opposed to the much more widespread distribution of Shaivite Hindu remains, this theory seems very plausible. It is possible that Buddhism remained the religion of the nobility, while Shaivism had a much broader popular base among the common people.

The Buddhism described in the inscriptions of the period is very clearly Tantric in nature. The sanctuary mentioned in one such inscription is dedicated to the Tantric deity Tara. Moreover, this inscription records that the sanctuary was also a dwelling place for Buddhist monks who followed the Mahayana monastic code. Another inscription of the same era is dedicated to the *bodhisattva* Avalokiteshvara. In the inscription of Karang Tengah, dated 832, we see an example of a religious pattern common to the mainland as well—a princess of the Shailendra dynasty recording the establishment of a sanctuary to the Buddha. But the merit that was believed to accrue from such an act was dedicated not to the foundress, but rather to her father, the king.

Of all the Buddhist remains found in central Java, the most magnificent are without doubt those of Borobudur, the largest Buddhist monument ever built in the Southern Hemisphere. The monument was constructed in about 800 and was designed to be a huge teaching tool in stone. It was built by overlaying a preexisting hill with a stone sheath to which carving and statuary were affixed in a series of ten levels of terraces. The lower six of these terraces are square in shape, while the four terraces above them are round. What they are meant to represent is nothing less than a map or *mandala* of the entire Buddhist cosmos, with the crowning statue of the Buddha seated in the center of its topmost level. The worshipper starts at the bottom of this colossal stupa and, while circling it in the approved clockwise fashion, slowly ascends the spiral of ramps and stairs that eventually lead to the top. Along the way, the pilgrim is presented with a constant flow of bas-relief pictures that lay out the life and philosophy of the Buddha. Many of the stories illustrated here can be traced to a number of specific Buddhist sources that give us a good idea of which texts were influential in the Shailendran kingdom.[3]

In Cambodia, a particular aspect of the Hinduism of the empire of Angkor was the Devaraja Cult. Of the many mysteries still surround the study of Cambodian history and culture, one of the most interesting is the origin and nature of this cult, which seems to have been established in about 800 by Jayavarman II, the founder of the Angkorean state. But if one examines the development of both religion and state apparatus in Southeast Asia as a whole, it becomes evident that Jayavarman II may not have been instituting a new state cult, but attempting to reestablish, albeit in a new form, an institution that was already an integral part of Southeast Asian life. Later monarchs of Angkor maintained the cult because of their desire to legitimize their rule. Thus the Devaraja cult might be seen as being at the same time an expression of earlier forms and a unique bridge between those forms and developing Angkorean institutions.

As we have seen, the veneration of the royal ancestral spirits as guardians of the land was a practice rooted in indigenous belief systems and clothed in Indic vestments. Its continuity was an essential and accepted part of the fabric of royal authority. Kings needed to be able to put forth the claim that they were the legitimate descendants of the spirits that controlled the fertility of the land, and thus were eligible to rule the country. What Jayavarman II may have been doing in setting up a new cult was to assert the primacy of his royal claims against competitors through establishing a more potent link with the previous regnal lines. The great monuments of the dynasty, such as Angkor Wat, were physical representations of the ruler's links with his ancestral past and the powers that controlled the fertility of the land, and of his domination of the world that these monuments symbolically represented.

The approach to Angkor Wat. Angkor Wat, originally dedicated to Vishnu, represents the pinnacle of Southeast Asian temple building in the classical period.

This act of channeling the powers of the royal ancestors was something that was proper to the king alone. The common people were not, and could not be, involved in the process except as pious spectators. Thus the Tantric ceremonies that served as the core of the Devaraja cult were seen as being applicable only to the king. In that sense, at least, it was a private religious devotion. But the supernatural power of the sovereign, generated and sustained by the rituals of the Devaraja cult, had political applications as well. The sovereign was able to confer supernatural benefits that would be realized by their recipients in the world to come, thus cementing their recipients' allegiance to the person of the king. But when all is said and done, Hinduism does not seem to have penetrated very deeply into Cambodia or any other Southeast Asian country at the local level except for certain limited magical rites and formulas; nor, at least in this early period, did Buddhism. In the innumerable small villages that dotted the region, the old religion of the local spirits ruled.

Vietnam and the Adaptation of the Chinese Worldview

Just as most other parts of Southeast Asia took the Indian worldview as their template for socioreligious change, the Vietnamese, because of history and geographical proximity, adapted the Chinese worldview to the developing needs of their own society. But as was the case elsewhere, they did so on their own terms and with results unique to their particular situation. Confucian and Daoist ideas no doubt entered the country very early in the van of the invading Chinese armies that forced Vietnam to acknowledge Chinese rule for almost a thousand years. Buddhism, however, appears to have entered the country not from China, but from the state of Champa to the south, coming along the sea routes from India. This Buddhism, heavily admixed with indigenous religious ideas, was influential in Vietnam from an early date.

Buddhist temples were soon established throughout the Red River delta, the core area of the early Vietnamese state. With the establishment of the independent Vietnamese monarchy under Dinh Bo Linh in 968 came a concomitant regularization of the Buddhist community. Dinh Bo Linh, following Chinese models, recognized Buddhism as an official religion in 971, but with this recognition came organization. Dinh Bo Linh standardized the different priestly grades in order to bring about religious conformity analogous to that of the military and civil service. A large number of Buddhist monks were involved in diplomatic and domestic affairs during this period. Indeed, one of the titles that was bestowed on monks at this time was Khuong Viet, "helper of the Viet country." Nor was their service purely pacific. As one source observes, monks were often "permitted to participate in the great military affairs of the nation." This was especially true during the early days of Vietnamese nation building.

But the Buddhism of the time was by no means the only religious tradition followed in Vietnam at this time, as the following story indicates:

> Ma Ha went to Ai Chau, and continued on till the outskirts of Sa Dang. The people there worshipped evil spirits and took great joy in slaughtering animals. The monk advised them to fast but the people replied, "Our spirits have the power to bless us or harshly punish us; we dare not provoke them." The monk responded, "you must abandon evil and do good. If anything bad happens, I will bear full responsibility." A villager answered, "In this village, a man has been stricken with leprosy for years.

Physicians and sorcerers can do nothing. If you could cure him, we will behave as you have said." The monk poured holy water on the leper and he was immediately cured.

SOURCE: Nguyen Tai Thi (ed.), *History of Buddhism in Vietnam* (Hanoi: Social Sciences Publishing House, 1992), p. 102

During this period, the different sects of Thien (Zen) Buddhism such as those introduced by Vinitaruci in about 600 C.E. began to gain ground. But these schools of Buddhism interacted with Tantric and Pure Land Buddhism as well. This was best illustrated by the Vietnamese interest in *dharanis*, magical formulas that were held to possess great power. The *Thien uyen tap anh ngu luc*, an early history of Vietnam, informs us that Ma Ha "recited the Buddhist scripture Dai Bi Tam [a Tantric text] continuously over a three year period," and thus came to master a method of meditation held to put the practitioner into a state of grace. Another such practice was the recitation of the *Mahakarunahridayadharani*. The study of this *dharani* seems to have been very widespread during the tenth and eleventh centuries. The *Thien uyen tap anh* records that one monk, Tu Dao Hanh, "recited this *dalani* [Vietnamese pronunciation of *dharani*] every day, one million eight thousand times." This and other incantations were used for many things, not all of them spiritual in nature. Monks recited the *dharanis* to cure disease, ward off evil spirits, and to ensure good weather and sufficient rain. There was also the widespread use of prophecy. Indeed, many monks, such as Van Hanh and Phap Thuan, were seen as being oracles, and their words were copied down and remembered.

With the founding of the Ly dynasty in 1010, Buddhism continued to flourish. The kings themselves tended to belong to the Thao Duong sect of Thien Buddhism or, less often, to the Wu Yan Tong sect of the same school. Likewise the principal families of the realm were lavish supporters of the *Dharma*, and many monks were of noble descent. There also seems to have been a program of missionary activity. An example of the result of this is the Bao Ninh Song Phuc temple, which was built in 1107 in an area inhabited by the non-Buddhist Tai peoples. The wealth of the Sangha increased enormously during this time, with the kings of the Ly dynasty donating large tracts of prime rice-growing land to the monasteries. These fields were farmed by tenant farmers who paid the monks a portion of their crop. In addition, particular monks were allowed to farm the tax revenues of allotted communities. Owing to the monastic prohibition on handling money, such funds were collected by lay temple bursars appointed by the king.

Under the Ly, the process of organizing the Sangha continued apace. The Sangha was divided into left- and right-side chief monks, and left- and right-side common monks. As before, many monks were elevated to important positions of trust in the government. Monks functioned as government officials in that they were formally charged with attending to religious affairs in particular regions. However change was in the air. As the Ly dynasty consolidated its position, it began to ease the monks out of actual power, becoming more Confucian in its orientation. This trend accelerated under the Tran dynasty. This is not to say, however, that Buddhism did not continue to prosper. But now criticism of the Sangha began to mount. Attempts were made to reform what was perceived as a growing laxness on the part of the monks. One provincial governor wrote:

At present the number of apprentice monks equals that of service people. By themselves they gather, name inconsiderately their chiefs for gangs and do many filthy actions. They publicly eat and drink in religious places or indulge in lewdness in nun rooms. They hide themselves in the daytime, and go out at night as fox and mice. They corrupt customs and deprave religion, all that becomes progressively habit. If it is not forbidden, it will grow worse.

SOURCE: Tai Thi, *History of Buddhism in Vietnam*, p. 180

Some emperors of the period, such as Tran Thai Tong, took a great interest in Buddhism and promoted a synthetic form of the religion that combined Zen and Pure Land ideas. He also strove to integrate Confucianism, Buddhism, and Daoism and was particularly interested in reconciling Buddhism and Confucianism. In 1299 this trend reached its peak when Emperor Tran Nhan Tong became a monk, founding the Truc Lam sect of Thien. The goal of this new sect was to reunite disparate strands of Vietnamese Buddhism into one unified school.

Foreign influences, especially the practice of Tantra, continued to play a role in Vietnamese Buddhism. In 1318, for example, a famous monk named Phap Loa was ordered by the king to search out a particular Indian monk and obtain the translation of a Tantric text. Phap Loa also wrote a commentary on Tantric *dharani*. This continued interest in Tantric Buddhism seems to have come from two sources. The first was an influx of Indian and Central Asian monks during the Tran period. The second was the prestige accorded to Tantric Buddhism in the Mongol-ruled China. This emphasis on the supernatural tended to weaken Buddhist prestige in Vietnam even further.

Confucianism had been steadily gaining ground ever since the period of the Ly dynasty. In 1070, a Temple of Literature dedicated to Confucius had been erected in what is now Hanoi. In 1075, national examinations on the Confucian Chinese pattern had been established, and in 1076 a national university had been created to train students for these examinations. Moreover, the class which had supported Buddhism in Vietnam began to decline in the mid-1300s. The great landholding nobles of the Tran dynasty were increasingly replaced in governmental circles by Confucian-trained small landlords. These new Confucians such as Truong Han Sieu and Le Quat launched campaigns that denigrated Buddhism and called on the throne to reform it. When a new dynasty assumed the throne in the mid-fifteenth century, one of their first acts was to return many of the monks to lay life. This marked the end of Buddhist domination of the religious life of Vietnam.

This is not to say that Buddhism ceased to play a role in the life of the nation. But it was being displaced by Confucianism as the official ideology of the state. This process was exacerbated by the accession to the throne of the Later Le dynasty, which wanted to draw a clear ideological line between itself and the previous Tran regime. In 1442, Le Thai To reorganized the examination system—indeed, he extended it. Henceforth monks had to take examinations if they wished to be issued certificates of higher ordination. Failure of these examinations resulted in a forced return to lay life. By 1500, Confucianism had completely replaced Buddhism as the official religion of the state, more for political than for religious reasons. Nevertheless, at the local level, Buddhism was, and remains today, a vital force in Vietnamese society.[4]

The Spread of Sri Lankan Buddhism in Mainland Southeast Asia

Of particular interest to students of both Buddhism and comparative religion is the study of how the Sri Lankan form of Theravada Buddhism—generally termed in the literature Sri Lankan Theravada Buddhism—spread throughout Mainland Southeast

Asia in the thirteenth and fourteenth centuries until it became the paramount religious tradition of all the countries of the region except for Vietnam. Early historians of religion held that the spread of Buddhism was a process that began in Myanmar and progressed eastward, gaining ground in areas that had formerly been non-Buddhist until it dominated virtually the whole of Mainland Southeast Asia.[5] The formerly Hindu areas of northeastern Thailand, central and southern Laos, and Cambodia were seen as having been particularly ripe for conversion owing to their economic and religious exhaustion that had been brought on through excessive taxation on the part of their rulers.[6] This exaction of money and labor had been used by these rulers for self-aggrandizing projects, particularly the erection of huge Hindu religious monuments. Buddhism, the classical theory holds, presented the peasants of these over-taxed areas with a simpler, purer form of religious faith than had previously been available to them, and as a consequence, the old religions and superstitions of the country, and the political system they supported, passed away as the peasants transferred their allegiance to the new Theravadin form of Buddhism.

But is this truly the case? If one examines this theory, one finds that it may have more to do with European ideas about the Protestant Reformation than it does with the spread of Buddhism in Southeast Asia. The historical data reveals that the religious world of Southeast Asia was, and continued to be, considerably more complex than previously supposed, as was the process of religious change within it. Rather than proceeding in a victorious sweep from west to east, and replacing preexisting

Theravadin monks collecting alms in Thailand. Theravada Buddhism is the predominant religious tradition of present-day mainland Southeast Asian countries such as Myanmar, Thailand, Laos and Cambodia.

cults completely with its own institutions, Sri Lankan Theravada Buddhism seems to have become the paramount religious tradition in Southeast Asia through a slow process of acculturation that included supplanting previously established forms of Buddhism. Moreover, a closer examination of the process suggests that it owes much of its success in the region to changing political conditions, its ability to adapt to indigenous religious beliefs, and to modifications in the Sangha-State relationship that first developed in Sri Lanka.

Buddhism, in a variety of forms, was present in Southeast Asia from at least the fifth century C.E. and probably considerably earlier. Both Buddhism and Hinduism, borne on the sea trade routes between India and China, penetrated quickly and deeply into the indigenous religious life of the area owing to their ability to complement the local religions and adapt themselves to local conditions. Consequently, we must look beyond a sudden discovery of Buddhism by a distressed peasantry for the factors that led to Sri Lankan Theravada Buddhism's ascendance in the region. The peasantry of much of Southeast Asia had certainly been aware of Buddhism, and committed to its support, long before the spread of the Sri Lankan tradition in the thirteenth and fourteenth centuries. The reasons for the change in religious attitudes that took place at this time are to be found not so much at the micro-social level of conditions of village society, but rather in conditions at the macro-social or state level of Southeast Asia society.

The impetus for this change originated from the reforms undertaken in 1164 by the Sri Lankan king, Parakramabahu I. He had succeeded to the throne of a country divided by many rivalries and competing power groups, some of the most powerful of which were the various schools (*nikayas*) of Buddhist monks. Accordingly, one of his first objectives was to bring these diverse segments of the Sangha to heel and subjugate them to the will of secular authorities. Parakramabahu's reforms were limited to matters of training and disciplining monks as well as the organization of the monastic institution itself. Nothing was said concerning either Buddhist doctrine or the position of Buddhism vis-à-vis other religious traditions in Sri Lanka. But the fact of the matter was that one school, the Theravadins, became the favored school of Buddhism; and it was from this group that government appointments were drawn and to whom government patronage was extended. Other groups persisted, but slowly withered away, as they were to do in Southeast Asia as well.

Parakramabahu's reforms, undertaken under the guise of "purifying" the Sangha, were notable both in what they did and what they did not do. On the positive side, they organized the *nikayas* and their component fraternities under a clear but initially relatively loose overarching organization with presiding officials loyal to the king. By establishing a clear hierarchical, bureaucratic structure within the Sangha, the central administration was now able to exert greater control over it and to reward clerics who served its interests. This control was also strengthened by the reiteration of the principle of the ruler as *Dharmaraja*, a personage who was karmically superior to those he ruled, and thus, by virtue of this superiority, the ultimate arbiter of Sangha as well as lay disputes. While this idea had originated at least as far back in time as Ashoka, Parakramabahu was among the first rulers to wed Buddhist ideology to concrete institutions.

On the other hand, these reforms did not demand a single uniform orthodoxy of belief and practice within the Sangha. Indeed, the competitors of the Theravada school continued for some centuries in Sri Lanka. This allowed the reformed Sri Lankan school of Theravada to accept local differences in Buddhist practice and gradually to assimilate their practitioners into their own tradition. Nor did the reforms attempt to purge Buddhism of the "non-Buddhist" elements that were so important to its adherents at the local level. It only required that they acknowledge the ontological and moral superiority of the Buddhist teachings, as well as the place of the king as administrator and ultimate arbiter of those values.

The reforms created a Sangha that was capable of forging well-defined links between the national macro-social interests of the central government and the local micro-social interests of the rural villages. This was a process essential to the functioning of a centralized bureaucracy. It also provided a mechanism for channeling wealth back into the rural areas to local Buddhist institutions through royal patronage, and it provided the government with a way of promoting education and the recruitment of talented individuals into administrative service. At the same time, it enabled the government to control in some degree the alienation of wealth from the national taxation base through donation to non-tax-paying religious institutions. In

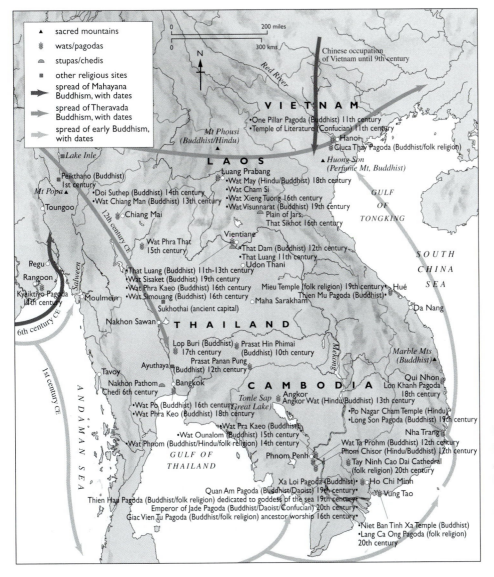

Religious sites in later mainland Southeast Asia. Southeast Asia has a large number of important religious sites that remain major influences on the cultural development of the region.

essence, the Sangha became a functional component in both the development and administration of the newly evolved centralized states of Sri Lanka, and soon of Mainland Southeast Asia as well.

Its combination of control and license gave the Sri Lankan Buddhist tradition the right balance between authority and flexibility that allowed it to prosper in the sometimes chaotic world of thirteenth century Mainland Southeast Asia. In Myanmar, it has been shown that the kings of the Pagan dynasty (despite being Theravada Buddhists already), supported the new Sri Lankan school to strengthen their control of the Sangha, purge it of elements unsympathetic to their interests, and recover property that had been previously alienated from the tax base. Consequently, even though they built magnificent temples such as Shwe Dagon to bolster the prestige of the new Sri Lankan form of Theravada Buddhism, the kings of Myanmar still benefited both financially and politically from the reform of the Myanmar Sangha.

In Thailand, competing rulers found that adherence to the new form, which was widely perceived as being morally stricter and hence purer than local Buddhism, both differentiated them from their former Khmer overlords and increased their claims to the status of *Dharmaraja*—the ruler who reigned through superior right-eousness. This, in turn, gave them political advantage over their rivals in the ongoing contest for political control of the country. In Cambodia, Sri Lankan Buddhism provided an ideologically acceptable substitute to the politically and religiously bankrupt Khmer Hindu theocratic government without deviating too severely from the original pattern. This eventually allowed Khmer kingship to be reinvented in a more centralized form, although this was not sufficient impetus in itself to allow the development of a more complex state governmental apparatus such as developed among Cambodia's neighbors.

Thus, for separate reasons in each of these different areas, Parakramabahu's reforms possessed institutional advantages that favored the spread and consoli-

Shwe Dagon Temple, Burma. The great Buddhist temples of Burma, Thailand and Cambodia play an important role in the daily religious practices of those countries despite the unsettled recent history of the region.

dation of the Sri Lankan Theravada Buddhist tradition in Mainland Southeast Asia. At the same time, it left alone those elements of local religion and belief that had come to define the religion for the common people. In due time, this combination of factors resulted in the preeminence of the Sri Lankan form of Theravada Buddhism throughout the whole of Mainland Southeast Asia except for Vietnam, which was more heavily influenced by Chinese rather than Indian cultural and institutional models.

Website References

1. For an overview of Southeast Asian culture, see www.seasite.niu.edu/

2. A general examination of ancient temples of Southeast Asia can be found at www.leidenuniv.nl/pun/ubhtm/mjk/intro.htm

3. Borobudur is extensively discussed at rubens.anu.edu.au/htdocs/bycountry/indonesia/borobudur/

4. www.quangduc.com/English/WorldBuddhism/22vietnam.html and www.quangduc.com/English/WorldBuddhism/27vietnam.html and www.quangduc.com/English/vnbuddhism/index.html all discuss Buddhism in Vietnam.

5. Information on Buddhism in Myanmar can be found at www.thanhsiang.org/education/dip3–11.htm and www.quangduc.com/English/WorldBuddhism/05burma.html and www.myanmars.net/travel/shwedagon.htm

6. www.thanhsiang.org/education/dip3–12.htm and www.quangduc.com/English/WorldBuddhism/19thai.html discuss Buddhism in Thailand. Buddhism in Cambodia is the subject of www.thanhsiang.org/education/dip3–13.htm

CHAPTER FOURTEEN

◆

Islam in South and Southeast Asia

As we have seen in chapter six, Islamic thought was influential in the development of Hindu devotionalism in South Asia from about the fifteenth century onward. But by that time, Islam had been in South Asia for almost six hundred years. In addition to the Middle East, Islam had become the predominant religion in Central Asia as well as a significant religious force in China, where it was said that one of the companions of Prophet Muhammad himself had led a delegation to bring gifts to the emperor in 650. In return, the emperor granted the Muslims the right to practice their religion, and ordered the establishment of China's first mosque at Changan. This still stands today, after thirteen centuries.

The Muslims who immigrated to China both by land (through Central Asia) and by sea (through Southeast Asia) soon began to have a great economic impact on the country. At the same time, they began to make local converts and integrated into Chinese society. Many Muslims who married Han Chinese women simply took on the name of their new wives. Others took the surnames of Mo, Mai, or Mu, Chinese adaptations of Muhammad, Mustafa, and Masoud. In time, the Muslims began to speak Han dialects and to read Chinese, but Islamic dress and dietary restrictions were consistently maintained. By the time of the Ming dynasty, the Muslims could not be distinguished from other Chinese people except by their unique religious customs.

During the time of Mao, Islam suffered the same repression as the other religions of China. However, since religious freedom was declared in 1978, Muslims are once again able to practice their religion. At present, there are 28,000 mosques in the People's Republic of China. Chinese Muslims were numbered at 15 million after the government census of 1982, but that figure may be as high as 20 million.

The Roots of South Asian Islam

It is in South and Southeast Asia, however, that Islam has had the greatest impact on the religious life of the people. Islam was first brought to India by the Arab Muhammad ibn al-Qasim in 711 when he invaded the far western Indian state of Sind. The people that he found there were mostly Buddhists, but they were ruled by a family of Brahmin descent. Muhammad, far from attempting any forced conversions, levied *jizya* or poll tax on the inhabitants. This was the Muslim practice when dealing with *ahl al-kitab* or People of the Books, as Christians and Jews were termed. That Muhammad should impose this tax in Sind suggests that he saw the Buddhists that he encountered there to be of equal status to non-Islamic monotheists. He also exempted Brahmins from paying the tax, a practice that was followed by many later Muslim rulers of India.

Although the Arab Muslims continued to rule in Sind from this time onward, Islam had little impact on the rest of South Asia for another three hundred years. Communities of Muslim merchants did spring up in the trading ports of India and Sri Lanka, as well as further east along the trade route to China in Southeast Asia. But these communities were self-contained, and had no particular interest in actively spreading their religion to the people among whom they lived. The next major Muslim incursion into South Asia was actually the result of Hindu aggression on the part of Jayapala of Waihind, a Hindu state located in the Punjab. Jayapala, fearing the growing power of the Muslim state of Ghazna in Afghanistan, invaded and attempted to destroy it. He was repulsed, and a protracted war developed between the two states. This led eventually to the final defeat of the Hindu forces at Peshawar in 1008. Mahmud, the ruler of Ghazna, could now raid into India with impunity, and he did so until his death in 1030.

Ghazna was soon replaced as the paramount Muslim state in the region by the neighboring state of Ghur in 1150. From this base, the first permanent Muslim presence in northern India was established when one of the Ghurid generals, Qutb al-Din Aybak (r. 1206–1211), proclaimed himself sultan at Delhi in 1206. The Delhi Sultanate became the most powerful state in northern India, and at times was able to bring large portions of the subcontinent under its control. One of the greatest of these north Indian Muslim rulers, Shams al-Din Iltutmish (r. 1213–1236), managed to avert a Mongol invasion of his domains and extend the sway of the Sultanate into the Deccan. He patronized the Sufi orders who now began to proselytize the Indian population and encouraged their missionary efforts throughout the regions that he ruled.

In 1290, the control of the Delhi Sultanate passed to the Khalji family. Like their predecessors, they patronized the various Sufi orders, and it was at this time that a number of influential Sufi *pirs* or saints began to be venerated by the emerging Muslim population in much the same way as outstanding Hindu holy men had been in the past. *Pirs* such as Nizam al-Din, the great saint of the Chisti Sufi order, were seen not only as guides to individual religious seekers in matters of faith and morals, but also as valuable instruments of state policy. Indeed, Nizam al-Din's prayers were widely seen as having turned back a Mongol invasion of northern India in 1303. Increasingly, the Sufis became a significant force in the religious and political life of India, and a counterbalance to the influence of the *ulama* or religious scholars who formed the formal governing body of the Muslim religious establishment. From time to time, this led to some friction between the two camps, since the Sufi orders were increasingly influenced by Hindu mysticism and philosophy. In general, however, each group had its own domain which the other respected and left to their control.

In general, the Muslim rulers of northern India took a mild and conciliatory attitude toward the religious practices of their non-Muslim subjects. Occasionally, however, this policy of toleration was strained by events. When Feroz Shah (r. 1351–1388) ascended the throne, he found that much of the populace, including the Muslim ruling elite, had been alienated by his predecessor Muhammad ibn Tughluq. In order to bolster his own power base, Feroz Shah had to accommodate the *ulama* who were pressing for a more Islamic form of state government. He demanded that Brahmins, who had previously been exempt from paying the *jizya* tax, should now be required to pay. This inflamed his Hindu subjects, many of whom threatened to burn themselves alive if he did not relent. Finally, a number of affluent Hindus decided to pay the tax on behalf of the Brahmins. But a precedent had been set, and some elements of the Islamic ruling class began to wonder why Islam was not being propagated more aggressively.

It is also around this time that Islam was introduced into areas which are today predominantly Muslim, such as Bengal and Kashmir. Islam definitely entered Bengal in 1415, when Ibrahim Shah of Jawnpur invaded at the instigation of the Muslim Sufi *pir* Qutb al-Alam. The hard-pressed Hindu ruler of Bengal had his son convert to Islam, and this son, Jalal al-Din Muhammad, presided over a golden age of Bengali culture when he ascended the throne. In Kashmir, Shah Mirza of Swat established a Muslim dynasty in 1339. His immediate successors were particularly intolerant of Hinduism, one of them being called *Butshikan* or Idol Breaker. But such policies were eventually seen as detrimental to the interests of the state, and subsequent Muslim rulers made many concessions to win back the allegiance of the mostly Hindu inhabitants of the country. In the south, a number of Muslim states began to emerge in central India as the power of the Delhi Sultanate began to decline. These states, such as Bijapur, Golkonda, and Bidar, continued to increase in power and prestige until they came under the control of the last great Muslim empire of India, the Mughals.

In 1526, the tottering Delhi Sultanate was replaced by the great Mughal dynasty. The replacement of one ruling house by another is always a difficult and perilous undertaking, and the Mughal rulers found that their seat on the Peacock Throne at Delhi was at first unstable. It was not until the reign of the third Mughal ruler, Akbar (r. 1556–1605), that the dynasty could be said to be firmly in control of the state. One of the ways that Akbar moved to secure the throne was to ally himself with his non-Muslim subjects. Consequently, he downplayed the Islamic faith, and even developed his own syncretic faith, the *Din-i Ilahi* or Divine Faith, that attempted to incorporate elements from many of the world's religions into a harmonious whole, with a conspicuous lack of success.

But the Mughals could not, in the end, rule without the consent of the Muslim aristocracy, and in the reign of Akbar's son Jahangir (r. 1605–1627) the Islamic establishment began to reassert itself. It was at this time that Shaykh Ahmad of Sirhind, a Naqshbandi Sufi leader, repudiated the Hindu tendency to monism that had for centuries influenced other Sufi orders such as the Shattariyya and the Qadiriyya. It was at this point that the high tide of Muslim–Hindu syncretism that had helped to transform northern Indian Hindu devotionalism began to recede. This syncretism would be carried forward by other groups, such as the Sikhs, but the Muslims themselves now started to shy away from incorporating Hindu ideas into their own philosophy. This return to Muslim orthodoxy found its fullest expression during the reign of Aurangzeb (1658–1707) who pursued a deliberate policy of militant intolerance toward non-Muslims.

Sufi teachers continued to play a central role in the religious life of later Mughal India. The most influential of these later Sufis was Shah Wali Allah of Delhi (1703–1762). He had made the Pilgrimage to Mecca, and he brought back to India a breadth of outlook that led him in new theological directions. His primary goal was the establishment of a state based on the principles of *Shari'a* or Islamic religious law. The model for this, he believed, could be found in the government of the first four successors of Muhammad in Arabia, the so-called "Righteous Caliphs," and he urged his compatriots to purge themselves of Hindu influences and return to the pure Islam of that early era. His son, Shah Abd al-Aziz (1746–1824), went so far as to call for holy war (*jihad*) against the British, although this came to nothing at that time. This question of how to build an Islamic society based on the very specific injunctions of Islamic law and tradition when most Islamic countries were under the domination of non-Muslim colonial powers was one that would shape the development of Islam in Asia for the next two centuries.

The Coming of Islam to Island Southeast Asia

Despite an abundance of stories concerning the conversion of Island Southeast Asia to Islam, the actual factual data is limited. But in general, this transference of religious allegiance away from the earlier syncretic Hindu-Buddhism of the Indonesian archipelago to the new Islamic faith seems to have had three distinct phases. The first of these was the arrival of Muslim traders in the seaports of the region. How early this occurred is still being debated, but it seems likely that Middle Eastern merchants may have been trading in Southeast Asia even before the advent of Islam. Certainly, Muslims were trading in China by the late eighth century, and so they were undoubtedly to be found throughout the many ports and harbors that lined the route between the Mediterranean and the Far East at that time.

How interested these traders were in converting the local populations to Islam is of course open to question. But their own religious needs no doubt contributed to the presence within their communities of religious functionaries who administered the laws of Islam, and of Muslim holy men and preachers. These holy men seem to have come primarily from India rather than from the original homelands of Islam further west, and their activities mark the second phase of Islam's penetration into the region. Known as *kiyayi*, *datu*, or *wali* in the indigenous Malay language, these itinerant preachers were continually on the move throughout the archipelago from about 1000, and served as advisors to local rulers, school teachers, and preachers. They would often rise to positions of great local influence, sometimes marrying into the local royal families. These royal families found that embracing Islam could often give them certain advantages in the fluid web of shifting allegiances that has always characterized the Southeast Asian political scene. As with the Indic religions that had preceded it, Islam could be used to increase a ruler's prestige and influence in a society where the control of supernatural power was always a prerequisite to exercising political power. Finally, the third phase of the conversion of Island Southeast Asia to Islam often took the shape of *jihad* or holy wars that served as much political as religious purposes.

The general pattern of the spread of Islam followed the trade routes. The first area in the region to embrace Islam was the northern part of Sumatra that became known as Acheh. Today one of the staunchest bastions of Islam in Indonesia, Chinese sources show that by 1282, the rulers of certain cities in this region bore Muslim names. By 1345, the Arab traveler Ibn Battuta was reporting favorably on the wealth and piety of the inhabitants of Pasai, one of the major towns of the region. Architecture still extant shows that the area was clearly influenced by Muslim cultural influences emanating from Gujarat in western India. Soon, Islam began to spread eastward from here down the straits running between Sumatra and the Malayan Peninsula.

One of the greatest of the early Islamic states of this region was Malacca. Originally founded in about 1400, the Malaccan royal family seems to have embraced Islam almost from the very beginning of their reign. From here, Islam spread up the coasts of the Malayan peninsula to the states of Trengganu, Kedah, Patani, and Kelantan. Malacca continued to be a center of Islamic influence up to its conquest by the Portuguese in 1511. Johore, the state that ruled at the tip of the Malayan Peninsula after Malacca's fall, continued to be a focal point for the dissemination of Islam to Kalimantan (Borneo), Brunei, the Sulu archipelago, and Mindanao in the southern Philippines. In these eastern regions, preachers such as Sharif Karim al-Makhdum, Abu Bakr, and Sharif Kabungsuwan built mosques, married the daughters of local rulers, and began the long process of accommodating Islam to local conditions.

The conversion of the principal island of the Indonesian archipelago, Java, seems to have come somewhat later. It is not until the early sixteenth century and the fall of the last great Hindu–Buddhist empire of Majapahit that we see a sustained Muslim presence in the island. This emanated from the northern coastal city of Demak. The trade cities of the northern coast of Java had earlier come under the control of Muslim rulers, and these rulers supported the missionary efforts of such charismatic preachers as Shaykh Ibn Mawlana who, in 1526, began to convert the western part of Java to Islam. In central and eastern Java, however, things did not progress so smoothly. It took much longer for these regions to accept Islam, and they only did so after the new religion had accommodated itself more closely to indigenous local beliefs. In the neighboring island of Bali, Islam made no headway whatsoever, and to this day the religion of Bali is a local form of Hinduism. The tension between *adat* or local custom, and *agama*, orthodox Islamic teachings, was to become a defining feature of Island Southeast Asian Islam. Many of the nominal adherents to Islam in the region continued to be heavily influenced by local beliefs. These *abangan* Muslims were looked down on by the more orthodox *santri* Muslims, who cleaved much more closely to the Islamic norms of the Middle East.

Despite the patronage extended to Muslim preachers by the rulers of the various Island Southeast Asian princes, Muslim teachers and holy men were often at odds with a secular authority that wore its Islam rather lightly. It is not surprising, therefore, that zealous Muslims often grouped together for mutual support. The institution of *perdikan-desa*, independent communities founded by *kiyayi* Muslim teachers in which pious Muslims could live under the rule of Islamic law, emerged, as well as *pesantren* schools. These schools, which in many ways resembled the ashram schools of the earlier Hindu–Buddhist tradition, served as focal points of Islamization. Their teachings included reading and writing in Arabic letters, the memorization of the Qur'an, and the study of *hadith*, theological treatises, and other religious material of sometimes rather dubious orthodoxy.

There also emerged in these schools a distinctive type of Southeast Asian Islamic mysticism which still persists in various forms today. This teaching, called collectively *Ingsun*, owed much to the monist thought of such Hindu religious teachers as Shankara. Its keynote idea was the unity of the microcosm and the macrocosm. It followed from this worldview that to know one's self is to know God, and various techniques evolved to facilitate such knowledge. As time went on, this indigenous mysticism was diluted with more orthodox Sufi doctrines from the Naqshbandiyya and Shattariyya schools. But these schools became suspect by the secular authorities, both indigenous and colonial, as hotbeds of resistance to government rule. This, combined with various local movements to bring Southeast Asian Islam more into line with the orthodox teachings of the larger Islamic world, diminished the influence of the *pesantren* schools in later years, but did not eliminate them entirely.

Islam in British Colonial India

The coming of the colonial powers to Asia brought with it great changes in the religious dynamics of the region. When the British assumed political power in India, the Muslim position in the subcontinent underwent a profound change. No longer the paramount power, Muslims now had to find ways of preserving their identity in a region where they were still a distinct minority despite significant conversions over the centuries. Although there were certain clear differences between the communities on such matters as dietary regulations, Muslims and Hindus in India shared many cultural similarities. They were virtually indistinguishable in terms of dress, and they spoke very similar languages. The major linguistic difference that separated the two was that Muslims employed a vocabulary more influenced by Arabic and Persian than by classical Sanskrit. Over time, the Muslim dialect of Hindustani, the language of northern India, became known as Urdu and the version spoken by Hindus as Hindi.

In many ways, Indian Muslims shared far more in common with their Hindu neighbors than with their new rulers, the British. As we have seen, by 1800 the British controlled much of India, and they were acutely aware that their success had been largely at the expense of the Muslims. Moreover, the transfer of power had inevitable consequences for the economic and social standing of the upper classes. Many Muslims were deprived of their posts in the higher reaches of the administrative and judicial systems and replaced by British officials. At first, Persian was retained as the official language of government and the courts, as it had been under the Mughals, but increasingly the British came to believe that their best course of action was to administer India through English-speaking intermediaries. Another consequence of this change in policy was that government patronage of Muslim scholars, which had been significant in the early days of British rule, began to be withdrawn. Clearly, Islam faced a crisis of identity under India's new rulers.

Two responses to this threat to Islamic culture were possible. The first was confrontation and revolt. One of the causes of the first Indian War of Independence in 1857 (which the British called the Great Indian Mutiny), was the Muslim desire to return to the glories of ancient days, and to protect their religion from perceived British threats. When the revolt failed, many Muslims chose withdrawal from society, content to nurture their religious culture in self-contained communities. The other response to the times was to confront the changes that were sweeping through South Asia head on, and adapt to them. One of the most vigorous proponents of this course of action was the author and educator Sayyid Ahmad Khan (1817–1898).

A staunch supporter of the British, Sayyid Ahmad Khan emerged from the war of 1857 with a reputation for loyalty that he was able to exploit in the years to come. He believed that the key to successful Muslim–British relations lay in education, and so he spent considerable time and effort in establishing schools for Muslims that would expose them to Western culture and ideas. In 1870, he founded a journal in Urdu to educate the general Muslim public about modern trends and ideas. But by far his greatest achievement was the establishment of the Anglo-Oriental College at Aligarh in 1875. For the first time, Muslims in South Asia had their own institute of higher learning where they could combine the study of modern subjects with traditional Muslim ones. His educational reforms were supported by such modernist theologians as Hali (1837–1914), Shibli (1957–1914), and Nadhir Ahmad (1831–1911) who applied Western scholarly methodology to the study and application of Islam in the South Asian environment.

Naturally, not all sectors of the Muslim community saw these developments as positive ones. Traditional theologians were concerned by the activities of both Christian missionaries and Arya Samajists. Such conservative scholars as Mawlana Mahmud Hasan (1851–1921) and Mirza Ghulam Ahmad (1839–1908) taught a more traditional interpretation of Islam than the modernists. Mirza Ghulam Ahmad's followers, known as the Ahmadiyya, eventually became a separate religious cult when their founder declared himself the *Mahdi*, the Muslim Messiah, in 1889. Their message of the restoration of the purity of Islam, and emphasis on dealing with social and economic problems facing the faithful gave their movement wide appeal not only in South Asia, but in Africa and the West as well.

Despite these promising beginnings, political events eventually came to control the course of South Asian Islam. In 1885, the All-India Congress was established. Many Muslims, including Sayyid Ahmad Khan, believed that this was merely a vehicle for the Bengali Hindus to dominate the political life of India, and so he and others opposed Muslim involvement in the new organization. Eventually, this led to the establishment of the Muslim League in 1906. The League and the Congress were able to work together on many issues for the next forty years. But as it became clearer in the 1940s that the British would soon be quitting India, fissures in the alliance between the two groups began to appear regarding the shape of the new South Asia.

Some Muslims favored remaining within the soon-to-be-created state of India, confident that Gandhi's promises of complete equality would be kept by the Hindu majority population. Other Muslim leaders were not so sure of their place in an India dominated by Hindus. The great South Asian Muslim poet and philosopher Muhammad Iqbal (1873–1938) had suggested the creation of a separate Muslim state as early as 1930. The leader of the Muslim League, Muhammad Ali Jinnah (1876–1948), not a particularly pious man, had been trained as a lawyer in England and initially favored a Hindu-Muslim India. But by 1937, Jinnah was no longer convinced that Muslim interests would be best served by inclusion in the new state of India. He began to agitate for a separate Muslim state of Pakistan formed from the five Muslim states of northwest India to which was later added the Muslim area of east Bengal. Although bitterly opposed by the Congress politicians, the new state of Pakistan came into being on August 14, 1947—a day ahead of the formation of the new state of India.

Islam under Dutch Colonial Rule in Indonesia

In general, Dutch colonial rule bore harder on the regions of Southeast Asia controlled by the Netherlands than did British rule in India. This no doubt was partially a result of the two different approaches to colonialism adopted by these countries, but part of the difference also lay in the geographical differences in the countries they occupied. Whereas India was a single, albeit large, unit, and so could be traversed relatively quickly by military forces when necessary, the islands of the Indonesian archipelago made troop movements difficult. Consequently, the Dutch needed to stop insurrection whenever possible, and this naturally led to oppression of the local populations. Nor were Dutch fears unfounded, since rebellions were constantly flaring up in their colonial possessions. In Indonesia, Islam often contributed significantly to such insurrections against Dutch rule.

One of the most serious of these rebellions was that of the Javanese prince Dipa-Negara in 1825. The son of the Sultan of Jogjakarta, Dipa-Negara was a devout Muslim who opposed Dutch policies. He became a rallying point for much of the resentment that permeated Java in the aftermath of the Napoleonic Wars and the restoration of Dutch rule over the islands. When hostilities broke out, many peasants flocked to Dipa-Negara's banner because of his reputation as a devout Muslim. This gave the insurrection a quasi-religious air, and some religious leaders tried to portray it as a *jihad*. After the Dutch crushed the rebellion, they were even more suspicious of Islam, and this colored all of their subsequent policies in Indonesia.

However, not all religious conflict in Indonesia came from clashes between the local people and the colonial powers. In the area of central Sumatra known as Minangkabau, a local reform movement, the *Padri* movement, clashed with local authorities in the first third of the nineteenth century. This movement was begun by three local religious leaders who had made the Pilgrimage to Mecca in 1803, and had been impressed with the purity and vigor of the Islam that they found there. They returned to their native land determined to reform the local version of Islam. They proscribed cock fighting, smoking, and drinking, while at the same time demanding strict adherence to the prayer times, the veiling of women, and other facets of Islamic custom. They were prepared to enforce their views with violence if necessary, and conflict raged throughout Minangkabau for the next twenty years. As their reform progressed, they installed their own religious functionaries in the villages that they controlled, thus overturning the traditional lines of authority in their community. Eventually, the hereditary leaders of the region appealed to the colonial authorities, and the so-called Padri War ensued until 1837, resulting in the suppression of the Islamic purists and the restoration of the authority of the local elites.

The tension between Islam and the state intensified with the emerging anticolonialist movements of the twentieth century. On one hand, the Dutch saw Islam as a focal point for resistance against their rule. But the leaders of the anticolonialist movement were uneasy with Islam as well. Often from the *priyayi* or old aristocratic class of Java, they wore their Islam lightly, and were far more products of a European education than of the *pesantren* schools. But Islam and organizations based on it could not be ignored in the anticolonial struggle, a good example of this being two influential organizations that emerged in the early twentieth century, Muhammadiyah and the Sarekat Islam, the Islamic League.

Muhammadiyah had been founded by a pious businessman by the name of Kiyayi Hajji Ahmad Dachlan (1869–1923). He did not want to found a political organization, but rather one that would purify Javanese Islam of its *abangan* elements. But by 1938, the organization had grown and operated some 1,700 schools and teachers' colleges throughout all of Indonesia, and was very influential in the intellectual life of the country. The success of the Muhammadiyah in education was duplicated by the Sarekat Islam in the field of politics. Drawing on the same basic constituency of urban petty bourgeoisie as the Muhammadiyah, Sarekat Islam soon expanded from a league of businessmen and small landowners located in central Java to a mass movement with decidedly political ambitions. Although the movement soon faltered as a result of the personal ambition of some of its leaders, it set the pattern for the association of Islam and nationalism that persists to the present day in Indonesia.

Islam in Modern South and Southeast Asia

One of the striking features of Islam in the newly independent states of South and Southeast Asia was that the early leaders of these states had no desire whatsoever to install Islam as the official religion of their respective states. Jinnah had seen the problems of Muslims in India as an ethnic rather than a religious question. Under his leadership and that of his immediate successors, Islam was given a privileged position in the new state of Pakistan, but efforts were made to safeguard the religion and customs of minority religions as well. In Indonesia, the official philosophy of the new state, the so-called *Pancasila*, called for a belief in God on the part of Indonesia's citizenry, but left the expression of that belief up to the individual. Indeed, the leaders of the South and Southeast Asian states were distrustful of Islam, seeing it as a potentially disruptive political force.

After independence, however, Islam began to reassert its power in both regions. In Pakistan, various religio-political organizations pressed for a constitution based on the Muslim law codes of *Shari'a*. Although the country's political elites resisted this, going only so far as declaring Pakistan an "Islamic Republic" in the 1956 constitution, religious groups continued to press the government for further official Islamicization. Pakistani politicians such as Ayub Khan and Z. A. Bhutto both clearly supported the idea of a secular state, but increasingly they yielded to pressure from Islamic groups on such issues as banning horse racing and the drinking of alcohol and declaring Friday, the Muslim day of prayer, an official day of rest. No doubt one of their reasons for making these concessions was to attempt to defuse regional rivalries and differences that were emerging in the Pakistani state through an appeal to Islam as a national ideology. This did not work, however, and in 1971 East Pakistan separated from West Pakistan after a bitter civil war, becoming the new country of Bangladesh.

When general Zia al-Haqq took over the reins of power in Pakistan after a coup in 1977, he used Islam as one of the major props for his own personal power. Laws passed by the Pakistani parliament were now reviewed to make sure that they were not "repugnant to Islam." The paying of alms, *zakat*, was made compulsory in 1980. The money was funneled into the building and maintenance of *madrassas* or religious schools. Even in secular schools, Islam became an essential part of the curriculum. At the same time, intolerance against other religions increased, with attacks being made against their schools and places of worship. Blasphemy laws were put into place that made it an offense punishable by imprisonment to speak against Islam and the Prophet.

All of these changes over the years had been the direct result of a rise in Islamic fundamentalism in Pakistan that began in the 1970s. The conflict with India over Kashmir took on an increasingly religious tone during this time. Moreover, events such as the Arab–Israeli War, the overthrow of the Western-oriented regime of the Shah of Iran, and the Soviet invasion of Afghanistan all contributed to the feeling in Pakistan that Islam was in danger. Various groups arose to defend their religion, and increasingly Pakistani politicians had to make concessions to the more fundamentalist elements in Pakistani society—a process that continues to the present day.

A similar phenomenon can be seen in Indonesia as well. Despite the best intentions of Indonesian leaders to create a secular state, Islam was from the beginning a major factor in Indonesian politics. The cataclysmic events of 1965, when hundreds of thousands of Indonesians were killed in the aftermath of an attempted Communist coup, opened the door for Islamic groups to increase their influence in the government. Anti-Christian rioting broke out in 1967 in Sumatra and Sulawesi as organizations such as Dewan Dakwah Islamiyah Indonesia promoted Islamic evangelism and opposed Christian missionary activities. In response, the government moved to restrain the efforts of the Muslim activists. President Suharto attempted to have *kebatinan*, a blend of Islam and indigenous Indonesian religion, declared an official religion in an effort to reduce the number of registered Muslims in the census. The government also severely restricted the Muslim Partai Persatuan Pembangunan (PPP) from campaigning outside urban areas, and secular marriage laws were passed despite extreme Muslim opposition.

In the 1980s, radical Islamic activity increased. Political rallies became more violent. While the government still tried to maintain the secular nature of the Indonesian state, they began to make concessions to Muslim sensibilities. In 1988, foreign missionary activities were restricted, and certain measures such as the banning of the *jilbab*, the Muslim woman's headscarf, in high schools were repealed. But as the 1990s progressed, Islamic fundamentalist elements continued to grow in Indonesia, fueled by that country's economic and political woes.

At present, it seems safe to say that Islam will continue to be a major factor in South and Southeast Asian society and politics in the foreseeable future. The general populations of the region have a strong commitment to the faith, which in turn sees as its ultimate objective the creation of societies completely organized along guidelines set down in the Qur'an. The real question with regard to Islam in Asia is whether the more aggressive fundamentalist form of the religion will predominate, or a more moderate ideology will prevail.

South and Southeast Asian Religions Timeline

DATE	SOUTH ASIA	SOUTHEAST ASIA
B.C.E.		
c. 6500	First Neolithic villages develop at Mehrgarh in the hills surrounding the Indus Valley.	Austro-Asiatic peoples spread south and east into Mainland Southeast Asia. Austronesian peoples move into Island Southeast Asia from Taiwan.
c. 3500	Rise of Indus Valley (Harappan) civilization.	
c. 2000	Aryan peoples drift into northern South Asia. Vedic hymns begin to be composed and collected.	
c. 1900	Decline and fall of the Indus Valley civilization.	
c. 1500–900	Four Vedas composed and collected.	
c. 900–500	Composition of the Brahmanas and the major Upanishads.	
c. 600–527	Life of Mahavira.	
c. 600–200		Dong Son culture flourishes in northern Vietnam.
c. 563–483	Life of the Buddha.	
c. 500–500 (C.E.)	Composition of Vedic literature and the *Dharmashastras*.	
c. 480	First Buddhist Council at Rajagriha.	
327–325	Alexander the Great invades India.	
c. 300	Gautama's Nyaya Sutra and Kanada's Vaisheshika Sutra. Mauryan Empire established.	
c. 273–237	Reign of Ashoka.	
c. 247–207	King Divanampiya Tissa of Sri Lanka converted to Buddhism.	
c. 200–100 (C.E.)	Age of Invasions. Numerous foreign peoples invade northern India. Manusmriti composed.	
c. 200– 200 (C.E.)	Peak period of Buddhist and Jain expansion in India.	First Indian trade contacts with Southeast Asia. Possible first Buddhist missions to Burma.
111–939 (C.E.)		Chinese rule northern Vietnam.
c. 100–500 (C.E.)	Patanjali's Yoga Sutra.	
c. 100–100 (C.E.)	Composition of the Bhagavad Gita and Badarayana's Vedanta Sutra. Beginnings of Mahayana Buddhism.	
C.E.		
c. 79	Jains divide into Shvetambara and Digambara sects.	
c. 100	First Christians in southern India.	Foundation of Champa and Funan.
c. 100–200	Rise of Nagarjuna's Madhyamika School.	
c. 200–500	Composition of the Vishnu Purana.	Buddhism and Hinduism from India spread through Mainland and Island Southeast Asia. Beginnings of Chinese influence in Vietnam.
c. 250–500	*Samkhya Karika* of Ishvara Krishna.	
c. 300–600	Composition of the older Puranas.	Shiva worship becomes religion of Champa.
c. 320–540	Gupta Empire.	
c. 400	Spread of Krishna cult.	
c. 500	Composition of the *Devi-mahatmya* section of the Markandeya Purana and the spread of Shaktism (Goddess worship).	Increasing Buddhist influence in Funan.

DATE	SOUTH ASIA	SOUTHEAST ASIA
c. 600	Development of Vedanta. Buddhist Tantra appears.	Founding of Srivijaya, first major empire in Island Southeast Asia.
c. 600–800	Hindu renaissance; decline of Buddhism and Jainism.	Hinduism becomes the official religion of Chenla.
c. 788–820	Life of Shankaracarya, founder of Advaita.	Borobudur built on Java.
c. 850–1100	Composition of the Shiva Purana and *Ramayana*.	Major temple construction at Angkor.
c. 900–1000	Sahajayana school marks last phase of Indian Buddhism.	
c. 1000–1200	Muslims invade India., where Buddhism disappears.	
1025–1137	Life of Ramanuja.	
c. 1100	Composition of the Hindu Tantra literature.	
c. 1150		Suryavarman II builds Angkor Wat. Parakramabahu I reforms Buddhism in Sri Lanka.
c. 1178–1200	Jayadeva writes *Gita Govinda* in praise of Krishna.	
c. 1197–1276	Life of Madhvacarya.	
c. 1200	Muslims now rule over large parts of India.	Jayavarman VII builds Angkor Thom.
1257–1285		Mongol invasions disrupt the political structure of Mainland Southeast Asia.
c. 1300		Sri Lankan Theravada Buddhism spreads throughout Myanmar, Thailand, and Cambodia.
1431		Fall of Angkor.
1440–1518	Life of Kabir.	
c. 1469–1539	Life of Guru Nanak.	
1498	Europeans reach India.	
1510	Portuguese occupy Goa. Christianity imposed on resident population.	
c. 1526–1858	Mughal Empire, the last great Indian native state.	
c. 1600		Spanish begin missionary work in the Philippines. Dutch begin colonial rule in Island Southeast Asia
1651	English East India Company establishes first factory in Bengal.	
1675–1708	Tegh Bahadur, last of the Sikh Gurus.	
1828	Death of Ram Mohan Roy.	
1834–1886	Life of Ramakrishna.	
1857	First Indian War of Independence ("Great Indian Mutiny").	
1867–1948	Life of Mahatma Gandhi.	
c. 1900		Emergence of Cao Dai sect in Vietnam.
1942	Foundation of militantly Hindu Rashtria Svayamsevak Sangh party.	
1947	Partition of India into the independent states of India and Pakistan.	
1950	Death of Sri Aurobindo and Ramana Maharshi.	
1960–1963		Vietnamese Buddhists persecuted by Vietnamese Catholic ruling elite.
1984	Armed conflict between Sikhs and Indian government. Golden Temple severely damaged. Indira Gandhi assassinated by Sikh bodyguards.	
1992	Hindu nationalists destroy a mosque in Ayodhya that is believed to sit on the birthplace of Rama.	

Scenes of Hermits' Long Days in the Quiet Mountains, Tang Yin, Ming dynasty, 16th century. The Daoists believed that an appreciation of nature brought one into closer contact with Dao.

◆

PART TWO

The Religions of China

CHAPTER FIFTEEN

✦

The Archaic Foundations of Chinese Religion

China, like India, presents the student of religions with a vast patchwork quilt of geographical features and the multiplicity of cultural expressions that result from them. But perhaps the single most important feature of Chinese physical geography is the vast number of its people and the relatively small area of land that they occupy. Despite being the third largest country in the world, China has only half as much inhabitable land as the United States, and on that land live five times as many people. Moreover, only a third of the land can be cultivated, and so some 85 percent of China's population live on 35 percent of its land area. This is over two thousand people per square mile of cultivatable land. China became heavily populated at an early date, and much Chinese thinking, both religious and philosophical, has been influenced by the problems arising from such a large population.

Broadly speaking, China is divided into a northern agricultural zone, where wheat and millet are grown, and a southern zone, where rice is grown. The line of this division lies roughly half way between the great Yellow River in the north and the Yangzi in the south. The source of this division is the tremendous difference in the climates of the two regions. The northern climate is determined by the huge Central Asian landmass, which gives rise to frigid winters and dry, cool summers. The southern climate, on the other hand, is dominated by oceanic influences that provide a much milder range of temperatures and heavy, dependable rainfall. Northern China's climate is marked by extreme variability in rainfall, which can fluctuate as much as 30 percent, and the attendant high possibility of drought and famine.

This variability in climate, along with other geographic factors and an extraordinarily high population density, has meant that agriculture developed in ways that are peculiarly Chinese. The first of these particular features has to do with the control of water. Not only are large areas of China subject to drought, they are also prone to flooding by its numerous rivers, especially in the north. Consequently, large-scale irrigation and flood-control projects were necessary from an early date so that the northern China plain, the center of early Chinese civilization, could support its ever-increasing population. This, in turn, demanded the mobilization and direction of huge workforces. This need, in conjunction with other political and social forces, began to favor the development of more complex governmental institutions than the simple village councils of early Chinese history. The problem of government, in the broad sense of the term, became, as we shall see, a central preoccupation with China's ruling class, and to a very large degree shaped many of their subsequent religio-philosophical speculations. Likewise the constant and unremitting demands of peasant agricultural life also shaped China's lower-class population's interaction with the world around them.

In addition to the climatic and socioeconomic factors that divided China, there were other factors to be considered. China is split by rivers and mountains into a number of discrete regions that in early days were relatively isolated from one another by the nature of the terrain. Moreover, these regions were often populated by groups that were ethnically and linguistically different from the Han Chinese people who came to dominate Chinese life. Coming to China during one of its periods of political unity in the late eighteenth century, Euro-Americans tended to conceive of China as a single monolithic cultural unit. Certainly, this was an ideal that the ruling class attempted to impose on the vast sociocultural mosaic they administered, but for most Chinese the concept of "China" was nothing more than a big idea. Their reality was the village, and perhaps the nearest city. They spoke their own dialect of Chinese—if they spoke Chinese at all—which was often unintelligible to speakers of other dialects, and they had their own distinctive foods, dress, and customs. This regionalism has always been both a blessing, in terms of its fostering a tremendous cultural vitality, and a curse, in that it encouraged political disunity. Indeed, many of the preoccupations of the ruling class centered around the production of a standardized culture designed to bind the country together under a single ideological aegis.

At most, the Chinese saw themselves as a cohesive group only in relation to non-Chinese. The great intellectual division for the Chinese was between the land of China and all other lands. China was seen as the "Middle Kingdom," sitting in the center of the world surrounded by deserts, mountains, and seas that effectively cut it off for most of its history from contact with the outside world. What contact that did occur was between the Chinese and ethnic groups such as the Mongols and Tibetans, who were seen by the Han Chinese as being at a much lower level of cultural attainment than themselves. This resulted in the development among many Chinese of a worldview in which China was civilized and all the other countries of the world were not. This idea was so firmly entrenched in the Chinese mind that for many years in the nineteenth century they were unable to deal effectively with the newly arrived Europeans and Americans, much to their cost.

The reaction of the two major divisions of society, the rulers and the ruled, to their sociogeographical reality has shaped their religious thinking quite profoundly. For the ruled peasant class, nature became a central preoccupation, since it controlled their lives and deaths remorselessly—in a way that it did not do with their Euro-American counterparts. People in Europe and America usually lived not too far from a water source that not only facilitated agriculture, but also provided relatively abundant protein sources through fishing, hunting, or animal husbandry. But virtually 90 percent of the Chinese peasants' diet came directly from the growth of grain, supplemented by relatively small amounts of protein from pigs, chickens, and fish, since they lacked the open rangeland and abundant water needed to raise cattle for food. This, coupled with a burgeoning population, meant that even the slightest variation in natural conditions was catastrophic. It has been estimated that in any given year in China, some 10 percent of the population died for reasons other than that of natural death by old age. Consequently, the central concern of the Chinese peasant became one of mitigating the vagaries of nature by any means possible—natural or supernatural. The central concern for the Chinese ruling class was the

The Immortal Han Shan, 14th century. Many local and regional deities were absorbed into the Daoist pantheon where they were organised in a manner reminiscent of the Chinese imperial hierarchy.

control of the people they ruled. Hence their preoccupation with what we would today consider to be political philosophy and ethics.

This has led to some significant problems in the study of Chinese "religion." In the West, religion had always been associated with the human being's relation to the divine. When Europeans went to India, they found that the Indian idea of religion was essentially the same as theirs, even though the Indians had reached some radically different answers to the great questions of life and death. But this was not the case in China. Here the central concerns of European and Indian society were of little or no interest. The Chinese, both rulers and ruled, were much more concerned with essentially practical questions about existence in this world than in speculation concerning the ultimate human fate and life after death. The Chinese had a certain interest in metaphysical speculation, but this was strongly mitigated and shaped by practical, this-worldly concerns and their experience of the natural world. Thus neither **Daoism** (Taoism) nor Confucianism concentrated on questions that were, for other cultures, central ones. This does not mean that the Chinese lacked "religion" but rather that they approached the great questions of human existence from a very different perspective than did the Europeans or Indians.

The Chinese Family: The Social Basis of Chinese Religion

The foundation of Chinese cultural thinking lay in neither the national nor even the ethnic group, but in the family and, to a lesser extent, the local grouping of families in the village. When we speak of the Chinese family, however, we are not speaking about the relatively small nuclear unit familiar in Euro-American society. We are speaking instead about a fairly large unit that existed widely dispersed in time and space, whose members were distributed throughout the local village and the villages that surrounded it. It was this extended family unit, which often included three or four generations living under the same roof, that was seen as the basic building block of Chinese society, and not the individual; and it was seen as perfectly appropriate that individual desires be sacrificed for the larger good. Consequently, filiality, the

The Temple of Heaven in Beijing. The Chinese emperor was required to periodically perform state rituals on behalf of the people as a whole.

respect of younger family members for older ones, was a highly regarded virtue throughout all strata of Chinese society.

This had some very practical ramifications. It meant that theoretically the head of the household—in most cases the oldest living male—reigned supreme. He inspired not so much what we would call love as awe, respect, and often not a little fear, since his word was law. As long as he lived, presuming that he retained his faculties, he was the undisputed arbiter of his family's life. This did not diminish with age, since in the Chinese worldview age and wisdom were seen as inexorably linked. Far from glorifying youth, the Chinese saw advanced age as increasing one's prestige inside and outside the family. The head of the family's dictatorial powers were mitigated both by his natural love for his children and by a variety of social mores that demanded reciprocity in family relationships.

Nor should the role of women in Chinese society and the societies influenced by it be minimized. Theoretically, women in Chinese society occupied a place inferior to men. Marriage was considered by many Chinese to be a contractual arrangement aimed at the production of offspring, preferably male, to carry on the family name, and so should not be the result of fickle human emotions but hard-headed calculation by the family elders instead. Thus marriages were not love matches between individuals in the Euro-American pattern, but business deals between families. Polygamy was perfectly acceptable in the Chinese view, especially when the primary wife had failed to produce the requisite male heir—although economic circumstances often made it impossible to support more than one wife. Moreover, wives were supposedly under the complete domination of their husbands' mothers, and the "wicked mother-in-law" occupies a place in Chinese folklore equivalent to the Euro-American "wicked stepmother."

That being said—and these views about marriage were reiterated at length throughout Chinese history in numerous didactic works on the subject by generations of Chinese moralists—anyone who has spent time in Asian societies knows that the reality of the situation can often be quite different. While a wife is still careful to defer to her husband in public, she often rules the home with a steady hand. She administers the family finances, with her husband dutifully turning over his entire paycheck to her and receiving back an allowance for his own personal use. Moreover, her relationship with her children, particularly her sons, is often the dominant emotional relationship in both their lives, and sons tend to defer to their mothers rather than their wives when family differences of opinion arise. It would be unwise, therefore, to take the official version of Chinese womanhood as passive and subordinate completely at face value. Certainly, Chinese women faced, and continue to face, severe handicaps compared to males in Chinese society. But they have managed, as in other societies, to carve out areas of responsibility and even dominance for themselves.

The Chinese family, in sharp contrast to most modern Euro-American families, had tremendous historical depth. It was seen as descending from a founding ancestor to whom it and other related families traced their origins. These families were patrilineal, reckoning descent through the male members of the family. Ranking within the family was complex and, as we have seen, usually age-based. Thus one was always in a system of dynamic relationships in which one was superior to some members of the family and subordinate to others. Rulership of the family always passed to the eldest son, but property did not. Early in their history, the Chinese abandoned the idea of primogeniture—the standard pattern in Euro-American societies, whereby all family property passed to the eldest son—and tended to replace it with the idea of corporate ownership of family assets. This had tremendous

Adoration scene at the ancestral altar, 19th century. The home shrine forms the focal point of their religious activities for many Chinese people.

practical consequences. As long as the family stayed together, then their patrimony stayed intact. But if they split up for any reason, so too did the family assets. Consequently, land and property in China was constantly being divided and subdivided. This in turn meant that the peasants often lacked enough land to win more than a meager subsistence living for their families, and that the ruling class often had difficulty in transforming political power into economic strength. The only alternative to this was to vest the ownership of property in the hands of the family rather than the individual, and this naturally increased the importance of the family unit and its dominance over the desires of the individual.

The Local Religious Matrix

This emphasis on the family had direct implications for the development of Chinese religion. In essence, the Chinese recognized three classes of supernatural beings—gods, ghosts, and ancestors. As was the case in mundane Chinese society, these beings had a strict social hierarchy. The gods were the "mandarins," the government officials of the spirit world; the ancestors were the family carried into eternity; and ghosts were those elements of Chinese society that disrupted its orderly flow—the counterparts of beggars and thieves in the natural world. Each supernatural agent had his or her part to play in the drama of existence, but the Chinese understanding of these terms and the beings they represented differs quite markedly from that of other religions. The most important of these differences was the Chinese belief that the unseen aspects of Reality originated from this world, not the reverse. The supernatural was seen as an extension of the structures and realities of the natural world and was taken notice of only so far as it aided one's worldly concerns. In general, metaphysics interested the Chinese very little until a relatively late date and then mostly because of the stimulus of external influences, although such concerns can occasionally be found in earlier indigenous writings such as the *Daodejing* and the works of Wang Bi.

Uppermost in the Chinese religious consciousness was the cult of the ancestors. In a sense, this worship represented the best chance of gaining immortality, since it was believed that as long as people were remembered and revered by their descendants, they would in some sense continue to survive after death. Ancestors were seen as being able to influence events in this world. But they were also prone to anger if the social norms were not observed and the interests of the family transgressed. Regular worship was directed toward these supernatural figures in the form of offerings of food, incense, and spirit money. It was, and is, a simple set of rituals that took place at home and did not require the services of a priest or attendance at a temple. Indeed, most Chinese religious observance still dispenses with the services of religious specialists—the only exception being in cases of urgent difficulty. Family worship takes place in the home in front of a family altar, which may be of greater or lesser opulence, depending on the family's circumstances. Indeed, one of the few places that it is considered appropriate to make an ostentatious display of wealth is through one's family altar.

The Chinese attitude to ancestors is perhaps best summarized in Ode 279, a poem from the ancient *Book of Odes*, a collection of the earliest poetry in Chinese:

> Abundant is the year, with much millet and much rice,
> And we have tall granaries,
> With hundreds of thousands and millions of units.
> We make wine and sweet spirits
> And offer them to our ancestors, male and female,
> Thus to fulfill all the rites,
> And bring down blessings to all.
>
> SOURCE: Wang-tsit Chan, *A Sourcebook in Chinese Philosophy*, (Princeton: Princeton University, 1963), p. 6

Temples do, of course, exist in China and are often quite magnificent, but they are seen as being not so much a focus of individual or family religious piety as that of the larger community. Consequently, they are not so much the domain of ancestral spirits as of the **shen** or gods. However, when we use this term we must nuance it in accordance with Chinese thinking. The Chinese do not see the gods as totally omnipotent beings in the way that Westerners tend to do. Gods and humans were linked in the sense that they were both composed of the same material—*qi* (*ch'i*). It was true that the powers and knowledge of these gods far exceeded that of human beings; but their power was by no means as absolute as that ascribed to God in the Jewish, Christian, and Muslim worldviews.

Gods are distinctly geographically limited in their influence and tend to be efficacious in only one village or urban neighborhood, although from time to time in

Chinese history certain gods have developed a much larger range of influence. The limit of their power is not administratively fixed, but depends instead on a complex constellation of factors, including the god's perceived efficacy, social divisions, and other factors. Each local god, usually the earth god or *tudigong* (*t'u ti kung*), has his own shrine, with shrines and temples reflecting the economic prosperity of the locality. Indeed, communities often vie with one another to construct the most opulent temple for their local deity as a display of their wealth and prestige in much the same way as individual families lavish great expense on their personal family altars.

Earth gods are only the most local of a whole hierarchy of divinities that closely resembles the former Chinese imperial hierarchy swept away by the revolution of 1911. Even today, deities are often depicted as dressed in court robes similar to those worn by real-life imperial officials in the old days. This hierarchy of gods culminates in the Jade Emperor, a sort of king of the gods and the apex of the divine organizational chart. But other gods, and particularly goddesses such as Xiwangmu, the Queen Mother of the West, and Tianhou Mazu, the Empress of Heaven, have many more devotees. In all, goddesses play a very important role in popular devotion.

While the gods are generally benevolent, if somewhat distant from human affairs, the same cannot be said for the final category of traditional Chinese spirits—ghosts. The Chinese concept of the metaphysical constitution of the human being is distinctly fuzzy. The generally held viewpoint sees a number of souls inhabiting the average person. These divide into two basic categories—the *hun*, or positive soul, and the *po* (*p'o*), or negative soul. If the family conducts the proper funeral ceremonies and maintains the required ancestral worship, the souls will ascend to heaven. Otherwise, the person becomes a ghost, a **gui** (*kuei*). *Gui* are, if not actively malevolent, certainly not well-disposed to humans. Hence they must be propitiated with the proper rituals, including offerings of food and other goods, at the appropriate times of the year in order to minimize their disruptive influence.

What would cause a soul to become a *gui*? First would be the lack of an appropriate family to perform the requisite rituals at and after death. This underscores the fundamental importance in the Chinese mind for producing sons. Without sons, the appropriate rites cannot be conducted. Another way that these *gui* are produced is through an untimely or inappropriate death. Thus death in childbirth or by drowning, murder, or suicide are all thought of as prime conditions for the production of *gui*, who can bring about illness, bad fortune, and even insomnia. Their influence is so strong that there is a Hungry Ghost festival on the fifteenth day of the seventh lunar month in Chinese-influenced societies that has the specific purpose of mollifying all the dissatisfied spirits in the area. A public altar for the unknown deceased is erected and goods offered. In addition to public ceremonies, there are numerous private ceremonies performed to avert the malevolent influences of evil spirits. Children are seen as particularly vulnerable, and thus every effort is made to distract such spirits away from them—including by the bestowal of unattractive nicknames, the deflection of praise, and the use of amulets and magic formulas.

Chinese Religion in Pre- and Proto-History

Present-day northern China possesses a semi-arid, cool continental climate that at first glance seems extremely unpromising for the development of agriculture. But the climate and topography of the region some twelve thousand years ago, when agriculture began to develop in what was one of the primary cradles of Chinese civilization, were far different from those of today. In those days, northern China enjoyed a warm, damp climate that favored the cultivation of grains, as well as the domestication of dogs and pigs. Indeed, there was almost too much water. Much of the area—today almost a desert—was swamps and fens. While this land was of little agricultural use, it provided an abundance of wild foods that supplemented the diet of the early ancestors of the Chinese.[1]

The first concentrations of population in this region took place below the southern bend of the Yellow River starting around 4000 B.C.E. Here, in the area of what was to become Xian—often the capital city of the Chinese Empire in its various incarnations—there arose villages. The villagers grew millet as their staple crop, although they constantly supplemented it with foods gained through hunting and fishing. Their grain was stored in pottery jars that bore markings which suggest the existence of distinct family lineages within the village. This culture, known as Yangshao, was paralleled in other parts of China by similar cultures, based on rice cultivation, in the lower Yangzi River valley and on the southern coast bordering the South China Sea.[2]

It might be useful here to say a word about the ethnic composition of the area that was to become China. Today, we see this region as a single unified cultural unit speaking one language and possessing a single cultural heritage. This is because many generations of Han Chinese intellectuals have labored to project this image. In fact, the ethnic history of China has numerous distinct strands that were only later amalgamated into a single unit. Even today, although the population of China supposedly speaks a single language—"Chinese"—the dialects of that language are so different as to be virtually unintelligible to any but those who speak them. Thus, for example, the standard language of China, *putung hua*, or "Mandarin" as it is called in the West, has four tones or ways of pronouncing the basic sound of the word. But Cantonese, the predominant dialect of southern China, has nine, and there are several other important dialects found in other regions that differ significantly from both of them.[3]

We can identify a number of distinct prehistoric cultures that ringed the homeland of the Han Chinese—zhongguo (the Middle Country)—and that contributed to the core culture which came to dominate China. In the northeast were the pig-raising Tungus peoples. Slightly to their west were the cattle-herding ancestors of the Mongols. To the west of them were the ancestors of the Turkic peoples who probably domesticated the horse, with all that that implies for the progress of human history, and who nowadays stretch from the borders of China to Turkey in the west. South of these proto-Turkic people lived the ancestors of the Tibetans, who herded sheep. These four groups were always seen by the Han as being culturally inferior. But this was not the case with those groups living to the south of the core Han region.

These peoples not only contributed to the development of Han culture but also created their own not inconsiderable civilizations in Southeast Asia. In the period under discussion, we can identify four distinct cultures in what is now southern China. In the far southwest were the Liao people who were of Austro-Asiatic background and had little effect on emerging Chinese culture. But to their east lay two cultures, the Yao and the Tai, later joined together into a single unit—the Yue, who invented rice agriculture as well as a number of other distinctive cultural elements now associated with Chinese culture. Today, the descendants of these cultures have been marginalized by the Han majority, but their contribution to Chinese civilization as a whole is considerable.

But it is from the ethnically Han peoples of the Yangshao culture that the primary impetus for the development of Chinese culture sprang. From their original homeland south of the great bend of the Yellow River, these peoples began to expand east-ward along that river's flood plain. The later Chinese probably retained folk memories of this period. Chinese histories speak of an early period of cultural development under semi-divine "emperors" who taught the people agriculture, industrial arts, and techniques of flood control and irrigation. They were replaced by the first Chinese "dynasty"—the Xia (Hsia). Until recently, scholars have dismissed the existence of this state as a backward projection of the Chinese political system by later historians. But recent discoveries suggest that a later phase of the Yangshao culture, known as the Longshan (Lungshan) culture, may have possessed at least rudimentary political organization—as witnessed by the existence of fairly substantial walled villages that emerged in about 2000 B.C.E. Perhaps the Xia rulers did exist, but on a much less grandiose scale than that envisaged by their descendants.

What were the religious beliefs of these various peoples that populated the vast area of China in these early days? The fact of the matter is that we know very little on this question. Given its current dispersal and the survival of many of its traits in modern Chinese folk religion, it would probably be safe to say that early Chinese religion resembled Shamanism in many respects. But we must be careful not to see early Chinese religion as unalloyed shamanic religion, such as is still practiced by isolated tribes to the northeast of China proper in what is now Russia. Shamanic religion does not usually survive the transition of a culture from a hunting-and-gathering mode of production to an agricultural one. When this economic change occurs, religions tend to become more formal and to develop rituals and beliefs tied to the cyclical patterns of the agricultural year.

Likewise, religion becomes more closely allied with institutions of political control. This was the case in China as well. It is fairly likely that the rulers of the various emerging petty states of the Yellow River valley began to arrogate to themselves some or all of the religious functions of their societies, as we shall see more clearly delineated in the slightly later Shang culture considered below. This increased emphasis on ritual in early northern China is exemplified by the emergence of ritual implements cast in extremely valuable bronze. The working of this metal seems to have occurred earlier in the south than in the north; and it was probably imported from the north as well as from the Siberian Turkic tribes of the northwest. These bronze vessels bear motifs that suggest some shamanic beliefs, such as veneration of animal spirits, but we do not possess enough information to do more than conjecture about their possible significance.

But with the emergence of the first reasonably well-documented civilization in this region, that of the Shang, our knowledge becomes much more firmly established. The Shang, who probably arose in about 1600 B.C.E., built imposing cities and defensive works that suggest that they were able to command human resources on a much greater scale than their predecessors. Although their capitals changed fairly frequently—as many as seven times in some five hundred years—they were built in an enduring style with techniques still practiced today. The Shang had craftsmen of impeccable skill and artistic vision—indeed many of the bronze implements cast in this period have never been surpassed. The Shang kings used writing—albeit of a somewhat primitive nature—as their archives that have come down to us clearly demonstrate. But all this development came at a price. Evidence suggests that the Shang were despotic rulers who clearly differentiated between a small privileged aristocracy and the vast mass of the common people. Control was exercised through a harsh system of punishment that, if we are to believe later historians, eventually led to the dynasty's downfall, although other factors no doubt played a role as well.

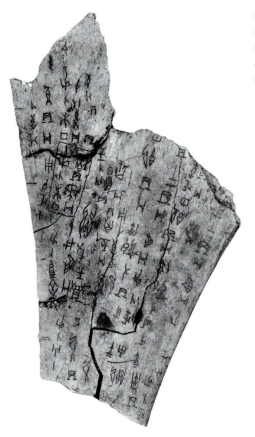

Oracle bone, Shang dynasty, c. 1200 B.C.E. Oracle bones were used by the early Chinese to uncover the course of future events and to discern the will of the deities such as Shangdi.

Much of the source of Shang power seems to have been religious in nature. One of the Chinese words for God as the ultimate principal of Reality is **Shangdi** (Shang-ti). Literally translated, this means "God on high." The Shang rulers claimed to be the direct descendants and representatives of the divine. This pattern of believing that a special and unique relationship existed between the ruler and the divine continued throughout Chinese history. One of the most often-used imperial titles was "the son of heaven," although this is a later term that was not used by the Shang. Most likely, the Shang king was seen as being the most effective intercessor for the common people in consequence of this close family relationship. Certainly the king consulted his ancestors on a constant basis, as evidenced by the vast collection of "oracle bones" that have come down to us.

These oracle bones, which number some hundred thousand examples, provide us with an unparalleled glimpse into the concerns and preoccupations of the Shang rulers, as well as into the more mundane aspects of their lives and those of their subjects. This use of oracle bones as a form of divination known as scapulamancy was not a Shang innovation. It dates as far back as the Fuhe culture of the eastern Mongolian plateau that flourished in about 3700 B.C.E. Oracle bones were the shoulder bones of cattle and, later, sheep, or the bottom bones (plastrons) of tortoises on which were inscribed questions to be answered by the spirits of the king's ancestors with either a "yes" or a "no." A red-hot bronze rod was touched to the inscribed bone and the subsequent pattern of cracks was interpreted. All manner of questions were posed, from whether or not to institute a war down to when the king's headache would disappear. After the question was asked and answered, the bone was "put on file" for future reference. These rediscovered bones provide a window into the lives of the early Chinese.[4]

This interest in divination would persist in Chinese society and find its fullest expression in the book of the *Yijing* (*I Ching*) or, as it is more commonly known in China, the *Zhouyi* (*Chou-I*). The *Yijing*, which was compiled during the Zhou dynasty, was the interpretation of the sixty-four hexagrams that were formed by various combinations of six solid and broken lines. These hexagrams were randomly generated, using a variety of methods, in an attempt to ascertain the course of the future. Originally intensely practical in nature, the *Yijing*, under the impetus of Daoist and even Confucian thought, began to evolve—in its fullest manifestation it became a road map to the fluctuation of the Dao, the Supreme Reality that gives rise to the world, discussed below, and thus a sort of scripture of continuous revelation that held tremendous existential importance. But all of this lay far in the future.[5]

The ritual life of the Shang seems to have revolved around a cult of the royal ancestors. The honored royal dead were interred in large underground tombs filled with innumerable precious objects and surrounded by their animals and servants—who were sent to the next world with their master to serve him there as they had done in this life.[6] Sacrifice seems to have held an important place in Shang religious life, as evidenced by its extensive dispersal throughout the Shang cultural sphere, particularly in association with the erection of public buildings. These funerary sacrifices were only the final act in a continuing ritual drama that governed the life of the upper classes and the royal family in particular. We know from the oracle bones

"Man and beast" motif on ceremonial axe, Shang dynasty, c. 1200 B.C.E. Early Chinese religion appears to have incorporated human sacrifice in its rites, but this died out as a religious practice relatively early.

that there were many outlying principalities—the bones name about a thousand towns altogether—governed by younger members of the royal family who held their power by virtue of their relationship to the high king of the Shang. Possibly these rulers not only officiated at religious ceremonies, but also participated in the rituals as mediums for their deceased royal ancestors. The animal motifs on the surviving bronze ritual vessels suggest that animal spirits also played a part in Shang religious life.

The final phase of this religio-political development found its fullest expression in the next dynasty to rule the northern China plain—the Zhou (Chou) who reigned from about 1040 to 221 B.C.E. The Zhou people, originally vassals of Shang living in the far western reaches of the kingdom, revolted against their masters' harsh rule and overthrew them. Like their predecessors, they used a hierarchical structure based on family ties and a system of vassalage. But this governmental structure presented them with a problem. They had been the vassals of Shang and had rebelled: what was to prevent their feudal underlings from doing the same? The answer that the Zhou evolved was the concept of **tianming** (*t'ien ming*), the "Mandate of Heaven." According to this theory, Heaven (*tian*) bestowed the right to govern the

Shang ceremonial vessel, c. 1200 B.C.E. Early Chinese society developed elaborate rituals designed to pay homage to their ancestors and to influence the course of events in the physical world.

state on a particularly virtuous and worthy family. If this family should decline in virtue, however, then the Mandate of Heaven could be withdrawn and conferred on another, more deserving family. To quote Ode 267 from the *Book of Odes* again:

> The Mandate of Heaven,
> How beautiful and unceasing!
> Oh, how glorious
> Was the purity of King Wen's [the founder of the Zhou dynasty] virtue!
> With blessings he overwhelms us.
> We will receive the blessings.
> They are a great favor from our King Wen.
> May his descendants hold fast to them.

SOURCE: Chan, *A Sourcebook in Chinese Philosophy*, p. 6

The implications of this theory were to have far-reaching effects in Chinese thought.

Other than this, there seems to have been little change in the general religious pattern of Chinese life for another five hundred years. But forces had been set in motion that would cause Chinese thought to develop in new directions. Most important among these was the development of the Chinese writing system, which allowed the free flow and exchange of ideas. Slowly but surely, Chinese thinking about human society, human happiness, and the ultimate meaning of human existence began to coalesce and deepen.[7]

Website References

1. www.china-window.com/wenwu/Pal/indexe.htm gives information on Paleolithic Chinese culture.

2. Neolithic China's culture is covered at www.china-window.com/wenwu/Neo/indexe.htm

3. For an overview of the Chinese language, see encarta.msn.com/index/conciseindex/37/03705000.htm?z=1&pg=2&br=1

4. Oracle bones are discussed at faculty.juniata.edu/atwill/or_bones.html

5. For more information on the *Yijing*, see acc6.its.brooklyn.cuny.edu/~phalsall/texts/lopez.html

6. Shang burial practices are examined at www.nga.gov.education/chinatp-fu.htm and depts.washington.edu/chinaciv/archae/2fuhbron.htm

7. Xia, Shang, and Zhou culture is discussed at www.china-window.com/wenwu/xia/indexe.htm

CHAPTER SIXTEEN

Philosophical Daoism

The constellation of Chinese beliefs that grew out of the experience of the natural world is collectively termed Daoism. But as we have seen, the appearance of religions in Asia can be deceptive. As is the case with Hinduism, the term Daoism is an "umbrella" under which different religious expressions find shelter; and, again like Hinduism, these various religious expressions share certain core characteristics but often differ quite significantly. Broadly speaking, however, they can be divided into two groups. The first is what might be called philosophical Daoism, Daojia (Tao Chia), the School of the Way. Here, there was an attempt to codify wisdom gained from the natural world into a coherent philosophy. The second, and much larger, division of Daoism is what might be called Daoist religion, Daojiao (Tao-chiao). Philosophical Daoism had only a brief period of activity from about 500 to 200 B.C.E., but it was to have long-lasting effects on Chinese thought. It formed the counterpoint to the more active politico-ethical systems of thought such as Confucianism, Mohism, and Legalism. The two sets of philosophical systems were originally conceived for a similar purpose—the regulation of society, and they were aimed at a similar audience, namely the ruling class of the states that made up the China of the Warring States period. Daoist religion was a later development, with its first texts appearing around 100 C.E.

The style and distribution of the texts of these two expressions of Daoism differed considerably. The texts of the philosophical school—the primary ones being the *Daodejing*, attributed to Laozi (Lao-tzu), and the *Zhuangzi* (*Chuang Tzu*) of Zhuangzi—were meant to be read by as wide an audience as possible. The texts of the religious Daoists were more esoteric and originally aimed at a small group. Their transmission was hedged in with oaths of secrecy, and they had at first only limited circulation. Nevertheless, by the fifth century C.E., moves were afoot to collect this growing literature. The canon of texts that emerged, known as the **Daozong** (*Tao-tsung*), was fixed by the fifteenth century and ran to almost 1,500 titles.[1] Consequently, scholars of Daoism have a tremendous wealth of material. Despite this, Euro-American study of Daoist religion has lagged far behind that of philosophical Daoism and is still very new.

Laozi and the *Daodejing*

With the exception of Confucius, the influence on Chinese thought of Laozi is greater than that of any other single figure. His accomplishment is even more impressive given the fact that he probably never existed. But this has never been a bar to the wielding of wide religious influence in any of the world's religions, and his non-existence in no way diminishes the impact that he has had on Chinese thought. The traditional view held by Chinese scholars was that the *Daodejing* was the work of Laozi, an older contemporary of Confucius. Sima Qian (Ssu-ma Ch'ien), the great early historian of China, included a fairly detailed biography of Laozi in his monumental *Shi Ji* (*Shih-chi*), the *Records of the Historian*. Here, he identifies Laozi's home town in the state of Qu and records that he was the historian in charge of the archives of the Zhou emperors. He also records encounters between Confucius and Laozi, when the younger Confucius, in the appropriate Chinese style, goes to the older Laozi for instruction. Later Laozi is said to have resigned his post and disappeared into the west, pausing only long enough to compose the *Daodejing* (also known as the *Laozi*) at the behest of the guardian of China's western border.

The figure of Laozi probably developed to give the emerging Daoist school of philosophy credibility and a sense of focus. In China it was the custom, as it was in India, to trace schools of thought back to definite founders. Laozi means literally "old master," a title rather than a name *per se*. The fictitious nature of Laozi is further suggested by the fact that the next great philosopher of Daoism, Zhuangzi, never mentions him. Nor do other writers of the time, including Mencius, who went out of his way to catalog and refute schools of thought that were not orthodox Confucianism. Whatever its provenance, the *Daodejing* has been immensely influential, and not just in its Chinese homeland. It has been translated into more languages than any book of scripture except the Bible. Why is this? The answer lies in the nature of the text itself. It is extremely brief, running to only some five thousand Chinese characters. Moreover, the aphoristic style in which it is written gives the text a cryptic nature that is succinct to the point of obscurity. Hence, translators and commentators have been able to manipulate the text to get it to yield whatever viewpoints they desire, no matter how contradictory they are to one another. Strangely enough, this is not really contrary to the spirit of the text, which focuses on change and transformation. Its compilers could hardly complain, therefore, if the text that they had produced exhibited such changes and transformations in the hands of its later redactors.[2]

The *Daodejing* itself is traditionally divided into two sections, the first containing thirty-seven chapters, the second forty-four. We can assume with a fair degree of certainty that the book is an anthology of related aphorisms collected by various compilers at an uncertain date probably between 500 and 200 B.C.E. If this is the case, then it would be a flawed enterprise to look for a coherent philosophy in the work. Even so, there are a number of powerful themes that run through it that continue to be echoed in later Chinese philosophy. The central concept of Daoism is the idea of the Dao, which literally translates as the "way" or "path." But the term is resonant with many other meanings. Perhaps the best way to conceptualize it is to say that the Dao is the essential source or ground of the universe. Consequently, it totally transcends any human ability to describe it. As the *Daodejing* says in the very first verse:

The Tao (Way) that can be told of is not the eternal Tao;
The name that can be named is not the eternal name.
The Nameless is the origin of Heaven and Earth;
The Named is the mother of all things.
Therefore let there always be non-being so we may see their subtlety,
And let there always be being so we may see their outcome.
The two are the same,

But after they are produced, they have different names.
They both may be called deep and profound.
Deeper and more profound,
The door of all subtleties!

SOURCE: Chan, A Sourcebook in Chinese Philosophy, p. 139

In addition to the contention that the basic motivating force in the universe is essentially indescribable, a number of seminal themes may be seen emerging from this initial passage. The most important of these is the concept of polarity—what would later be called **yin** and **yang**. The ancient Chinese saw all things as being composed of opposites. Yin was the dark principle of the universe. It was female, cold, moist, passive, and yielding. Its counterpart, yang, was the light principle and was male, hot, dry, active, and thrusting. But these two absolute principles were never present anywhere in the universe in their pure state. Rather, all things were composed of the interaction of the two principles which was initiated in response to the movement of the Dao.

The second important point alluded to in the first verse of the *Daodejing* is that the Dao both brought everything into being and continues to sustain that being. It necessarily follows that the Dao must have preceded the universe. To quote the *Daodejing* again:

There is something undifferentiated and yet complete,
Which existed before heaven and earth.
Soundless and formless, it depends on nothing and does not change.
It operates everywhere and is free from danger.
It may be considered the mother of the universe.
I do not know its name; I call it Tao.
If forced to give it a name, I shall call it Great.
Now being great means functioning everywhere.

SOURCE: Chan, A Sourcebook in Chinese Philosophy, p. 152

This, then, is ultimate Reality for the Daoist—a constantly moving, ineffable process of change, interaction, and adaptation that is undergirded and motivated by an eternal but indescribable principle that operates according to its own set of unknowable dictates. But if that is so, where does this leave the individual human being in his or her quest for the ultimate meaning of life? Even if the universe is not random at its core, its unknowability and consequent unpredictability would seem to leave human beings adrift in a world that is essentially meaningless—at least from their point of view. The Daoists came to the conclusion that the greatest human happiness must necessarily lie in achieving congruency with this first principle in which the material universe lived, moved, and had its being. Thus:

The best (man) is like water.
Water is good; it benefits all things and does not compete with them.
It dwells in (lowly) places that all disdain.
This is why it is so near to Tao.
[The best man] in his dwelling loves the earth.
In his heart, he loves what is profound.
In his associations, he loves humanity.
In his words, he loves faithfulness.
In government, he loves order.

In handling affairs, he loves competence.
In his activities, he loves timeliness.
It is because he does not compete that he is without reproach.

SOURCE: Chan, A Sourcebook in Chinese Philosophy, p. 143

Herein lies the essence of Daoist thought: To live a simple, spontaneous life close to nature that does away with the usual human preoccupations with wealth and power. As another verse puts it:

Which does one love more, fame or one's own life?
Which is more valuable, one's own life or wealth?
Which is worse, gain or loss?
Therefore he who has lavish desires will spend extravagantly.
He who hoards will lose heavily.
He who is contented suffers no disgrace.
He who knows when to stop is free from danger.
Therefore he can long endure.

SOURCE: Chan, A Sourcebook in Chinese Philosophy, p. 161

As the Daoist saw it, the fortunes of life were ever-changing. One might possess wealth and power one day, yet see it all dissipate the next. To have possessions and power was to tempt Fate. The wisest course, therefore, was to "keep one's head down," so to speak, since the person who had nothing had nothing to lose. This was certainly not to say that the Daoists advocated living in a cave without any creature comforts whatsoever. Seeing the natural world as good, they saw the pleasures of the body that flowed from that natural world as being good as well. No other world religion appreciates, as it were, a good wine as much as Daoism. But the Daoists would caution against becoming so fond of that wine as to leave the security of the simple life to procure it—they would much prefer a bottle of cheap table wine to the most costly French vintage, if that vintage somehow required them to renounce following the Dao.

Following the Dao meant being sensitive to its shifts and changes, and this implied the need for flexibility. This has often been misinterpreted by non-Daoists as meaning that Daoists should be passive and simply allow life to "happen." This is an incorrect interpretation of the Daoist term *wuwei* (non-action). Rather than meaning that one should not act, *wuwei* implies that one should not act in a manner contrary to that of the Dao at any given moment. For the Daoists, inappropriate action comes from too much thought founded purely on self-interest. Appropriate non-active action comes from the non-reflective, intuitive knowledge that is gained through being close to the Dao.

Nowhere is this concern for non-reflective action so apparent as in the *Daodejing*'s treatment of the conduct of government. Like all philosophies of this period, Daoism was profoundly concerned with the question of how the state was to be managed. The Warring States period (c. 770–221 B.C.E.) during which philosophical Daoism developed, was, as its name implies, a time of great instability. The central Zhou control of the northern Chinese plain, if it had ever existed at all, had broken down completely, and the region had divided into an ever-changing patchwork of petty states that were constantly trying to expand their influence at the expense of their neighbors. In a search for better means of achieving this dubious goal, the rulers of these states were searching for ideas and methodologies that would give them better administrative control of their domains. Consequently, this was a period of tremendous philosophical activity, as thinkers from all over China flocked to the courts of these petty rulers, anxious to present their solution to the chaos of the time. Not only Daoism, but Confucianism, and such now defunct creeds as Mohism and Legalism, arose in, and were shaped by, this environment.

The Daoist answers to the political problems of this era are consistent with its understanding of human perfection. As we have see, the best person is the person who is most in touch with the Dao. In opposition to Confucianism, the Daoist advocates:

Abandon sageliness [Confucian principles] and discard wisdom;
Then the people will benefit a hundredfold.
Abandon humanity and discard righteousness;
Then the people will return to filiality and deep love.
Abandon skill and discard profit;
Then there will be no thieves or robbers.
However, these three things are ornament and not adequate.
Therefore let people hold on to these:
Manifest plainness,
Embrace simplicity,
Reduce selfishness,
Have few desires.

SOURCE: Chan, *A Sourcebook in Chinese Philosophy*, p. 149

If this was the standard of conduct for the average person, how much more so for that supreme exemplar, the ruler? On how the state should be governed, the *Daodejing* observes:

Govern the state with correctness.
Operate the army with surprise tactics.
Administer the empire by engaging in no activity.
How do I know that this should be so?
Through this:
The more taboos and prohibitions there are in the world,
The poorer the people will be.
The more sharp weapons the people have,
The more troubled the state will be.
The more cunning and skill man possesses,
the more thieves and robbers there will be.
Therefore the sage [emperor] says:
I take no action and the people of themselves are transformed.
I love tranquillity and the people of themselves become correct.
I engage in no activity and the people of themselves become prosperous.
I have no desires and the people of themselves become simple.

SOURCE: Chan, *A Sourcebook in Chinese Philosophy*, p. 167

From the Daoist standpoint, he governed best who governed least. This, then, was the Daoist prescription for government: frugality and restraint on the part of the ruler, natural day-to-day actions on the part of the ruled. If both sides acted in a natural manner, the state would rule itself. It goes without saying that no sane ruler in Warring States China had even the remotest intention of trying to apply such a utopian system of governance. Daoism was never more than a theoretical curiosity in the realm of practical government. Nevertheless, it resonated deeply in Chinese minds, even among those in the upper classes who would never have dreamed of applying its principles in the practical arena. Daoism came to be a sort of alternate "shadow" philosophy among the intelligentsia of the upper classes. They would be Confucian during the day at the office, but they would become Daoist at night in the privacy of their own homes, as they pursued the pleasures of art and literature. Daoist motifs constantly run through Chinese literature and the plastic arts, informing both the creation of the art and theories of artistic criticism.

Zhuangzi

After the *Daodejing*, Daoists hold the *Zhuangzi*, written by Zhuangzi, to be the greatest book of the Daoist philosophical tradition. The two books differ greatly in their style. Whereas the *Daodejing* is terse and aphoristic, the *Zhuangzi* is a masterful blend of poetry and prose that is deservedly considered to be a milestone in the development of Chinese literature. In addition, the *Zhuangzi* is clearly the work of a single author, at least in its core text, although extrapolations by other hands appear to have been added later. Despite their differences, however, the two texts are very close to one another in their fundamental premises about the nature of Reality and the human response to it. Both texts are more evocative than discursive, their authority coming not so much from a coherent philosophical program—at least in the case of Laozi—as from the emotional states and the intuitive vistas that the writing opens up to the reader. This, of course, makes it very difficult for commentators to summarize Laozi's or Zhuangzi's "philosophy" of Daoism. Thus one must be content with elucidating some key concepts for the student and then referring them to the texts themselves.

Our main source of biographical information concerning Zhuangzi is once again the *Shi Ji* of Sima Qian. Although it is clear from this account that Zhuangzi, unlike Laozi, was an actual person, the information is still very sparse. Zhuangzi is recorded as being a native of the state of Meng, where he was said to have been an official "in the lacquer garden." He is supposed to have lived in the middle part of the fourth century B.C.E., thus making him a contemporary of the great Confucian scholar Mencius. His masterwork is noted and then little more is said—it is clear from this minor excerpt that Sima Qian had very little verifiable information about Zhuangzi, and so his book must speak for him. It is composed of thirty-three sections or chapters. These are divided into "inner," "outer," and "miscellaneous" chapters. Of these groups, the seven "inner" chapters probably represent the original work of Zhuangzi. These contain all the major ideas of the text and are written in a brilliant and elegant style. The remaining twenty-six chapters of the work seem to be later accretions to the text.[3]

The *Zhuangzi* presents a variety of ideas and concepts throughout its some hundred thousand words, but there is a central theme that knits them all together—that of freedom. This was not just freedom from existence, since, unlike the Indian philosophers, Zhuangzi did not see the world as intrinsically evil and something to escape from, so much as freedom from everything that hinders the individual from following the spontaneous movements of the Dao. Most other Chinese philosophers, such as the Mohists and the Legalists, answered the challenges of the troubled Warring States period by proposing a concrete plan of action designed to reform the individual and society. Zhuangzi rejected this enterprise entirely, holding that such a wide-ranging program of reform was impossible, given the nature of the world and of human beings. He concentrated his efforts on the individual, and his answer to the great questions of human existence was the answer of the mystic and not the philosopher.

The *Zhuangzi*'s answer to the great existential questions was simple and very similar to that of the Indian schools of thought—free yourself from the bondage of the world. But how are we to do this? The solution lies in one of the stories given in the *Zhuangzi*. A person who is perplexed and afflicted with a multitude of worries goes to see Laozi. When he encounters him, the sage asks, "Why did you come with this crowd of people?" The man is confused by this, since he came alone to see the philosopher. But what Laozi is really saying is that each of us carries with us old ideas, concepts of right and wrong and good and bad, and so on that condition our thinking and hold us back from spontaneously following the Dao. Only by freeing ourselves of these things can we be truly free.

Zhuangzi took the radical position—one very hard to defend from the standpoint of conventional logic—that the evils that befall human beings are only evils if we hold them to be so. For Zhuangzi, evils exist because of human labeling, so to speak. They arise because we have the habit, acquired from our families and society at large, of drawing distinctions between things and assigning them values. But, said Zhuangzi, these labels form a sort of cage that constrains us, and so we are the authors of our own bondage. To free ourselves from this cage of values and preconceptions is to free ourselves from the bondage of the world.

Zhuangzi approached the question of how this is to be achieved by using two literary devices to shake readers out of their bondage to concepts and values. The first of these is the paradoxical anecdote. This device was so effective that it became a standard tool employed by other schools of thought, notably the Chinese and Japanese schools of Zen Buddhism, to jolt their students out of entrenched thought structures. The second device was the use of a narrative style that starts out sounding completely rational and logical, but ends up reducing language to an absurd mishmash of meaning, thus demonstrating its innate senselessness. But perhaps the most telling weapon in Zhuangzi's pedagogic arsenal was his sense of humor. Unlike most philosophical discourse, both Eastern and Euro-American, Zhuangzi not only made use of humor but placed it at the very center of his style.

For Zhuangzi, only people who have freed themselves from the tyranny of conventional standards of judgment can be considered truly free. Such people do not see poverty as being inferior to wealth, death as less desirable than life, or fame superior to obscurity. Nor do they withdraw from the world, since to do so is to make a judgment of the world based on residual bondage to it. Rather, truly free individuals remain in the world, but not of it. They no longer act out of the motives that lead ordinary people to struggle for wealth, power, fame, or success. As he puts it in the seventh chapter of the *Zhuangzi*:

> Do not be the possessor of fame. Do not be the storehouse of schemes. Do not take over the function of things. Do not be the master of knowledge (to manipulate things). Personally realize the infinite to the highest degree and travel in the realm of which there is no sign. Exercise fully what you have received from Nature without any subjective viewpoint. In a word, be absolutely [empty] (*hsü*).
>
> SOURCE: Chan, *A Sourcebook in Chinese Philosophy*, p. 207

In this state, all actions become spontaneous and Dao-driven.

One who has achieved this state, says Zhuangzi, has achieved the state of *yu*—free and spontaneous wandering. Such a person now journeys freely through creation, guided only by the dictates of the Dao. Zhuangzi describes such a person as possessing magical powers, inhabiting a trancelike state, and being immortal and impervious to harm. Does he mean this literally, as many later commentators have assumed? More likely, what we see here is Zhuangzi attempting to convey to his readers, through a vocabulary familiar to them from preexisting Chinese religion, a state of being that transcends conventional language. His language is not meant to be descriptive so much as evocative and metaphorical.

But this is not how many subsequent readers of the text took its meaning. After Zhuangzi, Daoism largely ceased to function as a philosophical school, if it had ever been one to start with. It began to evolve in different directions. Some segments of the tradition gave rise to organized religions in the sense used in Euro-American thought. Some segments, fixated on the quest for immortality seemingly described by Zhuangzi, began to experiment with potions, exercise, diet, and other physical means in order to achieve that end. Still others, influenced by new ideas imported from India, attempted to form monastic organizations. All these groups continued to adhere to the basic vision of the great books of the school, the *Laozi* and the *Zhuangzi*, but they developed the ideas in these texts in their own unique ways.

Website References

1. helios.unive.it/~dsao/pregadio/tools/daozang/dz_0.html is an extensive site devoted to the Daoist canon of texts.

2. The *Daodejing* is translated at www.clas.ufl.edu/users/gthursby/taoism/ttc–list.htm

3. www.coldbacon.com/chuang/chuang.html gives excerpts from the work of Zhuangzi.

CHAPTER SEVENTEEN

Daoist Religion

Whereas Daojia—philosophical Daoism—became an integral component of the intellectual milieu of the upper classes, Daojiao (Tao-chiao)—Daoist religion—was more widespread throughout all levels of Chinese society. But in saying this we must again make clear that we are again not talking about a single tradition, but rather a constellation of traditions sharing common elements. These traditions take as their starting points the texts revealed to their various founders by the divinized Laozi and other figures of the Daoist pantheon, and develop them in ways particular to themselves. The differences in these Daoist traditions have little to do with doctrine *per se*, but rather with divergences in practice.

Early Daoist Traditions in Qin and Han Religion

With the unification of China under a central government in 221 B.C.E., a new phase opened up in Chinese intellectual history. Power was now totally in the hands of the First Emperor and the ruling elite that surrounded him. This in turn led to the concentration of philosophers and scholars of vaguely Daoist bent at the royal court, with everyone vying for royal favor. One such group, which came from the eastern coasts of China, where Daoism and shamanic religion mixed freely, described the fabulous islands of Penglai (P'eng-lai) that supposedly lay off those coasts and which were inhabited by *xian* (*hsien*)—human beings who had become immortal through following the natural principles of the Dao. So impressed was the First Emperor with these tales and with the possibility of obtaining the secrets of immortality that he outfitted several sizable expeditions to search for these islands. Strangely enough, none of these expeditions returned to inform the despotic emperor of their failure to fulfill his wishes, though folk legend indicates that their crews may have settled in lands peripheral to China, such as Japan and Korea.

Another Daoist movement that seems to have had its origins in this eastern region was less well received by the emperors of early China. In about 100 B.C.E., one Gan Zhongke (Kan Chung-k'o) appeared at the court of the then-ruling Han emperor, and presented him with a book entitled *Taipingjing* (*T'ai-p'ing Ching*), the *Classic of Great Peace*. Gan claimed that the book had been revealed to him by a god, who had ordered him to use it to renew the Han dynasty. Although Gan was promptly beheaded, various copies of this document continued to circulate. As Han rule became less effective, groups of dissidents began to coalesce into millenarian secret societies aimed at restoring "the good old days," or at least what their leaders thought the good old days had been. Some of these took their cue from the *Classic of Great Peace*, and thus the text could be said to be the charter for a form of "apocalyptic Daoism" that continued to persist for many centuries.

In 184 C.E., this unrest exploded into the great Yellow Turban Rebellion, the first, but not the last, such disruption to shake Chinese society. Many of its leaders claimed to be descendants of Laozi, and some actually claimed to be Laozi himself, reincarnated. One such leader in particular, Li Hong, became a recurrent figure in the Daoist messianic cults that continued to flourish long after his death and the suppression of the Yellow Turbans. In fact, the last "Li Hong" was executed in 1112. These messianic religious movements with their heavily Daoist elements continued to arise throughout Chinese history to trouble the peace of the empire and the stability of the current occupant of the Dragon Throne.

The Celestial Masters

The second century C.E. saw another important development in Daoist religion: the establishment of a Daoist "church." Unlike the various movements that characterized early Daoist religion, which came mainly from eastern China, this movement originated in the western frontier region of Sichuan. In 142, one Zhang Daolin (Chang Dao-lin) received a revelation from Taishang Laojun (Lord Lao the Most High). This was none other than Laozi himself—now envisioned as a divine being embodying the Dao—who gave Zhang two books designed to renovate society, ordering him to use them to reform the religious and ethical practices of the people. He also conferred on Zhang and his descendants the title of *dianshi (t'ien-shih)*, Celestial Master, and the school that Zhang founded became known as the *dianshi dao*, the Way of the Celestial Masters.

Zhang quickly formed an organization that became a sort of alternate government in the lightly administered western part of China. He and his descendants divided the area under their control into thirty-six "parishes" or *zhi (chih)*. Each *zhi* had a *jingshi (ching-shih)*, a "chamber of purity," that was its ritual center. This chamber of purity was also the headquarters of the *jijiu (chi-chiu)* or "libationer," who functioned as the chief priest of the *zhi*. These ritual centers were supported by a household tax of five pecks of rice per year from the faithful, hence another name for the movement—*wudoumi dao (wu-tou-mi tao)*, the Way of the Five Pecks of Rice.

Zhang seems to have taught that illness and misfortune were the direct results of evil deeds. The only way to mitigate the effects of such deeds was through an appeal to the ruling hierarchy of heaven, which mirrored the one found on earth at the imperial court. The appeal or *jang (chang)* was written by the libationer on a piece of paper that was burned. The ashes of the appeal were then mixed with water and drunk by the appellant. If this did not work, the libationer would produce amulets and talismans aimed at negating the evil influences plaguing the suppliant. The libationer also functioned as a moral instructor of his flock, teaching the sect's allegorical interpretation of the *Daodejing* and explicating the other texts of the tradition.

The Celestial Masters advocated right action and good works, as well as the performance of communal rituals such as the He Qi (Ho Ch'i), Union of Breaths, a ritual that appears from later commentators to have been a group sexual rite. Unfortunately, the only descriptions of such rituals that have come down to us were written by individuals hostile to the sect, and consequently it is not certain that we possess an accurate description of either their practice or their intents. In 215, the grandson of the founder of the sect submitted to the authority of the Han successor state of Wei, thus ensuring its survival. The sect has persisted to the present day in Taiwan where Zhang Daoling's direct descendant still presides over the faithful.

The Development of Daoism in South China

As new ideas began to penetrate China, particularly in the south, Daoism started to adapt and change. One important new influence was Buddhism, whose first presence in China is dated at 65 C.E., although it may well have appeared earlier, perhaps arriving in southern China via the Southeast Asian maritime trade routes before it traveled the Silk Road from Central Asia to northern China. Interestingly enough, the first verifiable reference to Buddhism is associated with the court of a Han prince renowned for his adherence to Daoism. The paths of the two religions in China remained intertwined, and at first Buddhism was viewed and interpreted through the lens of Daoist ideas.

The earliest texts of Buddhism to be translated were those that reflected the Daoist preoccupations with meditation and rules of conduct. Even the words used in such translations were ones that were used primarily in Daoist texts, since specific words for uniquely Buddhist terms had yet to be created. So, for example, Buddha's achieving enlightenment was literally translated as "the Buddha obtained the Dao." There was even an idea current during this period that Laozi, who was believed to have left China for the west at the end of his life, was in fact the Buddha. As we shall see, however, this interaction between the two religions was not just one way. Buddhism also supplied Daoism with ideas such as the concept of the afterlife that it had previously lacked.

The south of China came into the Han cultural sphere at a relatively late date. As a result of this, it was still poorly integrated into the empire, and one of the first areas to assert its independence as the Han dynasty began to disintegrate. Soon it had its own imperial court, that of the Wu emperors. Anxious to legitimize their rule, these emperors were lavish patrons of the various religious and philosophical groups that flourished in their territory. Although it was Buddhism that was to benefit most from the patronage of the Wu, other groups did so as well. It is here in the south that Daoism evolved new expressions. Two such developments were to affect radically the directions in which the religion began to move: the alchemical tradition; and a visionary and ecstatic form of Daoist religion known after its place of origin as Maoshan Daoism.

The alchemical search for an elixir of immortality has a long and venerable history in Daoist thought. Since immortality was one of the few things that the emperors of China did not possess, they were lavish in their patronage of those who claimed to be able to induce it. In this, the Wu emperors were no exception, and wonderworkers and alchemists flocked to their court. Of these, one Ge Xuan (Ko Hsüan) gained particular fame. But it was his great-nephew, Ge Hong (Ko Hung), who was to produce the definitive text on the subject—the *Baopuzi (Pao-p'u-tzu)*, *He Who Holds to Simplicity*. Despite its title, this text was about neither philosophy nor ethics. It was a text devoted entirely to the various technical means of achieving immortality as advocated by the various schools of Daoism, none of which Ge Hong seems to have utilized personally with any degree of success. Taking his great-uncle's alchemical formulas as his starting point, Ge Hong wrote an extensive commentary and evaluation of their efficacy. He made no pretense to originality, and scrupulously documented the origins of the various techniques. Thus his work provides not only information on Daoism in his own time but also a valuable window on the practices of the past.

The primary alchemical means of achieving immortality described by Ge Hong was "aurification." This involved the drinking of *jindan* (*chin-tan*), gold elixir, or *jinyi* (*chin-i*), gold in liquid suspension, and the use of elixirs made of cinnabar, a compound made of mercury and sulfur. These techniques were identified by Ge Hong as coming from the earlier Taijing (T'ai Ching) or "Great Purity" tradition. They involved extensive labor and costly ingredients—as did most other forms of alchemical Daoism—that were clearly not available to the average person, and so the practice of alchemical Daoism tended to be an upper-class preoccupation. But Ge Hong identified less expensive ways of prolonging life. A proper diet, avoiding grain products and alcohol, was seen as being effective, as was the ingestion of the "essences" of the sun, the moon, and various stars through ritual means. Gymnastic exercises, from which developed the present art of Taiji Zhuan (T'ai Chi Chuan), and the conservation of bodily fluids through a variety of sexual techniques were also advocated. The essence of all these practices was to harmonize and bring into balance the five elements of fire, water, earth, wood, and metal, which were the building blocks of the material world, and to facilitate the production and flow of *qi*, the essence of the life force animating the body. The balancing of these elements led to long life and even immortality. The traditions of the Celestial Masters, such as the use of talismans and the practice of good deeds, were commended to the earnest seeker, as were efforts to purge all disease from the body by means of herbs and plants.

But even as the *Baopuzi* was being finished in 317, changes were overtaking the Wu Empire. The last indigenous Chinese dynasty of the north, the Western Jin, fell to barbarian invaders in 316 and triggered a mass exodus of the royal family and upper-class families to the south. They brought with them new currents of Daoist thought, principally through the medium of the school of the Celestial Masters, which, for the first time, made inroads into the southeastern part of China. This region was well known for its ecstatic and mediumistic forms of religion, which may have been holdovers from the earlier religious traditions of the peoples who now inhabit Southeast Asia. True to the original mandate given to the sect's founder, the Celestial Masters vigorously opposed all such religious expression. As the new immigrants from the north began to gain political ascendancy in the southern kingdoms, many of the older southern aristocratic families, who by now had embraced the northern forms of Daoism, found themselves increasingly marginalized. But as time went on, these families were to play a major part in the development of a new phase of Daoist religious development—the Maoshan school.

This school, a synthesis of the teachings of the Celestial Masters and the indigenous traditions of the southeastern region of China, takes its name from Mount Mao (Maoshan), where the aristocratic Xu (Hsü) family maintained a retreat, and where the new school had its origins in the middle of the fourth century C.E. The Xu family was closely related to the family of Ge Hong and had provided officials to the administration of the Wu emperors for many years. One of their retainers was Yang Xi (Yang Hsi), who between 364 and 370 received a number of visions from a group of perfected immortals or *zhenren* (*chen-jen*) living in the Shangqing (Shang-ch'ing), "Supreme Purity," heaven. These visions were addressed to his employers Xu Mi (Hsü Mi) and his youngest son Xu Hui (Hsü Hui). Yang's visions resulted in a radical new interpretation of the older Celestial Masters' tradition, along with the generation of a voluminous new religious literature, which, apocalyptic in nature, held that the world was going to end in 392.

The world of the Maoshan revelations was not an optimistic one. The present time (fourth century)—so Yang informed his employers—was a time of trial; and presiding over these trials were the demonic residents of the Six Heavens or *liutian* (*liu t'ien*), who were scourging the earth with war, pestilence, and the worship of false gods. Eventually, the whole earth would be cleansed of the evildoers who plagued it. However, those who were virtuous would be saved. They would be sheltered in great caverns that existed beneath China's sacred mountains such as Maoshan. There, this remnant of humanity would perfect its studies in immortality and prepare for the coming of Lord Li Hong, who would usher in a new utopian age of peace and prosperity. Needless to say, the Xu were slated for high office in the new dispensation and would rule over a renewed world peopled by the elect.

Such a bare outline of the new sect's basic philosophy does little justice to the work of Yang Xi, whose artistic talent gave the new faith a corpus of literature remarkable for its consistency and high literary form. In addition to earlier Daoist

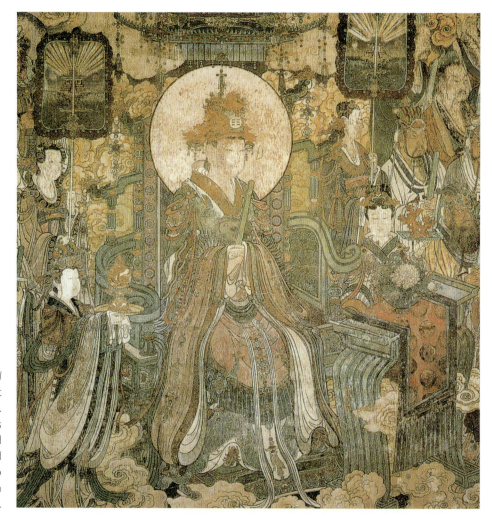

Detail from *A Celestial Court Audience*, Daoist temple at Yongle, c. 1325 C.E. Many Daoists saw the invisible world as being organised along similar lines to those found on earth in the Imperial court.

ideas and concepts garnered from indigenous southeastern Chinese religious traditions, Yang Xi also displays a clear understanding of Buddhism, especially with regard to the concepts of the action of karma and reincarnation. Indeed, one of the texts that he produced was a Daoist version of a Buddhist scripture, the *Sutra in Forty-Two Sections*, that had been translated into Chinese at an early date. One of the distinguishing hallmarks of Maoshan Daoism is its all-inclusive nature that attempted to assimilate and synthesize all the diverse spiritual currents abroad at the time of its inception.

The school was particularly concerned with moral purity. Consequently, considerable emphasis was placed on eliminating those elements of earlier traditions that were now seen as being objectionable. Of special concern to the practitioners of Maoshan Daoism was the suppression of the Union Of Breaths ritual. This was practiced by the Celestial Masters cult on each new moon and seems to have been a communal sexual ritual based on the linkage of agricultural and human fertility, an idea widespread among the world's early agricultural societies. In the Maoshan tradition, it was stigmatized and replaced with a more spiritual union with a celestial partner conjured up in the minds of the faithful through meditation. Other Celestial Masters' rituals were retained, but relegated to a minor position in Maoshan thinking. This tendency toward all-inclusiveness was very pronounced in Maoshan Daoism, where all strands of the tradition, including alchemy, were incorporated and transfigured in the light of the new revelation. This had some unforeseen effects. For example, the younger Xu probably died from ingesting an alchemical elixir of immortality, which had the opposite effect from that desired.

Maoshan Daoism found many adherents, but some thought that it had not gone far enough down the road of purifying Daoism of undesirable elements and practices. The next phase of Daoism's southern development is attributed to yet another member of the Ge family, Ge Chaofu (Ko Ch'ao-fu), who flourished at the beginning of the fifth century C.E. In 397, he began composing the *Classic of the Sacred Jewel* or *Lingbaojing* (*Ling-pao Ching*). Claiming that it had been revealed originally to the famous Ge Xuan, Ge Chaofu created a series of texts in which the Dao is personified through the medium of a series of *tianzun* (*t'ien-tsun*), "celestial worthies." These beings were worshipped in a series of complex liturgies that came to absorb the simple older rituals of the Celestial Masters. Since each of these "worthies" incarnated a different aspect of the Dao, each ritual had a specific goal that was reached through specific means. These rituals were known collectively as *zhai* (*chai*) or "retreats." They lasted from one to seven days and were presided over by a group of up to six officiants.

One of the most important of these retreats was associated with a person's ancestors. Known as the Retreat of the Yellow Register or *huanglu zhai* (*huang-lu chai*), it took place in the open air at an altar specially designated for that purpose. It was seen as the most effective way of ensuring the salvation of the dead. Similar rituals included the Retreat of the Golden Register, designed to promote the good luck and prosperity of the living; and the Mud and Soot Retreat, which was a rite of collective contrition meant for the aversion of punishment through confession and repentance.

As time went on, the Lingbao school of Daoism increased its influence in southern China. By the fifth century C.E., influential leaders such as Lu Xiujing had established important cult centers at such places as Lushan in Jiangsu province and at Qiongxu Guan (Ch'iung-hsü Kuan) in the capital city of Nanking. Despite the persecution of Daoism that took place in 504, it continued to thrive in southern China, with the Maoshan and Lingbao schools dominating the scene. One master,

Dao Hongjing (T'ao Hung-ching), who flourished in the last decades of the fifth century, established a state Daoist cult that attempted to synthesize Lingbao ritualism with the individual religious practices of the Maoshan school, and this pattern of synthesis came to predominate in southern Daoism.

Daoism in Northern China

Northern China presents a somewhat different pattern of development conditioned by the very different political realities that existed there. Here, rulership was vested

□	capitals of China from 4th century BCE
—	border of Zhou China, c.550BCE
▨	border of Han China, 206-220 BCE
⊔⊔⊔	Great Wall under the Han
▬	border of Qing China, 1644-1911CE
▨	countries with Confucian/Neo-Confucian presence/influence
▨	regions with Cao Dai
🛕	important Confucian temples
◇	important Confucian academies
—	modern borders

Important Chinese temples in South and Southeast Asia. The Chinese Diaspora from their homeland has resulted in the eatablishment of a number of important temple complexes outside China, particularly in Southeast Asia.

in foreign dynasties that were primarily concerned with dominating the vast mass of Han Chinese over whom they ruled. In 415, Kou Qianzhi (K'ou Ch'ien-chih) received a new revelation from Laozi in which he was designated a Celestial Master and ordered to reform the degenerate Daoism of his time. He was instructed to suppress all popular messianic movements and to purge Daoism of the abuses, such as sexual rituals and taxes used in supporting priests, that had corrupted the school. This program appealed to the king of the state of Northern Wei, whom Kou had recognized as the incarnation of a Daoist deity and who supported his reforms wholeheartedly. Kou was placed in charge of the religious affairs of the state and Daoism was made the state religion. Unfortunately, with Kou's death in 448, Daoism's preeminence in northern China was lost.

As China threw off the foreign yoke, and indigenous dynasties reunited the country, Daoism's prospects revived. The founder of the Tang dynasty which presided over what was perhaps the most glorious period of art and learning that China ever enjoyed, claimed direct descent from none other than Laozi himself. It is not surprising, therefore, that Daoism flourished during the reigns of the Tang emperors. Candidates for government office not only needed a comprehensive knowledge of Confucianism, but of Daoist texts such as the *Daodejing* as well.

Maoshan Daoism dominated the religious life of the period, particularly after the suppression of Buddhism in 845. Through their rites of initiation, the Maoshan school built up powerful connections with the ruling elites of the empire. Daoist texts proliferated widely, and the treasure trove of texts found in this century at Tunhuang in western China contains a large selection of the Daoist texts extant during this period. Copies of the *Daodejing* circulated far outside the borders of China at this time, with copies being sent to Tibet and the king of Kashmir, who had it translated into Sanskrit. Texts of both philosophical Daoism and Daoist religion penetrated into Korea and Japan in the seventh century C.E. and were to have considerable impact on the religious life of those countries as well.

A Daoist funeral. One of the major functions of Daoist priests was to conduct funeral rituals that would assure the deceased a favourable position in the afterlife.

With the fall of the Tang dynasty in 906, Daoism entered another period of change. Under the Song (960–1279) and the foreign Mongol Yuan dynasty (1279–1368), Daoism faced new challenges. Despite this, the Celestial Masters movement gained a new lease on life and was transformed into the Xin Zhenyi (Hsin Cheng-I) or New Orthodox Unity school. After the fall of the Song, breakaway sects of Daoism proliferated in both the north and the south, germinating as a result of the harsh rule of the foreign Mongol regime. One group, the Chuanzhen (Ch'uan-chen) or Perfect Realization school, gained the favorable attention of the Yuan rulers and, heavily influenced by Buddhist practices, established a series of monasteries populated by celibate monks, of which those of the White Cloud Monastery of Beijing were the most famous. This trend toward syncretism with Buddhism, as well as with Confucianism, continued with the establishment of the Pure and Luminous Way of Loyalty and Filial Obedience school, as well as the Three Religion school.

Daoism continues to have considerable influence on the Chinese religious mind. The philosophical texts of the religion still command a wide and varied readership, and the Daoist religions still flourish. In 1949, Zhang Enbu (Chang En-pu), the sixty-third patriarch of the Celestial Masters and a direct descendant of the founder, decided to flee Communist rule on the mainland and go to Taiwan. The movement transferred there intact, and Daoist priests or **daoshi** (*tao shih*) with their distinctive dress are still in evidence on the island. The liturgy of medieval times is still chanted, and there have been great activities since the 1960s in temple building and restoration. Meanwhile, Daoism is reasserting itself on the Chinese mainland as the old state philosophy of Maoist Communism begins to lose the allegiance of the common people. This, in addition to the continued vitality of the tradition in all the areas of the world where the Chinese have settled, suggests that Daoist religion and rituals will continue to be an integral part of Chinese culture into the foreseeable future.

CHAPTER EIGHTEEN

Confucius and the Origins of Confucianism

Of all the philosophies of China, the one that has had the greatest impact on the development of Chinese civilization is, without a doubt, Confucianism. But Confucianism did not appear fully formed from the mind of its founder, nor was it immediately embraced by the Chinese people. Rather, Confucianism was for many years only one of a number of competing ideologies—and not the most successful one at that. Only under the Han dynasty did Confucianism become the official state ideology in 136 B.C.E., and even then there were nearly two thousand years of development and change ahead of it.

Chinese History from Zhou to Qin

As with all the great philosophies of China, with the exception of the foreign faith of Buddhism, Confucianism was the product of the Warring States period. The first three hundred years of the reign of the Zhou rulers who succeeded the Shang dynasty seem to have been a period of relative stability and peace. But as the strength of the Zhou dynasty declined, its vassals began to become more and more independent. Eventually, even though the Zhou remained nominally on the throne, China disintegrated into a welter of small states, each competing with the others for control of China. As we have seen, it was within this context of political confusion, social unrest, and economic uncertainty that the great ideologies of China developed. Consequently, it is first necessary to understand the events of this period in some detail if we are to grasp the major themes of Confucius's thought.

The process of state absorption began to reduce the number of petty states—numbering some sixteen separate ones at the time of Confucius—in northern China. By about 360 B.C.E., the state of Qin had begun to emerge as the strongest state in the area. The reason for this was that Qin, from which we get the name "China," completely reorganized itself during this period with the sole aim of increasing its effectiveness as a military state. Economic reforms made Qin attractive to the peasantry, who began to migrate to the state and thus increase its agricultural potential. As the population grew, Qin, aided by its favorable position to the south and west of the great bend of the Yellow River and by extremely fertile soil, was able to mobilize greater and greater armies. These armies were governed by a harsh code that lavishly rewarded success and savagely punished failure. Noble birth ceased to be the major criterion for advancement in the government, being replaced by an emphasis on talent.

By 325 B.C.E., Qin had become so powerful that its ruler could flout the conventions of China and the authority of the Zhou dynasty and style himself king (*wang*) instead of the previously used title of duke. In 300 B.C.E., Qin began to build a wall to defend itself from the raids of the nomads on its western borders. Eventually about a hundred thousand people would be employed in its building, and it would become known to subsequent generations as the Great Wall of China. In 285 B.C.E., Qin began to complete its assimilation of the other states of northern China; and by 221 B.C.E., King Zheng, the ruler of Qin, controlled the whole region and declared himself Qinshi huangdi (Ch'in-shih huang-ti)—the First Emperor of Qin.

The period of the first true unification of China under an imperial system is important in that many of the cultural norms that were to govern Chinese society henceforth were established during this period. Law, writing, weights and measures, and currency were all standardized. A nonhereditary bureaucracy governing a centrally organized state was established, with its members being chosen, at least theoretically, on the basis of merit. The Civil Service and the military were designed to maintain checks and balances on each other, and the rule of law became paramount within the empire. Unfortunately, the laws of Qin were established according to the tenets of Legalism. Consequently, they were of such severity that opposition to the ruling dynasty surfaced almost immediately. Several assassination attempts were made against the First Emperor, and rebellion destroyed the dynasty completely during the reign of his son.

But a pattern had been established that was to persist. Despite the hatred that most Chinese felt for the first dynasty of Qin, later rulers adopted many of the ideas introduced by its rulers. However, the Han dynasty that succeeded them realized that the philosophy of Legalism was untenable as the official ideology of the state and that a change was necessary. The solution that the Han emperors arrived at was to make the doctrines of Confucius the official creed of their empire. With only a few periods of disruption, Confucianism was to maintain its intellectual ascendancy over the official class of China up to the abolition of the imperial system in 1912. This is not to say that at various times in Chinese history, there were not elements of the intelligentsia that were bitterly opposed to Confucianism and its values. Particularly after the fall of the empire many Chinese intellectuals turned to other systems of thought as the remedy for China's woes. But at least some elements of Confucian thought and morals had penetrated so deeply into the fabric of Chinese society that even today to be Chinese is, in some sense at least, to be Confucian.

Confucius: The Life of a Cultural Prototype

A considerable amount of solid biographical material on Confucius has come down to us, but it must be treated with care. Given his subsequent importance to Chinese culture, it is not surprising that later chroniclers of the life of Kung Zhongni (Kung Chung-ni) or Kung Fuzi (K'ung fu-tzu)—Confucius's family name (this Latin form was coined by sixteenth-century Jesuits) and an honorific title in Chinese—should endeavor to ascribe to him the most elevated pedigree possible. It was generally held that Confucius was descended from the Zhou royal family through the dukes of

Song. However, none of the early sources mention Confucius's father. Later sources seem to indicate that he was a famous warrior of the period, and this, combined with the allegedly humble economic circumstances of Confucius's youth, suggest that he was not the descendant of any particularly eminent lineage.

Concerning the man himself, we know that he was a citizen of the medium-sized state of Lu, located near the eastern coast of China. The traditional date of his birth is either 552 or 551 B.C.E. In the *Analects* (IX, 6, p. 35), he himself observes of his youth that, "[w]hen young, I was in humble circumstances, and therefore I acquired much ability to do the simple things of humble folks." Likewise his later disciple Mencius records in the *Mencius* (VB, 5) that, "Confucius was once a minor official in charge of stores. He said, 'all I have to do is to keep correct records.' He was once a minor official in charge of sheep and cattle. He said, 'All I have to do is to see to it that the sheep and cattle grow up to be strong and healthy.'" His humble origins notwithstanding, Confucius made a determined effort to master the classical culture of his day, and in 525 B.C.E. he was called to attend a visiting ruler from another state in order to instruct him on ancient government practices. His reputation as a teacher would seem to date from about this time. His renown increased in 518 B.C.E., when the de facto ruler of Lu, Meng Xizi (Meng Hsi-tzu), engaged him to tutor his sons in the proper ritual etiquette to be observed at the great state religious ceremonies. Shortly after this, Confucius began a peripatetic life, moving from one northern Chinese court to another, in the hope that one of these rulers would adopt his ideas and make them the basis of state policy. Unfortunately, this was never to happen in his lifetime, although some of his disciples were to achieve significant office in Lu and elsewhere. In 502 B.C.E., he returned to Lu.

On his return to Lu, Confucius was not immediately offered any government appointment at all. Apparently, he was later appointed to the relatively minor post of *sikou* (*ssu-k'ou*) or police commissioner. It is likely, however, that this post was a mere sinecure. In 498 B.C.E., Confucius was again on the road, this time traveling to

Celebrating Confucius's birthday. Despite his humble beginnings, Confucius's thought had a decisive effect on the subsequent development of Chinese civilisation.

the kingdom of Wei. The reason for this departure, according to Mencius, was set out as follows:

> Confucius was the police commissioner of Lu, but his advice was not followed. He took part in a sacrifice, but, afterwards, was not given a share of the meat of the sacrificial animal. He left the state without waiting to take off his ceremonial cap. Those who did not understand him thought he acted in this way because of the meat, but those who understood him realized that he left because Lu failed to observe the proper rites. For his part, Confucius preferred to be slightly at fault in thus leaving rather than to leave for no reason at all. The doings of a gentleman are naturally above the understanding of the ordinary man.
>
> SOURCE: Dobson (trans.), *Mencius* (Toronto: University of Toronto Press, 1963), p. 176

Whether or not Confucius left on a matter of principle or in a fit of pique, he now undertook a period of travel that seems to have lasted until 484 B.C.E. Sometimes his representations were merely ignored; sometimes, as in the state of Song, they were met with outright antagonism. Confucius's travels were at times harrowing. In the state of Chen, he and his followers seem to have actually been in danger of starving to death, probably as the result of the state of Wu's invasion of Chen at this time. In Song, the rival philosopher Huan Sima (Huan Ssu-ma) plotted to kill him, and he had to flee the state precipitately. Finally, Confucius abandoned his hopes of preferment from foreign potentates and returned to Lu, never to leave it again.

It may be that after his return to Lu, Confucius was again granted official rank, but if so, it was as a counselor of the lowest order. By this time approaching the age of seventy, he occupied himself by editing the five great classical texts from antiquity. These were the *Shujing* (*Shu Ching*), the *Classic of History*; the *Shijing* (*Shih Ching*), the *Classic of Poetry*; the *Yijing* (*I Ching*), the *Classic of Changes*; the *Lijing* (*Li Ching*), the *Classic of Rites*; and the *Chunqiu* (*Ch'un Ch'iu*), the *Spring and Autumn Annals*. These books were considered to be seminal by later Confucian scholars, and formed the basis for all subsequent Confucian studies along with such specifically Confucian books as the *Analects* and the *Mencius*. Confucius died in 479 B.C.E. Later traditions were to elevate him and his accomplishments far beyond anything that the philosopher himself ever claimed to have achieved. In later texts, he is said to have been, among other things, the prime minister of Lu, a rank that he certainly never achieved in life. But Confucius's legacy was secure. It lay not in what he achieved in his lifetime, but the transformative effect that his ideas were to have on an entire civilization.[1]

The Texts and Doctrines of Early Confucianism

The core text of Confucianism is the *Analects* or *Sayings*—the *Lunyu* (*Lun-yü*) of Confucius.[2] The philosopher seems to have never committed his own ideas to writing. Rather, he conveyed them through the medium of discussions with his students, in much the same manner as his near-contemporary Socrates did in Greece. Confucius based his entire system of thought on three basic presuppositions. The first was that the most worthwhile goal to which a human being could aspire was to become the most morally evolved person possible. For Confucius, such a goal was a good thing in itself, rather than a mere stepping stone to other things. He made no pretense that a person who pursued this goal of moral perfection would necessarily reap any material or spiritual reward in this life or the next—the only value of pursuing it was its own attainment. The second of Confucius's presuppositions was that when people were shown the correct way to act, they would act that way, no matter what their innate nature might be in itself. The third was that since the family unit was the fundamental building block of human society, a person who had been trained to interact properly with his or her family would, in Confucius's estimation, inevitably act correctly in all other social relationships.

Confucius warned his disciples not to expect any supernatural rewards or assistance in this life. The *Analects* (II, 11, p. 36) records a dialogue with a student on this question: "Chi-lu (Tzu-lu) asked about serving the spiritual beings. Confucius said, 'If we are not yet able to serve man, how can we serve spiritual beings?' 'I venture

Bells likely used for court ceremonies. Confucianism saw rituals as one of the best ways for individuals to cultivate personal virtues and reenforce communal mores.

to ask about death.' Confucius said, 'If we do not yet know about life, how can we know about death?'" Should we infer from this passage that Confucius was an atheist? Probably not. It is more likely that he believed in the existence of the various spiritual entities in much the same way as anyone else in his time. But in Confucius's opinion, the world of the spirits differed so very much from the physical world that it was effectively separate from it. The rituals that Confucius advocated might or might not have a supernatural effect, but what was certain was that they had an improving effect on the moral character of those who performed them with reverence. All cause-and-effect morality was questionable in Confucius's opinion, and the moral human being might very well see no discernible reward for his or her efforts at all.

Confucius realized that "goodness," the goal of moral perfection, came by degrees. This meant that at any given time, a broad spectrum of moral behavior could coexist amongst different people in society. The epitome of moral development was personified by the *shengren* (*sheng-jen*), the sage. This elevated rank was seldom seen, and Confucius denied the title to any living person, including himself. Lower down the scale was the *shanren* (*shan-jen*), the good man, and then the *chengren* (*ch'eng-jen*), the complete man. Both these types were also rare. In everyday life, the most morally evolved individual that one was likely to meet was the **junzi** (*chün-tzu*), the gentleman (literally, "the son of the prince"). Finally, there were the *xiaoren* (*hsiao-jen*), those people whose grasp and application of moral principles was extremely tenuous and who needed the instruction and examples of their betters in order to behave in a proper manner. It must be remembered, however, that Confucius believed that everyone, including the *xiaoren*, was capable of improvement, but only at the cost of considerable hard work and constant application.

All this hard work was designed to cultivate a clearly defined set of Confucian virtues. The most fundamental of these was **ren** (*jen*). Like many pivotal religio-philosophical terms, *ren* is a slippery concept that is very difficult to translate into other languages. The most common English translation of it is "humanity," but other terms such as "human-heartedness," and "compassion" have been used. No term is completely satisfactory in itself, but "compassion" comes close to what Confucius had in mind when he employed it. He believed that the essence of this virtue was that you should not do to others what you did not want done to yourself (compare *Analects* XII, 2 and XV, 23). Essential to this is the practice of *shu* (reciprocity) and *zhong* (*chung*), loyalty to oneself and one's superiors.

One way that Confucius saw of cultivating these virtues was through the medium of ritual (**li**). As we have seen, ritual for Confucius had little or nothing to do with the efficacy of religious observances in themselves. Rather, Confucius saw ritual as promoting social cohesion and individual morality. Communal rituals gave people a sense of continuity with the past, a common focus in the present, and a sense of group goals for the future. As such, they provided one of the strongest forms of social "glue" that helped to overcome the natural human tendency to favor the individual's, or at most the individual's immediate group's, interests over the common good of the society at large. Consequently, ritual was one of the most important vehicles for the Confucian virtues and a vital training ground for their development.

In addition to *ren*, the gentleman needed two other virtues—*zhi* (*chih*) or wisdom, and *yong* (*yung*) or courage. Wisdom meant for Confucius not only the command of facts, although Confucius certainly valued intellectual knowledge as such, but rather an understanding of human nature. For Confucius, the most random element in human existence was human nature itself. Only through a deep knowledge of human nature, garnered painfully over many years, could the gentleman have even the slightest hope of predicting the course of events and thus influencing them. To accomplish this, one must, first and foremost, be honest with oneself. As Confucius observed to a student, "Yu, shall I teach you [the way to acquire knowledge]? To say that you know when you do know and say that you do not know when you do not know—that is [the way to acquire] knowledge" (*Analects*, II, 17, p. 24).

Likewise, the gentleman must possess courage. As Confucius observes, "To see what is right and not to do it is cowardice" (*Analects*, II, 24, p. 24). Indeed, Chinese history has numerous examples of virtuous officials who opposed the will of the emperor on moral grounds and lost their lives as a result. Nevertheless, Confucius did not make the mistake of assuming that courage in itself led to *ren*. "A benevolent (*jen*) man," he noted, "is sure to possess courage, but a courageous man does not necessarily possess *jen*" (*Analects*, XIV, 4). Confucius knew that courage needed to be tempered with other virtues if it was to lead to real moral improvement.

Finally, the Confucians recognized three more primary virtues: trustworthiness or *xin* (*hsin*); reverence or *jing* (*ching*); and **xiao** (*hsiao*) or filiality—or, as it is also known, filial piety. *Xin* was the virtue of keeping one's word, of doing what one had undertaken to do. But the concept had deeper implications than that. For example, one had an obligation not to say something that might not be true, even if it seemed to be true at the moment. Thus true Confucians were very sparing with their words, since they did not wish to say anything that was untrue or might

Offerings to the Ancestors on *Ch'ing Ming*. One of the core principles of Confucianism is respect for one's parents and other ancestors not only in this world, but after their death as well.

become untrue. In general, Confucius advised that "the superior man wants to be slow in words, but diligent in actions" (*Analects*, IV, 24, p. 28). *Jing*, reverence, is roughly equivalent to what is termed in Christianity (rather misleadingly) as "fear of the Lord." Here the word "fear" is much better translated as "awe," that feeling of tremendous importance or gravity that some people or situations engender. For Christians, this supposedly comes from a sense of the presence of God. For Confucians, such emotions were associated with the awareness of the immensity of one's responsibilities toward both one's ancestors and promoting the welfare of the common people. *Xiao* was to show one's parents, and by extension one's ancestors, the devotion and obedience that both their seniority and position in the family deserved.

The virtues of *ren, shu, zhong, zhi, yong, xin, jing*, and *xiao* were all developed within the framework of the five Confucian relationships, which in turn defined the concept of *yi*—duty. These relationships were those between parent and child; between elder and younger siblings; between husband and wife; between ruler and subject; and between friends. With the exception of the last of these relationships, all of them were unequal, with one person being naturally dominant over the other. Both sides, however, were bound by rights and obligations. Moreover, each relationship was linked with all the other relationships. For Confucius it followed naturally that if certain people were good and obedient children, then they must inevitably be good subjects to their ruler, good husbands or wives, and loyal friends.

The fundamental organic relationship in Confucius's thought was that between parent and child. The essence of this relationship was *xiao* (filiality). By this Confucius meant that children, by virtue of the care given to them by their parents, had an unconditional duty of obedience and respect for them. This, of course, was based on the tacit assumption that parents would treat their children with love and consideration. Likewise, one owed one's elder siblings the duty of respect or *ti* (*t'i*). Both these relationships within families took precedence over all other obligations; and even today, the family forms the fundamental social unit in Chinese society and societies based on the Chinese model, such as those found in Vietnam, Korea, and Japan. Of course, these relationships only worked if both sides faithfully observed their part of the bargain. This in turn led to the Confucian concept of *zhenming* (*cheng-ming*) or the "rectification of names." By this, Confucius meant that it was not enough for a man simply to be called a father and receive the respect due to that position—he must actually function as a father. If rectification of names had indeed taken place, then there would be no dissonance between theory and reality. The negative side of this emphasis on the family lies in the fact that the social bonds become progressively weaker the farther one moves from the center of the family unit. This problem, despite the best efforts of Confucian philosophers to extend their core principles to the level of the nation state, has plagued Chinese rulers for millennia and hindered their efforts to establish complex administrative structures. As a result, considerable consideration has been given to ways of binding small groups together into larger units with significant cohesive ties.

All these virtues were centered in the primary concern for the continuation of the state as the guardian of human culture. Confucius subscribed very strongly to the concept of *tianming*, the Mandate of Heaven, even though the term itself is found only twice in the *Analects*. For Confucius, however, the Mandate of Heaven was not simply applicable to the emperor. Each individual was in some sense subject to the decrees of heaven. Certain things were brought about by destiny, not by human agency. This being the case, the reflective individual realized that many things were beyond his or her control. This made it all the more imperative that people, if they were to give their lives real meaning in the existential sense of the word, concentrated on those things, such as personal morality and individual development, that they could influence.

Private morality needed to find expression in public service. As Confucius's disciple Zixia observed, "A man who has energy to spare after study should serve his state. A man who has energy to spare after serving his state should study" (*Analects*, XIX, 13, p. 48). The obligation to engage in government was compelling for the earnest Confucian, but so too was the obligation to abstain from government office if policies contrary to Confucian principles were undertaken by the state's rulers. The goal of government service was to improve the lot of the common people. When asked about how this could best be accomplished, Confucius replied that good government resulted in "sufficient food, sufficient armament, and sufficient confidence of the people" (*Analects*, XII, 7, p. 39). While the common people could not be coddled if the state was to survive and prosper, Confucius felt that their general welfare was the state's paramount duty and, by extension, the paramount duty of the Confucian gentleman.

In keeping with this general principle and his understanding of the limited perfectibility of human nature, Confucius opposed rule by severe laws and draconian punishments. As he noted, "Lead the people with governmental measures and regulate them by law and punishment, and they will avoid wrong-doing but will have no sense of honor and shame. Lead them with virtue and regulate them by the rules of propriety (*li*), and they will have a sense of shame and, moreover, set themselves right" (*Analects*, II, 3, p. 22). How was this to be accomplished without a detailed law code? It was by the moral example of the gentleman. "If a ruler," said Confucius, "sets himself right, he will be followed without his command. If he does not set himself right, even his commands will not be obeyed" (*Analects*, XIII, 6, p. 41).

For a man to be sufficiently cultured to take office and serve as a moral exemplar for the common people, it was necessary that he cultivate *wen*, which, in its original meaning, refers to a type of pattern that was impressed or engraved on pottery. It came to mean an adornment or ornament and, by extension, good breeding and culture. Just as the clay of a pot, no matter how fine a material it was in itself, needed to be worked by human hands if a beautiful pattern was to emerge on it, so too did human beings need to be shaped through long and hard work if they were to become cultured. One may have a natural capacity for proper action (acquired, Confucius would argue, from the efforts of one's parents), but if one lacked the knowledge to put that capacity into action, nothing significant would be accomplished. Conversely, simply to go through the motions without sincerity was unacceptable as well. A combination of the two was necessary.

Confucius did not despise any form of knowledge, but he tended to privilege certain forms that seemed to him to have the broadest applicability in developing human potential. His beliefs in this matter diverge widely from the commonly held ideas of contemporary Euro-American culture. Confucius did not believe in a narrow technical education designed to fit the individual for a single form of employment. The gentleman was not, he scornfully observed, a mere tool fit only for one task. Rather, the gentleman's education should train him in making moral judgments consistent with the ideals and mores of his society in any situation. This was done by immersing the gentleman in the finest cultural products of that society, such as art, music, and literature, and exposing him to the historical development of the society through the study of past events. Ideally, this would result in a person who could make the proper judgments about future developments in the society and implement them with the help of technicians trained in specific occupations.

Confucius saw a very close correlation between beauty, truth, and goodness—concepts that he shared with his near contemporary, Plato. Indeed, the search for their true essence was imperative if one were to grasp fully the essence of reality and modify one's behavior and attitudes accordingly. For Confucius, beauty, truth, and goodness overlapped and illuminated one another. The manifestation of these primary philosophical values within a society could be discerned through a careful study of its cultural products such as music and poetry. This process was *xue* (*hsüeh*) or learning. For Confucius, learning meant initially committing the material being studied to memory—only then could one reflect on it at leisure. When the material was safely stored in the memory, the student could begin to draw comparisons and conclusions from it as a whole, rather than as individual blocks of information, and so arrive at what we today would call "the big picture." On this process, Confucius noted, "He who learns but does not think is lost; he who thinks but does not learn is in danger" (*Analects*, II, 15, p. 24). It is only after this process of acquisition and intellectual digestion is completed that people are in a position to put into practice what has been learned in a reasoned and coherent manner, thus transforming both themselves and, ultimately, their society.

Website References

1. The life of Confucius is examined at **www.confucius.org.uk/**

2. The *Analects* are translated at
   www.human.toyogakuen-u.ac.jp/~acmuller/contao/analects.htm

CHAPTER NINETEEN

Early Confucianism and its Rivals

After the death of Confucius, the school of thought that he founded began to develop in different ways. The basic doctrines of the school were elaborated in such texts as the *Great Learning* and the *Doctrine of the Mean*. But undoubtedly the most influential text of this first period of Confucian elaboration was the *Mencius* of Meng Ke Zi (whose name the early Jesuit missionaries to China rendered into Latin as Mencius).[1]

Mencius

About Mencius himself, we have very little real biographical material. We think that he was born in what is now Shandong province and that he lived between approximately 371 and 289 B.C.E. He studied with disciples of Confucius's grandson and seems to have spent much of his life as a professional teacher of Confucianism. Like his revered master, he spent much of large periods of his life moving from court to court in China, trying to persuade various rulers to implement his program of moral and political reform. He appears to have served as an official for several years in the court of Qi, but he resigned this position to enable him to perform the requisite three years of mourning when his mother died. Beyond this scant information we cannot reliably go, and it seems particularly meager in light of the fact that Mencius's considerable influence on the development of Confucian thought is second only to Confucius himself.

Mencius began his analysis of the human condition from the standpoint that human beings were essentially good. This viewpoint has traditionally always been attributed to Confucius, but in point of fact Confucius seems to have paid little attention to the question of the basic nature of human beings. His primary concern was the end product of the human developmental process, rather than its beginnings. For Mencius, however, the study of the foundations of human behavior formed the indispensable basis on which he would erect the entire framework of his system of thought. In doing so, he elaborated on many ideas that had been only lightly touched on in the *Analects*, and discussed many fundamental questions that were not even considered in that earlier text. Consequently, it can be confidently asserted that subsequent Confucian philosophy is as much the thought of Mencius as it is of Confucius. In later years, the *Mencius*, along with the *Analects*, the *Doctrine of the Mean*, and the *Great Learning*, became a core set text for those wishing to pass the official government examinations that led to power and prestige in Chinese society. No book in Euro-American society—with the obvious exception of the Bible—has ever exercised such a decisive effect on its society as the *Mencius* did on China.

Mencius's entire philosophical program revolved around his concept of **xin** (*hsin*)—the heart or mind. By this, he did not mean the organ that pumps blood to the body, but rather the emotions and cognitive abilities that distinguish human beings from animals. This is not to say that Mencius did not recognize that the human constitution contained many components inherited from the animal. But Mencius believed that these drives need not rule the human being, and that a person could rise above them and become their master, not their slave. By exercising the thinking and discerning powers of *xin*, one could avoid being drawn blindly to the instinctual objects of desires. But this human capacity, denied to lower forms of life, was only effective when it was exercised; and it could only be effectively exercised after a rigorous course of training.

What, then, were the characteristics of *xin* upon which Mencius based all of his subsequent thinking? Mencius identified four primary characteristics. The first of these was what he termed "the heart of shame." By this he meant the human capacity to reflect morally on one's actions. This sense of right and wrong was essential to any subsequent moral development. As Mencius observed, "Only when a man will not do some things is he capable of doing great things" (IVB, 8). A sense of shame not only resulted in moral development, but also the development of ambition, for "If a man is not ashamed of being inferior to other men, how will he ever become their equal?" (VIIA, 7).

Next, there was the "heart of right and wrong." This concept had two meanings for Mencius. First, it referred to the human capacity to distinguish between what was right and what was wrong. Second, it referred to the active and conscious acceptance of the "right," and a concurrent active and conscious rejection of the "wrong." Mencius would concur wholeheartedly with the sentiment that evil triumphs when good people do nothing, and with Confucius's dictum that to know what was right and not to do it was cowardice. Here the sense of shame played an integral part in a person's recognition of his or her own moral failures, and in the development of the desire to do better. But the individual's development did not take place in a vacuum, but rather within the matrix of society. Consequently, for social interactions to proceed harmoniously, it was necessary to possess the "heart of courtesy and modesty." Modesty prevented one from claiming credit unduly, and courtesy involved yielding to the desires of others. Obviously, this system of human interaction would only function properly when everyone involved in the system acted in a similar manner. Since this scenario seldom, if ever, came about, this "heart" might be seen as being more theoretical than practical. But like the concept of world peace in our own day, it represented an ideal to be sought after and a goal to be aimed at by the true Confucian.

These three "hearts" find their fullest collective expression in the fourth, "heart of compassion." It is on this innate natural tendency, whereby we find the suffering of others unbearable, that Mencius based his contention that human beings are by nature good. This is not to say that he felt that all humans possessed an equal measure of this "heart"—the compassion of Mother Teresa could not be compared to the compassion of Adolf Hitler. But Mencius felt that every human being possessed at least the germ of compassion, and that this germ of compassion gives rise to the other "hearts." As he observed in a famous passage of the *Mencius*: (IIA, 6, p. 65)

> When I say that all men have the mind [heart] which cannot bear to see the suffering of others, my meaning may be illustrated thus: Now when men suddenly see a child about to fall into a well, they all have a feeling of alarm and distress, not to gain friendship with the child's parents, nor to seek the praise of their neighbors and friends, nor because they dislike the reputation [of lack of humanity if they did not rescue the child]. From such a case, we see that a man without the feeling of [compassion] is not a man; a man without the feeling of shame and dislike is not a man; a man without the feeling of [courtesy and modesty] is not a man; and a man without the feeling of right and wrong is not a man. The feeling of [compassion] is the beginning of humanity [*jen*]. The feeling of shame and dislike is the beginning of righteousness [*yi*]; the feeling of [courtesy and modesty] is the beginning of propriety [*li*]; and the feeling of right and wrong is the beginning of wisdom [*chih*].

> SOURCE: Chan, *A Sourcebook in Chinese Philosophy*, p. 65

All these feelings and the attitudes that they subsequently engender—which we have already encountered as essentially integral components of Confucius's own thought—may be embryonic and wither without cultivation, but they are all present in the human being at birth.

The difference, then, between the "gentleman" and the "small man" lies in the degree to which the individual nourishes and develops the sparks of goodness inherent in his or her nature. Mencius agreed with Confucius that such a quest was at best difficult. He notes that "a man whose mind is set on high ideals never forgets that he may end in a ditch; a man of valor never forgets that he may forfeit his head" (5B:7). This should not be taken to mean that self-interest and morality are necessarily opposed to each other. It is only when self-interest becomes an obstacle to the development of goodness that it must be sacrificed. But in the ordinary course of events, a person has a duty to act prudently and with a modicum of self-interest.

One central problem related to the interaction of self-interest and moral duty that absorbed Mencius was the question of how to prioritize actions. Being in common with most of the Chinese philosophers, a practical man, he recognized that some aspects of human existence were beyond the control of the individual. These things were controlled by *ming*, fate or destiny, which for Mencius included virtually all external material possessions and honors. It followed that the only things that were truly under the individual's control were internal. Consequently, a person's interior capacities were the only things worth discovering and cultivating. Indeed, the real value of the search to find out more about oneself lay more in the search itself than in the objects of the search, although they too were of great value.

But what were the practical parameters of such a search? To understand this, we need to consider briefly the cosmology of Mencius's day. It was generally believed that the universe was composed of *qi*. As in Indian thought, this foundational constituent of the universe was seen as being essentially material. The nature and quality of this material was variable, ranging from being very thin and subtle to the point of invisibility to the gross and dense *qi* that can be perceived. Human beings were a mixture of these two kinds of *qi*. The gross *qi* constituted the body, the subtle *qi* formed the "inner person." Two different interpretations developed in Mencius's time concerning this subtle *qi*. The first held that as one matured, more *qi* could be acquired, and thus the inner person could be developed over the course of one's lifetime. The second interpretation denied this, holding that when the finite fund of *qi* one possessed at birth was exhausted, then death ensued. For those who held this viewpoint, thinking was considered to use up *qi* faster, so it was better to not do it. But Mencius held to the first interpretation, from which evolved his concept of the *hao ran zhi qi*—the "strong, moving power." It was by nourishing this power and augmenting it that moral development was achieved.

Mencius felt very strongly about his ideas and those he had inherited from Confucius. This led him to become one of the greatest controversialists of his day, with many of his writings being polemics against other schools of thought. He was particularly opposed to the teachings of Yang Zhu, and also Mo Zi, whom we will

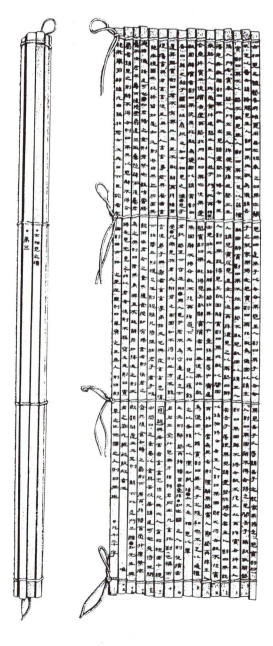

Bamboo Confucian book. Literacy and familiarity with the classical writings of Chinese culture were seen as essential to the development of the Confucian gentleman.

consider in some detail below. Mencius was most incensed by Yang Zhu's thought, which, in some significant senses, can be compared with that of the Hellenistic sage Epicurus. Yang Zhu's system stems from the concept of *weiwo* or egotism. Yang Zhu observed that the only thing that one could be absolutely sure one possessed was one's life. But it did not follow, as the hedonists suggested, that this meant one should sate one's desires before all else. To do this, said Yang Zhu, would be to waste one's life. Since life itself was the greatest good, no matter the circumstances in which it was lived, one should do absolutely nothing to imperil it, either for pleasure or profit.

Mencius opposed Yang Zhu's view because, as he understood it, it implied that individuals should completely turn their backs on society. The famous dictum attributed to Yang Zhu that he would give not one hair of his arm in exchange for the possession of the universe was seen by Mencius as the seed of the destruction of society. Likewise, Mencius saw the Mohist doctrine of universal and equal love for all as destructive of the family, since in his opinion it would lead to the elimination of *xiao* (filiality) and, above all else, the love of one's parents. This in turn would inevitably lead to the total dissolution of society, since Mencius agreed with Confucius that the foundation of all social order lay in the bond between parent and child.

It was from this viewpoint that Mencius began his construction of a political philosophy. Like his predecessor Confucius, Mencius saw rulership as being the manifestation on earth of the will of heaven. The primary function of the ruler was to make concrete on earth heaven's benevolent designs for humanity. It naturally followed for Mencius that the Mandate of Heaven was mutable. Should the ruler fail to carry out his duty toward his subjects, then he could and should be removed. Mencius wrote that, "[in a state] the people are the most important; the spirits of the land and grain (guardians of territory) are the next; the ruler is of slight importance ... When a feudal lord (a ruler) endangers the spirits of the land and grain (territory), he is removed and replaced" (VIIB, 14).

Mencius held the view, also espoused by Abraham Lincoln, that it was impossible for rulers to manipulate the people and hide their defects from them forever. You could fool all the people some of the time, and some of the people all the time, but you could not fool all the people all of the time. People knew when their rulers were governing with their best interests at heart, even if harsh measures were necessary, and when they were not. Again following Confucius, Mencius saw the relationship of the ruler and the ruled as being analogous to that of parent and child. Thus, he believed, perhaps quixotically, that "if the services of the people were used with a view to sparing them hardship, they would not complain even when hard driven. If people were put to death in pursuance of a policy to keep them alive, they would die bearing no ill-will toward the man who put them to death" (VIIA, 12).

For Mencius, the ruler occupied the same place in the body politic as the heart did in the body; so it is not surprising that Mencius saw the ruler as being the single most indispensable member of the state and advocated that he deserved special reverence and privileges. But he was less forbearing toward other members of the government, and particularly toward the military. Confucius, himself possibly the son of a soldier, made no references, slighting or otherwise, to the military. However, Mencius, who saw war as the single most heinous fate that could befall a state, was not so lenient. He recognized that war was sometimes necessary, and felt that if certain strict conditions were met war could be seen as equivalent to criminal punishment and thus justifiable. But in general, he felt that these conditions were seldom, if ever, met, and that most wars were fought for money and personal aggrandizement. He believed that "death is not enough for such a crime [of waging war]. Therefore those who are skillful in fighting should suffer the heaviest punishment"

(IVA, 14, p. 74). This antimilitary bias was increasingly to permeate Chinese society from this point onward.

How, then, can we sum up Mencius's contribution to the history of Confucian thought? First, he addressed fundamental questions, such as the problem of human nature, that had not been sufficiently addressed in Confucius's time. Second, he proposed a theory of human nature that successfully carried Confucian thought to the next level of its development and allowed it to triumph over other systems of thought that vied for influence with it. Third, he initiated the inquiry into the fundamental metaphysics of the universe that later blossomed into the Neo-Confucian synthesis. He accomplished all these goals within the framework of a complex system centered on the concept of the human heart—that is, the interior constituents of human nature. This lent Confucianism a sustainable structural framework. Mencius's work provided later Confucian thinkers with the material to advance Confucian thinking and to defend Confucian ideas from the encroachments of other domestic and foreign thought systems.

Xun Zi

But one should not assume that Mencius's ideas were adopted wholeheartedly by other Confucians without debate. Some, like Xun Zi (Hsün Zi), disagreed with his basic presuppositions; and even though Mencius's ideas became what we might term Confucian orthodoxy, Xun Zi's ideas continued to influence later thinkers—indeed, they seemed destined at first to dominate Confucian discourse. But the flow of events conspired to subtly discredit Xun Zi's philosophical conclusions, and later Confucians tended to rally to the Mencian interpretation of Confucius's thought.

Xun Zi was probably born in about 312 B.C.E., in the central northern state of Zhao (Ch'ao). His early life is obscure, and he does not step into the spotlight of history until he was about fifty. We can assume that this dark period of his life was spent in study and in either government service or teaching, but actual biographical details are lacking. In about 264 B.C.E., he was invited to the court of the state of Qi, where he was initially well received with honors, a government pension, and the king's confidence. However, his success was the envy of others, who slandered him, forcing him to leave Qi for the southern state of Qu (Ch'u). Here he was appointed a magistrate; but when his political patron was assassinated, he was removed from power. By now an old man, Xun Zi chose to remain in his former judicial district of Lanling, in what is now southern Shandong province, and there he died. He was survived by his literary work and by two famous disciples, Han Fei Zi and Li Si (Li Ssu), who subsequently became leading lights of the Legalist school of philosophy, the great nemesis of early Confucianism.

Xun Zi was a scholar of broad knowledge and ecumenical sympathies. Consequently, his philosophy shows marked syncretic leanings. In it are Daoist quietism, Legalist realism, the precision of the Logicians, and numerous other strains of thought. Despite these many different sources of ideas, Xun Zi produced perhaps the most systematic philosophical presentation in the early history of Chinese thought. At its heart were the fundamental Confucian concerns with ethics and politics. But it is the elaboration of these core ideas that makes Xun Zi such a seminal thinker. Most of the later opposition to his ideas arose from a misinterpretation of his fundamental understanding of human nature. In general, we would like to think that Mencius was right when he held that human nature is essentially good. But the opposite position espoused by Xun Zi—that human beings are essentially bad—is equally tenable. Nor should we read too much into either Xun Zi's thesis of human evil or Mencius's thesis of human goodness. Xun Zi did not see human beings as monsters of depravity. Rather, he asserted that, given a choice between doing the right thing in small matters and doing the wrong thing but gaining a profit, people would chose profit. Neither Xun Zi nor Mencius saw the moral nature of human beings as being very pronounced in most cases. The Mother Teresas and Adolf Hitlers of the world occupied the far ends of the spectrum of human morality and were not very abundant. Most of us are clustered in the middle.

But even if Xun Zi believed that people tended toward petty immorality, he had tremendous faith in their ability to reform through study and moral training. Such training was to be completely in the traditional Confucian mode. Through the perusal of classical texts, performance of the rituals, immersion in the fine arts, and contemplation of the successes and failures of Chinese history, a person became fit to take office in the government. But Xun Zi, for all his reliance on traditional Confucian educational models, was something of an innovator in these matters. An example of this is his contention that not only figures from the distant past, but also more recent figures should be used as instructional models. He was no blind believer in a golden age to which China should return. He knew full well that political, social, and economic conditions were always in a state of flux. What he desired, and what he believed that the tried and true Confucian educational program inevitably achieved, was a return to the moral certainly and direction of olden times, not to the social and political conditions of those times *per se*.

Xun Zi advocated political realism. He recognized that the old feudal system was proving inadequate to the needs of the Chinese people of his time. Like Confucius and Mencius, he felt that the people were the ultimate arbiters of the Mandate of Heaven, but that the day-to-day needs of government demanded a single ruler to implement that mandate. The future of government in his time, he believed, lay in strong, central hierarchical government. As a result, his political writings center around the figure of the *ba*, the hegemon. Xun Zi did not ascribe to this figure the moral stature of the true king or emperor. Instead, he seems to have believed that the stable rule of a dictator would produce conditions allowing the rise of such a moral ruler, who would offer not only political stability but moral guidance as well.

One of the more interesting aspects of Xun Zi's thought is his relative antipathy to what we might call religion. He carried this to its logical conclusions when he opposed all beliefs and practices that dealt with the supernatural. He condemned superstition and magic, allowing only grudgingly such time-honored forms of divination as those using the *Yijing*. He denied the existence of evil spirits and held that the primary effects of ritual were on the moral development of the participants, not the supposed recipients of the ritual action. It naturally followed for Xun Zi that any form of speculation that did not lead directly to moral development was essentially a waste of time, and he campaigned assiduously against them.

Mo Zi and Mohism

If Mencius and Xun Zi could be said to agree completely on any one subject, it would be their belief in the pernicious nature of the Mohist school of thought founded by Mo Zi (Mo Tzu). The reason for this was simple. Mo Zi advocated universal love or **jianai** (*chien-ai*). On the face of it, this would not seem to be a bad thing, but rather a necessary principle for advancement to the next level of human moral development. After all, Christianity, like many other religions, teaches that we must love our neighbors as ourselves. But the Confucians thought otherwise. To them, Mohist doctrine shattered the natural relationship that existed within the family by placing family and non-family on an equal basis in the affections of the individual. Thus it threw into question the entire hierarchical balance of society and, from the Confucian point of view, led to anarchy. But nobody attacks something that has no power. Mencius and Xun Zi wrote venomously about Mohism precisely because it appealed to the Chinese of their day. Consequently, it deserves closer examination.

Mo Di Zi, the founder of Mohism, was probably born slightly before Confucius died and flourished between approximately 478 and 438 B.C.E., dying just before the birth of Mencius. His home state was thought to have been either Lu or Song. The latter is more likely, in that his emphasis on economic development and his anti-militarism seem to have been characteristic of prevailing thought in Song during this period. Moreover, when he made his appeal to history, as all Chinese philosophers inevitably did, the period that he looked to was not that of the Zhou but of the semi-mythical Xia (Hsia) who supposedly flourished from about 2183 to 1752 B.C.E. No doubt this was because the Zhou traditions were essentially aristocratic, whereas the traditions of the Xia were supposedly more democratic. Presuming that the Xia existed, as we now are beginning to believe, and that their society was organized on smaller, more corporately ruled units, as would probably have been the case in the Neolithic China of the period, then Mo Zi's presuppositions may not be as unfounded as some later scholars have believed.

One thing that is certain is that Mo Zi's agenda was very different from that of Confucius—even though he might have been a Confucian at the outset of his career and many of his views on economy and religion continued to parallel Confucian views closely. As was the case with other teachers of the period, he peregrinated throughout northern China, looking for a ruler who would implement his philosophy. He was apparently accompanied on these journeys by a band of some three hundred followers sworn to follow his orders to the death. These bands of Mohists became a standard feature of the school. They were organized groups under the direct and absolute control of a leader, even after they had finished their studies, and they contributed a portion of their earnings to the maintenance of their units. Unlike the more aristocratic Confucians, the Mohists seem to have been drawn from all strata of society, including the lowest.

The key concept of Mohism was "universal love" moderated through the influence of asceticism and utilitarianism. Mo Zi strove not for *ren*, but for *yi* (righteousness), which he believed was directly mandated by the will of heaven (*tian*). Thus for Mo Zi, "heaven" played a much more active role than it did for the Confucians. Universal love was defined in his system as a nonhierarchical, uniform regard for all human beings, not simply those close at hand, such as one's family. All of the world's problems, said Mo Zi, came from a lack of love between individuals. One must regard all people as one's self. But we must be clear as to what Mo Zi means by the term "love." He does not mean an emotional state, but rather an intellectual disposition. "Love" stems from an appreciation of the benefits that accrue from mutual cooperation, not from any emotional attachment to individuals. Indeed, such particular attachments must be guarded against and totally extirpated from individuals if they are to develop true universal love. Emotions were dangerous and uncontrollable. It was best to train one's self to have none.

Universal love, like all Mohist doctrines, was always being tested against the Mohist touchstone of utility. Mo Zi opposed certain practices and ideas, not because they were evil in themselves or went against some divinely sanctioned code of conduct, but because they were not useful or profitable (*li*). Only those practices that benefited the realm in a tangible and practical way were to be encouraged. Those practices that did not, such as war, music, and expensive funeral rituals, were to be ruthlessly suppressed. Profit was defined in simple terms—the increase of population and wealth. Anything that increased either of these—such as practicing frugality and eliminating extravagance—was to be encouraged. Another thing that Mo Zi encouraged was religion, not because he had any particular belief in its metaphysical reality or its efficacy, but because it provided a useful and powerful form of social control. He supported the concept of a supreme god, who rewarded good and punished evil, and the idea of lesser gods and spirits who were his agents. Conversely, he strongly opposed the Confucian idea of fate, since it allowed an element of randomness into the conduct of human affairs that totally undermined his entire system.

Mo Zi held to the same basic ideas of government that other philosophers of his day advocated. Just as there was a supreme god in heaven, there should be a supreme ruler on earth, and governmental institutions existed to stave off chaos. Only the emperor could truly apprehend the will of heaven and so must necessarily be the arbiter of all earthly ideas and institutions. In the perfect state, the will of the government would become the will of the people, not vice versa. To deviate from the will of the ruler in the slightest degree was to bring the return of chaos, darkness, and confusion. Everything must be subordinated to the common good as embodied in the state, and, more particularly, in its ruler.[2]

The Legalists

As draconian as the Mohist concept of the absolute power of the ruler sounds to modern Western ears, it found considerable support among the Chinese people, not only as expounded by Mo Zi but also by other schools, of which the most influential was Legalism. In fact, the origins of Legalism (Fajia) can be traced back to Confucian roots, namely the teachings of Xun Zi. As we have seen, Xun Zi held that human nature tended toward the evil rather than the good, as exemplified in the human desire for profit. This desire resulted in strife and misery unless restrained by education and moral discipline. Nor were these negative personality traits ameliorated by beneficent natural influences. The cosmos was neither moral nor immoral, and there were no supernatural forces dedicated to improving the human condition. There was a tendency toward chaos in the tide of human affairs, and it was the duty of the gentleman to oppose this tendency by the institution and application of laws and governmental measures. If such measures had to be enforced by harsh punishments, so be it.

These themes in Xun Zi's thought were taken up and amplified by Han Fei Zi (d. 233 B.C.E.), who might rightly be termed the father of the Legalist school. A prince of the state of Han serving the ruler of Qin who later became the First Emperor of China, Han Fei Zi composed a comprehensive and systematic exposition of the human condition that became the manifesto of Legalism. Han Fei Zi disagreed with his teacher Xun Zi that moral cultivation was capable of reforming corrupt human nature, which could only be controlled—not reformed. This was accomplished through the application of the "two handles" of reward and punishment. These "two handles" were controlled by the ruler, who had to utilize them ruthlessly: "If the ruler does not see to it that the power of reward and punishment proceeds from him but instead leaves it to his ministers to apply reward and punishment, then everyone in the state will fear the ministers and slight the ruler, turn to them and away from the ruler. This is the trouble of the ruler who loses the handles of punishment and kindness" (*Han Fei Zi*, Ch. 7, II, 4a–5a, p. 256). But other than exercising the application of the "two handles," the ruler in Han Fei Zi's system is a very Daoist figure. He takes no part in the day-to-day running of the government, since that is the affair of the ministers of state.

The driving engine of government for the Legalists was the rule of law. Laws were devised and instituted by the ministers. They were to be written down, stored in government offices, and made known to the common people so that they would know what was expected of them. Han Fei Zi believed that these laws had to be universally and impartially applied, not simply left to the whim of government officials. Even the king was subject to the rule of law, with no heterodox opinions or ideas allowed. There were to be no opposition parties in a Legalist state. One might even say that in such a state, the ruler almost ceased to exist, except as the wielder of the "two handles." The aim of all of this was to produce a simple society geared toward simple goals. In such a state only two occupations were worthy of praise and support: farmers because they generated wealth, and soldiers because they protected it. Scholars, draft dodgers, merchants, artisans, and wandering soothsayers were labeled as the "five vermin," and were to be totally eradicated from the body politic.[3]

Initially, it was Legalism that triumphed in early China. The official philosophy of the state of Qin under the ministry of Li Si (d. 208 B.C.E.), Legalism became the official philosophy of the first Chinese empire. But it proved to be too harsh for the Chinese people to endure. The ruling dynasty of Qin was overthrown by the Han only some twenty years after the establishment of the empire. The Han maintained many features of the previous dynasty, but cloaked itself in the mantle of Confucianism. Thus Confucius's viewpoint, albeit much changed from his original vision, became the official philosophy of China and remained so for the next two millennia. But Confucianism still had much development and change ahead of it.

Website References

1. www.human.toyogakuen-u.ac.jp/~acmuller/contao/mencius.htm gives a translation of *Mencius*.

2. Mohism is discussed at hkusuc.hku.hk/philodep/ch/moencyred.html

3. hkusuc.hku.hk/philodep/ch/Legalism.htm examines Legalism.

CHAPTER TWENTY

◆

Neo-Confucianism

It had taken Confucianism nearly three hundred years to distinguish itself from the welter of philosophies that competed for dominance during the Warring States period. With the establishment of the Han dynasty, however, Confucianism (as defined by Mencius) became the official state creed, and its ideals were enshrined in the civil service examinations. For students who complain about modern exams, the Chinese ones would have been intolerable. They revolved around a core set of Confucian texts, including the *Analects* and the *Mencius*, that had to be committed to memory by the student. The exams themselves lasted for several days, during which the student was sequestered from the outside world, and required to write a series of extremely formalized essays.

But even if they passed, candidates had only reached the first rung of the governmental ladder that was the surest road to power and riches in imperial China. Success in the first round of the examinations only meant that they could proceed to the provincial capital for the second round. Success there allowed them to proceed to the imperial capital for the final round of examination by court officials, and sometimes even the emperor himself. Only after this third round of exams was completed were candidates actually admitted into the Civil Service and assigned to a government post, usually that of district magistrate. From there, they could advance farther if they demonstrated a practical skill for administration. Obviously, the road to government employment was long and arduous. Much has been made in Chinese literature of those individuals of humble origins who managed to navigate the system to become government officials. But the nature of the system weighed heavily against anyone who was not already a member of the ruling elite. The extraordinarily time-consuming demands of memorizing the requisite literary works and practicing the convoluted style of the official essay answers was not something that could be casually fitted into the grueling life of the average peasant. The pursuit of Confucian ideals, and the material rewards that accompanied them, was a uniquely upper-class occupation, although echoes of these ideals came to permeate all levels of Chinese society.

The peasants looked elsewhere for their spiritual sustenance, either to the indigenous spirit cults or to the emerging religions loosely based on Daoist principles. But Daoism offered little competition to Confucianism as an official ideology of the state. That came, at least initially, from other more politically oriented philosophies such as Mohism and Legalism. This is not to say, however, that these other philosophies did not influence Confucian thinking. Confucianism might have considerable practical value, and some of its proponents, such as Mencius for

Fragments of the Xiping stone canon of Confucian writings, Eastern Han dynasty, 1st century C.E. The core texts of the Confucian school became the basis for the examination system that staffed the Chinese civil service, and so led to fame and riches.

example, might be able to advance mystical interpretations of its key concepts. But for most Confucians, Confucianism was unable to nourish that side of human nature that grappled with great existential questions. This need was usually addressed by Daoism or, after about 65 C.E., by Buddhism.

Just as Mohism and Legalism had been Confucianism's greatest competitors in its early phase, so too did Buddhism become its great competitor in later centuries. But one should nuance what one means by competition. By then, the Chinese had long been adept at compartmentalizing their needs and feelings. One could be a Confucian at the office, a Daoist in the privacy of one's home study, and a Buddhist as the end of life approached. The Western notion of commitment to a single faith or worldview through thick and thin was not the Chinese way of approaching the problems of existence. It was inevitable, therefore, that there should be some over-lap and integration of ideas as these various thought systems rubbed together. This interaction with Buddhism in particular led to the next phase of Confucianism's development, the emergence of so-called Neo-Confucianism.

Zhou Dunyi and the Rise of Neo-Confucianism

Even though Confucianism was, and continued to be until 1911, the official phil-osophy of the ruling class, by the ninth century C.E. Buddhism was gaining more of a hold in upper-class circles. This led some Chinese intellectuals to mount cam-paigns to mitigate its influence or even have it suppressed entirely. Two of the most famous and influential of these early opponents of Buddhism, and as such the earliest precursors of Neo-Confucianism, were Han Yu (768–824) and Li Ao (fl. 798). Han Yu's critique of Buddhism was as simple as it was compelling. Speaking of the society of his day, he complained that, "now [the Daoists and Buddhists] seek to govern their hearts by escaping from the world, the state, and the family. They destroy the natural principles of human relations so that the son does not regard his father as father, the minister does not regard his ruler as ruler, and the people do not attend to their work" (*An Inquiry on the Way*, p. 455). Han Yu believed that to follow non-Confucian ideas led to anarchy, chaos, and the dissolution of civilization itself. His remedy for this was also simple and lay in a reexamination of Confucianism in the light of then current conditions, and a reapplication of Confucian principles to the specific ills of society.

Since Han Yu was a follower of Mencius, he held human nature to be basically good, and so he believed that it was possible for human beings to achieve *ren*. This, along with the other four virtues of ritual propriety, appropriateness, trustworthiness, and wisdom, constituted the five cardinal Confucian virtues on which social and intellectual reform could proceed. Society could, Han Yu believed, be classified into three broad groups according to the degree that these five virtues were actualized by the individual. At its apex stood the superior person, who was totally good. Next came the medium person, who was neutral and could be swayed by either the superior or the inferior person. Finally there was the inferior person, who was the incarnation of evil. The task of the good Confucian was to nourish the good, lead the medium to virtue, and suppress the inferior. This was to be done through practical rather than intellectual means. Han Yu particularly objected to the Daoist and Buddhist emphasis on metaphysics. Life, he contended, was a practical matter, and time spent in useless debate about unprovable principles could far better be expended in concrete action.

Han Yu's critique of non-Confucian thought systems was taken up by Li Ao, his younger contemporary and pupil. Li Ao clearly recognized that the Confucianism of his day, as admirable as it might be as a system of ethics and political theory, was not up to the task of providing metaphysical answers to those seeking the fundamental meaning of human existence. As he observed, "Everybody has joined the schools of Lao-tzu, the Buddha, Chuang-tzu, and Lieh-tzu. They all believe that the Confucian scholars were not learned enough to know about nature and the heavenly order, but that they themselves are. Before those who raise this hue and cry I do my best to demonstrate the opposite" (Carsun Chang, *The Development of Neo-Confucian Thought* [New Haven, CT: College and University Press, 1963], p. 36). For Li Ao, it was the failure to control one's feelings that diverted one from recognizing and nurturing the basic goodness of human nature. The Confucian virtues were therefore necessary in order to harness the natural exuberance of the emotions. Li Ao is vague about how this is to be accomplished, but his method of stilling the mind as the means of stilling the emotions seems to owe much to Buddhist thought.

These early attempts to demonstrate that Confucianism could be construed metaphysically found their culmination in the work of Zhou Dunyi (Chou Tun-i), who lived from 1017–1073. A native of central China, Zhou had a busy official career as well as being an influential teacher and philosopher. Possessing strong interests in metaphysics and aesthetics, he was well versed in Daoist and Buddhist thought, but nevertheless felt that Confucianism held within it a metaphysical depth not inferior to its two rivals. Zhou based his Neo-Confucianism on the premise that the world, being composed of real things, could not have its origins in nothing—a concept central to the negative Daoism of the *Daodejing* and the *Lie Zi* (*Lieh Tzu*). Consequently, Zhou Dunyi rejected the Dao as the ultimate source of things and proposed as an alternate principle "the Great Ultimate" (Taiji).

The Great Ultimate, according to Zhou, gave rise to yin and yang,

> [through] movement [it] generates yang. When it reaches its limit, it becomes tranquil. Through tranquillity the Great Ultimate generates yin. When tranquillity

reaches its limit, activity begins again. So movement and tranquillity alternate and become the root of each other.

SOURCE: Chan, *A Sourcebook in Chinese Philosophy*, p. 463

He goes on to explain that these two basic principles give rise to the five elements of wood, fire, water, metal, and earth from which all material creation is formed. But how do these constituent principles interact to bring forth creation? Zhou Dunyi believed that:

> When the reality of the non-ultimate [non-differentiated] and the essence of yin, yang, and the Five Agents comes into mysterious union, integration ensues, Ch'ien (heaven) constitutes the male element, and K'un (earth) constitutes the female element. The interaction of these two material forces engenders and transforms the myriad things. The myriad things produce and reproduce, resulting in unending transformation.

SOURCE: Chan, *A Sourcebook in Chinese Philosophy*, p. 463

Such thinking, and indeed the language itself, is very reminiscent of Daoist thought. The essence of Zhou's thinking is very close to this school, in that he admitted the basic unknowability of primary causes in the universe.

How do human beings fit into this model? In the following passage, Zhou further explains that:

> It is man alone who receives (the material forces) in their highest excellence, and therefore he is most intelligent. His physical form appears, and his spirit develops consciousness. The five moral principles of his nature (humanity or *jen*, righteousness, propriety, wisdom, and faithfulness) are aroused by, and react to, the external world and engage in activity; good and evil are distinguished; and human affairs take place.

SOURCE: Chan, *A Sourcebook in Chinese Philosophy*, p. 463

Following Confucius, Zhou Dunyi saw that sage as being the epitome and focal point of this process of interaction between humanity and the universe. He taught that a person must act in accordance with the metaphysical principles of the universe because they are the foundational causes of his being. But these foundational causes are also ethical imperatives. Hence to be true to the highest principles of morality is to be congruent with the basic principles of the universe. In this manner Zhou Dunyi established a Confucian metaphysics based on ethical criteria.

Cheng Hao, Cheng Yi, and the Elaboration of Neo-Confucian Thought

Whereas Zhou Dunyi established a system of thought that sought to harmonize metaphysical and ethical speculation, it was the two brothers Cheng Hao (1032–1085) and Cheng Yi (1033–1107) who paved the way for the definitive expression of Neo-Confucian ideas in the works of Zhu Xi (Chu Hsi). The problem that the Cheng brothers had with Zhou Dunyi's thought was that they found it entirely too Daoist. The Cheng brothers were relatively satisfied that Zhou

Dunyi had established a reasonable explanation of the metaphysical foundations of reality in the concept of the Great Ultimate, but they thought it was too nebulous an idea to act as a practical basis for moral action. Consequently, the Chengs elaborated on the idea of *li* (principle), a concept first advanced by Wang Bi in the third century C.E. In the Chengs' system of thought, principle was the framework that undergirded reality. It was monistic in that the principle from which all things emerged was the same as the principle inherent in individual entities. But the Chengs ultimately faced the same problem that the proponents of all monistic systems face: how can there be a single unifying principle that is at once one and many?

The Chengs believed that all reality originated from the interaction of *qi*, which they conceptualized as the material element of reality, and *li*, the form or organizational framework that gave definition to the inchoate mass of matter. But if the *li* which gives organization to matter is the same at all times and in all places, why were there such manifest differences in things? The answer to that, said the Chengs, lay in the different functions of things. Function modified principle so that things took on different aspects. Thus to understand the reason why something was one way and not another was to understand its foundational principles. The Chengs then extended this idea of foundational principles from the metaphysical sphere to the ethical one. Just as there was a universal principle that ordered the universe—albeit one that adapted itself to necessary differences in things based on function—so too must there be an overarching ethical principle that ordered and gave shape to human society based on that universal principle but adapted to individual circumstances.

This led to the belief that the principle of a thing was the source of that thing's essential activity. It also followed for the Chengs that it was fruitless to examine the details of things since they were only superficial characteristics imposed by transient conditions. What was essential was to understand their principles. This meant that to understand the motivating principle of a single member of a set of things allowed one to understand the set as a whole. One did not need to understand the particular details of the individual relationships of a million parents and children: to understand the motivating principle behind the relationship between one parent and child was to know it in all such relationships. But this premise led to yet more questions. What was the nature of the principle that gave rise to the substance and function of the universe? How is that principle related to human beings? Is the phenomenon of the mind different from this principle or the same? All these questions had practical implications for understanding the human condition and maximizing human potential.

The key to these questions for the Chengs was to understand the concept of *ren*, since it was from this that all other virtues derived. They believed that *ren* was primarily applicable to the human sphere, while *li*, the universal principle from which *ren* proceeded, structured the larger stage of the universe. Hence to cultivate *ren* was to establish a link with the foundation of reality. This led Cheng Hao to hold that there was absolutely no difference between human beings and nature (in the broad sense of the term). As in all religions, the Chengs drew a very clear distinction between knowing *ren* as information and existentially experiencing it. Cheng Yi observed that:

> True [existential] knowledge and ordinary [informational] knowledge are different. I once saw a farmer who had been wounded by a tiger. When someone said that the tiger was hurting people, everyone was startled. But in his facial expression the

farmer reacted differently from the rest. Even a young boy knows that tigers can hurt people, but this is not true knowledge. It is true knowledge only when it is like the farmer's. Therefore when men know evil and still do it, this also is not true knowledge. If it were, they would surely not do it.

SOURCE: Chan, *A Sourcebook in Chinese Philosophy*, p. 551

To truly know *ren* is to practice its cultivation and experience it in everyday life. Any other manner of investigation is artificial and hence, ultimately doomed to failure.

To undertake such a formidable task is to attempt to become a sage. But is such a goal practicable? Is not the figure of the sage an unattainable heuristic device designed to lure the student forward, but not actually reachable in the real world? After all, Confucius himself only identified mythical or semimythical figures from the Chinese past as sages, never any living person or indeed any person in living memory. Cheng Yi answered this question in a positive manner:

From the essence of life accumulated in Heaven and Earth, man receives the Five Agents (Water, Fire, Wood, Metal, and Earth) in their highest excellence. His original nature is pure and tranquil. Before it is aroused, the five moral principles of his nature called humanity, righteousness, propriety, wisdom, and faithfulness, are complete. As his physical form appears, it comes into contact with external things and is aroused from within. As it is aroused from within, the seven feelings, called pleasure, anger, sorrow, joy, love, hate, and desire ensue. As feeling becomes strong and increasingly reckless, his nature becomes damaged.

SOURCE: Chan, *A Sourcebook in Chinese Philosophy*, pp. 547–548

Given that the essential temperament possessed by all human beings is by nature "pure and tranquil," it was entirely possible for everyone to return to this state, which was enjoyed by the sage. This could be achieved through a program of controlling the feelings.

Individuals are in the final analysis the microcosm of the universe, since they contain in themselves the same essential principle that structures and motivates the larger reality. Cheng Hao believed that human nature represents the original essence of humanity, and that it must follow that human nature is identical with *li*, since morality is the hallmark of the human being, and that *ren* is the natural manifestation of *li*. So, to reach perfection of this human nature and to become a sage, we must be true to this original principle by practicing *cheng* (sincerity) through the cultivation of propriety, wisdom, and righteousness. In short, we must follow the ethical path laid out by Confucius.

Zhu Xi and the Flowering of Neo-Confucianian Tradition

But it was not the Cheng brothers who were to be remembered as taking Neo-Confucianism to its fullest state of development. That distinction is held by Zhu Xi (1130–1200). In fact, Zhu Xi is held to be the next most important figure after Confucius himself and Mencius for the elaboration of the Confucian system. Zhu Xi's significance lies in his ability to reinterpret earlier Neo-Confucian thinkers into a philosophical system that was true both to the vision of the school's founders and to the emergent metaphysical speculations of his immediate predecessors. Just as the work of Zhou Dunyi was centered around the question of the origins of the universe, and just as the Cheng brothers' philosophy centered around questions of how metaphysics and ethics were related, Zhu Xi took as the core of his inquiry the question of how, given the essential goodness of human nature, the clouding effects of *qi*, which gave rise to evil, could be overcome.

Zhu Xi started from the premise that the central goal of philosophical inquiry was the cultivation of *ren*, the establishment of the five basic human relationships as defined by Confucius, and the development of the Confucian virtues. If this were accomplished, he believed, then goodness would flourish and evil would be removed from the world. But why was there evil in the world at all? Mencius taught that it was because of the deficiencies of society and culture. Xun Zi's explanation was even simpler: people were just plain bad. But he was still a Confucian in that he believed that they could be made better. Despite the fact that this viewpoint held the virtue of being the simplest explanation that fitted the facts, it did not satisfy later Confucians, who generally preferred to adopt Mencius's explanation of the problem of evil.

Even so, this explanation of the problem was still unsatisfactory to many. Zhang Zai (Chang Tsai), who lived between 1020 and 1077, had attempted to address the deficiencies in Mencius's viewpoint by differentiating between human and physical nature. Human nature, Zhang believed, was essentially good, but it was clouded and obscured by contact with the physical world. Zhang differed from Daoist and Buddhist thinkers who held similar viewpoints on this subject in that he did not hold that evil existed because of the nature of the physical world. Rather, he saw evil arising as the result of human failure to adhere to proper principles in dealing with physical reality. But this explanation of the problem of evil was undercut by the Cheng brothers' contention that human nature and the physical world were both grounded on a common principle. Thus it fell to Zhu Xi to reconcile these philosophical inconsistencies.

Zhu Xi began his discussion of how these difficulties could be resolved by distinguishing between principle in itself, and principle as it is embodied in concrete entities. Again following the Chengs, he believed that principle was at first undifferentiated and harmonious. But as it adopted different forms in response to different functions, it became, in his words, "confused and mixed." This led to the differentiation of good and evil. He believed that principle was corrupted by its association with matter. Human beings are a mixture of the two, but their principle is identical with the principle of the universe and so by definition pure. It is the feelings that are generated in the human being as a result of principle's embodiment in matter that give rise to the passions, which in turn are the source of evil.

It naturally followed that the relationship between principle and matter needed to be carefully explicated. On this question, Zhu Xi held that:

> Throughout the universe there are both principle and material force. Principle [*li*] refers to the Way [Dao], which exists before physical form [and is without it] and is the course from which all things are produced. Material force [*qi*] refers to material objects, which exist after physical form [and is with it]; it is the instrument by which things are produced. Therefore in the production of man and things, they must be endowed with principle before they have their nature, and they must be endowed with material force before they have physical form.

SOURCE: Chan, *A Sourcebook in Chinese Philosophy*, p. 636

For Zhu Xi, nothing can exist without being a combination of principle and material force.

What then was the source of these two components of existence? He accepted Zhou Dunyi's concept of the Great Ultimate as their source, but he interpreted the Great Ultimate to be nothing more in the final analysis than principle. If this was so, then principle was both the origin of things and the ground of their being. Given that human beings have this ultimate principle as their source, that this ultimate principle is good in itself, and that the embodiment of this ultimate principle in human nature is *ren*, the next important question for Zhu Xi was how *ren* was to be realized in the individual's life.

Zhu Xi saw two practices as being fundamental to such a quest. The first was to rediscover one's true nature, since *ren* naturally existed there. The second was to investigate the actual functioning of principle in daily life so as to root out any deviations from one's essential goodness. This naturally led to the practice, in various ways, of love for others, since love was the primary manifestation of *ren* in actual human affairs. Zhu Xi believed that:

> If we truly practice love and preserve it, then we have in it the spring of all virtues and the root of all good deeds. This is why in the teachings of the Confucian school, the student is always urged to exert anxious and unceasing effort in the pursuit of *jen*.
>
> SOURCE: Chan, *A Sourcebook in Chinese Philosophy*, p. 596

In practice, Zhu Xi felt that to be sincere, humble, courteous, and calm is the absolute foundation of the practice of love, and to love others as we love ourselves is to truly practice love. It was toward these ideals that the true Confucian should strive, even if they were by their very nature unattainable in a perfect form in this life.

Wang Yangming and the Refutation of Zhu Xi's Synthesis

Although Zhu Xi had definitively fixed the direction of Neo-Confucian thought, and his system was declared in 1313 to be the official orthodox version of Confucian thought, it did not remain static and there were still areas of ambiguity within it. Of the philosophers who followed Zhu Xi and attempted to clarify his vision, undoubtedly the most influential was Wang Yangming (1472–1523). Although he enjoyed a relatively brief life, Wang was not only a brilliant scholar, but a successful general and statesman as well. But it is for his contributions to Neo-Confucian philosophy that he is best remembered by posterity.

Wang was motivated by two factors to question Zhu Xi's interpretation of Confucian thought. The first was that the adoption of Zhu Xi's system of Neo-Confucianism as the official form of state Confucianism had led to an inevitable ossification of his thought. Confucian scholarship had degenerated into a scholastic examination of minutiae that failed to grapple with new ideas and to reexamine basic concepts. The second factor was that in their zeal to "investigate things"—a procedure advocated by Zhu Xi as a means of understanding the deeper principles that motivated and maintained reality—later Neo-Confucians had moved away from the consideration of morality that Wang believed formed the core of Confucian thought.

Wang Yangming attempted in his work to redress what he considered to be aberrations of later Neo-Confucian scholasticism. Consequently, his philosophy, aimed as it was on a return to the basic investigation of moral values, was based on two overarching principles: a consideration of the character of the mind, and an attempt to establish the unity of knowledge and action. From these two principles arose his doctrine of the extension of the innate knowledge of the good (*zhi liangzhi*). As he wrote:

> The learning of the great man consists entirely in getting rid of the obscuration of selfish desires in order by his own efforts to make manifest his clear character, so as to restore the condition of forming one body with Heaven, Earth, and the myriad things, a condition that is originally so, that is all. It is not that outside of the original substance something can be added.
>
> SOURCE: Chan, *A Sourcebook in Chinese Philosophy*, p. 660

For Wang, knowledge and action are inseparable.

Wang Yangming chose to base his interpretation of Confucianism not on knowledge but on will. This meant that in his system practical knowledge, the necessary ingredient in making informed choices, superseded theoretical knowledge, but only to the degree that it facilitates action. This viewpoint, and the concepts that arise from it, are best exemplified in Wang's examination of the classical Confucian text, the *Great Learning*. Here three principle themes emerge. The first is an emphasis on manifesting clear character; the second is the necessity of loving people; and the third is the virtue of abiding in the highest good. What does Wang mean by these ideas? We must realize at the outset that all of these concepts are undergirded by a presupposition, common to all Confucian thinking, that the family is the primary model of reality. It naturally follows from this that all reality, like the family, even though constituted of a number of diverse parts, forms an organic whole. Just as it is the bond of familial love, generated by the individual *ren* of its members, that binds the family into one unit, so it is the bond of universal love generated by the foundational *ren* that is the basis of the universe that binds reality together into a single entity. The ideal in Wang Yangming's system is for individuals to actualize in their selves the unity of the universal and the individual *ren*. Hence we must strive to love all parents as though they were our own parents.

To "manifest clear character" is to return to this original character of purity and goodness. Its natural expression is a love of all creation. Wang observed that:

> Everything from ruler, minister, husband, wife, and friends to mountains, rivers, spiritual beings, birds, animals, and plants should be truly loved in order to realize [one's] humanity that forms one body with them, and then my clear character will be completely manifested, and I will really form one body with Heaven, Earth and the myriad things.
>
> SOURCE: Chan, *A Sourcebook in Chinese Philosophy*, p. 661

This led to the third characteristic of Wang's philosophy:

> The highest good is the ultimate principle of manifesting character and loving people. The nature endowed in us by Heaven is pure and perfect. The fact that it

is intelligent, clear, and not beclouded is evidence of the emanation and revelation of the highest good. It is the original substance of the clear character which is called innate knowledge of the good.

SOURCE: Chan, *A Sourcebook in Chinese Philosophy*, p. 661

This emphasis on the intrinsic goodness of human nature was what set Wang Yangming's thought apart from that of other Neo-Confucians. He saw no need for any external aid or support to realize this goodness. To know the good is nothing more than to do good, since knowledge of the good is already infused in the human mind. By actualizing that goodness through action, knowledge of it became manifest in the human consciousness and the goal of the Neo-Confucian quest was achieved.

CHAPTER TWENTY-ONE

The Chinese Transformation of Buddhism

While Confucianism and Daoism form the indigenous framework of Chinese thought, it is impossible to consider the course of Chinese religious history without making reference to Buddhism. Even though it had been imported from outside China and was based on presuppositions that were often very foreign to Chinese sensibilities, Buddhism not only took root in Chinese soil but subsequently flourished there.

The Origins of Chinese Buddhism

Buddhism evolved in China in ways that it never had in India. There are a number of major schools of Buddhism, such as Chan and Huayan, that were supposedly elaborations of preexisting Indian schools but were in reality wholly Chinese creations. Given the tremendous missionary impulse of early Buddhism, it would be surprising if the religion had not penetrated China at a fairly early date. However, it would also be surprising if more than a few monks had been able to cross the thousands of miles of harsh deserts and frigid mountain ranges that separate India and China. More accessible would have been the sea route through Southeast Asia. But the dates for the establishment of contacts between Southeast Asia, India, and China are still a matter of conjecture. Consequently, the earliest reliable date for the arrival of Buddhism in China is placed fairly late.

But there are suggestive, although ultimately unverifiable, stories that may indicate earlier dates for this first contact. The earliest of these stories concern a "foreign magician" carrying a staff and a begging bowl who created a three-foot-tall stupa on his fingertips at the court of Prince Zhao of Yen in 317 B.C.E. Another tale recounts that the foreign monk Shi Lifang had brought Buddhist scriptures to China in the reign of the First Emperor around 220 B.C.E. Other Chinese Buddhist writers have suggested that Buddhism came to China during the early second century B.C.E. It could have been brought by Chinese ambassadors on their return from diplomatic trips to Central Asia, or by nomadic raiders on the western borders of China who had been converted to Buddhism through contacts with Buddhist monks farther west in Central Asia.

But the earliest reliable information about Buddhism in China is dated 65, and refers to the existence of Buddhist monks and laypersons in the eastern area of China near the seacoast. It also involves a member of the ruling Han family, who is recorded as being a patron of, and probably a convert to, Buddhism. This record is interesting for a number of reasons. The first is that it indicates that by 65, Buddhism was held in high enough esteem for a member of the royal family, Prince Ying of Qu, to espouse the religion. Likewise, there can be little doubt that the community described had been in existence for some time, given the eastern placement of the Buddhist community mentioned in the record and the presence of laypersons who would undoubtedly be native Chinese, even if the monks were immigrant foreigners. It is likely, therefore, that the first penetration of Buddhism into China predates 65, perhaps by a significant period of time.

If the timeline for the arrival of Buddhism is vague, so too is the geographical path that it followed to reach China. The traditional theory has been that Buddhism reached China from Central Asia along the Silk Road, which connected China with the great markets of the Mediterranean world.[1] There can be little doubt that this was a significant source of Buddhist influence in early China, as it continued to be in later times. But records also indicate that by the time of the Han dynasty there were distinct patterns of Buddhist influence in China that would suggest other points of entry as well. The first was at the capital of Chanyan, which was not only the center of government, but also the Chinese terminus of the Silk Road. The second was at Pengcheng in the lower Yangzi valley; and the third was in what is now northern Vietnam, at that time the southernmost province of the Chinese Empire.

Transmission via the Silk Road would certainly explain the presence of Buddhism in the northern capital region, but not the strong early presence of Buddhism in the distant south. Buddhism was so well established in southern China at an early date that it is here where we see the earliest references to Buddhist images and temples. The most plausible explanation for this strong presence of Buddhism in southern China, far distant from the imperial capital and the Silk Road, is to postulate an early sea route between the region and South Asia. Such a route no doubt existed from a fairly early period, possibly as early as 200 B.C.E. If so, Buddhism likely traveled initially from the area now known as Vietnam to China, and not the other way around—as Chinese writers on the history of Buddhism have long contended.

But it is understandable that the Buddhist community established at the imperial capital should be the most influential of the early Buddhist communities. It was here that the earliest Buddhist monasteries, the Baima (White Horse) monastery and the Xuchang monastery (named after a cousin of Prince Ying), were founded in the early decades of the first century C.E. It was here as well that the first moves were made to accommodate Buddhism to Chinese sensibilities. Since the Chinese lacked the technical terms for describing Buddhist religious concepts, the early Chinese Buddhists tended to frame their discussions of Buddhism in terms borrowed from Daoism. This had the dual effect of giving non-Buddhist Chinese the impression that Buddhism was a form of Daoism, and allowing an early penetration of Daoist concepts into the indigenous interpretations of Buddhist ideas. While Buddhism was eventually able to overcome the first difficulty, the influence of Daoism was to have a profound and lasting effect on some aspects of Chinese Buddhist philosophy.

It was in some ways inevitable that for many Chinese, Buddhism should appear to be a form of Daoism. Daoism had evolved a concept of the soul. It had developed a complex set of physical practices designed to improve the individual's future prospects. It had advocated a simple lifestyle, divorced from the pomp and passions of human society. All this it shared with Buddhism. The association of the two religions in the Chinese mind was further strengthened by the fact that the first Buddhist converts had usually begun life as Daoists, and so had preexisting Daoist sympathies. They tended, therefore, to translate texts that reinforced Daoist similarities with Buddhism, and not those that emphasized the differences between the two faiths. As a result, very few early Buddhist texts translated into Chinese deal with what we know to be core Buddhist ideas, such as the Four Noble Truths, interdependent causation, or nonself. Rather, they concentrate on physical techniques such as meditation, breath control, and practical rules for living—all subjects of particular interest to Daoists.

This led to another question that was central to Chinese thinking: to what degree should the Chinese allow foreign ideas to influence their thought and actions? Did China really need them at all, given the riches of its own traditions? One viewpoint that developed and emerged periodically in Chinese history was that all non-Chinese ideologies should be suppressed as being incompatible with the basic nature of Chinese civilization. The second possibility, and the one most adopted in the early period, was to claim that Buddhism *was* Daoism. This school of thought, known as *huahu*, or "the conversion of the barbarians," held that after Laozi had left China, he went to India and became the Buddha. Hence Buddhism was nothing

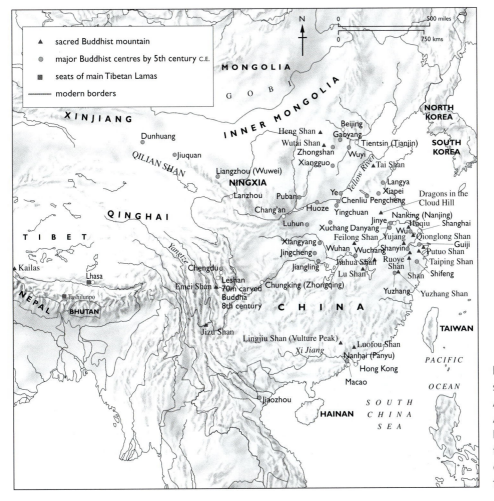

Important Buddhist sites in China. Although of South Asian origins, Buddhism became an important feature of Chinese culture from around the 3rd century C.E.

more than degenerate Daoism, albeit with certain useful developments that could be profitably incorporated into "real" Daoism.

This is not to say that the two religions were always amicable to one another. In the Daoist *Taipingjing* (the *Classic of Great Peace*), which was very influential in China in the second century C.E., there is a concentrated attack on Buddhist doctrine that echoes throughout the rest of Chinese history. Buddhism was deprecated on a series of interlinking counts that look far more Confucian in nature than Daoist—the major charge against Buddhism being that it encouraged people to be monks and alienated people from their duties both toward their parents and toward their wives and children. The text also disapproved of the Buddhist practice of drinking urine as medicine, and its promotion of begging through the solicitation of alms. In fact, Chinese disapproval of almsgiving was so great as to cause the elimination of this practice in later Chinese Buddhism altogether.

One of the primary intellectual problems that early Buddhism faced in China was that indigenous Chinese thought had little interest in the human fate after death. At best, there existed the concept of a shadowy afterlife in a place known as the Yellow Springs, which was a pale and unsatisfactory reflection of earthly existence. Humans

Seated Bodhisattva, 5th century. Although the Theravada tradition continued in China, most Chinese favoured Mahayana forms of Buddhism.

must exist in some sense after death, otherwise what point would there be in venerating the ancestors? But the nature of this existence held little interest for the practical-minded early Chinese philosophers, who were concentrating on how to order the present life and not the one to come. It was left to the Buddhists to articulate a plausible theology of the afterlife that resonated in the Chinese mind. Chinese intellectuals were especially troubled by the apparent contradiction between the concepts of karma and rebirth and the absence of a permanent soul—an essential concept in a society with such an emphasis on ancestor veneration. Hence early Chinese Buddhism evolved the concept of *shenling*, the "numinous spirit," which in some ways was similar to the concept of a permanent and eternally existing soul. From this concept it was not difficult to argue that there was an endless series of births and rebirths, and that people's actions affected these births in either a positive or negative manner.

The idea of an enduring soul accorded well with prevailing Daoist beliefs, as well as the indigenous belief in ghosts and ancestors. But how did one assure this soul a favorable rebirth? The earliest Buddhist text translated into Chinese, the *Sutra in Forty-Two Sections*, taught that this was accomplished through the restraint of the passions, an idea that was certainly present in some Daoist texts, such as the *Daodejing*, and that was consistent with Confucian ideas of self cultivation. Both those Chinese systems of thought, however, lacked a practical program by which this restraint could be accomplished. The Buddhists, on the other hand, offered two methods of suppressing the passions. The first was to observe the rules of conduct laid down for monks in the *Vinaya* literature, particularly as summarized in the two hundred and fifty *patimoksha* rules followed by Buddhist monks. The second method was through concentration and meditation.

A number of traditional Buddhist meditation techniques were known at an early date, such as meditating on a decaying corpse to develop detachment from the body. But many of the more traditional practices aimed at demonstrating the transitory nature of the body and lessening one's attachment to it tended to offend the delicate sensibilities of the Chinese intelligentsia, who preferred to follow the breath-control exercises described in such texts as the *Anban shouyi jing* (*The Sutra on Concentrating by Practicing Respiratory Exercises*). Charity and compassion were also emphasized to a greater degree than in early Indian Buddhism, and this favored the development in China of Mahayana expressions of Buddhism over Theravada ones. These attitudes were put into practice by donations of food, land, and money to monastic communities and through the cultivation of nonviolence in various forms toward all other living things. This latter ideal came to find expression in such ways as the practice of vegetarianism and the freeing of captured birds and animals.

Post-Han Developments in Early Chinese Buddhism

With the decline and fall of the Han dynasty in 220 C.E., China entered into a period of political decline and foreign domination that was to last until the rise of the Sui dynasty in 581. Most of northern China succumbed to non-Chinese invaders from the west, while those Chinese states that did survive in southern China were often weak and ineffectual. Even so, they became havens for Chinese intellectuals fleeing the north and, as such, the seedbeds for the next phase of

Chinese cultural growth. It is no surprise, therefore, that Buddhism's next Chinese transformation should take place here.

Paradoxically, it was hard times that allowed Buddhism to flourish. Whereas the Chinese of the Han period, who enjoyed stable government and general economic prosperity, were disinclined to listen to the pessimistic tones of Buddhism, the disruptions of later centuries made the Buddhist message more plausible. Now the idea that life was essentially unsatisfactory fell on fertile ground as millions were dispossessed and their comfortable lives turned upside down. The loss of the Chinese heartland to barbarian invaders cast doubts on the viability and worth of traditional Chinese creeds. The intelligentsia was ripe for fresh ideas and new viewpoints. They turned to Buddhism for inspiration and direction, and they were not disappointed. Meanwhile, different social and political conditions caused northern and southern Chinese Buddhism to begin to develop in two somewhat different directions. In the south, where government control was weak, the monastic and cultural aspects of Buddhism predominated and flourished. In the north, Buddhist monks came to play significant roles within the government of the foreign-ruled states that dominated the region.

Intellectually, post-Han Buddhism displayed two major currents of thought. The first was the meditation school, which emphasized the control of the mind and the suppression of the passions. This school, based on the early Buddhist translations of the monk An Shigao, drew primarily on Theravada traditions for its inspiration and was monastic in its orientation. The second major trend in Buddhist thought was the Prajna school, which was Mahayana in orientation. This school displayed the classic hallmarks of Mahayana thought and concentrated its efforts on penetrating to the core of reality and on realizing the true nature of the Buddha in ways that were more accessible to laypersons. As time went on, it was this second school that came to dominate Buddhist thought in southern China. This eventually resulted in the proliferation of Mahayana texts in China, and a closer interaction between Buddhist scholar monks, such as Daoan (312–385), and the Chinese literati.

This rapprochement between these two groups was not one sided. Just as the Buddhism of the period reflects Daoist influences, the Maoshan texts of Daoism clearly reflect Buddhist influence. Both traditions embrace the concept of emptiness—although their understanding of that term was somewhat different—and the unique contributions of the sage in whom all dualism has been eliminated. Both the Daoists and the Buddhists were concerned with *benti* (*pen-t'i*), the essential nature of things, with an attendant deprecation of the visible world of the senses. To realize this essential nature and to embrace it was to have achieved *fanben*—to have reverted to the original and to be one with reality. The Buddhists equated this with the achievement of Nirvana, while the Daoists saw it as merging with the Dao. In either case, one was free from the pains and disappointments of the transitory physical world.

This connection between later Daoism and Buddhism was further strengthened by the fact that both groups drew their members from the gentry class of southern China. This group, the effective rulers of the southern Chinese states, was the chief source of all the prominent monks and Daoist practitioners of the period. This is not to say that foreign monks did not continue to contribute to the development of Buddhism, since the indigenous Chinese grasp of Sanskrit and Pali, the canonical languages of early Buddhism, was still fairly weak during this early period. As a result, the bulk of translation of Buddhist scripture appears to have been done by, or at least under the tutelage of, Buddhist monks who came primarily from Central Asia or perhaps from Southeast Asia. But as time went on, the influence of these foreign monks waned and was replaced by native Chinese scholarship.

A good example of the melding of Buddhist and Daoist thought can be seen in the person of the eminent monk Zhi Dun (Chih Tun, 314–366). Even after taking ordination, he continued to interact with Daoist scholars; and one of his best-known works is a Buddhist commentary on the *Zhuangzi*. According to the Daoist viewpoint of Zhuangzi, the individual was justified in leading any type of life, so long as it was true to his or her inner nature. Zhi Dun, on the other hand, rejected this view, since he held that the law of karma allowed one to change one's nature through direct personal effort. This, he believed, negated the essential fatalism of the Daoist viewpoint. Zhi Dun was also among the first Chinese philosophers to endow the term *li* with a metaphysical meaning similar to that commonly associated with it in Neo-Confucian thinking. In his system of thought, *li* came to signify the absolute nature of the universe, in contradistinction to *shi*, the manifestations of the phenomenal world of the senses—with *shi* being understood in a manner similar to that of *qi* in later Neo-Confucianism.

But monks were not the only driving force in early southern Chinese Buddhism. Significant contributions to the development of the religion were also made by laypersons such as Sun Zhuo (c. 300–380). A prolific author, he wrote works of both biography, such as his *Treatise on Monks and Worthies*, and philosophy, such as his *Treatise Illustrating the Dao*. In this latter work, he made some of the first attempts to reconcile Buddhism and Confucianism. To Sun Zhuo, the difference between the two thought systems was mainly one of emphasis. Buddhism explicates the inner nature of things, while Confucianism shows how these inner principles are to be manifested in the everyday world. Their divergences, then, were more a matter of different circumstances than of essence, and a Chinese gentleman could simultaneously espouse both creeds without exposing himself to the charge of inconsistency.

The spread and development of Buddhism in southern China was further aided by the cordial relations that the religion enjoyed with the region's royal courts—the clans that dominated political life from the fall of the Han to the rise of the Sui came and went, but they all tended to promote Buddhism at court. This was especially true under such great statesmen as He Chong (292–346) who spent vast sums of public money on building monasteries for Buddhist monks. He did so on the premise that the monks' benign influence was a supernatural safeguard for the state. Indeed, the first mention of Buddhist nuns is found associated with him, as he is recorded as having built the first Buddhist nunnery in China shortly before his death. By 380, even some of the rulers of the southern Chinese states had formally become Buddhist laymen.

Given this special favor in the highest corridors of power, it is not surprising to find that Buddhism flourished. It has been estimated that by about 400, there were 1,785 temples and 24,000 monks and nuns in the region. The prodigality of the imperial clan and the aristocracy was so great that Confucian scholars protested what they saw as the ineffective use of public funds. The huge amounts of wealth expended on temples, and the maintenance of monks and nuns, they argued, did not contribute to the material prosperity of the court or to the health of the people. They were particularly incensed by what they perceived as meddling by Buddhist monks in affairs of state. This was especially evident in the reigns of the last emperors of the Eastern Jin state, who delegated virtually the entire administration of their country to Buddhist monks. Indeed, even Buddhist nuns such as Zhi Miaoyin became prominent in government councils of the time. Their influence may not have always been benign, and some scholars have argued that Buddhist interference in the state government may have led to the downfall of the ruling dynasty.

This tension between Confucians, who believed themselves to be the only legitimate government party, and the Buddhist monastic order came to be a dominant feature of Chinese life for the next thousand years. Traditionally, the Buddhist Sangha had seen itself as an autonomous entity. While this had not always been the actual case in India, it was the idealized paradigm of Buddhism's relationship to the state that had been brought to China. This of course ran totally contrary to the Confucian principle of the emperor as the supreme ruler of the state and the absolute arbiter of the actions of all its inhabitants. This conflict was exemplified in the dispute that arose in Eastern Jin in 340 over whether or not Buddhist monks should render homage to the emperor by means of prostration. The Buddhist monks held that not only should they be exempt from this, but that the emperor should prostrate himself to them, as was the custom in India and Southeast Asia. This caused a vigorous debate to rage at court. The major Confucian spokesman was Yu Bing, the regent for the young emperor of the time. He was opposed by the powerful Buddhist layman He Chong, who argued that far from undermining the state by their actions, as Yu Bing contended, Buddhist monks' observance of the Buddhist moral principles actually reinforced Confucian values. Moreover, in conducting rituals for the accumulation and distribution of merit, monks were in fact expressing their devotion to the emperor and their benevolent intentions toward the common people. Although the Buddhists carried the day on this occasion, the question continued to arise.

In 403, we see another instance of conflict between the state and the Buddhist order. The newly installed emperor of the southern Eastern Jin dynasty, Huan Xuan, proposed to purge the Buddhist order of undesirable elements. This practice was prevalent in India and Southeast Asia, and was seen in these areas as a legitimate function of the ruler. In Jin, however, Huan Xuan was opposed by the famous monk Huiyuan, who contended that the Buddhist monks and nuns had opted out of society and were therefore no longer subject to its rules and strictures. Consequently, the emperor had no jurisdiction over them. For whatever reason, the emperor bowed to Huiyuan's protest, and the proposed purification of the Buddhist monastic order did not take place.

Buddhism in Northern China from the Fall of the Han to the Rise of the Sui

While southern China enjoyed relative peace and security during the three hundred years of political fragmentation that followed the fall of the Han, northern China was not so fortunate, since it became the battleground over which contending foreign armies of Turks, Tibetans, and Mongols struggled for dominance. Amid these unsettled conditions, Buddhism developed in ways significantly different from those in the south. These conditions made the traditional Buddhist practice of proselytizing at the grassroots village level impractical. The only viable alternative for spreading the religion seemed to be through the ruling aristocracy of the petty states that characterized the region. So prominent Buddhist monks such as Daoan attached themselves to the retinues of the northern rulers.

These monks served not only as religious advisors, but as military, diplomatic, and administrative ones as well. Their ability to conduct Buddhist rituals for the prosperity of the state and particular individuals, along with their supposed talents

Standing Buddha, Northern Wei dynasty, 477 C.E. Buddhism was able to make the transition from being a South Asian religion to being a Chinese religion, but only after a period of adaptation to local conditions.

for fortunetelling and magic, made them honored guests in the halls of power. Whether the monks' magic powers were real or simply an expedient means of leading the credulous to a deeper understanding of Buddhism, their exercise of such powers resulted in the rise of many monks to the highest levels of command and influence. This royal favor, combined with the unstable nature of northern Chinese society, provided the Buddhist missionaries of the region with a fertile missionary field, since their influence at court allowed them to offer material as well as spiritual inducements to prospective converts. Under the patronage of Fu Jian of the Former Qin dynasty, which held sway in northern China from 351 to 394, famous monks from Kashmir, such as Sanghabhuti, Dharmanandi, and Sanghadeva, traveled to China to preach and translate the scriptures of the Sarvastivada school of Theravada Buddhism into Chinese. Monks whom they trained became the core of a new effort to translate the Buddhist scriptures into Chinese in a more accurate and less Daoist manner than before. But the real instigator of this push for better translations was Kumarajava (344–409/413), another foreign monk from Central Asia.

Our knowledge of Buddhism in this period was greatly enhanced by the discovery in the early twentieth century of a large cache of texts hidden near the northwestern oasis town of Dunhuang (Tun-huang). A strategic point on the Silk Road just inside what were then the borders of China, Dunhuang had from relatively early times been the home of a flourishing community of Buddhist monks. By the end of the third century, it was the home of such prominent translator monks as Dharmaraksha, who translated 154 texts into Chinese, including the Lotus Sutra, a text of tremendous importance to the subsequent development of Buddhism in China. As political dislocation increased in the fourth century, more monks fled to the relative safety of Dunhuang. There they not only translated texts but created magnificent murals on the walls of the cave temples that dotted the town. The dry air preserved these murals and a large cache of texts that had been hidden several centuries later when the town was overrun and destroyed by foreign invaders. Consequently, the Buddhist art of Dunhuang is not only a valuable record of the development of early Chinese art but also provides us with some of the earliest and best preserved examples of Chinese Buddhist literature.

Vimalikirti and the Doctrine of Non-Duality, Wang Zhenpeng, 1308 C.E. Chinese Buddhist thought emphasized certain elements of Buddhism that had little importance in India, thus creating a distinct Chinese Buddhism.

Another important facet of Buddhism during this period was the development of the pilgrim monk. The first of these famous figures was Faxian, who in 399 left China to travel to India. This tremendously difficult undertaking was motivated by two factors. The first was to actually visit the sites of the Buddha's earthly life. The second and more far-reaching motivation was to search for better copies of the Buddhist scriptures than those available in China at the time. Faxian left a detailed description of his journey that provides historians with vital information not only about China, but also India and Southeast Asia.

Faxian was not the first Chinese monk to attempt the journey, but earlier travelers had died on route, or stopped in Central Asia, or remained in India and never returned to China. Faxian was the first monk to go to India, study, and return. What motivated him was his desire to acquire and translate into Chinese the first complete recension of the *Vinaya* literature that formed the rulebook for Buddhist monks. In point of fact, Kumarajava translated the entire *Vinaya* of the Sarvastivadin school into Chinese, having begun his task in 401; but by then, Faxian had been on his way to India for some two years, traveling via the Silk Road route through Central Asia. He eventually reached Pataliputra, where he obtained copies of the *Vinaya* of both the Mahasanghika and the Sarvastivada school, as well as copies of other key scriptures. Perhaps dismayed by the arduous nature of the land route, Faxian elected to return to China by sea. He went first to Sri Lanka, where he acquired yet more texts, and then on to Java, where he embarked for Canton. But he was blown off course and ended up on the Shandong peninsula of eastern China sometime in 414. He had been gone from China for sixteen years. On his return, he dedicated the remainder of his life to translating the texts that he had gathered with such difficulty.

As the result of the work of these dedicated monks of early Chinese Buddhism, the groundwork was laid for the development of the religion in later times. By the beginning of the sixth century, most of the major texts had been translated in a manner that eliminated excessive Daoist leanings. A new technical vocabulary had arisen that was purely Buddhist in nature. Moreover, the key concepts of Buddhism, such as the Four Noble Truths, the Eightfold Path, Nirvana, and so forth, had become an accepted part of the evolving texture of Chinese intellectual discourse.

Cave 285 of the Megao Caves, Dunhuang. Buddhist influences that came to China over the Silk Road often contained artistic elements borrowed from Central Asia.

The time was right for the next step in the evolution of Chinese Buddhist thought. But that next step presupposed a stable and prosperous socioeconomic climate. With the establishment of the Sui Dynasty (581–618) and its successor, the Tang dynasty (618–907), the conditions were at last favorable for the efflorescence of new forms of Buddhism that were uniquely Chinese.

Website References

1. The Silk Road is discussed in detail at **www.silk-road.com**. For a comprehensive examination of the great Buddhist center of Dunghuang, see **idp.bl.uk**

CHAPTER TWENTY-TWO

The Consolidation and Expansion of Chinese Buddhism

As Buddhism developed and accommodated itself to the conditions and intellectual milieu of China, it began to evolve in directions that were different from those found in India and Southeast Asia. The first such development was the Sanjie Jiao (San-chieh Chiao), or School of the Three Stages, of Xinxing (540–594). Based on such texts as the Lotus Sutra and the Avatamsaka Sutra, Xinxing argued that the propagation of Buddhism followed a three-stage pattern. At first, the teachings of the Buddha were properly understood and rigorously followed. In the next stage, however, innovations and false doctrines crept into the religion and inauthentic expressions of Buddhism became the norm. Finally, in the third stage, the true teachings of the Buddha disappeared altogether, and it was necessary for a new Buddha to manifest himself in order for the cycle to repeat itself.

For Xinxing, the pure teachings of the first period were embodied in the teachings of the Buddha as exemplified in the Pali Buddhist canonical literature. In the second period, divisions in the teaching caused the development of different schools of thought, such as the Theravada and the Mahayana schools. In the third period, which Xinxing believed to include his own time, only his own teachings preserved the authentic message of the Buddha. During this hideous third period, the original forms of achieving enlightenment were no longer effective. The dedicated aspirant to enlightenment now needed to practice the rule of asceticism, which was designed to purge individuals of their imperfections, and to follow strict adherence to monastic discipline.

Xinxing's followers were the first to display a behavior and certain characteristic attitudes that were unique to Chinese Buddhism. They did not live in monasteries, but in secular surroundings. They mixed freely with laypersons in public places such as markets. They had little respect for the traditional trappings of Buddhism, such as images and the scriptures, which they saw as being merely artificial outward symbols with little or no salvific value in themselves. They believed that all existence and all beings were permeated with the Buddha nature, and so they advocated respect for everyone and the performance of altruistic actions, especially almsgiving, as the way to enlightenment. This emphasis on charity found expression in the establishment of the Inexhaustible Treasury at the Huada Temple in the Tang capital city of Changan between 618 and 627. This institution served as a focal point for the extensive social work of the school, with one third of donations to it going to the repair of temples, one third to helping the sick and destitute, and one third to ceremonies dedicated to worship of the Buddha.

Despite the school's many fine qualities, certain aspects of its teachings soon brought it into conflict with the authorities and with other schools of Buddhism. The School of Three Stages claimed, like so many religious groups before and since, to possess the sole means of achieving salvation. Its emphasis on the corrupt and decayed nature of the current age led it to the natural conclusion that in general people were lawless and depraved, a charge that the recently installed Tang dynasty necessarily rejected, since it undercut the legitimacy of their rule. This official distrust of the school was increased by its contention that no government existed that was capable of restoring the true religion. In the end, the school was declared heretical by Wu Zetian (Wu Tse-t'ien)—the only woman to rule China as empress in her own right—and it went into a serious decline, eventually disappearing in the great persecution of Buddhism of 845. But the School of Three Stages was not the only school of Buddhism to flourish in early Tang China. Schools with their origins in India also prospered in the new climate of peace and security that marked the beginnings of the new era. Some important examples of these schools were the Disciplinary school (*Lü-Zong*) and the Kosa school.

The Disciplinary school was founded by Daoxuan (Tao-hsüan, 596–667) and took its name from its adherence to the *Vinaya* texts. Using a new translation of these texts—*The Vinaya in Four Parts*, compiled in 412—the school had its headquarters at the Zhongnan Shan monastery near the Tang capital of Changan and so is often referred to as the Southern Mountain (Nanshan) school. But the rigor of the school's adherence to the monastic rules and regulations of Indian Buddhism did not attract a large following in China. The Kosa school based its teachings on Vasubandhu's Abhidharmakosha as translated by Paramartha between 563 and 567. This school followed closely the teachings of its Indian predecessor as well. Again, it attracted few Chinese followers, withering on the vine and disappearing as an independent school by 793.

The Tiantai School and Indigenous Chinese Buddhist Thought

Far more important to Chinese religious history were the new schools of Buddhism that arose in China and that owed little or nothing to Indian models other than their basic assumptions about the nature of reality. The first such school was the Tiantai (T'ien-t'ai) school founded by Zhiyi (Chih-i), who lived from 538 to 597. Zhiyi's biography is a pious litany of miracles and wonders. His mother supposedly conceived him after swallowing a white mouse in a dream, thus echoing the story of the Buddha's birth after his mother dreamed that a white elephant had entered her side. Zhiyi's birth was allegedly marked by a supernatural light in the sky and two monks appearing on the family doorstep to proclaim the newborn's glorious destiny. Whatever the truth of these stories, Zhiyi did indeed enter the Buddhist order and made his way to a monastery on Tiantai (Heavenly Terrace) mountain in present-day Zhejiang province—from which the name of the school that he founded was derived. Zhiyi wrote little, but his devoted disciple Guanding (Kuanting, 561–632) preserved his master's lectures for future generations. Zhiyi took for his text the Lotus Sutra, which had its origins in India. By the time of Zhiyi, however, it had undergone numerous emendations and additions in the Chinese environment.

Zhiyi began his approach to Buddhism by tackling a perennial problem in Chinese Buddhist thought. This was the tremendous number and variety of Buddhist texts then extant in China. Which one, wondered the Chinese, was the authoritative text? Zhiyi cut through this problem by postulating that this unwieldy mass of material could be arranged and classified according to what he called *banjiao* (*p'an-chiao*), a division of the literature into a series of historical periods and levels of metaphysical profundity. Zhiyi identified "five periods and eight teachings" in his examination of the question. Later Buddhist scholastics continued to debate the specific arrangement and relative importance of the main Buddhist texts, but the basic principles laid down for the analysis and interpretation of those texts by Zhiyi became normative in all later schools of Chinese Buddhism. Zhiyi held that there were five periods of Buddhist thought: the Huayan (Hua-yen) or Flower Garland period; the Ahan or Scripture period; the Fangdeng or elementary Mahayana period; the Da banruo (Ta pan-jo) or Perfection of Wisdom period; and the Fahua nieban (Fa-hua nieh-p'an) or Lotus/Great Decease period. Each of these periods, ranged from earliest to latest, represented the progressive teachings of the Buddha as he strove to communicate his experiential discoveries after his enlightenment.

The earliest Huayan period represented the highest level of the teaching, but it was too complex to be grasped by the average person, and so after three weeks the Buddha modified his message in order to be understood by the laity. The next period of teaching, the Ahan, lasted, according to Zhiyi, for twelve years. During this time, the Buddha taught a modified doctrine designed to accustom the average person to the fundamental truths of Buddhism. It was not, however, the full teaching. In the third period, which lasted some eight years, the Buddha began to introduce more material on the true nature of reality through the vehicle of Mahayana concepts, such as the *bodhisattva*, that elaborated on the earlier, Theravada teachings. This period was called "broad and equal" because the Buddha's teachings at this time were broad in the sense of universal, and equal in the sense that the sutras taught the equality and sameness of all things.

During the fourth period of twenty-two years, the Buddha began to teach complex metaphysical questions. From this emerged the Prajnaparamita literature that reconciled the apparent differences between the Theravada and the Mahayana schools. During this period, the Buddha also taught the essential nonduality of existence. All divisions were illusory and disappeared as one apprehended the higher levels of truth. Everything was *shunyata*, essential emptiness. But this doctrine was, at least in Zhiyi's mind, too negative. It had to be balanced with a concomitant positive message, which was encapsulated in the teachings of the Lotus Sutra that the Buddha expounded in the final eight years of his life. Here he taught the absolute identity of all phenomena in the *ekayana*, the One Vehicle. By this means, he accomplished the great task that he had set himself—the salvation of the human race from the wheel of suffering and rebirth. Of course, such a classification of the Buddhist literature ran into problems. Even the most committed of the followers of the Tiantai school were forced to admit that the Buddha had not followed a strict pattern in his teaching. He sometimes taught the teachings of the five periods simultaneously according to the capacity of his audience.

This reaction gave rise to attempts to classify further the Buddha's message in terms of both teaching method and the teachings themselves. Tiantai held there to

The Buddha Preaching on the Vulture Peak, Dunhuang, Tang dynasty, 8th century. Originally a religion of the gentry and aristocracy, Buddhism was spread to the common people of China through the efforts of Pure Land and Zen preachers.

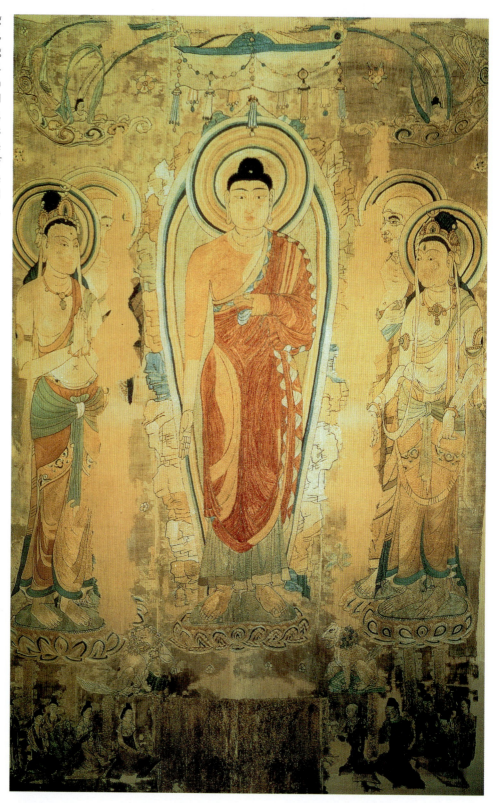

be four teaching methods. The first was the abrupt or sudden method, as taught in the Flower Garland (Huayan) scripture, that was suitable for beings of the highest capacity and led to immediate understanding of the true nature of reality. The second method was the gradual doctrine, suitable for audiences with only limited capacity, which led beings by gradual steps to a realization of the truth. Using both the Theravada and early Mahayana scriptures, this method was taught in the Ahan and Fengdeng periods of the Buddha's mission. The last two divisions were the secret method, used by the Buddha to address someone secretly; and the indeterminate method, for an audience of mixed capacity.

So much for method—what about the teachings themselves? Again, the Tiantai school believed there to be a fourfold division. The first was the teachings particular to the Theravada interpretation of the Buddhist scriptures. Next there was the common doctrine that applied to all the schools of Buddhism. The third type of teaching was the special doctrine: it was only for those beings that had become *bodhisattvas* and stood poised on the brink of becoming fully fledged Buddhas. Finally, there was the round or perfect doctrine that showed how all things arose and depended on one another. This was the epitome of the Buddha's teachings. Zhiyi then proceeded to associate these four teaching methods and four types of teachings with his scheme of five historical periods of the Buddha's mission. The earliest period, Huayan, was termed the twofold period since it was special and perfect. Next came the Ahan, or simple period of the scriptures. This was followed by the Fengdeng period, when all the doctrines were taught; the period of the Prajnaparamita; and finally the period of the Lotus Sutra, the perfection of the Buddhist teachings.

The Tiantai school appears to modern observers to be a somewhat artificial and forced systemization of Buddhist intellectual history, but it serves as an excellent example of the differences in approach between Chinese and Indian Buddhists. For the Indians, there was no need to explain the differences in Buddhist schools and doctrine. They existed side by side, coming into existence as a result of new interpretations of existing scriptures or the promulgation of new scriptures claiming to be revelations from an eternal Buddha resident in higher levels of universal reality. Their coexistence, and even their contradictory teachings, presented no problem to the Indian mind. One simply picked the interpretation that fitted one's personal view of reality and ignored the others. The Chinese, on the other hand, needed their intellectual universe to be more ordered. Unwilling to say that the Buddha's doctrine was not perfect at its inception, they needed to reconcile the perfection of the Buddha with developments in Buddhist thought over the thousand years that separated them from his death. Zhiyi was able to present a system that did just that, while at the same time justifying his adherence to the teachings of the Lotus Sutra. This made the Tiantai school very appealing to subsequent generations of Chinese Buddhists.

In its metaphysics, the Tiantai school held very closely to the teachings of Nagarjuna. Consequently, it believed that all phenomena were empty and without intrinsic existence. Phenomena existed by virtue of their interdependence on one another. To understand the interplay of being and nonbeing was to understand the fundamental nature of the universe, which was a balance of the two. This the Tiantai school extrapolated into the so-called three truths: the truths of emptiness, transience, and the mean or balance. The Tiantai worldview was one of vast vistas of interactive phenomena. It was summed up in the saying *yinian sanqian* (*i-nien san-ch'ien*), "one thought equals the three thousand worlds." Yet far from deprecating the visible world, such a view sacralizes it so that the life of the average Buddhist layperson becomes as real and important as that of the Buddha.

This interpenetration of the noumenal and the phenomenal worlds was further developed in the Tiantai doctrine of the absolute mind. This was the underlying framework of the universe that gave coherence and shape to the myriad elements of existence. It has two natures, the pure nature and the impure. The Buddha is the manifestation of the pure aspect of the universal mind, while the phenomena of day-to-day existence come into being as a result of the impure aspect. Since all things are merely aspects of the universal mind, it naturally follows that they are, in their essential core, all the same thing. Hence the position of later Tiantai leaders such as Zhanran (711–782), who argued that even inanimate objects such as mountains and rivers possessed the Buddha nature.

So much for theory, but how is the individual to realize this identity in actual fact? Tiantai developed an elaborate system of meditation that was aimed at addressing this question, which consisted of two elements. The first was *zhi* or concentration. The second was *guan* or insight. Concentration was aimed at producing the realization of the emptiness of all phenomena and their lack of real existence. Insight produced the realization that phenomena do exist within the universal mind. When these two streams of meditation merged, the individual gained true knowledge of the nature of the universe, and that knowledge liberated him or her from the round of birth and death.[1]

The Huayan School and the Elaboration of Chinese Buddhist Thought

The Tiantai system of classifying and analyzing Buddhist thought became the generally accepted framework within which Chinese Buddhist thought continued to evolve. But new interpretations of the scriptures and of previous philosophical efforts continued to develop. One of the most interesting of these was the Huayan school, which based its teachings on the Avatamsaka or Flower Garland Sutra. Despite the fact that elements of this scripture had their origins in India, much of the text was composed in China, and the interpretation and elaboration of the ideas found in the work are primarily Chinese in nature. The essence of the Huayan Sutra was translated in about 420 by Buddhabhadra, but it did not find a sympathetic commentator until Dushun (557–640) began lecturing on the text more than a century later. Dushun, a jack-of-all-trades as a youth, was a master of meditation and reputed to be the possessor of magical powers. Whatever the case may be, he must have been a magnetic preacher, since he was given high rank by the Sui dynasty and is accounted the originator of the Huayan school.

He was followed by Zhiyan (602–668), and then by Fazang (Fa-tsang, 643–712), who was the most able and original philosopher of the school. Fazang was followed by Zhengguan (733/737–820/838), then by his disciple Zongmi (Tsung-mi, 780–841). Zongmi is interesting in that he was at first a devotee of Chan Buddhism and only later embraced the Huayan school after reading a commentary on the Huayan Sutra by Zhengguan. Like his predecessors who had been heads of the school, Zongmi received high honors from the ruling emperor and was buried with great ceremony. But shortly after his death, Buddhism was suppressed by the court, and in the general decline of the religion that followed, the Huayan school was relegated to a minor position in Chinese intellectual life from which it never recovered.

However, during its heyday from about 620 to 840, Huayan Buddhism was the premier philosophical system of China. The foundational teaching of the school was centered on the theory of causation arising from the *dharmadhatu* or Realm of the Dharmas. In essence, Huayan held that the universe was self-creating and that all phenomena, while devoid of any intrinsic self, arose simultaneously. From this premise, the school then postulated that all phenomena were identical and that they interacted and interpenetrated one another. Needless to say, this theory of "everything is everything" was somewhat difficult for the average person to grasp. It was left to the great Huayan teacher Fazang to explain this doctrine in comprehensible terms. He did so in a famous lecture given for the Empress Wu. Asked to expound the Huayan doctrine to this formidable ruler in 704, Fazang composed the famous *Essay on the Golden Lion* to illustrate his philosophy. Taking a statue of a lion made of gold, Fazang made the following argument. First, he said, one must imagine that the gold symbolized the essence of things, their *li*. The shape of the parts of the statue represented *shi*, the form that conditions impose on this essence. The various parts of the lion were identical in that they were all made of the same essence, the gold. In a similar sense, the myriad phenomena of the universe, formed as they were of a single principle, were all identical as well. But, Fazang argued, no phenomenon could exist independently. The various parts of the statue of the lion could not exist without the existence of gold, but the gold was not the statue *per se*, unless it had been formed into the various parts of that statue. Thus phenomena were simultaneously the same and different.

Like Tiantai, Huayan divided the Buddhist teachings into various levels of profundity. At the bottom lay the doctrines of the Theravada school, which Huayan held to have been a necessary but now outmoded step in the understanding of the message of the Buddha. It was followed by the elementary doctrines of the Mahayana school that advanced Buddhist thinking, but were elementary in that they did not recognize the existence of the Buddha nature, as recognized by the Tiantai school, which had formed the third level of the final doctrine of the Mahayana. But this school still had not come to a perfect understanding of the teachings of the Buddha. The Chan school, which advocated abrupt enlightenment, had almost perceived the true nature of the teachings and so formed the fourth level of Buddhist teaching. However, it was only the fifth level of understanding, reached of course by the Huayan school with its full understanding of the interpenetration and interdependence of all phenomena, that fully encapsulated the true Buddhism of the Buddha.

The Persecution of Buddhism in the Later Tang

From the above discussions, the Tang period would seem to be a period of unprecedented prosperity for Chinese Buddhism, and indeed it was. But according to the Chinese theory of yin and yang, when something is at the height of its power and influence it contains within itself the seeds of its decline. This was certainly true in the case of Buddhism. As the Tang dynasty aged, it also began to decline—a trend that many Chinese statesmen saw as being rooted in the Tang emperors' support of the foreign Buddhist religion that flouted some of the most entrenched mores of Chinese culture. Consequently, they launched a campaign to purge what they viewed as unhealthy Buddhist influences from the court in an effort to halt the decline of the dynasty. While this did not ultimately destroy Chinese Buddhism, it did radically change the direction of its development and of the development of Buddhism in all East Asia as well.

During the Tang period, the Chinese tendency to control social institutions—something which has always been a major facet of government thinking—began to be applied to Buddhism with new vigor. Under previous dynasties, all except the most serious crimes committed by monks had been dealt with through internal discipline within the Buddhist monastic order. Now, for the first time, all crimes committed by monks, be they great or small, were tried in civil courts. This was symptomatic of an ever-increasing subordination of Buddhist religious institutions to civil authority. It was not long before these authorities began to tighten their grip on what they, as good Confucians, saw as a pernicious influence on Chinese morals and society.

The first major offensive against Buddhism was launched by the Daoist Fu Yi (554–639), who lived at the time of the first Tang emperor, Gaozu. The Tang imperial family claimed descent from the Daoist sage Laozi, and so was inclined to listen to the views of Daoist leaders such as Fu Yi. He attacked Buddhism for its extravagances, its deprecation of civil institutions, and its bad effects on Chinese morals owing to its downplaying of filiality and the institution of marriage. Moreover, since Buddhist monks were exempt from military service, and Buddhist institutions and land were exempt from taxation, the growth of Buddhism meant a threat to the state through diminished manpower and loss of tax revenues. The emperor, while not anti-Buddhist, did see the need to curb the growing power of the religion, and so limited the number of Buddhist establishments that could exist in any given province as well as the number of monks allowed to be ordained. But internal governmental conflicts ensured that these measures were never actually implemented.

The ambivalence that the first emperor of the Tang dynasty showed toward Buddhism was subsequently continued by his successors, but Buddhism flourished nonetheless. By the middle of the ninth century, it had reached unprecedented heights of considerable wealth and influence in China. This moved the Confucian philosopher and statesman Han Yu to compose his famous address to the throne, decrying what he saw as Buddhism's essentially anti-Chinese nature. In 819, a relic, supposedly a bone of the Buddha from the Famen Temple in the Tang imperial capital, was brought in an annual procession to the palace, where it was received with great pomp and ceremony by the emperor himself. Han Yu took this occasion to protest the great influence that Buddhism was having on China and so to call for its suppression.

Although Han Yu's petition to the throne seems to have had little direct effect, it represented the tip of the iceberg of Confucian disapproval of Buddhism's growing influence. In 845, this erupted into a full-fledged persecution of Buddhism. Whether this suppression of the religion was purely the result of the reigning emperor Wuzong's personal inclinations or, as is more likely, a manifestation of a more generalized power struggle between the Confucian bureaucrats and the eunuchs of the imperial household who supported Buddhism, the effects were catastrophic. Wuzong broke up the great Buddhist estates and forced about a quarter of a million monks and nuns to return to private life. Buddhist images were melted down for coins or weapons. Previous persecutions, such as those of 446 and 574, paled by comparison. But within a year, Wuzong died and the persecutions waned under the rule of the next emperor, Xuanzong. But the damage had been done. Monastic Buddhism never recovered from the blows it had been dealt, and the schools of Chinese Buddhism that were supported by that institution declined with it. It was left to new forms of Buddhism, such as Pure Land and Chan, to carry on the rich Buddhist traditions of China.

Pure Land Buddhism

At a relatively early point in Chinese history, Buddhism began to separate into two distinct camps, one appealing to the aristocracy, the other to the common people. The form of Buddhism espoused by the common people was the Pure Land school, which based its teachings on the Sukhavativyuha Sutra. In essence, this sutra spoke of a "pure land," a universe where a Buddha still lived and where it was possible to achieve enlightenment—unlike the universe in which we live, where the Buddha had departed physical existence as a result of human error. The Buddha of the Pure Land, Amitabha, had taken a vow that he would save all beings who called on his name with perfect faith by causing them to be reborn in his universe. In the Pure Land there were no demons, ghosts, or animals. Rich jeweled trees and fragrant flowers grew in abundance. Nothing impure, unpleasant, or painful existed there. It was a paradise as well as the gateway to escape from the cycle of life and death.

Unlike other schools of Chinese Buddhism that emphasized learning and monastic discipline, the Pure Land school gave primary importance to faith. One's own efforts, ineffective in themselves, were aided by the efforts of Amitabha. As such, the school held tremendous appeal for the lower classes, who could not spare any time from their harsh lives to devote themselves to meditation and study, and would not abandon their familial responsibilities by entering the monkhood. For the vast mass of the toiling peasantry, the only hope lay in the compassion of the Buddha Amitabha and the aid of his chief lieutenant, Avalokiteshvara, the *bodhisattva* of compassion who had vowed to lead suffering beings to the Pure Land. This being, known in China as Guanyin, "the one who perceives the sounds [of human prayers]," became one of the greatest objects of devotion in the Chinese mind; even today she remains one of the most venerated and supplicated figures in the Chinese pantheon.

The Pure Land school, although existing in embryonic form in India, found its fullest expression in East Asia. The core Sukhavativyuha Sutra seems to have been translated into Chinese no less than ten times and to have expanded considerably in the process.[2] The earliest references to the Pure Land teachings would seem to indicate that they were present in China by about the middle of the third century but did not achieve prominence until sometime later. The first *zu* (*tsu*), the patriarch or leader of the school, is accounted to be Huiyuan, a recluse living in the early fifth century who did no preaching, except by his example of devotion to Amitabha. But it was with Tanluan (476–542) that we see Pure Land Buddhism emerging as a formal Chinese Buddhist school. In about 530, following a serious illness, the middle-aged Tanluan met a Buddhist monk named Bodhiruci who sparked a religious conversion in him. Tanluan then devoted his remaining years to popularizing the new school.

Tanluan immediately realized that Pure Land Buddhism, unlike so much Chinese Buddhism of his day, was not the exclusive preserve of the educated classes. Consequently, he popularized one of the great devotional vehicles of world religious history—the Amitabha mantra or *koucheng nianfo* (*k'ou-ch'eng nien-fo*). By reciting the simple formula, "I rely on the name of Amitabha," Tanluan introduced a devotional technique that could be used everywhere and at all times. Peasants could chant it as they labored in the fields. Merchants could murmur it as they moved around their stalls. The government official could mentally repeat it as he waited hour upon hour for an imperial audience. No longer were religious activities shackled to specific times and places or to the ministrations of professional clergy. By a simple stroke, Tanluan liberated Buddhism, or at least one form of Buddhism, from a small group of specialists and presented it to society at large.

Guanyin, Sung dynasty, 13th century. Guanyin was the most popular *bodhisattva* in the Pure Land pantheon and the object of intense popular devotion.

The next great Pure Land teachers were Daozhuo and his student Shandao (613–681). Daozhuo advocated such devices as using beans to mark the number of times one repeated the name of Amitabha. While practices such as these might look like empty formalism, they could also be very effective in focusing the mind on religious matters. But it was Daozhuo's student, Shandao, who codified the methods of Pure Land devotion. These he considered to be five in number: uttering the name of the Buddha; chanting the Pure Land sutras; meditating on the Buddha; worshipping images of the Buddha; and singing the praises of the Buddha. He still believed that the primary means of attaining the Pure Land was through the repetition of the *nianfo* mantra, but he also realized that human nature demanded supports in the religious life that meditation alone did not provide—hence his regard for outward religious ceremonies and worship.

As Pure Land Buddhism became more popular, it naturally came into conflict with other forms of Buddhism. Under such leaders as Cimin (680–748) and Fazhao (fl. 763–804), attempts were made to harmonize the Pure Land teachings with the teachings of other schools, particularly the emerging Chan school. But it was the persecutions of 845 that allowed Pure Land to emerge as one of the two principal schools of later Chinese Buddhism. Beloved and supported by the peasantry, the Pure Land monks needed no governmental assistance to continue their missionary

Altarpiece with Amitabha and attendants, Sui dynasty, 593 C.E. The Pure Land school of Buddhism appealed to the common people who could not afford to spend a great deal of time or money on religious observances and practices.

activities. As a result, they suffered little in the brief but catastrophic period that spelled doom for many more powerful, richer, and well-established schools. The same could be said of the Chan school—the other tradition that emerged virtually unscathed from this time of trial.

Chan Buddhism

Chan Buddhism, which is better known in the West by its Japanese name of Zen, was another school that chose to follow a different path from those of the Chinese Buddhist schools that had preceded it. Chan Buddhism reflects the Chinese practical nature, which is oriented toward immediate results, rather than the speculative and patient nature of its Indian founders. Although Chan claims to have existed in India, it was in China that it truly originated and where it developed the authority and prestige that it continues to enjoy. The essence of the Chan, as its Indian name Dhyana or Meditation implies, is the practice of meditative introspection into the nature of one's own consciousness. Following other schools of Chinese Buddhism, Chan believed that all beings possessed the Buddha nature and that the key to salvation lay in gaining access to this preexisting condition within one's self. When this was accomplished, the cycle of life and death was broken. Of course, this was more easily said than done, and a range of meditative techniques evolved to aid the seeker in his or her quest for liberation. Two of the earliest Chinese monks to introduce these techniques into Chinese Buddhism (although without systematizing them into a distinctive school) were Daoan (312–385) and Huiyuan (334–416). These early pioneers labored to collect texts related to meditation and to disseminate information on the practice. They were aided in this by the arrival in China of a number of Indian meditation masters, such as Buddhabhadra and Buddhasanta; but it was not until the arrival of the great Indian monk Bodhidharma that Chan could be said to have become a major force in Chinese Buddhist thought.

As is the case with many other important religious figures, our knowledge about the life of Bodhidharma is somewhat obscure. According to traditional Chinese sources, he arrived in China in either 520 or 526. He then went north to the kingdom of Wei, where he sat in front of a wall meditating for nine years, only agreeing to teach when his disciple Shenguang cut off his own arm as evidence of his dedication to his master's teachings. Modern scholarship, however, seems to indicate that Bodhidharma may have arrived in China several years earlier than is traditionally supposed. In any event, he established a lineage of teachers that continued to propagate his teachings on meditation. Although later Chan vehemently denies the value of scripture as a source of true insight, at least in any ultimate sense, Bodhidharma seems to have based his teaching on the Lankavatara Sutra. This text, written in about 350, emphasized the doctrine of inner enlightenment, which eliminated all false perceptions of duality. Moreover, the text also argued that words were not essential to the communication of great truths, which could be communicated by a variety of means—such as the Buddha's communication of the essence of Chan doctrine to the monk Kashyapa through the medium of giving him a flower.

Central to this idea of communication of the truth through personal experience was the figure of the teacher. Consequently, there grew up in Chan, as in other Chinese Buddhist schools, an emphasis on the head of the school, the so-called patriarch, although how formal this institution actually was in early Chan is hotly debated. After Bodhidharma's death, his mantle supposedly descended on

Shenguang (whom he renamed Huike), who passed it on to Sengcan (d. 606), Daoxin (580–651), Hungren (602–675), and finally Shenxiu (600–706). The core teachings of Chan on the goal of enlightenment and the basic means of gaining it through meditation never changed, but there were numerous differences of opinion that soon arose over doctrinal and practical questions. The most important of these was whether enlightenment was a gradual process or an abrupt one. This question, apparently innocent enough, seems to have split the Chan school.

Chan Abbot Wuzhun, Southern Song dynasty, 1238. The Chan and Pure Land schools became the predominate schools of later Chinese Buddhism.

The immediate cause of this rupture was the contention of Shenhui (670–762), a monk from southern China, that the true line of transmission of Bodhidharma's teachings was not via Hungren through Shenxiu, but via Hungren through another monk, Huineng (638–713). In this version of the Chan school's development, Hungren had accepted Huineng's belief that enlightenment was instantaneous and, repudiating the gradual enlightenment theory of Shenxiu's followers, conferred the mantle of the patriarchy of the Chan school on Huineng, and his disciples who lived in south China. The northern followers of Shenxiu did not, of course, accept this interpretation of Chan history; but the Southern school flourished at their expense and, by 760, it was victorious in its campaign to be considered the premier school of Chan.

With the triumph of the Southern school of Chan, internal discussion shifted away from metaphysical toward practical questions. As a result, two main schools of practice developed. The first of these was the Linji (Lin-chi) school founded by Yixuan (d. 867). The second was the Caodung (Ts'ao-tung) school founded by Liangjie (807–869) and Benji (840–901). The Linji school was notable for its use of the *gongan* (*kung-an*), meaning a "case" or "problem." This was a pithy saying that was designed to "knock" the mind out of its usual patterns of thought and thus allow it to perceive its own nature clearly without the residue of conceptual thought that usually obscured this nature. Its use of non sequitur, the juxtaposing of disparate ideas, and shocking images by this school owes much, directly or indirectly, to the writings and philosophy of the Daoist master Zhuangzi. Since it saw enlightenment as an all-or-nothing proposition, the Linji school advocated a sort of "shock therapy" technique of meditation that used a variety of methods—including that of beating the meditator! The Caodung school, which advocated simple sitting meditation and quiet introspection interspersed with verbal instruction and discussion, was viewed as being considerably less radical; and it could be seen as a partial return, in a new guise, of the gradual enlightenment doctrine of the now defunct Northern school of Chan.[3]

But the development of the Chan School was not yet complete. With its freedom from the bonds of scripture, its advocating that its monks work to support themselves (thus escaping the charge that its members were parasites living on the labor of others), and its de-emphasis of the traditional trappings of Buddhism such as large monastic establishments and long courses of formal study, made Chan a very appealing option for a certain segment of the Chinese intelligensia and for the common people as well. Moreover, without scriptures, images or any other ritual paraphenalia, Chan could travel light and unencumbered by the traditional trappings of monastic Buddhism. This would serve the school well in the great persecution of Buddhism in the late 840s. It not only survived but even prospered in the aftermath of the persecution of 845, becoming one of the two predominate forms of Buddhism in post-Tang China. After the fall of the Tang dynasty, the Song emperors patronized the Chan School lavishly. This patronage resulted in the development of the Five Mountains and Ten Temples system. In essence, this was a series of Chan monasteries and temples, all belonging to the Yangqi branch of the Linji School that were assigned official ranks and grading and patronized accordingly. Although this increased institutionalization did limit to some extent the spontaneous nature of the school, it also afford it a favorable climate in which to develop before the Mongol storm overwhelmed China in the 1200s.

Another major development of this period was the syncretism that began to be evident between the Chan School and other forms of thought. This tendency is first evident in the thought of the Huayan master Zongmi. Originally a Chan monk, he melded the practical side of Chan with the more philosophical aspects of Huayan.

During the Song period, this tendancy intensified. Chan monks now associated themselves with Tiendai teachings, and the study of the Mahayana scriptures. Nor were the teachings of the Pure Land School ignored. Such monks as Yongming Yanshou (904–975) advocated the recitation of the Amida mantra (*nianfo*) as a prop to Chan meditation, and the simultaneous practice of the two disciplines became common. Nor were other Buddhist schools the only forms of thought appropriated by the Chan monks. A lively dialogue ensued in the late Song between the Chan thinkers and the Neo-Confucians, with both sides gaining much from the discussion. Many Chan thinkers took a lively interest in Confucian thought, incorporating Confucian ethics into their teaching and even writing commentaries on Confucian texts such as the one by Qisong (1007–1072) on the Doctrine of the Mean.

During the Ming period, the Yangqi branch of the Linji School absorbed all of the other schools of Chan, including the Caodung school, and propagated its syncretic version of the Chan teachings. But formal Chan was in decline. After the Ming period, all originality was lost and the age of the great Chan teachers was past. Chan began increasingly to merge into an undifferentiated "folk" Buddhism. Even though the school did not disappear entirely, its years of creativity were over. But it had planted its thought and doctrines in many parts of Asia, and so, in Vietnam, Korea, and especially Japan, Chan ideals and practices continued to flourish and make great contributions to the religious life of those countries.

Website References

1. An example of Tiantai writings can be found at
   hjem.get2net.dk/civet-cat/zen-writings/tien-tai/index.htm

2. villa.lakes.com/cdpatton/Dharma/Canon/T0367-e.html gives a translation of the smaller Pure Land Sutra.

3. Many Chinese and Japanese Chan/Zen texts can be found at
   hjem.get2net.dk/civet-cat/zen-writings.htm#sutras

Chinese Religions Timeline

DATE	
B.C.E.	
6000	First civilization begins to emerge around the bend of the Yellow River in northern China.
c. 1766–1122	Shang dynasty—ruler seen as "son of heaven" who can intercede for the people at large. Oracle bones used.
c. 1122–403	Zhou dynasty—doctrine of *tianming*, the "Mandate of Heaven," evolves.
c. 770–221	Warring States period.
c. 552–479	Kung Fuzi, founder of Confucianism.
c. 500–200	Beginnings of philosophical Daoism. *Daodejing* compiled.
c. 485–430	Mo Zi, founder of Mohist school.
c. 371–289	Meng Zi, founder of the idealistic school of Confucianism.
c. 350	Zhuang Zi writes the Daoist text that bears his name.
c. 312–250	Xun Zi, founder of the "legalist" school of Confucianism.
233	Death of Han Fei Zi, founder of Legalism.
221–207	Qin dynasty—the First Emperor patronizes Daoist alchemists who promise to find the elixir of immortality for him.
202–220 (C.E.)	Han dynasty.
c. 179–104	Dong Zhongshu, leading Confucian philosopher.
c. 145–90	Sima Qian, historian of early China.
136	Confucianism strengthened at court through the appointment of Doctors of the Five (Confucian) Classics.
124	Increased use of written examinations based on the Confucian classics to select government officials.
c. 100	Gan Zhongke presents Han emperor with the supposedly Daoist book entitled the *Taipingjing*. Despite Gan's being instantly beheaded, this book continues to circulate and inspire "apocalyptic Daoism."
C.E.	
c. 27–97	Wang Chong, Confucian rationalist.
c. 65	First written reference to Buddhism in China.
79	Confucian scholars create critical edition of the Five Classics.
142	Zhang Daoling establishes the Daoist Way of the Celestial Masters (*Tianshi Dao*).
c. 150	An Shigao, early Buddhist missionary.
175	Confucian classics and the *Analects* engraved in stone.
220–280	Three Kingdoms period.
280–589	Period of multiple northern and southern Chinese states.
317	Northern China abandoned to foreign invaders. Ke Hong writes the Daoist alchemical classic, the *Baopuzi*.
344–413	Kumarajiva, the great translator of Buddhist texts into Chinese.
364–370	Yang Xi has visions that result in the foundation of the Maoshan school of Daoism.
397	Ke Chaofu begins to compose the Classic of the Sacred Jewel (*Lingbao Jing*), which becomes the central text of the Daoist school of the same name.
399–414	Faxian travels to Central Asia and India in search of Buddhist texts.
403	Huiyuan argues that Buddhist monks should be exempt from bowing to the emperor.

DATE	
415	Kou Qianzhi receives a revelation ordering him to reform Daoism in northern China.
440	Beginnings of state patronage of Daoism in both the north and south.
476–542	Tanluan, popularizer of Pure Land Buddhism.
504	Daoism persecuted in southern China.
531–597	Zhikai, founder of the Tiantai school of Buddhism.
549–623	Jizang, exponent of Madhyamika school of Buddhism.
575	Tiantai school founded.
589–618	Chinese national unity restored under Sui dynasty.
596–664	Xuanzang, Buddhist pilgrim to India (629–645) and text translator.
618–906	Tang dynasty.
641	Chinese princess marries king of Tibet. First penetration of Chinese Buddhism into that country.
638–713	Huineng, sixth Chan patriarch and founder of the Southern school of Chan popularized by Shenhui (d. 760).
643–699	Fazang, third patriarch and real founder of the Huayan school of Buddhism.
666	Laozi canonized by Tang emperor (who claims to be his descendant) as Most High Emperor of Mystic Origin.
671	Yijing makes a pilgrimage to India.
786–824	Han Yu, Confucian revivalist.
807–869	Liangjie, founder of the Caodong school of Chan Buddhism.
845	State persecution of Buddhism. Beginning of decline of Buddhism in China.
867	Death of Yixuan, founder of the Linji school of Chan Buddhism.
932	Block printing of the Confucian classics begins.
960–1279	Sung dynasty.
972	Printing of the Buddhist Canon begins.
c. 1000	Daoist school of the Celestial Masters reformed under the name of the "New Orthodox Unity" (Xin Zhenyi).
1017–1073	Zhou Dunyi, proto-Neo-Confucian.
1032–1085	Cheng Hao, Neo-Confucian thinker.
1033–1107	Cheng Yi, Neo-Confucian thinker.
1130–1200	Zhu Xi, pivotal Neo-Confucian thinker.
1260–1368	Yuan (Mongol) dynasty.
1368–1644	Ming dynasty.
1416	Zhu Xi's commentaries on Confucian texts officially adopted as authoritative by the Ming government.
1472–1529	Wang Yangming.
1644–1912	Qing dynasty.
1912	Imperial system abolished and republican government inaugurated.
1925–1950	Mao Zedong formulates his theory of Communism by synthesizing Marxist and Chinese thought.
1949	Communists take over rule of China under Mao Zedong. Zhang Enbu, sixty-third patriarch of the Celestial Masters school, flees to Taiwan. Traditional religions and philosophies suppressed in China proper, but continue to flourish in Chinese communities outside mainland China.

Portrait of the monk Shinran, Japanese school. Shinran was a disciple of Honen and did much to spread Pure Land Buddhism, founding a school based on its teachings.

PART THREE

✦

The Religions of Northeast Asia

CHAPTER TWENTY-THREE

Religion in Korea

Korea, like Southeast Asia, is another point of religious transition. A physically rugged land with a relatively harsh climate, Korea often found itself caught between the political ambitions of its two larger neighbors; China and Japan. But as is the case in Southeast Asia, it would be unwise to see Korea as being swayed by every passing intellectual breeze. The Koreans were certainly influenced by external religious ideas, principally those originating in China. But they took each of these new systems of thought and transformed it in accordance with their own needs and native genius. Consequently, Korean religion exhibits many facets that are unique to that country, while at the same time it has made real contributions to the philosophical development of the traditions involved.

The Indigenous Religious Traditions of Korea

Early Korean society was formed from a number of different ethnic elements, each with its own religious and cultural traditions. The original inhabitants of the peninsula were probably members of the Paleo-Siberian peoples. They were followed by the group known as the Neo-Siberian people, and finally by Tungusic peoples. By 600 B.C.E., these groups had melded together into a single group, although vestiges of their diverse origins are still evident in Korean religion. The earliest tangible religious artifacts that remain from this period are a series of monolithic burial monuments, which, as is the case with similar remains elsewhere, tell us very little about the day-to-day religious beliefs of the people who built them. They obviously believed in some sort of afterlife, and the prevalence of horse, tiger, and bird motifs in the ornaments that they deposited in these tombs reflects symbolic motifs still used in current shamanic cultures of northeastern Asia. The tombs also reflect a society that was already highly stratified into nobles and common people, who were buried in much humbler circumstances.

From the evidence of present-day Shamanism in Korea, we can make some general extrapolations about its practice on the peninsula in ancient times. The first thing that becomes apparent is that the primary religious functionaries in Korean Shamanism, as in Japanese shamanic religion, were women. These *mudang* are a common feature of Paleo-Siberian society, whereas in Neo-Siberian shamanic religion the practitioners are usually men. In modern Korean shamanic religion there are still some male functionaries, the *paksu*, but their role in the tradition is limited, with women forming the majority of its religious specialists. There are a number of other Paleo-Siberian and Neo-Siberian elements in the modern Korean tradition as well. The female shaman wears men's clothing during rituals, as in the Paleo-Siberian tradition; and, in the Neo-Siberian tradition, these clothes are covered with dangling objects that clang together, with the drum being used to induce a trance. Unlike these Siberian traditions, however, the shaman does not journey into the spirit world, but is possessed by the spirit that she is trying to contact. This is a common feature in Southeast Asian shamanic religion and may reflect influences from the region. All in all, it seems likely that in early Korean shamanic religion a mixture of Siberian traditions was evident at an early date.[1]

As in all shamanic traditions, the world of Korean indigenous religion was populated by a vast number of spirits. At the apex of these spirits stood Hanüllim, the Ruler of Heaven. Everything in the world was seen as emanating from him, although he had delegated most of the authority for the day-to-day running of the world to lesser spirits. Also high in this spiritual hierarchy was Ch'ilsŏng-nim, the Seven Star Spirit, who was associated with the constellation of the Great Bear. This spirit may not have been a separate entity in his own right, but rather an alternate name for Hanüllim. Below these spirits were those of the air, the waters, and other geographical features. The most prominent of these was San-sin, the Mountain God, who was intimately associated with the legendary founder of the Korean people, Tangun. The Mountain God was seen as the protector of the people and the land, as well as a source of fertility. In addition to these spirits the Koreans venerated local spirits of the fields, village, and individual households, including Sŏngju, the chief guardian of the home, Chowang, the Kitchen Spirit, and even Pyŏnso kakssi, the guardian of the toilet. Finally, there were the spirits of the ancestors.

The rituals for the spirits were by their nature very local affairs, but by the fourth century C.E., we can see that a number of well-defined rituals had emerged in the distinctive tribal groups that characterized Korean society at that time. Among the northern Puyŏ people, who lived on the border between Korea and China, the most important festival was the *Yŏnggo-je*, which celebrated the end of the grazing season. At this festival, the Puyŏ would sacrifice an ox and read the future by interpreting the cracks in one of its hoofs—in much the same way as the early peoples of China had tried to read the future in cracks on oracle bones. Slightly farther south in Koguryŏ, the northernmost Korean peninsular state of the time, the harvest festival known as *Tongmaeng-je* was celebrated in honor of the male reproductive deity, Susin. In the southern part of the peninsula, the Han people celebrated spring (*Suritnal*) and fall (*Sangdal*) agricultural festivals. The officiants at these ceremonies were termed Ch'ŏn-gun, Prince of Heaven, and were seen as being *sinin* or divine men. They probably had secular as well as religious authority within their tribes.

As with all early peoples, early Korean rites tended to take place in the open air wherever a convenient location could be found. In southern Korea, however, sacred precincts called *sodo* began to evolve. These were groves of trees marked off by a bell and drum suspended on a pole, symbolizing the presence of divine beings within the sacred precinct. As certain families began to dominate the political life of larger and larger areas, their particular clan *sodos* became associated with their founding ancestors, who were often seen as being of divine origin. The Korean people's belief in their divine origin is clearly embodied in the national foundation myth of Tangun, who was the offspring of a tiger who later became a woman and Hwanung, the son of Hanüllim, who had descended to the earth on the mountain peak of T'aebaek-san. Tangun then proceeded to establish the earliest recorded Korean state, Chosŏn.

The various proto-states of early Korea all had myths very similar in structure to the Tangun myth, harking back to a divine origin for the ruler of the particular state in question.

The shamanic elements inherent in early Korean kingship are evident from the material remains found in the great tumulus tombs of the kings of Silla. Dating from the sixth century C.E. and later, their occupants were buried in three items of dress that were considered essential to the regalia of a shaman—the crown, the belt, and the shoes. The crown of the Silla kings was formed in the shape of trees and deer antlers. From these branches dangled comma-shaped beads of jade called *kogok*, which are very similar to the Japanese *magatama*, or sacred jewels, and probably represent either bear or tiger claws. Similar objects dangled from the gold belts of the Silla kings—in much the same way as they do on the regalia of present-day shamans. It would not be unreasonable to conclude from all this that the origins of Korean kingship, as in China, Japan, and Southeast Asia, were intimately linked with religious functions inherited from, and patterned on, shamanic antecedents.

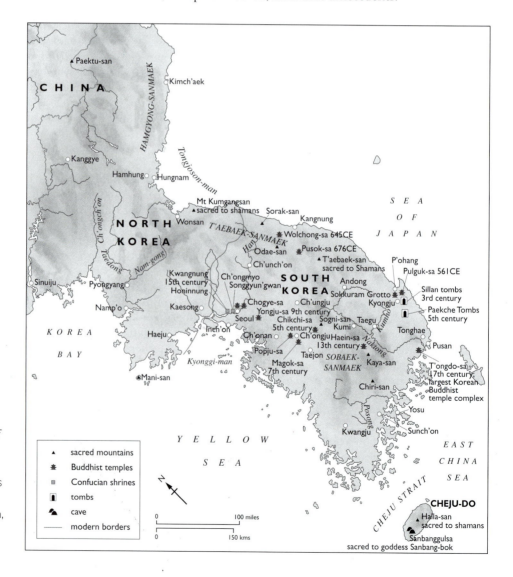

Important Korean religious sites. Korea has a large number of religious sites, representing a broad spectrum of traditions including Buddhism, Confucianism, Daoism, and indigenous traditions.

The Early Development of Confucianism and Daoism in Korea

As the states of the Korean peninsula began to coalesce, they came under the influence of China, their great neighbor to the south and west; and, for a period of its early history, much of Korea was under the direct political control of the Han dynasty. One would naturally expect, therefore, to see the beginnings of Buddhism, Confucianism, and Daoism at this time (c. 100 C.E.). But it is not clear to what extent a significant exchange of religious ideas actually took place during this early period. When we speak of Confucianism and Daoism in early Korea, at least up until about 650, we are not speaking of the development of a specific religious tradition so much as of a general influence on thought and literature that flowed from China into the peninsular states. In Koguryŏ, the first instance in which we can see such influence at work is in the establishment in 372 of the T'aehak, a national college for the education of sons of the aristocracy. This new institution, which owed its origins to Koguryŏ's disastrous defeat a few years previously by Paekche, another state located in the southwestern part of the peninsula, was not so much an attempt to promulgate the ideas of Confucius for moral or philosophical purposes as it was an effort to improve the state's governmental efficiency. Of course by this time in East Asia, such an institution was by definition a Confucian one. The new academy taught the Confucian classics, Chinese literature, and the martial arts, but its effectiveness as a vehicle for the transmission of Confucian ideals to the Korean people at large was restricted by an admission policy that allowed only aristocratic youths through its doors.

The situation was much the same in Paekche. Confucianism seems to have become established in the country at about the same time as Buddhism had. But, unlike Koguryŏ, Paekche seems to have developed a tradition of Confucian scholarship relatively early. As was the case with Buddhism, it was from Paekche that Confucianism was first exported to Japan. Between about 350 and 380, two scholars named A Chikki and Wang In traveled to Japan, where A Chikki became the tutor to the crown prince. A Chikki then requested that Wang In come to Japan to assist him. The latter arrived carrying copies of the *Analects* as well as a copy of the *Thousand Character Classic*, a basic text for the teaching of Chinese writing. It is probably from this date that we can trace the origins of literacy in Japan. Wang In's influence on Japanese society was extensive in that one of his descendants, Gyogi, became one of the most influential figures in early Japanese Buddhism.

Daoism, the other great tradition of China apart from Confucianism, had a much less extensive effect on Korean society, both in this early period and later in Korean history, and it left little in the way of organized institutions in Korea. But as was the case in China, Daoism's influence was considerably more subtle. Korean scholars were undoubtedly aware of the tenets of its philosophy and strongly influenced by its simple yet compelling assessment of the nature of reality. But if it is possible to assert that philosophical Daoism had a marked, if unobtrusive, effect on Korean intellectual development, the same cannot be said for Daoist religion. This was too close to indigenous Korean beliefs to commend it to the Korean people at large. If they felt drawn to this particular manifestation of the religious impulse, their own cultural heritage provided plenty of scope for such expression: they had no need to import foreign forms.

Of course, formal expressions of Daoism were not completely absent from Korea. Between about 625 and 650, institutional Daoism made considerable headway in

Koguryö. Whether this was due to the intrinsic merits of the religion, or, as is more likely, to the fact that the Tang rulers of the newly reunified empire fancied themselves as the descendants of Laozi, is debatable. Whatever the motivation, a number of Daoist adepts were now dispatched by the Chinese emperor Gaozu to the Koguryö court at the insistence of its principal noble, Yön Kaesomun. These adepts lectured on the *Daodejing* and other Daoist texts, and established the rudiments of a religious Daoist cult. Daoist influence waxed at the expense of Buddhism, and a number of Buddhist temples were transferred to the use of the newly arrived Daoists. Their influence was present in other states as well, but in a considerably less organized way. But Daoism's influence was transitory, and was never to become a distinct force in the Korean religious mind.

Buddhism in Early Korea

The earliest concrete indication that we have for the introduction of Buddhism into Korea is in the middle of the third century C.E. Buddhism was officially accepted as a state religion in the northern state of Koguryö in 372, and in the southwestern state of Paekche in 384, as a result of the teachings of an Indian monk named Malananda. The southeastern state of Silla, the farthest from Chinese influence, did not adopt Buddhism as an official state religion until almost a century later.

At first, Buddhism was very much a court religion, and found acceptance primarily among the aristocracy, coming as part and parcel of the general inroads of Chinese culture into the Korean states. But soon efforts were underway to spread the new religion beyond the circle of the capital. King Kogugyang of Koguryö (r. 384–391) and his successor Kwanggaet'o worked to transform Koguryö and its southern capital P'yöngyang into thoroughly Buddhist societies. Monks were dispatched to China to secure knowledge and scriptures. One such monk, Süngnang, studied with the famous Kumarajiva. He returned home to teach the doctrines of the San-lun school and seems to have espoused Huayan teaching before it became widely fashionable in China. As Buddhism took root in Korea, the Korean states began to send out missionaries of their own to the emerging nation of Japan. King Söng (r. 523–554) of Paekche was the first Korean ruler to dispatch monks and literature to Japan in 538, 545, and 552. This project was carried on by his successors. The Korean monks were accompanied by artisans and workmen who possessed a technical expertise far superior to their Japanese counterparts, and it is fair to say that early Japanese art and culture owed much to Korean models and technology. Koguryö also participated in the Buddhist evangelization of Japan. Indeed, the tutor to one of the most important figures of early Japanese history, Prince Shotoku Taishi, was Hyech'a, a Koguryö monk, and he was only one of several such missionaries who left northern Korea for the "barbaric" islands to the east.

The ambivalent reaction of the aristocracy of Silla toward Buddhism becomes all the more interesting in the light of this wholehearted and rapid acceptance of Buddhism elsewhere on the Korean peninsula. Here again, the first missionaries may have been of Indian ancestry, since the Silla records note that the first missionary to arrive there in about 430 was named Hükhoja (Black Barbarian), perhaps in reference to his dark south Indian skin. In any event, Buddhism's reception in Silla was decidedly chilly. This may have been because Silla's relatively isolated position had allowed it to retain more of its shamanic traditions than elsewhere in Korea.

Whatever the reason, it was a dangerous business to try to proselytize Silla, as the records show that some early Buddhist missionaries were martyred for their efforts. It is not until the reign of King Pöphüng (r. 514–539) that Buddhist regnal names appear in the Silla records, indicating the formal adoption of the religion by the royal family. In 539, Pöphüng built a great temple, the Taewang hüngnyun-sa, and on its completion he abdicated the throne to become a Buddhist monk.

Once Buddhism became part of Silla culture, however, it began to make significant inroads into the national consciousness. One notable example of this was connected with the establishment of the elite warrior corps of Silla, the Hwarang. These aristocratic young men were charged with protecting the country and lived by a code of chivalry known as the *Hwarang-do*. This was supposedly the work of the famous Silla monk Wön'gwang, who composed it after returning from an extensive period of study in China. He became not only a major religious leader, but an important civic figure as well. The code that he gave the Hwarang was a blend of Buddhism, Confucianism, and indigenous ideas, and it seems as if these warriors also developed a particular cult of the future Buddha Maitreya within their ranks. It was during the early 600s as well that Silla monks began to go on pilgrimage to India. According to one famous Chinese Buddhist work by I-tsing (635–713), virtually one sixth of all of the monks who traveled from China to India were in fact from Silla.

The later period of Silla history produced three eminent monks who had a decisive effect on the subsequent development of Korean Buddhism—Chajang (c. 600–655), Wönhyo (617–681), and Uisang (625–702). A member of a royal family, Chajang became a monk and traveled to China in 636. While there, he apparently had a vision of the Buddhist *bodhisattva* Manjushri. On returning to Silla, he was granted the highest title bestowed on Buddhist monks, that of *taegukt'ong* or supreme cleric. He immediately left the capital and went into the mountains, where he again had a vision of Manjushri, which led him to name the mountain range in which it occurred Odae-shan—after Manjushri's famous mountain shrine at Wutai (Wu-t'ai) in China. This story reflects the beginning of a trend that was to continue in Korea—the Buddhist appropriation of indigenous shrines of San-sin, the Mountain God.

Chajang now returned to the capital and began the task of reorganizing the Buddhist establishment. He implemented an intensified study of the scriptures, and made it compulsory for monks to attend a twice-yearly seminar on doctrine, followed by mandatory examinations based on the contents of those lectures. He consolidated the ordination of monks in the T'ongdo-sa Temple, making it the only place in Silla where monks could be ordained. Finally, he established a government department whose job it was to oversee the maintenance of Buddhist temples, images, and other such property. He was also the creator of the Yul-chöng or the Disciplinary school of Korean Buddhism, which emphasized monastic discipline as the way to enlightenment—although he himself also had a lively interest in the rituals of esoteric Buddhism.

It is hard to imagine a greater contrast than that between Chajang and Wönhyo, the next great figure in Silla Buddhism. Wönhyo was born into a provincial family of no great importance in 617, and appears to have become a Buddhist monk at an early age. After studying the Lotus and Nirvana Sutras in Silla, he arranged to go to China with his friend Uisang. The two set off, and at one point on their journey they were caught in a rainstorm and forced to spend the night in a cave. While they were there, a terrible thirst overcame Wönhyo, but, while groping around in the dark, he came upon a vessel filled with rainwater from which he drank eagerly. The next day, however, the two monks were horrified to discover that they had spent the night in a grave that had been opened by robbers, and that the vessel from which Wönhyo

Buddhist sculpture, South Korea. Buddhist influences in early Korea were closely tied to the development of organized states in the peninsula.

had drunk was in fact a skull. But after an initial feeling of revulsion, Wŏnhyo suddenly realized the relativity and temporary nature of all things, and thus achieved enlightenment. At this point, he felt that going on to China was irrelevant and left Uisang to return to Silla.

On returning home, Wŏnhyo began to work to unite the divergent schools of Korean Buddhism that were developing at that time. He no longer believed in the effectiveness of the scriptures, meditation, or monastic discipline as the sole roads to enlightenment. Rather, he felt that a balanced approach to practice and learning was the appropriate way of pursuing Buddhism. Consequently, he opposed the use of only isolated scriptures and practices within the narrow context of exclusive sects. His movement to unify Buddhism into a single entity became known as Ilsŭng pulgyo, Buddhism of the Single Vehicle, or T'ong pulgyo, Unified Buddhism. Particularly concerned with spreading Buddhism to the common people, Wŏnhyo eschewed the cloistered life style of the average Buddhist monk in favor of a peripatetic life wandering through the countryside. He preached Buddhism wherever he could find a crowd, be it in the marketplace, the tavern, or the country fair. The Buddhism he now taught was not the heavily philosophical Buddhism of his youth, but rather Chŏngt'o pulgyo, the Buddhism of the Pure Land. This did not mean, however, that he ceased his scholarly efforts. He continued to write, composing important commentaries on the Lotus, Nirvana, and Diamond Sutras as well as a commentary on the Mahayana Shraddhotpada Shastra, a manual on Buddhism for the layperson. Wŏnhyo differed from other monks in regards to his personal morality as well. He is reported to have abandoned the traditional Buddhist monastic emphasis on celibacy and fathered a child with Princess Yosŏk-kung of Silla. His son, Sŏl Ch'ong, became one of the great Confucian scholars and literary figures of the next generation, and he is credited with inventing *Idu*, the earliest form of indigenous Korean script.[2]

Uisang never approached his friend Wŏnhyo's level of eccentricity, but his contributions to the development of Korean Buddhism were substantial nevertheless. Uisang was another person who chose the monastic life at an early age, entering the Sangha in 644 at the age of nineteen. He reached China in 650 and there began to study the Huayan doctrine alongside a young Chinese monk named Fazong, who was to become the third patriarch and greatest philosophical thinker of the school. The two remained friends for life. After twenty years in China, Uisang returned home, where he became a hermit for the next six years in the eastern Sŏrak Mountains. Finally, in 676, at the age of fifty-one, he began to teach, and

Early pagoda at Chong Nimsa Temple, South Korea. When Korea was unified for the first time under the Silla dynasty, Buddhism was organized as a branch of the government.

also established the Hwaöm (Huayan) school in Korea. He went on to found a number of important monasteries, some of which are still active today. While the Hwaöm school never became entirely popular in its own right, it has had a considerable effect on the intellectual development of various other Buddhist schools in Korea over the years.

But philosophical and monastic Buddhism were not the only forms of Buddhism that flourished in Silla. Under the influence of Chajang's nephew Myöngnang, esoteric Buddhism gained a strong following as well. In 679, Myöngnang's efforts culminated in the building of the Sach'önwang-sa, the Temple of the Four Deva Kings. This sacred building was designed as a huge *mandala* that would afford magical protection to the kingdom of Silla through the esoteric Buddhist rituals performed in it. However, it is another monk, Hyet'ong, who is credited with formally establishing the Chinön school of esoteric Buddhism. Yet another monk, Myönghyo, came under the influence of the famous Indian monk Vajrabodhi in China during this period, and returned to Silla to teach esoteric Buddhism based on the Mahavairocana Sutra, a scripture that was also to be influential in seventh-century Japan. All in all, esoteric Buddhism flourished, and absorbed into itself many aspects of indigenous religious practice and belief, as it tended to do wherever it was practiced.

Buddhism in Later Silla and Koryö

The story of the religious life of Korea from approximately 700 to 1400 is very much the story of Buddhism. The early part of this period saw the development of the basic shape of Korean Buddhism with the establishment of the so-called Five Orthodox Schools (the O-gyo). The impetus for these five different interpretations of Buddhist doctrine came originally from China, but their elaboration in Korea gave them a distinctive aspect that transformed them from being imported ideas to concepts that were an integral part of Korean intellectual life.

The first of these Five Schools was the Yul-chöng school established by Chajang. As we have seen above, this Disciplinary school had been promulgated in China by Daoxuan and was based on the *Vinaya in Four Parts*. This text went into minute details as to how Buddhist monks should conduct their lives, giving 250 rules that needed to be observed, as well as 348 rules that were incumbent on Buddhist nuns. This school never really caught on in China, and its acceptance was limited in Korea. Its significance lay in its influence on the general development of state control of religious affairs, as noted above. The second school, the Hwaöm, established by Uisang, also had little popular appeal, but its influence was widespread among other Buddhist schools of thought, who adopted its profound metaphysical analysis of reality almost completely. As was the case in both China and Japan, this school virtually disappears from official records after only a generation or so of prominence, undoubtedly because, despite its intellectual profundity, it had little to offer the average monk in terms of practical religious training.

The third school had been established by the eccentric monk Wönhyo. Called the Haedong-jong (East of the Sea) or Pöpsöng-jong (Dharma Nature) school, it reflected Wönhyo's concern to weave the disparate strands of Korean Buddhism back into a single doctrine, as it had been in the time of the Buddha. Wönhyo saw value in all the various manifestations of the Buddhist *dharma* and opposed a narrow sectarian viewpoint. By adopting this attitude, he established the first distinctively Korean school of Buddhism. The fourth school, the Pöpsang-jong or Mind Only school, was inspired by the work of the Yogacara philosophers Asanga and Vasubandhu. The final school, the Yölban-jong or Nirvana school, was based on the work of the Chinese monk Daosheng (c. 360–434), who had a particular veneration for the Nirvana Sutra. Here again, we have a school that was intellectually influential, but which never attracted a large number of followers.

Outside the orbit of the Five Schools lay a number of other Buddhist schools that were to attract considerably more followers than the purely intellectual schools that preceded them. One of these was the Ch'önt'ae-jong, the Tiantai school, which emerged as a distinctive entity during the reign of king Hyegong (r. 765–779) and taught essentially the same doctrines as those promulgated by its Chinese counterpart. But after a brief period of flourishing, it sank into obscurity and never came near wielding the power and prestige that it did in nearby Japan. The Yoga-jong (Yoga) school was somewhat luckier. It was based on the principles of esoteric Buddhism that were influencing the development of Shingon Buddhism in Japan at about the same period. A form of Tantric Buddhism, Yoga-jong was allied to the similar Sinin-jong and Chinön-jong schools. Its founder was the monk Chinp'yo, who had received a vision of Manjushri in which the latter had given him a new scripture, the Manbun'gye, a set of 189 divination sticks, and a book of divination called the *Chan-ch'a Ching*. The group of monks that Chinp'yo gathered around him spent their time constructing *mandalas* and performing esoteric rituals. This school was very much a synthesis of Buddhism and the indigenous religious beliefs of the Silla people.

But by far the most important development in the later Silla period was the rise of Sön (Zen) Buddhism. The first monk to transmit this school to Silla was Pömnang, who is said to have studied under Daoxin (580–651), the fourth patriarch of the Chan lineage. Pömnang established the first Sön monastery at Koho-san in the 650s where he trained a number of successors—the most famous of whom was Sinhaeng. The Southern school of Chan was brought to Silla around 821 by To'üi, who settled at Chinjön-sa. But none of these founders were to have much of a following. The popularity of Sön did not emerge until the end of the Silla period, when the Ku-san or Nine Mountains of Sön emerged. Named after the mountain peaks on which their principal monasteries rested, these nine schools of Sön have dominated Korean Buddhism up to the present day.

When the state of Koryö overthrew Silla in 918 and assumed the rule of the Korean peninsula, one of the first things that T'aejo, the founder of the new dynasty, did was to throw his influence behind Buddhism. In his *Ten Injunctions* to his successors, he advocated state support of Buddhism as a prop to the authority of his newly established dynasty, while also advising them to limit severely the wealth of the Buddhist order. His successor quickly moved to accomplish both goals by establishing a set of official examinations for Buddhist priests. A separate series of examinations was established for the doctrinal and the Sön schools in which candidates were expected to demonstrate mastery over the various elements of their studies. Successful candidates were promoted in the Buddhist hierarchy and assigned as state teachers, with a higher rank than their Confucian counterparts. Two supreme ranks were created, the *kuksa* or National Teacher, and the *wangsa*, Teacher to the King, and the possessors of these titles wielded considerable political as well as religious influence.

Attempts were also made to try to bring some order to the burgeoning number of Buddhist schools that flourished in Koryö Korea. King Kwangjong tried to reunify all these groups under the aegis of the Ch'önt'ae-jong school, but such efforts were doomed to eventual failure, royal patronage notwithstanding. The movement to unify Korean Buddhism into a single entity gained strength with the work of Uich'ön (1055–1101). The fourth son of King Munjon (r. 1046–1083), Uich'ön became a monk at an early age and reached the highest level of the national examinations at the tender age of fifteen. After studying in China, he returned to Korea in 1086 to concentrate on acquiring new books on Buddhism and having them reprinted in Korea using woodblock printing. Uich'ön's influence and prestige was so great that he almost single-handedly transformed the institutional landscape of his time. Soon the Sön schools amalgamated into a single order, leaving Buddhism in Koryö a three-sided institution consisting of the Sön, the doctrinal or Kyo, and the Ch'önt'ae schools. It was at this time as well that one of the landmark events in Korean Buddhism occurred. This was the forty-year effort—started by King Hyönjong (r. 1009–1031) and completed by his successor, King Munjon—of publishing the Koryö changgyöng, the Great Canon of Koryö. This was nothing less than the transferring of the entire Buddhist canon to woodblock printing type. Although destroyed in the subsequent Mongol invasions of Korea, the Great Canon served as the model for similar later efforts, notably the mammoth *Tripitika on 80,000 Printing Blocks*, which was completed in 1256.

Undoubtedly the most original and influential Korean Buddhist thinker of the twelfth century was the Sön monk Chinul (1158–1210). The son of a Confucian academic, Chinul became a monk at the age of seven as the result of a vow made by his father. He passed all his examinations by the age of twenty-four, but, disturbed by what he perceived to be the corruption and worldliness of the contempoary Sön establishment, he chose to set up a *kyölsa* or religious fraternity with a few friends. At first thwarted from achieving this goal, he traveled to various Sön monasteries, where he had a number of spiritual breakthroughs. In 1190, he attempted, with more success this time, to establish a *kyölsa* at Köja-sa Temple. As the fraternity started to grow, it became evident that a new, larger site needed to be found to house it. In 1200, Chinul established the monastery of Songgwang-sa, where he stayed until his death ten years later. Despite his wandering life style, Chinul wrote a number of seminal Buddhist texts on a wide range of subjects. Not limiting himself to Sön, since he believed in the efficacy of all forms of Buddhism, he even wrote texts on Pure Land Buddhism.

But in many ways, Chinul marks the high watermark of Korean Buddhism. After the Yi dynasty took power in 1398 and established Chöson, the last kingdom of Korea, moves were made to curtail the power and prestige of Buddhism. The first king of the new dynasty established the *toch'öp-che* system that registered the names and residences of all of the Buddhist monks in Korea. Under his successor, the persecution of Buddhism intensified. Old Buddhist ranks and privileges were abolished, and the number of permitted temples limited to only 242.[3] The Buddhist schools were forced to amalgamate into either the Kyo or Sön schools, with no others being permitted, and these two branches were allowed only eighteen major temples each. While individual monarchs might be Buddhist in their personal orientation, the official thrust of the dynasty was toward Confucianism.

What kept Buddhism alive was the devotion of the common people to folk Buddhism. This form of Buddhism—heavily mixed with indigenous religious beliefs, such as veneration of the Mountain God as a protector of the *dharma*, and focused on Pure Land motifs such as the worship of Amitabha—persisted despite official displeasure. But increasingly, Buddhism slipped into decline. The situation was not helped by invasions from Japan and other disruptions of the state from the 1550s on. Increasingly, the control of the moral authority of the state slipped away from the Buddhists and was taken up by the Confucians.

Confucianism in Later Korean History

While Confucianism had been pushed into the background of Korean intellectual life by Buddhism until the advent of the Yi dynasty, it had by no means been completely moribund. At first only part and parcel of the general flow of Chinese culture to Korea, Confucianism soon found a place in the evolving intellectual life of the nation. When King Sinmun unified the country under the rule of Silla, he established a national academy in 682 for the training of aristocratic youth. This school, whose curriculum extended over nine years, taught the Confucian classics and led to advanced opportunities in the government. Unlike its Chinese counterparts, however, it did not admit nonaristocratic students, and this tended to slow the diffusion of Confucian ideas outside of the court circle. This trend toward "Confucianization" was accelerated somewhat under King Söngdök (r. 702–736), who established a shrine for Confucius and his seventy-two disciples where rituals for venerating the sage were performed.

During the Koryö period, Confucianism, while still subordinate to Buddhism, began to become a more integral part of Korean intellectual life. Under King Kwangjong, the *kwagö* or State Examination, based on Confucian texts, was established in 958. King Söngjong established the *Kukhak-kam* or Confucian College, and began the building of libraries to house books on Confucianism. Indeed, Confucianism became such a central part of a successful government career that private colleges were established to teach the classics, forcing the government to create *haktang*—official Confucian schools—in the provinces to counteract their influence. Later in the Koryö period, Neo-Confucianism—*Chuja-hak* or Zhu Xi Philosophy in Korean—made its appearance in Korea and, in the aftermath of the Mongol invasion, became very popular with younger scholars.

But it is with the establishment of the Yi dynasty and the state of Chosön that Confucianism truly came into its own and that we see the development of indigenous expressions of Confucian philosophy. The first such expression was found in Kwanhak-p'a, the School of Administrative Philosophy, popularized by Chöng Tojön, who died in 1398, and Kwön Kün (1352–1409). They advocated a complete repression of Buddhism and strict adherence to the philosophical concepts of Zhu Xi. They also began to write introductory and commentarial literature. Coming as they did at the interstice between two dynasties, they were particularly concerned with the shape that the new Korean polity would take, and believed that it should be based on logical and orderly principles. Parallel to the Kwanhak-p'a school there emerged the Sarim-p'a school of idealistic young scholars, established by the tutor of King Söngjong, Kim Chongjik (1431–1492). He, believing that commitment to one's sovereign must be absolute and complete, refused to accept the establishment of the new dynasty. However, as time went on, this school reconciled itself to the new rulers, seeing them as its best chance to impose its Confucian idealism on Korean society as a whole.

Although later there was a backlash on the part of the landed aristocracy against the excessive Confucianism of the Sarim-p'a school, it did accomplish its goal of radically transforming Korean society. By the mid-sixteenth century, distinctly Korean schools of Confucian philosophy such as the Principle First school and the Matter First school were debating fundamental points of Neo-Confucian thought. The foremost Principle First scholar was T'oegye (1501–1570), who believed that the virtues and emotions of the individual had their origins in the two basic forces of the universe, principle (*li*) and matter (*qi*), but that principle directed the action of matter—

hence the school's name. T'oegye was opposed in this viewpoint by members of the Matter First school, particularly Yi Yi (1536–1584), who gave primacy to matter as the foundational principle of the universe. The school that developed from his thought, the Pukhak-p'a or School of Northern Learning, increasingly influenced young Confucian scholars with its emphasis on the here and now, rather than on ephemeral metaphysical abstractions.

The trend toward idealism soon ran its course in Korea and was replaced by the Sirhak-p'a or School of Practical Knowledge, which built on the material foundations elucidated by the School of Northern Learning. After the period of the wars with Japan in the late sixteenth century, philosophers of this school felt that what the nation needed was practical, not theoretical, expertise. They advocated a complete reform of agriculture and commerce as a way to stimulate the rebuilding of the nation. Not surprisingly, this school favored research into science and technology. They also believed in leveling class distinctions and the prioritization of commerce, an idea that was totally anathema to traditional Confucians. Scholars of this school were at the forefront of calls to increase contacts with the West in order to profit from trade and technological innovation. Some of the more radical of their thinkers, such as Chŏng Yagyong (1762–1836), even went so far as to suggest the collectivization of land, in anticipation of classical Marxist economic theory.

But just as Confucianism had advocated the suppression of Buddhism, so too was its own influence curtailed. As the Yi dynasty began to weaken, extraordinary steps were taken to bolster the power and prestige of the throne. During the reign of King Kojong in the latter half of the nineteenth century, his father, the prince regent, moved to demolish the influence of the Confucians in Korea: academies were banned, shrines closed, and leading scholars sent into exile. He decreed the taxation of the important independent Confucian academies, the *sŏwŏn*, which had previously functioned as tax-exempt institutions. It should be noted, however, that these steps were not so much the expression of any government hostility toward Confucianism as they were attempts to limit the economic and intellectual influence of the institutions themselves. Confucianism remained the government philosophy of choice, but the institutions that supported it were seen as being too powerful, and thus a threat to the throne. Even at the cost of undercutting national institutions, the Yi family was determined to hang on to its power at all costs.

Website References

1. Shamanic ceremonies in Korea are described at faculty.vassar.edu/infenkl/knives

2. www.kwanumzen.com/primarypoint/v01nl-1984-winter-MuSoeng-TheLifeAndTimesOfWon Hyo.html examines the life of Wŏnhyo.

3. Buddhist temples in Korea are illustrated at www.media.granite.k12.ut.us/curriculum/korea/religion.htm

CHAPTER TWENTY-FOUR

Early Japanese Religion and the Development of Shinto

At the far eastern edge of the Asian continent is found the last of the major Asian cultural areas—the islands of Japan. Isolated from many of the main currents of Asian history by its geographical position, Japanese culture has always been in an especially favorable position to either assimilate new ideas from abroad or reject those ideas in favor of indigenous cultural norms. Consequently, Japanese culture—and religion in particular—has developed in such a way that, while owing much to other cultures, it is still uniquely Japanese.

The Geographical Setting of Japanese Religion

Japan is an archipelago consisting of four main islands and a large number of smaller islands that lie to the east of China and Korea. Originally connected to the East Asian mainland by a low marshy plain, the retreat of the glaciers after the last ice age and the subsequent rise of sea levels cut Japan off from continental Asia in much the same way as it did the islands of Southeast Asia. It is likely therefore that the earliest inhabitants of the area walked to their new homes. Later immigrants—and there were a number of distinct waves of such peoples—were carried to Japan by the ocean currents that wash its shores.

The land that these first inhabitants encountered was one of mixed potentials. On the one hand, Japan was a tremendously fertile land. Its proximity to the sea meant that there was an abundance of seafood available to the hunters and gathers that made up the first Japanese human populations. Even today, the Japanese diet leans heavily on such marine protein sources. Likewise, hunting was good in the abundant forests that covered much of the islands, as was foraging. But all this rich natural bounty came at a price. The thick foliage was a result of the volcanic soils that had been deposited by the many active volcanoes that dotted the Japanese countryside, since Japan formed part of the Pacific "Ring of Fire." This also meant that Japan was subject to devastating earthquakes, and many aspects of Japanese life, such as their wooden architecture, reflect this unpleasant reality. The prevailing climatic factors that blessed the islands with a reliable rainfall also made it subject to typhoons, the tremendous Pacific counterparts of the American hurricane. This combination of plenty and peril made life in Japan uncertain and resulted in the consciousness of the ephemeral nature of life that strongly infuses Japanese art and religion.

As Japanese culture developed, other limitations were imposed on it by the environment. Japan was an extremely mountainous land that had few river valleys or alluvial plains. As a result, when Japanese society advanced to the agricultural stage, lands that had been very productive for hunters and gatherers were now useless for agriculture. Likewise, the climate of Japan varied widely along its length, from semitropical in the extreme south of the island chain to the cold temperatures of the northern islands. This meant that much of Japan could not be successfully cultivated, which led to a concentration of the population on the two major rice-growing plains in the south of the island of Honshu, and on Kyushu and Shikoku, the two lesser southern islands. Thus from an early period the Japanese faced an expanding population and a limited resource base. Moreover, the Japanese islands were not blessed with mineral resources, so Japan was, even in early times, dependent on external sources of raw materials. In the modern period, with the advent of industrialization, this problem has become much more pressing.

The Early Cultures of Japan

Who were the people who became known to us as the Japanese? For most of their history, the Japanese believed themselves to be the unique descendants of the gods, homogeneous in makeup, and different from all other human beings. Certainly their language seemed to argue for this idea. Japanese is not closely related to any other of the world's languages, with the sole exception of Korean. It is very different from Chinese, having a different pronunciation and using a complex system of prefixes and suffixes to convey grammatical information. But owing to historical factors, it has been heavily influenced by Chinese, particularly regarding vocabulary and script. This led to the adoption of Chinese characters as a medium of writing. But because Chinese does not have the phonetic flexibility necessary to convey grammar in Japanese easily and accurately, two phonetic writing systems were developed alongside the Chinese characters to address this problem. The end result is perhaps the single most complex writing system still in use today.[1]

But were the Japanese truly a homogeneous people with no connections to others, as they believed? A detailed examination of the Japanese archaeological record and of Japanese culture and historical linguistics suggests quite the opposite. From this we find that Japanese society is made up of many layers of immigrants, superimposed one upon the other, as wave after wave of people washed over Japan. Each of these new groups was to leave its imprint on Japanese culture and religious beliefs. The final result is a rich and complex tapestry of beliefs that, despite their external origins and connections to other peoples and cultures, is uniquely Japanese.

Even though the present-day Japanese peoples are predominately Mongolian in race, there remains in northern Japan a tiny remnant of a group who may have been the earliest inhabitants of the Japanese islands—the Ainu. Displaying racial characteristics more reminiscent of the Caucasian than of the Mongolian group, the Ainu are now reduced to a few small government reserves—in much the same way as the Native Americans are in the United States. But in the early periods of Japanese history, they contended fiercely with the now-dominant Japanese people for control of the northern parts of the country. They still practice a shamanic religion centering on reverence for bears as messengers of the spirits. This religion seems to be of great antiquity, having many points of similarity with the hunting and gathering cultures of mainland northeastern Asia.

Whether or not the Ainu are the modern descendants of the first culture to inhabit Japan, we do have a fairly good picture of the nature of that culture from archaeological research. This earliest period of Japanese cultural history, which is termed the Jomon era, stretched from almost 10,000 to 300 B.C.E. and saw the first modern human populations reach the islands. The Jomon people were formed from an amalgam of different ethnic sources and lived a hunting and gathering life style that did not differ markedly from that still practiced by some isolated tribes on the adjacent northeastern Asian mainland. They hunted and fished using bone, wooden, and stone implements. They had domesticated dogs, and their equipment suggests that they fished in open waters as well as along the coastline. They lived in small, local, extended family groups.

So much for the bare physical details of life in Jomon Japan—but what of this people's religious life? This question is closely tied up with questions of the ethnic composition of early Japan, a matter that is still somewhat complicated by the Japanese national origin myth of the unique nature of the Japanese people. However, archaeology shows that the earliest stratum of populations seems to be, as we have noted, Siberian in nature; and the earliest Jomon remains show considerable similarity to cultural artifacts from the Angara culture of Siberia. If this is the case, the earliest forms of religion in Japan would likely have closely resembled the shamanic religion which is described in chapter one. Indeed, the native religion of historical Japan still retains a considerable number of characteristics that link it to this religious tradition.

But this Paleo-Siberian population was soon joined by others. Japan lies in the path of powerful ocean currents that move up the coast from Southeast Asia. This meant that groups from this area could, if they possessed the requisite sailing skills, reach the Japanese islands with relative ease. This indeed seems to have been what happened. The next layer of culture to be added to the Japanese mosaic is similar to that found in the Melanesian area of the southwestern Pacific region. This culture is characterized by the cultivation of root crops such as yam and taro; by adherence to a matrilineal descent tradition (many of the surviving Jomon figurines are of women who may represent fertility deities, as elsewhere in the world); and by a strong emphasis on group solidarity through belonging to "secret societies"—organized to their members' age group, each of which had their own secret ceremonies and traditions. In terms of cosmology, this type of society has a "horizontal orientation"— that is to say, its members see the next world or land of the dead as being over the sea beyond the horizon.

The next group to reach Japan seems to have spoken Austro-Asiatic languages similar to those still spoken in Vietnam and Cambodia. This group was also matrilineal, and one of the most interesting features of early Japanese religion—the dominance of the female medium-priestess/tribal chief—was probably introduced at this time. The central Japanese origin myths of **Amaterasu** Omikami and of brother-sister deities who incestuously begot other gods are characteristic of this group. Although it too adhered to a "horizontal cosmology", the next people, who were probably Tungusic speakers from the northeastern Asian mainland, did not. They had a "vertical cosmology," which placed the gods and the land of the dead in the heavens. Again, their religion was most likely shamanic in nature, although they seem to have had a particular reverence for mountaintops and trees, which they saw as pathways for the descent of the deities from the heavens.

Tumulus tomb of Emperor Nintoku. Some of the earliest information that we have concerning Japanese religion comes from archaeological data such as that found in this tomb of one of the earliest emperors of Japan.

The next people to appear on the Japanese scene were again from Southeast Asia. They were Austronesian speakers related to the present-day inhabitants of the islands of Indonesia and the Philippines, and they brought the cultivation of rice in paddies which allowed for the development of sufficient surplus to support the larger political units that would eventually coalesce into the Japanese state. It is not surprising, therefore, that many of the agricultural rituals practiced in premodern Japan can be traced to their influence. Burial practices became much more elaborate, and funeral urns, stone cists, and dolmens began to characterize the burials of important members of society. That the deceased were thought to persist in the spirit world in some form can be seen by the offerings of food and drink left in some of the burials of this period. It is at this point that archaeologists mark the change from the earlier Jomon era to the new Yayoi period (c. 300–250 C.E.).[2]

This Yayoi culture can be further divided into two branches: an eastern one, which seems to have placed an emphasis on bronze bells and sacred jewels (*maga-tami*) as cult offerings; and a western one, in which cult offerings consisted of blunt bronze weapons, such as halberds and swords. It is interesting to note that even in the present day, the imperial regalia of the Japanese emperor centers around a sacred sword, a mirror, and a necklace of jewels that have the same bearclaw shape as their Yayoi predecessors. Other artifacts were found that may have religious significance, such as burnt deer bones, which might have been used in divination, and shell ornaments that may be special marks of female shamans and mediums. However, in the absence of more evidence, any analysis of the religious significance of such material is tentative.

Finally there arrived the last great migration of peoples from northeastern Asia, a horse-riding Altaic-speaking group organized around the political unit of the patrilineal clan or *uji*. Each *uji* claimed descent from a deity, with the chief god being not

Amaterasu but the god Takamimusubi. Now begins the Kofun period, which ran from about 300 to 600 when the first written Japanese records appear. This period produced the great tombs attributed to the earliest emperors of Japan that are clearly the elaboration of ideas introduced in the earlier Yayoi period. The largest of these, the tomb of Emperor Nintoku, covers some eighty acres. Built in the shape of a key-hole and surrounded by a moat, it measures some 2,695 feet in length and testifies both to the religious fervor of its builder and to the increasing capacity of the Japanese elite to mobilize larger and larger workforces.[3]

Early Japanese Myths and Religion

The diversity of elements that went toward forming the present-day Japanese people is evident in the early mythology of Japan. No less than three origin myths coexist side by side in the classical collections of Japanese mythology and early history, the *Kojiki* and the *Nihonshoki* (*Nihongi*). In the first origin myth, the first god appears from a reed that grows out of chaos and is followed by two other gods and then a myriad divine beings. The second myth presents a similar motif, but with a differ-ent god; and in the third, a trio of gods appears. Although all three show individual differences, the basic motif is probably of Southeast Asian origin.

The primal origin story of the absolute beginnings of the world seems to have engaged the early Japanese far less than the elaboration of that story. Of much more impact was the story of Izanagi ("he who invites") and Izanami ("she who is invited"). These two deities, who were seen as brother and sister, mated. From them sprang not only all the gods, but the very islands of Japan themselves. In the process of giving birth to the god of fire, Izanami dies and the distraught Izanagi descends to the underworld to recover his spouse, but ultimately fails to do so. He returns to the Plain of Heaven, where the sun goddess Amaterasu is born from his left eye, Tsukiyomi the moon god from his right, and Susanoo the storm god from his nose.

The next cycle of Japanese myths—the Izumo myths—focuses on the exploits of Susanoo in the central Izumo region of the Japanese island of Honshu. Even today this area is held to be particularly sacred, no doubt as a result of its early political importance. Here Susanoo slays an eight-headed snake, rescues a fair maiden, and begets a line of rulers who govern Izumo. Eventually, this area was coopted by the clan that is the foundation of the present-day Japanese royal family, and Susanoo is subordinated to their titular progenitor, Amaterasu. She sends her grandson Ninigi to rule this new land. He is the offspring of Amaterasu's son and the daughter of another god, Takamimusubi ("the god who descends upon a tall tree"). The relation-ship between Amaterasu and Takamimusubi is interesting. As we have seen, Amaterasu's origins are distinctly Austro-Asiatic. But Takamimusubi has Altaic characteristics that were likely imported at a fairly late date. It has been suggested that Takamimusubi was the original titular god of the imperial clan, who had Altaic origins, but for political reasons connected with their relationship to the conquered peoples they ruled, they adopted Amaterasu as their titular ancestor.

Whatever the case may be, Ninigi is said to have descended to Japan on the mountain of Hiuga on Kyushu, the island closest to the Asian mainland. He mar-ries a local princess and has two sons. His great grandson, Jimmu Tenno, is reckoned to have led the Japanese people from Kyushu to the region of Yamato on the island of Honshu, and to have been the first emperor of Japan and the direct ancestor of the current occupant of the Japanese imperial throne.[4]

Early Japanese Religion as Shown in the Chinese Records

The earliest indications that we have about the state of Japanese religion before the introduction of writing and the Buddhist beliefs that accompanied it, come from the accounts of early Chinese travelers to Japan. These travelers, who usually came to Japan for commercial purposes, starting arriving around the end of the Yayoi period and the beginning of the Kofun. What they found was a society that had already become highly stratified. The basic political unit was the *uji*, communities claiming common descent from a divine ancestor called the **kami** *no uji*. This was the god, or perhaps better the spirit, whose worship was orchestrated and led by the clan chieftain. It should be noted that this was not, strictly speaking, ancestor worship in the Southeast Asian or Chinese sense, since only the *kami* who had founded the ruling lineage was worshipped—not subsequent ancestors in the royal lineage.

The *uji* was supported by the *be* or *tomo*, an association of unrelated families usually grouped together by occupation and probably representing previously conquered inhabitants of the land. Eventually, these two groups would merge in later Japanese history. Below them were the undifferentiated group of slaves and the increasing numbers of Koreans and Chinese who came to Japan fleeing the chaotic conditions that often prevailed in their homelands at this time. By the time that the Chinese reached Japan, the Yamato *uji* had asserted its dominance in the islands and become the predominant clan, but that authority was often more ceremonial than actually real. The head of the Yamato clan was seen as possessing the divine mandate to rule the islands of Japan, supposedly by virtue of his direct descent from the sun goddess. But this moral superiority needed to be buttressed by more concrete

The Grand Shrine of Ise. The Ise Shrine was built by the Japanese Imperial family for their supposed ancestress, Amaterasu, the Sun Goddess.

means of enforcing his authority, and this could only be accomplished through strategic alliances with other *ujis*, who became in time the ancestors of the great aristocratic families of Japan.

Among these families were several who clearly gained their prominence through religious means. The Nakatomi and the Imibe families were thought to be descended from gods who had performed religious rituals for the sun goddess. So they became the chief performers of the religious rituals sponsored by the Yamato clan as a means to maintaining its prestige. Consequently, the Nakatomi became more and more prominent as the power of the Yamato clan was extended throughout Japan. In fact, under the name of Fujiwara, which they adopted at a later date, members of the Nakatomi family were often the de facto rulers of Japan as the power of the imperial family waxed and waned. These indigenous aristocratic families were aided in their efforts by immigrants, who brought much-needed technical skills to Japan, and who were absorbed into the power structure. A seventh-century book of the peerage shows that by the time it was written, virtually one third of the noble families in Japan claimed descent from a Chinese or Korean founding ancestor.

Archaeological remains from the Kofun period show that there was no abrupt break between it and the Yayoi period, although changes were evident. By the Kofun period, established cult sites were beginning to appear. In these were found the stone mirrors, swords, and sacred jewels of the previous period, along with votive offerings of the images of horses and boats. We can probably conclude from this that the *kami* or spirits were thought of as descending to the human world on boats or horses. Boat effigies are also found in a number of tombs of this period, and this is consistent with the worldview of many Southeast Asian peoples, who see them as vehicles to ferry the souls of the dead to the afterlife. Likewise, there seems to have remained an emphasis on the figure of the female shaman, as evidenced by the discovery of a *haniwa* or clay tomb figure of a female with a characteristic cloth draped over her right shoulder—reminiscent of present-day shamanic attire.[5]

It also seems likely that—then as now—the central supernatural entities in the religious life of the people of the Kofun era were the *kami*. This word, of debated etymology, is often translated as "gods," but such a translation obscures the local and specific nature of these entities. The term "spirit" also falls somewhat short of the mark. Rather, the term is a blanket designation for someone or something that is infused with "divine power." As such, it can refer to a spirit in the classical sense of the word; the human soul; spirits of the ancestors; and physical phenomena that engender a sense of awe, such as mountains, strangely shaped trees, or waterfalls. Perhaps the best way to define it is to say that it signifies all that is mysterious and "awesome" in human experience—those things that send a shiver up the spine. As such, the *kami* had a variety of origins and functions.

The most prominent of these entities in the Kofun period were the *uji-kami*, the titular deities of the great clans that ruled Japan. They were seen as the progenitors of the clansmen and women of the group, and their veneration was the primary responsibility of the clan chief, assisted by his wife or sister. The existence of other *kami* was never disputed, but they played little or no role in the religious life of the given clan, which was almost exclusively centered on their own deity. Since the clan's fortunes were directly linked to the whims of this deity, it was imperative that its wishes be known. The only way that this could be accomplished was through spirit possession, which was the almost exclusive domain of the women of the chieftain's family. The term used for such a diviner in the Kofun period was *miko*, a word that still exists in Japanese but which now means a "witch" or female shaman. But for much of Japanese history, *miko* meant a female attendant at a **Shinto** shrine, and this clearly shows the connections between later formalized Shinto and the practices of this earlier period.

The *miko* seems to have been a universal feature of early Japanese religion and was found not only in the mansions of the rich but in the humble houses of the common folk as well. There were various types of mediums and female shamans who were called upon for fortunetelling, the transmission of spirit messages, and healing. They were intermediaries between this world and the unseen world of the spirits, in much the same way as were their northeastern Asian mainland cousins. All the calamities to which the human being was heir were seen as stemming from the influence of the *kami*. Through resorting to the trance state, the shamanic mediums of early (and later) Japan could divine the desires of these spirits, and so appease them.

But the power of the Kofun mediums began to wane under the influence of new ideas from the Asian mainland. As the Yamato clan moved to consolidate its political power, it also moved to limit the power of the clan priestesses, including those of its own clan. Increasingly they became mere shrine attendants, who sang, danced, and assisted with the rituals, but who no longer prophesied. The control of the religious tradition now passed to hereditary male priesthoods, some of whom became extremely powerful. It is at this point that we can say that the archaic religion of Japan begins to assume the shape in which it has come down to us today. As such, we can now start to talk of a distinctive Japanese national religion. This was Shinto.

Shinto: A Brief Overview of the National Religion of Japan

Shinto is the Japanese pronunciation of two Chinese characters (*shendao*) which mean "Way of the Gods." But the term was not used before the sixth century C.E. It seems to have come into use not to describe some organized religion, but rather to distinguish the indigenous traditions of Japan from the imported religions of Buddhism and Daoism, which were entering the country at that time from China and Korea. But even at this early date, the main outlines of this belief system were clear. It was, and remained, a religion of practice and not speculation. The world of Shinto was a vibrant one permeated with the life force. All things—stones, natural features, plants, animals, and of course human beings—were held to be alive. From this perception of the world as a living being grew not only religious sentiment, but also the roots of the uniquely Japanese aesthetic sensibility that has made Japanese art and literature so distinctive.[6]

By the sixth century, the rudimentary religious sentiments of the Japanese people were being systematized and subordinated to the ambitions of the imperial clan, as it moved to consolidate its control over the islands of Japan. What evolved was a state-subsidized cult centered on the imperial divine ancestress Amaterasu Omikami, the Heavenly Shining Great Deity. This cult was served by three hereditary priestly families. No longer did the imperial family preside over any except the most important of the yearly ceremonies, such as the first plowing ceremony. Now their religious duties were delegated to others. Each of the three families performed a different function in the emerging rituals of Shinto. The Imbe family was responsible for the ritual purity of implements used in rites and of the people who took part in them. This was very important. Very early in Shinto's development the idea arose that the *kami* were particularly repulsed by impurity, which could be simple dirt—hence the Japanese emphasis on cleanliness that permeates their entire culture even today—or it could be a substance, such as blood, which was impure in and of itself. Naturally, the participants of a Shinto ceremony intended to avoid ritual pollution, but the rules of rituals became so complicated that such pollution could take place unawares. Since the slightest mistake would render the ceremony ineffective, it became necessary to have priests whose only function was to eliminate all forms of pollution.

The second family of priests was the Nakatomi, later known as the Fujiwara, whose job it was to communicate with the *kami*. At first this was done through spirit possession. But as time went on, the focus of the ritual shifted away from possession toward a more sedate ceremony based on the recitation of liturgies and symbolic sacrifices. Nevertheless, the prestige of the Nakatomi family persisted. Not only were they central participants in the all-important state Shinto ceremonies, but powerful political allies to the ruling Yamato clan as well. As a result, they often intermarried with members of the imperial family, and for a period of time they were the actual rulers of Japan. Their former function as diviners of the will of the *kami* passed to the third great family of Shinto priests, the Urabe.

Shinto in the first stage of its development was a relatively unformed collection of folk beliefs from various sources and ethnic traditions that coexisted in easy interaction with one another over a long period of early Japanese history. This situation began to change with the introduction of Daoist, Buddhist, and Confucian ideas from the Asian mainland, beginning in the sixth and seventh centuries C.E. Now, religious ideas began to be expressed in Chinese terms and concepts. Shinto—or perhaps more accurately at this point indigenous Japanese religious tradition—began to lose its unique position in Japanese life. Having no philosophy or organization to support it, since most of its former priesthood were now Buddhists, it survived only as an adjunct to the newly dominant religion. Shinto gods were identified with Buddhist deities, and Shinto shrines, or *jinjas*, underwent an ever increasing "Buddhification." This trend continued until the middle of the nineteenth century.[7]

The change in Shinto's fortunes came not as a reaction to its intrinsic worth, but as the result of momentous political changes that rocked Japan at that time. From the eighth century onward, Japan had ceased to be directly ruled by the imperial family and had been governed instead by a series of families, such as the Fujiwaras, the Minamotos, and the Tokugawas, who held the real reins of power. But the prestige of the emperor and the royal family was such that they could not be done away with entirely. So the emperor was maintained on his throne, but had little or no actual political power for over a thousand years. During this period, Shinto languished. All this changed in 1868, when a group of powerful officials, dismayed by what they saw as the impending colonization of Japan by America and the powerful countries of Europe, staged a coup that dethroned the ruling Tokugawa family and restored the emperor to power in the so-called Meiji Restoration.

Along with this restoration of imperial power came a restoration of Shinto. The rising tide of nationalism that prompted the imperial restoration also brought about a reaction to the "foreign" religions, such as Buddhism and Confucianism. The imperial family was closely associated in the popular mind with Shinto and was still seen as being of divine descent. What happened next was a Shinto revival that was to last until the end of the Second World War, when the emperor was forced to renounce his divine status. Although the end of the war saw the disestablishment of

Shinto as the official state religion, a position that it had held since the Meiji imperial restoration, the fabric of the religion had been sufficiently repaired so that it once again became part of mainstream Japanese culture.

The Rites and Rituals of Shinto

Given its origins and functions in Japanese life, it is not surprising to find that Shinto has very little of what we would call intellectual apparatus. Rather, it is primarily a religion of practice and, with the exception of the mythological material already discussed, the first Shinto writings are collections of religious ceremonies such as the *Engishiki* (Ceremonies of Engi), which was written down early in the tenth century in some fifty volumes. While many of these rituals have fallen out of use, some elements of Shinto ceremony, such as the twenty-seven chants found in the eighth book of this work, the *Norito*, are still central components of Shinto ritual. As is the case with shamanic religion, whose basic worldview it shares, Shinto was originally a religion aimed at propitiating the spirits (*kami*) or gaining their aid. This was accomplished through the medium of sacrifice, which could take the form of offerings of rice and rice wine (saki) or, in earlier times, animals or even human beings. Nowadays, given Shinto's aversion to pollution through blood, such sacrifices are done through the use of effigies and ritual meals. Originally, Shinto rituals were a private affair, conducted in the home or out in the open in the vicinity of a sacred object, such as a tree, rock, or waterfall. Indeed, the term for a Shinto shrine is *miya*, which means "honorable house," and the Shinto shrines that dot the modern Japanese landscape differ only slightly from the simple wooden houses of ancient Japan.[8]

As with most ancient religions, a great deal of Shinto is hidden from those not of the initiated priesthood. The central feature of the Shinto shrine is the *go-shintai* (the "god-body"), which is an object such as a sword, mirror, or some other thing in which the *kami* is believed to reside. This "god-body" is never revealed to the general public, and even when taken outside the shrine in ritual processions it is shrouded in a curtain. Also considered sacred are the *gohei*, folded strips of cloth attached to a stick and placed on the shrine's altar. These objects, however, can be taken home by the faithful and are believed to have imbibed some of the "holiness" of the *kami* from whose altar they come. The same belief is held about *nusa*, strips of paper and hemp fiber tied to straw ropes and hung from the ceiling of houses as protection from evil influences.

Although Shinto ceremonies can and do take place at any time of the year, the religion became more and more tied to the cycle and concerns of the agricultural year as the Japanese moved away from the hunting and gathering culture that characterizes most of the surviving shamanic societies. As a result, Shinto religious observance came to be concentrated in a number of annual **matsuri** or festivals. The most important of these is the Dai-josai, the Great Harvest Festival, which is enacted only once in each imperial reign, when the newly enthroned emperor offers food to the *kami*. Next in importance comes the festival of praying for a good harvest in February, then the festival of the new rice harvest. Finally, there are numerous small festivals meant to prevent disaster and propitiate the souls of the deceased.[9]

Despite the differences in the avowed intention of the various Shinto festivals, the actual ritual actions associated with them are fairly similar and follow a prescribed pattern of three stages. The first stage is that of preparing for the ritual, since even the slightest deviation or mistake in the ritual renders it invalid. The head priest who officiates at the ceremony must therefore ensure that he is completely free of pollution. This is done through *kessai* or avoidance, which could be of two types, depending on the importance of the ceremony that it precedes. "Rough" avoidance, which can last for up to a month, involves avoiding all ordinary occasions of pollution, such as handling a corpse or touching blood—but the priest can still engage in shrine business and ordinary worship. In the period of "strict" avoidance, which lasts for about three days just prior to the ritual, the priest is much more limited in his actions. He must bathe frequently, not eat spicy food or drink alcohol, and as far as possible avoid contact with other people. The actual preparation of the ritual meal that will be served to the *kami* is left to his assistant priests. Here again, elaborate care is taken to ensure that the food is unpolluted. A new fire is kindled by means of the ancient method of using a flint, and the cooked and uncooked food, which is known as *shin-sen* ("god-food") and must be totally untainted by blood, is carefully arranged on special trays.

But it is not only the priest who must be ritually pure. The laypeople who attend the ceremony must be pure as well. The means of achieving this purity varied from place to place and century to century. In ancient times, the prescribed method was to bathe in a river at the point where it emptied into the sea. The individual was presumably purified both by the running water of the river and by the salt in the ocean water. As Japanese society moved inland, it became acceptable to bathe in running water alone. Today, ritual purification, except in the case of extreme forms of pollution or with the priests, only involves pouring water over the hands and rinsing the mouth from a source of running water before entering the shrine. In addition, other forms of purification came into use. Some of these included purification by *harai*—whereby a stick to which strips of white paper have been attached is waved over the participant—and the sprinkling of salt or salt water on the assembled faithful.

The Mikoshi shrine being carried in front of the Narita-san temple. Shinto is highly ritualistic and festivals such as this are enacted throughout the year.

After all the participants have been ritually cleansed, the ceremony proper may proceed. Originally, all Shinto ceremonies took place at night and ended near dawn. This was no doubt an echo of their shamanic origins, since even today, in many shamanic cultures, the night is seen as the appropriate time to enter a shamanic trance and talk with the spirits. By about 1200, however, the rule became to hold Shinto ceremonies in the daytime. The heart of the ceremony was the calling of the *kami* to attend the ceremony. Today, this takes place in the inner shrine (*honden*) of the Shinto shrine. But in olden times, there were no such shrines and the ceremony took place outdoors at places deemed particularly holy for one reason or another. Usually this place had an evergreen *sakaki* tree called a *himorogi*—the term still used in Japan for an outdoor shrine, only a few of which still exist—and was marked off for the ceremony by being enclosed with a straw rope and evergreens. The *kami* was believed to descend onto this tree in imitation of the myth of the descent of the imperial ancestor Ninigi-no-mikoto from the Plain of Heaven to rule Japan. At present, the focus of the Shinto ritual is not a tree but the *go-shintai*, which is believed to house the spirit of the shrine *kami*.

The ceremony opens with the calling of the *kami* and the opening of the door to the inner shrine, which is usually kept shut. When the *kami* has taken up residence in the *go-shintai*, the central portion of the ritual can commence. This involves the offering of a meal to the newly resident spirit. The food is presented on a small, unpainted stand, which is passed along a line of priests until it reaches the head priest waiting at the steps of the inner shrine. He enters the shrine, and places the food before the *go-shintai*. After this meal has been served (and the *kami* is presumably in a good mood), the head priest kneels and chants a **norito** or ritual prayer. As we have seen, these prayers are of great antiquity and are still intoned in ancient Japanese, which is unintelligible to the average modern person. The prayers petition the spirit for good crops, protection of the imperial household, good weather, and so forth. In ancient times, they would be followed by a rite of mediumistic possession in which the spirit's reply to the requests would be given, but this part of the ceremony is no longer observed.

After the petitions have been presented to the *kami*, the spirit is deeply reverenced by all the priests. It is then entertained by a type of ritual dancing called *kagura*, which can take two forms. The first is a formal classical style developed at the imperial court and still practiced in the larger shrines associated with the imperial family. The other form is "village" *kagura*—that is, as its name suggests, a more freeform artistic expression reflecting local peasant traditions. Owing to the expense involved, this aspect of the Shinto ritual is becoming rarer. In the larger shrines where it is still relatively common, the dance takes place in a separate building near the main shrine and is performed by special female dancers, the *miko*. They are the last vestige of the ancient female priestesses who acted as mediums and were possessed by the *kami* during Shinto rituals. After the entertainment, the food is removed from the inner shrine—the door to which is then shut.

While the main part of the ceremony is now over, there are still ritual actions to be accomplished. The food that has been offered to the spirit is now distributed to the assembled participants in a rite called *norai*. In ancient times, this was probably a full-blown feast, with considerable social importance. At present, it has dwindled in most cases to a simple drinking of a cup of the saki offered to the *kami*. Worshippers may also offer the *kami* a *tamagushi*, a small branch of the *sakaki* tree to which strips of white paper have been attached. After thus paying their respects to the spirit of the shrine and perhaps praying for some personal matter, worshippers depart the shrine.

Shrine maidens dancing in front of the Gagaku-Sagimari shrine. The primary religious functionaries of early Shinto appear to have been women. Today, women play only a minor role in Shinto ceremonies.

Shinto and the Japanese Imperial Family

It is impossible to consider Shinto without looking at its associations with the Japanese imperial family and the system of government that they represented. Indeed, the term for ritual, *matsuri-goto*, is the same term used to denote government in early Japan. Likewise, the term *miya*, used as we have seen to describe a shrine, also referred to the imperial court. Until the time of the tenth emperor of the present dynasty, Sujin, the imperial residence was also the shrine of the emperor's divine ancestors, as *kyujo*, the term for palace in Japanese, demonstrates, since it too can refer to both a palace and a shrine. Since the primary function of the emperor was to perform those rituals that would protect the country and assure its economic prosperity—even when he possessed no real political power at all—the Japanese imperial family has persisted up to the present day because no Japanese government has ever felt comfortable with the idea of abolishing it.

But for most of Japanese history, the emperor was little more than a figurehead. After the imperial capital was moved to Kyoto from Nara in 794, the aristocratic Fujiwara family began to dominate the court. By 858, they ruled Japan in all but name. This institution of indirect rule persisted in one form or another for the next thousand years, until the Meiji Restoration of 1867. Although the revival of Shinto had been advocated since the middle of the eighteenth century by such influential thinkers as Kamo Mabuchi (1697–1769) and Motoori Norinaga (1730–1817), it was this return to more direct imperial rule that led to the real revival of Shinto. Thus began the period of *saisei ichi*, "the unity of religion and politics," that was to dominate Japanese thought up to the end of the Second World War. During this period, Buddhism, which had effectively supplanted Shinto in the popular mind as the predominant Japanese religion, was suppressed. All Japanese people had to be associated with a local Shinto shrine. A cult of the emperor developed that made him a living god; and to die for the emperor became the ideal of many Japanese. Likewise, the expansion of Japanese influence in East Asia became for many an almost divine mission—with tragic results. Then, with its disestablishment in 1945, Shinto became a "private belief," albeit one that still deeply affects the older generation of Japanese. So, once again, the role of the emperor was reduced to a purely ceremonial one.

Shinto, based as it is on the earliest beliefs of the Japanese peoples, had, and continues to have, an important part to play in Japanese religious life. But it is not the only piece in the Japanese religious mosaic. Confucianism, Daoism, and the other philosophies of China have had important roles to play in the development of Japanese intellectual history. But it is Buddhism, adapted to the particular conditions of Japan, that has had the strongest effect on Japanese religious sensibility.

Website References

1. Japanese language is discussed at www.japan.mit.edu/articles/JapaneseLanguage.html

2. Jomon and Yayoi culture are discussed at www.wsu.edu/~dee/ANCJAPAN/YAYOI.HTM

3. www.nara-wu.ac.jp/bungaku/soramitsu/kofun.html illustrates the great tombs of the Kofun period.

4. Shinto mythology is covered at www.uwec.edu/academic/philrel/shinbutsudo/amaterasu.html

5. *Haniwa* figures are examined at www.art.unt.edu/ntieva/artcurr/asian/haniwa.html

6. www.religioustolerance.org/shinto.htm gives a good overview of Shinto.

7. www.japan-guide.com/e/e2059.html and www.arthistory.sbc.edu/sacredplaces/ise.html show a number of important Shinto shrines.

8. Basic Shinto terms are discussed at www.kokugakuin.ac.jp/ijcc/wp/bts/index1.html

9. festivals.com/search/map_country_events.cfm?RID=JP describes a number of Japanese festivals.

CHAPTER TWENTY-FIVE

✦

Japanese Buddhism to about 1200 C.E.

As might be expected from its geographical position, Buddhism came to Japan relatively late in the country's history. The traditional date ascribed to this pivotal event is 552. It was then, according to the early Japanese chronicle, the *Nihonshoki*, that a Korean monk arrived in Japan from the kingdom of Paekche with Buddhist scriptures and a gilded image of the Buddha. He hoped to foster an alliance between the two states, but that enterprise, as well as the Buddhist evangelization of Japan, was unsuccessful at that point. It is likely, however, that Buddhism had arrived in Japan before the traditional date, since we know that many Korean workmen were already well established in the country by then.

The reason that Buddhism did not immediately prosper in Japan is not hard to discern. Buddhist missionary efforts of the period in Korea, and later in Japan, were not aimed at converting the common people at the expense of their ancestral beliefs. The lower classes were inconsequential in the eyes of the Buddhist monks who made the long and arduous journey from the Asian mainland to Japan, and they remained so for almost another five hundred years. In keeping with the missionary traditions that had arisen in northern China during the period of foreign invasion and political division that had followed the fall of the Han dynasty, Buddhist monks tended to concentrate their efforts among the ruling families and the aristocracies of the areas in which they found themselves. But in Japan, they faced special circumstances. The imperial family had only recently been able to establish its hegemony over the other aristocratic *ujis* that ruled the country, and it had done so partly by an appeal to its superior divine ancestry and personal relationship with Amaterasu, the principal *kami* of the indigenous pantheon. To accept this alien Buddhist faith officially into the Japanese court was not only an intellectual decision, but a political one as well. However, the imperial family was anxious to establish ties outside of Japan with the largely Buddhist courts of Korea and China. It is not surprising, therefore, that the court adopted a neutral attitude toward the new religion, extending it patronage only in a backhanded way through intermediaries.

This neutrality did not extend to the clans vying for power in the new system. Two of these were especially involved in the fortunes of the newly arrived faith. The Mononobe clan vigorously opposed it, partially from religious conviction, but more from political motivation. They were a *shimbetsu* clan that claimed descent from a *kami* other than Amaterasu. Believed to be of divine descent themselves, they had contended with the Yamato family for the leadership of Japan and stood to profit from retaining the status quo. Their position was supported by other segments of the aristocracy, notably the Shinto priestly family of the Fujiwara. Conversely, the Soga clan was a *kobetsu* family that had, despite also claiming divine descent, acknowledged the subordination of their titular *kami* to Amaterasu and the Yamato family. Moreover, they were the managers of the imperial family's estates and so relied heavily on the foreign expertise of immigrants from the continent. As a result, they were much more open to cultural influences from that direction, including Buddhism. A compromise of sorts was arrived at when Emperor Kimmei (r. 531–571) allowed the Soga clan to embrace Buddhism officially.

It would be wise at this point to consider the Japanese understanding of Buddhism in this early period. First of all, we must realize that the Japanese aristocracy had absolutely no understanding of, or interest in, the religious or philosophical aspects of the new religion. Rather, they saw it in practical terms as a sort of superior magic that could be used for worldly advantage—the more advanced civilizations of the continent practiced Buddhism, so the Japanese should practice it as well. But by "practice," they did not mean following Buddhism in any personal sense. Rather, they merely imported Buddhist monks to conduct Buddhist ceremonies for the good of the state. If the new religion did not assure prosperity and protect the realm, then it was of no further use. The Soga had to contend with this attitude several times in the later sixth century, when natural disasters convinced many aristocrats, including the reigning emperors, that the indigenous gods were angry at the presence of the new religion. Despite this rocky start, Buddhism did make inroads among the upper classes. Finally, in about 586, Emperor Yomei formally converted to the new faith, thus securing it an official place in Japanese court life.

It was Yomei's son, the renowned statesman Prince Shotoku Taishi, who firmly established Buddhism in Japan. Perhaps the first aristocrat to actually understand and espouse the philosophy of the Buddha, the prince was deeply versed not only in Japanese culture, but in the culture of China as well; and, in addition to his many practical abilities, he was highly esteemed by his contemporaries as a scholar and a man of culture. He is alleged to have not only produced the great "Seventeen Article Constitution," which profoundly affected Japanese institutional development and led to the Taika Reform of 645, but to have written commentaries on Buddhist scriptures, such as the Lotus Sutra. Assuming the regency of Japan at the age of nineteen, he ruled the country for the next thirty years, during which time he enacted a series of sweeping reforms that altered the face of Japanese culture and government in ways that were to affect the country for the next millennium.

Prince Shotoku began his rule by opening up official relations with the newly established Tang dynasty of China. Students and monks began to travel back and forth to China, bringing with them new ideas and techniques that would eventually lead to the development of centralized governmental institutions in Japan. In the process, the Chinese language and writing system became the favored medium of cultural expression. Shotoku also accelerated the process of temple building. He is supposed to have been the driving force behind the building of Horyuji and Shitennoji, the great temples of the day. Whatever the prince's personal involvement was in the process of building temples, his regency saw the construction of forty-six temples, mostly in the style of the Korean state of Paekche. The Horyuji Temple housed a famous image of Yakushi, the Buddha of Healing, while Shitennoji memorialized the definitive victory of the Soga clan—to which Shotoku's mother belonged—over their Mononobe rivals in 587.[1]

Despite Prince Shotoku's advanced grasp of essential Buddhist principles, the Buddhism of this early period continued to be viewed mostly as magic. The images of the Buddha that were now entering Japan from the continent were venerated not as representations of a revered teacher, but as powerful magic talismans that could bestow material prosperity on the upper classes and avert natural disasters. Native-produced images show no indication that the artisans who carved them even understood that they could portray different individuals, so it is often impossible to differentiate statues of the various Buddhas and *bodhisattvas* without recourse to the inscriptions carved on their bases. The first Buddhist cult to gain wide acceptance was the veneration of Yakushi Nyorai, the so-called Medicine Buddha. The origins of this cult, which had a corresponding cult in Indian Tantric Buddhism, probably resulted from the amalgamation of a number of elements. It was never very influential in India, but it did blossom in seventh-century Japan. The Yakushiji Temple, which was finished in 680 and is one of the earliest temples constructed under imperial auspices, houses some very fine examples of early Tang sculpture. Extensive celebrations were held in this temple throughout the seventh century to petition for the health and welfare of the imperial family and the country as a whole.

Other Buddhist rituals became important fixtures of court life during this period as well. The Ritual of Repentance (*keka*) was a ceremony that in Japan closely resembled the purification rites that attended Shinto worship. Originally a ceremony of personal repentance and regeneration, in Japan it was seen mainly as a way to reap material benefits. The same may be said of the *ango* or retreat—a ritual that had its origins in the annual three-month rainy season retreat still observed in Theravada countries. In Japan, however, the *ango* became the occasion for large aristocratic gatherings in which monks and nuns would discourse on the Buddhist scriptures,

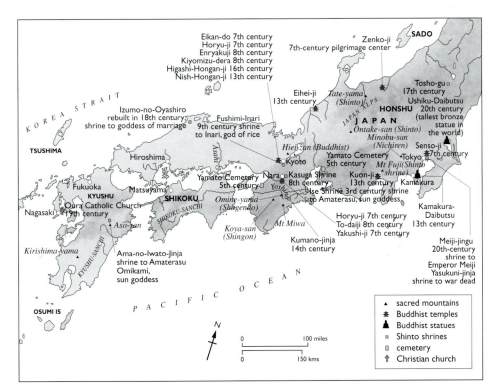

Important religious sites in southern Japan. Significant religious sites here include Buddhist, Shinto, and Christian places of worship.

and while some members of the audience may have been morally edified, the primary point of the gathering was to generate merit and its attendant material benefits. The same was true of the *hojo-e*, the "liberation of captive creatures," and the *sai-e*, "vegetarian feast." These two ceremonies celebrated the nonviolent aspects of the Buddha's teaching, but here again the emphasis was not on moral uplift but on prosperity-generating merit.

The *Ritsuryo* Government: Buddhism as an Appendage of the State

After the death of Prince Shotoku in 622, popular resentment of the ascendancy of the Soga clan grew and finally reached a crescendo in 645. In the ensuing revolt, the Soga clan leaders were killed and the clan toppled from power. They were replaced by the Fujiwara clan. Under the great statesman Fujiwara Kamatari, a new system of government was instituted through the Taika Reform. The aim of this new governmental system was to make Japan a more centralized state based on the model of the Tang state of China. Most of the Buddhist clergy of the time enjoyed the direct support of the Soga clan, and so moves were immediately implemented to regulate the number of Buddhist monks and to bring them under state control. This, in turn, caused the new regime to tilt its patronage heavily in favor of those monks who had been to China and had returned steeped in the Chinese culture and ideas that the government was trying to promote. It is not surprising, therefore, that Japanese Buddhism began to resemble the various forms of Chinese Buddhism.

The government, quartered in the city of Nara from which this period takes its name, established government boards to oversee various aspects of Buddhism in Japan. It also moved to establish the emperor as the supreme leader of the Buddhist faith. Thus there was a marked increase in court rituals, at which, even though the emperor could not officiate in person—as he had in Shinto rituals—he participated vicariously through his monk-representatives. Some emperors were in fact enthusiastic Buddhists. One of them, Emperor Temmu (r. 673–686), was actually ordained as a Buddhist monk for a period of time. He increased Buddhist ceremony in the imperial palace and commissioned the building of the temples. Indeed, in 685, he ordered that Buddhist shrines be erected in every house in the country, although by this, he probably meant every aristocrat's house and not the houses of the common people.

The new government that was fully implemented with the promulgation of the Taiho Ritsuryo Code of 701, from which its name derives, was a vast centralized bureaucracy shaped like a pyramid. At its apex stood the emperor and the royal family, with the aristocracy standing just below him. Then came the civil servants, who presided over the mass of common people who formed the pyramid's base. Buddhism, while still officially subordinate to Shinto, was a political and social reality that needed to be fitted into the new system. A code of regulations for Buddhist monks and nuns known as the *Soniryo* was developed, and this document regulated the lives of the Buddhist clergy in some detail. The code makes it clear that one of the principal concerns of those who drew it up was to control and limit the political power of the Buddhist establishment. Unlike Shinto, which was by its very nature local and institutionally dispersed, Buddhism was inherently coherent, with all the political potentials that such a state of affairs implies. The *Soniryo* attempted to curtail severely any Buddhist activity outside of the government-sanctioned temples and to prevent the Buddhist clergy from interacting with the common people.

This goal was frustrated by Buddhism's natural missionary impulse. In Japan, this was first manifested by Gyogi (668–749), who seems to have been a member of a family that was originally of Korean origin and claimed descent from the scholar Wang In, who had helped to introduce Confucianism into Japan in the fourth century C.E. Whatever the truth of his family background, Gyogi entered the monastic life at the age of fifteen as a member of the Hosso sect of Buddhism—the Japanese manifestation of the Yogacara school—although the Buddhism that he subsequently practiced was always heavily tinged with shamanic and magical elements as well. But Gyogi was not satisfied to study Buddhism simply for his own edification. He believed that Buddhist doctrines demanded an active living out of their principles. This was to lead him into severe difficulties with the government.

Reading an account of his work makes this later government persecution all the more puzzling. The *Continued Chronicle of Japan* relates that:

> Gyogi traveled around the capital and countryside preaching to and converting the masses. He had a thousand followers, both laity and clergy. Wherever he went, when people knew he was coming the villages would empty and men and women would vie to show him reverence. He led all according to their ability and made them incline to good. With his followers, he built bridges and erected dikes in strategic places. Wherever news of him spread, people came and provided their labor, so that the structure was soon finished.

> SOURCE: Yusen Kashiwahara and Koyu Sonanda (eds.), *Shapers of Japanese Buddhism* (Tokyo: Kosei, 1994), pp. 4–5

In addition, Gyogi is reputed to have built forty-nine Buddhist chapels around the capital. Whatever else they may be, these actions certainly do not seem like those of a revolutionary, but rather those of a praiseworthy subject of the emperor. But the central government did not see it this way. The new bureaucratic system that had just been implemented imposed a tremendous financial burden on the small farmers of Japan. Moreover, a series of natural disasters had further afflicted the common people. Consequently, many were deserting their land, thus depriving the government of sorely needed revenues at a critical time in its development. Gyogi's activities were seen as encouraging the common people to pursue a religious life rather than concentrating on farming, and this, it was feared, might possibly lead to revolution and anarchy. To combat this perceived threat, an even stricter official code of conduct was enacted in 717 that aimed at controlling monks in general, and Gyogi in particular.

The government also started a policy of rewarding monks and nuns who supported the government and controlling the number of people who could ordain monks and nuns through the institution of a certificate system. Without the appropriate certificate, one could not be ordained, and these certificates were dispensed grudgingly. But despite this period of intense persecution, which lasted from 717 to 724, Gyogi and his followers were impossible to ignore. More farsighted statesmen came to realize that the forces he commanded could be of tremendous use to the government if properly channeled. By 740, the government was in desperate need of labor for huge building projects such as the Great Buddha of Todaiji, and there was a complete reversal in the government's attitude. Gyogi was now venerated as a senior priest and a "Dharma Master." His followers were coopted and became an important component of the government's plans. Ironically, Gyogi died a valued and respected member of the Japanese establishment.

The Six Schools of Nara Buddhism

By the 730s, it was becoming evident to the Japanese government that Buddhism was a necessary prop to their rule. Under Emperor Shomu, a new system of national temples—the *kokubunji* system—was inaugurated in 741. This institution, an imitation of a similar system of temples established by the Tang empress Wu Zhao, mandated the maintenance of official temples in all the provincial capitals. Each province was to construct a seven-storied temple and make copies of selected Buddhist scriptures to enshrine therein. In addition, a *Konkomyashitennogokoku no tera* (Temple for the Protection of the Nation by the Four Deva Kings of the Konkomyokyo) was to be established with a staff of twenty priests, whose sole task it was to intercede for the nation's protection and prosperity. These temples were supported by allocations of rice-growing land, and they were soon granted other forms of tax relief that caused them to become considerable local economic forces in their own right.

Shomu was also responsible for the building of the great image of Birushana—known in Sanskrit as Mahavairocana (Great Sun) Buddha—at Todaiji in Nara. His aim was to establish a Buddhist ritual center that corresponded to the nation's political center. Just as Birushana was the center of the many universes of Buddhist cosmology, so too would the emperor, through rites of magical association, be the center of the earthly domain, or at least the Japanese part of it. Indeed, at the dedication ceremony of his great project, Shomu took the religious name of "Roshana," the Japanese form of Locana, another name for Mahavairocana Buddha. Covered in gold leaf, the finished statue was 53½ feet high and weighed some 452 tons and represented a tremendous commitment of resources.[2] Before beginning construction, Shomu had sent Gyogi to the main imperial Shinto shrine at **Ise** to win the approval of his divine ancestress Amaterasu. Henceforth, Amaterasu and Mahavairocana became increasingly associated in the Japanese religious mind. Todaiji now became the Buddhist religious center of the nation, with the headquarters of the six principal schools of Buddhism being housed there. These institutions, known as the Six Schools of Nara Buddhism, were not the only schools of Buddhist interpretation that existed in Japan, but they were the ones that were officially favored by the government. Essentially, all these schools were academic institutions that had little or no concern with anyone outside the immediate aristocratic circles of the court. Nevertheless, their ideas set the philosophical tone of Japanese Buddhism for the next thousand years, with subsequent schools of Buddhist thought building on the foundations laid by them.

The first of these schools was based on the Abhidharmakosha school of Vasubandhu and called the Kusha-shu. Introduced into Japan in about 650 by monks who had recently returned from China, it did not differ markedly from its Indian and Chinese predecessors. The second of the Nara schools, the Jojitsu-shu or Investigation of Truth school, was based on a single text of the same name written in India in the third century C.E. by Harivarman. Despite a brief independent existence during the Nara period, this school soon merged with the more numerous Sanron school, which was an extension of the Madhyamika school of

Nagarjuna. The fourth school was the Hosso school; the fifth was the Kegon-shu, which followed the teachings of the Huayan school of Chinese Buddhism. The last of the Nara schools was the Ritsu-shu (Vinaya) school, which advocated very strict adherence to the monastic code of conduct, even to the exclusion of meditative practice.

This last school, although it had little long-term effect on the development of Japanese Buddhism, played an important role in the early history of the religion. This was due to the fact that it controlled the *kaidan* or ordination platform at Nara. The government had ordered that this was the only place where Japanese monks could be ordained. Emperor Shomu had sent the monks Eiei and Fusho to China in order to be sure that Japanese ordination practices were canonically valid. When they found that this was not the case, they invited the Vinaya master Jienzhen (Ganjin in Japanese) to return with them to Japan and establish proper ordination lineages. Despite considerable hardship, this worthy monk finally arrived in Japan and established the official ordination platform at Todaiji in 754. Later two subsidiary *kaidan* were established at Yakushiji and Kanzeonji temples.

Control of these three ordination platforms gave the government control of the creation of monks, since no such ordination could be performed anywhere else. Although the *kaidan* were administered by the Ritsu-shu school, each of the established Six Schools had a yearly quota of monks that it was allowed to ordain on the official *kaidan*. This meant that all Buddhist monks had to belong officially to one of the six government-approved schools. But what if a person did not belong to one of these schools, or wanted to introduce new teachings into Japanese Buddhism that were opposed by the six official schools? As things stood, this was not allowable. However, the entire status quo was to be challenged by a new school of Buddhist thought that was promulgated by one of the most forceful figures in Japanese Buddhist history.

Todaiji Temple. The Todaiji Temple served as the headquarters for all of the early schools of Buddhism in Japan.

Map of Mount Hiei, Edo
period, 18th century.
Mount Hiei was home
to the sacred temples
and centers of learning
established by Saicho.

Saicho and the Establishment of Tendai Buddhism

A pivotal figure in the development of Japanese Buddhism, Saicho—or, as he is also
known, Dengyo Daishi—was born Mitsu no Obito Hirono in 767. It was he who
led a revolution that broke the Six Schools' grip on monastic ordination, thus

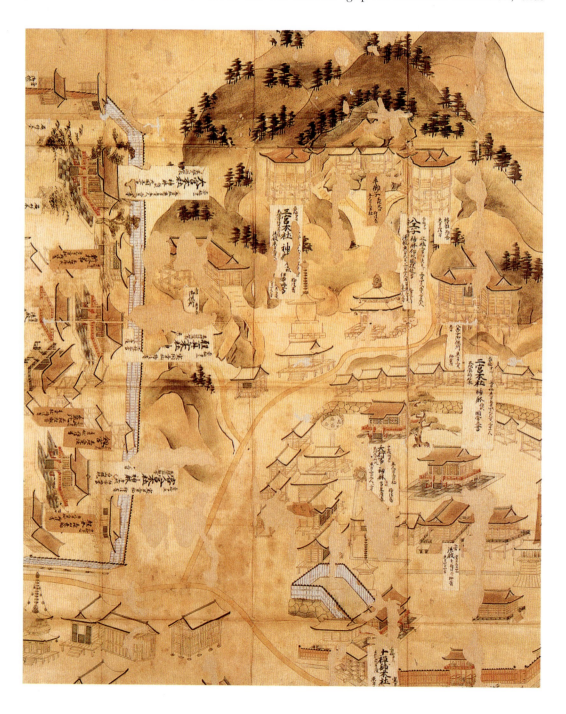

opening new directions for the development of Buddhism in Japan. Saicho came from a devoutly Buddhist family of Chinese descent and entered the Buddhist life at the age of thirteen, becoming ordained as a full Buddhist monk five years later in 785. In a sense, such an ordination was little more than a formal qualification for an official position in the religious arm of the government. But Saicho appears to have been assailed by genuine religious scruples at this prospect and subsequently withdrew to Mount Hiei, which lies to the northeast of the area in which Kyoto would be built in 794.

It was a time in Japanese history that might well have provoked religious reflection. Rebellion flared in the north, the oppressive tax system was breeding unrest among the peasantry, and the imperial capital was moved yet again. Saicho, perhaps despairing of the world, became a hermit on Mount Hiei for the next twelve years. There he studied and meditated. He seems to have trained in the Hosso sect, but as his studies progressed, he became more and more interested in the Chinese school of Tiantai. In 797, he was appointed to serve at court, and seven years later he sailed with an official Japanese embassy to China, where he made his way to Mount Tiantai in Zhejiang province. Tiantai was undergoing a revival when Saicho arrived at the headquarters of the school. He studied with the students of the sixth patriarch of the sect, Zhanian, and received the official transmission of the lineage. He spent the winter studying and copying religious texts, staying in China for only eight and a half months before returning to Japan. He spent his time well, however, bringing back some 230 Buddhist works in 460 volumes. The reigning emperor Kammu was pleased with Saicho's efforts, and granted the newly established Japanese Tendai school two ordinations per year. Saicho was also permitted to establish a monastic institution on Mount Hiei.

By the spring of 810, Mount Hiei had begun to become a center for Buddhist learning and discussion. New meditation techniques, such as the Lotus Samadhi or "half-sitting and half-walking practice," were introduced from China. It was at this time too that Saicho began his famous correspondence with the other great figure of early Japanese Buddhism, Kukai. As we shall see below, Kukai was also in the process of establishing a center of Buddhist learning on Mount Koya. At first, the two men got on well, but eventually they fell out. The essence of their disagreement lay in their different ideas about the route to enlightenment. Saicho believed that it could be entirely accomplished through study, while Kukai put his faith completely in practice.

But Kukai was not the only rival figure of the period with whom Saicho clashed. He also carried on a famous debate with the Hosso scholar Tokuitsu. Eventually, these increasingly acrimonious debates with other schools led Saicho to the conclusion that the Tendai school could only flourish if it possessed its own ordination platform beyond the control of rival sects. He therefore decided to petition the government for the establishment of a Mahayana ordination platform on Mount Hiei. In 818, he presented to the court his *Regulations for the Annual Quota of Students of the Tendai Lotus Sect*, in which he announced his intention to abandon the Theravada precepts and to establish a *kaidan* based on Mahayana principles. Naturally, both the Buddhist establishment and the government opposed such an attack on their control of Buddhist institutions. Nevertheless, Saicho pressed on with his demands, and his prestige was such that his request was finally granted. Sadly, this happened a week after his death on June 27, 822. But Saicho had managed through his efforts to free Japanese Buddhism from the complete control of the government. With the grip of the imperial bureaucracy broken, Buddhism could now branch off in new and innovative directions.[3]

Kukai's Journeys, Tomioka Tessai, 1924. Kukai introduced the Shingon school of Buddhism to Japan after being sent to China by the Japanese government.

Kukai and the Development of Esoteric Buddhism in Japan

The last great figure in the early history of Buddhism is Kukai (774–835), also known by his posthumous title, Kobo Daishi. He was born on the island of Shikoku, where his family, like Saicho's, belonged to the local aristocracy. At the age of fourteen, he was sent to the capital to foster his education under the patronage of his maternal uncle, who was the tutor to the crown prince. Three years later, he entered the imperial academy to study the Chinese language and literature that was the road to success in early Fujiwara Japan. During his studies, however, he met a Buddhist priest—who this priest was, history does not inform us—and immediately threw away a promising career in the civil service to become a reclusive mountain ascetic.

Unlike Saicho, whose initial religious formation was conditioned by his studies of the Hosso texts, Kukai was most influenced in his early days by the teachings of esoteric Buddhism. This form of Buddhism, whose main modern representatives are the various schools of Tibetan Buddhism, held a deep fascination for the Japanese of the eighth century. Its primary focus lay in mystical practice, elaborate ceremonies, and "secret knowledge" passed on from teacher to student through personal instruction. Incorporating diverse elements of local folklore, ritual, and magic, esoteric Buddhism seemed to the Japanese government to be the best means of achieving the magical protection of the country that was its primary objective for the religion. So, when the brilliant young Kukai showed an interest in the subject, the government hastened to foster it by sending him to China in 804. Esoteric Buddhism had not been established in China for very long at that point, having probably reached China from South India in the early part of the eighth century—the two most commanding figures in the early Chinese tradition were Shubhakarasimha and Vajrabodhi, who arrived in 716 and 720 respectively. Despite this late start, the esoteric tradition flourished in China, especially after the arrival of the school's most dominant figure, Amoghavajra.

Thus Kukai found that the Zhenyan (in Japanese Shingon, or "True Words") or esoteric school was extremely popular in the Tang capital. He immediately began to study Sanskrit, the key to the school's scriptures, and then proceeded to the school's most famous center of learning, the Qinglong Temple. There he met the patriarch of the school, Huiguo, who administered the three initiations required to empower Kukai to transmit the school's esoteric teachings. Kukai returned to Japan in 806 with 142 new texts of the esoteric school in his baggage, including forty-two Sanskrit texts that probably no one else in Japan could read. He settled in the southern island of Kyushu for the next two and a half years before returning to the capital where he began his famous and ill-fated association with Saicho.

Kukai soon established himself in the highest court circles. He exchanged calligraphy and poetry with Emperor Saga, and a genuine friendship seems to have sprung up between the two men. Utilizing these connections, Kukai established a temple on Mount Koya in 816. His aim was to emulate the great Indian teacher Amoghavajra, who had established a famous training center on Mount Wutai. Kukai was also granted a temple in the new capital of Kyoto that he immediately made an exclusively Shingon establishment. He was even granted permission to establish a chapel and a *mandala* in the palace itself. Thus, unlike Saicho, who harbored reservations about associating with the government aristocracy, Kukai embraced it enthusiastically. Most important, however, was the establishment of a Shingon chapel at the Todaiji in 822. From this foothold, Shingon soon extended its influence throughout the entire Nara Buddhist establishment. By 830, Kukai was at the height of his powers and influence. In this year, he finished his masterpiece, a commentary on the Great Sun Sutra—the key text of his school—entitled *The Ten Stages of Mind*. In this work, he divided religious consciousness into ten categories, each linked with various Buddhist and non-Buddhist philosophies. Of course, the highest religious consciousness was displayed by the Shingon school. But Kukai also believed that all religious thought was permeated by the presence of Mahavairocana Buddha, and this allowed Shingon to exhibit tolerance toward the other Buddhist groups of the period. This eventually resulted in their absorption into the school of Kukai. At the time, it was only Tendai and the incipient Pure Land sect who escaped the whirlpool of Kukai's influence, and only partially at that.

But Kukai's fame would not be as great as it is had he not also possessed a sizable following among the lower classes. Even today, he is associated with many areas of Japan where it is doubtful that he ever went, and his name has passed into popular folklore throughout the islands. This popular adulation stems from his involvement with, and support of, many public works, such as irrigation projects, that directly benefited the hard-pressed peasants of his time. As we have seen, other Buddhist monks, such as Gyogi, had similar concerns. But with his solid connections at court, Kukai was able to champion such projects with much more success, and considerably less adverse effects to his own career, than his illustrious predecessor. His work finally came to an end on April 23, 835, when he died on Mount Koya where he is believed to still sit in eternal meditation within the inner shrine of the temple. By that time, Shingon had been established as the premier school of Buddhism in Japan, and even today it still boasts many followers.[4]

Website References

1. www.kana.co.jp/okamoto/culture.htm gives examples of early Nara temples.

2. Todaiji is discussed at **www.jinjapan.org/atlas/historical/his11.html**

3. **www.tendai-lotus.org/** covers Tendai teachings.

4. Shingon Buddhism is discussed at **www.shingon.org/home.html**

CHAPTER TWENTY-SIX

Pure Land and Nichiren Buddhism

The Heian period of Japanese history was a time of unparalleled artistic development in Japan and could perhaps be called the Golden Age of Japanese literature. But this explosion of culture came at a high price to the common people of the islands. While the aristocracy lounged in Nara or Kyoto composing elegant verse in Chinese or playing refined parlor games, such as trying to guess the scent wafting from a hidden incense burner, rough-hewn warriors defended the harsh northern borders from the attacks of still-powerful indigenous groups such as the Ainu. The gorgeous many-layered silk robes that adorned the ladies of the court were purchased at the expense of the peasantry, who toiled under increasingly onerous tax burdens. In all, a very few profited from the labor of the many, but increasingly this minority gave little or nothing in return.

The Rise of Pure Land Buddhism

Buddhism was at this time a religion of the aristocracy. There were, of course, some gestures made toward the common people by isolated Buddhist monks, and these were greatly appreciated, as the legends that still circulate about Kukai bear witness. But the aristocracy was suspicious of any attempts by monks to evangelize the common people. They were well aware that the average citizen of Japan was dissatisfied with his or her lot and that it would only take a spark to ignite a rebellion. Such a spark could well come from the preaching of an itinerant monk. The best policy—at least from the aristocracy's point of view—was to contain Buddhism within the cocoon of court life. But for many truly devout Buddhist monks, this situation was unacceptable. The Buddha had explicitly given his followers the mandate to go out and spread the truth of the *dharma* for the good of all beings. It necessarily followed, therefore, that a true monk was under an obligation to preach to those who had not heard the saving truths of Buddhism. To do anything else was to fail in one's religious duty.

Gyogi had been the first Japanese monk to attempt to do this in a systematic way, but owing to bureaucratic interference and the type of relatively intellectual

Buddhism that he taught, his long-term influence was marginal. The problems of practicing Buddhism that were found in China were equally present in Japan. The back-breaking life of the peasants did not allow them much time for religious devotions, meditation, or study. This seemingly meant that Buddhist salvation was denied to such persons, at least in this life. Certainly, that is what the aristocracy believed. But, as we have already seen, there was a form of Buddhism that could be adapted to the conditions of the common laboring folk. These were the Pure Land teachings.

The first Japanese monk to popularize these teachings was Kuya (903–972), who is accounted the first Japanese patriarch of the Pure Land school. Also known as Amida Hijiri—Amida's Wandering Sage—Kuya traveled through Japan constantly repeating the words of the *nembutsu* (Chinese *koucheng nianfo*)—"I take refuge in Amida Buddha." His fervor and devotion to the salvation of all beings resonated strongly with all levels of Japanese society. In a period of increasing anarchy and revolution, Kuya offered a way out of chaos into a better existence.

Other than the fact that this seminal figure of Pure Land Buddhism was born in 903, we have no knowledge of his early years except that he was a lay practitioner of Buddhism from an early age. According to legend, he spent this time in doing pious good works, traveling throughout Japan to visit holy sites. At the age of twenty, he entered the Owari Provincial Temple, where he was ordained in about 923—but not as an "official" monk. This lack of official ordination barred him from holding office in the government. But this does not seem to have bothered Kuya at all: for him, ordination meant the chance to be a more effective apostle of the religion in which he fervently believed. He was not interested in a government career. Subsequently, in 948, he traveled to Mount Hiei to be initiated into the Tendai precepts, which made him an official monk. Kuya, however, chose to retain his training name rather than assume the new name bestowed on him at his official

Kuya. Kuya was among the first Japanese teachers of the *nembutsu* invocation of Amidabutsu.

ordination. This was entirely consistent with his mission up to this time, which was among the common people.

At an early date, Kuya had evolved the basic outlines of the practice that he would follow for the rest of his life. Instead of living comfortably in a monastery, he preferred to wander through the countryside, living on whatever alms people chose to give him and practicing asceticism and mortification of the body in the relatively mild tradition of the early Buddhist monks. He ceased to eat grains, he burned incense on his arms, and he went for extended periods without sleep and not moving. He also began to study the Buddhist scriptures intensively.

After several years of study and ascetic practice, Kuya began to travel in the wild northern parts of Japan, where Buddhism was only a distant rumor. There he preached the gospel of Buddhism until 938, when war drove him back to Kyoto and a new phase in his career. In the capital, he preached in the marketplaces and collected alms, which he then distributed to the poor and destitute. He also petitioned the government to relieve the economic suffering of the official outcasts and recently liberated government slaves. At the same time, by his life, work, and teaching, he popularized the use of the *nembutsu* as the primary spiritual exercise of the common people. Wandering through the streets and markets, he would sing songs of his own invention extolling the virtues of Amida and the Pure Land.

In the summer of 944, Kuya began to make images of Kannon Bodhisattva, the Chinese Guanyin. By the end of the year he had made thirty-three such images along with drawings of Amida's Pure Land, as well as of Mount Potalaka, the home of Kannon. He made more statues in 951. His purpose was no doubt twofold. First of all, the statues were believed to have magical power to avert disaster—and there were disasters aplenty during these years. But perhaps more important was their value as teaching tools. The vast mass of the Japanese people were illiterate. The complex Chinese writing system was imperfectly suited to expressing the very different grammar and phonology of Japanese, and so writing and reading were very much the preserve of the aristocracy. Consequently, Kuya recognized the value of art in communicating ideas to a population that could not read.

Despite his primary allegiance to the poor and dispossessed, Kuya found after his official ordination to the monkhood in 948 that he was now much more acceptable to the aristocracy. He soon formed a particular friendship with Fujiwara no Saneyori, the powerful Minister of the Left in the imperial government. Kuya continued to move between these two social spheres, but as he grew older he spent more of his time at the Saikoji Temple in Kyoto. It is likely that he died there in 972 after a long and productive life centered on communicating Buddhism to the common people of Japan. He advocated a much more relaxed and syncretic form of Pure Land Buddhism that attempted to integrate the religious concepts of Shinto as well as those of other Buddhist groups, than that of the more exclusivist followers of Honen and Shinran's form of Pure Land teachings. Kuya's particular teaching was adapted and carried on by later teachers such as Ippen-Shonin (1239–1289).

Honen and the Growth of Pure Land Buddhism

The next influential proponent of Pure Land teachings did not appear for more than a hundred and fifty years after the death of Kuya, and a very eventful period those years were. During this time, the aristocratic society of the Heian period was swept away, and the government came to reside in the hands of the warrior samurai class.

After a series of debilitating civil wars, the Minamoto family had triumphed over their rivals and secured the office of shogun, which gave them supreme political power in Japan. It was during the last acts of this violent drama that Honen (1133–1212) lived and precipitated the vigorous revival of the Pure Land tradition. He held that the practice of the *nembutsu* was the only hope of the poor, the stupid, or those unable to keep the formal precepts of Buddhism—that is, most human beings. For advocating this peaceful religious path that aimed at universal salvation, he was persecuted. His books and the wooden plates from which they were printed were publicly burned, and his grave was desecrated in 1227.

The man who engendered such passionate reactions among the religious establishment of his day began life innocently enough as the son of a minor provincial gentry family. Tragedy marred his early life, however, when in 1141 his father was murdered. He was sent to live with his mother's brother, a monk at the Bodai-ji Temple in his home province of Mimasaka. He remained there until 1147, when he traveled to Mount Hiei to study Tendai doctrine—the tradition in which he was eventually ordained. He was also exposed to the recitation of the *nembutsu* as it was practiced in the Kurodani practice hall on the western side of the mountain. He remained there for the next twenty years, during which time he not only recited the invocation of Amida, but is also said to have read through the entire Buddhist canon five times. At the age of forty-two, Honen decided to commit himself completely to the practice of the *nembutsu*. The year that he did so, 1175, is considered to be the date of the foundation of the Jodo (Pure Land) sect that subsequently evolved from his teachings.

Leaving Mount Hiei, Honen settled in Kyoto where he deepened his practice. Later, in 1186, he became engaged with members of other Buddhist orders in what became known as the Ohara Discussion over the efficacy of the various modes of Buddhist practice. Honen apparently got the better of his opponents, and his reputation began to spread throughout Japan. This process was accelerated when, in 1190, he gave a series of lectures on the three Pure Land sutras at the Todaiji itself. He now had the patronage of a former regent of the Fujiwara family, and his influence soon extended right into the imperial family itself. He was also attracting students, including the founders of the five major subsects of Jodo Buddhism that sprang up after his death. By 1198, Honen felt that he needed to set forth a definitive exposition of his religious views, which he did in a volume entitled *Collection of Passages on the Original Vow and the Nembutsu*.[1]

This book held the seeds of Honen's later persecution. In it, he abandoned the syncretic tendencies that had allowed the various Japanese Buddhist sects to coexist. Instead, he advocated the total renunciation of all practices other than the recitation of the *nembutsu*. All Theravada and non-Pure Land Mahayana practices and doctrines were declared useless. Meditation and ritual were to be abandoned. The world had degenerated since the time of the Buddha to a state where enlightenment was no longer possible. The other Buddhist paths might have worked in earlier times; but the recitation of the *nembutsu* was the only way that inhabitants of the present-day world could attain salvation through their rebirth in the Pure Land, where enlightenment was still possible—indeed, assured. Honen was not insensible to the furor that his words would provoke among the other Japanese Buddhist groups. There is even a clear indication that the *Collection of Passages on the Original Vow and the Nembutsu* was meant only for the eyes of Pure Land believers and not for the general public. Honen himself, in a postscript to the work, told the reader that "once you have perused this work . . . bury it beneath your walls and do not leave it before your window [where others might see it]."

A *mandara* painting, Muromachi period, 14th–15th century, showing Amida Buddha flanked by the *bodhisattvas* Kannon and Seishi. The *mandara* was the principal religious icon of the Pure Land sect of Buddhism founded by Honen.

The backlash that Honen feared was not long in coming. By 1204, clerics in his own Tendai sect were petitioning the head of the order to ban the practice of *nembutsu*. Honen retaliated with his *Seven Article Injunction* to his followers, which bound them not to disparage Tendai or Shingon, disregard the formal precepts, or dispute with other schools of Buddhism. But this did not dissuade other monks from petitioning the powerful retired emperor Go-Toba to ban the *nembutsu*. Criticism was particularly harsh against two disciples, Gyoku and Junsai, favorites of the ladies of the court. Honen expelled Gyoku from the movement, but it was too late. Both Gyoku and Junsai offended the emperor, and were executed in 1206.

Early the next year, Honen was forced to resign from the Buddhist priesthood and was exiled to the island of Shikoku under the lay name of Fujii Motohiko. Despite this, the terms of his banishment were not especially onerous, and he was permitted to continue preaching, which he did. He was allowed to return to the capital in 1211. But in the next year, the rigors of his life in exile began to catch up with Honen, who was by then seventy-nine years old. As his condition worsened, his disciples flocked to his bedside to witness their master's final moments. Chanting the *nembutsu*, he finally slipped away after dictating the *One Page Testament*, his final thoughts on the essentials of the *nembutsu* practice. The place where he died is now the site of the head-quarters of the Jodo sect that he founded—one of the largest schools of Buddhism in modern Japan. Honen's *One Page Testament* neatly encapsulates his doctrine of the Pure Land:

> The method of final salvation that I have propounded is neither a sort of meditation, such as has been practiced by many scholars in China and Japan, nor is it a repetition of the Buddha's name by those who have studied and understood the deep meaning of it. It is nothing but the mere repetition of the *"Namu Amida Butsu,"* without a doubt of His mercy, whereby one may be born into the Land of Perfect Bliss. The mere repetition with firm faith includes all the practical details, such as the three-fold preparation of mind and the four practical rules. If I as an individual had any doctrine more profound than this, I should miss the mercy of the two Honorable Ones, Amida and Shaka [the Buddha], and be left out of the Vow of Amida Buddha. Those who believe this, though they clearly understand all the teachings Shaka taught throughout his whole life, should behave themselves like simple-minded folk, who know not a single letter, or like ignorant nuns and monks whose faith is implicitly simple. Thus, without pedantic airs, they should fervently practice the repetition of the name of Amida, and that alone.
>
> SOURCE: Ryusaku Tsunoda *et al.*, *Sources of Japanese Tradition*, vol i (New York: Columbia University Press, 1964) pp. 202–203

Shinran and the Jodo Shin School

Honen's most prominent successor was Shinran (1173–1262), the founder of the Jodo Shin (True Pure Land) sect, who, with his relaxation of the rules of celibacy and meat-eating for the clergy, radically changed the entire perception of the Buddhist monk in Japanese society. Shinran's early life is obscure. Although it was claimed by later biographers that he was a descendent of the Fujiwara family that had previously ruled Japan, there is no doubt that he was of relatively humble origins. He seems to have entered the Tendai monastery on Mount Hiei at an early age, and there he was assigned to the perpetual recitation of the *nembutsu*. But in about 1201, at the age of twenty-eight, Shinran apparently had some sort of religious crisis. After a lengthy retreat at the Rokkaku-do Temple in Kyoto, he decided to throw in his lot with Honen. By doing so, he left the comfortable and protected life of a Tendai monk for the uncertainties of being one of Honen's followers. By 1205, he was in the select circle of Honen's personal disciples, as witnessed by his being one of the few who were allowed to make copies of the *Collection of Passages on the Original Vow and the Nembutsu*.

When Honen was sent into exile, so too was Shinran. But Shinran was compelled to go to the much harsher northern province of Echigo, where, for the first year, he was allotted a little rice and salt and allowed to plant vegetables. At the beginning of the second year, all government food assistance was withdrawn. Shinran endured this brutal life until 1211, when his banishment was rescinded along with that of his master. But when Honen died soon after, Shinran left the capital to preach the new faith in the eastern provinces of Japan, which were the stronghold of the now-dominant warrior clans that ruled the country. There, he not only spread the gospel of the Pure Land, but also completed his masterpiece—the book entitled *Teaching, Practice, Faith, Attainment*.[2]

Like Honen, Shinran believed that the teachings of the Buddha were no longer applicable in the degenerate age in which human beings found themselves. After a brief florescence, the *dharma* had steadily declined until the traditional practices advocated by the Buddha were totally ineffective. Only Pure Land Buddhism, Shinran believed, held an antidote for the evils of the present time or *mappo*. To attain salvation, one must reorient one's life. This was a process of conversion, Shinran thought, consisting of three distinct stages. The first was the impulse to perform good works and achieve purification through ascetic practice. However, although this might be of some use to those with money and leisure time, it was practically impossible for the vast laboring mass of the poor. In the second stage, people practiced the *nembutsu*, but they still clung to their pride in their own accomplishments—to "self-power" (*jiriki*)—and so did not possess faith in Amida or practice total surrender to his "other-power" (*tariki*). It was only with the entrance into the third stage, with its total faith in the saving grace of Amida Buddha, that salvation was possible. Of course it followed that if one held to any practice other than the *nembutsu*, this showed that one lacked the requisite faith in Amida. But with faith in "other-power," nothing was impossible. In another book, the *Tannisho*, Shinran taught that:

> People generally think . . . that if even a wicked man can be reborn in the Pure Land, how much more so a good man! This latter view may at first sight seem reasonable, but it is not in accord with the purpose of the Original Vow [of Amida Buddha], with faith in the Power of Another. The reason for this is that he who, relying on his own power, undertakes to perform meritorious deeds, has no intention of relying on the Power of Another and is not the object of the Original Vow of Amida. Should he, however, abandon his reliance on his own power and put his trust in the Power of Another, he can be born in the True Land of Recompense. We who are caught in the net of our own passions cannot free ourselves from bondage to birth and death, no matter what kind of austerities or good deeds we try to perform. Seeing this and pitying our condition, Amida made his Vow with the intention of bringing wicked men to Buddhahood. Therefore the wicked man who depends on the Power of Another is the prime object of salvation [not the good person].

> SOURCE: Tsunoda *et al.*, *Sources of Japanese Tradition*, p. 211

Shinran's *Teaching, Practice, Faith, Attainment* was not only a bold restatement of the fundamental principles of the Pure Land school, it was also a declaration of war by that school on the other sects of Japanese Buddhism. Shinran said publicly what his master Honen had believed but had concealed from the average person, namely that Pure Land Buddhism was the only way that one could be saved. Naturally, the other Japanese Buddhist schools took lively exception to this idea. Moreover, in 1221, the newly established shogunate government moved to consolidate its control over the peasantry. The general unrest that this caused, along with the popular influence of Shinran's teachings, resulted in the promulgation of a number of laws that made the exclusive recitation of the *nembutsu* illegal and condemned Shinran's relaxation of the monastic codes so that monks could eat meat and marry. At first, persecution of Shinran's followers was unorganized and sporadic, but by 1249 it had become very much more systematic, especially in the eastern provinces.

These persecutions went on until 1256. During this time there was considerable tension within the movement, and Shinran excommunicated his own son, Zenran, for failing to follow exactly in his footsteps. In the end, however, the persecutions died out, although it would be many years before the various branches of the Pure Land school were fully accepted by the Japanese Buddhist establishment. Shinran died at the ripe old age of eighty-nine in 1262, and control of both his school and that of Honen passed to less towering figures than their founders. But the age of innovation in Japanese Buddhism had not yet passed; it had merely moved on in other directions.

Nichiren

One of the most commanding and controversial figures in the history of Buddhism in Japan was Nichiren (1222–1282), the son of a common fisherman. Nichiren's Buddhism is uniquely Japanese in its associations and tone, owing to the religious and political preoccupations of its founder. Nichiren was obsessed with two questions. The first was whether or not he could be certain that he was saved. This is a common problem for people of a religious disposition worldwide, and it can lead the development of religious traditions in radical directions. The second question centered

Great Buddha of Kamakura, 1252. The soldier class increasingly became patrons of Buddhism as political power began to shift away from the imperial court in Kyoto to the military rulers based in eastern Japan.

around the person of the emperor: if he was of divine origin, as Nichiren believed, then why had the imperial forces been defeated and subjugated to the military clans that controlled the shogunate? Nichiren wrestled with these two questions during his term as a monk on Mount Hiei. Having joined the Tendai order in 1243 at the age of twenty-one, he had trained in the Tendai system for the next eleven years until he started his independent teaching at the age of thirty-two. His distinctive message blended complete faith in the Lotus Sutra with a fanatical belief in Japan's manifest destiny.[3]

Nichiren's aggressive campaign to propagate his version of Pure Land Buddhism was predicated on a pessimistic vision of the world. Nichiren held that all the calamities that were befalling Japan at this time—natural disasters, civil war, and, ultimately, foreign invasion by the Mongols—were the logical consequences of the decline of Buddhism that had started with the death of the Buddha. The only remedy for this decline lay in a return to the fervent practice of true Buddhism, and that was only possible through wholehearted adherence to the teachings of the Lotus Sutra (as interpreted by Nichiren, of course).[4] In 1261, Nichiren sent a memorial to the government detailing his views, prophesying that not only would the internal disasters that plagued Japan continue, but that there would be foreign invasion as well should the government not heed his advice to suppress all sects of Japanese Buddhism except his own.

Predictably, the shogunate did not look kindly on Nichiren's advice. In the course of his mission, he had made many enemies, some of whom had actually attempted to murder him. Deciding to return to the shogunate capital of Kamakura in eastern Japan in 1261, Nichiren was promptly sent into exile. Released in 1263, he immediately renewed his attack on other sects of Buddhism, including the Pure Land sects, which shared many of his beliefs but not his interpretations of them. He barely escaped assassination again in 1264. But the foreign invasion that he had prophesied materialized in 1268, when the Mongol rulers of China demanded that Japan submit to them, and consequently Nichiren's stock rose somewhat with the

Nichiren, Ichiyusai Kuniyoshi, c. 1800. Nichiren advocated a strongly nationalistic form of Buddhism. This print depicts him on the way to Sado, calming the storm at sea.

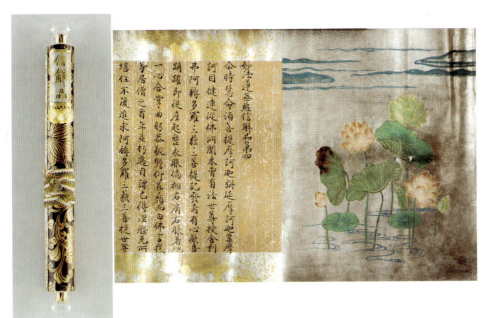

Chapter 4 of the Lotus Sutra, Tanaka Shinbi, 20th century. On the frontispiece the five lotus in a pond illustrate the development of five periods of the Buddha's teaching. Nichiren's teaching revolved around the first line of the Lotus Sutra.

ruling classes. This did not last long, however, and in 1271 we see Nichiren at odds with the government yet again. This time, he was to be executed for high treason. But as he was being led to his death, a blinding light supposedly terrified the executioner and the military escort, who ran away. His sentence was commuted to banishment on the desolate island of Sado, but in 1274 he was again released. He now retired to Mount Minobu. More convinced than ever of the truth of his teachings, he remained active in retirement, writing and teaching his disciples until his death in 1282.

What was Nichiren's message that so antagonized both the religious and secular authorities of his day? On the surface, it differed only slightly from that of other schools. Nichiren's metaphysics was essentially that of the Tendai school in which he had originally trained. He utilized Shingon ritual techniques. Most of all, he shared the basic views on human nature and salvation of the Pure Land schools. But unlike all these schools, he did not believe in the efficacy of ecclesiastical offices: religious leaders should gain their authority from their personal sanctity and attainment, not from the office that they held in a religious hierarchy. Leadership of a school, he believed, and the authoritative interpretation of a text, in this case the Lotus Sutra, depended on a "spiritual" succession. There could, therefore, be a long span of time between the appearance of true interpreters of any particular doctrine. Nichiren held himself to be the interpreter for his age, even going so far as to say that he was a *bodhisattva*.

This absolute—some might even say megalomaniacal—belief in himself and in his teaching led Nichiren to extreme positions. His antagonism toward other schools of Buddhist thought was uncompromising. He believed that "those who practice invocation to Amitabha [the *nembutsu*] are due to suffer continuous punishment in Hell; the Zen sect is the devil; the Shingon sect is the ruiner of the country; the Ritsu sect is the enemy of the country."

The core of his teaching revolved around the recitation not of the *nembutsu*, but of the **daimoku**, the first line of the Lotus Sutra—"reverence to the *Sutra of the Lotus* *of the Pure Truth"* (in Japanese, *namu myo-horenge-kyo*). His belief in the saving power of this mantra was absolute, not only in the spiritual sphere but in the material one as well; and his followers still believe that this incantation is the path to success, both in this world and in the next. Nichiren's goal was nothing less than to establish a Pure Land in the world. He believed that it was the destiny of Japan to be that Pure Land, and of the emperor to preside over it. Japan was to be the center of the world. Of course, the emperors were not to have the final say in religious matters—that was reserved for religious authority, that is to say the organization founded by Nichiren, since all other religious groups were to be repressed.

Despite the idiosyncratic nature of Nichiren's Buddhism, the unsettled nature of the times predisposed many people to listen sympathetically to his message. But the growth of the Nichiren school was far from being the peaceful development that one would naturally associate with a branch of Buddhism. The chaos into which Japan continued to slip for the next three hundred years resulted in the development of an increasingly militant Buddhism, not only in the case of Nichiren's followers, but among other Buddhists as well. Pitched battles were fought between advocates of the different groups. In one such battle in 1536, it is estimated that no less than 58,000 of Nichiren's followers were killed. After this, the influence of Nichiren Buddhism declined in the capital, but it continued to receive a hearing from the simple people of the provinces. Even today, Buddhist groups exist such as Soka Gakkai that look to Nichiren as their spiritual progenitor, and they still have a powerful voice in Japan.

Website References

1. www.jodo.or.jp/jsri/English/Main.html presents the teachings of Jodo Buddhism.

2. Shinran's writings are presented at www.shinranworks.com/

3. Nichiren Buddhism is discussed at www.nst.org/intro_to_ns.html

4. www.ezlink.com/~dozer/fc_sgi/lotus-sutra/lsoutlin.htm gives a translation of the Lotus Sutra.

CHAPTER TWENTY-SEVEN

Zen Buddhism in Japan

The last major Buddhist school to develop in Japan, Zen Buddhism is undoubtedly the one that has been most recognized in the West until recently. But in Japan, Zen is not, and never was, the most popular school of Buddhism. Why, then, did it have such an appeal to Westerners? The answer to this lies partly in the message of Zen itself, and partly in the social and intellectual conditions that prevailed in the West when Zen first made itself felt outside of Japan. Whatever the reason, there is no denying that Zen Buddhism, despite its relatively small number of practitioners, had a major effect not only on the religious life of the Japanese people, but on their intellectual and artistic lives as well.

Eisai and the Founding of the Rinzai School of Zen

Although Zen did not become an important part of Japanese life until the twelfth and thirteenth centuries C.E., it had a venerable history in Japan before that time. The earliest reference to Zen in Japan is associated with the monk Dosho, who came into contact with it during his visit to China in 653. He seems to have studied with Huiman, a disciple of Huike, the second patriarch of the school, and to have come into contact with the fourth patriarch, Daoxin. On returning to Japan, he opened the first Zen meditation hall at Nara. Later, in 737, the Chinese Buddhist teacher Daoxuan (702–760) arrived in Japan and taught Zen along with Vinaya and Kegon doctrines. His student Gyohyo (722–797) taught the meditative techniques to Saicho. In later years, Zen continued to be known in Japan; but it was not until the time of Eisai in the twelfth century that the school became prominent in the country in its own right.

Eisai was born into a family of hereditary Shinto priests in 1141. But instead of being brought up in that tradition, his education was entrusted to a family friend who was in charge of a nearby Buddhist temple. Thus, Eisai was trained in Tendai Buddhism and, in 1155, at the age of fourteen, he entered the Buddhist monastic life at Mount Hiei. A youth of exceptional mental powers, he quickly mastered the complex theories and ritual of the Tendai school. But he became dissatisfied with what he considered to be the empty formalism of Tendai and started to look for teachings that were more immediate in their results. He began to journey around Japan to learn from different teachers. In 1162, he studied with Shuzenbo Kiko, who was deeply versed in the Zen elements of Tendai teaching. But Eisai soon found that if he wanted to pursue such teachings further, he needed to journey beyond the confines of Japan to the Asian mainland.

Consequently, in 1168, Eisai took ship for China. He joined up with another Japanese monk, named Chosen, and together they traveled to Mount Tiantai, then on to Mount Ayuwang. These shrines lay in southern China, previously a stronghold of Tiantai teachings. But now the entire area was dominated by the Chan school of Buddhism. Despite this, Eisai's exposure to this new school was limited. At the insistence of his traveling companion, he returned to Japan after only six months,

Calligraphy, Tenjin Hackuin, Edo period, 18th century. This example of Zen calligraphy encapsulates the spirit of Zen Buddhism popularized by Eisei.

and he did not return to China for more than eighteen years. In 1187, Eisai once again took ship for China, with the intention of going on to India to reverence the relics of the Buddha. But unsettled conditions in Central Asia prevented him from making this journey, and he decided to return to Japan again. But his fate took yet another turn: the ship he was traveling on was blown off course, and he ended up in Wenzhou. Convinced that this was an omen that he should remain in China, Eisai returned to Mount Tiantai and undertook Zen training in the Linji tradition for three years under the meditation master Xuan Huaichang. After that period, he was recognized as being a *dharma* heir of his teacher and was authorized to return to Japan to teach.

Eisai returned home in 1191 and took up residence in the southern island of Kyushu, where he began expounding the doctrine of Zen. Soon he was ordaining monks in the pure Zen lineage. But as was often the case in Japanese history, such efforts to introduce new ideas into the country were met with hostility. A Tendai monk named Roben asked the imperial court to prohibit Eisai's teaching. This may have been a result of Eisai's association with another proponent of Zen, Daiichibo Nonin. Nonin advocated that Zen should be an exclusive practice, an idea that always stirred animosity among the established Buddhist sects. Eisai, now in the imperial capital city of Kyoto, did not hold to this viewpoint. He only wanted to resuscitate the moribund Tendai tradition by infusing it with new meditative techniques from the Huanglung Zen lineage to which he belonged. But once the gauntlet was thrown down, Eisai felt that he had to fight back.

He did so by writing his major work, *Propagation of Zen as a Defense of the Nation*. In this he argued that, since the principal function of the Tendai school was to generate religious merit for the protection of the Japanese homeland, anything that would buttress that function was not only allowable, but necessary for the good of the Japanese people. Zen techniques, he suggested, did just that. They increased the efficacy of the Tendai monks in self-cultivation, which, in turn, resulted in a surge of merit production that would keep the home islands safe from calamities. His arguments fell on fertile ground, and in 1195, he was granted an audience at court—thanks largely to the efforts of Honen's patron Kujo Kanezane.

At this interview, Eisai argued that the doctrine he was teaching was far from being a new innovation and in fact stretched back directly to the Buddha. This had been recognized by Saicho himself, and it was the reason why Zen methods had been appropriated by Tendai Buddhism. Thus, Eisai maintained, the rejection of Zen by Tendai monks was contrary to the intentions of the founder of their school. What Eisai neglected to mention, however, was that the debate between himself and Roben was not about the use of Zen in the Tendai setting, but rather about which Zen lineage to follow. Roben favored the traditional Ox Head lineage, learned by Saicho on Mount Tiantai, while Eisai naturally favored his own Huanglung lineage. It is not surprising that the court, living literally in the shadow of Mount Hiei, felt bound to support the traditional Tendai viewpoint. Eisai saw that his options in Kyoto were limited, so in 1197 he set out for Kamakura, the capital of the shogunate, near present-day Tokyo.

At Kamakura, Eisai found more scope for his teachings. In fact, he was soon a principal religious functionary for the ruling Minamoto family. One of his later works, *Drink Tea and Prolong Life*, was written specifically for the third shogun, Sanetomo. It is interesting to note that, unlike the period's other major proponent of Zen, Daiichibo Nonin, Eisai did not advocate the exclusive practice of Zen. During his time in Kamakura, he seems to have practiced an eclectic Buddhism very similar in nature to that of the Tendai school in which he had been trained. As was the case with all Japanese ruling elites, the shogunate was primarily interested in Buddhism as a form of supernatural protection rather than as a vehicle of personal growth. Consequently, Eisai seems to have spent much of his time conducting rituals aimed at protecting Japan in general, and the shogunate in particular.

This is, of course, entirely consistent with Eisai's vision of himself as a reformer, not an innovator. In 1202, he returned to the capital of Kyoto as chief monk in the newly established Kennin-ji Temple. But his luck in the capital was as bad as usual. In 1205, the population was clamoring for his expulsion on the grounds that a strong wind that had damaged the capital was the result of Eisai's introducing a new religion into Japan. Yet again the court was inclined to agree to his being expelled, but this time Eisai had the backing of the true ruler of Japan, the shogun. Indeed, instead of being shunned, Eisai now started to be courted by the imperial retinue. In 1206, he was appointed to supervise the reconstruction of the Todaiji and Hossho-ji temples. By 1213, Eisai was granted the title of provisional high priest, virtually the highest honor possible under the imperial system. Two years later he died in Kyoto.

Rinzai Zen

What was the nature of this new form of Buddhism that Eisai brought back from China? Some people said that it was not Buddhism at all. Others thought that it was Buddhism, but of a form so radically different from other branches of the religion that it should be classed as a separate division of it, in the same way that Theravada, Mahayana, and Vajrayana were. Was there any truth to these claims, or was Zen merely the logical conclusion of a process of development that stretched back to the Buddha himself, as its practitioners claimed? As we have seen, Zen developed in China in about the middle of the sixth century C.E. The Zen that was taught and practiced in China and Japan was in some senses an attempt to return to the primitive Buddhist ideal of personal religious development that undergirded the Buddha's original message. This, Zen practitioners felt, had been clouded by an overemphasis on institutions and scholarship. Buddhism, they argued, was not a matter of belief, but rather one of practice. Knowledge was not to be totally abandoned, particularly at the beginning of an individual's quest for enlightenment; but its uses were limited and provisional. It was through action and personal experience that enlightenment was won. If it could be gained through book learning, they suggested, then there would be far more enlightened people than there actually were in reality. As the great Soto Zen master Dogen observed, "as long as we only think about the Buddha-dharma with our minds, the Way will never be grasped, even in a thousand lifetimes."

Part of the problem inherent in the intellectual apprehension of Buddhism is inherent in other religions as well, namely the indescribability of their primary goal. All descriptions of the ideal afterlife are metaphorical. No Christian of mature faith believes that Heaven is populated by harp-strumming people floating around on wings with halos over their heads, nor do Muslims necessarily believe that Heaven is a giant garden replete with dancing girls and servants. Rather, they recognize in such descriptions a way of communicating, however imperfectly, the supreme joy and fulfillment of being in God's presence. Buddhists have always had a similar problem with describing Nirvana and the meditative states that lead up to it. Zen's answer to this difficulty was to not even try. Since all descriptions and speculations about enlightenment and the way thither were by definition imprecise and provisional, Zen thinkers thought it much better simply to eliminate speculation on the subject and strive for the practical experience of these ineffable states.

When this attitude was combined with the theoretical stance, developed in East Asia, that enlightenment and Nirvana were implicit in the everyday world, the distinctive synthesis of ideas and attitudes that define Zen emerged: a complete reliance on self-effort that discounted theory and emphasized practice and hard work. The Zen monks were not to sequester themselves in a monastery except for periods of intensive meditation practice and training, but were to go out and earn their living just as every one else did. This, of course, endeared the Zen monks to the peasantry, who resented having to support a Buddhist institutional establishment that brought them little or nothing in return.

But how, in practical terms, should Zen meditation be practiced? Over time, two principal methods emerged. In the first, the mediator allowed enlightenment to seep slowly into his or her consciousness. This was the method of the Soto Zen school taught by the great Japanese teacher Dogen that emphasized sitting meditation, **zazen**. The second major school of thought in Zen circles—that embraced by Eisai and his disciples—held that the mind had to be jolted out of its habitual patterns of thought. The device that this Rinzai school of Zen used to accomplish this end was the **koan**. The term *koan*, the Japanization of the Chinese term *gungan*, means literally a "public case" that sets a precedent. Originally a legal term, it came to mean in Zen parlance a phrase from the sutras, a teaching on Zen doctrine, an episode in the life of a Zen master, or a Zen *mondo* (story) that pointed to ultimate reality. At the heart of each of these types of teaching tools lay a paradox that transcended mundane logic, and so could not be solved through reason and the intellect. It would be mistaken, therefore, to see the *koan* as a riddle in the European sense of the word. The *koan* was meant not to exercise the mind, but to propel it out of its everyday habits of thought and force it to leap to the next higher level of comprehension.

Koans were often very simple and examples include the famous "What is the sound of one hand clapping?" and "Does a dog possess Buddha nature?" The "correct answer" or *wato* to this latter *koan* is *"mu"*—"NO!"—but the answer is not that simple. Is it, "No, the dog doesn't have Buddha nature"? This cannot be right, since Zen Buddhists argue that all creatures possess Buddha nature. Is it that the question itself is wrong? The real answer can only be experienced by someone who has wrestled with it existentially, not by one who has merely thought about it. Since the *koan* did not depend on logical reasoning, it naturally followed that its solution was not bound to a verbal answer. After all, words could only convey so much information, and the Zen master had to be certain that his disciple had indeed made the leap from one state of understanding to the next. Thus we often read in Zen literature about unconventional *dokusans*, meetings between Zen masters and their students in which the latter try to convey, by whatever means are appropriate at the time, proof of existential mastery of the problem exemplified in their *koans*. The use of the *koan* is actually a fairly late development in Buddhist pedagogic techniques. They start to be used in a methodical way in about the 950s in China. As the teaching method evolved, so too did the number of *koans*, until there were 1,700 of them. In the present day, however, only some five or six hundred are in actual use within the Japanese Zen schools. These have been compiled in numerous collections, of which the *Mumonkan* and the *Rinzai-roku* are the most famous. Of course, human nature being what it is, the "correct answers" to these *koans* have also been collected, and sometimes circulate covertly among Zen students. But a true Zen master has no trouble gauging whether or not the students have truly mastered their *koans* when they present themselves for *dokusan*.

One might wonder why there are so many *koans*. After all, would not solving one *koan* cause the student's consciousness to transcend the mundane and achieve *satori* or enlightenment? The Rinzai answer to this question is that enlightenment is a state that can be lost as well as achieved. Each small enlightenment, each *kensho*, is unique in itself, but not necessarily permanent or complete. One of the functions of the *koan* is to prevent a relapse to *bonpu-no-joshiki*, "everyman's consciousness," the state of awareness (or lack of it) that characterizes the average person. Consequently, an elaborate system of *koans* has evolved in the Rinzai school of Zen. For convenience, they are divided into five principal categories. The first of these are *Hosshinkoan*. These are what one might term "elementary *koans*," designed to lead the student to the fundamental realization of the nonduality of existence. This basic perception is reenforced by the second series of *koans*, the *kikan* or "support" *koans*, which are aimed at allowing the student to make distinctions within the present milieu of nonduality. The *gonsen-koans* link the student with his or her tradition's past and are a consideration of the sayings and teachings of the school's great past masters. At this point, the student is ready for stronger stuff. He or she is now set the *nanto-koans*, literally the "hard to solve *koans*." Finally, the student must solve the last of the five sets of *koans*, the *go-i koans* of Dungshan Liangjie (807–869), the great Tang organizer of Rinzai Zen. After *koan* work is completed, and the student's achievement assessed, he or she can receive *inka-shomei*, the seal of transmission of their lineage, and instruct students of their own.[1]

Dogen and the Establishment of the Soto School of Zen

Damma, Tenjin Hackuin, Edo period, 18th century. Dogen emphasized the practice of "just sitting" that characterizes Zen Buddhism in many people's minds.

Of all of the Zen masters of Japan, it is arguable that the most influential was Dogen. Born in 1200 in Kyoto into one of the most important aristocratic families at court, Dogen was an infant prodigy. By the age of four he could read Chinese, and only a few years later he was digesting both Chinese classics and difficult works of Buddhist philosophy. But his life took a decisive turn when his parents died while he was still very young. He went to live with an uncle, who wanted him to pursue a career in government service. Dogen, however, had other ideas. At the age of twelve, he left home secretly and went to Mount Hiei, where he began training under the auspices of Ryoken, another uncle. Ryoken tried to persuade the young boy to return to his secular life, but when this failed, he helped Dogen to begin training as a Tendai monk. However, Dogen was not satisfied with the teachings that he received on Mount Hiei, and soon began to travel about in search of the answers to his questions. Eventually, in 1217, he went to Kennin-ji Temple, where he began to train in the Rinzai Zen style established by Eisai. But he was still not satisfied. Finally, in 1223, he sailed for China, determined to find the answer to the doubts and questions that assailed his mind. There he had one of the defining encounters of his life—with a cook.

Soon after Dogen's ship arrived in China from Japan, the chief cook of the Zen temple on Mount Ayuwang came to the port hoping to buy Japanese mushrooms. He and Dogen began talking, and the young monk soon realized that he was in the presence of a deeply accomplished religious master. After talking long into the night,

Dogen invited him to remain with him overnight, but the old priest declined, saying that if he did not return to his temple, the next day's meals would not be prepared. Dogen then asked why the cook did not simply delegate the food preparation to someone else and devote all his time to meditation. The cook simply observed that Dogen did not really understand the practice of Zen and suggested that he should come to Mount Ayuwang for training. In later years, Dogen would observe to his students that although he did not realize it at the time, his encounter with the cook of Mount Ayuwang was his first meeting with a truly enlightened person, and that it had set him on the path of truly understanding Zen.

Dogen began to travel to the great centers of Rinzai Zen in China, but what he found there discouraged him. No longer was Chinese Zen interested simply in enlightenment. It had begun to be corrupted by its deepening ties with the Chinese upper classes. But fortune smiled on the earnest young monk when he encountered Rujing, the head of the Tiantung Temple and practitioner of Caodung (in Japanese Soto) Zen. This was the school of "just sitting" in *zazen*—without the *koan* study that the Rinzai school practiced. For the next three years, Dogen trained under the harsh regime of Rujing, who was an exacting master. In 1227, he received permission to return home and teach. At Kennin-ji Temple, believing that Soto practice was the only true Buddhist path, Dogen set out his thinking in his *General Advice on the Principles of Zazen* and in a series of lectures that were later collected and published under the title *Shobogenzo Zuimonki* or *Eye Treasury of the Right Dharma*. In these lectures, Dogen presented his interpretation of Zen and its practice. He totally rejected the belief, still implicit in much of Japanese Buddhism, that there was any "magical" value inherent in religious ceremonies, such as offering incense to the Buddha, chanting sacred texts, or bowing before Buddhist images. Only the practice of *zazen* led to enlightenment, nothing more and nothing less. But it would be wrong to assume that Dogen completely rejected the *koan* studies of his youth. He continued to use *koans* in his teaching, but where he differed from his contemporaries was that he rejected the formalized system of *koan* training that had evolved over time. Building on this viewpoint, Dogen now began to write manuals of Zen training advocating this new style of training.

Dogen was a vocal opponent of any division of Zen into schools. He believed that there was only one Zen and that any attempt to differentiate the *dharma* was wrong. Likewise, he was bitterly opposed to diluting Buddhism with other thought systems. He particularly opposed the idea, common for many centuries in China, Korea, and Japan, of the "unity of the three religions," in which Confucianism, Daoism, and Buddhism were seen as being complementary aspects of a single overarching truth. As for the intermixing of different schools of Buddhism, in the way that Eisai had allowed in his Zen temples, Dogen categorically rejected any other form of Buddhism within the walls of his monasteries. But he did not reject all aspects of the other Buddhist schools; nor did he have the "contempt" for the scriptures that is often ascribed to Zen Buddhism. He greatly valued the Lotus Sutra, and saw other texts as being useful to the degree that they advanced the student toward a true understanding of the nature of the universe. But of course such an understanding must come primarily from experience gained in *zazen*.[2]

Inevitably, Dogen's uncompromising stance led to trouble. As usual, this came from the Tendai Buddhist establishment on Mount Hiei. To avoid conflict, Dogen moved to an abandoned temple on the outskirts of Kyoto. Here the disciples of the Zen teacher Daiichibo Nonin, the opponent of Eisai who had advocated the practice of Zen to the exclusion of other forms of Buddhism, joined him on their master's death. But this increased popularity did not mitigate the Tendai opposition to

Dogen's teachings—quite the opposite in fact. Finally, in 1243, Dogen resolved to abandon the capital and to establish a training monastery, Eihei-ji, deep in the wilds of Echizen province. Why he decided to go to this particularly desolate location has been a question that scholars have long debated, most particularly in light of Dogen's own words. In his masterpiece, the *Shobogenzo Zuimonki*, Dogen presented the opinion that:

> Some say that the propagation of Buddhism in these latter degenerate days, on this remote island, would be facilitated if a secure and peaceful abode were prepared where monks could practice the teachings of Buddha without any worries over food, clothing, and the like. To me this seems wrong. Such a place would only attract men who are selfish and worldly, and among them could be found no one at all with a sincere religious intention. If we give ourselves over to the comforts of life and the enjoyment of material pleasures, then even though hundreds of thousands were induced to come here, it would be worse than having no one here at all. We would acquire only a propensity for evil, not a disposition for the practice of Buddha's Law.
>
> If on the contrary you live in spotless poverty and destitution, or go begging for your food, or live on the fruits of the field, pursuing your study of the Truth while suffering real deprivation, then if even one man hears of your example and comes to study with you out of genuine devotion to the Truth, it will be a real gain for Buddhism.

SOURCE: Tsunoda *et al.*, *Sources of Japanese Tradition*, p. 241

With the establishment of this new monastery, Dogen could begin training monks in earnest, using the strict, sometimes even harsh, discipline that he himself had trained under in China. He also implemented the ideals of the Zen cook whom he had encountered when he first stepped ashore in China. All the monk's activities were to lead to enlightenment—not just *zazen*. But at this point, his thinking on another subject suddenly changed. Previously, Dogen had believed that all beings, in whatever state of life they were living, be it lay or clerical, could achieve enlightenment. But in his later years at Eihei-ji he adopted the view that only monks could achieve enlightenment. Why he changed his mind is not clear, but it probably had to do with disputes between the followers of Rinzai and himself. Whatever the case, Dogen continued to practice an uncompromising Zen at Eihei-ji until his death in 1253.[3]

Dogen's Soto style of Zen can best be summed up in his own words:

> In the pursuit of the Way [Buddhism] the prime essential is sitting (*zazen*) . . . By reflecting upon various "public-cases" (*koan*) and dialogues of the patriarchs, one may perhaps get the sense of them but it will only result in one's being led astray from the way of the Buddha, our founder. Just to pass the time in sitting straight, without any thought of acquisition, without any sense of achieving enlightenment— this is the way of the Founder. It is true that our predecessors recommended both the *koan* and sitting, but it was the sitting that they particularly insisted upon. There have been some who attained enlightenment through the test of the *koan*, but the true cause of their enlightenment was the merit and effectiveness of sitting. Truly the merit lies in the sitting.

SOURCE: Tsunoda *et al.*, *Sources of Japanese Tradition*, p. 247

With Dogen's death, the Soto school continued to make gains, but the real creative impetus in Japanese Zen shifted back to the Rinzai school. This was the result of the influence of two great teachers, Takuin (1573–1645) and Hakuin (1689–1769), who was especially influential in that he melded *koan* training with *zazen*.

As time went on, Japanese religion continued to evolve. With the coming of the Europeans to Japan, Christianity entered the country and was for a time a significant force until the savage persecutions of the Tokugawa shoguns drove it underground. Buddhism continued to flourish, with the Tokugawas requiring all their subjects to belong—at least for administrative purposes—to one of the 469,934 Buddhist temples that had sprung up all over Japan.[4] Meanwhile, Neo-Confucian scholars such as Fujiwara Seika, Hayashi Razan, and Yamaga Soko pressed successfully for the adoption of Neo-Confucianism as the official governmental philosophy of the shogunate. Finally, in the eighteenth century, Kamo Mabuchi and Motoori Norinaga strove to renovate the Shinto tradition and return it to the prominence that it had enjoyed in earlier days. As Japan became more and more a part of the greater world of the nineteenth and twentieth centuries, all these currents of religious thought would play a role in its development.

Website References

1. www.easternreligions.com/text/zkoan-t.html gives several examples of Zen *koans*.

2. A selection of Dogen's writings can be found at hjem.get2net.dk/civet-cat/zen-writings/dogen-guidelines.htm

3. www.zendo.com/eiheiji.html provides a virtual tour of Eihei-ji.

4. photojapan.com/index.htm/temples.html gives examples of many Japanese temples.

CHAPTER TWENTY-EIGHT

East Asian Religions and the Challenge of the Modern World

With the coming of the Europeans to Asia in the mid-sixteenth century, the people of East Asia were presented with new worldviews that challenged their accepted conceptions of the nature of Reality and people's place within it. These intellectual challenges were exacerbated by the social and political challenges that European and American colonialism presented these ancient cultures. A detailed examination of how the various countries of the region dealt with these new challenges would require far more space than is available in the present work. However, it is possible to look at a few of the strategies used by East Asian religions to come to grips with the new ideas pressing in on them from outside the region. As we shall see, they did so by retaining many of the indigenous features of their religious traditions, but recasting them in new forms appropriate to the times. This allowed them to continue to address central concerns that had shaped their traditions from their beginnings in new and innovative ways.

Maoism

In China, the primary question that engaged intellectuals was, as always, the quest for political order and stability. In the nineteenth and twentieth centuries, the Chinese Empire had decayed and fallen apart. The Qing dynasty had been able to maintain the traditional sociopolitical system of imperial rule from the center for some two hundred years and had produced a number of highly competent and skilled rulers. However, internal dynastic quarrels and the continued encroachment of the European powers on Chinese sovereignty had brought about the effective collapse of the imperial system in the middle of the nineteenth century, and China was now largely a legal fiction propped up by the European powers for their own ends. Chinese intellectuals reluctantly came to the conclusion that Confucianism was no longer serving its primary function as an official ideology capable of knitting together the disparate regions of China. Indeed, Confucianism had never particularly appealed to the peasantry, who preferred to venerate the local deities of Daoist religion or follow the path of Pure Land Buddhism. Clearly, some new basis for Chinese unity needed to be found if the primary goal of Chinese civilization, cultural and political cohesion, was to be regained.

A number of different solutions were offered. The great statesman Kang Yuwei (K'ang Yu-wei, 1858–1927) advocated a return to traditional Confucianism, albeit in a more dynamic form. Zhang Dongsun (Chang Tung-sun, 1886–1962) believed that the answer to Chinese woes lay in adopting the philosophical assumptions of the West. Xiong Shili (Hsiung Shih-li, 1885–1968) believed that a renewed Neo-Confucianism would regenerate Chinese society through its moral influence. Fung Yu-lan (1890–1990), perhaps the most famous of the modern Chinese philosophers as the result of his classic study *The History of Chinese Philosophy*, experimented with a number of different approaches, eventually espousing a radical Maoist form of Marxism. However, none of these philosophies was able to mobilize public sentiment to the degree necessary to accomplish their goal. That achievement belonged to the thought of the most influential Chinese thinker of the twentieth century—Mao Zedong (Mao Tse-tung, 1894–1976).

Mao was the product of the intensely troubled times that engulfed China in the 1920s, 1930s, and 1940s. Superficially educated in traditional Chinese thought, Mao's concerns and thinking were primarily shaped by pragmatic considerations arising from his leading role in the revolutionary movements that were sweeping China at this time. In many ways, Mao's thinking represents a return of the indigenous philosophies of Mohism and Legalism, but cloaked in a new language borrowed from Euro-American Marxism. However, his synthesis of ideas from both Eastern and Euro-American sources produced a distinctly Chinese system of thought that resonated deeply with the average Chinese person. It was this resonance that gave Maoism its strength and allowed it to succeed in uniting China where other ideologies had failed, at least for a while.

Mao's philosophy is best epitomized by his 1937 work, *On Practice*. In this he laid out his basic assumption that all philosophy must, ultimately, be based on practical concerns and pragmatic goals. At one stroke, then, Mao dismissed the metaphysical speculations of the Neo-Confucians and the Buddhists. Metaphysical advancement, Mao reasoned, would be a natural outgrowth of social reintegration and material advancement. As he later said, the role of the Communist Party in China was "working hard to create the conditions in which classes, state power, and political parties will die out very naturally and mankind will enter the realm of the Great Harmony" (in Ann Freemantle, ed., *Mao Tse-tung: An Anthology of His Writings*, New York: New American Library, 1962; p. 185). Certainly this was a goal that would seem completely appropriate and acceptable to any Daoist, Confucian, Mohist, or Legalist thinker.

But how was this lofty state of affairs to be accomplished? Clearly it was the end goal of a long period of development. First of all, said Mao (paraphrasing the thought of the Neo-Confucian Zhou Dunyi), an investigation must be made of first principles, since all processes have a beginning and an end, and that end is understood and anticipated by the principles that govern their beginning. Moreover, borrowing from Daoist thought, he reasoned that all processes eventually transform themselves into their opposite. While Mao cloaked his analysis in Marxist terminology—partially out of conviction and partially to secure the continued material assistance that the Chinese Communist Party was receiving from the Soviet Union—the foundations of his analysis are profoundly Chinese. Since, for Mao, thinking and doing form an inseparable unity, a correct understanding and application of principle was essential. Thus, Mao held that "if man wants to achieve success in his work, that is, to achieve the anticipated results, he must make his thoughts correspond to the laws of the objective world surrounding him: if they do not correspond, he will fail in practice" (*Mao Tse-tung: An Anthology of His Writings*, pp. 201–202). Ideology was not just an intellectual exercise, it was an indispensable motivating force in social transformation. But this understanding of principle is ineffective if not embodied in action. Mao agreed completely with the Marxist belief in the centrality of matter and materiality as the true, fundamental, and complete explanation of the nature of ultimate reality. There was no supernatural world, no spiritual realm, and no divine beings poised to intercede for humanity. What one saw was what existed. Indeed, it was all that existed. Consequently, ideas that were not made flesh through action had no true reality, in the ultimate sense.

All this theory was geared to produce very specific practical social changes. Like the Mohists, Maoism saw the ultimate good to be material prosperity and the security of the state. As with the Mohists, this was to be achieved by stripping society of all extraneous frivolities and extravagances. Art and music, where they existed, were to serve the needs of the state or be eliminated. Like the Legalists, Mao believed that human beings, at least at the present moment, needed to be controlled by the two levers of punishment and reward, and so punishments became very public affairs, as they still are in Communist China. Again, like the Legalists, Mao established a government of ministers presided over by a shadowy supreme authority who only emerged into the light occasionally to correct the excesses of his subordinates and so protect the people. But like the Confucians, whom he publicly disparaged, Mao believed that in time education would reform the masses and that the rule of the state would cease to be only an external imposition and become internal reality for the people.[1]

These then were the foundations of Mao's philosophy, and they were very traditional Chinese foundations, both in their goals and their analysis of the principles that undergirded the process of achieving those goals. We can, therefore, see Mao's thought as an indigenous philosophy with foreign elements, rather than as an attempt to impose an alien philosophical system on the Chinese mind. The first goal was successful, at least in the short run. The second would likely have proved impossible in the Chinese context of the time, as the difficulty in developing democratic institutions along Euro-American lines in China clearly demonstrates. Despite its initial successes, Maoism was no more capable of remaining the primary ideological foundation of Chinese culture than the Legalism and Mohism from which it sprang. As time went on and the original true believers in Mao's thought died out, Maoism became viewed by the young people of China as outmoded. When Maoism lost its grip on the popular mind, old spiritual allegiances began to assert themselves. Sometimes these allegiances took the shape of a return to the old traditions of Daoism and Buddhism. But just as "new religions" that combined ancient traditions into new forms of spiritual expression grew up in Japan when state control on religion was relaxed, so too did such religions spring up in China.

One of the most influential of these is Falun Gong. An amalgam of Daoist and Buddhist ideas adapted to modern times, Falun Gong rapidly gained many followers in China and abroad. But the old Communist system of state control of religious organizations is not yet dead in China, and a concerted effort was made by the government to repress Falun Gong. It seems unlikely, however, that this campaign will ultimately be any more successful in controlling the religious sentiments of the Chinese people than similar attempts in the past.[2]

Cao Dai

In modern Vietnam, we see a good example of the syncretic process in religion that marks many areas of Asia and is particularly strong in Southeast Asia. There have been a number of movements exemplifying this tendency in Vietnam, but the most successful of these has been Cao Dai. The founder of Cao Dai, Ngo Van Chieu, was born in 1878 near Saigon. He was a brilliant youth, who rose through the French colonial civil service until he reached the high rank of administrative delegate for the island of Phu Quoc in the Gulf of Thailand. A man of pronounced religious tendencies, he studied all the world's religions and attended the spiritualist seances that were in vogue all over the world in the early twentieth century. In 1921, he was contacted at one of these events by the spirit "High Palace" or, in Vietnamese, Cao Dai. Ngo now started to receive messages from this spirit, who ordered him to found a new religion that would bring together all the world's warring faiths under the all-seeing eye of God. The symbol of the all-seeing eye became a distinctive mark of Cao Dai iconography.

Ngo continued to receive messages from the spirit, and on Christmas Eve of 1925 he instituted the new religion. Its adherents were mostly civil servants like himself. The centerpiece of the religion continued to be spiritualist seances, and in the course of one of these a new spirit, "A-A-A," revealed himself. This spirit, which the Cao Daists believed was the Holy Trinity of Christianity, commanded them to use a divination instrument called the "Crow's Beak," a small bag with a projection at one end, which was held by the chief medium of the seance and moved by the spirit to spell out its wishes. One of the first of these communications ordered the participants in the seance to go to Ngo Van Chieu for instructions on how to proceed accordingly.

The new religion was organized much along the administrative lines of the Roman Catholic Church, and its first "pope"(*Giao Tong*) was not Ngo Van Chieu, who declined the honor, but Le Van Trung, one of his first disciples. The new religion began to grow, primarily in the southern part of Vietnam, but eventually spreading to the north and to Cambodia as well. In the first two months of its official existence, the religion grew to some twenty thousand members and today numbers about two million adherents. In 1927, a "holy see" was established at Long Thanh in Tay Ninh province, some ninety miles northwest of Saigon. There, a magnificent temple was erected to serve as the religion's administrative and spiritual center.

The creed of the new religion was essentially monotheistic, with belief in a single all-powerful and all-knowing God. Just as God was one, so, it was thought, should all religions be one, and Cao Dai's primary mission was to reunite the disparate faiths of humanity. When this was accomplished, the divisions that plagued humanity would disappear by themselves, and a new world order of peace and justice would emerge. The unification of religions was to be accomplished by gathering the best features of each of the world's faiths and melding them into a harmonious whole. Consequently, the adherents of Cao Dai began to consciously appropriate ideas from other religions: from Daoism came the virtue of detachment from the material world; from Buddhism came compassion and tolerance; from Christianity came love and charity; from Confucianism came love of the good and of justice; and from the cult of the ancestors came respect for family and communion between the living and the dead.

Metaphysically, Cao Dai holds very closely to Buddhist ideas such as karma and *samsara*. In addition to God, Cao Dai followers venerate Quan Am (Guanyin), who they believed interceded with God on their behalf. Their moral code is also Buddhist in nature and resembles the classical Buddhist Five Precepts, since one needs to maintain a pure physical body to be worthy of receiving the gifts of God. But from those to whom much is given, much will be required, and Cao Dai followers hold that one needs to show fellowship and compassion not only to one's fellow human beings, but to all beings. Because all animal life needs to be respected, Cao Dai advocates vegetarianism and particular respect for trees.

Despite this pronounced inclination toward traditional East Asian expressions of faith, and despite the brutal rule of the French colonialists in Vietnam, Cao Dai also maintained a healthy respect for Christianity and European culture. Among the spiritual entities they channeled in their services were a number of figures from this tradition, including the French writer Victor Hugo. Also, they saw themselves as "the bridge thrown across the chasm that separates Christ from the Buddha who was his precursor." Nor did they abandon the traditional beliefs of the Vietnamese people. They stressed mediumistic communication with the spirits—a key component of indigenous religious ceremonies—and this emphasis continues. The followers of Cao Dai also forcefully advocate the practice of the cult of the ancestors and respect for the family, and especially the sanctity of the marriage bond.

As it grew, Cao Dai began to evolve a complicated ritual and administrative structure. Three categories of believers evolved: the Religious, the Mediums, and the Faithful. The Religious are priests and observe vows of chastity, obedience, and frugality, and abstain from sex, nonvegetarian foods, and alcohol. They are assisted in the rituals by the Mediums, who are the conduits by which messages are conveyed from the spirits. Unlike the Religious, these Mediums are laypeople who exercise a special gift. Finally there are the Faithful, the laypeople, who defer to the Religious and live lives based on the tenets of Cao Dai encapsulated in the *Phap Chanh Truyen*, or Religious Code, that has been revealed by the spirits. This code calls for a three-fold division of the Religious into three groups: the Executive Body, the Legislative Body, and the Administrative Body. The Executive Body, which is divided into a hierarchy of nine grades, handles the day-to-day administration of the institution. The Legislative Body pronounces on matters of faith and dogma, while the Administrative Body oversees the religion's many charitable activities.

On the day-to-day level, Cao Dai is particularly concerned with both public and private ritual. Believers are enjoined to pray four times a day between five and seven in the morning, eleven and one in the afternoon, five and seven in the evening, and eleven and one at night. This is done in front of a simple altar that every Cao Dai believer maintains in his or her home and on which are placed statues of the Buddha, Confucius, Jesus, Laozi, and various Cao Dai saints and spirits. There is also a perpetually burning lamp. Offerings are made to the divine, but unlike the meat, glutinous rice, and votive paper objects offered in traditional Vietnamese religious ceremonies, Cao Dai offerings consist of flowers, fruits, tea, water, and incense. Despite the relative simplicity of Cao Dai ritual at home, the rituals practiced at Cao Dai temples are both sumptuous and complex.[3]

Christianity in Korea

Christianity has a long and venerable history in Asia. The earliest Christians, who lived in what is now South India, probably reached that region within a hundred years of the death of Christ. Over the centuries, the Nestorian branch of the faith traversed all of Asia and made significant gains as far away as China. But with the advent of the Mongols and various other disruptions, Christianity had all but died out in East Asia by the beginning of the fifteenth century. The religion revived, however, under the patronage of the European traders and conquistadors who flocked to Asia in the wake of the Portuguese explorer Vasco da Gama. This revived missionary effort met with mixed success. In the places that the Europeans controlled directly, such as the Indian state of Goa and the Philippine islands, Christianity could be preached more forcefully than in those areas still independent of European rule. In these occupied territories, the new converts generally belonged to the Roman Catholic faith of the early Portuguese and Spanish colonialists; and it is no surprise that Christianity, imposed as it often was by force, soon became the dominant religion of the indigenous peoples, at least outwardly. Later European powers, the products of different conditions from those that had motivated their predecessors, were considerably less interested in proselytizing. They tended to officially ignore religious questions unless, as was the case with the French in Vietnam, they could be made to serve the greater imperial purpose of the state. Of course, that did not mean that Christian missionary work was totally ignored. Indeed, there were always men and women prepared to suffer and die to promulgate their faith in foreign lands.

Christianity in East Asia had an uneven reception. In seventeenth-century China, the Jesuits were welcomed with open arms by the imperial house. But this was not because of their religious beliefs. Rather, what the Chinese upper classes sought was access to the superior technological knowledge of the West, and this the Jesuits were able to give them. Such priests as Matteo Ricci (1552–1610) were highly respected and honored at court, and were often awarded official positions in the Chinese civil service. Nor were they completely unsuccessful in their primary goal of winning souls. Some very high-ranking Chinese officials, notably the minister of state, Xu Guangqi (Hsü Kuang-ch'i, 1562–1634), converted to Christianity and attempted to further its progress not only in China but elsewhere in East Asia.

But any chance that the Roman Catholic Church had to become a major religious force in China, or indeed elsewhere in East Asia, was dashed when the pope decreed that Asian Christians could no longer participate in the rituals of veneration for their ancestors. The so-called "Rites Controversy" eroded Jesuit influence at court and with the aristocracy. Without this official sanction, the church faded to a mere ghostly presence. It did not regain this lost ground until the coming of the European powers to China in force after 1840. At that point, the fortune of all the Christian churches revived under the aegis of the European powers, only to fade again under Communist rule, although in the areas of the Chinese diaspora not controlled by the Communists, there are still significant Chinese Christian communities.

In Japan, the situation was both similar and different. Early Portuguese and Spanish missionaries made notable gains among the aristocracy, with a number of powerful noblemen converting to Christianity along with most of their subjects. Christianity was so successful, in fact, that the military rulers of Japan became uneasy over its possible influence. After the first Tokugawa shogun took power in 1600, he closed Japan to outside trade—with the small exception of that with the Dutch—and moved to suppress Christianity. Many Japanese Christians preferred to die rather than renounce their faith, and the church in Japan went underground. It is a remarkable testimony to the faith of these underground Japanese Christians that when Japan was reopened to trade in the 1850s, Christian missionaries found them still practicing their faith—despite the terrible penalties that would befall them if they were discovered. While Christianity never became a major religious force in Japanese society, there is still a small but devout Christian presence in Japan.

But the difficulties that the missionaries faced in other parts of East Asia paled in comparison to those they faced in Korea. Despite their considerable efforts, Roman Catholic missionaries from China, Japan, and the Philippines could not gain a foothold in Korea, a land that they nicknamed "the Hermit Kingdom." This is not surprising in light of the Yi dynasty's determination to establish their state on Confucian principles. They could hardly be expected to welcome a rival religion such as Christianity at a time when they were moving to suppress even indigenous religions, such as Buddhism. But despite this, Roman Catholicism found its way into Korea, and the manner in which this took place set the pattern for the entire development of Christianity on the peninsula.

By the late eighteenth century, Roman Catholicism began to penetrate the Korean religious consciousness, not through the medium of missionary activity, but through the curiosity of certain Korean intellectuals. These young men, who tended to be disciples of the Confucian scholar Yi Ik (1681–1763), gathered together to examine and debate the doctrines put forth in a variety of Jesuit pamphlets on the Christian faith published in Chinese. But it was not until 1784 that the first Korean—a certain Yi Pyök (1754–1786)—went to Beijing to receive baptism from the Catholic priest resident there. He now began to evangelize their friends and neighbors. Soon Catholic Christianity began to spread.

The government, however, did not sit idly by. In 1785, it issued a decree banning the new faith and launched a series of persecutions aimed at repressing it. Completely cut off from outside assistance or information, the nascent Korean Catholic Church attempted to reproduce the church structures that it remembered from China, and in 1787 it elected a bishop and priests to lead it. It was about this time as well that the first Korean Christian martyrs were created. Eventually, in 1795, an officially ordained priest from China named Father Zhou Wenmu was dispatched to attend to the spiritual needs of the newly established Korean church. But the latter then suffered a series of vicious persecutions from 1801 to 1871. During the course of these, thousands of Korean converts were martyred, and a number of foreign missionary priests died as well.

Despite this, the church in Korea maintained itself. But since it drew its converts primarily from the lower classes, it was not looked on as a positive force in Korean society. In addition, missionary efforts were hampered by the fact that there was no complete translation of the Bible into Korean. Converts had to nourish their faith on those parts of the Bible that had been translated into Korean for use in the Mass, as well as on some devotional classics, such as *The Imitation of Christ* by Thomas à Kempis, that were ill-suited to the needs of their Korean readers. Despite all this, Catholicism maintained a foothold on the peninsula, albeit a precarious one. But by the last quarter of the nineteenth century a new spiritual force had come to Korea—Protestant Christianity.

Initially, Protestantism had as hard a time as Catholicism establishing itself in the "Hermit Kingdom." But as a result of the efforts of such dedicated servants of the Gospel as the missionary John Ross (1842–1915), the Bible was translated into Korean in its entirety, and copies were distributed throughout the peninsula, thus providing a focal point for the indigenous development of the religion. Many of the features of Ross's first translation are still authoritative to this day, such as his use of the Korean word *Hananim* to translate "God." Although European missionaries were still barred from Korean soil, indigenous Christian converts to Ross's Presbyterian faith and other forms of Protestantism began to propagate the religion by themselves. Thus from the very first, Korean Christianity was a homegrown faith that depended little on foreign support.

This pattern was reenforced when foreigners were finally allowed into Korea. The first missionaries to Korea came not to spread religious doctrine so much as to do charitable works. They established schools and hospitals, thereby gaining the respect of the common people and a hearing for their religious views. This bypassed the government's strict policy of not allowing the teaching of any religious faith that would conflict with the approved creed of Confucianism. But more and more foreigners entered Korea, ostensibly for humanitarian reasons. By 1908, the peninsula had been divided into missionary "spheres of influence," with the Presbyterians and Methodists being particularly well represented. Many young intellectuals flocked to the new faith, seeing it as an antidote to the conservatism and reactionary policies of the ruling regime. For them, Korea's future lay in adopting Euro-American ideology, and they saw Christianity as part and parcel of the Euro-American mindset.

Despite setbacks during the period of Japanese occupation and the Second World War and the Korean War, Christianity, particularly Protestantism, flourished and indeed grew rapidly after 1953. At present, Christians form some 20 percent of the population of Korea; Christianity has developed in ways that are uniquely Korean. A good example of this is the authority and prestige allotted to the presiding minister of a congregation—which far exceeds that of a clergyman in a similar setting elsewhere. Another feature of particular interest are the Korean concepts of *kibok* and the *kido-wön*. *Kibok* means a wish for blessings in this life. While Christianity often displays a "next worldly" orientation that emphasizes the rewards to be gained by its followers in the afterlife for their moral life style, Korean Christianity is strongly oriented toward the rewards in this life that its followers believe are the inevitable results of living a moral Christian life style. Attendance at church and a fervent prayer life are viewed as avenues to prosperity in the present. In this, we can see vestiges of Confucian morality, magical Buddhism, and the ritual orientation of shamanic religion.

Even more shamanistic is the Korean institution of the *kido-wön* or hall for prayer, which is a feature of virtually all large churches in Korea. This facility is not part of the church itself, but built at some distance from the main building, usually in the hills. Supposedly intended for religious retreats, the *kido-wön* mainly serves as a venue for faith-healing ceremonies. Indeed, a number of these halls are not even associated with a specific church, and some are so large that they have individual pastors who specialize in particular medical conditions. Korean experts in religion have described how the atmosphere and practices in the *kido-wön*, including the use of hypnotism, the laying on of hands, and the general atmosphere of the service hark back to shamanic practices. Likewise, the placement of the *kido-wön* resonates with the early Korean emphasis on mountains as places of divine power.

This is not to say that Korean Christianity is isolated from "real" Christianity, or that it has not contributed to the general development of the faith. Notable in this regard is Minjüng sinhak, or the Theology of the People, a theological school that is an outgrowth of the trend toward Liberation Theology that sprang up in many parts of the Third World in the 1960s. In essence, this school stresses God's love and ultimate concern for the poor and dispossessed of society. It advocates the hope that God gives such people, and calls Christians to live lives that actively make this hope a concrete force in the world.

Finally, it is interesting to consider one of the most interesting collateral phenomena to emerge from modern Korean religious thought: the Unification Church (T'ongil-gyo). Founded by Mun Sönmyöng (b. 1924) and claiming to be a Christian church, the "Holy Spirit Association for the Unification of World Christianity" sees itself as the culmination of Christian doctrine and the avenue of the Second Coming of Christ—a view vehemently rejected by all of the orthodox Korean Christian churches. Branded by others as a sect, the organization teaches that Eve had sexual relations with Satan, who took the shape of a serpent, and that sin has subsequently been physically transmitted to all generations of the human race through the centuries. Jesus, who was the son of God but not God himself, brought spiritual, but not physical, salvation to humanity. As a result of his failure, it is up to another person to complete the task of salvation.

That salvation can only come through the marriage of the perfect woman to the perfect man—the Lord of the Second Advent—and the subsequent physical eradication of sin from the human bloodline. Mun Sönmyöng is believed to be this Lord of the Second Advent, and his wife the Mother of the Universe. Their children are believed by members of the cult to be sinless. Mun's staging of vast wedding ceremonies at which people marry partners chosen for them by the church is merely another example of this attempt to purge humanity of its sin-tainted blood. Interestingly enough, in the course of this mission, the Unification Church has amassed a sizable business empire and has been branded a form of brainwashing and mind control. It has also been investigated all over the world for violations of both individual rights and laws of the countries in which it operates.[4]

The New Religions in Japan

In Japan, there have arisen in the last century and a half the so-called "new religions" or *shinto shukyo*. These expressions of religious faith have taken many elements of shamanic thought and ritual, Shinto, Buddhism, and even Christianity, and reshaped them to fit new social circumstances. In Japan, these "new religions" have grown tremendously in the last sixty years, partially in response to the Japanese defeat in the Second World War, and partially in response to the social dislocation that has resulted from Japan's meteoric industrial development and its attendant devaluing of traditional culture and mores. The essence of the new religions is to break decisively with old forms, and they have proved so popular that at present virtually one in every five Japanese belongs to one or another of them.

In all, about 170 new religions have sprouted up in Japan. Some have flourished, while others command at best a rather limited following. All of them tend to draw their members from the lower levels of Japanese society. However, some groups, such as Tenrikyo and Soka Gakkai, have made a concerted effort to recruit from the middle classes. As the Japanese economy has stalled over the last decade, increased hardship among members of these middle classes has led to an upswing in their enrollment in one or the other of the new religions. With this increase in middle-class enrollment has come a concomitant increase in the wealth of these religions, which in some cases was not inconsiderable to begin with. These new religions espouse a variety of creeds (one worships electricity as the supreme deity and has deified Thomas Alva Edison as one of their four primary gods), but they all tend to share some common characteristics.

The first of these is that they have a clearly discernible center. That is to say, there is usually an imposing headquarters in which various ceremonies take place, and which serves as a ritual center of the religion. Often, the followers of these religions aspire to make pilgrimages to these centers of their faith at every opportunity. All in all, these ceremonial centers imbue the faithful with a sense of pride and of participating in something bigger than themselves. The second characteristic is that they are easy to join. Lengthy periods of preparations or examinations are not necessary. The new converts are not required to serve a long period of conditional membership. There is no need for a promise of fidelity unto death. Rather, the aspirant pays a small fee, followed by monthly dues, and is often required to purchase the ritual trappings of the sect, which are usually not very expensive.

New members of the group are now ready to be taught the distinctive dogmas of their new religion. Usually extremely simple, this new doctrine is often driven home through the use of visual aids, and expressed physically through dance or some other form of ritual. The core concept here is to simplify religion to the level of the lowest common denominator, and to link it to social cohesion—a fundamental concern of Japanese society. Often the most important part of a new religious ritual is not the rite itself, but the social mixing that takes place after it. Here the doctrine is amplified with reference to everyday problems, and this leads to the third characteristic of these faiths: the fact that they are all relentlessly optimistic. There is no room for pessimism, as the numerous publications of these religions emphasize over and over.

This optimism is always linked to practical results. The new religions have as their goal nothing less than the complete renovation of society. Primarily, they promise an end to sickness, poverty, and unhappiness, and so far from being divorced from the material world, they embrace it with a vengeance. As one religious document avers, "We wish to overcome diseases and all other miseries of mankind by a true conception of man's life, by a true way of living, and by a true method of education; and we want to devote ourselves to propagating the idea that all men are children of God, in order to establish on earth the Heaven of Mutual Love and Assurance" (*Creed of Seicho no Ie*, 7th article).

Often this new kingdom is intimately associated with the end of illness and disease. Tenrikyo, a nineteenth-century new religion, owed its initial success to its claim to be able to end pain in childbirth, and even today faith-healing is one of the new religions' greatest drawing cards. This leads to the fifth characteristic of the new religions: their strong contention that all religion and life are one. This has led to an emphasis on social service, with members often being called on to perform community service. Several of the wealthier new religions have also undertaken a number of civic projects aimed at improving their communities.

These projects are implemented and directed by the groups' leaders: a factor that underscores the tremendous importance of charismatic leadership in these new religions. It is perhaps not an overstatement to say that this sixth characteristic, charismatic leadership, is the single most defining characteristic of these faiths. The emphasis on the equality of believers breaks down in respect of the leadership. Leaders are seen as being on a different level from the common people, very often being the conduits through which the gods or spirits reveal their new plans for humanity. Thus, given the tendency toward "easy divinity" in Japanese culture, these leaders are often considered as being "divine," although as we have seen, this does not mean as much in Japan as it would elsewhere. Succession of leadership has often remained in families, but there are also cases where, on the death of the founder, a group of leading figures within the faith has coopted the leadership role away from the founding family. This emphasis on the leader and his or her infallibility can have tragic results, as demonstrated by the actions initiated by the Aum Shinri Kyo cult's leader, Shoko Asahara.[5]

The new religions, like all the recent religious expressions examined in this chapter, were able to infuse new meaning and purpose into the lives of their followers after a difficult period in their country's history. All these traditions illustrate the tremendous powers of endurance and rejuvenation possessed by the religions of

Asia, as well as their continuing ability to grapple successfully with the great questions of human existence within the ever-changing matrix of global civilization. It is this combination of flexibility and efficiency that will propel the religions of Asia into the twenty-first century and beyond, and make them, for much of humanity, the preferred expression of our most deeply held yearnings and aspirations.

Website References

1. www.maoism.org/msw/mao_sw.htm gives an overview of Maoist thought.

2. www.falundafa.org/ presents the teachings of Falun Gong.

3. Cao Daism is discussed at www.caodai.org/

4. www.unification.org/ gives information on the Unification Church.

5. Japanese New Religions are examined at religiousmovements.lib.virginia.edu/profiles/listalpha.htm

Northeast Asian Religions Timeline

DATE	JAPAN	KOREA
B.C.E.		
c. 600		Korean people begin to emerge as a clearly defined ethno-linguistic group.
c. 300	Emergence of Yayoi culture. Consolidation of the various ethnic strands in Japan into a single people.	
c. 194		Rise of the first large-scale political units in Korea.
109		Korea annexed to the Han Chinese empire.
C.E.		
260	Possible date for the founding of the Ise Shrine.	
c. 300	Great tumulus tombs of the early emperors begin to be built.	
313		Chinese lose control of Korea.
c. 350	A Chikki and Wang In travel to Japan. They bring copies of Chinese texts, including the *Analects*.	
372		Buddhism adopted as official religion in Koguryö. School of Confucian studies established.
384		Buddhism adopted as official religion in Paekche.
527		Buddhism adopted as official religion in Silla.
538–552		King Sŏng of Paekche sends Buddhist texts and statues to Japan.
552	Introduction of Buddhism from Paekche.	
594	Buddhism proclaimed state religion.	
c. 600–655		Life of Chajang, reformer and codifier of Silla Buddhism.
607	First Japanese embassy to China.	
617–681		Life of Wŏnhyo; first attempts to unify divergent Buddhist sects in Korea.
625–650		Daoism briefly becomes the dominant tradition in Koguryö.
625–702		Life of Uisang, founder of Korean Hwaöm Buddhism which influences the philosophy of all subsequent schools.
645	The Taika Reform.	
c. 650		First Sön (Zen) monastery established in Silla by Pömnang at Kohi-san.
668		Silla becomes sole ruler of the Korean peninsula.
682		School of Confucian learning established in Silla.
c. 700		Establishment of the Five Orthodox Schools (O-gyo) of Buddhism in Silla.
712	*Kojiki* (Record of Ancient Matters).	
720	*Nihongi* (Chronicles of Japan).	

DATE	JAPAN	KOREA
727		Hyech'o returns from pilgrimage to China and India.
741	Golden Light Sutra distributed to all provinces by order of the emperor.	
c. 750		First printing of Buddhist texts in Korea.
752	Dedication of the Great Buddha at Todaiji in Nara.	
c. 770		Establishment of the Ch'önt'ae-jong (Tiantai) school.
788	Saicho (767–822) founds Enryaku-ji Temple on Mt. Hiei and establishes the Tendai school in Japan.	
805	Saicho rèturns from China.	
806	Kukai (774–835) returns from China.	
816	Kukai founds Koya-san Temple on Mt. Koya and establishes the Shingon school in Japan.	
818	Saicho codifies regulations for the monks of Mt. Hiei.	
847	Ennin returns from China to found esoteric branch of Tendai.	
c. 900		Emergence of the Nine Mountains (Ku-san) schools of Sön.
918		Koryö dynasty ascends the Korean throne. Buddhism supported but strictly controlled by the state.
927	First formal material on Shinto put down in the *Engishiki*.	
933	Internecine battles between Miidera and Hiei-zan sects of Tendai.	
c. 950	Kuya (903–972) begins to popularize the *nembutsu* of Pure Land Buddhism.	
998		Chinese civil service examinations instituted.
1011		First woodblock edition of the complete Buddhist scriptures.
1055–1101		Life of Uch'ön. Further attempts to unify the various schools of Korean Buddhism.
1158–1210		Life of Chinul, premier Sön philosopher of Korea.
1191	Eisai (1141–1215) returns from China and establishes Rinzai school of Zen.	
1206	Honen (1133–1212) exiled for teaching Pure Land doctrine.	
1222	Dogen (1200–1253), founder of Soto Zen school, goes to China.	
1251		New edition of the complete Buddhist scriptures printed.
1260	Nichiren (1222–1282) predicts foreign invasion.	
1262	Shinran (1173–1262), founder of True Pure Land school, dies.	
1268	Nichiren warns of Mongol invasion.	
1271	Nichiren sentenced to death but escapes.	
1274	First Mongol invasion.	
1281	Second Mongol invasion.	
1289	Ippen (1238–1289), popularizer of Pure Land Buddhism, dies.	

DATE	JAPAN	KOREA
1392		Yi dynasty ascends the Korean throne. Espouses Neo-Confucianism as the state ideology and suppresses Buddhism.
1420		Confucian academy of scholars founded on Chinese model.
1498–1545		Scholars unsympathetic to the regime purged.
1520–1604		Life of Hyujöng, the great promoter of the Pure Land *yömbul* prayer to Amitabha.
1542	Portuguese arrive in Japan, bringing Christianity.	
c. 1550		Emergence of distinctly Korean schools of Neo-Confucianism.
1593	Neo-Confucianism adopted as official philosophy of Tokugawa Japan.	
1610		Roman Catholicism arrives in Korea.
1617	Persecution of Christians.	
1640	All foreigners expelled from Japan and the country's borders closed. Christianity driven underground.	
1769	Death of Kamo Mabuchi (1697–1769), Shinto revivalist.	
1785		First anti-Catholic persecution.
1817	Death of Motoori Norinaga (1730–1817), most influential of the Shinto revivalists.	
1831		Establishment of first Catholic diocese and the arrival of French priests.
1866		Last large-scale persecution of Catholics.
1868	Meiji Restoration, official revival of Shinto, and suppression of Buddhism.	
1873	Edict against Christianity removed.	
c. 1880		Protestant Christianity begins to make significant inroads in Korea.
1910–1945		Japanese colonial rule. Attempts to impose Japanese Shinto and Buddhism.
1945	End of the Pacific War. Shinto disestablished as official religion of Japan. Rise of the New Religions.	
1947		South and North Korean states constituted. Christianity becomes significant minority religion.

Glossary

In the glossary, a guide to pronunciation follows most of the keywords. This gives an accepted pronunciation as simply as possible. Syllables are separated by hyphens, and in multi-syllable words stress marks (') indicate the main accent.

Indian Religious Terms

Hinduism

Advaita (uh-dvait'-ta): The philosophical subsystem of Vedanta taught by Shankara that is predicated on the premise that all visible phenomena are aspects of a single underlying reality. In Euro-American thought, the analogous term is monism.

asanas (ah'-suh-nuhs): The various physical postures of yoga that are believed to channel and harness the energies of the body. These energies can then be utilized either to gain special supernatural powers or for the purpose of liberation from the cycle of life and death.

ashvamedha (uh-shvuh-may'-duh): The horse sacrifice. This was one of the most expensive and longest running of the traditional Vedic sacrifices. It was designed to affirm and extend the ruling power of the king.

asuras (uh-soor'-uhs): The race of supernatural beings who opposed the gods of Hinduism. They were equivalent to the Titans of Greek mythology.

atman (aht'-muhn): An eternal fragment of Brahman that exists in every person and serves much the same function as a soul in other religions.

avatara (uh-vuh-tah'-ruh): The incarnation in the physical world of a god, usually Vishnu.

avidya (uh-veed'-ya): Ignorance of the true nature of the self and of the universe, the principal cause of bondage to the cycle of life and death in the wisdom mode of salvation of Hinduism.

bhakti (buhk'-tee): Faith in the saving power of a deity. The third and currently most popular mode of salvation in Hinduism.

brahmacharya (bruh-muh-chuh'-ryuh): The student stage of life. The first of the four stages of life in classical Hindu social thought.

Brahman (bruh'-muhn): The eternal Reality that undergirds and supports the visible universe. Differs from many other religions' understanding of Supreme Reality in that it is not in any sense personal.

Brahmanas (brah'-muh-nuhs): The texts which developed after the Vedas that describe in exact detail the various Vedic rituals. They also contain valuable information on other aspects of life in ancient India.

Brahmin (brah'-min): The highest of the four castes that make up the Hindu social order. Traditionally, its members were the priests of Hinduism.

caste (cahst): A Portuguese word meaning "color." In the Hindu context, it refers to the various class divisions of Hindu society.

devas (day'-vuhs): Literally "the shining ones," this is the generic term used to designate the various gods of Hinduism.

dharma (duhr'-muh): A concept found in all of the religious traditions of India, this term has many meanings. In the Hindu context, it refers to the individual's social and religious duties and obligations as well as to the proper manner in which society and the universe at large should function. In Buddhism, it tends to refer to the body of Buddhist teachings that lead to enlightenment.

Dvaita (dvai'-tuh): The Vedanta philosophical concept that the visible world and Ultimate Reality are separate and distinct entities. In Euro-American thought the analogous term is dualism.

grihastya (gree-huh'-styuh): The householder stage of a person's life. The second of the four Hindu stages of life.

gunas (goo'-nuhs): In Samkhya thought, the three primary components of matter. They are *sattva*, *rajas*, and *tamas*.

guru (goo'-roo): A religious teacher who, on the basis of his or her personal spiritual attainments, is able to lead the individual out of the cycle of birth and death.

japa (juh'-puh): The religious exercise of repeating the divine name.

jnana (jnyah'-nuh): The second of the three principal modes of salvation in Hindu religious thought. It aims at eliminating *avidya*.

karma (kuhr'-muh): Literally, "work." This is the concept that all actions have results that will effect the individual either in the present or in later lives.

kirtana (keer'-tuh-nuh): The religious exercise of singing hymns or *bhajans*.

kshatriyas (kshuh'-tree-yuhs): The second of the four traditional Hindu divisions of human society. It is composed of the warriors and rulers.

linga (lin'-guh): The cylindrical symbol of Shiva often considered to be phallic in origin.

mantra (muhn'-truh): A short formula used in all of the Indian religions as a support for meditation.

maya (mah'-yah): Illusion. The primary cause in many Hindu philosophical systems of bondage to the cycle of life and death.

moksha (mohk'-sha): Liberation. The state of having escaped from the cycle of reincarnation.

nirguna (neer-goo'-nuh): God or Supreme Reality as it is without any sensible characteristics.

prakriti (pruhk'-ri-tee): In Samkhyan philosophy, the eternally existing matter that interacts with *purusha* to form the visible world.

pramanas (pruh-mah'-nuhs): In Indian epistemology, the various ways of knowing objects and actions.

prana (prah'-nuh): Breath. The life force that animates living beings.

purusha (poo-roo'-shuh): In Samkhyan thought, pure consciousness or spirit that animates, but does not mix with, matter.

rishis (rish'-ees): The seers or sages to whom the Vedas were revealed.

rita (rit'-ah): The principle of cosmic order found in early Vedic Hinduism.

saguna (suh-goo'-nuh): Supreme Reality cloaked in characteristics that allow human beings to apprehend and interact with it.

samadhi (suh-mah'-dee): In yoga, the state of deep meditative absorption that leads to liberation from the cycle of life and death.

samnyasa (suhn-yah'-sin): The fourth stage of life in Hinduism in which the individual forsakes all ties with his former life and lives as a wandering holy man.

samsara (suhm-sah'-ruh): The cycle of life, death, and rebirth in which human beings are trapped.

satsang (suht'-sung): Association with others of like inclinations. A religious organization or school of thought.

satyagraha (suht-yah'-gruh-huh): Literally "an act of truth," this was the term used by Gandhi to refer to his program of nonviolent resistance to British rule in India.

Shakti (shuhk'-tee): The Goddess. The female principle or power of the universe.

shruti (shroo'-tee): Literally "that which is heard," this term refers to the revealed religious texts of Hinduism, the Vedas.

shudra (shood'-ruh): The fourth and lowest of the traditional divisions of Indian society. The servant class.

smriti (smri'-tee): Literally "that which is remembered," this term refers to the commentarial literature of Hinduism and includes all religious literature not associated with the Vedas. Some of the most influencial religious texts, such as the Bhagavad Gita, belong to this category and not that of revealed literature.

soma (soh'-muh): The drink offered to the gods and consumed at the traditional Vedic sacrifice. Although the original source of soma has been lost, it is speculated that the drink was made from a plant with halluciogenic properties.

vaishya (vaish'-yuh): The third of the four divisions of Hindu society. This group consists of the farmers and trades people.

vanaprastha (vah-nuh-pruhs'-tuh): The third of the traditional stages of the life of a Hindu. During this stage, a person begins to withdraw from active life and devote themselves to religious practice.

varnashramadharma (vuhr-nahsh-ruh-muh-duhr'-muh): The total systematic model of Hindu life and society.

yajna (yuhj'-nyuh): The first mode of salvation in Hinduism. The Hindu sacrifice which was the central feature of early Vedic Hinduism.

Islam and Sikhism

gurdwara (goor-dwah'-ruh): The local Sikh house of worship.

hadith (ha-deet): The sayings of the prophet Muhammad. Pious Muslims see them as second only to the Qur'an as a guide to the proper conduct of the religious life.

Hajj (hahj): The pilgrimage to Mecca that Muslims are required to make at least once in their lives if they can afford to do so.

kachh (kuhch): Short underclothes designed to remind the Sikh of the need for continence and moral restraint.

kanga (kuhn'-gah): In the Sikh religion, the wearing of a comb in the hair to hold it up.

kara (kuh-rah'): In the Sikh religion, a steel bangle worn on the right wrist to symbolize the wheel of dharma.

kesh (kaysh): The long hair that is one of the distinctive features of the observant Sikh. Its length requires the use of the kanga and of the turban to hold it up.

Khalsa (kahl'-sah): The "pure ones." The Sikh name for their own religious organization.

kirpan (keer'-pahn): In Sikhism, the sword (or its symbolic representation) that signifies the believer's willingness to fight for his beliefs.

langar (lahn'-gur): The kitchen attached to the *gurdwara*. A central symbol of Sikhism since all Sikhs traditionally dined communally without distinction to caste or class.

Jainism

ahimsa (uh-him'-suh): The fundamental Jain ethical value of noninjury to any living being.

anekanta (uh-nay-kahn'-tuh): Literally "many-sidedness." The Jain philosophical methodology of examining a question from a variety of angles.

astikas (ahs'-tee-kuhs): Those who say the Veda "is" divinely revealed literature. The followers of Hinduism.

Carvaka (chahr-vah'-kuh): Indian philosophical school of materialism that holds nothing to exist except the visible world.

jiva (jee-vuh): In Jainism, the eternal soul or life force possessed by all living beings. Some higher beings possess more then one.

nastikas (nahs'-tee-kuhs): Those who say that that the Veda "is not" divinely revealed literature. The Jains and Buddhists.

salakana (suhl-lay-kah'-nuh): Ritual suicide by fasting to death.

samyak darshana (suhm-yuk duhr-shah'-nuh): The momentary flash of insight that motivates and sustains the religious quest.

syatvada (see-yud-vah'-duh): Literally the "way of 'maybe,'" this concept reflected the Jain belief in the essential unknowability of many questions and the tentative nature of truth.

Buddhism

abhisheka (uh-bee-shay'-kuh): In Tibetan Buddhism, the ritual of initiation into various tantric texts and practices.

anatman **(Pali: *anatta*)** (uhn-aht'-mun/uhn-aht'-tuh): Nonself. The Buddhist belief that there is no permanent human soul.

anitya **(Pali: *anicca*)** (uh-neet'-yuh/uh-neech-chyuh): Impermanence. The Buddhist concept that all existence is in flux.

arya-satya **(Pali: *ariya-satta*)** (ahr'-yuh-suht'-yuh/ah-ree'-yuh-suh'-tuh): Four Noble Truths. The encapsulation of the Buddhist religion.

ashtangika-marga (uhsh-tuhn-gee'-kuh mahr'-guh): Noble Eightfold Path. The Buddhist practical program for salvation.

bodhisattva (boh-dee-suht'-tvuh): A being who has achieved enlightenment but postpones entering Nirvana until all other beings have been saved.

Dharma (duhr'-muh): The "Law" or teachings of the Buddha. The second of the "Three Jewels" of Buddhism.

duhkha **(Pali: *dukkha*)** (dook'-huh/duk'-huh): Literally "pain." The Buddhist concept of the ultimate unsatisfactoriness of existence.

Jatakas (jah-tuh'-kuhs): The stories of the Buddha's previous lives.

Mahayana (muh-hah-yah'-nuh): The form of Buddhism now found primarily in Vietnam and East Asia. In former times this form of Buddhism existed throughout Asia.

mandala (muhn'-duh-luh): In Tibetan Buddhism, a diagram or picture which functions as a mystic "road map" of reality in various forms of meditation and religious rituals.

Nirvana (neer-vah'-nuh): The indescribable goal of Buddhist practice. Liberation from the cycle of rebirth.

pratityasamutpada (pruh-teet-yuh-suh-moot-pah'-duh): Literally "interdependent arising," the Buddhist analysis of the cycle of causality that results in the bondage of the human being to *samsara*.

samsara (suhm-sah'-ruh): The cycle of life, death and rebirth.

Sangha (suhn'-guh): The third of the "Three Jewels" of the Buddhist religion. The order of Buddhist monks and nuns.

shamatha (shuh-muh'-tuh): Literally "calm abiding," this is the first of two steps in Buddhist meditation. Here the mind is calmed so that the second step, *vipassana*, can be accomplished.

Shramanas (shruh'-muh-nuhs): The movement in early Indian religion away from the religion of sacrifice toward a personal religion based on asceticism and the gaining of existential wisdom. This movement later split into a Hindu segment and a series of non-Hindu groups such as the Jains and Buddhists.

shunyata (shoon'-yuh-tuh): Emptiness. The Mahayana teaching that all phenomena are essentially empty of enduring real being.

stupa (stoo'-puh): An artificial mound built to house the relics of the Buddha.

Tantra (tuhn'-tru): A form of religious practice, found in both Hinduism and Buddhism, that uses a combination of physical and mental techniques to accelerate the process of escaping *samsara*.

Theravada (tay-ruh-vah'-du): The form of Buddhism now found primarily in Sri Lanka, Burma, Thailand, Laos and Cambodia.

trilaksana (tree-luk'-shuh-nuh): "Three Marks of Existence." The fundamental Buddhist analysis of the nature of existence.

Tripitaka (tree-pee'-tuh-kuh): The Buddhist scriptures which are divided into three "baskets" or divisions: the *Vinaya* (rules of conduct), the

Sutras (discourses of the Buddha), and the Abhidarma (philosophical analysis).

triratna (tree-ruht'-nuh): The "Three Jewels" or foundational elements of the Buddhist tradition. The Buddha, the *Dharma* and the Sangha.

trishna (trish'-nuh): Literally "thirst". The boundless desire for various objects and states of being that the Buddhists hold to be the root cause for human unhappiness.

tulku (tul'-koo): In Tibetan Buddhism, a reincarnated teacher generally held to be a bodhisattva or Buddha.

Vajrayana (vuhj-ruh-yah'-nuh): The form of Buddhism now found primarily in Tibet and Mongolia.

vipassana (**Sanskrit:** *vipashyana*) (vi-puh'-suhn-nah/vee-puhsh'-yuh-nah): "Insight" meditation. The second step in Buddhist meditation that led directly to enlightenment.

yidam (yee'-dahm): In Tibetan Buddhism, the particular deity used by an indivdual as a focal point for his or her meditative practice.

Chinese Religions

Daoism/Taoism (dow): A constellation of beliefs and practices aimed at bringing the practitioner into conformity with the Tao or Ultimate Reality, thus maintaining cosmic order and gaining a variety of practical benefits for the practitioner.

daoshi/tao shih (dow shee): A Daoist priest.

Daozang/Tao-tsang (dow dzahng): The Daoist canon of texts, organized into three sections or "Caverns."

gui/kuei (goo-ay) A ghost; a wandering spirit.

jianai/chien-ai (jee-an ay): The "universal love" that formed the foundation of the philosophy of the Mohists.

Junzi/chun-tzu (jun-dzuh): In Confucianism, the "gentlemen". One who follows the teachings of the Confucian school.

li (**different character from the "li" denoting ritual**) (lee): The underlying metaphysical form that shapes *qi* or matter into sensible objects in the world.

li (lee): Ritual.

oracle bones: The bones of various animals used for divination in early China.

qi/ch'i (chee): Matter or vital energy.

ren/jen (ren): In Confucianism, human heartedness or benevolence. The highest Confucian virtue.

Shangdi/Shang Ti (shang-dee): The "Lord on High". The supreme deity of the early Chinese pantheon.

shen: A god.

tianming/t'ien ming: The "Mandate of Heaven." The concept that the right to rule may be withdrawn from a royal family if they do not act in accordance with proper morality. When this happens, rebellion against their rule is justified.

wuwei (woo-way): In Daoism, the principle of spontaneous action without excessive reflection.

xiao/hsiao (shee-ow): Filiality or filial piety. A central virtue in Confucian thought.

xin/hsin (shin): Heart or mind. The seat of human reason and the source of human action.

yang: The active principle in nature. Always found in conjunction with yin.

yin: The passive principle in nature. Always found in conjunction with yang.

Japanese Religion

Amaterasu (ah-muh-tay-rha'-soo): The Sun Goddess. Ancestress of the Japanese Imperial family and chief deity of Shinto.

daimoku (day-moh-koo): Nichiren formula of "Hail to the Jewel in the Lotus." The first line of the Lotus Sutra.

Ise (ee-say) **Shrine:** The chief shrine of Amaterasu. Usually served by women of the Imperial family.

jinja: A Shinto shrine.

kami (kah-mee): In Shinto, a god or the "divine principle" found in various places and objects.

kamidana (kah-mee dah-nah): Household shrine for the *kami*.

koan (koh-an): In Buddhism, a "public case" or question that is aimed at jolting the mind out of its habitual patterns, thus leading it toward enlightenment.

matsuri (muht-soo-ree): A Shinto festival.

norito (noh-ree-toh): A hymn or formula chant used in Shinto ceremonies.

Shinto (shin-toh): The indigenous religious beliefs and practices of Japan, many of which predate the arrival of Buddhism and the Chinese systems of thought.

zazen: In Buddhism, the established practice of seated meditation.

Bibliography

Selected Bibliography

Early Human Religion and Shamanism

Carmody, Denise Lardner. *The Oldest God: Archaic Religion Yesterday and Today*. Nashville: Abingdon Press, 1981.

Clottes, Paul et al. *The Shamans of Prehistory: Trance and Magic in the Painted Caves*. Trans. by Sophie Hawkes. New York: Harry N. Abrams, 1998.

Davidson, D. Bruce. *The Dawn of Belief: Religion in the Upper Paleolithic of Southwestern Europe*. Tempe: University of Arizona Press, 1992.

Eliade, Mircea. *Shamanism: Archaic Techniques of Ecstacy*. Princeton: Princeton University Press, 1972.

Goodman, Felicitas. *Where the Spirits Ride the Wind: Trance Journeys and Other Ecstatic Experiences*. Bloomington: Indiana University Press, 1990.

Kalweit, Holger. *Dreamtime and Inner Space: The World of the Shaman*. Trans. Werner Wünsche. Boston: Shambhala Publications, 1988.

Lewis, I. M. *Ecstatic Religion: A Study of Shamanism and Spirit Possession*. 2nd ed., London: Routledge, 1989.

Hinduism

Basham, A. L. *The Origins and Development of Classical Hinduism*. Ed. and completed by Kenneth G. Zysk. New York: Oxford University Press, 1991.

Basham, A. L. *The Wonder that was India*. London: Sidgwick and Jackson, 1954.

Bhattacharji, Sukumani. *The Indian Theogony: A Comparative Study of Indian Mythology from the Vedas to the Puranas*. Cambridge: Cambridge University Press, 1970.

Chapple, Christopher and Mary Evelyn Tucker, eds. *Hinduism and Ecology: The Intersection of Earth, Sky and Water*. Cambridge: Center for the Study of World Religions, 2000.

Doniger O'Flaherty, Wendy, ed. and trans. *The Rig Veda: An Anthology, One Hundred and Eight Hymns*. Harmondsworth: Penguin, 1981.

Eck, Diana L. *Darshan: Seeing the Divine Image in India*. Chambersburg: Anima Books, 1981.

Embree, Ainslie T., ed. *Sources of Indian Tradition*. 2nd ed., 2 vols., New York: Columbia University, 1958.

Fuller, C. J. *The Camphor Flame: Popular Hinduism and Society in India*. Princeton: Princeton University Press, 1992.

Hawley, John S. *Devi: Goddesses of India*. Berkeley: University of California Press, 1996.

Hawley, John S. and Mark Jurgensmeyer, trans. *Songs of the Saints of India*. New York: Oxford University Press, 1988.

Hiriyanna, Mysore. *The Essentials of Indian Philosophy*. London: Allen and Unwin, 1985.

Klostermaier, Klaus K. *A Survey of Hinduism*. 2nd ed., Albany: State University of New York, 1994.

Leslie, Julia, ed. *Roles and Rituals for Hindu Women*. London: Pinter, 1991.

Lopez, Donald S., Jr., ed. *Religions of India in Practice*. Princeton: Princeton University Press, 1995.

Miller, Barbara Stoler, trans. *Love Song of the Dark Lord: Jayadeva's Gitagovinda*. New York: Columbia University Press, 1977.

Miller, Barbara Stoler, trans. *The Bhagavad-Gita: Krishna's counsel in time of war*. New York: Columbia University Press, 1986.

Mitchell, George. *The Penguin Guide to the Monuments of India*. vol. 1. London: Penguin, 1989.

Narayan, R. K. *Ramayana: A Shortened Modern Prose Version of the Indian Epic*. New York: Viking, 1972.

Olivelle, Patrick. *The Dharmasutras: The Law Codes of Atastamba, Gautama, Baudhyayana, and Vasishta*. New York: Oxford University Press, 1999.

Olivelle, Patrick. *The Pancatantra: The Book of*

India's Folk Wisdom. New York: Oxford University Press, 1997.

Olivelle, Patrick. *The Upanishads*. New York: Oxford University Press, 1996.

Orr, Leslie C. *Donors, Devotees, and Daughters of God: Temple Women in Medieval Tamilnadu*. New York: Oxford University Press, 2000.

Perrett, Roy. W. *Hindu Ethics: A Philosophical Study*. Honolulu: University of Hawaii Press, 1998.

Radhakrishnan, Sarvepalli and Charles A. Moore, eds. *A Source Book in Indian Philosophy*. Princeton: Princeton University Press, 1957.

Rajagopalachari, Chakravarti. *Mahabharata*. Bombay: Bharatiya Vidya Bhavan, 1953.

Renou, Louis. *Indian Literature*. New York: Walker, 1964.

Williams, Raymond Brady, ed. *A Sacred Thread: Modern Transmission of Hindu Traditions in India and Abroad*. Chambersburg: Anima, 1992.

Zimmer, Heinrich. *Myths and Symbols in Indian Art and Civilization*. New York: Pantheon, 1946.

Jainism

Dundas, P. *The Jains*. London: Routledge and Kegan Paul, 1992.

Jacobi, Hermann, trans. *Jaina Sutras*, Part I. Oxford: Clarendon Press, 1884.

Jacobi, Hermann, trans. *Jaina Sutras*, Part II. Oxford: Clarendon Press, 1895.

Jaini, Padmanabh S. *Gender and Salvation: Jaina Debates on the Spiritual Liberation of Women*. Berkeley: University of Californian Press, 1991.

Jaini, Padmanabh S. *The Jain Path of Purification*. Berkley: University of California Press, 1979.

Roy, Ashim Kumar. *A History of the Jainas*. New Delhi: Gitanjali, 1984.

Sangave, Vilas A. *Aspects of Jaina Religion*. New Delhi, Bharatiya Jnanpith, 1990.

Tobias, Michael. *Life Force: The World of Jainism*. Berkley: Asian Humanities Press, 1991.

Sikhism

Brown, Kerry. *Sikh Art and Literature*. London: Routledge, 1999.

Cole, W. Owen. *The Sikhs: Their Religious Beliefs and Practices*. London: Routledge and Kegan Paul, 1985.

Gill, Mahinda Kaura. *The Role and Status of Women in Sikhism*. Delhi: National Book Shop, 1995.

Khushwant, K. S. *A History of the Sikhs*. 2 vols., Princeton: Princeton University Press, 1963, 1966.

McLeod, W. H. *Guru Nanak and the Sikh Religion*. New York: Oxford University Press, 1968.

McLeod, W. H. *Historical Dictionary of Sikhism*. Lanham, MY: Scarecrow Press, 1995.

McLeod, W. H. *Popular Sikh Art*. Delhi: Oxford University Press, 1991.

McLeod, W. H. *Sikhism*. New York: Penguin Books, 1997.

McLeod, W. H. *Textual Sources for the History of Sikhism*. Manchester: Manchester University Press, 1984.

McLeod, W. H. *The Sikhs: History, Religion, and Society*. New York: Columbia University Press, 1989.

Singh, Harbans, ed. *The Encyclopaedia of Sikhism*. 4 vols., Patiala: Punjabi University, 1992-8.

Singh, Manmohan, trans. *Sri Guru Granth Sahib*. 8 vols., Amritsar: Shromani Gurdwara Parbandhak Committee, 1962.

Islam

Ahmad Ibrahim et al., eds. *Readings on Islam in Southeast Asia*. Singapore: Institute of Southeast Asian Studies, 1985.

Ali, Abdullah Yusuf. *The Meaning of the Holy Qur'an*. Brentwood, MY: The Amana Corporation, 1993.

Arberry, A. J. *The Koran Interpreted: A translation*. New York: Macmillan, 1955.

Awde, Nicholas, trans. *Women in Islam: An Anthology from the Quran and Hadiths*. New York: St. Martin's Press, 2000.

Bouhdiba, Abdelwahab. *Sexuality in Islam*. London: Routledge and Kegan Paul, 1985.

Encyclopedia of Islam. London and Leiden; E. J. Brill, 1913-1939.

Federspiel, Howard M. *A Dictionary of Indonesian Islam*. Athens: Ohio University Press, 1995.

Glassé, Cyril. *The Concise Encyclopedia of Islam*. San Francisco: HarperSanFrancisco, 1989.

Hillenbrand, Robert. *Islamic Art and Architecture*. London: Thames and Hudson, 1998.

Hodgson, Marshall G. S. *The Venture of Islam*. Chicago: University of Chicago Press, 1974.

Holt, P. M. and Bernard Lewis, eds. *Cambridge History of Islam : The Indian Sub-Continent, Southeast Asia, Africa and the Muslim West*. London: Cambridge University Press, 1977.

Lings, Martin. *Muhammad*. London: George Allen and Unwin, 1983.

Momen, Moojan. *An Introduction to Shi'i Islam.* New Haven; Yale University Press, 1985.

Nasr, Seyyed Hossein, ed. *Islamic Spirituality.* 2 vols., New York: Crossroads, 1997.

Nurbakhsh, Javad. *Sufi Women.* 2nd ed. New York: Khaniqahi Nimatullahi, 1990.

Peters, F. E. *A Reader on Classical Islam.* Princeton: Princeton University Press, 1993.

Rizvi, Saiyad Athar Abbas. *A History of Sufism in India.* Delhi: Munshiram Manoharlal Publishers Pvt. Ltd., 1983.

Schimmel, Annemarie. *Islam: An Introduction.* Albany: State University of New York, 1992.

Schimmel, Annemarie. *Mystical Dimensions of Islam.* Chapel Hill: University of North Carolina Press, 1985.

Trimingham, J. Spencer. *The Sufi Orders in Islam.* London: Oxford University Press, 1971.

Watt, W. Montgomery. *Islamic Philosophy and Theology.* Edinburgh: Edinburgh University Press, 1962.

Wilson, Peter Lamborn and Nasrollah Pourjavady. *The Drunken Universe: An Anthology of Persian Sufi Poetry.* Grand Rapids: Panes Press, 1987.

Buddhism

Cabezon, Jose Ignacia. *Buddhism, Sexuality, and Gender.* Albany: State University of New York Press, 1992.

Conze, Edward et al., eds. and trans. *Buddhist Texts through the Ages.* Oxford: Oneworld Publications, 1995.

Eppsteiner, Fred, ed. *The Path of Compassion: Writings on Socially Engaged Buddhism.* Berkeley: Parallax Press, 1988.

Fields, Rick. *How the Swans Came to the Lake: A Narrative History of Buddhism in America.* Boston: Shambhala Press, 1981.

Fisher, Robert E. *Buddhist Art and Architecture.* London: Thames and Hudson, 1993.

Friedman, Lenore. *Meetings with Remarkable Women: Buddhist Teachers in America.* Boston: Shambhala Press, 1987.

Harvey, Peter. *An Introduction to Buddhism: Teaching, History and Practice.* Cambridge: Cambridge University Press, 1990.

King, Winston Lee. *In the Hope of Nibbana: An Essay on Theravada Buddhist Ethics.* LaSalle: Open Court, 1964.

King, Winston Lee. *Theravada Meditation: The Buddhist Transformation of Yoga.* University Park: Pennsylvania State University Press, 1980.

Kraft, Kenneth. *The Wheel of Engaged Buddhism: A New Map of the Path.* New York: Weatherhill, 1999.

Lopez, Donald S., Jr., ed. *Buddhism in Practice.* Princeton: Princeton University Press, 1995.

Prebish, Charles S. *Luminous Passage: The Practice and Study of Buddhism in America.* Berkeley: University of California Press, 1999.

Queen, Christopher S. and Sallie B. King, eds. *Engaged Buddhism: Buddhist Liberation Movements in Asia.* Albany: State University of New York Press, 1996.

Robinson, Richard H. and Willard L. Johnson. *The Buddhist Religion: A Historical Introduction.* 4th ed., Belmont: Wadworth, 1997.

Strong, John S. *The Experience of Buddhism: Sources and Interpretations.* Belmont: Wadsworth, 1995.

Sulak Sivaraksa. *A Socially Engaged Buddhism.* Bangkok: Thai Inter-Religious Commission for Development, 1988.

Williams, Paul. *Mahayana Buddhism: The Doctrinal Foundations.* London: Routledge and Kegan Paul, 1989.

India

Gombrich, Richard. *Theravada Buddhism: A Social History from Ancient Benares to Modern Colombo.* London: Routledge and Kegan Paul, 1988.

Hirakawa Akira. *A History of Indian Buddhism: From Sakyamuni to Early Mahayana.* Honolulu: University of Hawaii Press, 1990.

Kalupahana, David J. *Ethics in Early Buddhism.* Honolulu: University of Hawaii Press, 1995.

Warder, A. K. *Indian Buddhism.* 2nd rev. ed., Delhi: Motilal Banarsidass, 1980.

Tibet

Goldstein, Melvyn C. and Matthew T. Kapstein, eds. *Buddhism in Contemporary Tibet: Religious Revival and Cultural Identity.* Berkeley: University of California Press, 1998.

Lopez, Donald S., Jr., ed. *Religions of Tibet in Practice.* Princeton: Princeton University Press, 1997.

Powers, John. *Introduction to Tibetan Buddhism.* Ithaca: Snow Lion Publications, 1995.

Southeast Asia

Gómez, Luis O. and Hiram W. Woodward, Jr. *Barabudur, History and Significance of a Buddhist Monument.* Berkeley: Asian

Humanities Press, 1981.

Ishii, Yoneo. *Sangha, State, and Society: Thai Buddhism in History*. Trans. by Peter Hawkes. Honolulu: University of Hawaii Press, 1986.

Kabilsingh, Chatsumarn. *Thai Women in Buddhism*. Berkeley: Parallax Press, 1991.

Kapur-Fic, Alexandra R. *Thailand: Buddhism, society, and women*. New Delhi: Abhinav Publications, 1998.

King, Winston Lee. *A Thousand Lives Away: Buddhism in Contemporary Burma*. Cambridge Harvard University Press, 1964.

Minh Chi et al. *Buddhism in Vietnam: from its Origins to the 19th Century*. 2nd impression. Hanoi: The Gioi Publishers, 1999.

Nhat Hanh, Thich. *Vietnam: the Lotus in the Sea of Fire*. London, S.C.M. Press, 1967.

Spiro, Melford E. *Buddhism and Society: A Great Tradition and its Burmese Vicissitudes*. 2nd expanded ed., Berkeley: University of California Press, 1982.

Swearer, Donald K. *The Buddhist World of Southeast Asia*. Rev. ed., Albany: State University of New York Press, 1995.

Tambiah, Stanley J. *Buddhism and the Spirit Cults in North-East Thailand*. Cambridge: Cambridge University Press, 1970.

Wells, Kenneth Elmer. *Thai Buddhism, its Rites and Activities*. New York: AMS Press, 1982.

China

Ch'en, Kenneth K. S. *Buddhism in China: A Historical Survey*. Princeton: Princeton University Press, 1964.

Ch'en, Kenneth K. S. *The Chinese Transformation of Buddhism*. Princeton: Princeton University Press, 1973.

Weinstein, Stanley. *Buddhism Under the T'ang*. Cambridge: Cambridge University Press, 1987.

Wright, Arthur F. *Buddhism in Chinese History*. Stanford: Stanford University Press, 1983.

Korea

Buswell, Robert E. *The Korean Approach to Zen: The Collected Works of Chinul*. Honolulu: University of Hawaii Press, 1983.

Buswell, Robert E. *The Zen Monastic Experience: Buddhist Practice in Contemporary Korea*. Princeton: Princeton University Press, 1992.

Lee, Peter H. *Lives of Eminent Korean Monks: The Haedong Kosüng Chön*. Cambridge:

Harvard University Press, 1969.

Lewis R. Lancaster and C. S. Yu, eds. *Introduction of Buddhism to Korea: New Cultural Patterns*. Berkeley: Asian Humanities Press, 1989.

Lewis R. Lancaster and C.S. Yu, eds. *Assimilation of Buddhism in Korea : Religious Maturity and Innovation in the Silla Dynasty*. Berkeley: Asian Humanities Press, 1991.

Lewis R. Lancaster, Kikun Suh and Chai-shin Yu, eds. *Buddhism in Koryo: A Royal Religion*. Berkeley: Institute of East Asian Studies, Univ. of Calif., 1996.

Lewis R. Lancaster and Chai-shin Yu, eds. *Buddhism in the early Choson: Suppression and Transformation*. Berkeley: Institute of East Asian Studies, University of California, 1996.

Japan

Andreasen, Esben. *Popular Buddhism in Japan: Shin Buddhist Religion and Culture*. Honolulu: University of Hawaii, 1998.

Bloom, Alfred. *Shinran's Gospel of Pure Grace*. Tucson: University of Arizona Press, 1965.

Bodiford, William M. *Soto Zen in Medieval Japan*. Honolulu: University of Hawaii Press, 1993.

Collcutt, Martin. *Five Mountains: The Rinzai Monastic Institution in Medieval Japan*. Cambridge: Harvard University Press, 1981.

Dumoulin, Heinrich. *Zen Buddhism: A History*. 2 vols., New York: Macmillan, 1988.

Machida, Soho. *Renegade Monk: Honen and Japanese Pure Land Religion*. Trans. by Joannis Mentzas. Berkeley: University of California Press, 1999.

Matsunaga, Daigan and Alicia Matsunaga. *Foundation of Japanese Buddhism*. 2 vols., Los Angeles: Buddhist Books International, 1974.

Yokoi, Yuho. *Zen Master Dogen: An Introduction with Selected Writings*. New York: Weatherhill, 1976.

Southeast Asia

Ariswara. *Temples of Java*. Jakarta: Intermasa, 1992.

Beatty, Andrew. *Varieties of Javanese Religion: An Anthropological Account*. New York: Cambridge University Press, 1999.

Coedès, George. *The Indianized States of Southeast Asia*. Ed. by Walter F. Vella., trans. by Susan Brown Cowing. Honolulu, East-West Center Press, 1968.

Desai, Santosh N. *Hinduism in Thai Life*. Bombay: Popular, 1980.

Geertz, Clifford. *The Religion of Java*. Chicago: University of Chicago Press, 1976.

Hefner, Robert W. *Hindu Javanese: Tengger Tradition and Islam*. Princeton: Princeton University Press, 1985.

Jacques, Claude. *Angkor: Cities and Temples*. Trans. by Tom White. London: Thames and Hudson, 1997.

Lustéguy, Pierre. *The Role of Women in Tonkinese Religion and Property*. Trans. by Charles A. Messner. New Haven: Human Relations Area Files, 1954.

Mus, Paul. *India Seen from the East: Indian and Indigenous Cults in Champa*. Trans. by I. W. Mabbett, ed. by I. W. Mabbett and D. P. Chandler. Clayton: Centre of Southeast Asian Studies, Monash University, 1975.

Oliver, Victor L. *Caodai Spiritism: A Study of Religion in Vietnamese Society*. Leiden: Brill, 1976.

Spiro, Melford E. *Burmese Supernaturalism*. Expanded ed., New Brunswick: Transaction Publishers, 1996.

Terwiel, B. J. *Monks and Magic: An Analysis of Religious Ceremonies in Central Thailand*. Lund: Studentlitteratur, 1975.

Unger, Ann Helen. *Pagodas, Gods and Spirits of Vietnam*. London: Thames and Hudson, 1997.

Chinese Religions

Bodde, Derk. *Festivals in Classical China*. Princeton: Princeton University Press, 1975.

Bodenkamp, Stephen R. *Early Daoist Scriptures*. Berkeley: University of California Press, 1997.

Burkhardt, Valentine R. *Chinese Creeds and Customs*. Hong Kong: South China Morning Post, 1982.

Chan, Wing-tsit. *A Sourcebook in Chinese Philosophy*. Princeton: Princeton University Press, 1963.

Ching, Julie. *Chinese Religion*. London: Macmillan, 1993.

Ching, Julie. *The Religious Thought of Chu Hsi*. New York: Oxford University Press, 2000.

De Bary, Theodore et al. *Sources of Chinese Tradition*. 2nd ed., 2 vols, New York: Columbia University Press, 1999–2000.

Ebray, Patricia and Peter Gregory. *Religion and Society in T'ang and Sung China*. Honolulu: University of Hawaii Press, 1993.

Fung Yu-lan. *A Short History of Chinese Philosophy*. New York: Macmillan, 1957.

Granet, Marcel. *The Religion of the Chinese People*. Oxford: Blackwell, 1975.

Hall, David and Roger Ames. *Thinking Through Confucius*. Albany: State University of New York Press, 1987.

Hook, Brian, ed. *The Cambridge Encyclopedia of China*. 2nd ed. Cambridge: Cambridge University Press, 1991.

Kohn, Livia. *The Taoist Experience: An Anthology*. Albany: State University of New York Press, 1993.

Lagerwey, John. *Taoist Ritual in Chinese Society and History*. York: Macmillan, 1987.

Lau, Dim C. *Mencius*. Harmonsworth: Penguin, 1970.

Lau, Dim C. *The Analects*. Harmondsworth: Penguin, 1979.

Lau, Dim C. *The Tao Te Ching*. Harmondsworth: Penguin, 1963.

Levenson, Joseph R. *Confucian China and Its Modern Fate: A Trilogy*. Berkeley: Univesrity of California Press, 1968.

Lopez, Donald S., Jr., ed. *Religions of China in Practice*. Princeton: Princeton University Press, 1996.

Macinnes, Donald E. *Religion in China Today: Policy and Practice*. Maryknoll: Orbis Books, 1989.

Overmeyer, Daniel L. *Religions in China: The World as a Living System*. San Francisco: HarperCollins, 1996.

Paper, Jordan and Lawrence G. Thompson. *The Chinese Way in Religion*. 2nd ed., Belmont: Wadsworth, 1998.

Robinet, Isabelle. *Taoism: Growth of a Religion*. Trans. by Phyllis Brooks. Stanford: Stanford University Press, 1997.

Shun, Kwong-Loi. *Mencius and Early Chinese Thought*. Stanford: Stanford University Press, 1997.

Sommer, Deborah, ed. *Chinese Religion: An Anthology of Sources*. New York: Oxford University Press, 1995.

Taylor, Rodney. *The Religious Dimensions of Confucianism*. Albany: State University of New York Press, 1990.

Thompson, Laurence G. *Chinese Religion: An Introduction*. 5th ed., Belmont: Wadsworth, 1996.

Tu Wei-ming. *Confucian Thought: Selfhood as Creative Transformation*. Albany: State University of New York Press, 1985.

Tucker, Mary Evelyn and John Berthong, eds. *Confucianism and Ecology: The Interrelation of Heaven, Earth and Humans*. Cambridge: Harvard University Press, 1998.

Waley, Arthur. *The Book of Songs*. London: Allen and Unwin, 1937.

Waley, Arthur. *The Nine Songs: A study of shamanism in ancient China*. London: Allen and Unwin, 1955.

Watson, Burton, trans. *Hsün Tzu: Basic Writings*. New York: Columbia University Press, 1963.

Watson, Burton, trans. *Mo Tzu: Basic Writings*. New York: Columbia University Press, 1963.

Watson, Burton, trans. *The Complete Works of Chuang Tzu*. New York: Columbia University Press, 1968.

Korean Religion

Clark, Donald N. *Christianity on Modern Korea*. Lanham: University Press of America, 1986.

Greyson, James Huntley. *Korea: A Religious History*. Oxford: Clarendon Press, 1989.

Guisso, Richard W. L. and Chai-shin Yu. *Shamanism: The spirit world of Korea*. Berkeley: Asian Humanities Press, 1988.

Ha, Te-Hung and Grafton K. Mintz, trans. *Samguk yusa: Legends and histories of the Three Kingdoms in ancient Korea*. Seoul: Yonsei University Press, 1972.

Harvey, Youngsook Kim. *Six Korean Women: The socialization of shamans*. St. Paul: West, 1979.

Introvigne, Massimo. *The Unification Church*. New York: Signature, 2000.

Janelli, Roger L. and Dawnhee Yim Janelli. *Ancestor Worship and Korean Society*. Stanford: Stanford University Press, 1988.

Kendall, Laurel and Griffin Dix. *Religion and Ritual in Korean Society*. Berkeley: University of California Center for Korean Studies, 1989.

Lee, Jung-young (Yi Chungyöng). *Korean Shamanistic Rituals*. The Hague: Mouton, 1981.

Lee, Peter, and William Theodore de Bary, eds. *Sources of Korean Tradition*. 2 vols., New York: Columbia University Press, 1997.

Yu, Chai-shin, ed. *Korean and Asian Religious Tradition*. Toronto: Korean and Related Studies Press, 1977.

Japanese Religion

Aston, William G., trans. *Nihongi: Chronicles of Japan from the Earliest Times to A.D. 197*. London: Kegan Paul, 1896.

Bellah, Robert Neelly. *Tokugawa Religion: The Cultural Roots of Modern Japan*. Boston: Beacon Press, 1970.

Blacker, Carmen. *The Catalpa Bow: A Study of Shamanistic Practices in Japan*. London: Unwin Paperbacks, 1989.

Bocking, Brian. *A Popular Dictionary of Shinto*. Richmond: Curzon Press, 1996.

Bowring, Richard and Peter Kornicki, eds. *The Cambridge Encyclopedia of Japan*. Cambridge: Cambridge University Press, 1993.

Davis, Winston Bradley. *Japanese Religion and Society: Paradigms of Structure and Change*. Albany: State University of New York Press, 1992.

Earhart, H. Byron. *Japanese Religion: Unity and Diversity*. 3rd ed., Belmont: Wadsworth, 1982.

Earhart, H. Byron. *Religion in the Japanese Experience: Sources and Interpretations*. 2nd ed., Belmont: Wadsworth, 1997.

Hardacre, Helen. *Shinto and the State, 1868–1988*. Princeton: Princeton University Press, 1989.

Hori, Ichiro. *Folk Religion in Japan: Continuity and Change*. Chicago: University of Chicago Press, 1968.

Kageyama, Haruki. *The Arts of Shinto*. New York: Weatherhill Press, 1973.

Kato, Genichi. *A Historical Study of the Religious Development of Shinto*. New York: Greenwood Press, 1988.

Kitagawa, Joseph M. *On Understanding Japanese Religion*. Princeton: Princeton University Press, 1987.

Kitagawa, Joseph M. *Religion in Japanese History*. New York: Columbia University Press, 1966.

Muraoka, Tsunetsuga. *Studies in Shinto Thought*. Trans. by Delmer Brown and James Araki. Tokyo: Ministry of Education, 1964.

Reader, Ian T. *Religion in Contemporary Japan*. Basingstoke: Macmillan, 1991.

Reader, Ian T. *Simple Guide to Shinto*. London: Global Books, 1998.

Schnell, Scott. *The Rousing Drum: Ritual Practice in a Japanese Community*. Honolulu: University of Hawaii Press, 1999.

Sered, Susan. *Women of the Sacred Grove: Divine Priestesses of Okinawa*. New York: Oxford University Press, 1999.

Tanabe, George J., Jr., ed. *Religions of Japan in Practice*. Princeton: Princeton University Press, 1999.

Thomsen, Harry. *The New Religions of Japan*. Rutland: Tuttle, 1963.

Tsunoda, Ryusuku, ed. *Sources of Japanese Tradition*. New York: Columbia University Press, 1958.

Primary Sources

The following is a representative selection of writings drawn from the various religious traditions of Asia. Although it provides insights into the ways in which Asian religions understand both themselves and the world around them, it is not exhaustive and the extracts have not been chosen to illustrate specific points of doctrine. Rather, they are meant to give an opportunity of sensing the rhythm and cadence of such writings. Thus the reader can experience the text in a form that would be familiar to the adherents of the various faiths. In general, I have opted for selections by translators other than those cited in the body of the book. This is to show how different translators approach the same text from different angles, and how the words they choose can alter the feel and even the meaning of the work.

The primary sources presented here can undoubtedly give only a cursory glimpse of the rich and varied religious literatures of Asia. For a much more detailed overview, consult the Penguin/Longman *Reader of Asian Religions*.

Contents

Hinduism

Rig Veda (c. 1400 B.C.E.)

Wendy Doniger O'Flaherty (tr.). *The Rig Veda, An Anthology*. London: Penguin, 1981.

Indra was the principal god to whom the Aryan people of India directed their sacrifices for much of the Vedic period. The king of the gods, he was the god most often mentioned in the Rig Veda. Today, he is virtually forgotten, and his cult has disappeared from present-day Hinduism.

The God Indra (2.12)

The god who had insight the moment he was born, the first who protected the gods with his power of thought, before whose hot breath the two world-halves tremble at the greatness of his manly powers—he, my people, is Indra. He who made fast the tottering earth, who made still the quaking mountains, who measured out and extended the expanse of the air, who propped up the sky—he, my people, is Indra. He who killed the serpent and loosed the seven rivers, who drove out the cows that had been pent up by Vala, who gave birth to fire between two stones, the winner of booty in combats—he, my people, is Indra. He by whom all these changes were rung, who drove the race of Dasas down into obscurity, who took away the flourishing wealth of the enemy as a winning gambler takes the stake—he, my people, is Indra. [5] He about whom they ask, "Where is he?," or they say of him, the terrible one, "He does not exist," he who diminishes the flourishing wealth of the enemy as gambling does—believe in him! He, my people is Indra. He who encourages the weary and the sick, and the poor priest who is in need, who helps the man who harnesses the stones to press Soma, he who has lips fine for drinking—he, my people, is Indra.

He under whose command are horses and cows and villages and all chariots, who gave birth to the sun and the dawn and led out the waters, he, my people, is Indra. He who is invoked by both of two armies, enemies locked in combat, on this side and that side, he who is even invoked separately by each of two men standing on the very same chariot, he, my people, is Indra. He without whom people do not conquer, he whom they call on for help when they are fighting, who became the image of everything, who shakes the unshakable—he, my people, is Indra. [10] He who killed with

his weapon all those who had committed a great sin, even when they did not know it, he who does not pardon the arrogant man for his arrogance, who is the slayer of the Dasyus, he, my people, is Indra. He who in the fortieth autumn discovered Sambara living in the mountains, who killed the violent serpent, the Danu, as he lay there, he, my people, is Indra. He, the mighty bull who with his seven reins let loose the seven rivers to flow, who with his thunderbolt in his hand hurled down Rauhina as he was climbing up to the sky, he, my people, is Indra. Even the sky and the earth bow low before him, and the mountains are terrified of his hot breath. He who is known as the Soma-drinker, with the thunderbolt in his hand, with the thunderbolt in his palm, he, my people, is Indra. He who helps with his favor the one who presses and the one who cooks, the praiser and the preparer, he for whom prayer is nourishment, for whom Soma is the special gift, he, my people, is Indra. [15] You who furiously grasp the prize for the one who presses and the one who cooks, you are truly real. Let us be dear to you, Indra, all our days, and let us speak as men of power in the sacrificial gathering.

Upanishads (c. 800–500 B.C.E.)

Patrick Olivelle (tr.). *Upaniṣads*. Oxford: Oxford University Press, 1996.

The Upanishads marked the first major movement away from the traditional sacrifice-oriented religion of the early Aryans. In these texts we see for the first time concerted speculation about the nature of the universe, the constitution of the human being, and the means necessary to gain liberation from the cycle of life and death.

Chandogya Upanishad (6.1.1)

6.1.1 There was one Śvetaketu, the son of Āruni. One day his father told him: "Śvetaketu, take up the celibate life of a student, for there is no one in our family, my son, who has not studied and is the kind of Brahmin who is so only because of birth."

Shvetashvatara Upanishad (1.8; 1.10–12; 1.15–16; 2.8–17)

1.8 This whole world is the perishable and the imperishable, the manifest and the unmanifest joined together—and the Lord bears it, while the self (*ātman*), who is not the Lord, remains bound, because he is the enjoyer. When he comes to know God, he is freed from all fetters. . . . .

1.10   The primal source is perishable, while Hara is immortal and imperishable. The one God rules over both the perishable and the self (*ātman*). By meditating on him, by striving towards him, and, further, in the end by becoming the same reality as him, all illusion disappears.

1.11   When one has known God, all the fetters fall off; by the eradication of the blemishes, birth and death come to an end; by meditating on him, one obtains, at the dissolution of the body, a third—sovereignty over all; and in the absolute one's desires are fulfilled.

1.12   This can be known, for it abides always within one's body (*ātman*). Higher than that there is nothing to be known. When the enjoyer discerns the object of enjoyment and the impeller—everything has been taught. That is the threefold *brahman*. . . .

1.15   Like oil in sesame seeds and butter in curds, like water in the river-bed and fire in the fire-drills, so, when one seeks it with truth and austerity, one grasps that self (*ātman*) in the body (*ātman*)—that all-pervading self, which is contained [in the body], like butter in milk.

1.16   That is *brahman*, the highest object of the teachings on hidden connections (*upaniṣad*), an object rooted in austerity and the knowledge of the self. . . .

2.8   When he keeps his body straight, with the three sections erect, and draws the senses together with the mind into his heart, a wise man shall cross all the frightful rivers with the boat consisting of that formulation (*brahman*).

2.9   Compressing his breaths in here and curbing his movements, a man should exhale through one nostril when his breath is exhausted. A wise man should keep his mind vigilantly under control, just as he would that wagon yoked to unruly horses.

2.10   Level and clean; free of gravel, fire, and sand; near noiseless running waters and the like; pleasing to the mind but not offensive to the eye; provided with a cave or a nook sheltered from the wind—in such a spot should one engage in yogic practice.

2.11   Mist, smoke, sun, wind, fire, fireflies, lightning, crystal, moon—these are the apparitions that, within yogic practice, precede and pave the way to the full manifestation in *brahman*.

2.12   When earth, water, fire, air, and ether have arisen together, and the body made up of these five becomes equipped with the attribute of yoga, that man, obtaining a body tempered by the fire of yoga, will no longer experience sickness, old age, or suffering.

2.13   Lightness, health, the absence of greed, a bright complexion, a pleasant voice, a sweet smell, and very little faeces and urine—that, they say, is the first working of yogic practice.

2.14   Just as a disk smeared with clay, once it is cleaned well, shines brightly, so also an embodied person, once he has perceived the true nature of the self, becomes solitary, his goal attained, and free from sorrow.

2.15   When, by means of the true nature of the self, which resembles a lamp, a man practising yogic restraint sees here the true nature of *brahman*, he is freed from all fetters, because he has known God, unborn, unchanging, and unsullied by all objects.

2.16   This God does pervade all quarters. He was born the first, yet he remains within the womb. He it is, who was born; he, who will be born. His face everywhere, he stands turning west towards men.

2.17   He who abides as God in the fire; who abides in the waters; who has entered every being; who abides in the plants; who abides in the trees—to that God adoration! Adoration!

The Laws of Manu (c. 200 B.C.E.–300 C.E.)

Wendy Doniger and Brian K. Smith (tr.). *The Laws of Manu.* London: Penguin, 1991.

Religion and the social order are inseparable in Hinduism. The following selections from the Laws of Manu, the most widely followed of the dharmashastras *or books of socio-religious rules and regulations, discuss questions of marriage.*

Chapter 3

[1] The vow for studying the three Vedas with a guru is for thirty-six years, or half of that, or a quarter of that, or whenever the undertaking comes to an end. [2] When, unswerving in his chastity, he has learned the Vedas, or two Vedas, or even one Veda, in the proper order, he should enter the householder stage of life. [3] When he is recognized as one who has, by fulfilling his own duties, received the legacy of the Veda from his father, he should first be seated on a couch, adorned with garlands, and honoured with (an offering made from the milk of) a cow.

[4] When he has received his guru's permission and bathed and performed the ritual for homecoming according to the rules, a twice-born man should marry a wife who is of the same class and has the right marks. [5] A woman who is neither a co-feeding relative on her mother's side nor belongs to the same lineage (of the sages) on her father's side, and who is a virgin, is recommended for marriage to twice-born men. [6] When a man connects himself with a woman, he should avoid the ten following families, even if they are great, or rich in cows, goats, sheep, property, or grain: [7] a family that has abandoned the rites, or does not have male children, or does not chant the Veda; and those families in which they have hairy bodies, piles, consumption, weak digestion, epilepsy, white leprosy, or black leprosy.

[8] A man should not marry a girl who is a redhead or has an extra limb or is sickly or has no body hair or too much body hair or talks too much or is sallow; [9] or who is named after a constellation, a tree, or a river, or who has a low-caste name, or is named after a mountain, a bird, a snake, or has a menial or frightening name. [10] He should marry a woman who does not lack any part of her body and who has a pleasant name, who walks like a goose or an elephant, whose body hair and hair on the head is fine, whose teeth are not big, and who has delicate limbs. [11] A wise man will not marry a woman who has no brother or whose father is unknown, for fear that she may be an appointed daughter or that he may act wrongly.

[12] A woman of the same class is recommended to twice-born men for the first marriage; but for men who are driven by desire, these are the women, in progressively descending order: [13] According to tradition, only a servant woman can be the wife of a servant; she and one of his own class can be the wife of a commoner; these two and one of his own class for a king; and these three and one of his own class for a priest. [14] Not a single story mentions a servant woman as the wife of a priest or a ruler, even in extremity. [15] Twice-born men who are so infatuated as to marry women of low caste quickly reduce their families, including the descendants, to the status of servants. [16] A man falls when he weds a servant woman, according to Atri and to (Gautama) the son of Utathya, or when he has a son by her, according to Śaunaka, or when he has any children by her, according to Bhṛgu. [17] A priest who climbs into bed with a servant woman goes to hell; if he begets a son in her, he loses the status of priest. [18] The ancestors and the gods do not eat the offerings to the gods, to the ancestors, and to guests that such a man makes with her, and so he does not go to heaven. [19] No redemption is prescribed for a man who drinks the saliva from the lips of a servant woman or is tainted by her breath or begets a son in her.

[20] Now learn, in summary, these eight ways of marrying women, that are for all four classes, for better and for worse, here on earth and after death: [21] the marriages named after Brahmā, the gods, the sages, the Lord of Creatures, the demons, the centaurs, the ogres, and, eighth and lowest, the ghouls. [22] I will explain to you all about which one is right for each class, and the virtues and vices of each, and their advantages and disadvantages for progeneration. [23] It should be understood that the first six, as they are listed in order, are right for a priest, the last four for a ruler, and these same four, with the exception of the ogre marriage, for a commoner or a servant. [24] The poets say that the first four are recommended for a priest, only one, the ogre marriage, for a ruler, and the demon marriage for a commoner and a servant. [25] But here, three of the (last) five are right, while two—those of the ghouls and the demons—are traditionally regarded as wrong and are never to be performed. [26] Two of the marriages mentioned above, those according to the centaurs and the ogres, are traditionally regarded as right for rulers, whether they are used separately or combined.

[27] It is said to be the law of Brahmā when a man dresses his daughter and adorns her and he himself gives her as a gift to a man he has summoned, one who knows the revealed canon and is of good character. [28] They call it the law of the gods when a man adorns his daughter and,

in the course of a sacrifice, gives her as a gift to the officiating priest who is properly performing the ritual. [29] It is called the sages' law when he gives away his daughter by the rules, after receiving from the bridegroom a cow and a bull, or two cows and bulls, in accordance with the law. [30] The tradition calls it the rule of the Lord of Creatures when a man gives away his daughter after adorning her and saying "May the two of you together fulfil your duties."

[31] It is called the demonic law when a man takes a girl because he wants her himself, when he has given as much wealth as he can to her relatives and to the girl herself. [32] It is to be recognized as a centaur marriage when the girl and her lover join with one another in sexual union because they want to, out of desire. [33] It is called the rule of the ogres when a man forcibly carries off a girl out of her house, screaming and weeping, after he has killed, wounded, and broken. [34] The lowest and most evil of marriages, known as that of the ghouls, takes place when a man secretly has sex with a girl who is asleep, drunk, or out of her mind. [35] For priests, the gift of a girl with (a libation of) water is the best (marriage); but for other classes (the best is) when they desire one another.

[36] Listen, priests, while I tell you fully about all the qualities of these marriages that Manu has proclaimed. [37] If a son born to a woman who has had the Brahmā marriage does good deeds, he frees from guilt ten of the ancestors who came before him, ten later descendants, and himself as the twenty-first. [38] A son born to a woman who had a marriage of the gods (frees) seven ancestors and seven descendants, a son born to a woman who had a marriage of the sages (frees) three (of each), and a son born to a woman who had a marriage of the Lord of Creatures (frees) six (of each). [39] The sons born from these four marriages, in order beginning with the Brahmā marriage, are filled with the splendour of the Veda and are esteemed by educated men. [40] Beautiful and endowed with the quality of lucidity, rich and famous, enjoying life to the fullest, most religious, they live for a hundred years. [41] But from those (four) other remaining bad marriages are born cruel sons, liars who hate the Veda and religion. [42] Out of the blameless marriages with women come blameless progeny. Blameworthy progeny come to men from blameworthy (marriages); therefore one should avoid the blameworthy ones.

[43] The transformative ritual of taking the bride by the hand is prescribed for women of the same class; know that this (following) procedure is for the marriage ritual with women of a different class. [44] When a woman marries a man of superior class, a woman of the ruler class must take hold of an arrow, a commoner girl a whip, and a servant woman must grasp the fringe of (his) garment.

[45] A man should have sex with his wife during her fertile season, and always find his satisfaction in his own wife; when he desires sexual pleasure he should go to her to whom he is vowed, except on the days at the (lunar) junctures. [46] The natural fertile season of women is traditionally said to last for sixteen nights, though these include four special days that good people despise. [47] Among these (nights), the first four, the eleventh, and the thirteenth are disapproved; the other ten nights are approved. [48] On the even nights, sons are conceived, and on the uneven nights, daughters; therefore a man who wants sons should unite with his wife during her fertile season on the even nights. [49] A male child is born when the semen of the man is greater (than that of the woman), and a female child when (the semen) of the woman is greater (than that of the man); if both are equal, a hermaphrodite is born, or a boy and a girl; and if (the semen) is weak or scanty, the opposite will occur. [50] A man who avoids women on the (six) disapproved nights and on the eight other nights is regarded as chaste, no matter which of the four stages of life he is in.

Puranas (c. 200–500 C.E.)

Wendy Doniger O'Flaherty (tr.). *Hindu Myths.* London: Penguin, 1975.

The Puranas are the mythological repositories of Hinduism. The first selection in this section tells the tale of the birth of the popular god Ganesha, the son of Shiva and Parvati, and the story of how he came by his elephant head. The second selection describes how the god Vishnu tricked the asuras out of their power through the creation of the non-Hindu Indian religions of Jainism and Buddhism.

From the Brhaddharma Purana

[Jaimini said,] This whole universe is filled everywhere with the descendants of Brahmā and Viṣṇu; tell me about the descendants of Śiva. [The sage replied,] Śiva is man and Pārvatī is woman; they are the causes of creation. All men have Śiva as their soul, and all women are Pārvatī. Śiva has the form of the male sign [*liṅga*], and the Goddess has the form of the female sign [*yoni*]; the universe, moving and still, has the form of the sign of Śiva and the Goddess. Thus this whole universe consists of Śiva's descendants and has Śiva for its soul, but Śiva has no separate descendants such as you are asking about, Jaimini . . .

Once, long ago, the daughter of the mountain made a request of Śaṅkara, who gives peace to the world; for she wished to have progeny even though, being the Goddess, she dwells in all progeny. She said, "No rituals are performed for a man who has no descendants; therefore you should have descendants to follow you. Unite with me this very day and beget a natural son." When Śaṅkara, who gives peace to the world, heard what the daughter of the king of the mountains said, he murmured honeyed words to her, saying, "Daughter of the mountain, I am not a householder, and I have no use for a son. The wicked circle of the gods presented you to me as a wife, but a wife is certainly the greatest fetter for a man who is free of passion; moreover, dear lady, progeny are described as a noose and a stake. Now, householders have need of a son and of wealth, and a wife is useful for a son, and sons are useful to give oblations to the ancestors. But I have no death, Goddess, and so I have no use for a son. Where there is no disease, what need is there for medicinal herbs? You are woman, and I am man; let us enjoy being the two causes from which progeny arise and rejoice in the pleasures of men and women; without progeny, let us always sport, taking pleasure in ourselves."

Pārvatī said, "Lord god of gods, blue-necked, three-eyed, what you have said is indeed true, but nevertheless I do wish for a little child. When you have begotten a child, you can do your yoga, great lord; I will bring up the son and you can be a yogi quite properly. An excessive yearning for the kiss of a son's mouth has arisen in me, and since you took me as your wife then you should beget a child in me. If you wish, your son will be averse to marriage, so that you will not have a son and grandson and subsequent descendants." When he heard this, the god became angry; he arose from his seat and went away. Then the Goddess became sad and brooded unhappily for a long time. Her two friends, Jayā and Vijayā, who had been staying with her, went to assuage Śiva's anger, and they won him over.

When Śaṅkara saw how sad the Goddess was, he said to her, "How can you be so sad just because you lack a son, beautiful goddess? If you want to kiss the face of a son all over, I will make a son for you; kiss him if you yearn to do so." As he said this, Śiva pulled at the gown of the daughter of the mountain and made a son with that fabric, and then Śaṅkara said, "Daughter of the mountain, take your son and kiss him as much as you wish." Pārvatī said, "How can this piece of cloth be the source of a son for me? This is my red dress. Stop teasing me, great lord Śiva; I do not have the mentality of a common beast. How shall I rejoice in a son obtained by means of a piece of cloth?" But when she had said this, the Goddess born of the mountain made the cloth into the shape of a son, and she held him to her breast, brooding upon the teasing words of her husband.

And when that cloth in the form of a son had touched the breast of the Goddess, it came to life and fell from her breast, and it quivered and quickened more and more. As she saw it quickening, Pārvatī cried out, "Live, live!", and she caressed it with the two lotuses which she held in her hands as she spoke before Śiva. Then the boy came to life, getting his life's breath at that very moment, and he made Pārvatī rejoice as he cried out indistinctly, "Mama! Mama!" The Goddess took the little boy and was filled with maternal love; she held him to her breast and gave him her breasts to suck, and milk flowed from her breasts. As the boy drank the milk, his lotus face broke into a smile, and he gazed up at his mother's face and she kissed his face all over.

When she had embraced him for a moment, she gave the beautiful little boy to her husband, the great lord, and said, "Husband, take my son. You gave me this son when your heart was softened by pity, and I want you too, Śaṅkara, to know how great is the happiness of having a son." When Śaṅkara heard what the Goddess had said, he smiled a little and said to the daughter of the mountain, who was now dearer to him, "Goddess, I gave you a son made out of cloth to tease you, but he became a true son by your good fortune. What is this miracle? Give him to me and let me see; he has indeed become a real son, but his body was made out of cloth; whence did life enter it?" As he said this, Śambhu, the lord of the mountain, took his son in his hands and laid him down; he looked at him carefully and minutely, inspecting all his limbs with an acute scrutiny. But then, remembering the flaw in his birth, Śaṅkara said to the goddess Pārvatī, "This son of yours was born with an injury wrought by the planet of suicides, and therefore your son will not live for a long time, but in a very short time an auspicious death will come to this short-lived son. The death of one who has acquired virtues causes the greatest sorrow." As Śambhu, the maker of the child, said this, the boy's head, which was pointing toward the north, fell from Śiva's hand.

When the little boy's head had fallen to the ground from her husband's hand, Pārvatī was overcome with grief; she took up the boy whose head had been cut off, and she wept copiously, crying out over and over, "My little baby, my baby" Śiva, astonished, took his son's head in his hand and spoke to the goddess Pārvatī with honeyed words, saying, "Do not cry, lovely Pārvatī, though you grieve for your son. There is no grief greater than the grief for a son, nothing that so withers the soul. Therefore stop sorrowing for your son; I will bring your son to life. Goddess, join this head onto his shoulders." The goddess Pārvatī joined that head on as he had told her to do, but it did not join firmly. Then Śiva thought about this, and at that very moment a disembodied voice in the sky said, "Śambhu, this head of your boy has been injured by a harmful glance, and therefore your little boy will not live with this head. Put the head of someone else upon his shoulders and revive him. Since the boy was held in your hand with his head facing north, therefore bring here the head of someone facing north and join it to him." When Śaṅkara heard this voice from the sky, he consoled the Goddess and summoned Nandin and sent him on this mission.

Nandin wandered over the triple universe and came to Amarāvatī, where he saw Airāvata, the elephant of Indra, with his head facing north. When the mighty Nandin saw Airāvata lying down facing north, he started to cut off his head, but the elephant began to trumpet and roar, and Śakra came there with the other gods and said, "Who are you who have come in this extraordinary form to kill the elephant? Who sent you, and why do you carry a sword in your hand?" Nandin said, "I am Nandin, the servant of Śiva, and I have come at Śiva's command. I will take the head of Airāvata and give it to Śambhu. The head of Śiva's son, who was facing north, fell from Śiva's hand because of his harmful fate, and a voice from the sky said, 'When the head of someone lying down facing north is fastened to his body, I will give the son of Śiva a head and bring him to life.' Therefore I will definitely cut off the head of your king of elephants. If you wish to keep your own life's breath, abandon your hope for Airāvata and go away, for no one is better suited than your Airāvata to give life's breath to the son of Śiva."

When the great Indra heard this speech of Nandin he became angry; he summoned all the gods and replied to Nandin, "How can you, the minion of Śambhu who lives in the wilderness, intend to cut up my elephant by force when I, the king of the gods, am alive?" And as he said this, Śakra took up a trident to kill Nandin, but Nandin attacked and reduced the trident to ashes with a roar. Then Indra took up a mace and hurled it violently, but Nandin took the mace playfully in his left hand, saying, "Take your own mace, Indra," and threw it at him. The mace fell on Indra's chest, fracturing it painfully, and Indra reeled in agony. He picked up another trident and hurled it at Nandin, but Nandin cut it into three pieces with his sword. Then Indra took up his thunderbolt and rushed again like the wind, and Nandin became even more horrible, unbearably frightening.

At this moment, the powerful driver of Śakra's elephant brought Airāvata, who was in rut, to Indra. The mighty Indra mounted the elephant and took his thunderbolt in his hand; aided by the army of the Maruts, he fought with Nandin. All the armies of the gods surrounded him, with their bows in their hands, and they sent a rain of arrows down upon the dreadful Nandin as clouds send rain down upon a great mountain in the violent time of the monsoon. But Nandin, whose monstrous body was a hard as a rock and marvellous to behold, withstood that rain of arrows, repelling them with parries of his left hand, with his sharp sword, and with fierce roaring snorts, stupefying them with his terrifying body. Then, while the gods looked on, he cut off the head of Airāvata, and the severed head of Airāvata fell to the ground when Nandin had struck it off. The gods were bewildered by this marvel; they cried out "Alas!" and did not move.

When Śiva heard of Nandin's deed of valour he embraced him joyfully, and he placed the elephant head on his son's shoulders, and the moment that the head was joined on, the boy became surpassingly beautiful. The god was rather short and fat, with the lotus face of a king of elephants; his face was bright as the moon, red as a China rose. He had four arms and was adorned by bees attracted by the perfume of his flowing ichor, and with his marvellous three eyes he shone in Śiva's presence. All the gods came there and saw the son of Śiva who had the auspicious head of the king of elephants, and Śambhu held the boy to his breast. Then Brahmā and the other gods anointed him, and Brahmā gave him names, calling him "Pot-bellied". The marvellous child shone [rarāja] in the midst of all the gods, and so they said, "Let him be king [rājā] of the gods, worshipped before all the gods." Then Sarasvatī gave him a writing pen with coloured inks, and Brahmā gave him a rosary of beads, and Indra gave him an elephant goad. Padmavatī gave him a lotus, and Śiva gave him a tiger skin. Bṛhaspati gave him a sacrificial thread, and the goddess Earth gave him a rat for his vehicle.

Then all the sages praised the red son of Śiva, and Brahmā said, "Śambhu, this is your son; you are he, there is no doubt, and he will be worshipped before all the gods except you, great lord, for you, great lord, are to be honoured first and last. The great-armed one has become the ruler of all the hosts [gaṇas] of the gods, and he is ruler of your hosts, too, and so let him be called Ruler-of the-hosts [Gaṇādhipa or Gaṇeśa]. Since he has the head of an elephant, let him be called Elephant-headed (Gajānana); and since, when Nandin performed his marvellous deed and conquered Indra and struck the elephant, the tusk of his head was broken, let him be called One-tusk [Ekadantaka]. Let him be called Heramba and always have the form of a seed, and because of his corpulence, Śiva, let this son of yours be called Pot-bellied [Lambodara]. By merely thinking of him, all those who would create obstacles become afraid, and so, Śaṅkara, let this son of yours be called Lord-of-obstacles [Vighneśa]. Anyone undertaking a journey or a worthy project should remember Gaṇādhipa and his journey will be fruitful, his undertaking successful in its outcome. Gaṇādhipa is to be honoured in all auspicious affairs, for when Gaṇeśa is honoured, the gods are honoured, and they will accomplish the affair."

Brahmā said this and stopped, but Indra, grieving at the absence of Airāvata, said to Śiva, "Greatest of gods, great god, three-eyed lord of Pārvatī, lord of the triple universe, I bow to you. Your powerful servant, Nandin, slew my elephant and in my ignorance I fought with him. Forgive me, O god, great lord. It is said, 'You should give even your own head to one who begs', but I did not wish to give my elephant's head to him. Forgive me for that." Then Śiva said, "Throw Airāvata, headless, into the ocean, and you will obtain your king of elephants again when he arises from the churning of the ocean. And since you gave Airāvata's head to my son, therefore I will also give you an immortal bull." When the god Indra, the son of Kaśyapa, heard this, he went to heaven, and Brahmā and the other gods received the veneration due to them and went to their own homes. Then the goddess Pārvatī, rejoicing, cared for Gaṇeśa, and Gaṇeśa became a great yogi, averse to worldly attachments, and all the sages assembled and praised Gaṇeśa . . . and went away again.

This, O Jaimini, is the meritorious story of the birth of Gaṇeśa. But there are no descendants of Śambhu, who is the very form of final universal destruction. His other son, mentioned first, is Kārttikeya, the youth [Kumāra]; he did not marry either, but kept his vow of chastity [kaumāra].

From the Visnu Purana

There was once a battle between the gods and the demons that lasted for a hundred celestial years, in which the gods were conquered by the demons commanded by Hrāda. The gods went to the northern shore of the ocean of milk and practised asceticism in order to propitiate Viṣṇu, and they sang a hymn of praise to him . . . When they had finished praising him, the gods saw the supreme lord Hari mounted on the Garuḍa bird, with his conch and discus and mace in his hands. All the gods prostrated themselves before him and said, "Have mercy, lord; protect us from the demons, as we have come for refuge. The demons under the command of Hrāda have stolen away our portions of the sacrifices of the triple world, but they have not violated the command of Brahmā, O supreme lord. Even though we and they are both born of portions of you, who are the essence of all creatures, nevertheless we see the universe as divided, a distinction caused by ignorance. They take pleasure in the duties of their own class, and they follow the path of the Vedas and are full of ascetic powers. Therefore we cannot kill them, although they are our enemies, and so you should devise some means by which we will be able to kill the demons, O lord, soul of everything without exception."

When the lord Viṣṇu heard their request, he emitted from his body a deluding form of his magic power of illusion, and he gave it to the supreme gods and said, "This magic deluder will bewitch all the demons so that they will be excluded from the path of the Vedas, and thus they will be susceptible to slaughter. For no matter how many gods, demons, or others obstruct the way of the authority of Brahmā, I will slaughter them all in order to establish order. Therefore go away and do not fear; this magic deluder will go before you today and assist you, gods." When the gods heard this they prostrated themselves before him and went back whence they had come, and the magic deluder went with the great gods to the place where the great demons were.

When the magic deluder, naked, bald, carrying a bunch of peacock feathers, saw that the great demons had gone to the banks of the Narmadā river and were practising asceticism, he spoke to the demons with smooth words, saying, "Lord of demons! Tell me why you are practising asceticism—do you wish for the fruits of asceticism in this world or in the world beyond?" The demons replied, "Noble one, we have undertaken this practice of asceticism in order to obtain the fruits of the world beyond. What is there here for you to dispute?" he said, "Do as I say, if you wish for release, for you are worthy of this *dharma* which is the open door to release. This is the *dharma* worthy of release, and there is none better than this; by following it you will obtain heaven or release. All of you, mighty ones, are worthy of this *dharma*." With many deductions, examples, and arguments of this sort, the magic deluder led the demons from the path of the Vedas: "this would be *dharma*, but it would not be *dharma*; this is, but it is not; this would give release, but it would not give release; this is the supreme object, but it is also not the supreme object; this is effect, but it is not effect; this is not crystal clear. This is the *dharma* of those who are naked; this is the *dharma* of those who wear many clothes." Thus the magic deluder taught a varying doctrine of more than one conclusion to the demons, who abandoned their own *dharma*. And they who took refuge in this dharma became Ārhatas, because the magic deluder said to them, "You are worthy [*arhata*] of this great *dharma*."

When the magic deluder had caused the demons to abandon the *dharma* of the triple Vedas, they themselves became his disciples and persuaded others; and yet others were persuaded by these, and still others by those, and so in a few days most of the demons abandoned the three Vedas. Then the magic deluder, who had subdued his senses, put on a red garment and went and spoke to other demons in soft, short, and honeyed words: "If you demons wish for heaven or for Nirvāṇa, then realize that you must stop these evil rites such as killing animals. Comprehend that all this universe is perceived only by means of knowledge; understand my speech properly, for it has been said by wise men. All this universe is without support and is intent upon achieving what it mistakenly believes to be knowledge; it wanders in the straits of existence, corrupted by passion and the other emotions." As he said to them over and over, "Understand! [*budhyata*]," the magic deluder caused the demons to abandon their own *dharma*, and with various speeches employing logic he made them gradually abandon the *dharma* of the triple Vedas. Then they spoke in this way to others, who addressed yet others in this way, so that they abandoned the highest *dharma* which is taught in the Vedas and lawbooks.

Then the magic deluder, capable of producing total delusion, corrupted other demons with many other sorts of heresy, and in a very short time the demons were corrupted by the magic deluder and abandoned the entire teaching of the triple path of the Vedas. Some reviled the Vedas; others the gods; and others the collection of sacrificial rituals and the twice-born. "This speech is not logical, that 'injury is conducive to *dharma*'." "It is the babbling of a child, to say that butter burnt as an oblation in the fire is productive of reward." "If the *śamī* fire-sticks and other wood are consumed by Indra, who has become a god by means of many sacrifices, then a beast who eats leaves is better than Indra." "If an animal slaughtered in the sacrifice is thus promised entry into heaven, why does not the sacrificer kill his own father?" "If the oblation to the ancestors which is eaten by one man satisfies another, then people travelling abroad need not take the trouble to carry food." "When you have understood what contemptible people will believe in, then the words I have uttered will please you. The words of authority do not fall from the sky, great demons; only the speech based upon logic should be accepted by men and by others like you."

When the magic deluder had made the demons free-thinkers with many speeches like this, not one of them took pleasure in the triple Vedas. And when the demons were thus set upon the wrong path, the immortals made the supreme effort and prepared for battle. Then the battle between the gods and demons was resumed, and the gods slew the demons, who now stood in opposition to the right path. The armour of their own *dharma* which had at first been theirs had formerly protected them, and when it was destroyed, they were destroyed.

Bhagavad Gita (c. 200 B.C.E.–200 C.E.)

Juan Mascaró (tr.). *The Bhagavad Gita*. London: Penguin, 1962.

The Bhagavad Gita is undoubtedly the most beloved scripture in modern Hinduism. In this selection, Krishna reveals himself as the supreme deity in response to his friend Arjuna's request to see him as he truly is.

Chapter 11

ARJUNA

1 In thy mercy thou hast told me the secret supreme of thy Spirit, and thy words have dispelled my delusion.

2 I have heard, in full from thee of the coming and going of beings, and also of thy infinite greatness.

3 I have heard thy words of truth, but my soul is yearning to see: to see thy form as God of this all.

4 If thou thinkest, O my Lord, that it can be seen by me, show me, O God of Yoga, the glory of thine own Supreme Being.

KRISHNA

5 By hundreds and then by thousands, behold Arjuna, my manifold celestial forms of innumerable shapes and colours.

6 Behold the gods of the sun, and those of fire and light; the gods of storm and lightning, and the two luminous charioteers of heaven. Behold, descendant of Bharata, marvels never seen before.

7 See now the whole universe with all things that move and move not, and whatever thy soul may yearn to see. See it all as One in me.

8 But thou never canst see me with these thy mortal eyes: I will give thee divine sight. Behold my wonder and glory.

SANJAYA

9 When Krishna, the God of Yoga, had thus spoken, O king, he appeared then to Arjuna in his supreme divine form.

10 And Arjuna saw in that form countless visions of wonder: eyes from innumerable faces, numerous celestial ornaments, numberless heavenly weapons;

11 Celestial garlands and vestures, forms anointed with heavenly perfumes. The Infinite Divinity was facing all sides, all marvels in him containing.

12 If the light of a thousand suns suddenly arose in the sky, that splendour might be compared to the radiance of the Supreme Spirit.

13 And Arjuna saw in that radiance the whole universe in its variety, standing in a vast unity in the body of the God of gods.

14 Trembling with awe and wonder, Arjuna bowed his head, and joining his hands in adoration he thus spoke to his God.

ARJUNA

15 I see in thee all the gods, O my God; and the infinity of the beings of thy creation. I see god Brahma on his throne of lotus, and all the seers and serpents of light.

16 All around I behold thy Infinity: the power of thy innumerable arms, the visions from thy innumerable eyes, the words from thy innumerable mouths, and the fire of life of thy innumerable bodies. Nowhere I see a beginning or middle or end of thee, O God of all, Form Infinite!

17 I see the splendour of an infinite beauty which illumines the whole universe. It is thee! With thy crown and sceptre and circle. How difficult thou art to see! But I see thee: as fire, as the sun, blinding, incomprehensible.

18 Thou art the Imperishable, the highest End of knowledge, the support of this vast universe. Thou, the everlasting ruler of the law of righteousness, the Spirit who is and who was at the beginning.

19 I see thee without beginning, middle, or end; I behold thy infinite power, the power of thy innumerable arms. I see thine eyes as the sun and the moon. And I see thy face as a sacred fire that gives light and life to the whole universe in the splendour of a vast offering.

20 Heaven and earth and all the infinite spaces are filled with thy Spirit; and before the wonder of thy fearful majesty the three worlds tremble.

21 The hosts of the gods come to thee and, joining palms in awe and wonder, they praise and adore. Sages and saints come to thee, and praise thee with songs of glory.

22 The Rudras of destruction, the Vasus of fire, the Sadhyas of prayers, the Adityas of the sun; the lesser gods Visve-Devas, the two Asvins charioteers of heaven, the Maruts of winds and storms, the Ushmapas spirits of ancestors; the celestial choirs of Gandharvas, the Yakshas keepers of wealth, the demons of hell and the

Siddhas who on earth reached perfection: they all behold thee with awe and wonder.

23 But the worlds also behold thy fearful mighty form, with many mouths and eyes, with many bellies, thighs and feet, frightening with terrible teeth; they tremble in fear, and I also tremble.

24 When I see thy vast form, reaching the sky, burning with many colours, with wide open mouths, with vast flaming eyes, my heart shakes in terror: my power is gone and gone is my peace, O Vishnu!

25 Like the fire at the end of Time which burns all in the last day, I see thy vast mouths and thy terrible teeth. Where am I? Where is my shelter? Have mercy on me, God of gods, Refuge Supreme of the world!

26, The sons of Dhrita-rashtra, all of them, with
27 other princes of this earth, and Bhishma and Drona and great Karna, and also the greatest warriors of our host, all enter rushing into thy mouths, terror-inspiring with their fearful fangs. Some are caught between them, and their heads crushed into powder.

28 As roaring torrents of waters rush forward into the ocean, so do these heroes of our mortal world rush into thy flaming mouths.

29 And as moths swiftly rushing enter a burning flame and die, so all these men rush to thy fire, rush fast to their own destruction.

30 The flames of thy mouths devour all the worlds. Thy glory fills the whole universe. But how terrible thy splendours burn!

31 Reveal thyself to me! Who art thou in this form of terror? I adore thee, O god supreme; be gracious unto me. I yearn to know thee, who art from the beginning: for I understand not thy mysterious works.

KRISHNA

32 I am all-powerful Time which destroys all things, and I have come here to slay these men. Even if thou dost not fight, all the warriors facing thee shall die.

33 Arise therefore! Win thy glory, conquer thine enemies, and enjoy thy kingdom. Through the fate of their Karma I have doomed them to die: be thou merely the means of my work.

34 Drona, Bhishma, Jayad-ratha and Karna, and other heroic warriors of this great war have already been slain by me: tremble not, fight and slay them. Thou shalt conquer thine enemies in battle.

SANJAYA

35 When Arjuna heard the words of Krishna he folded his hands trembling; and with a faltering voice, and bowing in adoration, he spoke.

ARJUNA

36 it is right, O God, that peoples sing thy praises, and that they are glad and rejoice in thee. All evil spirits fly away in fear; but the hosts of the saints bow down before thee.

37 How could they not bow down in love and adoration, before thee, God of gods, Spirit Supreme? Thou creator of Brahma, the god of creation, thou infinite, eternal, refuge of the world! Thou who art all that is, and all that is not, and all that is Beyond.

38 Thou God from the beginning, God in man since man was. Thou Treasure supreme of this vast universe. Thou the One to be known and the Knower, the final resting place. Thou infinite Presence in whom all things are.

39 God of the winds and the waters, of fire and death! Lord of the solitary moon, the Creator, the Ancestor of all! Adoration unto thee, a thousand adorations; and again and again unto thee adoration.

40 Adoration unto thee who art before me and behind me: adoration unto thee who art on all sides, God of all. All-powerful God of immeasurable might. Thou are the consummation of all: thou art all.

41 If in careless presumption, or even in friendliness, I said "Krishna! Son of Yadu! My friend!", this I did unconscious of thy greatness.

42 And if in irreverence I was disrespectful—when alone or with others—and made a jest of thee at games, or resting, or at a feast, forgive me in thy mercy, O thou Immeasurable!

43 Father of all. Master supreme. Power supreme in all the worlds. Who is like thee? Who is beyond thee?

44 I bow before thee, I prostrate in adoration; and I beg thy grace, O glorious Lord! As a father to his son, as a friend to his friend, as a lover to his beloved, be gracious unto me, O God.

45 In a vision I have seen what no man has seen before: I rejoice in exultation, and yet my heart trembles with fear. Have mercy upon me, Lord of gods, Refuge of the whole universe: show me again thine own human form.

46 I yearn to see thee again with thy crown and sceptre and circle. Show thyself to me again in thine own four-armed form, thou of arms infinite, Infinite form.

KRISHNA

47 By my grace and my wondrous power I have shown to thee, Arjuna, this form supreme made of light, which is the Infinite, the All: mine own form from the beginning, never seen by man before.

48 Neither Vedas, nor sacrifices, nor studies, nor benefactions, nor rituals, nor fearful austerities can give the vision of my Form Supreme. Thou alone hast seen this Form, thou the greatest of the Kurus.

49 Thou hast seen the tremendous form of my greatness, but fear not, and be not bewildered. Free from fear and with a glad heart see my friendly form again.

SANJAYA

50 Thus spoke Vasudeva to Arjuna, and revealed himself in his human form. The God of all gave peace to his fears and showed himself in his peaceful beauty.

ARJUNA

51 When I see thy gentle human face, Krishna, I return to my own nature, and my heart has peace.

KRISHNA

52 Thou hast seen now face to face my form divine so hard to see: for even the gods in heaven ever long to see what thou hast seen.

53 Not by the Vedas, or an austere life, or gifts to the poor, or ritual offerings can I be seen as thou hast seen me.

54 Only by love can men see me, and know me, and come unto me.

55 He who works for me, who loves me, whose End Supreme I am, free from attachment to all things, and with love for all creation, he in truth comes unto me.

The Teachings of Sri Ramana Maharshi (1879–1950 C.E.)

David Godman, ed. *Be As You Are: The Teachings of Sri Ramana Maharshi.* London: Arkana, 1985.

Ramana Maharshi was one of the greatest of the modern Hindu gurus. Although he never published any writings of his own, his disciples often took down his discussions with them, and passed them around among themselves. The following selection is a record of one such discussion between the guru and one of the disciples concerning religious practice.

Chapter 12: Life in the World

Q: *I have a good mind to resign from service and remain constantly with Sri Bhagavan (Ramana Maharshi).*

A: Bhagavan is always with you, in you, and you are yourself Bhagavan. To realise this it is neither necessary to resign your job nor run away from home. Renunciation does not imply apparent divesting of costumes, family ties, home, etc., but renunciation of desires, affection and attachment. There is no need to resign your job, only resign yourself to God, the bearer of the burden of all. One who renounces desires actually merges in the world and expands his love to the whole universe. Expansion of love and affection would be a far better term for a true devotee of God than renunciation, for one who renounces the immediate ties actually extends the bonds of affection and love to a wider world beyond the borders of caste, creed and race. A *sannyasi* who apparently casts away his clothes and leaves his home does not do so out of aversion to his immediate relations but because of the expansion of his love to others around him. When this expansion comes, one does not feel that one is running away from home, instead one drops from it like a ripe fruit from a tree. Till then it would be folly to leave one's home or job.

Q: *How does a* grihastha *[householder] fare in the scheme of* moksha *[liberation]? Should he not necessarily become a mendicant in order to attain liberation?*

A: Why do you think you are a *grihastha*? Similar thoughts that you are a *sannyasi* [wandering monk] will haunt you, even if you go out as a *sannyasi*. Whether you continue in the household or renounce it and go to the forest, your mind haunts you. The ego is the source of thought. It creates the body and the world and it makes you think of being the *grihastha*. If you renounce, it will only substitute the thought of *sannyasa* for that of *grihastha* and the environment of the forest for that of the household. But the mental obstacles are always there for you. They even increase greatly in the new surroundings. It is no help to change the environment. The one obstacle is the mind and it must be overcome whether in the home or in the forest. If you can do it in the forest, why not in the home? Therefore, why change the environment? Your efforts can be made even now, whatever the environment.

Q: *Is it possible to enjoy* samadhi *[awareness of reality] while busy in worldly work?*

A: The feeling "I work" is the hindrance. Ask yourself "Who works?" Remember who you are. Then the work will not bind you, it will go on automatically. Make no effort either to work or to renounce; it is your effort which is the bondage. What is destined to happen will happen. If you are destined not to work, work cannot be had even if you hunt for it. If you are destined to work, you will not be able to avoid it and you will be forced to engage yourself in it. So, leave it to the higher power; you cannot renounce or retain as you choose.

Q: *Bhagavan said yesterday that while one is engaged in search of God "within", "outer" work would go on automatically. In the life of Sri Chaitanya it is said that during his lectures to students he was really seeking Krishna within and he forgot all about his body and went on talking of Krishna only. This raises a doubt as to whether work can safely be left to itself. Should one keep part of one's attention on the physical work?*

A: The Self is all. Are you apart from the Self? Or can the work go on without the Self? The Self is universal so all actions will go on whether you strain yourself to be engaged in them or not. The work will go on of itself. Thus Krishna told Arjuna that he need not trouble to kill the Kauravas because they were already slain by God. It was not for him to resolve to work and worry himself about it, but to allow his own nature to carry out the will of the higher power.

Q: *But the work may suffer if I do not attend to it.*

A: Attending to the Self means attending to the work. Because you identify yourself with the body, you think that work is done by you. But the body and its activities, including that work, are not apart from the Self. What does it matter whether you attend to the work or not? When you walk from one place to another you do not attend to the steps you take and yet you find yourself after a time at your goal. You see how the business of walking goes on without your attending to it. So also with other kinds of work.[2]

Q: *If one holds the Self in remembrance, will one's actions always be right?*

A: They ought to be. However, such a person is not concerned with the right or wrong of actions. His actions are God's and therefore right.

Q: *How can my mind be still if I have to use it more than other people? I want to go into solitude and renounce my headmaster's work.*

A: No. You may remain where you are and go on with the work. What is the undercurrent which vivifies the mind, enables it to do all this work? It is the Self. So that is the real source of your activity. Simply be aware of it during your work and do not forget it. Contemplate in the background of your mind even whilst working. To do that, do not hurry, take your own time. Keep the remembrance of your real nature alive, even while working, and avoid haste which causes you to forget. Be deliberate. Practise meditation to still the mind and cause it to become aware of its true relationship to the Self which supports it. Do not imagine it is you who are doing the work. Think that it is the underlying current which is doing it. Identify yourself with the current. If you work unhurriedly, recollectedly, your work or service need not be a hindrance.

Sikhism

Japuji (c. 1500 C.E.)

Gurbachan Singh Talib (tr.). *Japuji: The Immortal Prayer-chant.* Munshiram Manoharlal Publishers Pvt. Ltd, 1977.

For Sikhs, the most important section of their scriptures, the Guru Granth Sahib, is the Japuji. This section of the scriptures, which is used daily in Sikh ritual and private devotions, is often memorized verbatim by pious Sikhs. Only selected portions of this long prayer are given here.

Mul Mantra (Fundamental Creed)

Ek Oankar Satti-Nam

The One Indivisible Supreme Being; Reality
Eternal; Creator-Purusha; Without Fear;
Without Rancour; Timeless Form; Unborn;
Self-Existent; Realized by Divine Grace.

Prayer-Chant
Adi Sach, Jugadi Sach

The Eternal, the Holy ever was; ever shall be.
Nothing is real but the Eternal.
Nothing shall last but the Eternal.

Stanza 1
Sochai soch na havaee je sochi lakh var

Ritual purification, though million-fold, may not
    purify the mind;
Nor may absorption in trance still it, however long
    and continuous.
Possessing worlds multiple quenches not the rage of
    avarice and desire.
A thousand and million feats of intellect bring not
    Emancipation.
How then to become pure in soul? How demolish
    the wall of Illusion?
Through obedience to His Command and Will—
Saith Nanak; This blessing too is pre-ordained.

2
Hukmin hovan akār Hukam na kahiya jāee

By Divine ordinance are all forms manifested;
Inexpressible is the Ordinance.
By Divine Ordinance are beings created;
By Ordinance is one exalted.
By Divine Ordinance are being marked with
    nobility or ignomiy;
By Ordinance are they visited with bliss or bale.
On some by Ordinance grace falls;
Some by Ordinance are whirled around in cycles of
    births and deaths.
All by Ordinance are governed, none exempt.
Saith Nanak: Should man realize the might of the
    Ordinance,
His ego he *most certainly* would disclaim.

3
Gāwai ko tān hovai kisai tān

Those endowed with might sing of God's might;
Those viewing marks of God's grace sing of His
    blessings.
Some sing of His noble attributes and exalted state.

Some express Him through philosophical
    intricacies and ratiocination.
Some tell of His giving life and taking it away.
Some sing of His transcendence;
To some is He ever manifest.
To singing of Him there is no end;
Millions upon millions sing endlessly of Him.
Eternally He doles out gifts;
Those receiving them at last can receive no more.
Infinitely the creation receives from Him
    sustenance.
He is the Ordainer;
By His Ordinance the universe He runs.
Saith Nanak: Ever is He in bliss.
Ever fulfilled.

4
Sāchā Sahib sach nāen bhākhiya bhāu apār

The Lord is holy; holy is His Name:
Infinite are the expressions of devotion to Him.
All creation seeks *boons* of Him;
Endlessly does He confer these.
What to offer Him in return?
How get a glimpse of His Court?
What words to utter to win His pleasure?
In the ambrosial hour of dawn
To meditate on His holy name, His Greatness!
By man's actions is acquired the vesture of human
    incarnation;
By God's grace is attained the Door of Liberation.
Nanak! Know the All-holy to be Almighty,
    Absolute.

5
Thāpiya na jāe kīta na hoe

Neither is He installed *in temples,*
Nor fashioned *by skill:*
He the Immaculate is self-existent.
Those devoted to him acquire *true* honour.
Such honour, saith Nanak, comes from chanting
    laudation of His inexhaustible attributes.
Those chanting His laudation, listening to it *with
    minds attentive*;
Those to Him devoted—
Their sorrows annulled,
Are into the House of Bliss ushered.
The Divine Word is mystic sound and true
    scriptural texts;
The Word is all-pervasive.
The Lord Supreme is all deities—
He is Shiva, Vishnu, Brahma,
And the *goddesses* Parvati, Lakshmi and Sarasvati.
Were I to realize His true greatness,
How may I utter it?

By what power may I express it?
My Master thus has enlightened me:
He alone is the Provider of all—
Never may I put Him out of my mind!

6

Tirath nhāwān je tis bhavan rin bhāne ke nhae kari

At holy bathing-spots would I dip my limbs, were
this to win God's approval—
Without His approval what good bathing!
No one out of God's creation finds fulfilment
except by His grace.
Absorbing the Masters' precept enriches the
seeker's mind
With qualities invaluable as pearls and rubies.
My Master thus has enlightened me:
He alone is the Provider of all—
Never may I put him out of my mind!

7

Je Juga chāre ārja hor dasūni hoe

Were someone to live the length of four Yugas,
And even ten times that;
Were he known in all the nine continents and
commanded universal following;
Were he to have fame and praise for all mankind—
Without Divine grace all may turn their faces
away from him,
And treat him as the most insignificant of worms:
The very reprobates may point accusing fingers at
him.
Nanak, he confers worth on the worthless:
All worth from Him proceeds.
None to equal Him, to share His qualities.

8

Suniyai Siddha, Pir, Sur, Nath

By absorbing holy teaching
The seeker may enter into the supreme state of
enlightenment and holiness.
To one absorbing holy teaching
Shall be revealed the cosmic esoteric mysteries of
the earth, the Bull and the sky;
The continents of the earth,
And its various realms and the nether regions.
Absorption of holy teaching
Makes man immune from Death.
Saith Nanak: God's devotees are ever in bliss;
Absorbing holy teaching annuls sorrow and sin.

9

Suniyai Ishar, Brahma, Ind

By absorbing holy teaching

The seeker is exalted to status of Shiva, Brahma
and Indra;
By absorbing holy teaching
The seeker is invested with praiseworthy qualities;
Absorption of holy teaching
Brings true knowledge of esoteric powers of the
personality,
And invests the mind with scriptural knowledge.
Saith Nanak: God's devotees are ever in bliss;
Absorption in holy teaching annuls sorrow and sin.

10

Suniyai Satt, Santokh, Gian

Absorption of holy teaching
Brings truthfulness, contentment and spiritual
illumination;
Absorption of holy teaching
Equals in merit bathing at the sixty-eight *holy
water-edges*;
Absorbing and study of holy teaching
Brings to *the seeker* true honour;
Absorption of holy teaching fixes the mind in God-
realization.
Saith Nanak: God's devotees are ever in bliss;
Absorption in holy teaching annuls sorrow and sin.

11

Suniyai Sarān Gurān ke gāh

Absorption of holy teaching
Brings knowledge of deep spiritual truths;
By absorption of holy teaching
May one attain to states of Supreme holiness;
By absorbing holy teaching
Those spiritually blind find the Path.
By absorbing holy teaching
Are fathomed deep secrets of the ocean of truth.
Saith Nanak: God's devotees abide ever in bliss;
Absorption of holy teaching annuls sorrow and sin.

12

Mannei ki gati kahi na jāe

Inexpressible is the state of faith. . . .

Jainism

*Jainism was the origin of a number of concepts that were
strongly to affect all subsequent religious thinking in
India. The following selections address three key points:
non-violence (ahimsa), whether or not there is a supreme
God, and the nature of the soul.*

Acaranga Sutra (c. 300 B.C.E.)

Ainslie T. Embree, ed. Translated by A. L. Basham. *Sources of Indian Tradition*, vol. 1. New York: Columbia University Press, 1988.

1.4.1

Thus say all the perfect souls and blessed ones, whether past, present, or to come—thus they speak, thus they declare, thus they proclaim: All things breathing, all things existing, all things living, all beings whatever, should not be slain or treated with violence, or insulted, or tortured, or driven away.

This is the pure unchanging eternal law, which the wise ones who know the world have proclaimed, among the earnest and the non-earnest, among the loyal and the not-loyal, among those who have given up punishing others and those who have not done so, among those who are weak and those who are not, among those who delight in worldly ties and those who do not. This is the truth. So it is. Thus it is declared in this religion.

When he adopts this Law a man should never conceal or reject it. When he understands the Law he should grow indifferent to what he sees, and not act for worldly motives. . . .

What is here declared has been seen, heard, approved, and understood. Those who give way and indulge in pleasure will be born again and again. The heedless are outside [the hope of salvation]. But if you are mindful, day and night steadfastly striving, always with ready vision, in the end you will conquer.

Mahapurana (c. 800 C.E.)

Ainslie T. Embree, ed. Translated by A. L. Basham. *Sources of Indian Tradition*, vol. 1. New York: Columbia University Press, 1988.

4.16–31; 4.38–40

Some foolish men declare that Creator made the world.
The doctrine that the world was created is ill-advised, and should be rejected.

If God created the world, where was he before creation?
If you say he was transcendent then, and needed no support, where is he now?

No single being had the skill to make this world—
For how can an immaterial god create that which is material?

How could God have made the world without any raw material?
If you say he made this first, and then the world, you are faced with an endless regression.

If you declare that this raw material arose naturally you fall into another fallacy,
For the whole universe might thus have been its own creator, and have arisen equally naturally.

If God created the world by an act of his own will, without any raw material,
Then it is just his will and nothing else—and who will believe this silly stuff?

If he is ever perfect and complete, how could the will to create have arisen in him?
If, on the other hand, he is not perfect, he could no more create the universe than a potter could.

If he is formless, actionless, and all-embracing, how could he have created the world?
Such a soul, devoid of all modality, would have no desire to create anything.

If he is perfect, he does not strive for the three aims of man,
So what advantage would he gain by creating the universe?

If you say that he created to no purpose, because it was his nature to do so, then God is pointless.
If he created in some kind of sport, it was the sport of a foolish child, leading to trouble.

If he created because of the karma of embodied beings [acquired in a previous creation]
He is not the Almighty Lord, but subordinate to something else. . . .

If out of love for living things and need of them he made the world,
Why did he not make creation wholly blissful, free from misfortune?

If he were transcendent he would not create, for he would be free;

Nor if involved in transmigration, for then he
would not be almighty.

Thus the doctrine that the world was created by
God
Makes no sense at all.

And God commits great sin in slaying the children
whom he himself created.
If you say that he slays only to destroy evil beings,
why did he create such beings in the first
place? . . .

Good men should combat the believer in divine
creation, maddened by an evil doctrine.

Know that the world is uncreated, as time itself is,
without beginning and end,
And is based on the principles, life and the rest.

Uncreated and indestructible, it endures under the
compulsion of its own nature,
Divided into three sections—hell, earth, and
heaven.

Ganadharavada (c. 800 C.E.)

Ainslie T. Embree, ed. Translated by A. L. Basham. *Sources of Indian
Tradition*, vol. 1. New York: Columbia University Press, 1988.

1.32–39

You should know that the chief characteristic of
the soul is awareness,
And that its existence can be proved by all valid
means of proof.
Souls may be classified as transmigrant and
liberated,
Or as embodied in immobile and mobile beings.

If the soul were only one,
Like space pervading all bodies,
Then it would be of one and the same character in
all bodies.
But the soul is not like this.
There are many souls, just as there are many pots
and other things
In the world—this is evident from the difference
of their characteristics.

If the soul were only one
There would be no joy or sorrow, no bondage or
freedom.

The awareness, which is the hallmark of the soul,
Differs in degree from body to body.
Awareness may be intense or dull—
Hence the number of souls is infinite.

If we assume the monist hypothesis, since the soul
is all-pervading,
There can be no liberation or bondage, [for the
soul is uniform] like space.
Moreover the soul is neither agent nor enjoyer, nor
does it think,
Nor is it subject to transmigration—again just
like space.

Again assuming monism, there can be no soul
enjoying final bliss,
For there are many maladies in the world, and
thus the world-soul can only be partly happy;
Moreover, as many phenomenal souls are in
bondage
The world-soul cannot be released from
transmigration, but only partly so.

The soul exists only within the body, just as space
in a jar,
Since its attributes are only to be detected
therein,
And since they are not to be found elsewhere,
As a pot is different from a piece of cloth.

Therefore action and enjoyment,
Bondage and release, joy and sorrow,
And likewise transmigration itself,
Are only possible on the hypothesis that souls
are many and finite.

Indian Buddhism

Dhammapada (c. 400 B.C.E.)

The Venerable Balangoda Ananda Maitreya (tr.). *The Dhammapada: The
Path of Truth.* Berkeley: Parallax Press, 1995.

*The message of the Buddha was to change profoundly not
only the Indian religious landscape, but that of all Asia
as well. In the following selections from the
Dhammapada, one of the earliest Buddhist scriptures,
the question of what makes a person wise, the value of the
Buddhist Eightfold Path, and a number of miscellaneous
Buddhist aphorisms are presented.*

Chapter 6: The Wise

1 If someone sees an intelligent person
   Who is skilfully able to point out
      shortcomings,
   And give suitable reproof,
   Let him cherish such a revealer of hidden
      treasures.
   Only good can come from such an association.

2 Let the wise one guide, correct,
   And deter others from what is base and vile.
   He will be treasured by the good and spurned
      by the evil.

3 Do not choose bad friends.
   Do not choose persons of low habits.
   Select good friends. Be discriminating.
   Choose the best.

4 Whoever drinks deeply of Dhamma lives
      happily,
   With a peaceful mind.
   The wise man rejoices in the Dhamma
   Taught by the holy ones.

5 Irrigators contain the flowing waters.
   Arrowsmiths fashion arrows.
   Carpenters shape wood to their design.
   Wise men mold their characters.

6 As a solid rock stands firm in the wind,
   Even so is a wise man unmoved by praise or
      blame.

7 As a deep lake remains still and clear,
   So do wise men, listening to the teachings,
   Attain a serene mind.

8 The good certainly cling to nothing.
   They do not talk aimlessly, concerned with
      personal gains.
   The wise, the saintly,
   Whether experiencing comfort or discomfort,
   Show neither elation nor depression.

9 Not for one's own or another's gain
   Should one commit an evil deed.
   Regardless of the desire for children, wealth,
      or kingdom,
   Or any other kind of success,
   One should remain virtuous, wise, and
      righteous.

10 The few cross over to the far shore.
   The many merely run back and forth
      fruitlessly
   Along the side of the stream.

11 But only those who follow the carefully taught
      law
   Can cross to the other shore,
   Beyond the grasp of death, so hard to
      overcome.

12, Let the wise man shun the cauldron
13   of confusion,
   And proceed on the path of light.
   Let him leave the comfort of home,
   Forsaking sensual pleasures,
   Freeing himself from all obstacles,
   Delighting in seclusion
   (Not an ordinary man's choice),
   And devote himself to cleansing the blemishes
      of the mind.

14 Those who have carefully cultivated their
      minds
   In tune with the elements of enlightenment—
   Who, without grasping, delight in
      detachment,
   Cleansed of all corruption and therefore
      shining brightly,
   Send forth brilliant light.

Chapter 20: The Way

1 The Eightfold Path is the best of ways.
   The Four Noble Truths are the best of truths.
   Freedom from desire is the best of states.
   Whoever is clear-eyed and wise is the best of
      men.

2 This is the one and only way.
   There is no other leading to the purity of
      vision.
   Follow this path;
   This bewilders Mara, the tempter.

3 Following this path, you shall put an end to
      suffering.
   Having myself realized the way that can lead
      to removal
   Of the thorns of defilements,
   I have shown it to you.

4 You, yourselves, must walk the path.
   Buddhas only show the way.
   Those who are meditative, who have gotten
      on the path,
   Will be free from the bonds of Mara.

5 All conditioned things are subject to change.
   When one realizes this truth,
   One feels wearied of these suffering heaps.
   This is the way of purification.

6 All conditioned things are unsatisfactory.
   When one realizes this truth,
   One feels wearied of suffering.
   This is the way of purification.

7 All things in the world are insubstantial.
   When one realizes this truth,
   One feels wearied of suffering.
   This is the way of purification.

8 The lazy man, weak in mental discipline,
   Indolent, prone to sloth,
   Unproductive, and though young and strong,
   Failing to move at the right time,
   Never finds the road to wisdom.

9 Curb your speech.
   Restrain your mind.
   Commit no evil deed.
   By these means,
   Accomplish the practice of the path
   Made out by the sages.

10 Wisdom is born from meditation.
   Not to meditate is loss.
   Know the difference between gain and loss.
   Make the choice to walk where wisdom grows.

11 Cut down the whole jungle of craving,
   Not just an isolated tree in the forest.
   The jungle of craving harbors dangers.
   Clear the trees of craving, both strong and
      weak,
   And find freedom.

12 As long as there is the least clinging to lustful
      thoughts,
   Man will remain in mental bondage,
   Like a nursing calf attached to its mother.

13 Cut off the love of ego with your own hands,
   As you would an autumn lily.
   Follow the peaceful path leading to nirvana,
   Guided by the one who has walked the path.

14 "I shall live here in the rains,
   There in winter,
   Elsewhere in summer," muses the fool,
   Not aware of the nearness of death.

15 Death carries the unaware man away,
   While he is still busily acquiring children and
      animals,
   Much as a rampaging flood engulfs a sleeping
      village.

16, When death comes,
17 Neither children, father, or other loved ones
   Can offer refuge.

Aware of this,
The wise behave well.
Don't postpone right action,
But clear the path to nirvana.

Chapter 21: Miscellany

1 If, by giving up lesser comforts,
   A greater happiness is to be found,
   The wise should give up the lesser comforts
   In view of the greater happiness.

2 How foolish to seek comfort
   Through someone else's pain.
   There is no escape from the trap of animosity.

3 The indolent and negligent
   Accrue unwholesome mind states
   By doing what should not be done,
   And failing to do what should be done.

4 Unwholesome mind states disappear
   Among those who are mindful of the nature of
      the body,
   Who stop doing what is right not to be done,
   And fulfill what needs to be done.

Sutras (c. 500 C.E.)

Wm. Theodore de Bary, ed. *The Buddhist Tradition in India, China and Japan.* New York: Vintage Books, 1972.

The Buddhist Sutras are some of the earliest examples of Buddhist argumentation in support of their understanding of the human predicament and the manner in which one achieves liberation. In the following selections, the question of what constitutes the human soul, states of meditative developments, and the last teaching of the Buddha are presented.

Digha Nikaya (2.64 ff.)

It is possible to make four propositions concerning the nature of the soul—"My soul has form and is minute," "My soul has form and is boundless," "My soul is without form and boundless." Such propositions may refer to this life or the next. . . .

There are as many ways of not making propositions concerning the soul, and those with insight do not make them.

Again the soul may be thought of as sentient or insentient, or as neither one nor the other but having sentience as a property. If someone affirms that his soul is sentient you should ask, "Sentience is of three kinds, happy, sorrowful, and neutral.

Which of these is your soul?" For when you feel one sensation you don't feel the others. Moreover these sensations are impermanent, dependent on conditions, resulting from a cause or causes, perishable, transitory, vanishing, ceasing. If one experiences a happy sensation and thinks "This is my soul," when the happy sensation ceases he will think "My soul has departed." One who thinks thus looks on his soul as something impermanent in this life, a blend of happiness and sorrow with a beginning and end, and so this proposition is not acceptable.

If someone affirms that the soul is not sentient, you should ask, "If you have no sensation, can you say that you exist?" He cannot, and so this proposition is not acceptable.

And if someone affirms that the soul has sentience as a property you should ask, "If all sensations of every kind were to cease absolutely there would be no feelings whatever. Could you then say 'I exist'?" He could not, and so this proposition is not acceptable.

When a monk does not look on the soul as coming under any of these three categories . . . he refrains from such views and clings to nothing in the world; and not clinging he does not tremble, and not trembling he attains Nirvāna. He knows that rebirth is at an end, that his goal is reached, that he has accomplished what he set out to do, and that after this present world there is no other for him. It would be absurd to say of such a monk, with his heart set free, that he believes that the perfected being survives after death—or indeed that he does not survive, or that he does and yet does not, or that he neither does nor does not. Because the monk is free his state transcends all expression, predication, communication, and knowledge.

Majjhima Nikaya (1.420 ff.)

The Lord was staying at Sāvatthī at the monastery of Anāthapindaka in the Grove of Jeta. One morning he dressed, took his robe and bowl, and went into Sāvatthī for alms, with the Reverend Rāhula following close behind him. As they walked the Lord, . . . without looking round, spoke to him thus:

"All material forms, past, present, or future, within or without, gross or subtle, base or fine, far or near, all should be viewed with full understanding—with the thought 'This is not mine, this is not I, this is not my soul.'"

"Only material forms, Lord?"

"No, not only material forms, Rāhula, but also sensation, perception, the psychic constructions, and consciousness."

"Who would go to the village to collect alms today, when he has been exhorted by the Lord himself?" said Rāhula. And he turned back and sat cross-legged, with body erect, collected in thought.

Then the Venerable Sāriputta, seeing him thus, said to him: "Develop concentration on inhalation and exhalation, for when this is developed and increased it is very productive and helpful."

Towards evening Rāhula rose and went to the Lord and asked him how he could develop concentration on inhalation and exhalation. And the Lord said:

"Rāhula, whatever is hard and solid in an individual, such as hair, nails, teeth, skin, flesh, and so on, is called the personal element of earth. The personal element of water is composed of bile, phlegm, pus, blood, sweat, and so on. The personal element of fire is that which warms and consumes or burns up, and produces metabolism of food and drink in digestion. The personal element of air is the wind in the body which moves upwards or downwards, the winds in the abdomen and stomach, winds which move from member to member, and the inhalation and exhalation of the breath. And finally the personal element of space comprises the orifices of ears and nose, the door of the mouth, and the channels whereby food and drink enter, remain in, and pass out of the body. These five personal elements, together with the five external elements, make up the total of the five universal elements. They should all be regarded objectively, with right understanding, thinking 'This is not mine, this is not me, this is not my soul.' With this understanding attitude a man turns from the five elements and his mind takes no delight in them.

"Develop a state of mind like the earth, Rāhula. For on the earth men throw clean and unclean things, dung and urine, spittle, pus and blood, and the earth is not troubled or repelled or disgusted. And as you grow like the earth no contacts with pleasant or unpleasant will lay hold of your mind or stick to it.

"Similarly you should develop a state of mind like water, for men throw all manner of clean and unclean things into water and it is not troubled or repelled or disgusted. And similarly with fire, which burns all things, clean and unclean, and with air, which blows upon them all, and with space, which is nowhere established.

"Develop the state of mind of friendliness, Rāhula, for, as you do so, ill-will will grow less; and of compassion, for thus vexation will grow less; and of joy, for thus aversion will grow less; and of equanimity, for thus repugnance will grow less.

"Develop the state of mind of consciousness of the corruption of the body, for thus passion will grow less; and of the consciousness of the fleeting nature of all things, for thus the pride of selfhood will grow less.

"Develop the state of mind of ordering the breath . . . in which the monk goes to the forest, or to the root of a tree or to an empty house, and sits cross-legged with body erect, collected in thought. Fully mindful he inhales and exhales. When he inhales or exhales a long breath he knows precisely that he is doing so, and similarly when inhaling or exhaling a short breath. While inhaling or exhaling he trains himself to be conscious of the whole of his body . . . to be fully conscious of the components of his mind, . . . to realize the impermanence of all things . . . or to dwell on passionlessness . . . or renunciation. Thus the state of ordered breathing, when developed and increased, is very productive and helpful. And when the mind is thus developed a man breathes his last breath in full consciousness, and not unconsciously."

Digha Nikaya (2.99 ff.)

Soon after this the Lord began to recover, and when he was quite free from sickness he came out of his lodging and sat in its shadow on a seat spread out for him. The Venerable Ānanda went up to him, paid his respects, sat down to one side, and spoke to the Lord thus:

"I have seen the Lord in health, and I have seen the Lord in sickness; and when I saw that the Lord was sick my body became as weak as a creeper, my sight dimmed, and all my faculties weakened. But yet I was a little comforted by the thought that the Lord would not pass away until he had left his instructions concerning the Order."

"What, Ānanda! Does the Order expect that of me? I have taught the truth without making any distinction between exoteric and esoteric doctrines; for . . . with the Tathāgata there is no such thing as the closed fist of the teacher who keeps some things back. If anyone thinks 'It is I who will lead the Order,' or 'The Order depends on me,' he is the one who should lay down instructions concerning the Order. But the Tathāgata has no such thought, so why should he leave instructions? I am old now, Ānanda, and full of years; my journey nears its end, and I have reached my sum

of days, for I am nearly eighty years old. Just as a worn-out cart can only be kept going if it is tied up with thongs, so the body of the Tathāgata can only be kept going by bandaging it. Only when the Tathāgata no longer attends to any outward object, when all separate sensation stops and he is deep in inner concentration, is his body at ease.

"So, Ānanda, you must be your own lamps, be your own refuges. Take refuge in nothing outside yourselves. Hold firm to the truth as a lamp and refuge, and do not look for refuge to anything besides yourselves. A monk becomes his own lamp and refuge by continually looking on his body, feelings, perceptions, moods, and ideas in such a manner that he conquers the cravings and depressions of ordinary men and is always strenuous, self-possessed, and collected in mind. Whoever among my monks does this, either now or when I am dead, if he is anxious to learn, will reach the summit."

THE LAST WORDS OF THE BUDDHA

"All composite things must pass away. Strive onward vigilantly."

Vajrayana Buddhism

Buddhism in India did not stand still. After developing into Mahayana mode (see Chinese Buddhism below), Indian Buddhism found its final expression in the ritual-oriented Vajrayana mode. The selections below illustrate this mode of Buddhism's particular orientation, which differed considerably from the austere religion advocated by the Buddha himself.

Cittavisuddhiprakarana (c. 600 C.E.; attributed to Arya Deva)

Wm. Theodore de Bary, ed. *The Buddhist Tradition in India, China and Japan.* New York: Vintage Books, 1972.

Passion as a Means of Salvation

They who do not see the truth
   Think of birth-and-death as distinct from
     Nirvāna,
But they who do see the truth
   Think of neither. . . .

This discrimination is the demon
   Who produces the ocean of transmigration.
Freed from it the great ones are released
   From the bonds of becoming.

Plain folk are afflicted
   With the poison of doubt. . . .
He who is all compassion . . .
   Should uproot it completely.

As a clear crystal assumes
   The color of another object,
So the jewel of the mind is colored
   With the hue of what it imagines.

The jewel of the mind is naturally devoid
   Of the color of these ideas,
Originally pure, unoriginated,
   Impersonal, and immaculate.

So, with all one's might, one should do
   Whatever fools condemn,
And, since one's mind is pure,
   Dwell in union with one's divinity.

The mystics, pure of mind,
   Dally with lovely girls,
Infatuated with the poisonous flame of passion,
   That they may be set free from desire.

By his meditations the sage is his own Garuda,
   Who draws out the venom [of snakebite] and
      drinks it.
He makes his deity innocuous,
   And is not affected by the poison. . . .

When he has developed a mind of wisdom
   And has set his heart on enlightenment
There is nothing he may not do
   To uproot the world [from his mind].

He is not Buddha, he is not set free,
   If he does not see the world
As originally pure, unoriginated,
   Impersonal, and immaculate.

The mystic duly dwells,
   On the manifold merits of his divinity,
He delights in thoughts of passion,
   And by the enjoyment of passion is set free.

What must we do? Where are to be found
   The manifold potencies of being?
A man who is poisoned may be cured
   By another poison, the antidote.

Water in the ear is removed by more water,
   A thorn [in the skin] by another thorn.
So wise men rid themselves of passion
   By yet more passion.

As a washerman uses dirt
   To wash clean a garment,
So, with impurity,
   The wise man makes himself pure.

Dohakosa (c. 800 C.E.; attributed to Saraha)

Wm. Theodore de Bary, ed. Translated by D. S. Snellgrove. *The Buddhist Tradition in India, China and Japan.* New York: Vintage Books, 1972.

Everything is Buddha

As is Nirvāna so is Samsāra.
   Do not think there is any distinction.
Yet it possesses no single nature,
   For I know it as quite pure.

Do not sit at home, do not go to the forest,
   But recognize mind wherever you are.
When one abides in complete and perfect
      enlightenment,
   Where is Samsāra and where is Nirvāna?

Oh know this truth,
   That neither at home nor in the forest does
      enlightenment dwell.
Be free from prevarication
   In the self-nature of immaculate thought!

"This is myself and this is another."
   Be free of this bond which encompasses you
      about,
And your own self is thereby released.

Do not err in this matter of self and other.
   Everything is Buddha without exception.
Here is that immaculate and final stage,
   Where thought is pure in its true nature.

The fair tree of thought that knows no duality,
   Spreads through the triple world.
It bears the flower and fruit of compassion,
   And its name is service of others.

The fair tree of the Void abounds with flowers,
   Acts of compassion of many kinds,

And fruit for others appearing spontaneously,
 For this joy has no actual thought of another.

So the fair tree of the Void also lacks compassion,
 Without shoots or flowers or foliage,
And whoever imagines them there, falls down,
 For branches there are none.

The two trees spring from one seed,
 And for that reason there is but one fruit.
He who thinks of them thus indistinguishable,
 Is released from Nirvāna and Samsāra.

If a man in need approaches and goes away hopes
  unfulfilled,
 It is better he should abandon that house
Than take the bowl that has been thrown from the
  door.

Not to be helpful to others,
 Not to give to those in need,
This is the fruit of Samsāra.
 Better than this is to renounce the idea of a self.

He who clings to the Void
 And neglects Compassion,
Does not reach the highest stage.

But he who practices only Compassion,
 Does not gain release from toils of existence.
He, however, who is strong in practice of both,
 Remains neither in Samsāra nor in Nirvāna.

Daoism

Zhuangzi: Basic Writings (c. 250 B.C.E.)

Burton Watson (tr.). *Chuang Tzu: Basic Writings*. New York: Columbia University Press, 1964.

Much of Daoism's appeal lay in its transfiguration of conventional values. No one was more adept at doing this than Zhuangzi (or Chuang Tzu, as below).

The Characteristics of a Sage

Jo of the North Sea said, ". . . the Great Man in his actions will not harm others, but he makes no show of benevolence or charity. He will not move for the sake of profit, but he does not despise the porter at the gate. He will not wrangle for goods or wealth, but he makes no show of refusing or relinquishing them. He will not enlist the help of others in his work, but he makes no show of being self-supporting, and he does not despise the greedy and base. His actions differ from those of the mob, but he makes no show of uniqueness or eccentricity. He is content to stay behind with the crowd, but he does not despise those who run forward to flatter and fawn. All the titles and stipends of the age are not enough to stir him to exertion; all its penalties and censures are not enough to make him feel shame. He knows that no line can be drawn between right and wrong, no border can be fixed between great and small. I have heard it said, 'The Man of the Way wins no fame, the highest virtue wins no gain, the Great Man has no self.' To the most perfect degree, he goes along with what has been allotted to him."

Action and Inaction

Men of ardour are regarded by the world as good, but their goodness doesn't succeed in keeping them alive. So I don't know whether their goodness is really good or not. Perhaps I think it's good—but not good enough to save their lives. Perhaps I think it's no good—but still good enough to save the lives of others. So I say, if your loyal advice isn't heeded, give way and do not wrangle. Tzu-hsü wrangled and lost his body. But if he hadn't wrangled, he wouldn't have made a name. Is there really such a thing as goodness or isn't there?

What ordinary people do and what they find happiness in—I don't know whether such happiness is in the end really happiness or not. I look at what ordinary people find happiness in, what they all make a made dash for, racing around as though they couldn't stop—they all say they're happy with it. I'm not happy with it and I'm not unhappy with it. In the end is there really happiness or isn't there?

I take inaction to be true happiness, but ordinary people think it is a bitter thing. I say: the highest happiness has no happiness, the highest praise has no praise. The world can't decide what is right and what is wrong. And yet inaction can decide this. The highest happiness, keeping alive—only inaction gets you close to this!

Let me try putting it this way. The inaction of Heaven is its purity, the inaction of earth is its peace. So the two inactions combine and all things are transformed and brought to birth. Wonderfully, mysteriously, there is no place they come out of.

Mysteriously, wonderfully, they have no sign. Each thing minds its business and all grow up out of inaction. So I say, Heaven and earth do nothing and there is nothing that is not done. Among men, who can get hold of this inaction?

Chuang Tzu's wife died. When Hui Tzu went to convey his condolences, he found Chuang Tzu sitting with his legs sprawled out, pounding on a tub and singing. "You lived with her, she brought up your children and grew old," said Hui Tzu. "It should be enough simply not to weep at her death. But pounding on a tub and singing—this is going too far, isn't it?"

Chuang Tzu said, "You're wrong. When she first died, do you think I didn't grieve like anyone else? But I looked back to her beginning and the time before she was born. Not only the time before she was born, but the time before she had a body. Not only the time before she had a body, but the time before she had a spirit. In the midst of the jumble of wonder and mystery a change took place and she had a spirit. Another change and she had a body. Another change and she was born. Now there's been another change and she's dead. It's just like the progression of the four seasons, spring, summer, fall, winter.

"Now she's going to lie down peacefully in a vast room. If I were to follow after her bawling and sobbing, it would show that I don't understand anything about fate. So I stopped."

Confucianism

The Analects (c. 450 C.E.)

D. C. Lau (tr.). *Confucius: the Analects (Lun yü)*. London: Penguin, 1979.

Confucius's teachings were not presented systematically, but rather in the form of aphorisms collected by his students from his talks with them. The following selections present these sayings in the format most familiar to Chinese students of the Master's thought.

Book 7

1 The Master said, 'I transmit but do not innovate; I am truthful in what I say and devoted to antiquity. I venture to compare myself to our Old P'eng.'

2 The Master said, "Quietly to store up knowledge in my mind, to learn without flagging, to teach without growing weary, these present me with no difficulties."

3 The Master said, "It is these things that cause me concern: failure to cultivate virtue, failure to go more deeply into what I have learned, inability, when I am told what is right, to move to where it is, and inability to reform myself when I have defects."

4 During his leisure moments, the master remained correct though relaxed.

5 The Master said, "How I have gone downhill! It has been such a long time since I dreamt of the Duke of Chou."

6 The Master said, "I set my heart on the Way, base myself on virtue, lean upon benevolence for support and take my recreation in the arts."

7 The Master said, "I have never denied instruction to anyone who, of his own accord, has given me so much as a bundle of dried meat as a present."

8 The Master said, "I never enlighten anyone who has not been driven to distraction by trying to understand a difficulty or who has not got into a frenzy trying to put his ideas into words.

"When I have pointed out one corner of a square to anyone and he does not come back with the other three, I will not point it out to him a second time."

9 When eating in the presence of one who has been bereaved, the Master never ate his fill.

10 On a day he had wept, the Master did not sing.

11 The Master said to Yen Yüan, "Only you and I have the ability to go forward when employed and to stay out of sight when set aside."

Tzu-lu said, "If you were leading the Three Armies whom would you take with you?"

The Master said, "I would not take with me anyone who would try to fight a tiger with his bare hands or to walk across the River and die in the process without regrets. If I took anyone it would have to be a man who, when faced with a task, was fearful of failure and who, while fond of making plans, was capable of successful execution."

12 The Master said, "If wealth were a permissible pursuit, I would be willing even to act as a guard holding a whip outside the market place. If it is not, I shall follow my own preferences."

13 Fasting, war and sickness were the things over which the Master exercised care.

14 The Master heard the *shao* in Ch'i and for three months did not notice the taste of the meat he ate. He said, "I never dreamt that the joys of music could reach such heights."

15 Jan Yu said, "Is the Master on the side of the Lord of Wei?' Tzu-kung said, 'Well, I shall put the question to him."

He went in and said, "What sort of men were Po Yi and Shu Ch'i?"

"They were excellent men of old."

"Did they have any complaints?"

"They sought benevolence and got it. So why should they have any complaints?"

When Tzu-kung came out, he said, "The Master is not on his side."

16 The Master said, "In the eating of coarse rice and the drinking of water, the using of one's elbow for a pillow, joy is to be found. Wealth and rank attained through immoral means have as much to do with me as passing clouds."

17 The Master said, "Grant me a few more years so that I may study at the age of fifty and I shall be free from major errors."

18 What the Master used the correct pronunciation for: the *Odes*, the *Book of History* and the performance of the rites. In all these cases he used the correct pronunciation.

19 The Governor of She asked Tzu-lu about Confucius. Tzu-lu did not answer. The Master said, "Why did you not simply say something to this effect: he is the sort of man who forgets to eat when he tries to solve a problem that has been driving him to distraction, who is so full of joy that he forgets his worries and who does not notice the onset of old age?"

20 The Master said, "I was not born with knowledge but, being fond of antiquity, I am quick to seek it."

21 The topics the Master did not speak of were prodigies, force, disorder and gods.

22 The Master said, "Even when walking in the company of two other men, I am bound to be able to learn from them. The good points of the one I copy; the bad points of the other I correct in myself."

23 The Master said, "Heaven is author of the virtue that is in me. What can Huan T'ui do to me?"

24 The Master said, "My friends, do you think I am secretive? There is nothing which I hide from you. There is nothing I do which I do not share with you, my friends. There is Ch'iu for you."

25 The Master instructs under four heads: culture, moral conduct, doing one's best and being trustworthy in what one says.

26 The Master said, "I have no hopes of meeting a sage. I would be content if I met someone who is a gentleman."

The Master said, "I have no hopes of meeting a good man. I would be content if I met someone who has constancy. It is hard for a man to have constancy who claims to have when he is wanting, to be full when he is empty and to be comfortable when he is in straitened circumstances."

27 The Master used a fishing line but not a cable; he used a corded arrow but not to shoot at roosting birds.

28 The Master said, "There are presumably men who innovate without possessing knowledge, but that is not a fault I have. I use my ears widely and follow what is good in what I have heard; I use my eyes widely and retain what I have seen in my mind. This constitutes a lower level of knowledge."

29 People of Hsu Hsiang were difficult to talk to. A boy was received and the disciples were perplexed. The Master said, "Approval of his coming does not mean approval of him when he is not here. Why should we be so exacting? When a man comes after having purified himself, we approve of his purification but we cannot vouch for his past."

30 The Master said, "Is benevolence really far away? No sooner do I desire it than it is here."

31 Ch'en Ssu-pai asked whether Duke Chao was versed in the rites. Confucius said, "Yes."

After Confucius had gone, Ch'en Ssu-pai, bowing to Wu-ma Ch'i, invited him forward and said, "I have heard that the gentleman does not show partiality. Does he show it nevertheless? The Lord took as wife a daughter of Wu, who thus is of the same clan as himself, but he allows her to be called Wu Meng Tzu. If the Lord is versed in the rites, who isn't?"

When Wu-ma Ch'i recounted this to him, the Master said, "I am a fortunate man. Whenever I make a mistake, other people are sure to notice it."

32 When the Master was singing in the company of others and liked someone else's song, he always asked to hear it again before joining in.

33 The Master said, "In unstinted effort I can compare with others, but in being a practising gentleman I have had, as yet, no success."

34 The Master said, "How dare I claim to be a sage or a benevolent man? Perhaps it might be said of me that I learn without flagging and teach without growing weary." Kung-hsi Hua said, "This is precisely where we disciples are unable to learn from your example."

35 The Master was seriously ill. Tzu-lu asked permission to offer a prayer. The Master said, "Was such a thing ever done?" Tzu-lu said, "Yes, it was. The prayer offered was as follows: pray thus to the gods above and below." The Master said, "In that case, I have long been offering my prayers."

36 The Master said, "Extravagance means ostentation, frugality means shabbiness. I would rather be shabby than ostentatious."

37 The Master said, "The gentleman is easy of mind, while the small man is always full of anxiety."

38 The Master is cordial yet stern, awe-inspiring yet not fierce, and respectful yet at ease.

Xun Zi: Basic Writings (c. 200 B.C.E.)

Burton Watson (tr.) *Hsün Tzu: Basic Writings.* New York and London: Columbia University Press, 1963.

Not all later Confucian scholars agreed in their interpretations of the Master's teachings. Although Mencius' interpretations came to dominate the official version of Confucianism, the interpretations of Xun Zi were also influential. Indeed, they led to the philosophy of Legalism which, though harsh, was directly responsible for the creation of the Chinese Imperial system that endured for over two millennia.

Improving Yourself

When you see good, then diligently examine your own behavior; when you see evil, then with sorrow look into yourself. When you find good in yourself, steadfastly approve it; when you find evil in yourself, hate it as something loathsome. He who comes to you with censure is your teacher; he who comes with approbation is your friend; but he who flatters you is your enemy. Therefore the gentleman honors his teacher, draws close to his friends, but heartily hates his enemies. He loves good untiringly and can accept reprimand and take warning from it. Therefore, though he may have no particular wish to advance, how can he help but do so? The petty man is just the opposite. He behaves in an unruly way and yet hates to have others censure him; he does unworthy deeds and yet wants others to regard him as worthy. He has the heart of a tiger or a wolf, the actions of a beast, and yet resents it when others look upon him as an enemy. He draws close to those who flatter him and is distant with those who reprimand him; he laughs at upright men and treats as enemies those who are loyal. Therefore, though he certainly has no desire for ruin, how can he escape it? This is what is meant by the lines in the *Odes*:

> They league together, they slander;
> It fills me with sorrow.
> When advice is good
> They all oppose it.
> When advice is bad,
> They follow all together.

This is the way with impartial goodness: use it to control your temperament and nourish your life and you will live longer than P'eng Tsu; use it to improve and strengthen yourself and you may become equal to the sages Yao and Yü. It is appropriate when you are in a time of success; it is profitable when you are living in hardship. It is in fact what is meant by ritual. If all matters pertaining to temperament, will, and understanding proceed according to ritual, they will be ordered and successful; if not they will be perverse and violent or slovenly and rude. If matters pertaining to food and drink, dress, domicile, and living habits proceed according to ritual, they will he harmonious and well regulated; if not they will end in missteps, excesses, and sickness. If matters pertaining to deportment, attitude, manner of movement, and walk proceed according to ritual, they will be refined; if not they will be arrogant and uncouth, common and countrified. Therefore a man without ritual cannot live; an undertaking without ritual cannot come to completion; a state without ritual cannot attain peace. This is what is meant by the lines in the *Odes*:

> Their rites and ceremonies are entirely according to rule,
> Their laughter and talk are entirely appropriate.

To make use of good to lead others is called education; to make use of good to achieve harmony with others is called amenity. To use what is not good to lead others is called betrayal; to use what is not good to achieve harmony with others is called sycophancy. To treat right as right and wrong as wrong is called wisdom; to treat right as wrong and wrong as right is called stupidity. To speak ill of good men is called slander; to do harm to good men is called brigandage. To call right right and wrong wrong is called honesty. To steal goods is called robbery; to act on the sly is called deceit; to go back on your word is called perfidy. To be without a fixed standard in your actions is called inconstancy. To cling to profit and cast aside righteousness is called the height of depravity. He who has heard much is called broad; he who has heard little is called shallow. He who has seen much is called practiced; he who has seen little is called uncouth. He who has difficulty advancing is called a laggard; he who forgets easily is called a leaky-brain. He whose actions are few and well principled is called orderly; he whose actions are many and disorderly is called chaotic.

This is the proper way to order the temperament and train the mind. If your temperament is too strong and stubborn, soften it with harmony. If your intellect is too deep and withdrawn, unify it with mild sincerity. If you are too courageous and fierce, correct the fault with orderly compliance. If you are too hasty and flippant, regulate the fault with restraint. If you are too constrained and petty, broaden yourself with liberality. If you are too low-minded, lethargic, and greedy, lift yourself up with high ambitions. If you are mediocre, dull, and diffuse, strip away your failings by means of teachers and friends. If you are indolent and heedless, awaken yourself with the thought of imminent disaster. If you are stupidly sincere and ploddingly honest, temper your character with rites and music. Of all the ways to order the temperament and train the mind, none is more direct than to follow ritual, none more vital than to find a teacher, none more

godlike than to learn to love one thing alone. This is called the proper way to order the temperament and train the mind.

If you will is well disciplined, you may hold up your head before wealth and eminence; if you are rich in righteous ways, you may stand unmoved before kings and dukes. Look well inside yourself and you may look lightly upon outside things. This is what the old text means when it says, "The gentleman uses things; the petty man is used by things." Though it may mean labor for the body, if the mind finds peace in it, do it. Though there may be little profit in it, if there is much righteousness, do it. Rather than achieve success in the service of an unprincipled ruler, it is better to follow what is right in the service of an impoverished one. A good farmer does not give up plowing just because of flood or drought; a good merchant does not stop doing business just because of occasional losses; a gentleman does not neglect the Way just because of poverty and hardship.

If you are respectful in bearing and sincere in heart, if you abide by ritual principles and are kindly to others, then you may travel all over the world and, though you may choose to live among the barbarian tribes, everyone will honor you. If you are the first to undertake hard work and can leave ease and enjoyment to others, if you are honest and trustworthy, persevering, and meticulous in your job, then you can travel all over the world and, though you choose to live among the barbarians, everyone will want to employ you. But if your bearing is arrogant and your heart deceitful, if you follow dark and injurious ways and are inconsistent and vile in feeling, then you may travel all over the world and, though you penetrate to every corner of it, there will be no one who does not despise you. If you are shiftless and evasive when it comes to hard work but keen and unrestrained in the pursuit of pleasure, if you are dishonest and insincere, concerned only with your own desires and unattentive to your work, then you may travel all over the world and, though you penetrate to every corner of it, there will be no one who does not reject you.

One does not walk with his arms held out like wings because he is afraid of soiling his sleeves in the mud. One does not walk with his head bent down because he is afraid of bumping into something. One does not lower his eyes when meeting others because he is overcome with fright. It is simply that a man of breeding desires to improve his conduct by himself and to cause no offense to his neighbors.

A thoroughbred can travel a thousand *li* in one day, yet even a tired old nag, given ten days to do it in, can cover the same distance. But will you try to exhaust the inexhaustible, to pursue to the end that which has no end? If you do, then you may wear out your bones and flesh but you will never reach your goal. If, however, you set a limit to your journey, then you may arrive there sooner or later, before others or after them, but how can you fail to arrive at your goal some time? Will you be an unwitting plodder who tries to exhaust the inexhaustible, to pursue to the end that which has no end? Or will you choose to set a limit to your journey? It is not that the propositions concerning black and white, sameness and difference, thickness and non-thickness are not penetrating. But the gentleman does not discuss them because he puts a limit to his goal. Therefore in learning there is what is called "waiting." If those who have gone before stop and wait, and those who are behind keep going, then, whether sooner or later, whether first or last, how can they fail all in time to reach the goal? If he keeps putting one foot in front of the other without stopping, even a lame turtle can go a thousand *li*; if you keep piling up one handful of earth on top of another without ceasing, you will end up with a high mountain. But if you block the source of a river and break down its banks, even the Yangtze and the Yellow River can be made to run dry; if they take one step forward and one step back, pull now to the left and now to the right, even a team of six thoroughbreds will never reach their destination. Men are certainly not as widely separated in their capacities as a lame turtle and a team of six thoroughbreds; yet the lame turtle reaches the goal where the team of thoroughbreds fails. There is only one reason: one keeps on going, the other does not. Though the road is short, if you do not step along you will never get to the end; though the task is small, if you do not work at it you will never get it finished. He who takes many holidays will never excel others by very much.

He who loves law and puts it into effect is a man of breeding. He who has a firm will and embodies it in his conduct is a gentleman. He who has a keen insight which never fails is a sage.

A man who has no laws at all is lost and guideless. A man who has laws but does not understand their meaning is timid and inconsistent. Only if a man abides by laws and at the same time comprehends their wider significance and applicability can he become truly liberal and compassionate.

Ritual is the means by which to rectify yourself; the teacher is the means by which ritual is rectified. If you are without ritual, how can you rectify yourself? If you have no teacher, how can you understand the fitness of ritual? If you unerringly do as ritual prescribes, it means that your emotions have found rest in ritual. If you speak as your teacher speaks, it means that your understanding has become like that of your teacher. If your emotions find rest in ritual and your understanding is like that of your teacher, then you have become a sage. Hence to reject ritual is to be without law and to reject your teacher is to be without a guide. To deny guide and law and attempt to do everything your own way is to be like a blind man trying to distinguish colors or a deaf man, tones. Nothing will come of it but confusion and outrage. Therefore learning means learning to regard ritual as your law. The teacher makes himself the standard of proper conduct and values that in himself which finds rest in ritual. This is what is meant by the lines in the *Odes*:

> Without considering, without thinking,
> He obeys the laws of God.

If a man is sincere, obedient, and brotherly, he may be said to have a certain amount of good in him. But if he adds to this a love of learning, modesty, and alertness, then he may be considered a gentleman. If a man is mean and lazy, lacking in modesty, and a glutton over food and drink, he may be said to have a certain amount of bad in him. But if in addition he is wanton, reckless, and disobedient, vicious and evil and lacking in brotherly feeling, then he can be called ill-omened, and no one can protest if he falls into the hands of the law and is executed.

If you treat old people as they ought to be treated, then young people too will come to your side. If you do not press those who are already hard pressed, then the successful too will gather around you. If you do good in secret and seek no reward for your kindness, then sages and unworthy men alike will be with you. If a man does these three things, though he should commit a grave error, will Heaven leave him to perish?

The gentleman is careless in the pursuit of profit but swift in avoiding harm. Timidly he shuns disgrace but he practices the principles of the Way with courage.

Though poor and hard pressed, a gentleman will be broad of will. Though rich and eminent, he will be respectful in his manner. Though at ease, he will not allow his spirit to grow indolent;

though weary, he will not neglect his appearance. He will not take away more than is right because of anger, nor give more than is right because of joy. Though poor and hard pressed, he is broad of will because he honors benevolence. Though rich and eminent, he is respectful in manner because he does not presume upon his station. Though at ease, he is not indolent because he chooses to follow what is right. Though weary, he does not neglect his appearance because he values good form. He does not take away too much in anger nor give too much in joy because he allows law to prevail over personal feeling. The *Book of Documents* says: "Do not go by what you like, but follow the way of the king; do not go by what you hate, but follow the king's road." This means that a gentleman must be able to suppress personal desire in favor of public right.

Chinese Buddhism

Despite its beginnings in India, Mahayana Buddhism found its fullest expression in China, Korea, Japan, and Vietnam. The following selections point out some of the new emphases that informed the Mahayana viewpoint, including the concept of Emptiness (Shunyata), the nature of reality, the Buddha Nature, and the figure of the Bodhisattva.

Lalitavistara Sutra (c. 750 C.E.)

Wm. Theodore de Bary, ed. *The Buddhist Tradition in India, China and Japan.* New York: Vintage Books, 1972.

Emptiness (Shunyata) (13.175–177)

All things conditioned are instable, impermanent,
　　Fragile in essence, as an unbaked pot,
Like something borrowed, or a city founded on
　　sand,
　　They last a short while only.

They are inevitably destroyed,
　　Like plaster washed off in the rains,
Like the sandy bank of a river—
　　They are conditioned, and their true nature is
　　frail.

They are like the flame of a lamp,
　　Which rises suddenly and as soon goes out.

They have no power of endurance, like the wind
　　Or like foam, unsubstantial, essentially feeble.

They have no inner power, being essentially empty,
　　Like the stem of a plantain, if one thinks clearly,
Like conjuring tricks deluding the mind,
　　Or a fist closed on nothing to tease a child. . . .

From wisps of grass the rope is spun
　　By dint of exertion.
By turns of the wheel the buckets are raised from
　　the well,
　　Yet each turn of itself is futile.

So the turning of the all the components of
　　becoming
　　Arises from the interaction of one with another.
In the unit the turning cannot be traced
　　Either at the beginning or end.

Where the seed is, there is the young plant,
　　But the seed has not the nature of the plant,
Nor is it something other than the plant, nor is it
　　the plant—
　　So is the nature of the Law of Righteousness,
　　neither transient nor eternal.

All things conditioned are conditioned by
　　ignorance,
　　And on final analysis they do not exist,
For they and the conditioning ignorance alike are
　　Emptiness
　　In their essential nature, without power of
　　action. . . .

The mystic knows the beginning and end
　　Of consciousness, its production and passing
　　away—
He knows that it came from nowhere and returns
　　to nowhere,
　　And is empty [or reality], like a conjuring trick.

Through the concomitance of three factors—
　　Firesticks, fuel, and the work of the hand—
Fire is kindled. It serves its purpose
　　And quickly goes out again.

A wise man may seek here, there, and everywhere
　　Whence it has come, and whither it has gone,
Through every region in all directions,
　　But he cannot find it in its essential nature. . . .

Thus all things in this world of contingence
　　Are dependent on causes and conditions.

The mystic knows what is true reality,
  And sees all conditioned things as empty and
    powerless.

Lotus Sutra (c. 300–600 C.E.; attributed to the Buddha)

Wm. Theodore de Bary, ed. *The Buddhist Tradition in India, China and Japan.* New York: Vintage Books, 1972.

Taisho daizokyo (9.8–9; 9.15): All Things Have the Buddha-Nature

The Buddha appears in the world
Only for this One Reality.
Both the Vehicle of the Direct Disciples and the
    Vehicle of the Private Buddhas are not real.
For never by the Small Vehicle
Would the Buddhas save all beings.
The Buddha himself abides in the Great Vehicle,
And in accordance with the Law he has attained,
By meditation and wisdom and the effort and
    ornament of virtue,
He saves all beings.
I have realized the Supreme Way.
The Law of the Great Vehicle applies to all beings.
If I converted by the Small Vehicle
Even one single human being,
I should fall into stinginess and greed.
Such a thing cannot be done.
If men turn in faith to the Buddha,
The Tathāgata will not deceive them.
O, Shāriputra! you should know that
From the very start I made a vow,
With the desire to enable all beings
To be the same as we are,

To convert all beings
And enable them all to enter the Path of the
    Buddha.
Although I preach Nirvāna,
It is not real extinction.
All dharmas from the beginning
Are always tranquil in themselves and are devoid
    of appearance.
When the Buddha-son fulfills his course,
He becomes a Buddha in his next life.

Because of my adaptability [to use every suitable
    means for salvation]
I reveal the Law of Three Vehicles.
Any among the living beings,
Who have come into contact with former
    Buddhas,

Have learned the Law and practiced charity,
Or have undergone discipline and endured
    forbearance and humiliation,
Or have made serious efforts at concentration and
    understanding, etc.,
And cultivated various kinds of blessing and
    wisdom—
All of these people,
Have reached the level of Buddhahood.

Those people who, for the sake of the Buddha,
Installed images,
Or have had them carved,
Have reached the level of Buddhahood.

Those who with a happy frame of mind
Have sung the glory of the Buddha,
Even with a very small sound,

Or have worshiped,
Or have merely folded their hands,

Or have uttered one "Namo" [Praise be . . .],
All have reached the level of Buddhahood.
About the Buddhas of the past—
After they passed away from this world,
They heard the Law,
And all reached the level of Buddhahood.
As to the Buddhas of the future,
Their number will be infinite.
All these Tathāgatas
Will preach the Law by all suitable means.
All these Buddhas,
With an infinite number of suitable means,
Will save all living beings,
And enable them to dwell in the Pure Wisdom of
    the Buddha.
Among those who have heard the Law,
None will fail to become Buddha.
All Buddhas have taken the vow:
"The Buddha-way which I walk,
I desire to enable all living beings
To attain the same way with me."
Although Buddhas in future ages
Preach hundreds and thousands and tens of
    thousands
Of methods, beyond number,
In reality there is only the One Vehicle.
All the Buddhas, past and future,
Know that dharmas have no [self-] nature,
And Buddha-seeds [all beings and defilements] are
    produced by causation.
Therefore they preach the One Vehicle.
All the direct disciples
And private buddhas

Cannot by their powers
Penetrate this scripture.
You, Shāriputra,
Can, into this scripture,
Enter only by faith.

Gandhavyuha Sutra (c. 300–600 C.E.)

Wm. Theodore de Bary, ed. *The Buddhist Tradition in India, China and Japan.* New York: Vintage Books, 1972.

The Vow to Live the Life of Samanta-bhadra

1   I sincerely salute with body, speech and mind all Lions of Mankind (Buddhas) residing in the past, present, and future in the ten quarters of the Universe.

2   I reverently prostrate myself before all the Victorious Ones (Buddhas), multiplying my obeisances as if with bodies as numerous as the dust particles in the earth, with my heart devoted to them on the strength of the vows that I live the life of Bhadra.

3   I rejoice in the belief that the entire Universe is filled with the Victorious Ones; even on the tip of a grain of sand, Buddhas as numerous as particles of dust exist, each of them sitting in the center surrounded by bodhisattvas.

4   I glorify all those who have attained bliss, and in unison with the eulogies offered by the ocean of all sounds, exalt the Victorious Ones' virtues, as inexhaustible as the sounds of the oceans.

5   And I make offerings to the Buddhas with the best of flowers, wreaths, musical instruments, ointments, umbrellas, lamps, and incense.

6   And I make offerings to the Buddhas, adorning them with the best of garments, perfumes, and containers of powdered incense like Mt. Meru.

7   And I earnestly devote myself to the acts of offering to the Buddhas, offerings exquisite and noble; I salute and make offerings by virtue of my earnest application to live the life of Bhadra.

8   And I confess whatever evil deeds I might have committed with my body, speech, and mind due to passion, anger, and delusion.

9   I feel sympathetic joy for all the meritorious deeds performed by people, disciples still to be trained, accomplished disciples, private buddhas, bodhisattvas, and all the Victorious Ones in the ten quarters.

10   And I entreat all the Lords, who are the Lights of the world in the ten quarters, who have awakened in Enlightenment and obtained non-attachment—to revolve the unsurpassed Wheel of the Law.

11   And also with clasped hands, I entreat those who expect to manifest Nirvāna that they should remain in the world for ages yet to come, as many as the particles of dust in the earth, for the benefit and welfare of all beings.

12   I apply toward Enlightenment whatever good I have accumulated through the practice of adoration, offering, confession, sympathetic joy, asking for instruction, and begging.

13   May all the Buddhas in the past be revered; may the Buddhas residing in the ten quarters of the world be honoured; may those who are yet to come be at ease and awaken to Enlightenment fulfilling their wishes.

14   May all the lands in the ten quarters be pure and extensive and filled with bodhisattvas and the Victorious Ones who have stayed under the Tree of Wisdom.

15   May all beings in the ten quarters always be happy and healthy; may they be endowed with the benefits of piety, may they be successful and their wishes be fulfilled.

16   And may I be able to remember my previous births in all paths of existence while practicing the way to Enlightenment; may I always remain a mendicant in the course of coming and going through all forms of life.

17   May I always practice a spotless life of morality, without defect and without interruption, imitating all the Victorious Ones and realizing the life of Bhadra.

18   May I be able to disclose the teachings of the Buddhas with all the kinds of voices that exist in the world—the voices of gods, Nāgas, Yakshas, Kumbhāndas, and mankind.

19   Let him, who applies himself steadfastly to the excellent virtues (*pāramitās*), never be confused in mind as to Enlightenment; let him be wholly free from evils that might obstruct his way.

20 Let him walk in the paths of the world, free from karma, defilement and the course of the Tempter, like the lotus floating free on the water, or like the sun and moon not fixed in the sky.

21 Allow me to work for the welfare of all creatures, as long as the lands and roads exist in the ten quarters, relieving anxieties, extinguishing pain, and assisting all beings in the Six Paths of transmigratory existence.

22 Allow me to work till the end of time, adjusting myself to the lives of beings, fulfilling the life of Enlightenment, and cherishing the life of Bhadra.

23 Allow me always to be associated with those who would be companions in living the life of Bhadra; and let me practice the same vows with my body, speech, and mind.

24 May I always be associated with those well-wishing friends who advocate the life of Bhadra and may I never be estranged from them.

25 May I always be in the presence of the Victorious Ones, the Lords surrounded by bodhisattvas; allow me to make extensive offerings to the end of time without wearying.

26 May I discipline myself to the end of time, upholding the Truth of the Victorious Ones, manifesting the life of Enlightenment, and living the life of Bhadra with purity.

27 May I be an inexhaustible storehouse of all excellences—wisdom, skillful devices, concentration, emancipation—transmigrating all paths of existence and becoming an indefatigable one because of my merits and wisdom.

28 May I see the Buddhas while practicing the course to Enlightenment; on the tip of a particle of dust there are fields as numerous as particles of dust, and in each of these fields there are innumerable Buddhas, each sitting in the midst of bodhisattvas.

29 Allow me to go deep into the oceans of Buddhas, of lands, and of aeons of devotional life, throughout time and everywhere without exception, even on paths as narrow as a hair.

30 Allow me always to comprehend the voices of the Buddhas and their speeches responding to the aspirations of all beings, pure in the quality of their sound, with an ocean of meanings in even one sound.

31 And allow me, while I turn the Wheel of the Law, to penetrate, on the strength of my understanding, into those everlasting utterances of the Victorious Ones residing in the past, present, and future.

32 May I instantly advance into all aeons of time to come, and may I instantly place myself in aeons of time past as long as the times of future, present, and past combined.

33 May I see at once the Lions of Mankind, staying in the three divisions of time, and may I always enter their realms on the strength of being emancipated from the course of Illusion (*māyā*).

34 May I produce on the tip of a particle of dust supernal arrangements of the lands in the past, present, and future, and may I enter the Victorious Ones' lands supernally arranged in the whole of ten quarters.

35 And may I reverently approach all the future Lords, the Lamps of the world, who would revolve the Wheel of the Law when enlightened, and who would reveal perfect peace in manifestation of Nirvāna.

36 By supernatural powers swiftly moving everywhere, by the power of vehicles turning to all directions, by the power of conduct, of perfect virtues, and of all-pervading goodwill;

37 By the power of the merits of complete purity, of wisdom free from attachment, of insight, clever devices, concentration, and of acquiring the force of Enlightenment;

38 Purifying the power of influences from past evil actions, crushing the forces of defilement, and rendering impotent the Tempter, may I utilize to the fullest of all of my energy toward living the life of Bhadra.

39 Purifying the ocean of lands, releasing the ocean of beings, observing the ocean of phenomena, plunging into the ocean of wisdom.

40 Purifying the ocean of conduct, fulfilling the ocean of vows, and honouring the ocean of Buddhas, may I discipline myself without growing weary throughout the ocean of aeons.

41 And may I awaken to Enlightenment by living the life of Bhadra, fulfilling completely in the

course of Enlightenment all the vows of the Victorious Ones in the past, present, and future.

42 May I extend all my merits to those who walk on the same path as the Wise One whose name is Samanta-bhadra, the most cherished son of all the Buddhas.

43 May I be like him, the Wise One, whose name Bhadra signifies purity of body, speech, mind, life, and the land [where he resides].

44 May I practice the vows of Manjushrī to consummate the living of the life of Bhadra; and may I perfect all disciplines without exception throughout aeons to come.

45 May I discipline myself through and through, and may I accumulate immeasurable merits; and making myself firm in countless disciplines, may I know all the supernatural powers of the Buddhas and bodhisattvas.

46 When space reaches non-existence, when all beings cease, and when karma and defilements are exhausted, only then should my vows come to an end.

47 May I offer the Buddhas the innumerable lands in the ten quarters adorned with gems; and may I give them excellences conducive to the happiness of gods and men, for aeons countless as the particles of dust in the earth.

48 By listening to this [hymn which may be called], "the king of merit-extending," one should be inspired at once to apply it earnestly; the merits acquired by seeking superb Enlightenment are the highest and most excellent.

49 Those who devote themselves to living the life of Bhadra will be kept away from evil states and bad friends, and be enabled instantly to perceive the Buddha Amitābha.

50 With ease will they obtain whatever is profitable and live most happily; they will be welcome when born among men; and before long they will be like Samanta-bhadra.

51 Should one commit any of the five deadly sins out of ignorance, if he recites this hymn of living the life of Bhadra, his sins will quickly be extinguished;

52 He will be endowed with wisdom, beauty, and auspicious marks, he will be born in a high caste, in a noble family; he will not be

attacked by the host of heretics and the Tempter, but will be honoured in all the three worlds;

53 He will go directly under the Tree of Wisdom, the king of trees, and there he will meditate for the sake of the welfare of mankind; overcoming the Tempter and his followers, he will awaken in Enlightenment and revolve the Wheel of the Law.

54 When one recites, preaches, and adheres to this "vow of living the life of Bhadra," the Buddha will know its consequences; have no doubt about [attaining] peerless Enlightenment.

55 The powerful Manjushrī knows, as does Samanta-bhadra; following them I will extend what is meritorious [toward Enlightenment].

56 I wish to extend all that is meritorious to the matchless living of the life of Bhadra; that "merit-extending" comes foremost has been preached, is being preached, and will be preached by the Buddhas of the past, present, and future.

57 When the time comes for me to die, may I come into the presence of Amitābha and, clearing away all hindrances, go to the land of bliss.

58 Having gone there, may all the vows be equally present in my mind; and fulfilling them completely, may I endeavor to work for the welfare of beings in the world as far as the world extends.

59 Being born in the glorious assembly of Buddhas, graceful and beaming with beautiful lotus flowers, may I be given the assurance [that I shall attain Enlightenment] in the presence of the Buddha Amitābha.

60 Having obtained that assurance, may I change myself into numberless forms and benefit the beings in the ten quarters by virtue of my wisdom.

61 By whatever merits I have accumulated reciting the vows of living the life of Bhadra, may all the pure vows of the world be fulfilled in a moment.

62 By the infinite and most excellent merit acquired through perfecting and living of the life of Bhadra, may those people drowned in the flood of calamities go to the most excellent city of Amitābha.

Shikshasamuccaya (c. 650 C.E.; attributed to Shantideva)

Wm. Theodore de Bary, ed. *The Buddhist Tradition in India, China and Japan.* New York: Vintage Books, 1972.

Faith in Emptiness

He who maintains the doctrine of Emptiness is not allured by the things of the world, because they have no basis. He is not excited by gain or dejected by loss. Fame does not dazzle him and infamy does not shame him. Scorn does not repel him, praise does not attract him. Pleasure does not please him, pain does not trouble him. He who is not allured by the things of the world knows Emptiness, and one who maintains the doctrine of Emptiness has neither likes nor dislikes. What he likes he knows to be only Emptiness and sees it as such.

All Depends on the Mind

All phenomena originate in the mind, and when the mind is fully known all phenomena are fully known. For by the mind the world is led . . . and through the mind karma is piled up, whether good or evil. The mind swings like a firebrand, the mind rears up like a wave, the mind burns like a forest fire, like a great flood the mind bears all things away. The bodhisattva, thoroughly examining the nature of things, dwells in everpresent mindfulness of the activity of the mind, and so he does not fall into the mind's power, but the mind comes under his control. And with the mind under his control all phenomena are under his control.

Nirvana is Here and Now

That which the Lord revealed in his perfect enlightenment was not form or sensation or perception or psychic constructions or thought; for none of these five components come into being, neither does supreme wisdom come into being . . . and how can that which does not come into being know that which also does not come into being? Since nothing can be grasped, what is the Buddha, what is wisdom, what is the bodhisattva, what is revelation? All the components are by nature empty—just convention, just names, agreed tokens, coverings. . . .

Thus all things are the perfection of being, infinite perfection, unobscured perfection, unconditioned perfection. All things are enlightenment, for they must be recognized as without essential nature—even the five greatest sins are enlightenment, for enlightenment has no essential nature and neither have the five greatest sins. Thus those who seek for Nirvāna are to be laughed at, for the man in the midst of birth-and-death is also seeking Nirvāna.

Lankavatara Sutra (c. 300 C.E.)

Wm. Theodore de Bary, ed. *The Buddhist Tradition in India, China and Japan.* New York: Vintage Books, 1972.

Nirvana is Here and Now

Those who are afraid of the sorrow which arises from . . . the round of birth-and-death seek for Nirvāna; they do not realize that between birth-and-death and Nirvāna there is really no difference at all. They see Nirvāna as the absence of all . . . becoming, and the cessation of all contact of sense-organ and sense-object, and they will not understand that it is really only the inner realization of the store of impressions. . . . Hence they teach the three Vehicles, but not the doctrine that nothing truly exists but the mind, in which are no images. Therefore . . . they do not know the extent of what has been perceived by the minds of past, present, and future Buddhas, and continue in the conviction that the world extends beyond the range of the mind's eye. . . . And so they keep on rolling . . . on the wheel of birth-and-death.

Shinto

Nihongi (c. 600 C.E.)

Terence Barrow and W. G. Aston (tr.). *Nihongi: Chronicles of Japan from the Earliest Times to AD 697.* Rutland, Vermont: Charles E. Tuttle Company, 1972.

Shinto never developed much in the way of formal scriptures such as are found in other religions. But many of its basic ideas can be found in the myths preserved in the earliest Japanese books of history. The following selection retells the story of how the Sun Goddess Amaterasu no Oho-kami—the supreme ruler of Heaven and the ancestress of the Japanese Imperial family—claimed the islands of Japan and sent her descendents to rule it. It is this myth that legitimized the Japanese royal family as the supreme priests of the Shinto religion.

2.14–16

After this Ama-terasu no Oho-kami united Yorodzu-hata Toyo-aki-tsu-hime, the younger sister of Omohi-kane no Kami to Masa-ya-a-katsu-katsu-no-haya-hi no Ama no Oshi-ho-mimi no Mikoto, and making her his consort, caused them to descend to the Central Land of Reed-Plains. At this time Katsu-no-haya-hi no Ama no Oshi-ho-mimi no Mikoto stood on the floating bridge of Heaven, and glancing downwards, said:—"Is that country tranquillized yet? No! it is a tumble-down land, hideous to look upon." So he ascended, and reported why he had not gone down. Therefore, Ama-terasu no Oho-kami further sent Takamika-tsuchi no Kami and Futsu-nushi no Kami first to clear it. Now these two Gods went down and arrived at Idzumo, where they inquired of Oho-na-mochi no Mikoto saying:—"Wilt thou deliver up this country to the Heavenly Deity or not?" He answered and said:—"My son, Koto-shiro-nushi is at Cape Mitsu for the sport of bird-shooting. I will ask him, and then give you an answer." So he sent a messenger to make inquiry, who brought answer and said:—"How can we refuse to deliver up what is demanded by the Heavenly Deity?" Therefore Oho-na-mochi no Kami replied to the two Gods in the words of his son. The two Gods thereupon ascended to Heaven and reported the result of their mission, saying:—"All the Central Land of Reed-Plains is now completely tranquillized." Now Ama-terasu no Oho-kami gave command, saying:—"If that be so, I will send down my child. She was about to do so, when in the meantime, an August Grandchild was born, whose name was called Ama-tsu hiko-hiko-ho-no-ninigi no Mikoto. Her son represented to her that he wished the August Grandchild to be sent down in his stead. Therefore Ama-terasu no Oho-kami gave to Ama-tsu-hiko-hiko-ho no-ninigi no Mikoto the three treasures, viz. the curved jewel of Yasaka gem, the eight hand mirror, and the sword Kusanagi, and joined to him as his attendants Ame no Koyane no Mikoto, the first ancestor of the Naka-tomi, Futo-dama no Mikoto, the first ancestor of the Imbe, Ame no Uzume no Mikoto, the first ancestor of the Sarume, Ishi-kori-dome no Mikoto the first ancestor of the mirror-makers, and Tamaya no Mikoto, the first ancestor of the jewel-makers, in all Gods of five Be. Then she commanded her August Grandchild, saying:—'This Reed-plain-1500-autumns-fair-rice-ear Land is the region which my descendants shall be lords of. Do thou, my August Grandchild, proceed thither and govern it. Go! and may prosperity attend thy dynasty, and may it, like Heaven and Earth, endure for ever.'"

2.23

At this time Ama-terasu no Oho-kami took in her hand the precious mirror, and, giving it to Ame no Oshi-ho-mimi no Mikoto, uttered a prayer, saying:—"My child, when thou lookest upon this mirror, let it be as if thou wert looking on me. Let it be with thee on thy couch and in thy hall, and let it be to thee a holy mirror." Moreover, she gave command to Ame no Ko-yane no Mikoto and to Futo-dama no Mikoto, saying:—"Attend to me, ye two Gods! Do ye also remain together in attendance and guard it well." She further gave command, saying:—"I will give over to my child the rice-ears of the sacred garden, of which I partake in the Plains of High Heaven."

Norito (c. 300–700 C.E.)

Donald L. Philippi (tr.). *Norito: A Translation of the Ancient Japanese Ritual Prayers.* New Jersey: Princeton University Press, 1991.

Chapter 25: To Drive Away a Vengeful Deyty (*Tataru Kami wo Utusi-yaru*)

By the command of the Ancestral Gods and
      Goddesses,
  Who divinely remain in the High Heavenly
     Plain,
  And who began matters,
The eight myriad deities were convoked in a divine
     convocation in the high meeting-place of
     Heaven,
  And consulted in a divine consultation, [saying]:
    "Our Sovereign Grandchild is to rule
    "The Land of the Plentiful Reed Plains and of
     the Fresh Ears of Grain
    "Tranquilly as a peaceful land."
Thus he left the heavenly rock-seat,
  And descended from the heavens,
    Pushing with an awesome pushing through
     the myriad layers of heavenly clouds
  And was entrusted [with the land]—
Then they consulted with a divine consultation,
    [saying]:
    "Which deity should first be dispatched
    "To expel with a divine expulsion and so pacify
    "The unruly deities in the Land of the Fresh
     Ears of Grain?"
Then the numerous deities all consulted and said:
   "Ame-no-ho-hi-no-mikoto should be sent to
     pacify them."
Then when he was dispatched down from the
    heavens,

He did not return to report on his mission.
Next Take-me-kuma-no-mikoto was also
    dispatched,
    But he also, obeying his father's words, did not
      return to report on his mission.
Again, Ame-waka-hiko was also dispatched,
    But he did not return to report on his mission,
    But because of woe from a bird of on high
    Immediately lost his life.
Hereupon by the command of the Heavenly
    Deities
    Another consultation was held,
And the two deities:
    Futu-nusi-no-mikoto
    And Take-mika-duti-no-mikoto
    Were caused to descend from the heavens;
They expelled with a divine expulsion the unruly
    deities
    And pacified with a divine pacification;
They silenced to the last leaf
    The rocks and the stumps of the trees,
    Which had been able to speak,
And when the Sovereign Grandchild descended
    from the heavens,
    Entrusted [the land to him].

The lands of the four quarters thus entrusted [to
    him when he] descended from the heavens,
    Great Yamato, the land of the Sun-Seen-on-
    High, was determined as a peaceful land;
The palace posts were firmly rooted in the bed-
    rock below,
    The cross-beams of the roof soaring high
    towards the High Heavenly Plain,
    And [the palace of the Emperor] constructed as
    a heavenly shelter, as a sun-shelter
    In this land which he is to rule tranquilly as a
    peaceful land.
May the Sovereign Deities dwelling within the
    heavenly palace
    Not rage and not ravage,
Because as deities they are well acquainted
    With the matters begun in the High
    Heavenly Plain;
May they rectify [their hearts] in the manner of
    [the rectifying deities] Kamu-naho-bi and
    Oho-naho-bi,
And may they go from this place
    And move to another place of lovely mountains
    and rivers
      Where they can look out over the four
      quarters,
    And may they reign over that as their place.

With this prayer I present offerings,

Providing garments of colored cloth, radiant
    cloth, plain cloth, and coarse cloth;
A mirror as something to see clearly with,
A jewel as something to play with,
A bow and arrow as something to shoot with,
A sword as something to cut with,
A horse as something to ride on;
Wine, raising high the soaring necks
    Of the countless wine vessels filled to the
    brim;
In rice and in stalks;
That which lives in the mountains—
    The soft-furred and the coarse-furred
    animals—
That which grows in the vast fields and plains—
    The sweet herbs and the bitter herbs—
As well as that which lives in the blue ocean—
    The wide-finned and the narrow-finned
    fishes,
    The sea-weeds of the deep and the sea-weeds
    of the shore—
I place these noble offerings in abundance upon
    tables
    Like a long mountain range and present them
Praying that the Sovereign Deities
    Will with a pure heart receive them tranquilly
      As offerings of ease,
      As offerings of abundance,
    And will not seek vengeance and not ravage,
But will move to a place of wide and lovely
    mountains and rivers,
    And will as deities dwell there pacified.
With this prayer, I fulfill your praises. Thus I
    humbly speak.

Japanese Buddhism

*Although Shinto produced little in the way of primary
texts, many of its central attitudes and beliefs can be seen
in the mythology preserved in the early histories such as
the Nihongi and in the norito, the ritual chants of
Shinto. Japanese Buddhism, despite owing a large debt to
Chinese models, soon developed in ways that were
distinctly Japanese as well.*

Saicho: Dengyo Daishi zenshu (c. 810 C.E.)

Wm. Theodore de Bary, ed. *The Buddhist Tradition in India, China and Japan.* New York: Vintage Books, 1972.

Vow of Uninterrupted Study of the Lotus Sutra (4.749)

The disciple of Buddha and student of the One Vehicle [name and court rank to be filled in] this day respectfully affirms before the Three Treasures that the saintly Emperor Kammu, on behalf of Japan and as a manifestation of his unconditional compassion, established the Lotus sect and had the *Lotus Sūtra*, its commentary, and the essays on "Concentration and Insight," copied and bound, together with hundreds of other volumes, and installed them in the seven great temples. Constantly did he promote the Single and Only Vehicle, and he united all the people so that they might ride together in the ox-cart of Mahāyāna to the ultimate destination, enlightenment. Every year festivals of the *Golden Light Sūtra* were held to protect the state. He selected twelve students, and established a seminary on top of Mt. Hiei, where the Tripiṭaka, the ritual implements, and the sacred images were enshrined. These treasures he considered the guardian of the Law and its champion during the great night of ignorance.

It was for this reason that on the fifteenth day of the second moon of 809 Saichō with a few members of the same faith, established the uninterrupted study of the *Sūtra of the Lotus of the Wonderful Law*.

I vow that, as long as heaven endures and earth lasts, to the most distant term of the future, this study will continue without the intermission of a single day, at the rate of one volume every two days. Thus the doctrine of universal enlightenment will be preserved forever, and spread throughout Japan, to the farthest confines. May all attain to Buddhahood!

Kukai: Kobo Daishi zenshu (806 C.E.)

Wm. Theodore de Bary, ed. *The Buddhist Tradition in India, China and Japan*. New York: Vintage Books, 1972.

Kukai and His Master (1.98–101)

During the sixth moon of 804, I, Kūkai, sailed for China aboard the Number One Ship, in the party of Lord Fujiwara, ambassador to the T'ang court. We reached the coast of Fukien by the eighth moon, and four months later arrived at Ch'ang-an, the capital, where we were lodged at the official guest residence. The ambassadorial delegation started home for Japan on March 11, 805, but in obedience to an imperial edict, I alone remained behind in the Hsi-ming Temple where the abbot Eichū had formerly resided.

One day, in the course of my calls on eminent Buddhist teachers of the capital, I happened by chance to meet the abbot of the East Pagoda Hall of the Green Dragon Temple. This great priest, whose Buddhist name was Hui-kuo, was the chosen disciple of the master Amoghavajra. His virtue aroused the reverence of his age; his teachings were lofty enough to guide emperors. Three sovereigns revered him as their master and were ordained by him. The four classes of believers looked up to him for instruction in the esoteric teachings.

I called on the abbot in the company of five or six monks from the Hsi-ming Temple. As soon as he saw me he smiled with pleasure, and he joyfully said, "I knew that you would come! I have been waiting for such a long time. What pleasure it gives me to look on you today at last! My life is drawing to an end, and until you came there was no one to whom I could transmit the teachings. Go without delay to the ordination altar with incense and a flower." I returned to the temple where I had been staying and got the things which were necessary for the ceremony. It was early in the sixth moon, then, that I entered the ordination chamber. I stood in front of the Womb Mandala and cast my flower in the prescribed manner. By chance it fell on the body of the Buddha Vairochana in the center. The master exclaimed in delight, "How amazing! How perfectly amazing!" He repeated this three or four times in joy and wonder. I was then given the fivefold baptism and received the instruction in the Three Mysteries that bring divine intercession. Next I was taught the Sanskrit formulas for the Womb Mandala, and learned the yoga contemplation on all the Honoured Ones.

Early in the seventh moon I entered the ordination chamber of the Diamond Mandala for a second baptism. When I cast my flower it fell on Vairochana again, and the abbot marveled as he had before. I also received ordination as an āchārya early in the following month. On the day of my ordination I provided a feast for five hundred of the monks. The dignitaries of the Green Dragon Temple all attended the feast, and everyone enjoyed himself.

I later studied the Diamond Crown Yoga and the five divisions of the True Words teachings, and spent some time learning Sanskrit and the Sanskrit hymns. The abbot informed me that the Esoteric scriptures are so abstruse that their meaning cannot be conveyed except through art.

For this reason he ordered the court artist Li Chen and about a dozen other painters to execute ten scrolls of the Womb and Diamond Mandalas, and assembled more than twenty scribes to make copies of the Diamond and other important Esoteric scriptures. He also ordered the bronzesmith Chao Wu to cast fifteen ritual implements. These orders for the painting of religious images and the copying of the sūtras were issued at various times.

One day the abbot told me, "Long ago, when I was still young, I met the great master Amoghavajra. From the first moment he saw me he treated me like a son, and on his visit to the court and his return to the temple I was as inseparable from him as his shadow. He confided to me, 'You will be the receptacle of the esoteric teachings. Do your best! Do your best!' I was then initiated into the teachings of both the Womb and Diamond, and into the secret mudrās as well. The rest of his disciples, monks and laity alike, studied just one of the Mandalas or one Honored One or one ritual, but not all of them as I did. How deeply I am indebted to him I shall never be able to express.

"Now my existence on earth approaches its term, and I cannot long remain. I urge you, therefore, to take the two Mandalas and the hundred volumes of the Esoteric teachings, together with the ritual implements and these gifts which were left to me by my master. Return to your country and propagate the teachings there.

"When you first arrived I feared I did not have time enough left to teach you everything, but now my teaching is completed, and the work of copying the sūtras and making the images is also finished. Hasten back to your country, offer these things to the court, and spread the teachings throughout your country to increase the happiness of the people. Then the land will know peace and everyone will be content. In that way you will return thanks to Buddha and to your teacher. That is also the way to show your devotion to your country and to your family. My disciple I-ming will carry on the teachings here. Your task is to transmit them to the Eastern Land. Do your best! Do your best!" These were his final instructions to me, kindly and patient as always. On the night of the last full moon of the year he purified himself with a ritual bath and, lying on his right side and making the mudrā of Vairochana, he breathed his last.

That night, while I sat in meditation in the Hall, the abbot appeared to me in his usual form and said, "You and I have long been pledged to propagate the esoteric teachings. If I am reborn in Japan, this time I will be your disciple."

I have not gone into the details of all he said, but the general import of the Master's instructions I have given. [Dated 5th December 806.]

Dogen: Shobo genzo zuimonki (c. 1235 C.E.)

Wm. Theodore de Bary, ed. *The Buddhist Tradition in India, China and Japan.* New York: Vintage Books, 1972.

The Importance of Sitting

When I stayed at T'ien-t'ung monastery [in China], the venerable Ching used to stay up sitting until the small hours of the morning and then after only a little rest would rise early to start sitting again. In the meditation hall he went on sitting with the other elders, without letting up for even a single night. Meanwhile many of the monks went off to sleep. The elder would go around among them and hit the sleepers with his fist or a slipper, yelling at them to wake up. If their sleepiness persisted, he would go out to the hallway and ring the bell to summon the monks to a room apart, where he would lecture to them by the light of a candle.

"What use is there in your assembling together in the hall only to go to sleep? Is this all that you left the world and joined holy orders for? Even among laymen, whether they be emperors, princes, or officials, are there any who live a life of ease? The ruler must fulfil the duties of the sovereign, his ministers must serve with loyalty and devotion, and commoners must work to reclaim land and till the soil—no one lives a life of ease. To escape from such burdens and idly while away the time in a monastery—what does this accomplish? Great is the problem of birth and death; fleeting indeed is our transitory existence. Upon these truths both the scriptural and meditation schools agree. What sort of illness awaits us tonight, what sort of death tomorrow? While we have life, not to practice Buddha's Law but to spend the time in sleep is the height of foolishness. Because of such foolishness Buddhism today is in a state of decline. When it was at its zenith monks devolved themselves to the practice of sitting in meditation (*zazen*), but nowadays sitting is not generally insisted upon and consequently Buddhism is losing ground." . . .

Upon another occasion his attendants said to him, "The monks are getting overtired or falling ill, and some are thinking of leaving the monastery, all because they are required to sit too long in meditation. Shouldn't the length of the sitting period be shortened?" The master became highly indignant. "That would be quite wrong. A monk who is not really devoted to the religious life may very well fall asleep in a half hour or an hour. But one truly devoted to it who has resolved to persevere in his religious discipline will eventually come to enjoy the practice of sitting, no matter how long it lasts. When I was young I used to visit the heads of various monasteries, and one of them explained to me, 'Formerly I used to hit sleeping monks so hard that my fist just about broke. Now I am old and weak, so I can't hit them hard enough. Therefore it is difficult to produce good monks. In many monasteries today the superiors to not emphasize sitting strongly enough, and so Buddhism is declining. The more you hit them the better,' he advised me."

Islam

Islam has had a wide-ranging effect on all areas of Asia. For the hundreds of millions of Asians who profess this religion, the ultimate sources of knowledge of God's will lie in the Qur'an and in the sayings of the Prophet Muhammad, known as hadith. *The Riyadh as-Salihin is one of numerous collections of such sayings. Ascertaining the authenticity of various collections of* hadith *(and of individual* hadith *themselves) is important amongst Muslim theologians.*

The Qur'an (c. 600 C.E.)

Arthur J. Arberry (tr.). *The Koran Interpreted.* New York: Macmillan, 1955.

Chapter 19: Mary

In the Name of God, the Merciful, the Compassionate

Kaf Ha Ya Ain Sad

The mention of thy Lord's mercy unto His servant Zachariah; when he called upon his Lord secretly saying, "O my Lord, behold the bones within me are feeble and my head is all aflame with hoariness. And in calling on Thee, my Lord, I have never been hitherto unprosperous. [5] And now I fear my kinsfolk after I am gone; and my wife is barren. So give me, from Thee, a kinsman who shall be my inheritor and the inheritor of the House of Jacob; and make him, my Lord, well-pleasing." "O Zachariah, We give thee good tidings of a boy, whose name is John. No namesake have We given him aforetime." He said, "O my Lord, how shall I have a son, seeing my wife is barren, and I have attained to the declining of old age?" [10] Said He, "So it shall be; thy Lord says 'Easy is that for Me, seeing that I created thee aforetime, when thou wast nothing.'" He said, "Lord, appoint to me some sign." Said He, "Thy sign is that thou shalt not speak to men, though being without fault, three nights." So he came forth unto his people from the Sanctuary, then he made signal to them, "Give you glory at dawn and evening." "O John, take the Book forcefully"; and We gave him judgment, yet a little child, and a tenderness from Us, and purity; and he was godfearing, and cherishing his parents, not arrogant, rebellious. [15] "Peace be upon him, the day he was born, and the day he dies, and the day he is raised up alive!"

And mention in the Book Mary when she withdrew from her people to an eastern place, and she took a veil apart from them; then We sent unto her Our Spirit that presented himself to her a man without fault. She said, "I take refuge in the All-merciful from thee! If thou fearest God. . . ." He said, "I am but a messenger come from thy Lord, to give thee a boy most pure." [20] She said, "How shall I have a son whom no mortal has touched, neither have I been unchaste?" He said, "Even so thy Lord has said: 'Easy is that for Me; and that We may appoint him a sign unto men and a mercy from Us; it is a thing decreed.'" So she conceived him, and withdrew with him to a distant place. And the birthpangs surprised her by the trunk of the palm-tree. She said, "Would I had died ere this, and become a thing forgotten!" But the one that was below her called to her, "Nay, do not sorrow; see, thy Lord has set below thee a rivulet. [25] Shake also to thee the palm-trunk, and there shall come tumbling upon thee dates fresh and ripe. Eat therefore, and drink, and be comforted; and if thou shouldst see any mortal, say, "I have vowed to the All-merciful a fast, and today I will not speak to any man.'" Then she brought the child to her folk carrying him; and they said, "Mary, thou has surely committed a monstrous thing! Sister of Aaron, thy father was not a wicked man, nor was thy mother a woman unchaste." [30] Mary pointed to the child then; but they said, "How shall we speak to one who is still in the cradle, a little child?" He said, "Lo, I am God's servant; God has given me the book, and made me a Prophet. Blessed He has made me, wherever I may be; and He has enjoined me to pray, and to give the alms, so long as I live, and likewise to cherish my mother; He has not made me arrogant, unprosperous. Peace be upon me, the day I was born, and the day I die, and the day I am raised up alive!" [35] That is Jesus, son of Mary, in word of truth, concerning which they are doubting. It is not for God to take a son unto Him. Glory be to Him! When He decrees a thing, He but says to it "Be," and it is. Surely God is my Lord, and your Lord; so serve you Him. This is a straight path.

But the parties have fallen into variance among themselves; then woe to those who disbelieve for the scene of a dreadful day. How well they will hear and see on the day they come to Us! But the evildoers even today are in error manifest. [40] Warn thou them of the day of anguish, when the matter shall be determined, and they yet heedless and unbelieving. Surely We shall inherit the earth and all that are upon it, and unto Us they shall be returned.

And mention in the Book Abraham; surely he was a true man, a Prophet. When he said to his father, "Father, why worshippest thou that which neither hears nor sees, nor avails thee anything? Father, there has come to me knowledge such as came not to thee; so follow me, and I will guide thee on a level path. [45] Father, serve not Satan; surely Satan is a rebel against the All-merciful. Father, I fear that some chastisement from the All-merciful will smite thee, so that thou becomest a friend to Satan." Said he, "What, art thou shrinking from my gods, Abraham? Surely, if thou givest not over, I shall stone thee; so forsake me now for some while." He said, "Peace be upon thee! I will ask my Lord to forgive thee; surely He is ever gracious to me. Now I will go apart from you and that you call upon, apart from God; I will call upon my Lord, and haply I shall not be, in calling upon my Lord, unprosperous." [50] So, when he went apart from them and that they were serving, apart from God, We gave him Isaac and Jacob, and each We made a Prophet; and We gave them of Our mercy, and We appointed unto them a tongue of truthfulness, sublime.

And mention in the Book Moses; he was devoted, and he was a Messenger, a Prophet. We called to him from the right side of the Mount, and We brought him near in communion. And We gave him his brother Aaron, of Our mercy, a Prophet.

[55] And mention in the Book Ishmael; he was true to his promise, and he was a Messenger, a Prophet. He bade his people to pray and to give the alms, and he was pleasing to his Lord.

And mention in the book Idris; he was a true man, a Prophet. We raised him up to a high place.

These are they whom God has blessed among the Prophets of the seed of Adam, and of those We bore with Noah, and of the seed of Abraham and Israel, and of those We guided and chose. When the signs of the All-merciful were recited to them, they fell down prostrate, weeping.

[60] Then there succeeded after them a succession who wasted the prayer, and followed lusts; so they shall encounter error save him who repents, and believes, and does a righteous deed; those—they shall enter Paradise, and they shall not be wronged anything; Gardens of Eden that the All-merciful promised His servants in the Unseen; His promise is ever performed. There they shall hear no idle talk, but only "Peace." There they shall have their provision at dawn and evening. That is Paradise which We shall give as an inheritance to those of Our servants who are godfearing.

[65] We come not down, save at the commandment of thy Lord. To Him belongs all that is before us, and all that is behind us, and all between that. And thy Lord is never forgetful, Lord He of the heavens and earth and all that is between them. So serve Him, and be thou patient in His service; knowest thou any that can be named with His Name?

Man says, "What, when I am dead shall I then be brought forth alive?" Will not man remember that We created him aforetime, when he was nothing? Now, by thy Lord, We shall surely muster them, and the Satans, then We shall parade them about Gehenna hobbling on their knees.

[70] Then We shall pluck forth from every party whichever of them was the most hardened in disdain of the All-merciful; then We shall know very well those most deserving to burn there.

Not one of you there is, but he shall go down to it; that for thy Lord is a thing decreed, determined. Then We shall deliver those that were godfearing; and the evildoers We shall leave there, hobbling on their knees. When Our signs are recited to them as clear signs, the unbelievers say to the believers, "Which of the two parties is better in station, fairer in assembly?" [75] And how many a generation We destroyed before them, who were fairer in furnishing and outward show! Say: "Whosoever is in error, let the All-merciful prolong his term for him! Till, when they see that they were threatened, whether the chastisement, or the Hour, then they shall surely know who is worse in place, and who is weaker in hosts."

And God shall increase those who were guided in guidance; and the abiding things, the deeds of righteousness, are better with thy Lord in reward, and better in return.

[*80*] Hast thou seen him who disbelieves in Our signs and says, "Assuredly I shall be given wealth and children"? What, has he observed the Unseen, or taken a covenant with the All-merciful? No, indeed! We shall assuredly write down all that he says, and We shall prolong for him the chastisement; and We shall inherit from him that he says, and he shall come to Us alone.

And they have taken to them other gods apart from God, that they might be for them a might. [*85*] No, indeed! They shall deny their service, and they shall be against them pitted. Hast thou not seen how We sent the Satans against the unbelievers, to prick them? So hasten thou not against them; We are only numbering for them a number. On the day that We shall muster the godfearing to the All-merciful with pomp and drive the evildoers into Gehenna herding, [*90*] having no power of intercession, save those who have taken with the All-merciful covenant.

And they say, "The All-merciful has taken unto Himself a son." You have indeed advanced something hideous! The heavens are wellnigh rent of it and the earth split asunder, and the mountains wellnigh fall down crashing for that they have attributed to the All-merciful a son; and it behoves not the All-merciful to take a son.

None is there in the heavens and earth but he comes to the All-merciful as a servant; He has indeed counted them, and He has numbered them exactly. [*95*] Every one of them shall come to Him upon the Day of Resurrection, all alone. Surely those who believe and do deeds of righteousness—unto them the All-merciful shall assign love.

Now We have made it easy by thy tongue that thou mayest bear good tidings thereby to the godfearing, and warn a people stubborn. And how many a generation We destroyed before them! Dost thou perceive so much as one of them, or hear of them a whisper?

Chapter 24: Light

In the Name of God, the Merciful, the Compassionate

A sura that We have sent down and appointed; and We have sent down in it signs, clear signs, that haply you will remember. The fornicatress and the fornicator—scourge each one of them a hundred stripes, and in the matter of God's religion let no tenderness for them seize you if you believe in God and the Last Day; and let a party of the believers witness their chastisement. The fornicator shall marry none but a fornicatress or an idolatress, and the fornicatress—none shall marry her but a fornicator or an idolator; that is forbidden to the believers.

And those who cast it up on women in wedlock, and then bring not four witnesses, scourge them with eighty stripes, and do not accept any testimony of theirs ever; those—they are the ungodly, [*5*] save such as repent thereafter and make amends; surely God is All-forgiving, All-compassionate. And those who cast it up on their wives having no witnesses except themselves, the testimony of one of them shall be to testify by God four times that he is of the truthful, and a fifth time, that the curse of God shall be upon him, if he should be of the liars. It shall avert from her the chastisement if she testify by God four times that he is of the liars, and a fifth time, that the wrath of God shall be upon her, if he should be of the truthful.

[*10*] But for God's bounty to you and His mercy and that God turns, and is All-wise—

Those who came with the slander are a band of you; do not reckon it evil for you; rather it is good for you. Every man of them shall have the sin that he has earned charged to him; and whosoever of them took upon himself the greater part of it, him there awaits a mighty chastisement. Why, when you heard it, did the believing men and women not of their own account think good thoughts, and say, "This is a manifest calumny"? Why did they not bring four witnesses against it? But since they did not bring the witnesses, in God's sight they are the liars. But for God's bounty to you and His mercy in the present world and the world to come there would have visited you for your mutterings a mighty chastisement. When you received it on your tongues, and were speaking with your mouths that whereof you had no knowledge, and reckoned it a light thing, and with God it was a mighty thing— [*15*] And why, when you heard it, did you not say, "It is not for us to speak about this; glory be to Thee! This is a mighty calumny"? God admonishes you, that you shall never repeat the like of it again, if you are believers. God makes clear to you the signs; and God is All-knowing, All-wise. Those who love that indecency should be spread abroad concerning them that believe—there awaits them a painful chastisement in the present world and the world to come; and God knows, and you know not.

[*20*] But for God's bounty to you and His

mercy and that God is All-gentle, All-compassionate—

O believers, follow not the steps of Satan; for whosoever follows the steps of Satan, assuredly he bids to indecency and dishonour. But for God's bounty to you and His mercy not one of you would have been pure ever; but God purifies whom He will; and God is All-hearing, All-knowing.

Let not those of you who possess bounty and plenty swear off giving kinsmen and the poor and those who emigrate in the way of God; but let them pardon and forgive. Do you not wish that God should forgive you? God is All-forgiving, All-compassionate.

Surely those who cast it up on women in wedlock that are heedless but believing shall be accursed in the present world and the world to come; and there awaits them a mighty chastisement on the day when their tongues, their hands and their feet shall testify against them touching that they were doing. [25] Upon that day God will pay them in full their just due, and they shall know that God is the manifest Truth.

Corrupt women for corrupt men, and corrupt men for corrupt women; good women for good men, and good men for good women—these are declared quit of what they say; theirs shall be forgiveness and generous provision.

O believers, do not enter houses other than your houses until you first ask leave and salute the people thereof; that is better for you; haply you will remember. And if you find not anyone therein, enter it not until leave is given to you. And if you are told, "Return," return; that is purer for you; and God knows the things you do. There is no fault in you that you enter houses uninhabited wherein enjoyment is for you. God knows what you reveal and what you hide.

[30] Say to the believers, that they cast down their eyes and guard their private parts; that is purer for them. God is aware of the things they work. And say to the believing women, that they cast down their eyes and guard their private parts, and reveal not their adornment save such as is outward; and let them cast their veils over their bosoms, and not reveal their adornment save to their husbands, or their fathers, or their husbands' fathers, or their sons, or their husbands' sons, or their brothers, or their brothers' sons, or their sisters' sons, or their women, or what their right hands own, or such men as attend them, not having sexual desire, or children who have not yet attained knowledge of women's private parts; nor let them stamp their feet, so that their hidden ornament may be known. And turn all together to God, O you believers; haply so you will prosper.

Marry the spouseless among you, and your slaves and handmaidens that are righteous; if they are poor, God will enrich them of His bounty; God is All-embracing, All-knowing. And let those who find not the means to marry be abstinent till God enriches them of His bounty. Those your right hands own who seek emancipation, contract with them accordingly, if you know some good in them; and give them of the wealth of God that He has given you. And constrain not your slavegirls to prostitution, if they desire to live in chastity, that you may seek the chance goods of the present life. Whosoever constrains them, surely God, after their being constrained, is All-forgiving, All-compassionate.

Now We have sent down to you signs making all clear, and an example of those who passed away before you, and an admonition for the godfearing.

[35] God is the Light of the heavens and the earth; the likeness of His Light is as a niche wherein is a lamp (the lamp in a glass, the glass as it were a glittering star) kindled from a Blessed Tree, an olive that is neither of the East nor of the West whose oil wellnigh would shine, even if no fire touched it; Light upon Light; (God guides to His Light whom He will.) (And God strikes similitudes for men, and God has knowledge of everything.) in temples God has allowed to be raised up, and His Name to be commemorated therein; therein glorifying Him, in the mornings and the evenings, are men whom neither commerce nor trafficking diverts from the remembrance of God and to perform the prayer, and to pay the alms, fearing a day when hearts and eyes shall be turned about, that God may recompense them for their fairest works and give them increase of His bounty; and God provides whomsoever He will, without reckoning.

And as for the unbelievers, their works are as a mirage in a spacious plain which the man athirst supposes to be water, till, when he comes to it, he finds it is nothing; there indeed he finds God, and He pays him his account in full; (and God is swift at the reckoning.) [40] or they are as shadows upon a sea obscure covered by a billow above which is a billow above which are clouds, shadows piled one upon another; when he puts forth his hand, wellnigh he cannot see it. And to whomsoever God assigns no light, no light has he.

Hast thou not seen how that whatsoever is in the heavens and in the earth extols God, and the birds spreading their wings? Each—He knows its prayer and its extolling; and God knows the things they do. To God belongs the Kingdom of the heavens and the earth, and to Him is the homecoming. Hast thou not seen how God drives the clouds, then composes them, then converts them into a mass, then thou seest the rain issuing out of the midst of them? And He sends down out of heaven mountains, wherein is hail, so that He smites whom He will with it, and turns it aside from whom He will; wellnigh the gleam of His lightning snatches away the sight. God turns about the day and the night; surely in that is a lesson for those who have eyes. God has created every beast of water, and some of them go upon their bellies, and some of them go upon two feet, and some of them go upon four; God creates whatever He will; God is powerful over everything.

[45] Now We have sent down signs making all clear; God guides whomsoever He will to a straight path. They say, "We believe in God and the Messenger, and we obey." Then after that a party of them turn away; those—they are not believers. When they are called to God and His Messenger that he may judge between them, lo, a party of them are swerving aside; but if they are in the right, they will come to him submissively. What, is there sickness in their hearts, or are they in doubt, or do they fear that God may be unjust towards them and His Messenger? Nay but those—they are the evildoers.

[50] All that the believers say, when they are called to God and His Messenger, that he may judge between them, is that they say, "We hear, and we obey"; those—they are the prosperers. Whoso obeys God and His Messenger, and fears God and has awe of Him, those—they are the triumphant. They have sworn by God the most earnest oaths, if thou commandest them they will go forth. Say: "Do not swear; honourable obedience is sufficient. Surely God is aware of the things you do." Say: "Obey God, and obey the Messenger; then, if you turn away, only upon him rests what is laid on him, and upon you rests what is laid on you. If you obey him, you will be guided. It is only for the Messenger to deliver the manifest Message."

God has promised those of you who believe and do righteous deeds that He will surely make you successors in the land, even as He made those who were before them successors, and that He will surely establish their religion for them that He has approved for them, and will give them in exchange, after their fear, security: "They shall serve Me, not associating with Me anything." Whoso disbelieves after that, those—they are the ungodly. [55] Perform the prayer, and pay the alms, and obey the Messenger—haply so you will find mercy. Think not the unbelievers able to frustrate God in the earth; their refuge is the Fire—an evil homecoming.

O believers, let those your right hands own and those of you who have not reached puberty ask leave of you three times—before the prayer of dawn, and when you put off your garments at the noon, and after the evening prayer—three times of nakedness for you. There is no fault in you or them, apart from these, that you go about one to the other. So God makes clear to you the signs; and God is All-knowing, All-wise. When your children reach puberty, let them ask leave, as those before them asked leave. So God makes clear to you His signs; and God is All-knowing, All-wise. Such women as are past child-bearing and have no hope of marriage—there is no fault in them that they put off their clothes, so be it that they flaunt no ornament; but to abstain is better for them; and God is All-hearing, All-knowing.

[60] There is no fault in the blind, and there is no fault in the lame, and there is no fault in the sick, neither in yourselves, that you eat of your houses, or your fathers' houses, or your mothers' houses, or your brothers' houses, or your sisters' houses, or the houses of your uncles or your aunts paternal, or the houses of your uncles or your aunts maternal, or that whereof you own the keys, or of your friend; there is no fault in you that you eat all together, or in groups separately. But when you enter houses, greet one another with a greeting from God, blessed and good. So God makes clear to you the signs; haply you will understand.

Those only are believers, who believe in God and His Messenger and who, when they are with him upon a common matter, go not away until they ask his leave. Surely those who ask thy leave—those are they that believe in God and His Messenger; so, when they ask thy leave for some affair of their own, give leave to whom thou wilt of them, and ask God's forgiveness for them; surely God is All-forgiving, All-compassionate. Make not the calling of the Messenger among yourselves like your calling one of another. God knows those of you who slip away surreptitiously; so let those who go against His command beware, lest a trial befall them, or there befall them a painful chastisement.

Why, surely to God belongs whatsoever is in the heavens and the earth; He ever knows what state you are upon; and the day when they shall be returned to Him, then He will tell them of what they did; and God knows everything.

Chapter 25: Salvation

In the Name of God, the Merciful, the Compassionate

Blessed be He who has sent down the Salvation upon His Servant, that he may be a warner to all beings; to whom belongs the Kingdom of the heavens and the earth; and He has not taken to Him a son, and He has no associate in the Kingdom; and He created every thing, then He ordained it very exactly. Yet they have taken to them gods, apart from Him, that create nothing and themselves are created, and have no power to hurt or profit themselves, no power of death or life or raising up.

[5] The unbelievers say, "This is naught but a calumny he has forged, and other folk have helped him to it." So they have committed wrong and falsehood. They say, "Fairy-tales of the ancients that he has had written down, so that they are recited to him at the dawn and in the evening." Say: "He sent it down, who knows the secret in the heavens and earth; He is All-forgiving, All-compassionate."

They also say, "What ails this Messenger that he eats food, and goes in the markets? Why has an angel not been sent down to him, to be a warner with him? Or why is not a treasure thrown to him, or why has he not a Garden to eat of?" The evildoers say, "You are only following a man bewitched!" [10] Behold, how they strike similitudes for thee, and go astray, and are unable to find a way!

· Blessed be He who, if He will, shall assign to thee better than that—gardens underneath which rivers flow, and he shall assign to thee palaces.

Nay, but they cry lies to the Hour; and We have prepared for him who cries lies to the Hour a Blaze. When it sees them from a far place, they shall hear its bubbling and sighing. And when they are cast, coupled in fetters, into a narrow place of that Fire, they will call out there for destruction. [15] "Call not out today for one destruction, but call for many!"

Say: "Is that better, or the Garden of Eternity, that is promised to the godfearing, and is their recompense and homecoming?" Therein they shall have what they will dwelling forever; it is a promise binding upon thy Lord, and of Him to be required.

Upon the day when He shall muster them and that they serve, apart from God, and He shall say, "Was it you that led these My servants astray, or did they themselves err from the way?" They shall say, "Glory be to Thee! It did not behove us to take unto ourselves protectors apart from Thee; but thou gavest them and their fathers enjoyment of days, until they forgot [20] the Remembrance, and were a people corrupt." So they cried you lies touching the things you say, and you can neither turn it aside, nor find any help. Whosoever of you does evil, We shall let him taste a great chastisement.

And We sent not before thee any Envoys, but that they ate food, and went in the markets; and We appointed some of you to be a trial for others: "Will you endure?" Thy Lord is ever All-seeing. Say those who look not to encounter Us, "Why have the angels not been sent down on us, or why see we not our Lord?" Waxed proud they have within them, and become greatly disdainful.

Upon the day that they see the angels, no good tidings that day for the sinners; they shall say, "A ban forbidden!" [25] We shall advance upon what work they have done, and make it a scattered dust. The inhabitants of Paradise that day, better shall be their lodging, fairer their resting-place. Upon the day that heaven is split asunder with the clouds and the angels are sent down in majesty, the Kingdom that day, the true Kingdom, shall belong to the All-merciful, and it shall be a day harsh for the unbelievers. Upon the day the evildoer shall bite his hands, saying, "Would that I had taken a way along with the Messenger! [30] Alas, would that I had not taken So-and-so for a friend! He indeed led me astray from the Remembrance, after it had come to me; Satan is ever a forsaker of men."

The Messenger says, "O my Lord, behold, my people have taken this Koran as a thing to be shunned." Even so We have appointed to every Prophet an enemy among the sinners; but thy Lord suffices as a guide and as a helper. The unbelievers say, "Why has the Koran not been sent down upon him all at once?" Even so, that We may strengthen thy heart thereby, and We have chanted it very distinctly. [35] They bring not to thee any similitude but that We bring thee the truth, and better in exposition. Those who shall be mustered to Gehenna upon their faces—they shall be worse in place, and gone further astray from the way.

We gave Moses the Book, and appointed with him his brother Aaron as minister and We said, "Go to the people who have cried lies to Our signs"; then We destroyed them utterly. And the people of Noah, when they cried lies to the Messengers, We drowned them, and made them to be a sign to mankind; and We have prepared for the evildoers a painful chastisement. [40] And Ad, and Thamood, and the men of Er-Rass, and between that generations a many—for each We struck similitudes, and each We ruined utterly. Surely they have come by the city that was rained on by an evil rain; what, have they not seen it? Nay, but they look for no uprising. And when they see thee, they take thee in mockery only: 'What, is this he whom God sent forth as a Messenger? Wellnigh he had led us astray from our gods, but that we kept steadfast to them.' Assuredly they shall know, when they see the chastisement, who is further astray from the way. [45] Hast thou seen him who has taken his caprice to be his god? Wilt thou be a guardian over them? Or deemest thou that most of them hear or understand? They are but as the cattle; nay, they are further astray from the way.

Hast thou not regarded thy Lord, how He has stretched out the shadow? Had He willed, He would have made it still. Then we appointed the sun, to be a guide to it; thereafter We seize it to Ourselves, drawing it gently. It is He who appointed the night for you to be a garment and sleep for a rest, and day He appointed for a rising. [50] And it is He who has loosed the winds, bearing good tidings before His mercy; and We sent down from heaven pure water so that We might revive a dead land, and give to drink of it, of that We created, cattle and men a many.

We have indeed turned it about amongst them, so that they may remember; yet most men refuse all but unbelief.

If We had willed, We would have raised up in every city a warner. So obey not the unbelievers, but struggle with them thereby mightily.

[55] And it is He who let forth the two seas, this one sweet, grateful to taste, and this salt, bitter to the tongue, and He set between them a barrier, and a ban forbidden. And it is He who created of water a mortal, and made him kindred of blood and marriage; thy Lord is All-powerful.

And they serve, apart from God, what neither profits them nor hurts them; and the unbeliever is ever a partisan against his Lord. We have sent thee not, except good tidings to bear, and warning. Say: "I do not ask of you a wage for this, except for him who wishes to take to his Lord a way."

[60] Put thy trust in the Living God, the Undying, and proclaim His praise. Sufficiently is He aware of His servants' sins who created the heavens and the earth, and what between them is, in six days, then sat Himself upon the Throne, the All-compassionate: ask any informed of Him!

But when they are told, "Bow yourselves to the All-merciful," they say, "And what is the All-merciful? Shall we bow ourselves to what thou biddest us?" And it increases them in aversion.

Blessed be He who has set in heaven constellations, and has set among them a lamp, and an illuminating moon. And it is He who made the night and day a succession for whom He desires to remember or He desires to be thankful.

The servants of the All-merciful are those who walk in the earth modestly and who, when the ignorant address them, say, "Peace"; [65] who pass the night prostrate to their Lord and standing; who say, "Our Lord, turn Thou from us the chastisement of Gehenna; surely its chastisement is torment most terrible; evil it is as a lodging-place and an abode"; who, when they expend, are neither prodigal nor parsimonious, but between that is a just stand; who call not upon another god with God, nor slay the soul God has forbidden except by right, neither fornicate, for whosoever does that shall meet the price of sin—doubled shall be the chastisement for him on the Resurrection Day, and he shall dwell therein humbled, [70] save him who repents, and believes, and does righteous work—those, God will change their evil deeds into good deeds, for God is ever All-forgiving, All-compassionate; and whosoever repents, and does righteously, he truly turns to God in repentance. And those who bear not false witness and, when they pass by idle talk, pass by with dignity; who, when they are reminded of the signs of their Lord, fall not down thereat deaf and blind; who say, "Our Lord, give us refreshment of our wives and seed, and make us a model to the godfearing." [75] Those shall be recompensed with the highest heaven, for that they endured patiently, and they shall receive therein a greeting and—"Peace!" Therein they shall dwell forever; fair it is as a lodging-place and an abode.

Say: "My Lord esteems you not at all were it not for your prayer, for you have cried lies, and it shall surely be fastened."

Imam Nawawi: Riyadh as-Salihin (c. 1250 C.E.)

C. E. Bosworth and Muhammad Zafrulla Khan (tr.). *Gardens of the Righteous: Riyadh as-Salihin of Imam Nawawi*. London: Curzon Press, 1975.

On Kindness towards Women (34.275–282)

275   Abu Hurairah relates that the Holy Prophet said: Treat women kindly. Woman has been

created from a rib and the most crooked part of the rib is the uppermost. If you try to straighten it you will break it and if you leave it alone it will remain crooked. So treat women kindly (Bokhari and Muslim). Another version is: A woman is like a rib; if you try to straighten it you will break it and if you wish to draw benefit from it you can do so despite its crookedness. Muslim's version is: Woman has been created from a rib and you cannot straighten her. If you wish to draw benefit from her do so despite her crookedness. If you try to straighten her you will break her, and breaking her means divorcing her.

276 Abdullah ibn Zam'a relates that he heard the Holy Prophet delivering an address. He mentioned the she-camel of Saleh, the Prophet, and the one who hamstrung her. He said: When the most wretched of them stood up (91.13), means that a distinguished, wicked and most powerful chief of the people jumped up. Then he mentioned women and said: Some of you beat your wives as if they were slaves, and then consort with them at the end of the day. Then he admonished people against laughing at another's passing the wind, saying: Why does any of you laugh at another doing what he does himself (Bokhari and Muslim)?

277 Abu Hurairah relates that the Holy Prophet said: Let no Muslim man entertain any rancour against a Muslim woman. Should he dislike one quality in her, he would find another which is pleasing (Muslim).

278 Amr ibn Ahwas Jashmi relates that he heard the Holy Prophet say in his address on the occasion of the Farewell Pilgrimage, after he had praised Allah and glorified Him and admonished people: Treat women kindly, they are like prisoners in your hands. You are not owed anything more by them. Should they be guilty of open indecency you may leave them alone in their beds and inflict slight chastisement. Then if they obey you do not have recourse to anything else against them. You have your rights concerning your wives and they have their rights concerning you. Your right is that they shall not permit anyone you dislike to enter your home, and their right is that you should treat them well in the matter of food and clothing (Tirmidhi).

279 Mu'awiah ibn Haidah relates: I asked the Holy Prophet: What is the right of a wife against her husband? He said: Feed her when you feed yourself; clothe her when you clothe yourself, do not strike her on her face, do not revile her and do not separate yourself from her except inside the house (Abu Daud).

280 Abu Hurairah relates that the Holy Prophet said: The most perfect of believers in the matter of faith is he whose behaviour is best; and the best of you are those who behave best towards their wives (Tirmidhi).

281 Iyas ibn Abdullah relates that the Holy Prophet admonished: Do not strike the handmaidens of Allah. Some time later Umar came to him and said: Women have become very daring vis-a-vis their husbands. So he permitted their chastisement. Thereafter a large number of women came to the wives of the Holy Prophet and complained against their husbands. The Holy Prophet announced: Many women have come to my wives complaining against their husbands. These men are not well-behaved (Abu Daud).

282 Abdullah ibn Amr ibn 'As relates that the Holy Prophet said: The world is but a provision and the best provision of the world is a good woman (Muslim).

On a Husband's Right concerning His Wife (35.283–90)

283 Abu Hurairah relates that the Holy Prophet said: When the husband calls his wife to his bed and she does not come and he spends the night offended with her, the angels keep cursing her through the night (Bokhari and Muslim). Another version is: When a woman spends the night away from her husband's bed, the angels keep cursing her through the night. Still another version runs: The Holy Prophet said: By Him in Whose hands is my life, when a husband calls his wife to his bed and she refuses him, He Who is in heaven is offended with her till her husband is pleased with her.

284 Abu Hurairah relates that the Holy Prophet said: It is not permissible for a woman to observe a voluntary fast when her husband is at home, except with his permission. Nor should she permit anyone to enter his house without his leave (Bokhari and Muslim).

285 Ibn Umar relates that the Holy Prophet said:

Every one of you is a steward and is accountable for that which is committed to his charge. The ruler is a steward and is accountable for his charge, a man is a steward in respect of his household, a woman is a steward in respect of her husband's house and his children. Thus everyone of you is a steward and is accountable for that which is committed to his charge (Bokhari and Muslim).

286 Abu Ali Talq ibn Ali relates that the Holy Prophet said: When a man calls his wife for his need, she should go to him even if she is occupied in baking bread (Tirmidhi and Nisai).

287 Abu Hurairah relates that the Holy Prophet said: Had I ordained that a person should prostrate himself before another, I would have commanded that a wife should prostrate herself before her husband (Tirmidhi).

288 Umm Salamah relates that the Holy Prophet said: If a woman dies and her husband is pleased with her she will enter Paradise (Tirmidhi).

289 Mu'az ibn Jabal relates that the Holy Prophet said: Whenever a woman distresses her husband his mate from among the *houris* of Paradise says to her: Allah ruin thee, do not cause him distress for he is only thy guest and will soon part from thee to come to us (Tirmidhi).

290 Usamah ibn Zaid relates that the Holy Prophet said: I am not leaving a more harmful trial for men than women (Bokhari and Muslim).

On the Obligation of Paying the Zakat (215.1212; 215.1215)

1212 Talha ibn Ubaidullah relates: A man from Nejd with rumpled hair came to the Holy Prophet. His voice reached our ears but we could not understand what he was saying till he approached close to the Holy Prophet and we understood that he was inquiring about Islam. The Holy Prophet said to him: There are five obligatory Prayers in twenty four hours. He said: Am I under obligation beyond these? The Holy Prophet answered: No, unless you were to offer voluntary Prayer; and went on to say: then there is the fast of the month of Ramadhan. The man asked: Am I under obligation beyond it? The Holy Prophet repeated: No, unless you were to observe voluntary fasts. Then the Holy Prophet mentioned to him the *Zakat* and he made the same inquiry and the Holy Prophets gave the same answer. The man then turned away saying: Allah is my witness that I shall not add anything to this, nor shall I detract anything from it. On this the Holy Prophet observed: He will prosper if he proves truthful (Bokhari and Muslim). . . .

1215 Abu Hurairah relates: When the Holy Prophet died and Abu Bakr became Khalifa of the Arabs some repudiated their obligations and Abu Bakr said he would fight them, Umar said to him: How will you fight them while the Holy Prophet said: I have been commanded to fight those who fight me till they should affirm: There is none worthy of worship save Allah. Then whoever affirms this, his life and property will be secure except to the extent of his obligations, and his responsibility is to Allah. Abu Bakr answered him: I shall certainly fight those who make a distinction between Prayer and *Zakat*. *Zakat* is obligatory in respect of wealth. Allah is my witness that if they hold back from me the nose-rope of a camel that they paid to the Holy Prophet, I shall fight them for their holding it back. Umar said thereafter: I then understood that Allah had made the matter of fighting plain to Abu Bakr and I recognised that he was in the right (Bokhari and Muslim).

Picture and Literary Credits

Picture Credits

The publishers would like to thank the following museums and photographers for permission to reproduce their material. Every care has been taken to trace copyright holders. However, if we have omitted anyone we apologise for this and will, if informed, make corrections in any future edition.

Front Cover Panos Pictures, London/Jean-Léo Dugast

Page xii British Museum, London, #OA 1962. 12–31.013 (42)
15   AKG London/Jean-Louis Nou
18   Robert Harding Picture Library, London
20   Archaeological Survey of India, New Delhi
41   Hutchison Library, London/David Brinicombe
42   AKG London/British Library, London
51   British Museum, London, #OA 1955. 10–18.1
53   AKG London/Jean-Louis Nou
54   British Museum, London, #OA 1990.12–17.010
56   British Museum, London, #OA 94. 2–16.10
57   British Museum, London, #OA 1966. 2–12.03
59   British Museum, London, #OA 1955.10–8.094
60   British Museum, London, #OA 1956. 7–14.017
63   Bury Peerless, Birchington on Sea, Kent
66   Christie's Images, London
67   AKG London/Paul Almasy
68   Robert Harding Picture Library, London
73   Bodleian Library, Oxford, Ms Pers B.1, f.33r
80   Panos Pictures, London/Daniel O'Leary
83   AKG London/Jean-Louis Nou
92   AKG London/Waldemar Abegg
95   Magnum Photos, London/Henri Cartier-Bresson
99   Hutchison Library, London/Christine Pemberton
102 British Museum, London, #OA 1872.7–1.99
107 Robert Harding Picture Library, London/Sassoon
109 British Library, London/Indian Museum, Calcutta, #1000/30 2262 OIE 51544R
111 Panos Pictures, London/Rod Johnson
117 Royal Scottish Museum, Edinburgh, #A.1993.155
118 Robert Harding Picture Library, London/Robert Harding
122 Robert Harding Picture Library, London/Alain Evrard
124 Musée Guimet, Paris/RMN-Richard Lambert #93DE3196
131 Panos Pictures, London/Neil Cooper
134 Asian Art Museum, San Francisco. Avery Brundage Collection, #B60S22+
135 Metropolitan Museum of Art, New York. Purchase Lila Acheson Wallace Gift, #1992–54. Photo © 1995
136 City of Birmingham Museum & Art Gallery. Gift of Samuel Thornton
138 Panos Pictures, London/Mark Henley
147 Ashmolean Museum, Dept of Eastern Art, Oxford, #EA X.7298
150 Musée Guimet, Paris/RMN-Thierry Ollivier, #00DE18120
152 Hutchison Library, London/Juliet Highet
153 Panos Pictures, London/Jim Holmes
157 Panos Pictures, London/Jean-Léo Dugast
160 Panos Pictures, London/Jeremy Horner
174 Bridgeman Art Library, London/Private Collection/Christie's
178 Bridgeman Art Library, London/Private Collection/Christie's
179 Robert Harding Picture Library, London/Bildagentur Schuster/Layda
181 Bridgeman Art Library, London/Bibliothèque des Arts Decoratifs, Paris. Photo Jean-Loup Charmet
186 LKP archives
187 Cultural Relics Publishing House, Beijing
188 Cultural Relics Publishing House, Beijing
202 Cultural Relics Publishing House, Beijing
205 Hutchison Library, London/Sarah Errington
209 Robert Harding Picture Library, London/Alain Evrard
211 Magnum Photos, London/Lise Sarfati
213 Robert Harding Picture Libary, London/Alain Evrard
220 Cultural Relics Publishing House, Beijing
228 Cultural Relics Publishing House, Beijing

240 Musée Guimet, Paris/RMN-Ravaux, #92CE3188
245 Metropolitan Museum of Art, New York. John Stewart Kennedy Fund, 1926, #26.123. Photo © 1983
246–247 Metropolitan Museum of Art, New York. Purchase the Dillon Fund Gift, 1980, #1980.276
248 Cultural Relics Publishing House, Beijing
252 Bridgeman Art Library, London/British Museum, London
258 Victoria and Albert Museum, London, #A.7–1935
259 Museum of Fine Arts, Boston. Gift of Mrs W. Scott Fitz, #22.407
261 Tofukuji, Kyoto
266 Bridgeman Art Library, London/Nara National Museum, Japan
274 Hutchison Library, London/Michael Macintyre
275 Panos Pictures, London/Jean-Léo Dugast
284 Japan Information & Cultural Centre, Japanese Embassy, London
286 Japan Information & Cultural Centre, Japanese Embassy, London
291 Hutchison Library, London/J. Burbank
293 Hutchison Library, London/Michael Macintyre
301 Robert Harding Picture Library, London/Christopher Rennie
302 Ancient Art & Architecture, Pinner, Middx
303 Musée Guimet, Paris/RMN-Arnaudet, #81EE125
307 Musée Guimet, Paris/RMN-P.Bernard #90DE1908
310 Christie's Images, London
313 Robert Harding Picture Library/Robert McLeod
314 Christie's Images, London
315 Christie's Images, London
318 Musée Guimet, Paris/RMN-Richard Lambert, #95DE13722
322 Musée Guimet, Paris/RMN-Richard Lambert, #98DE9130

Literary Credits

Every effort has been made to contact all copyright holders. The publisher would be pleased to rectify any omissions at the earliest opportunity.

Amana Publications: from *The Meaning of the Holy Qur'an*, Revised edition, translated by Abdullah Yusuf Ali (Brentwood, MD: The Amana Corporation, 1989).

Bharatiya Vidya Bhavan: from *Tiruvacakam*, translated by Ratna Navaratnam (Mumbai: Bharatiya Vidya Bhavan, 1963).

Columbia University Press: from *Sources of Japanese Tradition*, Volume 1, edited by Ryusaku Tsunoda et al. (New York: Columbia University Press, 1964); from *Sources of Indian Tradition*, 2/e, Volume 1, edited by Ainslie T. Embree (New York: Columbia University Press, 1988).

HarperCollins Publishers: from *The Bhagavadgita*, translated by Sarvipalla Radhakrishnan (London: George Allen & Unwin, 1960).

Kosei Publishing Co: from *Shapers of Japanese Buddhism*, edited by Yusen Kashiwahara and Koyu Sonada (Tokyo: Kosei, 1994).

Oxford University Press Inc: from *The Early Upanishads*, translated by Patrick Olivelle (New York: Oxford University Press, 1998).

Parallax Press: from *The Dhammapada: The Path of Truth*, translated by Ven. Ananda Maitreya, revised by Rose Kramer (Berkeley: Parallax Press, 1995).

Princeton University Press: from *A Sourcebook in Chinese Philosophy*, edited by Wing-tsit Chan (Princeton: Princeton University Press, 1963).

Ramakrishna Math: from *Vedarthasangraha* by Ramanuja, translated by S. S. Raghavacar (Mysore: Ramakrishna Math, 1956).

Random House Inc: from *The Sikhs* by Patwant Singh (New York: Alfred A. Knopf, 2000), © 1999 by Patwant Singh.

SUNY Press: from *A Survey of Hinduism*, 2/e by Klaus K. Klostermaier (New York: SUNY Press, 1994), © 1994, State University of New York. All rights reserved.

University of Toronto Press: from *Mencius: a new translation arranged and annotated for the general reader*, translated by W.A.C.H. Dobson (Toronto: University of Toronto Press, 1963).

Index